T0331076

Business
Sustainability
Framework

Providing a practical and accessible introduction to a complex yet essential area, *Business Sustainability Framework* enables readers to integrate and report on sustainability from business and accounting perspectives.

The author explores how organizations of all sizes can adopt an integrated strategic approach to business sustainability, encompassing planning, performance, reporting, and assurance. Grounded in the latest research, the book includes topics such as shareholder and stakeholder governance models, business sustainability factors and initiatives, sustainability theories, standards and best practices, the use of AI, and financial reporting and auditing initiatives.

An ideal introduction for advanced undergraduate and graduate students of sustainability governance, performance, risk, reporting, and assurance, this textbook equips readers with the knowledge and skills necessary to become successful business leaders in sustainability.

Zabihollah Rezaee is the Thompson-Hill Chair of Excellence and Professor of Accountancy at the Crews School of Accountancy, University of Memphis.

Business Sustainability Framework

Theory and Practice

Zabihollah Rezaee

Routledge
Taylor & Francis Group

LONDON AND NEW YORK

Designed cover image: ©Getty Images. Credit: Alexis Gonzalez Creative #:1264737466

First published 2025
by Routledge
4 Park Square, Milton Park, Abingdon, Oxon OX14 4RN

and by Routledge
605 Third Avenue, New York, NY 10158

Routledge is an imprint of the Taylor & Francis Group, an informa business

British Library Cataloguing-in-Publication Data
A catalogue record for this book is available from the British Library

ISBN: 978-1-032-78268-3 (hbk)
ISBN: 978-1-032-78267-6 (pbk)
ISBN: 978-1-003-48708-1 (ebk)

DOI: 10.4324/9781003487081

Typeset in Univers
by Deanta Global Publishing Services, Chennai, India

Access the Instructor Resources: www.Routledge.com/9781032782676

This book is dedicated to Dr. Rezaee's parents, Fazlollah and Fatemeh, sister Monireh, brother Heshmat, wife Soheila, and children Nick and Rose.

Contents

Contents

Preface

Business sustainability is becoming increasingly important in both the global business and academic communities. The Association to Advance Collegiate Schools of Business (AACSB) Accreditation has observed that topics related to business sustainability are gaining widespread acceptance and attention among business schools worldwide. Adequate coverage of these crucial topics will enable business colleges and accounting schools to effectively train competent and ethical students who will become future business leaders. Business sustainability encompasses economic, governance, social, ethical, and environmental (EGSEE) performance in creating shared value for all stakeholders. Investors now demand business sustainability information, regulators require it, and business organizations report it. Organizations around the world report their integrated financial economic sustainability performance (ESP) and non-financial environmental, social, and governance (ESG) sustainability performance, aiming to create shared value for stakeholders such as shareholders, customers, suppliers, creditors, employees, environmental agencies, communities, governments, and society. Several professional organizations, including the Global Reporting Initiative (GRI), the Sustainability Accounting Standards Board (SASB), the International Integrated Reporting Council (IIRC), the Corporate Reporting Dialogue (CRD), and the International Sustainability Standards Board (ISSB), have issued numerous sustainability reporting and assurance guidelines to help businesses disclose their financial ESP and non-financial ESG sustainability performance information to all stakeholders.

Business colleges and accounting schools can serve as vital conduits for producing and transferring knowledge about business sustainability and organizational ethics, ensuring a more sustainable future and contributing to society's well-being. They play a crucial role in preparing competent future business leaders who understand corporate governance, business sustainability, and ethical business practices. This book is the first to present a comprehensive framework for the theory and practice of business sustainability education. Currently, over 450 courses and programs on business sustainability are offered by colleges and universities worldwide, and more than 200 research centers on business sustainability, ethics, and corporate governance exist at high-profile universities. The number of universities offering standalone courses, programs, and research centers on business sustainability is expected to grow.

This book equips students with the knowledge and skills necessary to become successful business leaders and is intended for use at both undergraduate and graduate levels.

It adopts a holistic teaching approach, emphasizing the value-adding roles of all participants in the corporate governance process, who share the collective responsibility of creating shareholder value, protecting the interests of other stakeholders, complying with all applicable laws, rules, regulations, ethical standards, and best practices, and producing reliable, transparent, and high-quality financial information. The book can be used in a three-credit-hour course at either the undergraduate or graduate levels, or both, as it is designed to develop an awareness and understanding of the main themes, perspectives, frameworks, and issues related to business sustainability. Alternatively, different chapters of the book can be used separately in various undergraduate and/or graduate accounting and business courses.

This book is an essential reference for all business colleges, accounting schools, and other college programs offering business sustainability education. It is also valuable for professionals seeking an up-to-date understanding of emerging areas in business. Currently, no other comprehensive book covers all these critical contemporary issues of business sustainability, including the use of artificial intelligence (AI) and other technologies in identifying, measuring, classifying, and reporting key sustainability performance indicators. The book uses straightforward language to illustrate theoretical and practical concepts and procedures, aiding comprehension of complex business sustainability processes and exposing readers to various organizational ethics issues that shape corporate culture. It emphasizes the role of corporate culture in creating links between business sustainability, corporate governance, and organizational ethics.

Business sustainability education is of paramount importance and relevance in today's rapidly evolving global landscape. It equips future business leaders with the knowledge and skills necessary to navigate complex environmental, social, and economic challenges. By integrating sustainability principles and standards into business practices, education programs foster a deep understanding of corporate governance, ethical conduct, and stakeholder engagement. This holistic approach not only prepares students to drive long-term value creation but also ensures that they are capable of making decisions that benefit society and the environment. As businesses face increasing scrutiny from investors, regulators, and consumers, the demand for leaders who can implement sustainable practices and report on their sustainability performance has never been greater. Consequently, business sustainability education is essential for cultivating responsible, forward-thinking professionals who can lead organizations towards a more sustainable and equitable future. Organizations of all types, sizes, and complexities can benefit from comprehensive business sustainability. It is time for business colleges and accounting schools to renew and revitalize their commitment to providing education that integrates business sustainability with technology and trains the most ethical, competent, and socially and environmentally responsible future business leaders. Universities play a crucial role in preparing the next generation of business leaders, who will receive lifelong training in acting with integrity, upholding the highest level of ethical conduct, and bearing the significant burden of public trust. We hope you find this book relevant in educating future business leaders on undergraduate and/or graduate accounting and business courses.

Sincerely,
Zabi Rezaee

Chapter 1
The Role of Corporations in Financial Markets and Society

Learning Objectives

- Understand the roles and responsibilities of businesses in our society and financial markets.
- Exemplify the importance of reliable and transparent financial information.
- Identify corporate stakeholders, including shareholders and other stakeholders, and understand their roles and responsibilities.
- Understand corporate governance and accountability systems.
- Learn the importance of business sustainability in promoting shared value for all stakeholders.
- Develop an understanding of how public companies contribute to national economic growth, capital allocation, market efficiency, and innovation.
- Learn how corporations and their financial information contribute to the safety, integrity, and efficiency of capital markets.
- Recognize the importance of the free enterprise system in job and wealth creation, growth, innovation, and resource efficiency.
- Understand the role of the free enterprise system in promoting healthy and constructive competition among business organizations.

Introduction

This chapter presents the importance and dynamics of relationships between capital markets and businesses as influenced by corporate culture, perceived by stakeholders (including investors), and transformed through business sustainability and corporate governance. Many initiatives have been taken to establish standards and best practices for public companies and their directors, officers, accountants, auditors, legal counsel, financial analysts, investing banks, and others to effectively fulfill their responsibilities and discharge their accountability. Impactful corporate culture, a robust business environment, effective corporate governance, integrated business sustainability, and an enforceable accountability and compliance system can improve a corporation's strategic plan, decisions, actions, and

DOI: 10.4324/9781003487081-1

the reliability of its financial reports, as well as the efficiency of capital markets and the nation's prospects and growth. The free enterprise system is a bedrock principle of the global economy, and the capital markets are the backbone of that system. This widespread and global investment by individual and institutional investors has been accomplished by, and will continue to prosper from, investors receiving reliable and useful financial and nonfinancial information in making sound investment decisions. This chapter provides an introduction to the role of corporations and background for a plan for business sustainability and corporate governance presented throughout the book.

The Role of Corporations

Corporations are the main engines that drive a nation's economy and its financial markets to long-term sustainable performance and prosperity. Corporations have contributed to the creation of millions of jobs, they drive economic growth by producing goods and services that are beneficial to society, and they generate profits that contribute to the overall productivity and wealth of a nation. Corporations and their financial information contribute to the safety, integrity, and efficiency of capital markets. Well-managed and effectively governed public companies are the engines of a nation's economic growth and prosperity, as public companies can contribute significantly to employment, capital spending, capital allocation, social responsibility, globalization, and market efficiency. The free enterprise system in the United States has been developed and promoted with a keen focus on creating jobs and wealth, enabling growth, fostering innovation, rewarding initiatives and risks, and using resources effectively. This widespread and global investment by individual and institutional investors has been accomplished and will continue to prosper from investors receiving reliable and useful financial information in making sound investment decisions. The free enterprise system promotes healthy and constructive competition among business organizations without much government interference. The financial markets provide a means of ensuring retirement resources for senior citizens, college tuition funds for the younger generation, and sources of income for the workforce. Thus, the safety, integrity, and efficiency of capital markets can benefit society at large.

Corporations in the United States are viewed as creators of shared value for all stakeholders, as depicted in Exhibit 1.1. As distinct legal entities, corporations obtain their financial capital, human capital, skills (managerial capital), reputational capital (customer loyalty), environmental capital, and social capital, among others presented in Chapter 10, from their stakeholders; conduct their value-added activities; and generate sustainable and enduring value for their stakeholders. All stakeholders contribute to the successful operation of corporations in creating shared value from shareholders to creditors, suppliers, customers,

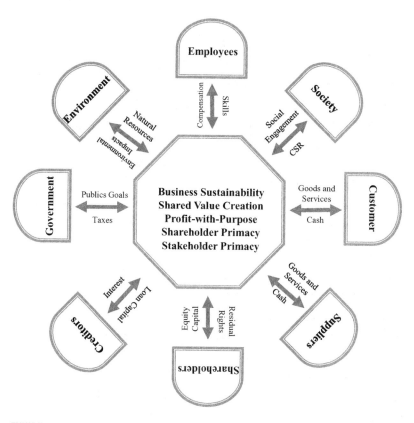

EXHIBIT 1.1 Corporations' role in society.

employees, society, and the environment. For example, equity and debt holders provide financial capital, employees offer human capital, management provides managerial skills, customers create reputational capital, boards of directors oversee corporate affairs and performance, and the government sets rules to protect stakeholders. In return, corporations grant (1) limited liability assurance for shareholders and (2) shared value in the normal course of their business, with shareholders having a residual claim. Public companies play an important role in both financial markets and society. The significant role of corporations in the financial markets includes (1) capital formation and allocation by raising capital from the investing public through the issuance of stocks and bonds in financial markets to invest in new projects and innovations and expand operations in generating wealth for investors; (2) enhancement of liquidity and efficiency in financial markets, enabling investors to buy and sell securities at fair prices; (3) allocation of resources and investment decisions by providing a platform for effectively assessing the value of corporations through price discovery; and (4) risk assessment and management by presenting mechanisms (swaps, options, futures) for corporations and their investors to effectively assess and manage risks related to fluctuations in interest rates, currency, and commodity prices. Corporations

The Role of Corporations

also play an essential role in our society by (1) creating jobs and employment opportunities for millions of people that contribute to economic growth and prosperity in the nation and worldwide; (2) development and innovation by investing in research and development (R&D) that drives economic progress and prosperity and improves the quality of life for society worldwide; (3) corporate social responsibility by engaging in initiatives and activities that have social and environmental impacts in addition to financial consequences; and (4) tax revenue by paying taxes to local, national, and international governments to fund public services including education, infrastructure, retirement benefits, and healthcare. These are the expected roles and responsibilities of corporations, and they have often been criticized for not effectively performing their duties in society and the financial markets. The next section describes corporate sustainability, accountability, and transparency in effectively and ethically fulfilling their roles in both financial markets and society.

The liquidity, integrity, safety, efficiency, transparency, and related dynamics of capital markets are vital to the nation's economic welfare and growth since the markets act as signaling mechanisms for capital allocation. The capital markets have been vibrant because investors have confidence in them and are able to obtain, analyze, and price securities based on the information provided about public companies and the economy. Information is the lifeblood of capital markets. Without such trusted information being available, stocks would be mispriced, capital markets would be inefficient, scarce resources (capital) would be inefficiently used and allocated, and the level of economic growth that we currently see would not be possible. The shareholder primacy with a profit-maximizing model of publicly traded companies has shaped the role and responsibilities of business organizations in our society and capital markets in creating value for shareholders. According to this model, a public firm's shareholders elect a board of directors, and the board then appoints managers to maximize the firm's profits and thus increase the firm's value and shareholders' wealth. The trends emerging in the past few decades, including the focus on protecting the interests of all stakeholders and the rise of indexing among shareholders, have raised questions about whether this model is still applicable and relevant. This emerging trend of moving away from the shareholder primacy model and moving toward the stakeholder primacy model has led to a debate centered around the profit-with-purpose mission of corporations and their roles in both financial markets and society.

The evolution of public companies in the United States indicates that in 1975 there were 4819 publicly listed corporations; that number increased to 7002 by 1995, reached its peak of 7507 in 1997, and dropped to 3766 by 2015.[1] As of 2017, that number had fallen further to approximately 3600.[2] In recent years, the number of public companies listed on major stock exchanges, such as the New York Stock Exchange (NYSE) and the NASDAQ, has fluctuated in the range of 4000 to 5000 because of factors such as mergers and acquisitions (M&A), initial public offerings (IPOs), companies going private and/or delisting. Thus, there are fewer corporations now than four decades ago, primarily because of the extensive mergers and acquisitions of recent decades and the high cost of compliance with regulatory reforms. These factors both encourage private companies not to go public and public companies to go private. However, these public corporations (Microsoft, Google, FedEx, Amazon) are now older and bigger and spread across larger industries with widespread and diversified shareholders. Their capital and asset structures are also different, with fewer physical and more intangible assets as well as a market capitalization that is seven times larger than it was 40 years ago.[3] Public corporations are now investing more in R&D and less in capital expenditures, with a substantial increase in institutional ownership, which was about 50.4% in 2015.[4] The percentage of institutional ownership in recent years is above 65%, with the "Big Three" asset management companies of BlackRock, Vanguard, and State Street Global holding more than 20% of S&P 500 shares in 2017, compared to 5% in 1998.[5] Institutional ownership is defined as the percentage of a company's shares that institutional investors hold, including pension funds, mutual funds, insurance companies, hedge funds, and other large investment entities. These institutional investors usually purchase large blocks of shares in publicly traded companies and often conduct thorough research and analysis before investing in a company. Thus, their trading activities can influence stock prices, market sentiment, and investor confidence. Investors can view high institutional ownership as a sign that the company is sustainable and growing, whereas low institutional ownership may raise concerns about the company's sustainable performance. Existing public corporations appear to be more sustainable, more concentrated, and more profitable, with substantial holdings in intangible assets.

Accountability System

Effective establishment of the accountability system for corporations consists of several key components to ensure a robust corporate governance structure that defines the roles and responsibilities of all corporate governance participants. This accountability system enables compliance with applicable laws, rules, and regulations, transparency in corporate disclosures, sustainable performance, and ethical conduct. The key components of an effective accountability system are:

- The properly defined corporate mission of profit-with-purpose ensures the achievement of financial performance in generating the desired rate of return for shareholders while creating shared value for other stakeholders (described in Chapter 3).

Accountability System

- Robust and comprehensive corporate governance structures that clearly define roles and responsibilities for all corporate governance participants, including the board of directors, executives, investors, regulators, and employees (presented in Chapter 4).

- Reliable, relevant, and transparent corporate disclosures of both financial economic sustainability performance (ESP) and nonfinancial environmental, social, and governance (ESG) sustainability performance provide stakeholders, including shareholders, creditors, employees, customers, suppliers, society, and regulators, with accurate and timely information about the company's ESP and ESG sustainability performance, risks, and governance practices (presented in Chapters 7, 8, 9, and 11).

- Sound corporate culture and a code of conduct and ethics that promote competent and ethical behavior throughout the company by specifying the company's culture, values, principles, and expected behavior for all corporate governance participants, including directors, executives, and employees (presented in Chapter 8).

  - An effective and efficient internal control system assesses and manages financial and nonfinancial risks to safeguard assets; ensure operational effectiveness, reliability, completeness, and accuracy of ESP and ESG reports; prevent fraud; and ensure compliance with all applicable laws, rules, regulations, standards, and best practices (presented in Chapter 9).

  - Independent external audits to audit financial statements relevant to ESP performance and assurance statements applicable to ESG sustainability performance and reports (presented in Chapter 11).

  - Continuous improvement of ongoing assessment and improvement of both ESP and ESG key performance indicators (KPIs) that are aligned with the company's mission, strategic objectives, and ethical standards fosters a culture of continuous improvement and accountability throughout the company (described in Chapter 12).

  - Stakeholder engagement involves establishing constructive interaction with all stakeholders, including shareholders, customers, employees, suppliers, creditors, communities, society, and the environment. This engagement aims to understand their insights, issues, challenges, and concerns, gather feedback, address issues proactively, and turn challenges into opportunities (presented in Chapter 4).

The above key components of the corporate accountability system enable corporations to integrate these components into their corporate governance structure and build a strong culture of accountability that promotes integrity, competency, compliance, and responsible business practices in achieving ESP and ESG sustainability performance. As depicted in Exhibit 1.1, corporations in the United States are viewed as creators of sustainable economic value. Public companies have a set of contractual relationships with a broad range of stakeholders, including shareholders, creditors, suppliers, customers, employees, governmental agencies, auditors, global communities, society, and the environment. Corporations are viewed as having a nexus of contracts with their stakeholders that have a stake in their companies and take risks. Stakeholders and contracting participants pursue their own goals and continue their relationships and interactions with the company only as long as there is a mutual interest, and the company creates shared value for them. Society in general, and the government in particular, creates an environment in which corporations are able to fulfill their fiduciary duties to their stakeholders, as well as their social responsibilities and tax obligations.

All stakeholders are provided with incentives and opportunities to reward corporations for good performance and discipline them for poor performance. For example, suppliers and customers reward good corporate performance by actively and favorably doing business with a company and discipline a company by restricting business with it in the case of corporate failures. Investors, including lenders and shareholders, reward good performance by investing in the company at a lower-than-desired rate of return on investment (cost of capital) and discipline poor corporate performance by disinvesting or demanding a higher rate of return on their investment. Employees provide human capital and skills and are expected to receive fair compensation. Thus, the role and responsibilities of each group of stakeholders are defined by a set of laws, rules, regulations, standards, norms, and commonly accepted business practices and contracts.

Public companies are vital to the nation's economic growth and prosperity. The sustainable performance of public companies depends on the willingness of investors to invest in them. Such willingness has been undermined by a loss of confidence in corporations and their directors and officers to look after the interests of investors. Public companies rely on public sources of funding through issuing stocks, as opposed to private funding from banks or select groups of investors. For this open financial system to function effectively, there should be an appropriate system of checks and balances, namely an effective corporate governance structure. The separation of ownership and control in the open financial system can result in the so-called agency problem, in which management's interests are not aligned with those of shareholders or where management withholds important information from shareholders (information asymmetry). Under an open system, shareholders invest in a corporation and elect the board of directors, which then hires management to run the corporation for the benefit of its owners.

Shareholders are responsible for providing needed capital to facilitate the effective operation of a company and have a right to elect their representatives: the company's board of

Accountability System

directors. The board of directors is authorized to make decisions on behalf of shareholders and is directly responsible for selecting and continuously monitoring management's decisions and actions without micromanaging. Management is authorized to run the company and is responsible and accountable for decisions made and actions taken, with the primary purpose of creating and enhancing sustainable shareholder value. Corporate governance provides the opportunity for shareholders to monitor the company's board of directors and enables the board to monitor management and facilitate management's decision-making process, which creates shareholder value. Corporate governance should create an appropriate balance of power-sharing that:

- Provides shareholder democracy in freely electing directors (e.g., the majority voting system).
- Enables the board of directors to make strategic decisions and oversee and consult with management without micromanaging.
- Empowers management to run the company for the benefit of its shareholders.

The separation of ownership and control in the modern corporate structure, the diffuse nature of ownership, and the focus on protecting the interests of a wide range of stakeholders (investors, creditors, employees, suppliers, customers, government, society, and the environment, among others) necessitate the need for an effective corporate governance structure that addresses, manages, and minimizes potential conflicts of interest among corporate governance participants. These conflicts of interest are commonly referred to as agency problems resulting from differences in incentives and goals of corporate governance participants, as well as information asymmetry among those participants. The primary goal of corporate governance is not simply to reduce agency costs, but to create an equitable balance of power and access to relevant information among all corporate governance participants, particularly shareholders, directors, and management. Recent financial scandals have raised serious concerns about how this balance is being managed and who is watching over the companies to ensure that shareholders' interests are being protected.

The management team – consisting of the chief executive officer (CEO), the chief financial officer (CFO), the controller, the treasurer, and other top executives – is appointed by the board of directors to work in the best interests of shareholders. However, information asymmetry can exist between management and investors regarding long-term strategic decisions, performance, and disclosures. Management has incentives to focus on short-term planning and performance, which can be detrimental to long-term and sustainable performance. Management may also be motivated to withhold damaging bad news from investors. This perceived information asymmetry can be minimized when management provides:

- Disclosure goes beyond mere compliance with regulatory requirements of annual financial reports and includes more corporate disclosures of both financial performance and nonfinancial environmental, social, and governance information (e.g., by adding to public information or presenting additional context for existing disclosures).
- Contextualized disclosures that enable investors to assess publicly disclosed financial ESP and nonfinancial ESG sustainability performance.
- Integrated reports on economic and financial sustainability performance information and nonfinancial environmental, social, ethical, and governance sustainability performance information.
- Forward-looking and futuristic disclosures for both financial and nonfinancial information.

Traditionally, public companies in the United States have operated under the corporate model known as "shareholder primacy." This corporate governance model posits that the primary purpose of a corporation is to generate returns for shareholders, and thus, managerial decisions and actions should be focused on creating shareholder value with the primary fiduciary duties to shareholders. This shareholder primacy model has served investors well in maximizing wealth for them but is being criticized for focusing on generating short-term profits at the expense of long-term sustainability, performance, innovation, growth, and not considering the social and environmental impacts of corporations. The focus on shareholder wealth creation may not benefit other stakeholders, such as employees, customers, creditors, suppliers, government, society, and the environment. Companies are given rights to operate and generate profits for their shareholders, but with these rights come public interests and societal responsibilities. The current corporate governance rules and measures do not guarantee that public companies advance the public interest and have social and environmental impacts in addition to financial consequences.

Corporations as legal entities are incorporated under state law with many privileges, enabling them to raise public capital and create wealth for their owners. However, in recent years, there has been a movement worldwide toward the stakeholder primacy model of corporations and related corporate governance measures intended to rebalance power among stakeholders fundamentally. The stakeholder primacy model holds that public companies should focus on corporate purposes beyond shareholder value and thus maintains that corporate governance measures and corporate decision-making should also consider every stakeholder who provides capital (including financial, operational, human, societal,

Accountability System

and environmental) and contributes to corporate success. This suggests that corporations, in the long term, must not only secure financial returns for shareholders but must also make a positive contribution to society and the environment. Business sustainability models of "Shareholder Primacy and Stakeholder Primacy, Shareholder Governance, and Stakeholder Governance" are described in detail in Chapter 4.

Several initiatives have been undertaken in moving away from the shareholder primacy model and toward the stakeholder primacy model under this new corporate governance structure, including:[6]

1. The board's fiduciary duty should be extended to all stakeholders, and the board of directors should be accountable to all stakeholders, not just shareholders.
2. Corporate purpose statements should focus on the profit-with-purpose mission (described in Chapter 3) by specifically stating that corporations positively benefit society in the context of creating shared value for all stakeholders.
3. The fiduciary duties of the board of directors should have been extended to all stakeholders, including shareholders.
4. Multiple stakeholders, including employees, should be represented on corporate boards.
5. Large corporations should be required to be organized under federal charters to facilitate governance reform accountability that requires responsibility to all stakeholders.
6. Management should be a steward of all corporate capital, including financial, human, social, reputational, strategic, compliance, and environmental, among others described in Chapter 10.

Corporate Challenges and Opportunities

In recent years, public companies worldwide have experienced a wide range of challenges that affect their operations, sustainability, and existence. These challenges include greater market volatility, increasing political, economic, and geopolitical uncertainty, artificial intelligence, social media, disruptive technologies, and cybersecurity incidents. Corporate challenges can vary depending on the corporate culture and business environment, including the industry, size of the company, and market conditions, among others. Some of the important challenges that corporations worldwide face that can be turned into opportunities are:

● Financial stability and viability are essential to ensure that fluctuations in interest rates, currency exchange rates, commodity prices, and stock market performance do not adversely affect corporate earnings, strategic plans, investment decisions, and financial stability.

- Sustainability performance focuses on the achievement of both financial ESP and nonfinancial ESG in generating a desired return on investment for shareholders and having social and environmental impacts.
- Regulatory compliance involves adhering to all applicable laws, rules, and regulations locally, nationally, and internationally.
- Technological advances include the use of artificial intelligence (AI) and related cyber-security measures to safeguard sensitive data and intellectual property from cyber threats such as data breaches, ransomware attacks, and phishing scams.
- Globalization provides both challenges and opportunities for operating in multiple countries or regions that may trigger complexities related to cultural differences, market infrastructure, legal frameworks, supply chain management, new market entrants, changing consumer preferences, and geopolitical events.
- Global supply chain disruptions triggered by factors such as trade disputes, natural disasters, supplier bankruptcies, and geopolitical tensions can impact production schedules, business sustainability, product availability, and costs.
- Creation of a unique brand and a positive corporate reputation and public perception of having social and environmental impacts.
- Attraction and retention of talent, reputation, human capital, and management of the ability to recruit, retain, and develop the human capital of skilled management and employees.

Identification of these challenges and turning them into opportunities often requires comprehensive and robust strategic planning, operational efficiency, risk assessment and management, investment in technology and talent improvements, stakeholder engagement, and a commitment to ethical and responsible business practices. These challenges should provide incentives for corporations to seek various opportunities for growth, innovation, and success. The important opportunities for corporations in this competitive, global, and technological environment are:

- Redefining their business goals with the profit-with-purpose mission of creating shared value for all stakeholders.
- Refocusing on business sustainability initiatives to create shared value for all stakeholders by generating ESP performance to achieve financial performance while having social and environmental impacts.

Corporate Challenges and Opportunities

- Utilizing technological advancements, including the use of artificial intelligence, Internet of Things (IoT), blockchain, and automation, to improve operational efficiency, drive innovation, and enhance customer reputation and experiences, as well as embrace e-commerce platforms and digital marketing strategies.

- Using data analytics and data science to make data-driven decisions can provide valuable insights into customer preferences, behavior, market trends, and operational efficiencies.

- Creating diversity in terms of product expertise and investing in employee training and talent development.

- Taking advantage of government incentives and regulations relevant to tax breaks, grants, and favorable regulatory environments can stimulate investment and innovation in certain industries or regions.

- Identifying and capitalizing on any emerging opportunities that can drive sustainable growth and performance, maintain competitiveness, and create long-term shared value for all stakeholders, including shareholders, employees, customers, suppliers, and communities.

Public companies in the United States have also been affected by the divided government, which reflects deep societal schisms and could impact the environment in which companies and their boards and executives operate. Public companies in the United Kingdom have also been impacted by the uncertainty surrounding Brexit, while public companies in Europe are dealing with economic downturns and hyperinflation. Thus, public companies face not only the traditional challenges relevant to financial performance, earnings growth, and investor relations, but also the emerging challenges of stakeholder issues, which run from environmental and social governance matters to long-term sustainability, global warming, climate change, the depletion of natural resources, water management, use of plastics, human capital management, gender pay equity, political and lobbying spending, the opioid crisis, diversity, gun control, and social media madness. These emerging issues impact the role of businesses, including corporations, in society. These issues – from climate change to political, societal, and environmental concerns – affect the risks facing corporations, as described in detail in Chapter 9. Ever-increasing risks cause investors to seek to understand the company's purpose, mission, and business strategy better to assess, manage, and mitigate these risks. Corporate purpose must be defined, strategic plans must be determined, and measures and processes must be established to implement strategic plans as described in Chapter 2. The composition and qualifications of the board of directors in terms of education, experience, skills, diversity, and business views and insights will be essential in overseeing the effective execution of strategy by management. This book focuses on the importance of the corporation of the future that can make capitalism sustainable by establishing and implementing corporate governance measures and reforms that promote the mission of profit-with-purpose described in Chapter 3, an alignment of corporate conduct with social purpose, ensuring that companies' strategic plans and their governance, measurement, and incentive systems as related to the environment, culture, ownership, and other social issues. The future of the corporation will focus on aligning corporate goals with social interests, an approach promoted by the British Academy, the United Kingdom's national body for the social sciences and the humanities.[7] In moving toward the implementation of this concept of profit-with-purpose of the future of the corporation, business organizations should (1) define their purpose with the goal of aligning the maximization of shareholder value with social and environmental purpose, (2) focus on fiduciary duties and commitments to all stakeholders, (3) design corporate governance mechanisms and measures to protect the interests of all stakeholders, and (4) disclose their accountability with respect to ownership, governance, and social and environmental performance measurements in achieving their stated purposes. This view of the corporation, based on the stakeholder primacy model rather than the shareholder primacy model presented in Chapter 4, promotes the main goal of creating shared value for all stakeholders rather than merely maximizing shareholder wealth.

The goal of companies has evolved from profit maximization to shareholder wealth enhancement, to the creation of shared value for all stakeholders. For many years, the focus on profit maximization for shareholders worked in US financial markets. Globalization and the rise of China, technological advances, and often disruption have forced corporations to focus on the short-termism of meeting or beating analysts' forecast expectations. However, corporations are now facing pressures from social activists and stakeholders to pay attention to the interests of customers, suppliers, employees, society, and the environment, among others, to create shared value for all stakeholders. Prioritization of shareholder wealth maximization has contributed to wealth inequity and populism in the nation to the extent that the nature, extent, and value of capitalism are being questioned. Policymakers and regulators worldwide also promote the move toward a more balanced-purpose model for public companies.

The three major index fund managers have criticized the short-term focus of many public companies on shareholder wealth maximization and promoted the long-term sustainable performance of shared value creation for all stakeholders. In 2019, managers of three major index funds, owning about 15% of the shares of publicly listed companies in the United States, sent an open letter to CEOs of major corporations demanding that corporations specify their purpose regarding profit and social impacts. For example, the statement

Corporate Challenges and Opportunities

by Larry Fink, the CEO of BlackRock, suggests that public and private companies should have a purpose beyond the focus on shareholder wealth maximization and have some social and environmental impacts.[8] In its letter to board members, State Street also promotes long-term investment value through achieving both financial and nonfinancial ESG performance objectives.[9]

The definition of corporate purpose is an emerging topic of discussion, suggesting that corporations should consider their financial, social, and environmental impacts. Under corporate law and in accordance with the shareholder theory, it has been well-defined and commonly accepted that shareholders are the owners of the firm and that the board of directors and management have a fiduciary duty to act in their best interests.[10] Historically, the primary goal of corporations has been to maximize profit and increase shareholder wealth. In the past decade, many firms (over 15,000 globally) that voluntarily focus on both profit-seeking and social missions have emerged. Called "social enterprises" or "hybrid corporations" (HCs), these entities pursue performance in all five EGSEE dimensions of sustainability performance. Recently, "benefit corporations" (BCs) have been chartered as legal entities by legislation in 21 states, including by the General Corporation Law in Delaware, which authorized the formation of public BCs on August 1, 2013.[11] Legally, BCs are for-profit entities incorporated as conventional corporations (CCs) under state law that have also chosen to adopt other ESG missions in their articles of incorporation. BCs are intended to minimize the conflicts between corporations and society caused by differences between private and social costs and benefits, as well as to align corporate goals with those of society under both the state corporate model and benefit statute. Examples of conflicts between corporations and society are related to environmental issues (pollution, acid rain, and global warming), wages paid by multinational corporations in poor countries, and child labor in developing countries. In pursuing their mission of protecting the interests of all stakeholders, BCs can raise companies' awareness of the social costs and benefits of their business activities. The major characteristics of the BC structure are (1) a requirement that a BC has the corporate purpose of creating a materially positive impact on society and the environment, (2) an expansion of the duties of directors to require the consideration of nonfinancial stakeholders as well as the financial interests of shareholders, and (3) an obligation to report on the overall social and environmental performance of the BC using a comprehensive, credible, independent, and transparent third-party standard.

Several benefits of BCs are the ability to (1) gain attention and market share from socially conscious investors, (2) use the power of business and resources to solve social and environmental challenges; (3) spur more trust in businesses by the public, shareholders, and potential employees, and attract more customers to a company's brands and products; (4)

improve business, operational, and investment efficacy; (5) assess, manage, and minimize strategic, operational, financial, reputational, and compliance risks; and (6) focus on human capital as the company's most significant asset. These benefits can improve the financial and nonfinancial performance of BCs, as reflected in their financial reporting quality, cost of capital, and firm value. The BC structure is administered on a state-by-state basis, with the state's BC statutes placed within existing state corporation codes. The justification for BCs is that existing law does not hold boards of directors fiduciarily responsible to stakeholders from considering the impact of corporate decisions on other stakeholders, the environment, or society at large. Thus, boards of directors of BCs are required to consider the impact of their decisions on specific corporate constituencies, including shareholders, employees, suppliers, and the community, as well as on the local and global environment. In the past several years, 35 states, including New York, New Jersey, California, Louisiana, Maryland, Vermont, Virginia, South Carolina, and Hawaii, have enacted laws allowing for the creation of BCs for businesses that wish to pursue profit and benefit society simulta-neously.[12] Delaware's General Corporation Law (1) allows entrepreneurs and investors to create for-profit corporations that are charged with promoting public benefits; (2) modifies the fiduciary duties of directors of BCs by requiring them to balance public benefits with the economic interests of shareholders; and (3) requires BCs to report to their shareholders with respect to the advancement of public benefits and/or other benefits to stakeholders.

Public companies are being criticized for focusing primarily on profit maximization (and thus shareholder value creation) with minimal attention to the impacts of their operations on society and the environment.[13] As corporate sustainability has gained more attention and has been integrated into the business culture and model, there has been a shift in empha-sis from the creation of shareholder value to the development of "sustainable shared value creation" to protect the interests of all stakeholders.[14] "Shared value" is defined as "poli-cies and practices that enhance the competitiveness of a company while simultaneously advancing the economic and social conditions in the communities in which it operates."[15] Under a shared value creation approach, management focuses on the continuous perfor-mance improvement of business operations in generating long-term value while maxi-mizing the positive impacts of operations on society and the environment by measuring sustainable performance in terms of both ESP (economic sustainability performance) and ESG (environmental, social and governance) sustainability performance. Thus, corporate objectives have advanced from profit maximization to increasing shareholder wealth, and now to creating shared value for all stakeholders.

Business sustainability requires business organizations to expand their mission to not only generate profit and create shareholder value but also ensure shared value for all

Corporate Challenges and Opportunities

stakeholders. The concept of shared value challenges the way we think about profits, philanthropy, sustainability, and development. Sustainable shared value creation enables business organizations to integrate financial ESP and nonfinancial ESG objectives into the corporate culture and environment. Porter and Kramer define the concept of shared value as "policies and operating practices that enhance the competitiveness of a company while simultaneously advancing the economic and social conditions in the communities in which it operates."[16] This definition suggests that shared value initiatives can be created in three ways: (1) producing products and services that increase shareholder wealth and meet societal needs, including improved nutrition, education, health, and general well-being; (2) redefining productivity in the supply chain by investing in training and resources to create high-quality suppliers and improve ESP and ESG sustainability performance; and (3) developing material indicator taxonomies to effectively measure the revenue, costs, and value of organizations.

Corporate Stakeholders

Corporate stakeholders are those individuals or groups that often provide capital to a company (financial, human, reputational, societal, environmental, among others presented in Chapter 10) and have an interest or stake in the activities and performance of a corporation (presented in Chapters 7 and 8) and take risks associated with the activities and affairs of a company (presented in Chapter 9). Business sustainability is a relatively broad concept related to the benefits of internal and external stakeholders. These stakeholders are those who have vested interests in a firm through their investments in the form of financial capital (shareholders), human capital (employees), physical capital (customers and suppliers), social capital (society), environmental capital (ecological), and regulatory capital (government). Stakeholders have a reciprocal relationship and interaction with a firm in the sense that they contribute to the firm's value creation, and in return, their well-being is also affected by the firm. Sustainability planning involves developing goals, strategies, and practices to establish the right balance between "shareholder value maximization," where management attempts to improve earnings for shareholders, and the broader "stakeholder/ society value creation," where management maximizes the sum of the various stakeholders' surpluses (e.g., creditors, employees, customers, suppliers, society, and the environment) in creating shared value for all stakeholders. All stakeholders are provided with incentives and opportunities to reward corporations for good performance and discipline them for poor performance. For example, suppliers and customers reward good corporate performance by actively and favorably doing business with a company and discipline a company by restricting business with it. Lenders and investors reward good performance by investing in a company at a lower-than-desired rate of return of investment (cost of capital) and discipline poor corporate performance by disinvesting or demanding a higher rate of return on their investment. The ten types of stakeholders are shareholders, creditors, employees, customers, suppliers, government, society/communities, competitors, NGOs and activist groups, and trade unions, as described in the next section. Thus, the role and responsibilities of each group of stakeholders are defined by a set of rules, laws, norms, standards, and commonly accepted business practices and contracts.

The rash of financial scandals at the turn of the 21st century and the 2007–2009 global financial crisis raised serious concerns about public companies' corporate governance, sustainability, and quality of financial disclosures. It contributed to the erosion of investor confidence in public company financial disclosures, raising relevant questions about whether companies are achieving their goal of creating sustainable shareholder value and how public company performance can be improved. The primary mission of public companies is regarded as creating shared value for all stakeholders, and the corporate governance structure is designed to ensure the accomplishment of this mission. The mission of corporate governance can be further classified into two goals: value creation and value protection. The value creation goal of corporate governance focuses on shareholder value creation and enhancement through the development of long-term strategies to ensure sustainable and enduring operational performance. The value protection goal concentrates on the accountability of the way the company is managed and monitored to protect the interests of shareholders and other stakeholders.

The concept of stakeholder capitalism has emerged in recent years in response to the emerging transformation of business, society, and governments.[17] The emerging move toward a profit-with-purpose business mission, ESG sustainability, and growing interest by a diverse group of market participants, including index funds and financial institutions, for creating long-term shared value for all stakeholders has resulted in a move toward business sustainability. There is a general move toward stakeholder capitalism, which creates long-term sustainable shared value for all stakeholders, from shareholders to creditors, employees, customers, suppliers, regulators, society, and the environment. Public companies, their board of directors, and executives can communicate the commitment to sustainability in creating shared value for stakeholders through integrated sustainability reporting, focusing on measuring and disclosing both financial ESP and nonfinancial ESG sustainability performance as presented in Chapter 4.

Corporate stakeholders are classified into ten layers/types, as depicted in Exhibit 1.2, and are categorized into three general tiers. The primary objective of any business organization is to achieve financial performance by creating shareholder value. Within this objective framework, companies that conduct their business ethically, have effective corporate

Corporate Stakeholders

EXHIBIT 1.2 Exhibit 1.2 contains ten layers/types of stakeholders.

governance, and pay attention to the well-being of society and the environment can be expected to be more sustainable and generate enduring financial performance. As corporate sustainability has gained more attention and has become integrated into business culture, there has been a shift in focus from the creation of shareholder value to the development of "sustainable shared value creation" to protect the interests of all stakeholders.[18] Under the shared value creation approach, management focuses on the continuous performance improvement of business operations in generating long-term value while maximizing the positive impacts of operations on society and the environment by measuring sustainable performance in terms of both ESP and ESG sustainability performance. Corporate stakeholders can be further classified into several tiers according to their extent of their interest, influence, and involvement in the decision-making, operations, and performance of a company. The following three tiers are described in the following sections.

The First Tier: Shareholders

The first tier of the stakeholder hierarchy is composed of shareholders who own a company. Shareholders are the primary stakeholders; without them, the company would not exist. Shareholders are individuals, entities, or financial institutions that own shares, provide financial capital, or have invested in the company. They are interested in and concerned with the financial performance and return on their investment. Many argue that the primary purpose of a company is to maximize shareholder wealth. Thus, the company's corporate governance structure should reduce agency costs, which are generated from the separation of ownership and control, by aligning the interests of management and shareholders. Shareholders provide capital to the company in return for a sustainable return on their investment in terms of periodic dividends and stock price appreciation. Payment of dividends reduces the amount of discretionary funds available to management and thus can be used as a deterrent to opportunistic managerial behavior and as a vehicle for controlling management actions. Shareholders participate and shape the company's corporate governance structure by exercising their voting rights to elect the members of the board of directors who are directly responsible for protecting their interests and are ultimately accountable to them for the company's business affairs.

Corporations are owned by shareholders who have a variety of risk and return preferences. Owners can be individual investors, institutional investors, banks, pension funds, industrial companies, and other entities. Conceptually, institutional investors represent small shareholders as pensioners or beneficiaries. To ensure that institutional investors effectively protect the interests of their beneficiaries or trustees, they should disclose their corporate governance and voting policies, as well as potential conflicts of interest and how they manage them. These owners have different identities, strategic interests, financial interests, and time horizons. Financial interest derives from the investor's motivation to obtain a desired return on investment, which can be achieved by either receiving dividends from the company's profits or the realization of capital gains through stock price appreciation. Institutional and individual investors are typically motivated by the maximization of financial return and exercise control through a shareholder voting process. Strategic interests are often motivated by nonfinancial objectives and are associated with attempts to exert control over a company via ownership stakes. Strategic interests can be pursued to secure markets, underwrite relational contracts, manage technological dependence, protect managerial autonomy, and regulate competition between firms.

Liquidity is another factor considered by investors when they invest in a company. Liquidity relates to investors' ability to sell their shares in a relatively short time without a reduction in price or substantial cost. The liquidity preference of investors may result in a diversified portfolio, fragmented shareholders, and stable capital markets that allow for exit without negatively affecting share prices. Ownership by individual and institutional investors is often motivated by financial interests and high liquidity, whereas ownership by

Corporate Stakeholders

governments, banks, and industrial corporations is typically focused on highly committed stocks with sustainable strategic interests.

Corporate governance and reforms, including state and federal laws, are aimed at protecting shareholder rights by allowing shareholders to (1) inspect and copy the company's stock ledgers, its list of shareholders, and certain books and records; (2) approve certain business transactions (e.g., mergers and acquisitions); (3) receive proxy materials; and (4) obtain significant disclosures for related-party transactions. Shareholder democracy, empowering shareholders to nominate, elect, or remove directors, has been extensively debated. Under the current plurality voting system of uncontested director elections, even a single vote for a nominee will elect that director to a board regardless of the number of withholding votes. The majority voting system, which requires a director who received a majority of "against" or "withhold" votes to resign, has received a great deal of attention. Despite its many legal concerns and complications (e.g., plurality voting is allowed under state law, while majority voting is not), the majority voting system is supported by many institutional investors and investor activists. A modified version of majority voting, better known as "majority voting lite" or "Pfizer majority voting," has been suggested. Under a majority voting lite system, directors who receive a majority of "against" or "withhold" votes are required to submit their resignation to the board. The company's board of directors then decides whether to accept the resignation and, if it does, appoints its candidate.

The Council of Institutional Investors (CII) recommends the following shareholder voting rights:[19]

- *Access to the proxy.* Companies should provide access to management proxy material for long-term investors (those owning shares for at least three years or a group of long-term investors owning in aggregate at least 5% of a company's voting shares) to nominate less than a majority of directors.
- *Voting Rights (One share, one vote).* Each share of common stock should have one vote. Companies should allow one vote for each share of their common stock and eliminate disparate voting rights for certain classes of common stock. The company's board should not issue authorized common stock with unequal voting rights without shareholder approval.
- *Confidential voting.* Companies shall have confidential policies and practices for proxy vote casting, counting, and verifying. All proxy votes should be confidential.
- *Voting requirements.* Supermajority votes should not be required in any circumstances. A majority vote should be adequate for amending the company's bylaws or for taking other actions requiring a shareholder vote. A majority vote of outstanding common

shares should be required to approve (1) major corporate decisions concerning a sale or pledge of the company's assets whose value exceeds 10% of the total consolidated assets; (2) the acquisition of 5% or more of the company's common shares at above-market prices, except for tender offers to all shareholders; (3) poison pills; (4) abridging or limiting the rights of common shares to take a variety of actions (e.g., election or removal of directors, nominations of directors, and a call for special meetings); and (5) decisions for the issuance of debt to the extent that it would excessively leverage the company.

- *Broker votes.* Broker nonvotes and abstentions should only be counted for a quorum.
- *Bundled voting.* Companies should permit shareholders to vote on unrelated issues separately, and no bundled voting should be permitted for actions concerning amendment of the company's charter, bylaws, or antitakeover provisions.

The Second Tier: Creditors

The two most common methods by which corporations finance investments are equity financing – where companies issue shares of stock in a public offering, and shareholders expect a desired rate of return on their investment – and debt financing – where companies raise money by borrowing or selling debt instruments, and creditors receive interest returns. A third way of financing is through internal growth and reinvestment. Lenders and creditors are the second tier of stakeholders in a company. Creditors are individuals or entities that have provided loans or credit to the company, and they are concerned with the company's ability to repay its debts and maintain financial stability. The typical ownership structure of a public company usually consists of three distinct components: debt securities held by creditors, internal equity securities held by directors and officers, and external equity held by shareholders. Debt and equity securities may not only have different impacts on the value of a company but also on the company's corporate governance structure. Total corporate debt in the United States has reached $9 trillion, which could cause financial challenges for many companies if interest rates continue to rise, and the economy continues to weaken.[20]

The proportion of debt equities to the total capital of a company will determine the extent of the financial capital financed by debtholders and their concerns that management may be motivated to maximize shareholder wealth at the expense of debtholders. It will also determine the agency costs assumed by debtholders and their demand for monitoring.[21] Thus, debtholders demand some control over managerial actions by entering into debt covenant contracts designed to protect their interests and determine whether breaches of contractual provisions have occurred.

Corporate Stakeholders

The extent to which an organization derives its funding from equity or debt may signifi-cantly affect the company's business decisions. For example, the United States and the UK rely on shareholder funding, while in Germany, a company derives a significant portion of its capital from creditors. As a result, companies in the United States and the United Kingdom tend to favor their shareholders, and those in Germany tend to favor creditors. Since creditors tend to be more conservative in weighing business risk (shareholders are usually more likely to encourage business decisions that will result in large capital gains, while creditors do not benefit from such gains), companies largely funded by creditors often choose to minimize risk instead of maximizing wealth.[22]

Debt financing has been more common than equity financing in recent years because of relatively low interest rates. Corporate governance measures are intended to protect the interests of all stakeholders, particularly the suppliers of finance (shareholders and credi-tors). Thus, bondholders and other creditors have the incentives and ability to monitor public companies through their engagement in corporate governance. Traditionally, credi-tors have played a passive role and have gotten involved with corporate governance only when a company violates the terms of the loan contract or misses a payment. Recently, creditors such as banks, institutional creditors, and underwriters of syndicated loans have played a more active role in corporate governance by influencing companies' borrowing, credit agreements and risk management to prevent a payment default or covenant viola-tion. Creditors can exercise control over the company when it encounters financial chal-lenges by insisting on elaborate covenants. Academic research suggests that companies in violation of a covenant often become more conservative in their financial and investment policies and practices, change senior management, and improve performance.[23]

The Third Tier: Others

Business organizations are now realizing that their stakeholders consist of more than just holders of corporate debt and equity. Stakeholders are now identified as those who have a stake in an organization and influence, or are influenced by, either directly or indirectly, organizational activities. Examples of these stakeholders are employees, suppliers, cus-tomers, society, the government, and competitors. Many companies today are reaching out to these stakeholders to overcome various challenges, such as improving customer perception and reputation, satisfying employees, entering viable markets, and resolving conflicts with stakeholder activists. Communication with all stakeholders of the organiza-tion is central to improving decision-making processes, strengthening relationships, gath-ering important information, and building an accord among dissimilar views.[24]

Stakeholders can influence corporate governance in many ways by providing human, social, and environmental capital. Corporations are increasingly under pressure from their stakeholders to integrate economic, social, and environmental sustainability into their managerial strategies and corporate governance framework. Stakeholders have a reciprocal relationship and interaction with a company in the sense that they contribute to the firm's value creation and that their well-being is affected by the firm's performance. Stakeholders other than shareholders and creditors that are considered as investors are: (1) employees, who are essential stakeholders providing human capital and employment skills that contribute to the company's success through their work in return for fair compensation and other benefits, as well as job security and a positive work environment; (2) customers, who are important stakeholders purchasing goods or services from the company and are concerned with product quality, pricing, customer service, and overall satisfaction with the company's products and services; (3) suppliers, who provide the raw materials, components, or services necessary for the company's operations and are concerned with timely payments, fair treatment, and long-term engagement with the company; (4) government agencies, which regulate businesses and collect taxes from them to provide public services and public welfare and a framework to generate sustainable performance; (5) the society and communities in which the company operates, which are important stakeholders interested in the company's impacts on society, the local economy, and the environment; (6) non-governmental organizations (NGOs) and activist groups, which are becoming vital stakeholders often advocate for specific causes or interests and impacting public opinion and government policies that affect the company's strategic decisions, activities, and performance; (7) trade unions, which can become stakeholders if the company's workforce is unionized in protecting employees' fair wages, working conditions, and labor rights; and (8) competitors, who are important stakeholders interested in the company's activities and performance including market share, competitive advantages, and pricing strategies. Effective corporate governance measures and sustainable initiatives can enable these stakeholders to work toward the achievement of the company's mission and ensure the long-term success, growth, and sustainability of the company.

Governance performance reflects the effectiveness of corporate governance measures in managing the company to achieve its objectives of creating shareholder value and protecting the interests of other stakeholders. Maintaining a good business reputation and meeting the expectations of stakeholders – from investors to creditors, suppliers, customers, employees, the environment, and society – is a major challenge for many businesses. The focus of corporations in our society has evolved from profit maximization to creating shareholder value to (in recent years) protecting the interests of all stakeholders. Corporate

Corporate Stakeholders

governance measures should recognize this emerging role and the rights of stakeholders as they are established through mutual agreements or by law. Corporate governance measures that enable employees to serve on the board of directors, promote diversity and customer satisfaction, and engage in social and environmental matters can encourage cooperation between companies and their stakeholders, which will create shared value for all stakeholders.

Corporate stakeholder tiers can be classified into primary stakeholders, secondary stakeholders, and tertiary stakeholders based on their stake and risk as well as the extent of influence, involvement, and interest in the decisions, operations, and performance of a company. The primary stakeholders are those individuals or groups directly affected by the company's decisions, actions, and performance and usually have substantial financial or operational interests in the company, such as shareholders, creditors, employees, customers, and suppliers. Investors, as primary stakeholders, prefer long-term, sustainable, and forward-looking financial and nonfinancial information on the company's strategy and performance. Public companies should provide investors with the company's mission, purpose, core drivers of growth and competitive advantages, long-term objectives, and the strategic plan for achieving them, as well as priorities for capital allocation and investment. The strategic plan should be used as a guideline to frame discussions of critical risk factors that could impact strategy and objectives related to core business drivers. KPIs relevant to operational and financial goals should be tied to the company's core drivers of growth. KPIs should be developed to achieve the company's objectives and cover short-term, medium-term, and long-term goals. To improve investor confidence and encourage them to focus on long-term investment strategy, BlackRock released a report describing its stewardship approach to engagement on long-term strategy, purpose, and culture in January 2019. The BlackRock report suggests that while the majority of investors focus on long-term investment strategies, many executives of public companies still press for the achievement of strong financial performance within two years or less. Sustainable performance and long-term investment with the purpose of creating shared value for all stakeholders enable business organizations of all types (public and private) and sizes (large, medium, and small) to succeed and build business and investor confidence. A managerial strategy that focuses on purpose and profit enables improved financial performance that enhances investor confidence. Purpose and profits are linked in the sense that purpose unifies the efforts of all corporate governance participants (directors, executives, employees, and investors) in achieving long-term performance that creates profits and, thus, shared value for all stakeholders. Strategy, purpose, and culture should be integrated into corporate governance, and BlackRock suggests covering the following six areas:

1. What are the main drivers for how the company's strategic framework has evolved (investor demands, customer needs, industry dynamics, global megatrends, and availability of resources)?
2. How does the company define long-term strategy, and why is that time frame most relevant?
3. Does the board of directors oversee the development of strategy, purpose, and culture?
4. Has management developed and implemented strategy, purpose, and culture policies and procedures that are aligned with operational, financing, and investment strategies?
5. Are managerial strategies adequately communicated to shareholders when assessing their investment performance?
6. Are the interests of all stakeholders (shareholders, employees, customers, and suppliers) considered in the development of long-term strategy?

The secondary stakeholders are those individuals and groups that are indirectly affected by the company's decisions, actions, and performance without having a direct financial interest in the company, such as communities, governments, media, and trade unions. The last category includes tertiary stakeholders who have a very minimal direct association with the company, and they could be affected by the company's decisions, actions, and performance with minimal ability to affect the company's directions, such as environmental groups, competitors, industry affiliates, and future generations. The overall classifications of corporate stakeholders into either tier 1, 2, and 3 or primary, secondary, and tertiary enable public companies to set priorities for the allocation of resources, engagement efforts, and management of relationships, and consideration of the needs, concerns, and interests of different stakeholders effectively.

Global Financial Scandals and Crises

Public trust and investor confidence in the nation's economy and its capital markets are the key drivers of economic growth, prosperity, and financial stability. The effectiveness of regulations and market mechanisms in protecting investors and maintaining efficient, transparent, and competitive capital markets can be the best measure of investor confidence in the markets. The existence and persistence of global financial scandals create poor corporate cultures that negatively affect corporate governance and business sustainability, thus affecting investor confidence in the global financial markets. Potential global challenges are the potential collapse of global debt in the United States, Europe, and China, the long-term durability of the Eurozone, the effects of Brexit, and rising interest rates. Thus, global policymakers and regulators must assess and monitor these challenges and mitigate their risks. In September 2016, Wells Fargo was fined $185 million for illegally, and without customers' consent and knowledge, opening 2 million bank and credit card accounts.[25] The CEO was forced to step down, and about 5300 employees who opened the unwanted and unneeded bank and credit card accounts were fired. This suggests that Wells Fargo has a corporate culture problem whose solution goes beyond just firing employees, dismissing executives, and paying fines. Corporate culture sets an appropriate tone at the top by promoting integrity and competency throughout the company, which influences the behavior of employees and guides executive decisions. Wells Fargo set the wrong tone and instituted a bad culture by putting pressure on employees to achieve the "Great 8" goal of an average of eight financial products per household, a goal initiated by top executives, communicated to employees through middle managers and translated into policies, processes, and practices. Although bad practices can be stopped, culture assessment and management are essential for minimizing the risk of unethical, self-serving, and fraudulent behaviors and actions, as the corporate culture determines how a company conducts its business.

The 2007–2009 global financial crisis and resulting economic meltdown were caused by a variety of factors, including ineffective corporate governance and troubled financial institutions. The overriding causes and effects of the global financial crisis may never be determined. US regulatory responses were aimed at reforming and strengthening the resilience of financial systems, reducing the broader and systemic effects of bank failure, protecting investors and consumers, improving intergovernmental and cross-agency cooperation, and preventing further financial crises. Traditionally, two general approaches have been suggested to address global financial crises and their resulting economic meltdowns. The first solution is through global market mechanisms, by allowing shareholders to vote on a company's legal jurisdiction in a country that has better investor protection laws and more corporate governance. However, this approach ignores the differences in legal systems, politics, culture, and financial systems among countries. The second solution is to develop effective and enforceable global governance and regulatory reforms that hold companies worldwide accountable to their shareholders. The author advocates a hybrid approach of global market mechanisms in which investors can freely invest in global financial markets that provide a higher return on investment and better protection, along with global regulatory reforms that monitor and discipline the global capital markets.

Causes and Effects of the Global Financial Crisis

The existence and persistence of the 2007–2009 financial crisis in the United States and the resulting global economic meltdown is commonly viewed as the most serious since the

Great Depression. The global competitiveness of US capital markets depends to a significant extent on the reliability of financial information in assisting investors in making sound investment decisions, cost-effective regulation in protecting investors, and efficiency in attracting global investors and companies. The US free enterprise system has transformed from a system in which public companies (including banks and other financial institutions) are owned and controlled by small groups of investors to a system in which global investors own businesses. The United States has achieved this widespread participation by adopting sound regulations, maintaining high-quality disclosure standards, and initiating enforcement procedures that protect the interests of global investors. Recent financial regulatory reforms, including the Sarbanes-Oxley Act of 2002 (SOX)[26] and the Dodd-Frank Wall Street Reform and Consumer Protection Act of 2010 (DFA),[27] are intended to protect global investors and consumers from incurring excessive risks and obtaining materially misstated financial reports.

Financial challenges and imbalances worldwide exacerbated the 2007–2009 global financial crisis initiated in the United States and have affected the entire world's economy and financial markets for the past decade. The global financial crisis did not happen overnight and its effects will not disappear soon. It was caused by many factors, including the subprime crisis in the United States and substantial public borrowing by EU members (Spain, Portugal, and Greece), and thus requires regulatory responses and bold, coordinated actions on the part of governments, central banks, regulators, and the business community worldwide. There has been much debate on the overriding causes of the 2007–2009 global financial crisis. The consensus is that a combination of many macroeconomic and microeconomic factors, as well as governmental and regulatory decisions, contributed to the crisis. Other contributing factors are greedy and incompetent executives, the subprime mortgage crisis, government policies promoting home ownership, securitization of mortgage-backed assets, inadequate risk assessment of business transactions, and ineffective global regulation and supervision of banks, among others.

The recent financial crisis caused a global economic meltdown and affected all aspects of global business – from unemployment to home foreclosures, bank failures, and international budget deficits. The wave of financial scandals at the turn of the 21st century eroded investor confidence in corporate America and its financial reports. The US Congress responded by passing SOX to restore investor confidence. The persistence of financial scandals and the subsequent 2007–2009 global financial crisis encouraged Congress to pass the new Restoring American Financial Stability Act of 2010 (RAFS), better known as the Dodd-Frank Wall Street Reform and Consumer Protection Act of 2010, which was signed into law on July 21, 2010. SOX and DFA were intended to prevent further financial

Global Financial Scandals and Crises

crises and promote a corporate culture of honesty, integrity, and competency. The lesson from the 2007–2009 financial crisis is that cost-effective, efficient, enforceable, and scalable regulations are needed to create a framework within which businesses can generate sustainable performance while they are prevented from defrauding investors and consumers. Lessons learned from the financial crisis and corresponding regulatory reforms are:

- It is important to understand the global nature of business markets and economies and the urgent need for convergence in corporate governance reforms, including regulations.
- A better understanding of both the magnitude and nature of financial risks by policy-makers, regulators, banks, financial institutions, and corporations.
- There is a need to make regulatory reforms globally enforceable. There is continued support for instituting more global regulations, lessening deregulation, and moving toward the use of International Financial Reporting Standards (IFRS).
- There is a need to strengthen the transparency of financial markets through enhanced disclosure of complex financial products, changing corporate culture and board structures, improving accountability by ensuring proper risk assessment and enhancing sound, cost-effective, efficient, and scalable regulations, and ensuring that all financial markets, products, and participants are regulated or subject to effective oversight (e.g., regulatory oversight over credit rating agencies and mutual funds).
- The responsibility is to promote integrity in financial markets to protect investors, avoid conflicts of interest, and prevent illegal market manipulations, fraudulent activities, and abuse. Such integrity can be advanced through convergence in international regulations and related enforcements and by promoting corporate cultures of integrity, competency, sustainability, and ethical behavior.
- There is a need to hold financial institutions and banks accountable for their lending activities. The fact that Bank of America allegedly committed $16.65 billion to financial fraud (for which it reached a settlement in 2014 with the Department of Justice) suggests issues in lending activities.
- There is a need for boards of directors to fulfill their oversight responsibility with respect to instituting healthy corporate cultures and ensuring legal compliance. Recent alleged instances of sexual harassment by senior executives, improper workplace practices, and unethical business practices have caused investors concern about corporate culture. Proper corporate cultures should be aligned with and support the company's long-term business strategy, which will mitigate the risks associated with the image and reputation of the business.

Corporate Governance and the Financial Crisis

The 2007–2009 financial crisis was caused by a myriad of different issues, one of them being corporate governance. However, it was not the lack of corporate governance per se that allowed the crisis to take place; it was the lack of proper application and compliance, specifically pertaining to risk management. In the wake of the financial crisis, a reexamination of corporate governance was called for, which necessitated a series of reforms in financial institutions, including enhancing the board's oversight of management, designating risk management as a top priority for the board, and establishing policies that would balance long-term goals with risks. Shareholder activism became strengthened through this crisis, as shareholders can hold the board accountable for their actions and influence corporate governance. Financial institution reforms inspired targeting prevalent corporate governance problems, even in nonfinancial institutions. Such reform efforts have inspired the international convergence of governance policies to tackle common problems. Having standard principles that can be applied internationally, nationally, and regionally promotes a drive toward convergence, allowing for a smoother governance evaluation process. While the reforms mainly targeted financial institutions, certain aspects of corporate governance (e.g., shareholder rights, concentrated ownership, and state of the owner) may also be applied to new corporations in emerging markets. Sustainability should be redefined specifically to incorporate corporate performance and embed it into effective stakeholder governance.

The importance of corporate governance to the global economy has been recognized and addressed by the United Nations Conference on Trade and Development (UNCTAD) many times in the aftermath of the 2007–2009 global financial crisis. Specifically, UNCTAD issued *Corporate Governance in the Wake of the Financial Crisis* in 2010.[28] The following insights and recommendations are made in the report:

1. Develop corporate governance reforms at financial institutions to strengthen board oversight of management and set a tone at the top. These reforms should require risk assessment and management as well as remuneration practices that balance risk and long-term performance criteria. Establish corporate governance reforms and regulations to improve the mechanisms that enable shareholders to influence corporate governance and take a more active role in the governance of companies in their portfolios.
2. Develop broader governance-related reforms that benefit both financial and nonfinancial institutions. Promote convergence in global corporate governance by designing principles-based guidance that is globally applicable but can be implemented in specific national and regional contexts.

Global Financial Scandals and Crises

3. Create flexibility in corporate governance reforms so that developing countries can customize reforms for their markets, and policymakers in emerging markets can consider factors such as concentrated ownership, rights of minority shareholders, problems in enforcement regimes, and the important role of the state as owner.

4. Transform the general concept of "sustainability" into more concrete measures of corporate performance and embed sustainability into a new model of stakeholder governance.[29]

Smart Regulations

Global bailouts in the United States, the United Kingdom, and other countries in response to the 2007–2009 financial crisis have cost trillions of taxpayer dollars without energizing and stimulating capital markets and economies. The general perception is that subsidizing troubled companies and their executives does not serve the global economy. In contrast, better accountability and corporate governance should improve it, as it is continuing to sink. Bailing out companies without effective accountability and corporate governance provides their executives with powerful economic incentives (i.e., outrageous compensation) to make decisions that destroy shareholder value.

Three general approaches are feasible to address the aftermath of the global financial crisis and resulting economic meltdown. The first solution uses global market mechanisms to allow shareholders to vote on placing a company's legal jurisdiction in a country that has better investor protection laws and more corporate governance. The second solution is to develop an effective and enforceable global corporate governance to hold companies worldwide accountable to their shareholders. The third solution is to develop smart regulations that are cost-effective, efficient, proactive, and scalable.

The Business Roundtable's Achieving Smarter Regulation[30] plan aims to begin reforms by improving the regulatory process to meet the needs of businesses without unnecessary costs. The main challenges that arise from federal regulatory policy are the expensive and rigid policies that impede innovation and competitiveness. The plan proposes that encouraging early public engagement and the use of quality information to promote objective analysis are two key principles that could serve as a guide for a well-functioning regulatory process. Since both the public and government share this responsibility, stakeholders need to work together to implement this plan. A new regulatory process is needed, as the current one does not always apply cost-benefit analysis to proposed regulations and does not always use the best available data and scientific methodologies. A stronger emphasis on objective analysis, earlier agency disclosure of costs, updates requiring rigorous promulgation, and streamlining the permitting process will help combat these challenges.

Technological advances such as blockchain and bitcoin, as well as global competition, have enabled investors to decide how, when, and where to invest – developments that have also allowed public companies to decide where and how to raise capital. Thus, companies can choose the regulatory regime they desire to operate under, and investors have a choice of safeguards and protections provided under different regulatory frameworks. Effective regulatory frameworks create an environment under which companies can achieve sustainable performance, be held accountable for their activities, and provide protection for their investors. Some argue that there is no need for corporate governance reforms, policy interventions, or regulations because competition provides incentives for public companies to adopt the most effective and efficient corporate governance structure. Companies that do not adopt effective corporate governance, the argument holds, are less efficient in the long term and are ultimately replaced. However, the rash of financial scandals in the late 1990s and the early 2000s proved that market-based mechanisms alone cannot solve corporate governance problems. The capital markets hit rock bottom in the early 2000s primarily because market correction mechanisms, lax regulations, and poorly developed disclosure standards failed to protect investors. They thus diminished public trust and investor confidence in the capital markets.

Furthermore, market correction mechanisms are often initiated and enforced after substantial management abuse and after shareholders sell their shares and depress stock prices. The sale of shares has transaction costs and does not directly remove assets from management control; therefore, their sale amounts to simply passing shares to other investors, who ultimately suffer from the same management malfeasance. Market correction mechanisms may affect corporate governance only after significant wealth is destroyed due to management misconduct and corporate malfeasance and after considerable transaction costs for other stakeholders – including employees, in the form of layoffs, lost wages, pension funds, and society, in the form of lost taxes. Market mechanisms failed to prevent the corporate debacles at Enron, WorldCom, and Global Crossing (among others), which were devastating to shareholders, employees, pensioners, and society, as almost all corporate wealth was destroyed. Thus, corporate governance reforms are expected to create an environment that promotes strong marketplace integrity and efficiency, as well as investor confidence and public trust in the quality, reliability, and transparency of financial disclosures.

US securities law (in the form of the Securities Act of 1933 and the Securities Exchange Act of 1934) was enacted almost 75 years ago to restore investors' confidence. It was the government's response to the perception that investors (a small group of wealthy investors) had been defrauded because of an offer of bad securities. Today, we face a similar problem of erosion of investors' confidence and public trust in corporate America

Smart Regulations

and its financial reports. The general perception is that a large group of investors (120 million Americans) has been defrauded by the executives of public companies who are not accountable to anyone. Regulatory reforms should create an environment in which public companies can create value for shareholders, protect the interests of other stakeholders, and rebuild investors' trust through effective enforcement of these reforms.

Regulations vary significantly throughout the world based on the country's economic, cultural, and legal circumstances — but with one emerging trend: a demand for protection of global investors. Effective regulations can align the interests of directors, management, and shareholders in achieving sustainable performance, which promotes market efficiency and economic prosperity. In a perfect global market, a company could be incorporated in one jurisdiction (Country A), be listed in exchange in a second country (Country B), operate in a third (Country C), be subject to corporate governance and the regulatory and financial services of a fourth (Country D), and be taxed in all of them. Technological advances, globalization, and cross-country investments demand that regulators worldwide cooperate in reducing regulator conflict and excessive corporate governance measures and regulatory reforms. Thus, there is a need for convergence in corporate governance reforms, with more emphasis on national regulations not relevant to emerging global investment, capital markets, or the economy.

The issues that need to be resolved are (1) what measures are considered good corporate governance practices, (2) how such practices can be converged while maintaining domestic market confidence in both national and global regulations affected by differences in legal, political, and cultural environments, and (3) to what extent effective corporate governance and global regulatory cooperation can facilitate the emergence of global corporate governance. Corporate and capital structure can also influence corporate governance and financial disclosure requirements. One of the key differences in corporate structure is ownership of the company. In the United States, ownership of shares is dispersed, whereas stock ownership in Europe is more concentrated, meaning that controlling shareholders are in a better position to influence corporate governance and business operations. Corporate governance in a dispersed-share ownership system is designed to align the interests of management with those of shareholders, as management may have incentives to engage in earnings management and focus on short-term considerations at the expense of sustainable shareholder-value creation and long-term performance. Conversely, in a concentrated ownership system, corporate governance creates the right balance between the interests of minority and majority shareholders.

The primary purpose of corporate governance in the United States is to enhance shareholder value creation while protecting the interests of other stakeholders (creditors, employees, suppliers, customers, and the government). In contrast, in Germany the focus is on protecting creditors, as banks play an important role in financing companies. This type of ownership structure can be influenced by the typical agency problem of separation of the decision control assigned to management and the ownership control retained by a wide range of shareholders. The integrity and efficiency of financial markets depend on the quality and reliability of financial information disseminated to the markets by public companies, as well as investor confidence in such information. Thus, smart regulations should create a framework within which public companies operate to generate legitimate, sustainable performance, create sustainable shared value for all stakeholders, and produce reliable, relevant, and useful financial information for all stakeholders.

Senator Warren's Accountable Capitalism Act includes several worthwhile provisions. It is premised on the federalization of all public corporations with revenues in excess of $1 billion, which suggests replacing shareholder primacy with stakeholder primacy and changing from shareholder-centric governance to stakeholder-centric governance.

Sources of Information for Capital Markets

Technological advances, including the internet, have enabled investors to have real-time access to a large volume of information about public companies – their governance, operations, and investment choices – and capital markets. The internet facilitates the flow of fair and transparent information to all investors, individuals, and institutions, small or large. Investors have online access to companies' financial disclosure filings and auditor and analyst reports, and they rely on information public companies disseminate to the capital markets when making investment and voting decisions. Information from public companies flows into the marketplace from three fundamental sources: regulated (mandatory) disclosures, voluntary disclosures, and research analyst reports.[31]

Mandatory Disclosures

The US Congress established capital markets as disclosure-based rather than merit-based systems. That is, the Securities and Exchange Commission (SEC) regulates capital markets by establishing rules and regulations that require public companies to disclose material information that may impact investors' investment decisions. The SEC does not regulate by determining the merits of whether it is appropriate for a company to be public and sell its stock to the public. Regulated disclosures include annual audited financial statements, which are filed with the SEC on Form 10-K; quarterly reviewed financial reports, filed on Form 10-Q; extraordinary transactions on a current basis (e.g., auditor changes, resignation or death of a director or an officer, bankruptcy), filed on Form 8-K; and internal control reports for large public companies (Sections 302 and 404 of SOX). SOX requires executive certifications of both financial statements and disclosure controls and procedures. Internal control reporting is valuable to investors in assessing financial risk and integrity and the reliability of financial reporting. Financial statements and internal control reports should be prepared from the perspective of shareholders, who have residual claims on a company's assets.

These regulated financial disclosures are a vital source of information for investors. These disclosures create a way for public companies to communicate with their shareholders about financial and corporate governance issues that affect their financial condition and results of operations. SEC-mandated filings have been criticized for encouraging public companies to focus on the short-term performance of meeting earnings forecast**s** and creating a check-box compliance mentality in order to ensure minimum compliance with SEC, rules rather than focusing on improving earnings quality and quantity.[32] In the United Kingdom, it has been found that short-termism is a problem for equity markets due to a lack of trust and misalignment of incentives; this reemphasizes the importance of corporate governance. It is recommended that rebuilding trust, increasing incentives to do well, reducing the pressures of frequent financial reporting, and measuring performance that incentivizes short-term decision-making would improve equity markets.[33]

PricewaterhouseCoopers LLP (PwC) reports that improved investor trust comes from an improved financial reporting system. They believe that the seven pillars of effective communication are (1) attaining objectives through explaining the available resources the company has, (2) describing risks and uncertainties that would affect long-term goals, (3) clarifying significant stakeholder relationships, (4) presenting trends that would affect prospects of the company, (5) clarifying any uncertainties affecting progressive information, (6) explaining business targets in conjunction with KPIs, and (7) linking long-term objectives with the strategies used to achieve them.[34]

Voluntary Disclosures

Public companies often voluntarily release earnings guidance regarding projected performance and other financial and nonfinancial information in addition to their mandated disclosures. Public companies have traditionally provided investors and analysts with earnings guidance. This practice was initiated during the 1970s when many companies began privately communicating their earnings forecasts to large investors. It became a common practice during the stock market boom of the 1990s, particularly when Congress protected companies from liability for their earnings forecasts.[35] Earnings announcements, even though not required, provide valuable information to market participants and motivate companies to meet their earnings expectations. Voluntarily released earnings guidance is thought to result in higher valuations, lower volatility, and improved liquidity.[36] However, a study reveals that while corporate earnings guidance may increase trading volumes in the short term, it does not increase valuations and has no lasting effect on stock price volatility or liquidity.[37]

Several prominent public companies (e.g., Coca-Cola, Intel, Ford, General Motors, Google, and Citigroup) have discontinued the practice of issuing earnings guidance and instead issued more detailed performance measures.[38] These companies have decided to focus on sustainable goals and long-term performance instead of short-term earnings targets. They are attempting to avoid both the costs associated with releasing earnings guidance and the possible negative impacts on stock price if earnings targets are not met. However, a majority of surveyed companies (83%) that are already issuing earnings guidance plans continue to do so. About 75% of the surveyed companies believe that earnings guidance helps to satisfy requests from investors and analysts, and over half report that the guidance facilitates management's focus on financial goals.[39]

Large public companies, their analysts, and fund managers are in favor of discontinuation of quarterly earnings guidance, which is influenced by executives' obsession with meeting earnings estimates. This is expected to change the relationship between the company's executives and financial analysts, as well as the way fund managers are evaluated and rewarded. Quarterly earnings guidance has historically been provided because it (1) assists management in focusing on short-term results, (2) makes forecasting by analysts easier, and (3) enables hedge funds to profit from discrepancies between actual earnings and forecasted earnings. However, earnings guidance, by focusing on the short-term performance at the expense of the long-term health of the company, has been detrimental to sustainable shareholder value creation and enhancement.

The disclosure of management earnings forecasts (MEFs) has recently received considerable attention from regulators, investors, and public companies. The accounting and finance literature provides several overriding reasons for firms releasing voluntary MEFs. The perceived benefits of earnings guidance disclosure are improved liquidity, reduced information asymmetry, lower stock volatility, and lower cost of capital.[40] The perceived costs of such practices are relevant costs of earnings, guidance disclosures, and the potential for encouraging management, financial analysts, and even investors to focus on short-term performance at the expense of long-term sustainable performance.[41] The issue of whether current MEF practices encourage short-termism and thus compromise financial reporting

Sources of Information for Capital Markets

quality or instead improve market efficiency has recently been debated within the business community and among policymakers, regulators, and standard setters. Proponents argue that MEFs improve market efficiency by reducing analysts' forecast errors and dispersions.[42] Opponents view MEFs as damaging to sustainable financial performance and reporting by encouraging short-termism.[43]

The short-termism phenomenon also affects asset managers' practices through (1) frequent trading of shares, (2) shortening holding periods of asset funds, (3) pressures from market traders and speculators encouraging corporate managers to produce short-term results, and (4) reduction of the sustainable, long-term return on investments.[44] Taken together, short-term practices of maximizing short-term reported performance are detrimental to long-term investment, R&D, training, and other sustainable, value-enhancing corporate activities. The short-termism phenomenon may create incentives for management to be more enthusiastic about issuing MEFs.

In December 2018, the SEC released its request for public comment on quarterly reporting and earnings release.[45] Specifically, the SEC is seeking comments on (1) the nature, timing, and frequency of earnings releases and interim reports that maintain investor protections while reducing the burden on public companies, (2) whether public companies should be allowed to use the information voluntarily provided in their earnings releases to satisfy the requirements of Form 10-Q, (3) whether the SEC should require semiannual reporting or allow public companies to select the frequency of their interim reporting as needed by their investors, and (4) whether the release of voluntarily forward-looking earnings guidance encourages short-term decision-making and what actions, if any, the SEC should take to discourage such practices.[46]

Research Analyst Reports

Financial analysts who follow and project companies' future earnings and evaluate their short-term quarterly performance are an important source of information and are essential to transparent and efficient capital markets. Analysts forecast for both long-term and short-term earnings quality and quantity. Focusing merely on short-term analyst forecasts and quarterly earnings guidance when such earnings numbers can be easily massaged through either acceleration of revenue recognition or deferral of investments (e.g., technology, research, and development) can create the illusion of value relevance for earnings releases. Management has traditionally manipulated earnings disclosures by establishing or promoting a low threshold for earnings forecasts and then attempting to beat the forecasts through actual lower-than-optimum performance or earnings management. This process can lead to the misallocation of investor capital when reported earnings are higher than management-forecasted earnings.

Academic research documents that sell-side analysts' earnings estimates and forecast revisions provide an important source of information to the marketplace, with a stronger market reaction to upward rather than downward forecast revisions.[47] During the economic and market boom of the 1990s, the objective and skeptical mental attitude of analysts became almost irrelevant. The perception was that investment banking concerns did not influence analysts' research. The current system of financial disclosures – which consists of mandated disclosures of quarterly, annual, and other filings with the SEC; voluntary disclosures of earnings guidance above and beyond the required disclosures by the SEC; and analyst reports – has served the capital markets, investors, public companies, and regulators well. Nonetheless, this model captures only financial information regarding financial conditions and results of operations. A corporate reporting model that captures both financial and nonfinancial KPIs is needed. Nonfinancial information disseminated to the capital markets by public companies includes market information (such as market growth, market share, and regulatory environment), corporate governance information (such as board of directors' composition, structure, and committees), strategic information about goals and objectives and management (such as record of accomplishment, compensation plans, and incentive plans), value-creating information (such as customers, employees, suppliers, innovative brands, and supply chain as well as environmental, ethical, and social information), and forecasts, projections, and other technical and quantitative market information. Investors demand forward-looking financial and nonfinancial information, and companies have strived to provide such information. Any improvements in this system – such as more timely and ready access to relevant information by using the XBRL format, greater focus on a principles-based approach to financial reporting, and less complexity in and convergence toward globally accepted accounting standards – enable public companies to provide better-quality financial information to investors.

The Role of Financial Information in the Capital Markets

The sustainability and financial health of public companies, public trust, and investor confidence in financial reports play a crucial role in the integrity and efficiency of the capital markets and the economic growth and prosperity of the nation. Investors, by investing in 401(k)s, mutual funds, and retirement accounts, or through actively playing the stock market, become more interested in public companies' governance and more sensitive to the companies' activities, the reputation of their directors, and officers (including their honesty, integrity, ethics, accountability, and reliability), and the transparent communication of this reputation to investors. The sustainability of public companies is key to keeping investor confidence high by presenting accurate financial reports to investors to make informed investment decisions.

The ever-increasing demand for high-quality financial information means that individuals involved in the corporate financial reporting supply chain — including the board of directors, the audit committee, management, and auditors — are under intense scrutiny. In underscoring the importance of financial reports to our society, former chairman of the Federal Reserve Board, Alan Greenspan, has testified that recent financial scandals by high-profile corporations have eroded public confidence in financial reports.[48] This has caused depressed valuations of equity securities, made new capital investment unattractive, and led to higher capital costs.[49] Financial disclosures under SEC regulations are necessary to provide investors with reliable, meaningful financial information so that they can make informed investment decisions.

Our society, particularly the investing community, relies on the quality of corporate financial reports in making rational decisions. Accurate financial information assists investors in making informed, sound investment decisions, whereas inaccurate financial information is likely to mislead them into making bad investment decisions. William McDonough, the former chairman of the Public Company Accounting Oversight Board (PCAOB), states that "confidence in the accuracy of accounting statements is the bedrock of investors being willing to invest, in lenders to lend, and for employees knowing their firms' obligations to them can be trusted."[50] A greater number of people are now investing through retirement funds or actively managing their portfolios, and they are affected by the financial information presented to the market.

Financial statements are a vital source of information to the capital markets and their participants. The quality of investment and voting decisions by investors depends on the accuracy, completeness, and reliability of financial information disseminated to them by public companies. Thus, high-quality financial information improves investor decisions and, in turn, the efficiency, liquidity, and safety of the capital markets, which may result in prosperity and economic growth for the nation. Financial disclosures under SEC regulations are necessary to prevent fraud and financial manipulation. Our society, particularly the investing community, relies on accuracy in corporate financial reporting to make rational decisions. However, there is an expectation gap between what users of financial reports expect to receive and what they actually receive. Several factors have contributed to this expectation gap, including (1) deficiencies in auditing and reporting standards, in the sense that they are not suitable for the existing knowledge-based economic environment of the Internet age, (2) lack of motivation on the part of corporate executives to completely adhere to standards in providing high-quality and reliable financial information, (3) lack of financial literacy and training of financial statement users to effectively utilize financial information in making decisions, and (4) complexity of accounting standards.

Summary

This chapter discusses the important role that corporate culture and the financial markets play in the nation's economic growth and prosperity as well as our society. Financial markets enable investors to invest their money by buying public company stocks and earning a desired return on investment. Investors pay cash now to obtain a desirable return on their investment. This chapter also discusses the importance and dynamics of relationships between capital markets and businesses as perceived by stakeholders, including investors, and transformed through corporate culture business sustainability. The objective of corporations has evolved from profit maximization, to increasing wealth for shareholders, to the creation of shared value for all stakeholders with a focus on profit-with-purpose mission in recent years. This chapter presents emerging issues in business organizations. The capital markets in the United States, the strongest in the world, cannot survive without public trust and investor confidence in the reliability of the financial information disseminated to them.

Financial scandals and financial restatements have underscored how vital these qualities are. The reliability, relevance, usefulness, and transparency of information disseminated to the marketplace depend on the personal integrity, competence, and organizational accountability of those involved in the financial reporting process. These participants are management, boards of directors (including the audit committee), independent auditors, and financial and legal advisors. Management is primarily responsible for the reliability and completeness of financial and nonfinancial reports. These gatekeepers play an important role in influencing the quality of information corporations disseminate to the marketplace. The concept of profit-with-purpose corporations has gained attention in recent years, which suggests that the objectives of public companies should be broader than just making profits for their shareholders, as considering social and environmental impacts can make them sustainable.

Key Points

- A vital financial system and reliable financial information are essential for economic growth and development worldwide.

- Investors prefer long-term, sustainable, and forward-looking financial and nonfinancial information on a company's strategy and performance.
- A healthy financial sector and efficient capital markets are vital to the nation's economic growth and prosperity.
- Corporations with an entrepreneurial spirit are the main engines that drive the nation's economy and its capital markets to long-term sustainable prosperity.
- Public companies have a set of contractual relationships with a broad range of participants, including shareholders, creditors, vendors, customers, employees, governmental agencies, auditors, and global communities and societies.
- Public companies should consider their financial, social, and environmental impacts.
- Sustainable shared-value creation enables business organizations to integrate financial and nonfinancial factors into the corporate culture and environment.
- The existence and persistence of global financial scandals create a poor corporate culture that negatively affects corporate governance and, thus, investor confidence in the global financial markets.
- Regulations must be proactive, cost-effective, efficient, and scalable.
- Information from public companies flows into the marketplace from three fundamental sources: regulated disclosures, voluntary disclosures, and research analyst reports.

Review Questions

1. **How has the mission of corporations evolved?**
2. **What is the focus of the free enterprise system in the United States?**
3. **How do corporations contribute to national economic growth?**
4. **What is the emerging trend in corporate governance models?**
5. **What are the main components of an effective accountability system for corporations?**
6. **What is the role of the board of directors in a public company?**
7. **What are the key challenges faced by public companies in recent years?**
8. **What are the primary components of a company's corporate governance structure?**
9. **What are the roles of shareholders in a public company?**
10. **What is the significance of voluntary disclosures by public companies?**
11. **What are the main objectives of corporate governance reforms?**
12. **What is the role of financial analysts in the capital markets?**
13. **What is the significance of corporate social responsibility (CSR) initiatives?**

14. **How does globalization impact corporate governance?**
15. **How can companies ensure the integrity of their financial reports?**

Discussion Questions

1. **How has the mission of corporations transformed over time?**
2. **How do corporations contribute to market efficiency?**
3. **How do capital markets benefit society at large?**
4. **How do corporations create shared value for stakeholders?**
5. **Why is stakeholder engagement important in corporate governance?**
6. **How can technological advancements benefit corporations?**
7. **What is the shareholder primacy model?**
8. **What is the importance of corporate governance in public companies?**
9. **What are the primary objectives of corporate governance?**
10. **What role do employees play as corporate stakeholders?**
11. **What is the impact of corporate social responsibility on society?**
12. **What are the benefits of the stakeholder primacy model?**
13. **What are the key components of an effective accountability system?**
14. **What are the responsibilities of corporate directors?**
15. **What is the significance of corporate culture in business sustainability?**

Multiple Choice Questions

1. **How has the mission of corporations transformed over time?**
   A) From focusing on stakeholder value to focusing on shareholder wealth
   B) From focusing on profit to focusing on regulatory compliance
   C) From shareholder wealth creation to achieving shared value for all stakeholders
   D) From innovation to financial stability
2. **What does the free enterprise system in the United States promote?**
   A) Government interference in business operations
   B) Healthy and constructive competition among business organizations
   C) Limiting innovation to reduce risks
   D) Reducing the number of public companies
3. **What is the primary goal of the free enterprise system?**
   A) To limit the creation of new businesses
   B) To create jobs and wealth

C)   To reduce market efficiency

D)   To increase government regulation

4.   **How do corporations contribute to national economic growth?**

A)   By creating jobs, driving innovation, and investing in research and development (R&D)

B)   By reducing the number of public companies

C)   By focusing on short-term profits

D)   By avoiding corporate social responsibility

5.   **What is the emerging trend in corporate governance models?**

A)   Moving from the stakeholder primacy model to the shareholder primacy model

B)   Moving from the shareholder primacy model to the stakeholder primacy model

C)   Increasing government control over corporations

D)   Reducing the role of corporate governance

6.   **What is the significance of corporate social responsibility (CSR)?**

A)   It focuses solely on financial performance

B)   It enhances a company's social and environmental impacts

C)   It reduces corporate accountability

D)   It limits the role of stakeholders

7.   **What are the components of an effective accountability system for corporations?**

A)   Reducing transparency in financial disclosures

B)   Limiting stakeholder engagement

C)   A well-defined corporate mission, robust governance structure, and transparent disclosures

D)   Focusing solely on short-term profits

8.   **What is the shareholder primacy model?**

A)   A model where the primary purpose of a corporation is to maximize shareholder wealth

B)   A model that focuses on stakeholder value

C)   A model that limits the role of corporate governance

D)   A model that focuses on short-term profits

9.   **How do public companies contribute to market efficiency?**

A)   By reducing liquidity

B)   By enhancing liquidity and enabling price discovery

C)   By focusing solely on short-term profits

D)   By limiting the role of stakeholders

10. **What is the role of the free enterprise system in the United States?**
    A) To reduce market efficiency
    B) To promote healthy and constructive competition among business organizations
    C) To limit the creation of new businesses
    D) To increase government regulation

11. **What is the emerging trend in corporate governance?**
    A) Moving from the stakeholder primacy model to the shareholder primacy model
    B) Moving from the shareholder primacy model to the stakeholder primacy model
    C) Increasing government control over corporations
    D) Reducing the role of corporate governance

12. **What is the significance of corporate social responsibility (CSR)?**
    A) It focuses solely on financial performance
    B) It enhances a company's social and environmental impacts
    C) It reduces corporate accountability
    D) It limits the role of stakeholders

13. **What are the components of an effective accountability system for corporations?**
    A) Reducing transparency in financial disclosures
    B) Limiting stakeholder engagement
    C) A well-defined corporate mission, robust governance structure, and transparent disclosures
    D) Focusing solely on short-term profits

14. **What is the shareholder primacy model?**
    A) A model where the primary purpose of a corporation is to maximize shareholder wealth
    B) A model that focuses on stakeholder value
    C) A model that limits the role of corporate governance
    D) A model that focuses on short-term profits

15. **How do public companies contribute to market efficiency?**
    A) By reducing liquidity
    B) By enhancing liquidity and enabling price discovery
    C) By focusing solely on short-term profits
    D) By limiting the role of stakeholders

16. **What is the role of the free enterprise system in the United States?**
    A) To reduce market efficiency
    B) To promote healthy and constructive competition among business organizations

Multiple Choice Questions

C) To limit the creation of new businesses

D) To increase government regulation

17. **What is the emerging trend in corporate governance?**

A) Moving from the stakeholder primacy model to the shareholder primacy model

B) Moving from the shareholder primacy model to the stakeholder primacy model

C) Increasing government control over corporations

D) Reducing the role of corporate governance

18. **What is the significance of corporate social responsibility (CSR)?**

A) It focuses solely on financial performance

B) It enhances a company's social and environmental impacts

C) It reduces corporate accountability

D) It limits the role of stakeholders

19. **What are the components of an effective accountability system for corporations?**

A) Reducing transparency in financial disclosures

B) Limiting stakeholder engagement

C) A well-defined corporate mission, robust governance structure, and transparent disclosures

D) Focusing solely on short-term profits

20. **What is the shareholder primacy model?**

A) A model where the primary purpose of a corporation is to maximize shareholder wealth

B) A model that focuses on stakeholder value

C) A model that limits the role of corporate governance

D) A model that focuses on short-term profits

21. **How do public companies contribute to market efficiency?**

A) By reducing liquidity

B) By enhancing liquidity and enabling price discovery

C) By focusing solely on short-term profits

D) By limiting the role of stakeholders

22. **What is the role of the free enterprise system in the United States?**

A) To reduce market efficiency

B) To promote healthy and constructive competition among business organizations

C) To limit the creation of new businesses

D) To increase government regulation

23. **What is the emerging trend in corporate governance?**
    A) Moving from the stakeholder primacy model to the shareholder primacy model
    B) Moving from the shareholder primacy model to the stakeholder primacy model
    C) Increasing government control over corporations
    D) Reducing the role of corporate governance

24. **What is the significance of corporate social responsibility (CSR)?**
    A) It focuses solely on financial performance
    B) It enhances a company's social and environmental impacts
    C) It reduces corporate accountability
    D) It limits the role of stakeholders

25. **What are the components of an effective accountability system for corporations?**
    A) Reducing transparency in financial disclosures
    B) Limiting stakeholder engagement
    C) A well-defined corporate mission, robust governance structure, and transparent disclosures
    D) Focusing solely on short-term profits

26. **What is the shareholder primacy model?**
    A) A model where the primary purpose of a corporation is to maximize shareholder wealth
    B) A model that focuses on stakeholder value
    C) A model that limits the role of corporate governance
    D) A model that focuses on short-term profits

27. **How do public companies contribute to market efficiency?**
    A) By reducing liquidity
    B) By enhancing liquidity and enabling price discovery
    C) By focusing solely on short-term profits
    D) By limiting the role of stakeholders

28. **What is the role of the free enterprise system in the United States?**
    A) To reduce market efficiency
    B) To promote healthy and constructive competition among business organizations
    C) To limit the creation of new businesses
    D) To increase government regulation

29. **What is the emerging trend in corporate governance?**
    A) Moving from the stakeholder primacy model to the shareholder primacy model
    B) Moving from the shareholder primacy model to the stakeholder primacy model

Multiple Choice Questions

C) Increasing government control over corporations

D) Reducing the role of corporate governance

30. **What is the significance of corporate social responsibility (CSR)?**

A) It focuses solely on financial performance

B) It enhances a company's social and environmental impacts

C) It reduces corporate accountability

D) It limits the role of stakeholders

Notes

1 Kale, K.M. and Stulz, R. (2017). Is the American public corporation in trouble? Finance Working Paper No. 495/2017, European Corporate Governance Institute. https://papers .ssrn.com/sol3/papers.cfm?abstract_id=2869301.

2 Bloomberg Editorial Board. (2018). Where have all the public companies gone? https://www .bloomberg.com/opinion/articles/2018-10-29/trading-on-news-before-it-s-published.

3 Bloomberg Editorial Board. (2018). Where have all the public companies gone? https://www .bloomberg.com/opinion/articles/2018-10-29/trading-on-news-before-it-s-published.

4 Bloomberg Editorial Board. (2018). Where have all the public companies gone? https://www .bloomberg.com/opinion/articles/2018-10-29/trading-on-news-before-it-s-published.

5 Hirst, S and Bebchuk, L. A. (2019). The specter of the giant three. Technical report, National Bureau of Economic Research. Available at https://scholarship.law.bu.edu/faculty_schol-arship/602/

6 Palladino, L. and Karlsson, K. (2018). Towards "accountable capitalism": Remaking corporate law through stakeholder governance (October). http://rooseveltinstitute.org/wp -content/uploads/2018/10/Towards-%E2%80%98Accountable-Capitalism%E2%80%99 -issue-brief.pdf.

7 Mayer, C. (2018). The future of the corporation: Towards humane business. Available at http://www.wlrk.com/docs/TheFutureoftheCorporationTowardsHumaneBusiness.pdf.

8 Lipton, Martin, Lipton, Wachtell, Rosen et al. (2019). It's time to adopt the new paradigm (February 11). https://corpgov.law.harvard.edu/2019/02/11/its-time-to-adopt-the-new -paradigm/#more-115585.

9 Lipton, Martin, Lipton, Wachtell, Rosen et al. (2019). It's time to adopt the new paradigm (February 11). https://corpgov.law.harvard.edu/2019/02/11/its-time-to-adopt-the-new -paradigm/#more-115585.

10 Jensen, M. and Meckling, W. (1976). Theory of the firm: Managerial behavior, agency costs and ownership structure. *Journal of Financial Economics* 3: 305–360.

11 Delaware Law Series. (2013). DGCL amended to authorize public benefit corporations (August 14). http://blogs.law.harvard.edu/corpgov/tag/delaware-law.

12 Hiller, J. S. (2013). The benefit corporation and corporate social responsibility. *Journal of Business Ethics* 118 (2) (December 2013): 287–301.

13 Porter, M.E. and Kramer, M.R. (2011). Creating shared value. *Harvard Business Review* January–February: 62–77.

14 Porter, M.E. and Kramer, M.R. (2011). Creating shared value. *Harvard Business Review* January–February: 62–77.

15 Porter, M.E. and Kramer, M.R. (2011). Creating shared value. *Harvard Business Review* January–February: 65.

16 Porter, M.E. and Kramer, M.R. (2011). Creating shared value. *Harvard Business Review* January–February: 2.

17 Klemash, S., J c. Smith and R. Doyle. (2019). Stakeholder capitalism for long-term value creation. Harvard Law School on Corporate Governance and Financial Regulation. June 13, 2019. Available at https://corpgov.law.harvard.edu/2019/06/13/stakeholder-capitalism-for -long-term-value-creation/

18 Porter, M.E. and Kramer, M.R. (2011). Creating shared value. *Harvard Business Review* January–February: 62–77.

19 Council of Institutional Investors. (CII). (2018). Corporate governance policies (October 24, 2018). Available at https://www.cii.org/files/10_24_18_corp_gov_policies.pdf

20 Cox, J. (2018). A $9 trillion corporate debt bomb is "bubbling" in the US economy (November 21). https://www.cnbc.com/2018/11/21/theres-a-9-trillion-corporate-debt-bomb-bubbling -in-the-us-economy.html.

21 Jensen, M., and Meckling, W. (1976). Theory of the firm: Managerial behavior, agency costs and ownership structure. *Journal of Financial Economics* 3 (October): 305–360.

22 Mintz, S.M. (2005). Corporate governance in an international context: legal systems, financing patterns and cultural variables. *Corporate Governance* 13 (5): 582–597. search .ebscohost.com/login.aspx?direct=true&db=buh&AN=18035531&site=ehost-live.

23 Nini, G., Sufi, A., and Smith, D.C. (2011). Creditor control rights, corporate governance, and firm value (December 11) https://papers.ssrn.com/sol3/papers.cfm?abstract_id=1344302.

24 Business for Social Responsibility (BSR). (2003). Stakeholder engagement. BSR Issue Brief. (April). www.bsr.org/CSRResources/IssueBriefDetail.cfm?DocumentID=48813.

25 Leonhardt, M. (2016). How to steer clear of a Wells Fargo-like toxic culture. *Money* (September 29).

26 Sarbanes-Oxley Public Company Accounting Reform and Investor Protection Act of 2002. http://www.whitehouse.gov/infocus/corporateresponisbility.

27 Dodd-Frank Wall Street Reform and Consumer Protection Act of 2010, Public Law 111-203.

28 United Nations Conference on Trade and Development (UNCTAD). (2010). Corporate governance in the wake of the financial crisis: Selected international views. http://unctad.org /en/Docs/diaeed20102_en.pdf.

29 United Nations Conference on Trade and Development (UNCTAD). (2010). Corporate governance in the wake of the financial crisis: Selected international views. http://unctad.org /en/Docs/diaeed20102_en.pdf.

30 Business Roundtable. (2011). Achieving smarter regulation. http://businessroundtable.org/ resources/achieving-smarter-regulation.

Notes

31 Lackritz, M.E. (2006). Testimony before the US House of Representatives Committee on financial services, subcommittee on capital markets (March 29). financialservices.house.g ov/media/pdf/071504ml.pdf.

32 Lackritz, M.E. (2006). *Testimony Before the US House of Representatives Committee on Financial Services, Subcommittee on Capital Markets* (March 29). financialservices.house.g ov/media/pdf/071504ml.pdf.

33 Harvard Law School Forum on Corporate Governance and Financial Regulation. (2012). UK equity markets and long-term decision making. file:///Z:/Sharefiles/Book%20Projec ts/Business%20Expert%20Press/Corporate%20Governance/Chapters/Chapter%201/ UK%20Equity%20Markets%20and%20Long-term%20Decision%20Making%20%E2%8 0%94%20The%20Harvard%20Law%20School%20Forum%20on%20Corporate%20Go vernance%20and%20Financial%20Regulation.htm.

34 PricewaterhouseCoopers. (PwC) (2012). Guide to forward-looking information. http://www .pwc.com/gx/en/audit-services/corporate-reporting/corporate-reporting-guidelines/for- ward-looking-information.jhtml.

35 *McKinsey Quarterly.* (2006). Weighing the pros and cons of earnings guidance: A McKinsey survey (April 2). www.mckinseyquarterly.com/article_page.aspx?ar=1752&62=5.

36 McKinsey & Company. (2006). Weighing the pros and cons of earnings guidance. (March). mckinseyquarterly.com/article_abstract.aspx.

37 Hsieh, P., Koller, T., and Rajan, S.R. (2006). The misguided practice of earnings guidance. *McKinsey Quarterly* (March). www.mckinseyquarterly.com/article_abstract_visitor.aspx ?ar=1759&L2=5&L3=5.

38 Roberts, D. (2006). Guidance falling out of favor on Wall Street. *Financial Times* (March 12).

39 *McKinsey Quarterly.* (2006). Weighing the pros and cons of earnings guidance: A McKinsey survey (April 2). www.mckinseyquarterly.com/article_page.aspx?ar=1752&L2=5&L3=5.

40 Healy, P.M. and Palepu, K.G. (1993). The effect of firms' financial disclosure strategies on stock prices. *Accounting Horizons* 7 (1): 1–11.

41 Fuller, J. and Jensen, M. (2002). Just say no to Wall Street. *Journal of Applied Corporate Finance* 14: 41–46.

42 Committee for Economic Development. (2007). Built to last: Focusing corporations on long- term performance. www.ced.org/docs/report/report_corpgov2007.pdf.

43 Committee for Economic Development. (2007). Built to last: Focusing corporations on long- term performance. www.ced.org/docs/report/report_corpgov2007.pdf.

44 Committee for Economic Development. (2007). Built to last: Focusing corporations on long- term performance. www.ced.org/docs/report/report_corpgov2007.pdf.

45 Securities and Exchange Commission (SEC). (2018). Request for comment on earnings releases and quarterly reports. Release No. 33-10588; 34-84842; File No. S7-26-18], December 18, 2018. Available at https://www.sec.gov/rules/other/2018/33 10588.pdf

46 US Securities and Exchange Commission (SEC). (2018). Request for comment on earn- ings releases and quarterly reports. *Release No. 33-10588; 34-84842; File No. S7-26-18* (December 18). https://www.sec.gov/rules/other/2018/33-10588.pdf.

47 Lang, M., and Lundholm, R. (1996). Corporate disclosure policy and analyst behavior. *Accounting Review* 71 (October): 467–491.

48 Greenspan, A. (2002). Testimony before the senate committee on banking, housing, and urban affairs. The Federal Reserve Board's Semiannual Monetary Policy Report to the Congress (July 16).

49 Greenspan, A. (2002). *Testimony Before the Senate Committee on Banking, Housing, and Urban Affairs: The Federal Reserve Board's Semiannual Monetary Policy Report to the Congress* (July 16).

50 Solomon, D., and Bryan-Low, C. (2003). "Tough" cop for accounting beat. *Wall Street Journal* (April 16): C1.

Chapter 2
An Introduction to Business Sustainability

Learning Objectives

- Present various definitions of business sustainability.
- Learn business sustainability factors such as planning, performance, risk, and disclosure.
- Understand the importance of business sustainability in the organization.
- Provide an overview of the dimensions of sustainability performance.
- Address the value relevance of sustainability performance.
- Address the risks and opportunities that are related to business sustainability.
- Provide an overview of sustainability reporting and assurance.
- Explain the management implications of sustainability programs and activities.
- Acknowledge how effective sustainability reporting can boost investor confidence.
- Recognize the primary intent of sustainability initiatives.
- Identify the challenges of sustainability reporting.
- Describe the principles underlying sustainability reporting and elaborate on them.
- Explain the relationship between the five performance dimensions of business sustainability and the accountability framework.
- Understand the purposes that KPIs serve within an organization.
- Identify the emerging issues in sustainability reporting and elaborate on them.
- Discuss how the integrity of sustainability reporting can be strengthened.
- List the five risks associated with business sustainability.

Introduction

Many initiatives and developments over the past several decades have shaped business sustainability. The topic of business sustainability has gained considerable attention from policymakers, regulators, investors, business organizations, and academics. Traditionally, business organizations have reported their financial economic performance in a set of financial statements. Business sustainability has transformed from greenwashing and branding to a business imperative by being integrated into business strategic plans, decisions,

DOI: 10.4324/9781003487081-2

operations, and accountability reports. In the era of technological advances and the move toward consideration of social and environmental impacts, these financial reports are no longer considered sufficient. In recent years, stakeholders, investors, regulators, global institutions and organizations, and the public at large have increasingly demanded information on both financial and nonfinancial key performance indicators (KPIs) in the platform of accountability and sustainability reporting. This chapter first introduces the emergence of business sustainability, followed by in-depth discussions of the definition of business sustainability and four important business sustainability factors in planning, performance, disclosure, and risk. It also provides guidelines for the complete and accurate measurement, recognition, and disclosure of financial economic sustainability performance (ESP) and nonfinancial environmental, social, and governance (ESG) dimensions of sustainability performance in an integrated reporting model.

Definition of Business Sustainability

Business sustainability has evolved from a focus on corporate social responsibility (CSR), corporate governance, and internal operational efficiencies to integration into organizations' strategies, culture, and practices toward long-term and multidimensional economic, governance, social, environmental, and ethical (EGSEE) sustainability performance.[1] Sustainability can have different meanings when perceived by different stakeholders. From the academic and practical aspects, business sustainability can be defined as a process of meeting the needs of the present without jeopardizing the needs of future generations through environmental preservation to create a better environment for all stakeholders. It can be viewed as fulfilling the company's CSR responsibilities beyond mandatory obligations. From a financial perspective, sustainability is considered as focusing on short-, medium-, and long-term financial performance to generate value for shareholders. It can also be viewed as conducting business activities ethically with effective corporate governance to ensure the continuity of the business.

Business sustainability has been defined in many ways. Agency/shareholder theory defines it as the process of aligning management interests with those of shareholders. In this regard, the main purpose of business sustainability is to enable management to focus on short-, medium-, and long-term strategic decisions to achieve high performance in creating shareholder value. It can be defined from the legal and compliance view as the process of complying with all applicable laws, rules, regulations, and standards, including those related to the environment, society, governance, ethical guidelines, as well as financial standards in achieving all five economic, governance, social, ethical, and environmental dimensions of sustainability performance. Until recently, the terms business sustainability,

Definition of Business Sustainability

corporate social responsibility, and triple-bottom-line of focusing on profit, people, and planet have been used interchangeably in the literature and authoritative reports. However, the concept of business sustainability is broader than just CSR or even ESG, and thus a more comprehensive definition of sustainability is needed. The Sustainability Accounting Standards Board (SASB) defines business sustainability in the broader context of activities that create long-term value across several sustainability dimensions of environment, social capital, human capital, business model and innovation, and leadership and governance.[2]

Business sustainability is a relatively new concept, which has been defined as a process of focusing on the achievement of all five EGSEE dimensions of sustainability performance.[3] In this context, sustainability focuses on activities that generate financial economic sustainability performance (ESP), and nonfinancial environmental, social, and governance (ESG) sustainability performance with ethics integrated into both ESP and ESG sustainability dimensions. In this context, business sustainability is regarded as being much broader than CSR and even ESG, and it has recently gained more acceptance.[4] Business sustainability has advanced from a main focus on CSR to being integrated into corporate culture, mission, strategy, business model, and management processes.[5] Recent research conducted by the *MIT Sloan Management Review*, the Boston Consulting Group, and the United Nations Global Compact (UNGC) suggests that business sustainability is moving away from isolated and opportunistic efforts with the main focus on CSR and toward a more integrated, holistic, and strategic approach of embracing all dimensions of sustainability performance and engaging diverse stakeholders.[6] The Global Reporting Initiative (GRI), in its G4 sustainability guidelines, promotes integrated reporting on these five EGSEE dimensions of sustainability performance, with the ethical dimension being incorporated into other dimensions.[7]

This book defines business sustainability as a process of achieving sustainability performance in all five EGSEE dimensions to create shared value for all stakeholders.[8] Business sustainability provides organizations with both challenges and opportunities to properly measure all five EGSEE dimensions of sustainability performance, effectively assess their related risks, and properly disclose them to all affected stakeholders. In this context, a model of business sustainability should incorporate activities that generate financial (long-term earnings, growth, and return on investment) and nonfinancial sustainability performance (governance, social, ethical, and environmental) that concern all stakeholders. In practice, business sustainability should be viewed as a collection of procedures that improve both financial ESP and nonfinancial ESG sustainability performance dimensions to create shared value for all stakeholders. Currently, several organizations are trying to address these sustainability factors by establishing practices in terms of mandatory and voluntary initiatives. However, these initiatives are still constantly being evaluated, as their effectiveness is still debatable. This text describes these initiatives and tries to assess their relative success. Attention is given to the interactions of all five EGSEE dimensions of sustainability performance and possible tensions among these dimensions. ESP is the primary dimension that practitioners should emphasize, while environmental, social, and governance sustainability may interact with economic sustainability and produce important effects that should not be ignored. It provides descriptions of current practices of sustainability reporting and assurance and how these practices can enhance the overall concept of business sustainability practice and performance.

Emergence of Business Sustainability

Business sustainability is a multidisciplinary function of accounting, economics, ethics, finance, management, marketing, law, science, and supply-chain management, among others, with a keen focus on improving economic vitality, ethical behavior, ecological health, governance measures, and social justice. It can "bring benefits in terms of risk management, cost savings, access to capital, customer relationships, human resource management, and innovation capacity."[9] It also facilitates engagement with stakeholders regarding sustainable growth and risks, building trust in the company and with shareholders by enhancing effective capital allocation and achieving long-term investment goals. The 2017 KPMG survey of corporate responsibility reporting indicates that (i) there is an increasing quantitative global trend in corporate responsibility accounting with a keen focus on nonfinancial ESG sustainability performance; (ii) investors, regulators, and stock exchanges worldwide are the main drivers of the move toward integrated sustainability reporting; (iii) integrated reporting takes off worldwide, particularly in Europe and Asia; (iv) assurance on sustainability reports continues steady growth; (v) GRI guide 4 (G4) is the most popular framework for sustainability reporting; and (vi) more public companies worldwide include nonfinancial ESG information in their annual financial reports.[10]

Business sustainability has evolved in the past three decades from an initial focus on sustainable development and leaving a better environment for future generations to CSR corporate governance. The main goal is to create shared value for all stakeholders, including shareholders. Business sustainability is not a single event; it is a journey to improve both financial ESP and nonfinancial GSEE performance to create shared values for all stakeholders. In this context, sustainability focuses on activities that generate financial (long-term earnings, growth, and return on investment) and nonfinancial sustainability performance (ESEG) that concern all stakeholders. The terms *business sustainability, corporate social responsibility*, and *triple bottom line* (focusing on ESG) have been used interchangeably in the literature and authoritative reports. Business sustainability can also be defined as a social objective with a keen focus on achieving the triple-bottom-line performance of profit, planet, and people.[11]

Business sustainability for organizations refers to not only providing products and services that satisfy customers but also operating in a socially responsible manner, protecting the environment, and presenting reliable and transparent sustainability reports. The focus on business sustainability can benefit business organizations in many ways, including higher market and accounting performance, improved business reputation, enhanced product innovation and earnings growth, customer and employee satisfaction, and the creation of more stakeholder value. Yet, sustainability can be viewed as a box-ticking compliance and risk-mitigation exercise. This book defines all the above definitions in creating synergy for business strategies, activities, and performance from ethical, environmental, social, compliance, legal, governance, and economic dimensions in creating shared value for all stakeholders. A report released by the International Federation of Accountants (IFAC, 2015:3) indicates that global business organizations are expected to "take responsibility for a broader range of sustainability issues, such as social and environmental aspects that will ultimately affect financial performance and an organization's ability to create value over time."[12] In summary, business sustainability is defined as a process of focusing on the achievement of all five EGSEE dimensions of sustainability performance in creating shared value for all stakeholders.

The ever-increasing interest in sustainability reporting on financial, economic, and nonfinancial information is a natural response to stakeholders who are seeking more information from businesses on governance, environmental, and social matters. Customers are becoming more aware and making decisions based on how environmentally friendly a company is. Investors demand sustainability information to assess companies' cost-effectiveness, efficiency, and long-term survival. The integration of five EGSEE dimensions of sustainability performance into corporate infrastructure, business models, and management processes enables companies to conserve scarce resources, optimize production processes, identify product innovations, achieve cost efficiency and effectiveness, increase productivity, and promote corporate reputation. Taken together, the persistent challenges of sustainability have been the proper identification, measurement, recognition, reporting, and assurance of financial and nonfinancial KPIs. The integration of five EGSEE dimensions of sustainability performance into managerial strategies and practices enables companies to conserve scarce resources, optimize production processes, identify product innovations, achieve cost efficiency and effectiveness, increase productivity, and promote corporate reputation.

The 2013 Global Corporate Sustainability Report released by the United Nations Global Compact addresses the current state of corporate sustainability and presents the actions taken by companies worldwide in integrating sustainability into their strategies, operations, and culture.[13] The report encourages companies to engage their suppliers in the establishment of more sustainable practices and integration of sustainability into their supply chain processes (UN Global Compact, 2013). The report finds that companies are increasingly focusing on business sustainability and making progress in setting expectations for their suppliers to integrate sustainability into their strategies and practices. Investors worldwide are demanding more information on sustainability when making informed investment decisions. Other benefits of sustainability reporting are improved reputation, increased employee loyalty, and customer satisfaction. However, there are several sustainability challenges that, if not addressed properly, can threaten business value. The 2015 report by the Corporate Economic Forum offers these examples of the challenges faced by companies:[14]

1. Operational resources: Integration of business sustainability into the company's supply chain management has presented a challenge when dealing with price volatility and availability of resources.
2. Government regulation: Management faces challenges of effectively complying with sustainability regulations, rules, and standards, as well as the rising costs of compliance.
3. Mergers and acquisitions: Business sustainability can generate and promote merger and acquisition activities and cause companies to add or divest assets. Management should recognize the impact of these changes on sustainability and make proper decisions.
4. Major investors: Institutional investors and socially responsible investors have recently shown much interest in business sustainability. Thus, management should recognize this continuous interest in sustainability and its possible impact on the cost of capital.
5. Activist shareholders: Shareholders are becoming more actively involved with sustainability activities, and many shareholder resolutions in recent years have been related to the environment and society. Management should address these resolutions to avoid reputational or financial damage.
6. Reporting requirements: Sustainability financial and nonfinancial information are becoming more popular and more broadly demanded by external stakeholders. Management should recognize such continuous interest in sustainability information and integrate it into corporate reporting.
7. Talent acquisition: Employees are becoming interested in business sustainability by showing their interest in working in environmentally friendly, diverse, and socially responsible companies. Thus, management should demonstrate a commitment to sustainability in attracting and maintaining talented employees.

Emergence of Business Sustainability

The concept of sustainability performance suggests that management must extend its focus beyond maximizing short-term shareholder profit by considering the impact of its operations and entire value chains on all stakeholders, including the community, society, and the environment. Disclosure of EGSEE dimensions of sustainability performance, while signaling management commitment to sustainability and establishing legitimacy with all constituencies, poses a cost–benefit trade-off that has implications for investors and business organizations. In creating stakeholder value, management should identify potential social, environmental, governance, and ethical issues of concern and integrate them into their strategic planning and managerial processes. There are many reasons and justifications for management to integrate sustainability performance into its processes and practices, such as pressure from the labor movement, the development of moral values and social standards, and the change in public opinion regarding the role of business in environmental matters, governance, and ethics. Companies that are, or aspire to be, leaders in sustainability are challenged by rising public expectations, increasing innovation, continuous quality improvement, effective governance measures, high standards of ethics and integrity, and heightened social and environmental problems. Thus, management should develop and maintain proper sustainability programs that provide a common framework for the integration of all five EGSEE dimensions of sustainability into their management processes, such as:

- Integration of financial and nonfinancial sustainability KPIs into the business and investment analysis, supply chain management, and decision-making process.

- Communication of the company's management sustainability strategies, practices, and expectations to major stakeholders, including suppliers and customers, helps mitigate risks and foster corporate values and culture.

- Continuous assessment of the company's sustainability initiatives and related managerial processes is necessary to monitor and improve sustainability performance and identify challenging areas and risks that need further improvement.

- Promotion of product innovation and quality, customer retention and attraction, employee satisfaction, talent attraction, and productivity through management sustainability processes.

- Development of ESG initiatives that will impact the company's ability to generate sustainable financial performance for shareholders and create value for all stakeholders.

- Establishment of financial and nonfinancial KPIs relevant to all five EGSEE dimensions of sustainability performance that support management's strategic decisions and actions.

- Develop integrated sustainability reports to ensure that relevant financial and non-financial sustainability performance information is disclosed to all stakeholders.
- Periodic certifications of both financial and nonfinancial sustainability KPIs, issuance of integrated sustainability reports, and securing external assurance reports on all five EGSEE dimensions of sustainability performance.
- Proper culture, governance, structure, mechanisms, and processes for sustainability achievement in all five EGSEE dimensions of sustainability performance.
- Strategic plan in aligning financial ESP with nonfinancial ESG sustainability performance.
- Vigilant oversight functions performed by the board of directors and a firm commitment by management to sustainability.

The ever-improving accountability for business organizations appears to be an international trend. The global investment community is holding public companies responsible and accountable for their business activities and their financial and nonfinancial reports. Organizations of all types and sizes are focusing on an integrated strategic approach to business sustainability planning, performance, risk, reporting, and assurance. Business sustainability is no longer about greenwashing and branding; it has become a business imperative as investors demand, regulators require, and companies report their sustainability information in areas of financial economic sustainability performance and nonfinancial environmental, social, and governancesustainability performance with the ethics component integrated into both ESP and ESG dimensions. Companies are now adopting the corporate mission of profit to create shared value for all stakeholders by shifting their goals to create shareholder value while fulfilling their social, environmental, and governance responsibilities. Shared value creation for all stakeholders can be promoted within the wealth-maximization framework to pursue the goal of profit-with-purpose for corporations. Corporations can create the right balance between wealth maximization for shareholders under the shareholder primacy concept while achieving welfare maximization for all stakeholders under the stakeholder primacy concept.

Several initiatives have recently been taken to promote the move toward more robust business sustainability. For example, the Sustainability Accounting Standards Board, the International Integrated Reporting Council (IIRC), and the Global Reporting Initiative have joined forces with the International Financial Reporting Standards (IFRS) to establish the International Sustainability Standards Board (ISSB) and issue a practical guide for the measurement and reporting of sustainability performance from a market participants perspective. The ISSB has issued two standards for the identification of key performance indicators for ESG activities and their measurement and reporting. As of August 2022, it integrated the GRI, SASB, and IIRC as the primary sustainability organization in establishing sustainability accounting and reporting standards.[15] The regulators worldwide, including the Securities and Exchange Commission (SEC) in the United States, will require more robust and relevant disclosures of sustainability-related issues, including climate change and human capital.[16] The European Union (EU) adopted the Corporate Sustainability Reporting Directive (CSRD), which requires companies to disclose historical and forward-looking information about sustainability factors in planning, reporting, risk, and other matters, including environmental, social, employee, human rights, and governance.[17] These initiatives will extend sustainability reporting beyond metrics, disclosures, and ratings to assigning monetary values to an organization's ESG issues and integrating them into ESP and financial statements. The American Institute of Certified Public Accountants (AICPA), the Public Company Accounting Oversight Board (PCAOB), and the International Accounting and Auditing Standards Board (IAASB) are working on the development of assurance standards for sustainability reports. These initiatives enable business organizations to generate desired financial returns for shareholders and achieve positive social and environmental impacts. Business colleges and accounting schools should provide education in these emerging initiatives.

Sustainability Attributes

Business sustainability has advanced from branding and greenwashing, focusing on CSR, to the strategic imperative of achieving both financial ESP and nonfinancial ESG sustainability performance in the past decade. Four primary attributes of sustainability present a framework for the five dimensions of business sustainability performance and ten sustainability principles.[18] First, the business sustainability framework is driven by and built on stakeholder theory, which is the process of protecting the interests of all stakeholders, with a keen focus on achieving long-term and enduring financial and nonfinancial performance for all corporate constituencies, from shareholders to creditors, employees, customers, suppliers, society, and the environment. Stakeholder theory implies that business organizations have obligations to a number of constituencies and thus add value for all stakeholders, as listed above.[19] This stakeholder view of business organizations and business sustainability is supported by researchers, regulators, and the business and investment community.

Second, the main goal and objective function of business organizations is to maximize firm value. The goal of firm value maximization under the business sustainability framework can be achieved when the interests of all stakeholders are considered. The focus is on long-term shareholder value creation and maximization while considering trade-offs among other apparently competing and often conflicting interests of society, creditors, employees, and the environment. Theoretically, management's engagement in nonfinancial ESG sustainability activities, performance, and disclosure can be viewed as value increasing or value decreasing for investors. On the one hand, companies should effectively manage and improve nonfinancial ESG sustainability performance, enhance their reputation, fulfill their social responsibility, and promote a corporate culture of integrity and competency.

On the other hand, companies can only survive and generate sustainable performance when they continue to be financially profitable and are able to create shareholder value. Nonetheless, financial ESP and nonfinancial ESG sustainability performance and reporting complement each other and are not mutually exclusive. Companies that are governed effectively, are socially and environmentally responsible, conduct themselves ethically, have a good reputation and customer base, and operate in a satisfying employee environment are expected to produce sustainable performance, create shareholder value, and gain investor confidence and public trust.

The third theme is the time horizon of balancing short-term, medium, and long-term performance with a keen focus on long-term performance. Business sustainability focuses on the achievement of long-term and enduring performance and enables corporations to focus on maximizing long-term performance instead of meeting periodic financial targets. Businesses can no longer focus only on short-term earnings performance to beat analysts' forecasts and generate positive stock movements.

The fourth theme is the multidimensional nature of sustainability performance in all EGSEE areas. The multidimensional EGSEE sustainability performance is interrelated and integrated. The relative importance of the EGSEE sustainability dimensions and their contribution to the firm's overall long-term value maximization is affected by whether these EGSEE dimensions are viewed as competing, conflicting, or complementary. One view is that these EGSEE dimensions are complementary because a firm that is governed effectively adheres to ethical principles and commits to CSR and environmental obligations, enabling sustainable generation of long-term financial performance. Another view is that corporations must do well financially in the long term to be able to do well in terms of CSR and environmental activities. On the one hand, corporations that are managed ethically, governed effectively, and are socially and environmentally responsible are expected to produce sustainable performance, create shareholder value, and gain public trust and investor confidence. On the other hand, more economically profitable and viable corporations are in better positions and have more resources to create jobs, generate wealth, and better fulfill their social and environmental responsibilities.

Sustainability Attributes

In this chapter, sustainability reporting refers to the ongoing process of promoting, measuring, recognizing, enforcing, reporting, and auditing sustainability performance in all five EGSEE dimensions of sustainability.[20] Business organizations have traditionally reported their performance in economic affairs, but their main focus on financial results has become insufficient. In recent years, stakeholders, investors, regulators, global organizations, and the public at large have increasingly demanded information on both financial ESP and nonfinancial ESG KPIs in this platform of MBL accountability and sustainability reporting. Sustainability performance and accountability reporting have gained new interest during the recent financial crisis and the resulting global economic meltdown, which has sparked widening concerns about whether big businesses (e.g., banks and car-makers) are sustainable in the long term in contributing to the economic growth and prosperity of the nation. The ever-increasing erosion of public trust and investor confidence. in the sustainability of large businesses, the widening concern about social responsibility and environmental matters, the overconsumption of natural resources, the global government bailout of big businesses, and the perception that the government cannot solve all problems in the business world underscore the importance of having a keen focus on sustainability performance and accountability reporting.

Principles

Business sustainability has been promoted in response to demands by investors, necessary compliance with requirements from regulators, and voluntary initiatives by corporations considering interdependencies between global financial markets, the business community, and investors in advancing sustainable performance. More than 15,000 companies in 140 countries have adopted the ten sustainability principles established by the UNGC and integrated these principles into their strategic planning and operations.[21] These ten sustainability principles are classified into the four general categories of human rights, labor, environment, and anti-corruption. They are, in turn, related to the three dimensions (social, environmental, and ethical) of sustainability performance, as explained in the prior section. The 2013 Sustainability Report of the United Nations Global Compact suggests two ways for companies to achieve business sustainability: (i) integrating the ten principles into their strategies and operations and (ii) taking actions that support continuous improvements in sustainability performance.[22] The UN Global Compact Report also provides the Global Compact Management Model as a practical tool for companies to improve their sustainability performance.[23] The suggested model consists of six managerial processes of committing to, assessing, defining, implementing, measuring, and communicating sustainability strategies, operations, and performance in ensuring alignment with the ten principles and compliance with applicable laws, rules, and regulations.[24]

Sustainability Development Goals

In September 2015, the United Nations proposed a holistic framework of the Sustainable Development Goals (SDGs) to design indicators and an integrated monitoring framework to address all three dimensions of economic development, social inclusion, and environmental sustainability.[25] The 17 Sustainable Development Goals build on the United Nations Millennium Development Goals of 2000–2015 and involve new areas such as climate change, economic inequality, innovation, sustainable production, consumption, and peace and justice.[26] These SDGs are relevant to three dimensions of sustainability development – economic, social, and environmental development – and thus can be linked to all EGSEE dimensions of sustainability performance. A total of 169 targets and 232 indicators support the SDGs, and they are aligned with GRI G4 performance indicators.[27] Corporations frequently use these goals and link them to sustainability performance from the sourcing of raw materials and inputs for production to product innovations that lead to positive environmental, health, or societal impacts; employee safety, training, and diversity; compliance with ethical principles and human rights standards; and community initiatives in the areas of health and well-being, education, employment, and economic empowerment. Exhibit 2.1 presents all 17 SDGs and their relevance to the five EGSEE dimensions of sustainability performance. For example, SDG 6 is a proxy for clean water and sanitation, a combination of SDGs 5, 10, and 16 focuses on human rights and equalities, SDG 13 is related to climate action, and SDGs 14 and 15 are applicable to the nature of life below the water and life on land.

The 17 SDGs are related to sustainability reporting and assurance as they address economic, social, ethics, governance, and ecological sustainability performance. In November 2016, the International Federation of Accounting published a policy document that considers many of the 17 SDGs relevant to the accounting profession, including those that address quality education, gender equality, economic growth, innovation, production, climate action, and societal issues.[28] The 2017 report of PricewaterhouseCoopers (PwC) suggests that the majority of global firms (over 62%) referred to the SDGs in their reporting.[29]

Sustainability Factors

Sustainability has gained the attention of global financial institutions and investors as they began to consider both financial ESP and nonfinancial ESG opportunities and risks that affect their investment portfolio value. Four sustainability factors areplanning, performance, risks, and disclosures. These four sustainability factors enable business organizations to create shared value for all stakeholders, including shareholders.[30]

Exhibit 2.1   United Nations Sustainability Development Goals (UNSDGs)

Goal	Title	Description
SDG 1	No poverty: A measure of social dimension	By 2030, ensure all make more than $1.25/day. Equal access to economic resources. Increase mobilization of economic resources. Economic and social protection measures by 2030.
SDG 2	Zero Hunger: A measure of social dimension	End hunger by 2030 via universal nutrition (Zero Hunger Challenge). End malnutrition by 2030. Increase investment in farming and agricultural endeavors. Adopt food commodity markets.
SDG 3	Good health and well-being: A measure of social dimension	Maternal Mortality Rate Ratio. Reduce infant mortality in all countries. End AIDS and other serious disease epidemics by 2030 (World Bank). Universal reproductive care. Universal health coverage.
SDG 4	Quality education: A measure of social dimension	Expected years of schooling (years) UNESCO (2016). Literacy rate of 15–24 years old, both sexes (%) 2001–2013 UNESCO (2016). Net primary school enrolment rate (%) 1997–2014 UNESCO (2016). Population aged 25–64 with tertiary education (%) (a) – 2011 OECD (2016). PISA score (0–600) 2012 OECD (2016). Population aged 25–64 with upper secondary and post-secondary non-tertiary educational attainment (%) 2011–2013 OECD (2016)
SDG 5	Gender equality: A measure of social dimension	The proportion of seats held by women in national parliaments (%) 2012–2014 IPU (2015). Female years of schooling of the population aged 25 and above (% male) – 2014 UNDP (2015). Female labor force participation rate (% male) – 2010–2014 ILO (2016). Estimated demand for contraception that is unmet (% of women married or in union, ages 15–49) 2015 WHO (2016). Gender wage gap (% of male median wage) – 2012 OECD (2016).
SDG 6	Clean water and sanitation: A measure of social dimension	Universal water access by 2030. Adopt universal sanitation rules by 2030. Universal management, ecosystems, and sanitation of water by 2030.
SDG 7	Affordable and clean energy: A measure of social dimension	Universal, modern energy by 2030. 2x energy efficiency by 2030. Infrastructure upgrades.
SDG 8	Decent work and economic growth: A measure of social dimension	Full employment for all by 2030. Increase youth employment. Create policies and technologies to increase economic growth and promote diversity. Promote the protection of international labor rights. Eliminate forced labor.
SDG 9	Industry innovation and production: A measure of social dimension	Create an international infrastructure that promotes diversity and inclusion. Increase global accessibility to the Internet. Encourage education in technology and research-related fields. Promote financial funding for the development of infrastructure.

(Continued)

Exhibit 2.1 (Continued)

Goal	Title	Description
SDG 10	Reduce inequality: A measure of social dimension	Increase income growth of the bottom 40%. Include all races and sexes in economic, political, and social systems by 2030. Reduce the cost of immigration. Improve regulations of the global marketplace. Work with the World Trade Organization to increase the well-being of developing nations.
SDG 11	Sustainable cities and communities: A measure of social dimension	Housing for all by 2030. Reduce death due to poverty or economic status. Improve settlement management globally by 2030. Transportation for all by 2030.
SDG 12	Responsible consumption and production: A measure of environmental dimension	Percentage of anthropogenic wastewater that receives treatment (%) 2012 OECD (2016). Municipal solid waste (kg/year/capita) – 2012 World Bank (2016). Non-recycled municipal solid waste (kg/person/year) 2009–2013 OECD (2016).
SDG 13	Climate change: A measure of Environmental dimension	Energy-related CO_2 emissions per capita (CO_2/capita) – 2011 World Bank (2016). Climate Change Vulnerability Monitor (0–1) – 2014 HCSS (2014).
SDG 14	Life below water: A measure of environmental dimension	Conserve and sustainably use the oceans, seas, and marine resources for sustainable development. Manage this vital resource, which is crucial to humanity and affects climate change. Manage and protect marine and coastal ecosystems from pollution.
SDG 15	Life on land: A measure of the social dimension	Red List Index of species survival (0–1) 2016. IUCN and BirdLife International (2016). Annual change in forest area (%) 2012 YCELP & CIESIN (2014). Terrestrial sites of biodiversity importance are completely protected (%) 2013. BirdLife International, IUCN & UNEP-WCMC (2016).
SDG 16	Peace and justice: A measure of social dimension	Homicides (per 100,000 people) 2008–2012 UNODC (2016). Prison population (per 100,000 people) – 2002–2013 ICPR (2014). The proportion of the population who feel safe walking alone at night in the city or area where they live. (%) 2006–2015 Gallup (2015). Corruption Perception Index (0–100) – 2014. Transparency International (2015). The proportion of children under five years of age whose births have been registered with a civil authority, by age (%) 2014 UNICEF (2013). Government efficiency (1–7) – 2015/2016 WEF (2015). Property rights (1–7) – 2014/2015 WEF (2015).
SDG 17	Partnerships for the goals: A measure of social dimension	International concessional public finance, including official development assistance (% of GNI) 2013 OECD (2016). For all other countries: Tax revenue (% of GDP) 2013 World Bank (2016). Health, education, and R&D spending (% of GDP) – 2005–2014 UNDP (2015).

Sustainability Factors

Sustainability planning involves developing goals, strategies, and practices to establish the right balance between "shareholder value maximization," where management attempts to improve earnings for shareholders, and the broader "stakeholder/society value creation," where management maximizes the sum of the various stakeholders' surpluses (e.g., creditors, employees, customers, suppliers, society, and the environment) in creating shared value for all stakeholders. Sustainability planning focuses on activities and processes that are sustainable in the long term without causing significant short-term negative impacts on economic resources, society, and the environment. Sustainability planning consists of (1) evaluation and assessment of business activities and priorities; (2) establishment of goals and objectives; (3) stakeholder engagement and communication; (4) implementation and monitoring; and (5) reevaluation, reassessment, and adaptation.

Sustainability performance consists of financial economic ESP and nonfinancial ESG sustainability performance, with the ethics component integrated into both ESP and ESG dimensions of sustainability performance. The focus on sustainability efforts indicates that companies that achieve nonfinancial ESG sustainability performance, including social and environmental performance, manage their activities more effectively with effective corporate governance, conduct their business ethically, and are more financially sustainable in terms of ESP, enabling them to stay in business longer to contribute to their bottom-line earnings. The voluntary or mandatory ESG performance disclosures demonstrate that "sustainability-centric" companies that focus on achieving financial ESP and nonfinancial ESG sustainability performance have more incentives to disclose information that will differentiate themselves from "non-sustainability-centric" companies that often do not focus on financial ESP and nonfinancial ESG to avoid a bad reputation. Therefore, disclosure of voluntary nonfinancial ESG sustainability performance may signal management's commitment to transparency in both financial ESP and nonfinancial ESG sustainability performance and thus can reduce information asymmetry and increase firm value. The sustainability risk factor determines stakeholder exposure to risks associated with failure to achieve sustainability performance.

Sustainability performance has received the attention of investors, and several dimensions of sustainability performance in social and environmental initiatives have gained widespread global acceptance. These initiatives include important sustainability matters such as global warming, climate change, ethical workspace, customer satisfaction, just and safe working conditions, non-discriminatory fair wages, workplace diversity and inclusion, safe and quality products, concern for the environment, fair and transparent business practices and environmental preservation, clean air and water, and minimum age for child labor. It is, however, important to realize that each industry has its own applicable set of financial and nonfinancial key performance indicators relevant to both financial ESP and nonfinan-cial ESG sustainability performance. Each business organization must carefully identify its profit-with-purpose mission of generating profit for shareholders while protecting the interests of other stakeholders, including social and environmental responsibilities and impacts in the context of its business culture and environment. The proper and relevant list of financial ESP and non-financial ESG sustainability KPIs should be determined accord-ing to corporate mission and strategy, industry best practices, legal regimes, corporate culture, diversity, political infrastructure, and managerial philosophy.

The sustainability performance factors underscore that firms that focus on their nonfinan-cial performance, including social and environmental performance, are managed more effectively with good corporate governance and are more financially sustainable. The sus-tainability performance attribute underscores that firms that focus on their nonfinancial performance, including social and environmental performance, and are managed more effectively with good corporate governance are more financially sustainable. Sustainability risks determine the relationship between risks and rewards assumed by shareholders. The sustainability risk factor determines stakeholder exposure to risks associated with busi-ness sustainability.

The voluntary or mandatory disclosure attribute of sustainability performance posits that more sustainability-centric, "good type," firms that focus on nonfinancial ESG and sustain-able financial performance have more incentives to disclose information to differentiate themselves from less sustainability-centric, "bad type," firms that do not focus on ESG and financial sustainability to avoid a bad reputation. Disclosure of ESG sustainability may signal management's commitment to both financial ESPand nonfinancial ESG sustain-ability performance, thereby reducing information asymmetry and increasing firm value. Disclosure of voluntary ESG sustainability may signal management's commitment to both financial and nonfinancial performance. to be more transparent and thus can affect infor-mation asymmetry and firm value. Business sustainability can be beneficial to both internal and external stakeholders. Stakeholders are those who have vested interests in a firm through their investments in the form of financial capital (shareholders), human capital (employees), physical capital (customers and suppliers), social capital (society), environ-mental capital (the environment), and regulatory capital (government). Stakeholders have a reciprocal relationship and interaction with a firm in the sense that they contribute to the firm's value creation, and their well-being is also affected by the firm.

Companies should strive to maintain good business sustainability in their everyday prac-tices to create shared value for stakeholders and to minimize information asymmetry among all stakeholders. If a company withholds information about its practices, whether

Sustainability Factors

intentionally in efforts to minimize its effect on the bottom line or unintentionally as a result of not performing due diligence on its processes, this may result in an increased perceived risk of the venture, decreased share price, concerns regarding the management's ability to lead the company, or even "black swan" events: unforeseen events that have a major, and usually negative, impact on the company and very often can be seen clearly in hindsight as turning points that could have been avoided if more attention had been paid. Thus, good sustainability is important for a company in the short run to ensure viability in the ever-changing marketplace. However, to build a strong company in the long run, business sustainability must be put into practice to prepare for the future and mitigate unforeseen or inescapable events. One of the key features of putting business sustainability into practice is that when faced with problems from multiple stakeholders, a company with good sustainability practices can pivot its position to address the problem in the best manner possible.

Sustainability Planning

Business organizations have recently focused on sustainable and long-term strategic plans to pursue their mission of profit-with-purpose, enabling them to implement short-term and long-term plans for making a profit while pursuing long-term strategic plans for social and environmental impacts. The concept of impact investing, which emphasizes corporate long-term investment strategies for creating returns on investment for shareholders and providing positive social and environmental impacts, is gaining acceptance among investors. Investment managers are trying to maximize financial performance and achieve positive and measurable effects on the environment and society. This section discusses strategic planning for business sustainability, including the role of corporate boards and executives in developing a strategy for business sustainability and how stakeholders' perception of sustainability reports and metrics influences those strategic plans. Business sustainability encourages management to establish synergy and congruence between short-term planning to make a profit and long-term planning to ensure the continuity of operations and integrate sustainability into the business environment, corporate culture, and strategic plans to generate earnings and social and environmental impacts.

Long-term sustainability planning takes into account many more factors beyond just profits and shareholder wealth maximization to create a shared value for all stakeholders. If companies want long-term success, they will need to factor in environmental consciousness, ethics, social impacts, diversity and inclusion, and customer satisfaction and reputation. They will need to ensure that their products and services are environmentally friendly and minimize negative impacts on society and the environment. Furthermore, companies should embrace their ESG activities and make it a practice to be active in their communities through neighborhood cleanups and volunteering with non-profit organizations that assist in communities' environmental and educational development. Fostering a workplace that encourages these actions can help sustain a company long-term through a symbiotic relationship and reputation enhancements. Companies that help protect the environment through eco-friendly business practices and involvement in community outreach projects can help communities progress and improve the environment for future generations. This, in turn, will create a sense of trust in their respective communities, and the chances of these communities conducting business with these companies will increase.

Strategic sustainability planning enables business organizations to focus on the profit-with-purpose mission of maximizing their positive impacts on all stakeholders, including shareholders, employees, communities, customers, society, and the environment, and to minimize the negative impacts on multiple stakeholders. In case of nonexistence of and/or inadequate "statement of purpose" and "strategic sustainability planning," the board of directors, in collaboration with management, should develop the statement of purpose and strategic sustainability planning. The statement of purpose should include the mission, which reflects the organization's strategic sustainability planning in achieving short-, medium-, and long-term sustainable performance. Companies are now adopting the corporate mission of profit with purpose and strategic sustainability planning to create shared value for all stakeholders by shifting their goals to create shareholder value while fulfilling their social, environmental, and governance responsibilities. The statement of purpose, along with strategic sustainability planning, should define objectives for survival in the short term, continuity of business in the medium term, and strategic sustainability planning in the long term. In collaboration with management, the board of directors should also design strategic sustainability planning to achieve new objectives by designing business continuity plans, long-term strategic plans, and crisis management strategies.

Sustainability planning consists of the following:

- Evaluation and assessment of business activities and priorities. Business organizations should evaluate and assess their activities, set priorities, and define strategies to determine their economic, environmental, and social impacts. There are currently several sustainability investment strategies: "Impact First," "Finance First," "Impact Investing," and "Anti-ESG." "Impact First" refers to an investment strategy that prioritizes the social, environmental, or ethical consequences and benefits of a decision or investment above financial considerations. "Finance First" is an investment strategy that prioritizes financial returns as the primary and often only consideration in

Sustainability Factors

decision-making. "Impact Investing" incorporates both "Impact First" and "Finance First" into investment portfolio assessment. "Anti-ESG" is an investment strategy that does not consider ESG factors. Investors typically use two approaches, positive screening and negative screening, in assessing ESG investment factors, and management uses the same approaches in managing ESG investment activities. Positive screening enables investors to actively consider investments that exhibit strong ESG performance or contribute to sustainability goals of renewable energy, diversity, and inclusion practices by assessing the ESG ratings or scores of the selected investments and comparing them to relevant benchmarks. Negative screening involves excluding certain industries or companies from the investment portfolio based on ESG factors and criteria avoiding investments in fossil fuels, tobacco, or weapons manufacturing. Management uses measurement to track the percentage of excluded sectors in the portfolio and compare it to the overall market.

- Establishment of goals and objectives. Business organizations should establish specific, attainable, relevant, measurable short-term and long-term goals aligning with sustainability priorities. There can be multiple goals of balancing profit, people, planet, and prosperity to achieve the corporate mission of profit-with-purpose.

- Stakeholder engagement and communication. Business organizations should engage diverse stakeholders, including local communities, employees, customers, and environmental groups, and collect their input to better understand better their sustainability opportunities, preferences, concerns, and expectations. Sustainability goals and progress should be effectively and timely communicated to all stakeholders, as transparency builds trust and support.

- Implementation and monitoring. Sustainability strategic plans should be implemented and monitored continuously to ensure the effective achievement of sustainability goals. Business organizations should monitor the implementation of (1) measures to reduce energy and water consumption through energy-efficient technologies, renewable energy sources, and water-saving practices; (2) processes for minimizing waste generation and promoting recycling and reuse; (3) consideration of the entire life cycle of products and services; (4) engagement in initiatives that contribute positively to local communities, such as job creation, education, and healthcare; and (5) ensurance that sustainability plans and operations promote diversity, equity, and inclusion both within the organization and in the broader community.

- Compliance, reassessment, and adaptation. Compliance with applicable sustainability laws, rules, regulations, standards, and best practices ensures the achievement of sustainability goals and missions. Business organizations should reevaluate and reassess their success and progress toward achieving their sustainability purposes by identifying key performance indicators for all five economic, environmental, ethical, social, and governance dimensions of sustainability performance. These KPIs should be regularly monitored to track progress toward sustainability goals. This continuous monitoring and assessment assists in identifying areas for improvement and adapting plans based on changing circumstances. Technological innovation enables businesses to apply cutting-edge technologies and embrace innovative technologies that can improve sustainability performance. Adaptability provides flexibility and responsiveness to changing economic, environmental, and social conditions.

Investors can use various quantitative and qualitative metrics to effectively assess and measure sustainability investment strategies, such as: (1) ESG ratings and scores by using third-party ESG rating agencies to assess the sustainability performance of investments and portfolios; (2) financial performance by analyzing risk-adjusted returns, volatility, and other financial metrics of sustainable investment portfolios compared to the benchmarks; (3) specific ESG metrics relevant to the investment strategy, including carbon intensity, water usage, employee turnover, and board diversity; (4) impact metrics to measure the social and environmental impact of investments through indicators like greenhouse gas emissions avoided, lives improved, and jobs created; (5) stakeholder engagement by evaluating the effectiveness of engagement activities by assessing changes in company behavior or performance in response to stakeholder preferences and investor pressure; and (6) regulatory compliance to ensure compliance with all applicable laws, rules, relevant regulatory frameworks, and standards governing sustainable investing practices.

Dimensions of Sustainability Performance

Sustainability performance is typically classified into financial and nonfinancial performance and grouped into five dimensions: Economic (E), Governance (G), Social (S), Ethical (E), and Environmental (E), abbreviated as EGSEE.[31] Although business sustainability continues to evolve, several dimensions of sustainability performance pertaining to social and environmental initiatives have gained widespread global acceptance. These initiatives include an ethical workplace, customer satisfaction, just and safe working conditions, nondiscriminatory fair wages, workplace diversity, environmental preservation, clean air and water, minimum age for child labor, safe and good-quality products, concern for the environment, and fair and transparent business practices. Each industry has its own applicable set of sustainability financial and nonfinancial KPIs. Each business organization must carefully identify its own social and environmental responsibilities, given the context of the industry and community in which it operates. The list of financial and nonfinancial sustainability KPIs depends on a variety of factors: industry, legal regimes, cultural background,

Sustainability Factors

corporate mission and strategy, corporate culture, political infrastructure, and managerial philosophy. Despite these disparate sustainability performance dimensions and their KPIs, sustainability has become an integral component of business. This section describes each of the EGSEE sustainability performance dimensions and their related KPIs.

Financial Economic Sustainability Performance

The most important and commonly accepted dimension of sustainability is financial economic sustainability performanceThe primary goal of any business organization is to create shareholder value through generating sustainable economic performance. Business organizations should focus on activities that generate long-term corporate profitability rather than short-term performance. The financial ESP dimension of sustainability performance can be achieved when business organizations focus on long-term sustainability performance and improved effectiveness, efficiency, and productivity. Long-term ESP should be communicated to shareholders through the preparation of high-quality financial reports in compliance with global accounting standards as well as the Global Reporting Initiative guidelines.[32]

The ESP sustainability involves ensuring the long-term viability and profitability of a business while contributing to environmental protection and the overall economic well-being of society. It requires sound strategic financial management, responsible investment practices, and adherence to ethical business standards. The financial ESP dimension of sustainability also involves considering the impact of business decisions on local economies and communities, as well as global markets and society. The ESP dimension of sustainability should reflect the financial strengths and concerns of an organization as well as the economic impacts on its stakeholders and society.[33] ESP can be measured directly through financial activities between an organization and its stakeholders or indirectly through non-financial costs and benefits of economic relations and their effects on stakeholders. The financial ESP dimension of sustainability is further presented in Chapter 7.

Although the conventional measures of cash flows, earnings, and return on investment are essential in evaluating financial performance, they don't reflect sustainable performance and future growth. The report also identifies the key measures of sustainable performance as operational efficiency, customer satisfaction, talent management, and innovation that should be derived from internal factors of strategy, risk profile, strengths and weaknesses, and corporate culture, as well as external factors of reputation, technology, competition, globalization, and utilization of natural resources.[34] Business sustainability demands an integrated effort by management and a change in managerial focus from the short-termism of tangible quick wins to the achievement of long-term, sustainable, nonfinancial performance. Sustaining sustainability requires an understanding of both performance and risks and their integration into the corporate culture, as well as management strategies, decisions, and actions. This integrated approach to sustaining business sustainability enables management to compete effectively in the global marketplace.

Nonfinancial Dimensions of Sustainability Performance

Nonfinancial dimensions of sustainability performance (governance, social, ethical, and environmental) are briefly described in this section and thoroughly explained in Chapter 8. Nonfinancial dimensions of sustainability, also referred to as environmental, social, and governance with ethics, are integrated into other dimensions.

Governance Sustainability Performance

The corporate governance landscape has changed significantly in the aftermath of the passage of the Sarbanes-Oxley (SOX) Act of 2002 and the global 2007–2009 financial crises. The lack of effective corporate governance has been mentioned frequently as an overriding contributing factor to the global financial crisis. Internal and external corporate governance measures have since been established by policymakers, regulators, and corporations to improve the quality of corporate governance and, thus, stakeholder trust and investor confidence in corporate sustainable performance and reporting. Regulatory reforms in the United States, such as the Sarbanes-Oxley Act of 2002[35] and the Dodd-Frank Act of 2010,[36] are designed to improve the quality and effectiveness of corporate governance. Effective corporate governance promotes accountability for the board of directors and executives, enhances sustainable operational and financial performance, improves the reliability and quality of financial information, and strengthens the integrity and efficiency of the capital market, which results in economic growth and prosperity for the nation. Effective corporate governance sustainability requires setting an appropriate tone at the top, defining roles and responsibilities of all corporate gatekeepers, from the board of directors and executives to internal and external auditors and legal counsel, and promoting accountability for them. The effectiveness of corporate governance is also affected by legal, regulatory, internal, and external mechanisms and best practices to create shared value for all stakeholders, as further explained in Chapter 8. Effective corporate governance is vital for business sustainability and involves establishing transparent decision-making processes by the corporate board of directors and executives, accountability mechanisms, and ethical standards. Comprehensive and strong corporate governance practices help create opportunities, mitigate risks, build trust with stakeholders, and ensure compliance with all applicable laws, rules, regulations, and standards.

Corporate governance mechanisms are multidimensional, and it is important to consider all dimensions when examining governance sustainability performance. The corporate governance landscape has also changed significantly in the aftermath of the global 2007–2009 financial crisis. The lack of effective corporate governance has been identified frequently as an overriding contributing factor in the global financial crisis. For example, a rising trend in corporate governance is the matter of "Say on Pay." As businesses become more transparent regarding their inner workings, not to mention the stark realization of the income gap brought to light throughout the Great Recession, shareholders are asking for more say in how companies reward their executives. Over time, different internal and external corporate governance measures have been established by policymakers and regulators to improve the quality of corporate governance. As a result, these measures have enhanced stakeholders' trust and investors' confidence in sustainable corporate performance and reporting. It is important to note that the governance dimension of sustainability performance is affected by legal, regulatory, internal, and external mechanisms, as well as best practices to create shareholder value while protecting the interests of other stakeholders. For example, regulatory reforms are designed to improve the quality and effectiveness of corporate governance, which are demanded by the business community. In summary, effective corporate governance sustainability performance promotes accountability for the board of directors and executives, enhances sustainable operational and financial performance, improves the reliability and quality of financial information, and strengthens the integrity and efficiency of the capital market, which results in economic growth and prosperity for the nation.

Social Sustainability Performance

The social dimension of sustainability performance reflects the transformation of social goals into practices that benefit an organization's stakeholders. Social performance measures an organization's social mission and its alignment with the interests of society. The social dimension of sustainability performance ranges from ensuring the high quality of products and services, better customer satisfaction, and improved employee health and well-being to adding a positive contribution to the sustainability of the planet and the quality of life for future generations. Social sustainability performance involves establishing and maintaining positive relationships with stakeholders, including shareholders, creditors, employees, customers, suppliers, and the communities in which a business operates. It encompasses employee satisfaction, fair labor practices, diversity and inclusion, employee well-being, community engagement, and customer service. Socially sustainable businesses prioritize issues such as fair wages, healthy and safe working conditions, and ethical operation and sourcing practices.

Socially responsible investment (SRI) is becoming an increasingly important part of business. Though the mantra of business has long been to increase shareholders' profits, the advent of benefit corporations (or B-corporations) has brought with it a chance for shareholders to affect businesses' methods to increase their desire for social change instead of personal enrichment. The UN's Principles of Responsible Investing (PRI) was initiated in 2005 to encourage global investors to integrate ESG into their investment decisions.[37] Recently, under sustainable and SRI principles, investors have considered various sustainability issues in their investment analyses, and SRIs have increased by more than 22% to $3.74 trillion in managed assets during the 2010–2012 period,[38] and it is estimated to exceed $53 trillion in 2025.[39] The social dimension of sustainability performance is typically viewed as CSR and is further explained in Chapter 8.

Ethical Sustainability Performance

The ethical dimension of sustainability performance, particularly corporate ethical culture, plays an important role in ensuring business continuity and the achievement of corporate goals and financial sustainability. The effectiveness of ethical sustainability performance depends on a corporate culture of integrity and competency and an appropriate tone at the top by the corporate board of directors and executives. Characteristics of an ethical organizational culture are codes of conduct for directors, officers, and employees, a system of responsibility and accountability, and a workplace that promotes honesty, mutual respect, fair practices, and freedom to raise concerns. The persistence and existence of corporate scandals and financial crises have shown that companies that conduct their business ethically are more sustainable in the long term and can generate high quality and quantity of earnings, economic growth, and development. The ethical dimension of sustainability performance is often integrated into the business environment and corporate culture to achieve financial ESP.

Environmental Sustainability Performance

Sustainability performance with respect to the environmental dimensions has gained attention from the business community. Stakeholders are demanding clearer and more transparent information about the impacts of an organization's activities and operations on the environment beyond what is legislated by law. Corporations cannot solely focus on corporate profitability and ignore their impacts on the environment. The environmental dimension of sustainability performance includes creating a better work environment, reducing the carbon footprint, improving air and water quality, and maximizing the positive effects of an organization on natural resources and the environment. The main goal of the environmental sustainability performance dimension is to minimize the environmental impact of business operations by reducing resource consumption, mitigating pollution, and minimizing waste generation. Strategies for environmental sustainability include the effective and efficient use of natural resources, adopting renewable energy sources, implementing energy-efficient practices, reducing water usage, and minimizing carbon emissions. Currently, there are a number of global organizations trying to encourage corporations to consider their impact on the environment when making business decisions. For example, the Coalition for Environmentally Responsible Economies (CERES) and the UN Environment Program, in collaboration with the UNGC, promote environmental initiatives.[40] Governments throughout the world are also instituting measures to ensure that the environment is better protected at the behest of society at large. For example, the Chilean government recently canceled a $10 billion dam project in Patagonia due in part to inadequate environmental impact assessments and in part due to pressure from citizens who did not want the natural beauty and usability of their land to be devastated. In this case, the government decided to forego the economic benefits of the project in consideration of not only the current impact it would have on the environment but also future known and unknown ramifications.

Stakeholders are demanding clearer and more transparent information about the impacts of an organization's activities and operations on the environment beyond what is legislated by law. The environmental dimension of sustainability performance includes creating a better work environment, reducing the carbon footprint, improving air and water quality, and maximizing the positive effects of an organization on natural resources and the environment. Effective achievement of environmental sustainability performance requires businesses to create the right balance in maximizing their economic profits, protecting the environment, and ensuring a better environment for future generations. Climate change and greenhouse gas emissions affect organizations of all types and sizes worldwide and thus should be integrated into sustainability initiatives, decisions, actions, and performance measures. The environmental dimension of sustainability performance will be discussed in detail in Chapter 8.

Business Sustainability Risk

The third factor of business sustainability is sustainability risk, which is important to all stakeholders, particularly investors, in the assessment of their investments. Five risks are associated with business sustainability. These risks are strategic, operational, compliance, financial, and reputation.[41] One more emerging risk that currently threatens the sustainability of all types and sizes of organizations is the risk of potential cyberattacks and security breaches. Consideration and proper assessment and management of those six risks are becoming increasingly important and play an effective role in achieving EGSEE sustainability performance.

The most important risk relevant to business sustainability is strategic risk. Strategic risks should be identified, assessed, and managed with a keen focus on minimizing their negative effects and building upon the opportunities provided by addressing these risks. Operational risks are associated with all five EGSEE dimensions of sustainability performance, including the integration of all sustainability performance dimensions into operating activities across operational units, operation technology, supply chain, information technology, and other functional areas. Many companies are facing the challenges of complying with these regulatory measures, and noncompliance may cause significant risks of interruption and/or discontinuation of their business. Compliance risks need to be assessed and managed, and their negative impacts need to be minimized. To achieve this objective, many companies have created either a board compliance committee or an executive position as compliance and risk officer. All five EGSEE dimensions of sustainability performance are associated with business reputation, customer satisfaction, and the ethical workplace. The company's reputation and its related risks should be evaluated on an ongoing basis, and any damage to the reputation should be minimized. The financial risk of issuing materially misstated financial reports is detrimental to the sustainability of corporations. Sustainability reports are expected to be value-relevant to both external and internal users of such reports. Cyber hacking and security breaches of information systems are becoming a reality for many businesses (e.g., Sony, Target, Morgan Chase), and their risk assessment and controls demand significant IT investment and commitment by directors and offices to prevent their occurrences.

The International Organization for Standardization (ISO) published its new standard, ISO 31000: Risk Management – Principles and Guidelines, in 2009, which provides principles and guidelines on risk management.[42] These ISO 31000 risk guidelines assist business organizations in developing, implementing, maintaining, assessing, monitoring, and continuously improving their risk management system to minimize the negative effects of strategic, operational, financial, compliance, and reputation risks.[43] These risks are interrelated and, thus, should be properly assessed and managed. For example, excessive strategic risk can also cause operational, financial, compliance, and reputational risks. The compliance risk directly or indirectly associated with business sustainability – including noncompliance with regulatory reforms, health and safety, human rights and labor laws, corporate governance measures, antibribery, and environmental risks – can vary among organizations and across countries. For example, environmental risks can include direct effects (e.g.,

Environmental Sustainability Performance

emissions trading cost exposures) and indirect consequences (e.g., energy price increases and accompanying reporting and compliance costs) of noncompliance with environmental laws, rules, and regulations. Business organizations also assess and manage their financial risk of producing and disclosing materially misstated financial reports. Minimization of reputational risk is vital to the success of sustainability programs and related performance, as stakeholder satisfaction is essential to a sustainable business.

Sustainability Disclosure

Sustainability disclosure is another important factor in business sustainability. Sustainability disclosure provides financial information on ESP and nonfinancial information on ESG sustainability performance. Authoritative reports (GRI, IIRC) and academic research often classify sustainability dimensions into financial ESP and nonfinancial ESG, while the ethics dimension is integrated into both ESP and ESG sustainability dimensions. As of now, disclosure of ESP information is mandatory in many countries, whereas ESG information is typically disclosed on a voluntary basis, except for large European companies starting in 2017 and Hong Kong-listed companies in 2016.[44] Voluntary disclosure is considered any financial and nonfinancial information disclosed by management beyond mandatory financial reports, consisting of strategic information (product, competition, customers), financial information (management earnings forecast, stock price), and nonfinancial ESG information.

Global public companies today face the challenges of adapting proper sustainability strategies and practices to effectively respond to social, ethical, environmental, and governance issues while creating sustainable financial performance and value for their shareholders. Business sustainability has recently evolved from the focus on short-term financial performance and fulfillment of CSR to the achievement of long-term financial performance and ESG sustainability performance in creating shared value for all stakeholders. In September 2014, the European Commission adopted the Council Directive on the disclosure of nonfinancial sustainability information for more than 6,000 companies for their financial year 2017.[45] The Directive provides nonbinding guidelines in facilitating the disclosure of nonfinancial environmental, social, anticorruption, and diversity information by large public companies. The Directive also provides large companies with significant flexibility to disclose nonfinancial information either as a separate report or an integrated report along with financial information. The primary objectives of the Directive are to (i) increase transparency in sustainability reporting, (ii) increase sustainability performance on social and environmental matters, and (iii) contribute effectively to long-term economic growth and employment. Affected companies should report their:[46]

- Environmental performance.
- Social and employee-related materials.
- Human rights policies.
- Anticorruption and bribery issues.
- Diversity on the board of directors.

The European Commission, on September 29, 2014, endorsed the adoption by the Council of the Directive on the disclosure of nonfinancial sustainability information for more than 6,000 companies for their financial year 2017. The Directive provides nonbinding guidelines for facilitating the disclosure of nonfinancial information by large public companies. Thus, stakeholders, including investors and society at large, are intended to benefit from this increased transparency of nonfinancial sustainability information by these affected companies. The Directive also provides large companies with significant flexibility to disclose nonfinancial information either as a separate report or an integrated report along with financial information. It is expected that other countries will follow the European suit in requiring the disclosure of sustainability information on all or some of the five EGSEE dimensions of sustainability performance.

Arguments about the detrimental effects of conventional financial reporting focusing only on economic performance are mounting. While financial information may have a short-term impact on market efficiency and thus require interim trading updates, in the long term, it will lead to substantial pressures on management from the market to meet short-term targets. There are basically two detrimental effects of conventional financial reporting: (i) it encourages short-termism, and (ii) it compromises the quality of financial reporting. Short-termism is defined as a phenomenon that leads managerial decisions and actions disproportionately toward achieving short-term earnings targets at the expense of sustainable performance. Conventional financial reporting encourages management to focus on short-term performance and the goal of meeting or exceeding short-term targets or analysts' forecast estimates. Such an impact on management behavior prevents management from directing its resources toward sustainable and enduring plans, activities, and EGSEE sustainability performance. Uncertainty about the future, including government policies, regulations, markets, and other unforeseeable factors, drives managerial planning to short-term considerations rather than long-term sustainable performance.

The European Commission has long promoted CSR and its integration into corporate strategic decisions by defining CSR as "a concept whereby companies integrate social and environmental concerns in their business."[47] This definition of CSR suggests companies take social actions above and beyond their mandatory requirements toward society and

Environmental Sustainability Performance

the environment. Business sustainability with a keen focus on CSR can "bring benefits in terms of risk management, cost savings, access to capital, customer relationships, human resource management, and innovation capacity."[48] Thus, disclosure of such information promotes interaction with all stakeholders on important nonfinancial ESG sustainability performance. Disclosure of nonfinancial ESG sustainability performance demonstrates companies' commitment and move toward achieving the European Union's treaty objectives of "the Europe 2020 strategy for smart, sustainable, and inclusive growth, including the 75% employment target."[49] It also facilitates engagement with stakeholders regarding sustainable growth and risks, building trust in the company and shareholders regarding the allocation of capital and achievement of long-term investment goals.

Voluntary Sustainability Disclosure

Corporate disclosure, either mandatory or voluntary, is the backbone of financial markets worldwide. Public companies are required to disclose a set of financial information as long as the public holds their securities. The primary purpose of corporate disclosure is to provide economic agents (e.g., shareholders and creditors) with adequate information to make appropriate decisions. Mandatory corporate reporting, including financial reports disseminated to investors and filed with regulators, is designed to provide investors with relevant, useful, and reliable information for making sound investment decisions. A moral hazard can occur in the presence of information asymmetry, wherein management knows more about its actions and their effects on financial reports and chooses to withhold proper financial information from investors. Voluntary sustainability reports are usually considered as any disclosures outside of financial statements that regulators and standard-setters do not require.

Voluntary disclosure often takes the form of corporate responsibility reports and responses to surveys or data requests. The proposed fourth generation (G4) of GRI's guidelines covers economic, governance, social, and environmental performance. The GRI reporting process enables organizations to self-declare sustainability information based on one of three application levels (A, B, or C), depending on the extent of the information provided. The GRI initially focused on a triple-bottom-line of economic, social, and environmental performance with version 3.1 (G3) of its sustainability framework. However, in 2011, the GRI developed version 4.1, or the fourth generation (G4) of guidelines, which covers economic, governance, social, and environmental performance. Unlike audit reports on financial statements, assurance reports on sustainability information are neither standardized nor regulated or licensed.

The Sustainability Accounting Standards Board, in its 2013 Conceptual Framework for Sustainability, suggests that sustainability performance disclosures be made as a complete set in the Management's Discussion and Analysis of Financial Condition and Results of Operations (MD&A) section of Form 10-K, in a subsection titled "Sustainability Accounting Standard Disclosures" filed with the SEC and disseminated to shareholders. The IFAC released its revised "International Standard on Assurance Engagements Other Than Audits or Reviews of Historical Financial Information" 3000 (ISAE 3000). Specifically, ISAE 3410 deals with assurance engagements for an organization reporting greenhouse gas (GHG) statements. Alternatively, GRI can examine the content provided by sustainability reporters and express an opinion on the extent of compliance with GRI guidelines but not the quality and/or reliability of disclosed sustainability information.

Global and national stock exchanges have promoted sustainability performance reporting by adopting laws, regulations, and listing standards that specifically mandate sustainability reporting. In recent years, many countries, including Australia, Austria, Canada, Denmark, France, Germany, Malaysia, the Netherlands, Sweden, Hong Kong, and the United Kingdom, have adopted stand-alone ESP and ESG sustainability performance reports.[50] It is expected that regulators in other countries will follow suit, moving toward mandatory sustainability performance reporting. Stock exchanges worldwide either require or recommend that their listed companies report sustainability information (e.g., Singapore Stock Exchange, 2011; Toronto Stock Exchange, 2014 [TSX, 2014]; Hong Kong Stock Exchange, 2015 [HKEx, 2015]), and more than 6,000 European companies will be required to disclose their non-financial ESG sustainability performance and diversity information for their financial year 2017.[51]

The Delaware Certification of Adoption of Transparency and Sustainability Standards Act (the "Act") was signed into law on June 27, 2018.[52] The Act became effective on October 1, 2018, and represents Delaware's initiative to support sustainability practices by enabling Delaware-governed entities to disclose their commitment to CSR and sustainability. It reflects Delaware's recognition that sustainability is a business imperative rather than greenwashing and should be integrated into the business environment and corporate culture to promote innovation, long-term financial growth, societal benefits, and environmental protection. The Act is intended to demonstrate a firm commitment to sustainability and a proper response to the increasing calls from investors, customers, and clients for greater transparency in sustainability practices. The Act is voluntary and applies only to Delaware-law-governed entities that seek to become certified as reporting entities. It also gives entities much flexibility in developing their sustainability strategies and practices to meet their sustainability goals and needs. However, several mandatory features of the Act require the entity's governing body to approve its standards and assessment measures and

Voluntary Sustainability Disclosure

for those standards and measures to be made publicly available. The Act also recommends that sustainability practices be addressed at the highest levels of the organization.

To meet this requirement, the board of directors must adopt resolutions creating "standards," including the principles and guidelines to assess and report the impact of the firm's activities on society and the environment. Top executives must establish proper measures and assess their effectiveness in evaluating sustainability performance to meet the requirements of sustainability standards approved by the board. The Act provides much flexibility for reporting entities to select their standards and tailor them to the specific needs of their industry or business. Entities and their governing body (the board of directors) may seek insight from investors, clients, and customers and obtain advice from third-party experts and advisors in establishing their sustainability standards and assessment measures. Participating entities can obtain a certification of adoption of transparency and sustainability standards from the Delaware Secretary of State by (i) establishing and preparing a standards statement, including the standards and assessment measures; (ii) submitting the payment of relatively nominal fees to the Delaware Secretary of State; (iii) agreeing to the entity's becoming and remaining a reporting entity; and (iv) filing a renewal statement annually to continue as a reporting entity. The certification allows the reporting entity to disclose its participation in Delaware's sustainability reporting regime. The renewal certification statement requires disclosure relevant to changes to the entity's standards and assessment measures and an acknowledgment that its most recent sustainability reports are publicly available on its website and the related link to that site.

The 2018 Delaware Act is a voluntary disclosure regime requiring adopted reporting entities to provide reports on their sustainability and related standards and metrics. Reporting entities are provided with the flexibility to report on their financial as well as nonfinancial sustainability performance while maintaining their privileged information, trade secrets, or competitively sensitive information. Thus, Delaware entities that decide to disclose their sustainability performance information can obtain certification from the Delaware Secretary of State under the Act as to their transparency in sustainability reporting. This certification demonstrates the entity's commitment to sustainability efforts and compliance with related sustainability standards and measures and is a signal to investors, clients, and customers that the entity is taking its sustainability efforts seriously.

Mandatory Sustainability Disclosure

Until the late 1990s, sustainability reports were largely voluntary and included in a firm's supplementary disclosures. In recent years, many countries, including Australia, Austria, Canada, Denmark, France, Germany, Malaysia, the Netherlands, Sweden, Hong Kong, and the United Kingdom, have adopted mandatory reporting on financial ESP and nonfinancial ESG sustainability performance.[53] The issue of whether sustainability disclosures should be uniform and standardized has been debated by authoritative bodies (GRI, IIRC, SASB, regulators) worldwide, and it is expected that as investors demand such information, more companies will disclose their sustainability performance information and regulators provide guidelines for standardizing sustainability disclosures to make them more consistent, comparable, and thus more value-relevant to all stakeholders, including shareholders.

In the past several decades, growing concerns regarding financial scandals (e.g., Enron, WorldCom, Parmalat, Satyam, Volkswagen), the environmental impact, CSR, governance, and ethical behavior of corporations have encouraged policymakers and regulators to address these concerns by establishing laws and regulations to minimize their negative impacts. One example in the United States is the passage of the Sarbanes-Oxley Act of 2002 to combat financial statement fraud and prevent further occurrences of financial scandals by improving corporate governance measures and financial reporting and audit processes.[54] SOX (2002) and related Securities and Exchange Commission (SEC) regulations also require public companies in the United States to establish and maintain effective internal control over financial reporting to combat fraud and irregularities in reporting related to governmental laws and SEC regulations. The SEC, in the past several decades, has issued numerous regulations for the disclosure of environmental liabilities, including Releases Number 5170 in 1971, Number 5386 in 1973, the climate change interpretive guidance in 2010, and conflict minerals rules in 2012.[55]

In January 2023, the EU Corporate Sustainability Reporting Directive was issued, requiring mandatory sustainability reporting for European companies that could apply to their counterparts and trading partners worldwide.[56] The CSRD is intended to complement existing sustainability-focused regulations and voluntary frameworks and standards of the GRI and the ISSB and will have a global implication. The CSRD requires covered companies to disclose historical and forward-looking information relevant to sustainability matters, including ESG issues and information about sustainability risk management, metrics, and value chain due diligence for EU companies. The reliability and credibility of sustainability reports can be enhanced by assuring such reports. However, the 2017 survey conducted by Ernst & Young (EY), one of the Big Four international auditing firms, indicates that (i) investors are increasingly considering the important role that nonfinancial ESG sustainability dimensions play in their investment decision-making; (ii) CEOs should present annual long-term board reviews of sustainability; (iii) a majority of surveyed companies have not considered environmental and social issues, their related risks, and the opportunities they present as core to their business; (iv) generating sustainable financial ESP returns over time requires a sharper focus on nonfinancial ESG sustainability performance; and

Mandatory Sustainability Disclosure

(v) nonfinancial ESG issues have real and quantifiable impacts over financial ESP sustainability over the long term.[57] The European Sustainability Reporting Standards (ESRS) were adopted in July 2023 by the European Financial Reporting Advisory Group (EFRAG) under the Corporate Sustainability Reporting Directive of the European Union.[58] These standards aim to enhance and harmonize the reporting of ESG factors by companies within the EU, ensuring greater transparency and consistency in sustainability reporting.

Summary

Business sustainability requires organizations to focus on achieving all five EGSEE dimensions of sustainability performance by taking initiatives to advance social good beyond their interests, compliance with applicable regulations, and enhancement of shareholder wealth. Simply put, business sustainability means enhancing corporations' positive impacts and minimizing their negative effects on society and the environment while creating positive impacts on shareholders, the community, the environment, employees, customers, and suppliers. The true measure of success for corporations should be determined not only by their reported earnings but also by their governance, social responsibility, ethical behavior, and environmental performance. Business sustainability has received considerable attention from policymakers, regulators, and the business and investment community over the past decade, and it is expected to be the main theme for decades to come. Business sustainability initiatives, programs, activities, and best practices presented in this chapter should assist business organizations worldwide in integrating the five EGSEE dimensions of sustainability performance into their corporate culture, business environment, strategic decisions, and supply chain management to improve their KPIs as well as the quality of financial and nonfinancial sustainability information disseminated to their stakeholders. This chapter addresses the increasing focus on business sustainability and its factors of performance, disclosure, and risk and their implications for business practice, education, and research. Proper measurement of sustainability performance, as well as accurate and reliable disclosure of sustainability performance and effective assessment of sustainability risks, remain major challenges for organizations of different types and sizes, as discussed in detail in the next several chapters.

Key Points

- Business sustainability is the process of achieving financial and economic performance to create shareholder value while generating nonfinancial governance, social, ethical, and environmental sustainability performance in protecting the interests of other stakeholders.

- Constituencies and stakeholders should be identified, and policies and procedures to achieve strategies and goals should be developed.
- A clear linkage between KPIs, business models, strategy and risk management, and disclosures is required for the effective implementation of business sustainability.
- Strategies models to improve governance and board effectiveness and to strengthen relationships with all key stakeholders should be developed.
- Integration of five EGSEE dimensions of sustainability performance into management processes enables companies to conserve scarce resources, optimize production processes, identify product innovations, achieve cost efficiency and effectiveness, increase productivity, promote corporate reputation, and create stakeholder value.
- Effective implementation of all five EGSEE dimensions of sustainability performance is essential in creating sustainable value for all stakeholders.
- Sustainability managers should understand that shareholder value can be improved by enhancing value creation for other stakeholders.
- The integration of sustainability concepts into managerial decision-making processes related to strategy development, corporate governance, risk assessment, and performance management.
- The collaboration of people, businesses, and resources in the business sustainability and accountability model, along with best practices of business sustainability, is explained.
- Guidance to organizations to properly integrate all five EGSEE dimensions of sustainability into their business models, strategic plans, and practices should be established.
- Guidelines for the complete and accurate measurement, recognition, and disclosure of all five EGSEE dimensions of sustainability performance in an integrated reporting model should be established.

Review Questions

1. **How has business sustainability evolved in recent years?**
2. **What is the primary mission of corporate sustainability?**
3. **What are the primary components of sustainability planning?**
4. **What is the role of corporate governance in business sustainability?**
5. **Why is it important for companies to disclose sustainability performance?**
6. **What are the main objectives of the EU Corporate Sustainability Reporting Directive (CSRD)?**
7. **How do sustainability performance and risk management relate?**
8. **Why is stakeholder engagement crucial in sustainability planning?**

Review Questions

9. **What is the role of voluntary sustainability disclosure?**
10. **What are some of the emerging trends in business sustainability?**
11. **What are the components of an effective accountability system for corporations?**
12. **What is the primary focus of long-term sustainability planning?**
13. **What are the benefits of effective corporate governance?**
14. **What are the challenges of sustainability reporting?**
15. **What are the emerging issues in sustainability reporting?**

Discussion Questions

1. **How has business sustainability evolved in recent years?**
2. **Why is transparency in sustainability reporting important?**
3. **What is the primary mission of corporate sustainability?**
4. **What are the emerging issues in sustainability reporting?**
5. **What are the primary components of sustainability planning?**
6. **What are some benefits of good sustainability practices for companies?**
7. **What is the role of sustainability reporting in achieving business sustainability?**
8. **What is the significance of stakeholder theory in business sustainability?**
9. **What is the impact of effective corporate governance on business sustainability?**
10. **What are some global initiatives promoting sustainability reporting?**
11. **What are the main objectives of the EU Corporate Sustainability Reporting Directive (CSRD)?**
12. **How do sustainability performance and risk management relate?**
13. **Why is stakeholder engagement crucial in sustainability planning?**
14. **What is the role of voluntary sustainability disclosure?**
15. **What are some of the emerging trends in business sustainability?**

Multiple-Choice Questions

1. **What has business sustainability evolved from?**
    A) From regulatory compliance to strategic imperative
    B) From branding and greenwashing to strategic imperative
    C) From financial performance to environmental performance
    D) From social responsibility to economic responsibility

2. **Why is transparency in sustainability reporting important?**
   A) It helps in creating shared values for stakeholders and enhances investor confidence
   B) It reduces regulatory compliance costs
   C) It focuses solely on financial performance
   D) It limits stakeholder engagement

3. **What are the primary components of sustainability planning?**
   A) Developing goals, strategies, and practices to balance shareholder value maximization and stakeholder value creation
   B) Reducing transparency in financial disclosures
   C) Limiting stakeholder engagement
   D) Focusing solely on short-term profits

4. **What is the role of sustainability reporting in achieving business sustainability?**
   A) It reduces regulatory compliance costs
   B) It provides a platform for accountability and transparency of sustainability performance
   C) It limits stakeholder engagement
   D) It focuses solely on financial performance

5. **What is the significance of stakeholder theory in business sustainability?**
   A) It focuses solely on financial performance
   B) It protects the interests of all stakeholders and focuses on achieving long-term and enduring financial and non-financial performance
   C) It reduces regulatory compliance costs
   D) It limits stakeholder engagement

6. **What is the impact of effective corporate governance on business sustainability?**
   A) It reduces transparency and limits stakeholder engagement
   B) It promotes accountability, enhances operational and financial performance, and strengthens stakeholder trust
   C) It focuses solely on short-term profits
   D) It limits regulatory compliance

7. **Why is it important for companies to disclose sustainability performance?**
   A) To demonstrate commitment to transparency and enhance firm value by reducing information asymmetry
   B) To limit stakeholder engagement and reduce regulatory compliance costs

C) To focus solely on financial performance

D) To minimize the impact of sustainability initiatives

8. **What are the main objectives of the EU Corporate Sustainability Reporting Directive (CSRD)?**

A) To reduce transparency and limit stakeholder engagement

B) To increase transparency in sustainability reporting, enhance sustainability performance, and contribute to long-term economic growth

C) To focus solely on financial performance and short-term profits

D) To minimize regulatory compliance and reduce costs

9. **How do sustainability performance and risk management relate?**

A) Sustainability performance focuses solely on financial performance

B) Effective sustainability performance requires identifying, assessing, and managing sustainability risks to minimize negative impacts and capitalize on opportunities

C) Sustainability performance reduces transparency and limits stakeholder engagement

10. **Why is stakeholder engagement crucial in sustainability planning?**

A) It limits transparency and reduces regulatory compliance

B) It helps in understanding stakeholder preferences and expectations, which inform the development of effective sustainability strategies

C) It focuses solely on financial performance

D) It minimizes the impact of sustainability initiatives

11. **What is the role of voluntary sustainability disclosure?**

A) It focuses solely on financial performance

B) It demonstrates a company's commitment to transparency and can differentiate it from less sustainable firms

C) It reduces regulatory compliance and limits stakeholder engagement

D) It minimizes the impact of sustainability initiatives

12. **What are some of the emerging trends in business sustainability?**

A) Integration of sustainability into corporate strategies, increased stakeholder engagement, and enhanced sustainability reporting and assurance

B) Focus on short-term profits, reduced transparency, and limited stakeholder engagement

C) Increased regulatory compliance, reduced costs, and minimized sustainability initiatives

D) Focus solely on financial performance and short-term gains

13. **What are the components of an effective accountability system for corporations?**
    A) Reducing transparency and limiting stakeholder engagement
    B) A well-defined corporate mission, robust governance structure, and transparent disclosures
    C) Focusing solely on short-term profits
    D) Minimizing regulatory compliance and reducing costs

14. **What is the primary focus of long-term sustainability planning?**
    A) To ensure the continuity of business operations and integrate sustainability into the business environment, corporate culture, and strategic plans
    B) To focus solely on financial performance
    C) To reduce transparency and limit stakeholder engagement
    D) To minimize regulatory compliance and reduce costs

15. **What are the benefits of effective corporate governance?**
    A) It promotes accountability, enhances operational and financial performance, and strengthens stakeholder trust
    B) It reduces transparency and limits stakeholder engagement
    C) It focuses solely on financial performance
    D) It minimizes regulatory compliance and reduces costs

16. **What are the challenges of sustainability reporting?**
    A) Proper identification, measurement, recognition, reporting, and assurance of all five dimensions of sustainability performance
    B) Reducing transparency and limiting stakeholder engagement
    C) Focusing solely on financial performance
    D) Minimizing regulatory compliance and reducing costs

17. **What are the emerging issues in sustainability reporting?**
    A) The need for better measurement, recognition, and disclosure of all five dimensions of sustainability performance
    B) Reducing transparency and limiting stakeholder engagement
    C) Focusing solely on financial performance
    D) Minimizing regulatory compliance and reducing costs

18. **What is the role of sustainability reporting in achieving business sustainability?**
    A) It reduces regulatory compliance costs
    B) It provides a platform for accountability and transparency of sustainability performance

Multiple-Choice Questions

C)   It limits stakeholder engagement

D)   It focuses solely on financial performance

19. **What is the significance of stakeholder theory in business sustainability?**

A)   It focuses solely on financial performance

B)   It protects the interests of all stakeholders and focuses on achieving long-term and enduring financial and non-financial performance

C)   It reduces regulatory compliance costs

D)   It limits stakeholder engagement

20. **What is the impact of effective corporate governance on business sustainability?**

A)   It reduces transparency and limits stakeholder engagement

B)   It promotes accountability, enhances operational and financial performance, and strengthens stakeholder trust

C)   It focuses solely on short-term profits

D)   It limits regulatory compliance

21. **Why is it important for companies to disclose sustainability performance?**

A)   To demonstrate commitment to transparency and enhance firm value by reducing information asymmetry

B)   To limit stakeholder engagement and reduce regulatory compliance costs

C)   To focus solely on financial performance

D)   To minimize the impact of sustainability initiatives

22. **What are the main objectives of the EU Corporate Sustainability Reporting Directive (CSRD)?**

A)   To reduce transparency and limit stakeholder engagement

B)   To increase transparency in sustainability reporting, enhance sustainability performance, and contribute to long-term economic growth

C)   To focus solely on financial performance and short-term profits

D)   To minimize regulatory compliance and reduce costs

23. **How are sustainability performance and risk management related?**

A)   Sustainability performance focuses solely on financial performance

B)   Effective sustainability performance requires identifying, assessing, and managing sustainability risks to minimize negative impacts and capitalize on opportunities

C)   Sustainability performance reduces transparency and limits stakeholder engagement

D)   Risk management focuses solely on short-term profits

24. **Why is stakeholder engagement crucial in sustainability planning?**
    A) It limits transparency and reduces regulatory compliance
    B) It helps in understanding stakeholder preferences and expectations, which inform the development of effective sustainability strategies
    C) It focuses solely on financial performance
    D) It minimizes the impact of sustainability initiatives

25. **What is the role of voluntary sustainability disclosure?**
    A) It focuses solely on financial performance
    B) It demonstrates a company's commitment to transparency and can differentiate it from less sustainable firms
    C) It reduces regulatory compliance and limits stakeholder engagement
    D) It minimizes the impact of sustainability initiatives

26. **What are some of the emerging trends in business sustainability?**
    A) Integration of sustainability into corporate strategies, increased stakeholder engagement, and enhanced sustainability reporting and assurance
    B) Focus on short-term profits, reduced transparency, and limited stakeholder engagement
    C) Increased regulatory compliance, reduced costs, and minimized sustainability initiatives
    D) Focus solely on financial performance and short-term gains

27. **What are the components of an effective accountability system for corporations?**
    A) Reducing transparency and limiting stakeholder engagement
    B) A well-defined corporate mission, robust governance structure, and transparent disclosures
    C) Focusing solely on short-term profits
    D) Minimizing regulatory compliance and reducing costs

28. **What is the primary focus of long-term sustainability planning?**
    A) To ensure the continuity of business operations and integrate sustainability into the business environment, corporate culture, and strategic plans
    B) To focus solely on financial performance
    C) To reduce transparency and limit stakeholder engagement
    D) To minimize regulatory compliance and reduce costs

29. **What are the benefits of effective corporate governance?**
    A) It promotes accountability, enhances operational and financial performance, and strengthens stakeholder trust
    B) It reduces transparency and limits stakeholder engagement

Multiple-Choice Questions

C) It focuses solely on financial performance

D) It minimizes regulatory compliance and reduces costs

30. **What is the significance of stakeholder engagement in sustainability planning?**

A) It reduces transparency and limits stakeholder engagement

B) It helps in understanding stakeholder preferences and expectations, which inform the development of effective sustainability strategies

C) It focuses solely on financial performance

D) It minimizes regulatory compliance and reduces costs

Notes

1 Much of the material presented in this chapter comes from three books published on sustainability by Zabihollah Rezaee, including Brockett, A. and Rezaee, Z. (2012). *Corporate Sustainability: Integrating Performance and Reporting.* Wiley; Rezaee, Z. (2015). *Business Sustainability: Performance, Compliance, Accountability and Integrated Reporting.* Greenleaf Publishing; and Rezaee, Z. (2024). *The Sustainable Business Blueprint: Planning, Performance, Risk, Reporting and Assurance.* Routledge/Taylor and Francis.

2 Sustainability Accounting Standards Board (SASB). (2017). SASB conceptual framework. https://www.sasb.org/wp-content/uploads/2017/02/SASB-Conceptual-Framework.pdf.

3 Brockett, A. and Rezaee, Z. (2012). *Corporate Sustainability: Integrating Performance and Reporting.* Wiley.

4 United Nations Global Compact (UN Global Compact). (2013). Global corporate sustainability report 2013. https://www.unglobalcompact.org/docs/about_the_gc/Global_Corporate _Sustainability_Report2013.pdf.

5 Global Reporting Initiative (GRI). (2013). G4 exposure draft. 2013. Frequently asked questions about the G4 Exposure Draft and the second G4 Public Comment Period. https://www .globalreporting.org/resourcelibrary/G4-ED-PCP2-FAQs.pdf.

6 Kiron, D., Kruschwitz, N., Haanaes, K., Reeves, M., Fuisz-Kehrbach, S. and Kell, G. 2015. Joining Forces: Collaboration and Leadership for Sustainability. *MIT Sloan Management Review*, the Boston Consulting Group, and the United Nations Global Compact (UNGC), Available at: http://marketing.mitsmr.com/PDF/56380-MITSMR-BGC-UNGC-Sustainability2015.pdf?cid=1 (accessed July 08, 2017).

7 GRI (2013).Global Reporting Initiative (GRI). (2013). G4 exposure draft. 2013. Frequently asked questions about the G4 Exposure Draft and the second G4 Public Comment Period. https://www.globalreporting.org/resourcelibrary/G4-ED-PCP2-FAQs.pdf.

8 Rezaee, Z. (2015). *Business Sustainability: Performance, Compliance, Accountability and Integrated Reporting.* Greenleaf Publishing Limited.

9 European Commission (EUC). 2011. Communication from the Commission to the European Parliament, the Council, the European Economic and Social Committee and the Committee of the Regions, Brussels, 25.10.2011, COM(2011) 681 final.

10 KPMG. (2017). The road ahead: The KPMG survey of corporate responsibility reporting, 2017. https://home.kpmg/content/dam/kpmg/nz/pdf/November/KPMG_NZ_Supplement _Corporate_Responsibility_Reporting%202017.pdf.

11 Cruz, N. and Marques, R. (2014). Scorecards for sustainable local governments. *Cities* 39: 165–170.

12 International Federation of Accountants (IFAC). (2015). Accounting for sustainability: From sustainability to business resilience (July). https://www.ifac.org/publications-resources/ accounting-sustainability.pdf.

13 United Nations Global Compact (UN Global Compact) (2013). Global corporate sustainability report 2013. https://www.unglobalcompact.org/docs/about_the_gc/Global_Corporate _Sustainability_Report2013.pdf.

14 Nidumolu, R., Simmons, P.J., and Yosle, T.F. (2015). Sustainability and the CFO: Challenges, opportunities, and next practices. Corporate Eco Forum, April 2015. http://www.corpora- teecoforum.com/wp-content/uploads/2015/04/CFO_and_Sustainability_Apr-2015.pdf.

15 International Sustainability Standards Board (ISSB). (2021). https://www.ifrs.org/groups/ international-sustainability-standards-board/

16 Securities and Exchange Commission (SEC). (2022). SEC proposes rules to enhance and standardize climate-related disclosures for investors. https://www.sec.gov/news/press -release/2022-46

17 European Union (EU). (2023). Corporate Sustainability Reporting Directive (CSRD). https:// finance.ec.europa.eu/capital-markets-union-and-financial-markets/company-reporting -and-auditing/company-reporting/corporate-sustainability-reporting_en.

18 Rezaee, Z. (2015). *Business Sustainability: Performance, Compliance, Accountability and Integrated Reporting*. Greenleaf Publishing Limited.

19 Jensen, Michael C. (2001). Value maximization, stakeholder theory, and the corporate objective function. *Journal of Applied Corporate Finance* 14 (3): 8–21.

20 Brockett, A. and Rezaee, Z. (2012). *Corporate Sustainability: Integrating Performance and Reporting*. Wiley.

21 United Nations Global Compact (UN Global Compact). (2013). Global corporate sustainability report 2013. https://www.unglobalcompact.org/docs/about_the_gc/Global_Corporate _Sustainability_Report2013.pdf.

22 United Nations Global Compact (UN Global Compact). (2013). Global corporate sustainability report 2013. https://www.unglobalcompact.org/docs/about_the_gc/Global_Corporate _Sustainability_Report2013.pdf.

23 United Nations Global Compact (UN Global Compact). (2013). Global corporate sustainability report 2013. https://www.unglobalcompact.org/docs/about_the_gc/Global_Corporate _Sustainability_Report2013.pdf.

24 United Nations Global Compact (UN Global Compact). (2013). Global corporate sustainability report 2013. https://www.unglobalcompact.org/docs/about_the_gc/Global_Corporate_Sustainability_Report2013.pdf.

25 UN Sustainable Development Goals Report (UNSDGs). (2015). Indicators and a monitoring framework for the sustainable development goals launching a Data Revolution for the SDGs. http://unsdsn.org/wp-content/uploads/2015/03/150320-SDSN-Indicator-Report .pdf (accessed 10 August 2017).

26 UN Sustainable Development Goals Report (UNSDGs) (2015). Indicators and a monitoring framework for the sustainable development goals launching a Data Revolution for the SDGs. http://unsdsn.org/wp-content/uploads/2015/03/150320-SDSN-Indicator-Report .pdf (accessed 10 August 2017).

27 Global Reporting Initiative (GRI). (2017). Linking the GRI Standards and the European Directive on nonfinancial and diversity disclosure. https://www.globalreporting.org/standards/resource-download-center/linking-gri-standards-and-european-directive-on-non-financial-and-diversity-disclosure/.

28 International Federation of Accountants. (2016). The 2030 agenda for sustainable development: A snapshot of the accountancy profession's contribution. International Federation of Accountants, New York, NY. https://www.ifac.org/publications-resources/2030-agenda-sustainable-development.

29 PWC. (2017). SDG Reporting Challenge 2017. Exploring business communication on the Global Goals 2017. https://www.pwc.com/gx/en/sustainability/SDG/pwc-sdg-reporting-challenge-2017-final.pdf.

30 Much of the discussion presented in this section comes from Chapter 1 of Rezaee, Z. (2024). *The Sustainable Business Blueprint: Planning, Performance, Risk, Reporting and Assurance.* Routledge/Taylor and Francis.

31 Brockett, A. and Rezaee, Z. (2012). *Corporate Sustainability: Integrating Performance and Reporting.* Wiley.

32 Global Reporting Initiative (GRI). (2013). G4 exposure draft. 2013. Frequently asked questions about the G4 Exposure Draft and the second G4 Public Comment Period. https://www .globalreporting.org/resourcelibrary/G4-ED-PCP2-FAQs.pdf.

33 Global Reporting Initiative (GRI). (2013). G4 exposure draft. 2013. Frequently asked questions about the G4 Exposure Draft and the second G4 Public Comment Period. https://www .globalreporting.org/resourcelibrary/G4-ED-PCP2-FAQs.pdf.

34 KPMG. (2013). Beyond quarterly earnings: Is the company on track for long-term success? Spring 2013 Audit Committee Roundtable Report. auditcommittee@kpmg.com.

35 Sarbanes-Oxley Act 2002, Pub. L. 107–204, enacted July 30, 2002, adding 15 U.S.C. § 7201 *et seq.* and adding and amending other provisions of the United States Code, as explained in the notes accompanying 15 U.S.C. § 7201, hereinafter in this portfolio the "Sarbanes-Oxley Act" or "SOX."

36 Dodd-Frank Wall Street Reform and Consumer Protection Act of 2010 (2010) (pp. 111–203). Pub. L.

37 United Nations Principles of Responsible Investing (UN PRI). (2005). The fresh fields report. www.unepfi.org/fileadmin/documents/freshfields_legal_resp_20051123.pdf.

38 Social Investment Forum (SIF) (2012). 2012 Report on sustainable and responsible investing trends in the United States. US SIF Foundation: The Forum for Sustainable and Responsible Investment (November).

39 Bloomberg. (2021). Bloomberg professional services: ESG assets may hit $53 trillion by 2025, a third of global AUM. Bloomberg Intelligence, February 23, 2021. https://www.bloomberg.com/professional/blog/esg-assets-may-hit-53-trillion-by-2025-a-third-of-global-aum/

40 CERES and Environmental Defense Fund.

41 Brockett, A. and Rezaee, Z. (2012). *Corporate Sustainability: Integrating Performance and Reporting*. Wiley.

42 International Organization for Standardization (ISO) (2009). *ISO 31000: Risk Management – Principles and Guidelines, 2009*. ISO. www.iso.org.

43 International Organization for Standardization (ISO) (2009). *ISO 31000: Risk Management – Principles and Guidelines, 2009*. ISO. www.iso.org.

44 Rezaee, Z. (2015). *Business Sustainability: Performance, Compliance, Accountability and Integrated Reporting*. Greenleaf Publishing.

45 European Commission (2014). Disclosure of nonfinancial information: Europe's largest companies to be more transparent on social and environmental issues (September 29, 2014). http://ec.europa.eu/internal_market/accounting/nonfinancial_reporting/index_en.htm.

46 European Commission (2014). Disclosure of nonfinancial information: Europe's largest companies to be more transparent on social and environmental issues (September 29, 2014). http://ec.europa.eu/internal_market/accounting/nonfinancial_reporting/index_en.htm.

47 European Commission (EUC). (2011). Communication from the Commission to the European Parliament, the Council, the European Economic and Social Committee and the Committee of the Regions, Brussels, 25.10.2011, COM(2011) 681 final.

48 European Commission (EUC). (2011). Communication from the Commission to the European Parliament, the Council, the European Economic and Social Committee and the Committee of the Regions, Brussels, 25.10.2011, COM(2011) 681 final.

49 European Commission (EUC). (2011). Communication from the Commission to the European Parliament, the Council, the European Economic and Social Committee and the Committee of the Regions, Brussels, 25.10.2011, COM(2011) 681 final.

50 Rezaee, Z. (2015). *Business Sustainability: Performance, Compliance, Accountability and Integrated Reporting*. Greenleaf Publishing.

51 Rezaee, Z. (2015). *Business Sustainability: Performance, Compliance, Accountability and Integrated Reporting*. Greenleaf Publishing.

52 Delaware General Assembly. (2018). House Bill 310: An Act to Amend Title 6 of the Delaware Code Relating to the Certification of Adoption of Sustainability and Transparency Standards by Delaware Entities. (June 27, 2018). https://legis.delaware.gov/BillDetail/26304.

Notes

53 Rezaee, Z. (2015). *Business Sustainability: Performance, Compliance, Accountability and Integrated Reporting.* Greenleaf Publishing.

54 Sarbanes-Oxley Act 2002, Pub. L. 107–204.

55 Rezaee, Z. (2015). *Business Sustainability: Performance, Compliance, Accountability and Integrated Reporting.* Greenleaf Publishing.

56 European Commission (EC). (2023). The Corporate Sustainability Reporting Directive (CSRD), January 5, 2023. https://finance.ec.europa.eu/capital-markets-union-and-financial-markets/company-reporting-and-auditing/company-reporting/corporate-sustainability-reporting_en

57 Ernst & Young (EY). (2017). Is your nonfinancial performance. revealing the true value of your business to investors? https://www.ey.com/Publication/vwLUAssets/EY_-_Nonfinancial_performance_may_influence_investors/$FILE/ey-nonfinancial-performance-may-influence-investors.pdf.

58 European Commission (EC). (2023). The Commission adopts the European Sustainability Reporting Standards, July 31, 2023. https://finance.ec.europa.eu/news/commission-adopts-european-sustainability-reporting-standards-2023-07-31_en

Chapter 3
Business Sustainability

Profit-With-Purpose, Shared Value, and Strategic Plans

Learning Objectives

- Understanding the shift in business purpose from profit maximization to creating shared value for all stakeholders with a profit-with-purpose mission.
- Recognizing the importance of integrating both financial economic sustainability performance (ESP) and nonfinancial environmental, social, and governance (ESG) sustainability performance into corporate environment and business culture.
- Examining how business sustainability with a profit-with-purpose mission influences strategic planning and decision-making.
- Learning about the role of corporate directors and executives in developing strategies for business sustainability.
- Understanding how stakeholders' perception of sustainability reports and metrics can influence strategic plans.
- Discussing the adoption and implementation of shared value concepts and their significance in the current business environment.

Introduction

The recent moves toward business sustainability require business organizations to refocus their objectives, goals, and strategies on the profit-with-purpose mission of creating shared value for all stakeholders. Thus, the conventional goal of profit maximization that only achieves shareholder value creation may no longer be desirable and sustainable for business organizations and needs to adopt the mission of profit-with-purpose to generate shared value for all stakeholders. Thus, public companies should pay attention to the impacts of their operations on society, communities, and the environment. The latter purpose can be achieved when corporations focus on the profit-with-purpose mission of generating desired financial returns for their shareholders while protecting the interests of other stakeholders, including customers, employees, suppliers, communities, society, and the environment, as well as having social and environmental impacts.

DOI: 10.4324/9781003487081-3

The global economy, prosperity, stakeholder expectations, business environment, and corporate culture have changed in recent years, and thus, business organizations are adopting new missions and purposes. Purpose determines why the organization exists, its mission, who the stakeholders are, its objectives and strategies for achieving the objectives, and their matrixes in measuring success. The main objective function for any business organization has been and continues to be the achievement of sustainable performance in creating shared value for all stakeholders, including shareholders, customers, suppliers, employees, creditors, government, society, and the environment. Changes in business organizations' purpose, mission, objectives, and strategies are needed to achieve financial ESP and non-financial ESG sustainability performance.

The profit-with-purpose mission for business organizations integrates traditional profit-making activities with a commitment to social or environmental impact. Unlike conventional commitment for-profit models that focus mainly on maximizing shareholder value, the profit-with-purpose mission prioritizes creating positive social or environmental outcomes alongside financial viability and profitability. The shared value creation concept means that the interests of all stakeholders should be protected, and thus, corporate resources and activities should be managed to create shared value for all stakeholders.[1] To effectively achieve sustainability ESP and ESG performance, corporations' boards of directors should promote the shared value concept in fulfilling their responsibility to protect the interests of all stakeholders. Management, as the steward of business resources and capital (financial, operational, human, social, and environmental), should promote the shared value concept, has the primary role of improving sustainability performance and managing related risks, maximizing utilization of all capital from strategic to operational, financial, reputational, manufactured, human, social, and environmental to create shared value for all stakeholders. The other corporate gatekeepers, including accountants and auditors, should consider sustainability in enabling opportunities to create shared value by focusing on the continuous improvements of short-term and mid-term strategic plans as well as reliable and transparent reporting of ESP and ESG sustainability performance information. This chapter examines the business sustainability mission of profit-with-purpose in designing strategic plans to create shared value for all stakeholders, including obtaining the desired rate of returns for shareholders while achieving social and environmental impacts. This chapter also examines the importance and relevance of the profit-with-purpose concept and related strategic plans in promoting business sustainability and creating shared value for all stakeholders.

Profit-With-Purpose Mission

The concept of profit-with-purpose represents a business strategy of integrating financial success and viability with a commitment to social and environmental impacts by aligning business strategies with broader societal goals, environmental outcomes, and ethical practices. The concept suggests that the corporate mission should go beyond simply maximizing profits for shareholders and be extended to creating shared value for various stakeholders, including investors, employees, customers, suppliers, communities, society, and the environment. This concept indicates that while the main objective function for any business organization is to earn profit for its owner, it should also have a purpose specified in the article of incorporation (e.g., serving the community, promoting diversity, and having social and environmental impacts). The mission of profit-with-purpose enables businesses to demonstrate that profitability and positive social or environmental outcomes are not mutually exclusive and competing but can complement and reinforce each other. This mission has gained traction as investors, consumers, employees, suppliers, and communities increasingly prioritize sustainability and social responsibility, viewing businesses as powerful agents for positive change in society and the environment.

The global move toward adopting a profit-with-purpose mission is inevitable as sustainability initiatives are integrated into the business environment, corporate culture, strategies, supply chain, decisions, actions, and performance. The board of directors should review and reevaluate the Statement of the purpose from the conventional shareholder primacy model to the emerging stakeholder primacy model of assuming fiduciary duties to all stakeholders. Under the stakeholder primacy model, the board is responsible for protecting the interests of all stakeholders, including shareholders, employees, customers, suppliers, communities, society, and the environment. The stakeholder primacy model promotes the nexus between corporate financial performance and societal well-being and increases the public perception and awareness of corporate social responsibility and business sustainability. It defines the new purpose of securing employees, customers, and suppliers' safety, health, and well-being, making a profit for shareholders, and moving toward the "profit-with-purpose" concept discussed in the next section.

Business organizations are being criticized for paying a keen focus on profit maximization for their shareholders with minimal or no attention to the impacts of their operations on society, communities, and the environment. As business sustainability is gaining more attention and being integrated into the business environment and corporate culture, there has been a shift from creating shareholder value to developing "sustainable shared value creation" to protect the interests of all stakeholders with a keen focus on the profit-with-purpose mission. Under the shared value creation concept, the board of director's fiduciary duties are to protect the interests of all stakeholders and oversee management activities of focusing on the continuous performance improvement of business operations in generating long-term value while maximizing the positive impacts of operations on society, communities, and the environment by measuring sustainable performance in terms of both ESP and ESG sustainability performance. Thus, corporate objectives have advanced from profit maximization to increasing shareholder wealth and creating shared value for all stakeholders. Companies implementing a profit-with-purpose mission often integrate social and environmental considerations into their strategic planning and decision-making processes to positively impact society and the environment while being financially successful.

This profit-with-purpose mission represents a growing acceptance that businesses can significantly address environmental and societal challenges. Every company should have its unique purpose determined in its charter of incorporation to maximize its positive impacts on all stakeholders, including communities, society, and the environment, and to minimize the negative impacts on multi-stakeholders. In case of a nonexistent and/or inadequate "Statement of Purpose," the board of directors, in collaboration with management, should develop the Statement of Purpose and obtain approval by majority shareholders. The Statement of Purpose should include the mission, which reflects the organization's determination to stay with its purpose and its short, medium, and long-term achievement. Companies are now adopting the corporate mission of profit with the purpose of creating shared value for all stakeholders by shifting their goals to create shareholder value while fulfilling their social, environmental, and governance responsibilities. The Statement of Purpose should also define objectives that have substantially evolved to survive in the short term, continuity in the medium term, and sustainability in the long term. The board of directors pays more attention to the well-being, safety, and health of their employees, customers, and suppliers. In collaboration with management, the board of directors should also design strategies to achieve new objectives by designing business continuity plans, deliberate decisions, and crisis management. This chapter introduces the concept of profit-with-purpose for creating shared value for all stakeholders.

There has been much debate over the Business Roundtable's updated Statement of Corporate Purpose, published in August 2019 and signed by more than 180 CEOs.[2] The Statement of Corporate Purpose suggests a move away from shareholder primacy as a guiding principle and outlines a move toward stakeholder primacy with a modern corporate responsibility standard that commits to all stakeholders. The shareholder primacy model suggests that corporations exist principally to serve shareholders, and the interests of other stakeholders are not considered. Thus, society and all stakeholders deserve an economy that allows people to succeed through hard work, dedication, commitment, and creativity and to lead a life of meaning, fairness, and dignity. Stakeholder capitalism focuses on the free-market system, which promotes hard work and quality performance, creating good jobs, a strong and sustainable economy, innovation, economic opportunity, a healthy environment, and social justice for all. Businesses play a vital economic role by creating jobs, fostering innovation, and providing essential goods and services. Businesses make and sell consumer products, create jobs, manufacture equipment and vehicles, grow and produce food, support the national defense, generate and deliver energy, provide health care, and offer financial and other services that underpin economic growth and prosperity for the nation.

On February 23, 2022, the European Union Commission launched its Corporate Sustainability Due Diligence Directive proposal. However, there were a few issues related to this Directive that the Commission is working to address, including the ongoing debate about the definition of stakeholders versus shareholders. This allows companies to fall into a primacy model that puts too much emphasis and energy on maximizing value for one group and not the other, leading to inequalities in power dynamics. An example of this would be maximizing shareholder wealth and not factoring in the interests of other stakeholders. Another issue was not changing company law to incorporate sustainability in business decision-making and the possibility of "box-ticking" instead of thoroughly evaluating sustainability principles.[3]

A survey shows increasing evidence for defining corporate purpose and that it is in investors' interest to hold companies accountable for the defined purpose rather than viewing it as an unnecessary distraction.[4] Furthermore, the survey indicates that (1) the majority of investors (93%) agree that it is important for a company to define its purpose, especially to set a long-term business strategy that creates value and strengthens corporate culture and that this was the responsibility of the board; (2) about the 75% of the respondents suggest that companies should disclose and implement sustainability information through their key performance indicators (KPIs); and (3) more than 59% agree that these KPIs may be included in new executive pay programs.[5] French legislation on the corporate purpose of "Pacte Statute" regarding the "Development and Transformation of Businesses" states that each French company must now be managed "in furtherance of its corporate interest" and "while taking into consideration the social and environmental issues arising from its activity."[6]

Sustainability Trends Toward Profit-With-Purpose

The World Economic Forum (WEF) advocates the stakeholder governance concept with a focus on "profit-with-purpose" that has been promoted by the stakeholders to protect the interests of all stakeholders, including shareholders, employees, customers, suppliers, governments, and society.[7] The International Business Council (IBC) of the WEF, in

Profit-With-Purpose Mission

collaboration with the Big-Four accounting firms, has released its final recommendations for a set of ESG sustainability performance metrics and disclosures that can be globally accepted and implemented.[8] These recommendations provide guiding principles and metrics for focusing on the ESG sustainability factors of performance, risk, and disclosures relevant to governance, people, planet, and prosperity.

The IBC/WEF framework defines a set of "Stakeholder Capitalism Metrics" pertaining to ESG sustainability factors of performance, risk, and disclosure that affect public companies' governance, people, planet, and prosperity. These metrics also determine a company's compliance with and contributions to achieving the Sustainable Development Goals (SDGs) that the United Nations has promoted. These recommendations and related metrics reflect the insights of many regulators, standard-setters, and professional organizations promoting business sustainability and its ESG components. The recommendations encourage companies to report on their core ESG metrics using a "disclose or explain" approach by focusing on a "materiality test" of reporting ESG information that is material, important, and relevant to achieving "profit-with-purpose in creating long-term shared value for all stakeholders.

Profit-with-purpose strategies consist of a range of approaches that businesses can adopt to accomplish financial success while having some social and environmental impacts. Business organizations can adopt metrics relevant to (1) governance issues, including corporate purpose; shared value, quality of governing body; composition, competencies, and diversity of the board of directors and board committees; stakeholder engagement and participation; and ethical behavior and practices of all corporate governance; (2) people core values including dignity and equality (diversity, inclusion, and fair compensation); skills for the future (training hours and expenses); health and safety and well-being; (3) planet concerns including climate change and climate-related financial disclosures; freshwater availability; nature loss; and (4) prosperity issues including earnings quality and quantity; employment and wealth generation, innovation and growth through offering the best products and services.

Business sustainability requires business organizations to expand their mission to generate profit, create shareholder value, and ensure shared value for all stakeholders. The concept of shared value challenges how we think about profits, the planet, people, philanthropy, sustainability, and development. Sustainable shared value creation enables business organizations to integrate financial ESP with nonfinancial ESG into business culture and corporate environment. Shared value creation for all stakeholders can be achieved when business organizations advance their competitiveness in improving the quality and quantity of earnings and, thus, financial returns for shareholders while contributing to the well-being of employees, customers, suppliers, society, the environment, and the communities in which it operates.[9] Share value creation with the profit-with-purpose mission for business organizations requires: (1) producing products and services that are not detrimental to society and the environment, increase shareholder wealth, and meet customers and societal needs; (2) improving productivity in the supply chain by investing in training and resources to create high-quality products and enhance ESP and ESG sustainability performance; (3) developing key performance indicators to effectively measure and report revenue, costs, and value of the organizations; and (4) periodically accessing the selected KPIs and related matrices.

Purpose determines why the organization exists, its mission, who the stakeholders are, and its objectives and strategies for achieving the objectives. The main objective function of any business organization has been and continues to be creating shared value for all stakeholders, including shareholders, creditors, customers, suppliers, employees, government, society, and the environment. Changes in business organizations' purpose, mission, objectives, and strategies need to be assessed and modified by focusing on achieving sustainable financial-economic and nonfinancial ESG sustainability performance.

Traditionally, business organizations and their board of directors and executives have focused mainly on the bottom line of maximizing profit for investors under the shareholder primacy model. In recent years, public companies have moved toward the mission of profit-with-purpose in creating shared value for all stakeholders. The Business Roundtable (BRT), in August 2019, released a new "Statement on the Purpose of a Corporation" that promotes the move toward ESG sustainability of creating shared value creation for all stakeholders.[10] The concept of purpose suggests that business organizations should determine their mission of creating shared value for all stakeholders, including employees, customers, suppliers, society, and the environment, as a fundamental reason for their existence.

The Statement of Purpose should include the mission, which reflects the organization's determination to stay with its purpose and its short, medium, and long-term achievement. Companies are now adopting the corporate mission of profit with the purpose of creating shared value for all stakeholders by shifting their goals to create shareholder value while fulfilling their social, environmental, and governance responsibilities. The Statement of Purpose should also define objectives that have sustainably changed in the post-COVID-19 pandemic to include survival in the short term, continuity in the medium term, and sustainability in the long term. The board of directors pays more attention to the well-being, safety, and health of their employees, customers, and suppliers. In collaboration with management, the board of directors should also design strategies to achieve new objectives by designing business continuity plans, deliberate decisions, and crisis management.

Profit-With-Purpose Mission

Improving the quality of ESG disclosures requires a close look at the transparency of the financial information and the perceptions of the short- and long-term strategies related to addressing these material risks and opportunities. Deloitte suggests that companies must navigate societal and environmental trends to begin integrating ESG into their business while preparing transparent and high-quality ESG disclosures. The key steps for ESG integration and disclosure strategy include governance and organizational structure, benchmarking and roadmap development, materiality assessment, integration into strategy, data and process management, target setting and alignment with business goals, internal audit and external assurance, and disclosure preparation.[11] The public and investors are demanding enhancements to sustainability disclosure and ESG accountability. To answer the call to transparency, companies should develop a robust governance structure, further integrate internal audits and boards of directors, and obtain external assurance to improve the related disclosure of information and ultimately reduce risks related to omitted or misleading disclosures.

Business organizations should adopt long-term sustainable strategies focusing on the profit-with-purpose mission of creating shared value for all stakeholders. The board of directors should review management's vision and decision for long-term sustainable strategic planning and the direction in areas of operational, investment, and financing activities, including investments in technology, manufacturing plans, research and development, and workforce training and other initiatives to ensure safety, health, and well-being of employees, suppliers, and customers in the aftermath of the COVID-19 pandemic. Business purposes should be integrated into long-term strategic planning, and benchmarks should be provided against which performance is evaluated and decisions are made. Business organizations should communicate their mission of profit-with-purpose through the means of:

1. The revised article of incorporation with profit-with-purpose statement.
2. A letter to shareholders by the chair of the board of directors clearly states the purpose statement and strategic sustainability planning.
3. Management discussion and analysis (MD&A) report showing management commitment to achieving profit-with-purpose through strategic sustainability planning.
4. Corporate website under the general heading of business sustainability.
5. Corporate public filings such as Form 10-K, 10-Q, and proxy statements.

BlackRock Investment Stewardship suggests the following topics to be addressed in the Statement of strategy, purpose, and culture:[12]

1. The evolution of the company's strategic framework and the drivers of such (e.g., changing customer needs, resources/input constraints, industry dynamics, and global megatrends).
2. The definition of a "long-term" strategic plan and whether that time frame is most appropriate.
3. The board's engagement in strategy, purpose, and culture and its oversight function of overseeing and approving management's implementation of the agreed plans and policies.
4. The strategic milestones against which shareholders should assess long-term strategic performance.
5. Employee engagement in shaping strategy, purpose, and culture and the feedback in improving its implementation.
6. Assessment of the compatibility of the company's culture, purpose, and strategy by the board of directors and management.
7. Alignment of the short-term dynamics in the business with the long-term strategy.
8. Short-term pressures on the company and how management and the board deal with it for a long-term focus.

Best Practices of Sustainability-Driven Profit-with-Purpose

Business organizations define their Statement of purpose and the mission of profit-with-purpose incentives to disclose the achievement of their ESP and ESG sustainability performance information to demonstrate their commitment to financial viability and social and environmental outcomes. Business companies should follow the guidelines of the "Statement of Purpose" released by the Business Roundtable and assess whether they have adequately adopted a clear corporate purpose that focuses on their long-term strategic goals, implemented ESG policies and practices that advance those goals, have communicated those goals and objectives effectively and have held their board of directors and executives achieving the stated purposes.[13] The updated BRT Statement on the Purpose of a Corporation declares that companies should not only serve their shareholders but also deliver value to their customers, invest in employees, deal fairly with suppliers, and support the communities in which they operate.[14] Stakeholders, including shareholders, should demand a clear Statement of Purpose and raise their concerns directly with the Company's directors and officers. The European Union is updating the EU Non-financial Reporting Directive and is considering developing nonfinancial reporting standards. The World Economic Forum has released its paper on common metrics and consistent reporting for sustainable value creation, defining 21 core metrics.

Profit-With-Purpose Mission

The International Financial Reporting Standards (IFRS) Foundation's consultation on estab-lishing a global nonfinancial reporting framework has already received strong support from other organizations.[15] The IFRS, in consultation with a cross-section of stakeholders involved in development sustainability reporting, including global policymakers, regulators, standard-setters, investors, businesses, auditing firms, and other service providers, is pro-moting business sustainability and sustainability reporting. The IFRS, while realizing that sustainability is gaining considerable attention and sustainability reporting is continuing to be important and relevant, there are differences in the scope and nature of sustain-ability reports, and thus, it calls for the improvement in standardization, comparability, and consistency in sustainability reporting. The IFRS concludes that a set of globally accepted, consistent, and comparable accounting and assurance standards is needed to foster public trust and investor confidence in sustainability performance information. This move toward reliable, relevant, and transparent sustainability performance information enables busi-ness organizations to focus on achieving their profit-with-purpose mission. Indeed, the following best practices of ESP and ESG sustainability with a keen focus on the concept of profit-with-purpose are gaining considerable attention and acceptance:

- **Purpose Statement**: Develop a concise and clear corporate purpose statement with a keen focus on the profit-with-purpose mission and ensure that the Statement of Purpose is broadly communicated and understood across the organization. There is a renewed interest in the Company's purpose in society and responsibility to all stake-holders, including producing the goods and services that meet basic needs, promote innovation, and are not detrimental to society and the environment.
- **Sustainability Strategy**: Establish a sustainability strategy that aims to achieve both financial ESP and nonfinancial ESG sustainability performance and shift empha-sis from shareholder primacy to stakeholder primacy to protect the interests of a broader set of stakeholders.
- **Priorities:** Identify ESP and ESG priorities for the business as a roadmap for achiev-ing organizational goals and objectives. Accelerating interest in nonfinancial ESG per-formance and matters by addressing social issues, including racial diversity, inclusion and gender equality, and social justice.
- **Commitment and Responsibility**: Set a tone at the top for the board of directors and commitment by executives to achieving the mission of profit-with-purpose.
- **Social or Environmental Commitment**: Establish a clear mission to address spe-cific social or environmental issues by reevaluating business activities and decision-making processes.

- **Accountability**: Hold the board of directors, executives, and employees accountable for working toward achieving the profit-with-purpose mission. The development of business models and accountability processes that address concerns about business continuity.
- **Governance**: Establish proper and effective governance measures for directors and executives to ensure the achievement of goals and objectives, focusing on the value of human capital and related improvements in work and the workplace.
- **Stakeholder Engagement**: Establish effective two-way communication channels with all stakeholders, including shareholders, customers, suppliers, employees, and others.
- **Multiple Bottom Line**: Establish strategic plans and policies to measure success not only by financial performance but also by social and environmental impacts by focusing on people, the planet, profit, and prosperity.
- **Ethical Practices**: Promote ethical business practices, including fair labor practices, customer satisfaction, supplier services, sustainable sourcing, and transparent operations.
- **Measure both ESP and ESG performance:** KPIs for properly measuring, recognizing, and reporting sustainability performance information.
- **Impact Measurement and Reporting:** Establish accountability systems to measure properly, effectively recognize, and reliably report social and environmental outcomes.
- **Innovation for Impact:** Design innovative products, services, and business models to achieve and maintain financial performance while effectively addressing social and environmental challenges.
- **Communications:** Provide a uniform, consistent ESP and ESG narrative, and tell your sustainability stories and messaging across all communications channels with all stakeholders.
- **Partnerships and Collaboration:** Collaborate with not-for-profits, governments, and other non-governmental organizations to amplify their impacts and address complex societal and environmental issues collectively.
- **Sustainability Rating and Ranking**: Ensure that sustainability ranking and rating organizations include your sustainability matrices in their indexes.

Sustainable Shared Value Creation

The shared value concept has been promoted as an idea that business organizations should simultaneously generate economic value for themselves and create societal value by advancing from creating shareholder value to developing "sustainable shared value creation" to protect the interests of all stakeholders.[16] The shared value concept promotes the alignment of business goals with societal needs. Shared value is defined as "policies and practices that enhance a company's competitiveness while advancing the economic and social conditions in the communities in which it operates."[17] Under the shared value creation concept, the board of directors' fiduciary responsibility is extended to all stakeholders to protect their interests. Management focuses on the continuous performance improvement of business operations in generating long-term value for shareholders while maximizing the positive impacts of operations on society and the environment. Operational performance is measured in terms of both financial ESP and nonfinancial ESG sustainability performance. Thus, corporate objectives have advanced from profit maximization to increasing shareholder wealth and creating shared value for all stakeholders.

Management should manage multidimensional aspects of sustainability performance, which could be viewed as complementary or conflicting as the interests of shareholders may not be congruent with those of other stakeholders. Thus, management approaches to sustainability can vary among organizations in terms of creating the right balance between apparent conflicts of interest among stakeholders. Investors and public companies now focus on financial ESP and market long-term performance indicators such as long-term stock prices, return on investment, return on assets, earnings growth, and research and development. Recently, KPMG uploaded a "Market Insights" survey to demonstrate efforts toward value creation in private equity firms. Several insights were discovered in this survey. Only a few private equity firms have reached their potential in terms of their investment value. Thus, value creation continues to impact businesses and their decision-making as improved analytics help drive deal processes. The top metrics for value creation involve innovation and people. Private equity firms utilize external advising at earlier stages to maximize investment value as over 70% of ESG factors get evaluated at the start of evaluating deals, during the due diligence and investment decision-making process.[18]

Academic research suggests that ESP is crucial in creating shareholder value by finding that firms with better ESP exhibit better financial and market performance and lower cost of equity, and such link between ESP and cost of equity is more pronounced in the presence of ESG.[19] However, the 2020 global COVID-19 pandemic crisis has caused a significant decline in CEO confidence in global growth within their companies, around one-third (32%), whereas only 17% are less confident in the future of their company altogether. The crisis has accelerated digital growth for most of the responses, as 75% say that the pandemic has accelerated the creation of a seamless digital customer experience, with over 1 in 5 (22%) of those saying progress "has sharply accelerated, putting us years in advance of where we expected to be."[20] As companies plan for their strategic shift for long-term growth, many business leaders are now recognizing a shortage in talent and keeping their workforce productive. Talent risk was rated at 2% in 2019 but shot up to 21% in July/ August of 2020, which makes it the highest risk to most businesses, according to their CEOs.[21]

In shared value creation, stakeholders are classified as internal stakeholders, shareholders, and employees with direct interest (stake) and bear risks associated with business activities and other external stakeholders. Other stakeholders, including creditors, customers, and suppliers, have reciprocal relationships and interactions with a firm because they contribute to firm value creation (stake), and their well-being is affected by the firm's activities (risk). Stakeholder interests in a firm are equity capital, human capital, social capital, compliance capital, and reputational capital, as presented in Chapter 6. Stakeholders' sustainability-related risks are strategic, financial, operational, compliance, and reputational risks, as presented in Chapter 7. Agency theory, in defining the relationship between the agent (management) and principals (shareholders), has traditionally been the dominant theory in corporate finance, management, and governance research in creating shareholder value.[22] While agency theory has been used to explain the principal–agent relationship and interest divergence for individualistic utility maximization and motivation, this theory may be irrelevant and undesirable under the emerging complex organization structure oriented toward stakeholders and the corporate strategy of shared value creation. Under stakeholder and stewardship theories, management, considering interests (stakes) and risks to shareholders (its main and direct stakeholders), may engage in nonfinancial ESG sustainability performance activities to protect non-shareholding stakeholders' interests and ensure the firm legitimacy and reputation.[23]

Business sustainability and shared value concepts can be combined to create business strategies and practices that not only drive economic success but also contribute positively to social and environmental sustainability. Shared value creation can be promoted within the wealth-maximization framework and implemented in the context of welfare maximization to pursue the goal of profit-with-purpose for corporations that protect the interests of all stakeholders. Corporations can balance wealth and wealth maximization for shareholders under the shareholder primacy concept while achieving welfare maximization for all stakeholders (e.g., safety, health, and well-being of employees, suppliers, and customers) under the stakeholder primacy concept. The concept of impact investing, focusing on the importance and relevance of corporate investment strategies in creating the desired returns on investment for shareholders and providing positive social and environmental impacts, is gaining acceptance. Business organizations must attain sustainable financial performance that has positive and measurable effects on the environment and society. Positive effects on the environment, communities, and society can be achieved when corporations invest in ESG activities, which may require allocating scarce resources that could otherwise be used to maximize firms' financial and economic performance. The board of directors and executives are important in promoting business sustainability performance, assessing and managing continuity and sustainability risk, and properly disclosing sustainability information in an integrated sustainability report.

Move Toward Shared Value Creation Concept

There has been a global move toward shared value creation for all stakeholders in the past two decades, either under the mandatory ESG initiatives in Europe and Asia or the voluntary ESG initiatives in the United States. For example, large European companies have been required to disclose their ESG activities that reflect information on shared value creation for all stakeholders since the 2017 annual report. In August 2019, the Business Roundtable (BRT) announced the adoption of a new Statement on the Purpose of a Corporation, signed by 181 high-profile chief executive officers (CEOs), promoting sustainability by creating shared value for all stakeholders.[24] Many business organizations have voluntarily considered the BRT Statement in the past year in creating shared value for their stakeholders. The BRT Statement emphasizes the significance of shareholders in business development, the need for companies to maintain values for shareholders in the long run, and the need to protect the interests of other stakeholders such as customers, employees, and communities.

A major concern is whether BRT CEOs want to change stakeholder governance to avoid accountability. There are also concerns regarding political and social objectives in the BRT Statement and whether business organizations should consider societal goals higher than shareholders. Nonetheless, the BRT Statement does not prioritize societal objectives over shareholders. The BRT Statement acknowledges the importance of meeting the expectations of a wider range of stakeholders to maintain the company's "long-term success." Thus, the BRT Statement does not require CEOs to consider a major change in the way they operate their business and take care of their shareholders. Indeed, the Statement suggests that public companies pay attention to all stakeholders, including shareholders, to create and maintain sustainable performance and maximize shared value for all stakeholders. The BRT Statement suggests moving away from the shareholder primacy concept toward the stakeholder primacy concept that promotes sustainability and creates shared value for all stakeholders.[25] Corporate purpose and stakeholder considerations have gained recognition in the business community worldwide. Stakeholder primacy challenges companies to put stakeholders at the heart of their purpose. A shift in corporate purpose from shareholder primacy to stakeholder primacy, reinforced by the US Business Roundtable's Statement on the Purpose of a Corporation. This focus, combined with public pressure for CEOs to engage in social and political topics (e.g., human capital, diversity, immigration, gun control, gender pay equity) encourage the move toward shared value creation for all stakeholders.

The interests and values of shareholders play a crucial role in value creation. On November 2, 2021, The Securities and Exchange Commission put out a bulletin concerning the processes for proposals for shareholder consideration in Rule 14a-8 and the exceptions to the rule. One exception was Rule 14a-8(i)(7), also known as the "ordinary business" exception, which excludes proposals relating to a business's ordinary operations to keep that at the discretion of management and the board of directors. Another exception is Rule 14a-8(i)(5), also known as the "economic relevance" exception, which excludes proposals that affect operations that account for less than 5% of the Company's total assets and/or net income or gross revenue. Another rule concerning 14a-8 was Rule 14-a8 (d), which requires proposals and supporting statements to be 500 or fewer words.[26]

Bain and company outlined information in their 2021 Global Private Equity Report about the growing importance of ESG initiatives in private equity firms. ESG is paramount to improving shareholder value and reducing risk. According to the report, Europe is leading the world in valuing global standards in sustainability. 80% of European funds were committed to Principles for Responsible Investment, Net-Zero Asset Owner Alliance, or Task Force on Climate-related Financial Disclosures. In the last few years, the highest EcoVadis scores for Europe and the US centered around the ESG categories of environment, labor/human rights, and ethics. The report took data from various stakeholders, including customers, employees, partners, creditors, and regulators. The report also outlines methods companies can use to execute ESG initiatives successfully. This includes a clear and focused direction of where companies want to go, complete integration from top to bottom, and continuous building upon results.[27]

Several examples of the new purpose mission for high-profile companies are BP, International Paper, Microsoft, and FedEx, among others. For example, in its 2019 Annual Report, BP defines its corporate mission as "Energy with Purpose," "Our purpose is reimagining energy for people and our planet," and "We want to help the world reach net zero and improve people's lives." In its 2019 Annual Report, the Swedish private equity firm EQT defines its "Statement of Purpose" as "To future-proof companies and make a positive impact, To be the most reputable investor and owner" with the mission of "With the best talent and network around the world, EQT uses a thematic investment strategy and distinctive value creation approach to future-proof companies, creating superior returns to EQT's investors and making a positive impact with everything we do." Corporations are moving toward purpose strategies that drive value for all stakeholders. With these

Sustainable Shared Value Creation

emerging "profit-with-purpose" mission, the finance function leads of the CFO is an integrated strategic, operating. and finance activities and performance, which is tasked with achieving specific financial and performance reporting objectives that can be measured, held accountable, and rewarded.

The concept of shared value sustainability recognizes that business organizations have a role to play in creating a more sustainable and equitable world by integrating sustainability into their core strategies and creating long-term value for both them and society. The combined sustainability and shared value concepts enable businesses to:

1. Develop products or services that are not detrimental to society and address pressing social or environmental issues.
2. Implement sustainable business strategies and practices that reduce negative environmental impacts.
3. Engage with communities in meaningful and impactful ways to address social issues and improve quality of life.
4. Invest in renewable energy, resource efficiency, natural resources, or waste reduction initiatives.
5. Collaborate with stakeholders to find innovative solutions to complex sustainability issues.
6. Set tone at the top by the board of directors in promoting stakeholder primacy and shared value creation models by signing the Statement of Purpose pledging to operate their business in the interests of all stakeholders, including shareholders, employees, suppliers, customers, and communities. This can be achieved by having a sustainability-centric board, a director interested in ESG sustainability, and/or a sustainability board committee.
7. Ensure fair treatment of workers throughout the supply-chain process.
8. Ensure commitment by senior executives, including the CEO and CFO, to sustainability and stakeholder primacy with a shared value focus. This can be achieved by either linking executive compensation to sustainability achievement and/or creating the executive position of the Chief Sustainability Officer.
9. Consider opting-in as a benefit corporation with a specified purpose statement in the corporate charter of incorporation.

The Role of the Board of Directors in Shared Value Creation

The board of directors plays an essential role in fostering shared value creation within the context of sustainability. The board's role in the shared value creation under stakeholder primacy/capitalism as opposed to shareholder primacy/capitalism is to oversee the managerial function of achieving the long-term ESP and ESG sustainability performance and effectively communicating sustainability performance information to all stakeholders. The board should be vigilant and understand the stakeholders' objectives and rationales for focusing on sustainability factors of performance, risk and disclosure, managerial, strategic planning, sustainable operational performance, and executive compensation in promoting long-term corporate value. The board should also provide oversight, insight, and foresight function on the achievement of both financial ESP and nonfinancial ESG sustainability performance driven by financial, human, social, environmental, and manufacturing capitals as well as innovation, culture, corporate governance. The board of directors and senior executives, especially the CFO, play an important role in promoting business sustainability performance, assessing and managing sustainability risk, and properly disclosing sustainability information in an integrated sustainability report.

The primary oversight function of the board of directors remains protecting the interests of multi-stakeholders during this challenging time and appointing competent, responsible, accountable, and ethical executives (e.g., CEOs, CFOs, and other C-suite executive) to manage the business for the benefit of all stakeholders. It is expected that the boards of directors engage more proactively in the oversight function in setting strategic priorities in dealing with global economic and political uncertainties and challenges caused by the pandemic and the potential risk of substantial interruptions in business operations and supply chain. The fiduciary duties of the board of directors are expected to be extended to multi-stakeholders, including shareholders, creditors, customers, suppliers, employees, government, society, and the environment with the move toward profit-with-purpose mission. The expanded fiduciary duty to all stakeholders requires the board of directors to establish proactive strategic profit-with-purpose missions, goals, and objectives to ensure business continuity and sustainability in creating long-term shared value and oversee managerial decisions and actions in effectively implementing these strategic goals.

The board of directors should set an appropriate tone at the top of reserving and promoting the corporate culture of competency, integrity, and transparency. Revising and reinforcing the corporate purpose of protecting the interests of all stakeholders becomes more relevant and important to the board of directors. The board of directors should review and revisit executive compensation by creating the right balance between managerial efforts and compensation on surviving the pandemic and ensuring the safety, health, and well-being of employees, customers, suppliers, supply-chain partners, communities, shareholders, and other stakeholders. There should be a move away from the traditional fiduciary loyalty model of the board of directors to shareholders under the shareholder capitalism and shareholder primacy and a move toward the board fiduciary due to all stakeholders

Sustainable Shared Value Creation

under the stakeholder capitalism and stakeholder primacy model. There is an alternative to changing corporate law on the fiduciary duties of the board of directors as it relates to board composition, adding the corporate purpose statement, and allowing non-shareholder stakeholders to be represented on the board.

In summary, the board of directors plays an important role in driving shared value creation within an organization by setting the strategic direction, overseeing managerial decisions, actions, and risk assessment, engaging stakeholders, overseeing both ESP and ESG sustainability performance, ensuring accountability and transparency, and providing leadership and advocacy. By fulfilling these responsibilities effectively, boards can help companies generate sustainable shared value for all stakeholders. Specifically, the board of directors should:

- Set Strategic Direction: The board should set the strategic direction of the company, including its mission of profit-with-purpose and approach to shared value creation by establishing goals and priorities that align business goals with societal needs and environmental concerns.

- Oversee Management Decisions and Activities: The board should oversee the decisions and activities of the management team, including the CEO, CEO, and other senior managers, to ensure that shared value initiatives are integrated into the company culture, business environment, operations, and business strategies as well as monitoring progress, providing guidance, and hold management accountable for achieving shared value goals.

- Monitor Risk Management: The board of directors should assess and mitigate risks related to shared value initiatives, including strategic risks, reputational risks, regulatory risks, and operational risks, by ensuring that shared value initiatives and efforts are aligned with the company's overall risk management framework as explained in *Chapter* 9.

- Ensure Stakeholder Engagement: The board of directors should engage with key stakeholders, including investors, suppliers, customers, employees, and communities, to understand their needs and expectations regarding shared value creation and integrate stakeholders' sentiments into board discussions and decision-making processes.

- Conduct Performance Evaluation: The board of directors should evaluate the company's ESO and ESG sustainability performance in relation to shared value creation, using KPIs and other metrics to measure progress over time and assess the effectiveness of shared value initiatives and adjust as needed to drive continuous improvement.

- Ensure Accountability and Transparency: Boards promote accountability and transparency in shared value efforts by requiring clear reporting and disclosure of relevant information to stakeholders. They ensure that the company communicates its shared value activities accurately and effectively.

- Provide Leadership and Advocacy: The board of directors should provide leadership and advocacy for shared value creation, both within the company and in the broader business community, by promoting the importance of integrating social and environmental considerations into corporate culture business environment and advocating for policies that support shared value initiatives.

Management Role Under Shared Value Concept

Management plays a pivotal role in driving the integration of social and environmental considerations into business strategy and operations under the shared value concept in several ways. First, management, as the steward of business capital and resources, has the primary role of improving ESP and ESG sustainability performance and managing related risks, maximizing utilization of all capital from strategic to financial, reputational, manufactured, human, social, and environmental, as explained in Chapter 10 to create shared value for all stakeholders. Second, business organizations' main goal and objective function is to maximize firm value. The goal of firm value maximization can be achieved through continuous improvements of both financial ESP and nonfinancial ESG sustainability performance. The ESP and ESG sustainability performance dimensions are interrelated and complement/complete each other, and thus, they should be integrated into supply-chain management. Third, the focus of business sustainability should be on creating long-term and sustainable shared value for all stakeholders, including investors, creditors, suppliers, customers, employees, the environment, and society. Finally, companies should effectively and transparently communicate their business sustainability with all stakeholders by periodically releasing their sustainability reports.

The shared value concepts require the precise definition and establishment of an organization's purpose. Every company should have its unique purpose determined in its charter of incorporation to maximize its positive impacts on all stakeholders, including society and the environment, and to minimize the negative impacts on multi-stakeholders. In case of the nonexistence of and/or inadequate "Statement of Purpose," management should work with the other executive in the C-suite under the oversight function of the board of directors and approval by majority shareholders to establish an appropriate stakeholder-inclusive "Statement of Purpose." Management should work effectively with other executives under the oversight function of the board of directors to implement and achieve the adopted "Statement of Purpose. Finally, the CFO should collaborate with the CEO in preparing and certifying the integrated sustainability reports and disclosing the achievement of the adopted "Statement of Purpose." This integrated sustainability report can disclose

Sustainable Shared Value Creation

the achievement of both financial returns and social and environmental impacts. This integrated report enables shareholders and other stakeholders to learn and assess the company's success in achieving its adopted purpose. This assessment can positively impact investor risk-premium and their willingness to invest in the company's stock. This is the only path forward toward stakeholder capitalism rather than societal socialism to achieve long-term, durable, and sustainable growth and performance. It is obvious that the challenge is not whether a "Statement of Purpose" is desirable and achievable, but the hurdle is whether high-profile corporate executives, including CEOs, CFOs, and institutional investors, collaborate to make it happen. Policymakers, investor activists, regulators, and rating agencies continuously monitor management, demanding real action on financial ESP and nonfinancial ESG sustainability performance goals and achievements. Time has passed for using sustainability as a greenwashing and branding tool for companies and their management to write climate, sustainability, and diversity reports without firm commitments to pursue the mission of profit-with-purpose in creating shared value for all stakeholders. Management should be held accountable for failure to achieve ESP and ESG sustainability.

In summary, management plays a vital role in driving shared value creation within an organization by developing strategies, engaging stakeholders, driving innovation, measuring performance, managing the supply chain, empowering employees, managing risks, fostering collaboration and partnerships, and integrating social and environmental considerations into business decision-making processes. Management should establish the following policies and procedures to obtain the profit-with-purpose mission under the shared value concept that contributes to shared value creation for all stakeholders, including the company and society:

- Develop a Statement of Purpose that is commonly acceptable by all stakeholders and is fair, transparent, and attainable.
- Design and implement the profit-with-purpose mission to achieve the adopted Statement of Purpose goal.
- Develop strategies that align business objectives with societal needs and environmental concerns by identifying opportunities to create shared value by addressing social and environmental issues while driving business growth and profitability.
- Focus on achieving both financial ESP and nonfinancial ESG sustainability performance.
- Hold individuals throughout the organization accountable for contributing toward achieving the profit-with-purpose mission by fostering a culture of shared value within the organization, engaging employees in sustainability initiatives, providing

opportunities for professional development, and empowering employees to contribute to shared value creation.

- Design sustainability metrics and effectively measure key performance indicators relevant to financial ESP and nonfinancial ESG sustainability performance by establishing KPIs and other metrics to measure the company's progress toward shared value goals and tracking performance, analyzing data, and reporting results to stakeholders transparently.

- Prepare and report integrated sustainability reports presenting both financial ESP and nonfinancial ESG sustainability performance.

- Assess and manage risks associated with shared value initiatives, including reputational risks, regulatory risks, and operational risks; by conducting thorough risk assessments and implementing risk mitigation strategies, management can minimize potential negative impacts on the business and society, as described in depth in Chapter 9.

- Communicate the Statement of Purpose, the profit-with-purpose mission, and both financial ESP and nonfinancial ESG sustainability performance with all stakeholders.

- Talk about sustainability stories and both financial ESP and nonfinancial ESG accomplishments by providing a consistent ESG narrative and messaging across all communications channels, collaborating with external partners, including other businesses, not-for-profit organizations, governments, and academia, *and* leveraging the expertise and resources of diverse stakeholders; management can amplify the impact of shared value initiatives and drive systemic change.

- Engage with key stakeholders, including shareholders, creditors, customers, employees, suppliers, and communities, to understand their needs and expectations and incorporate stakeholder preferences into decision-making processes by identifying shared value opportunities and building stronger relationships with stakeholders.

- Drive innovation and product development efforts to create solutions that address social and environmental issues and challenges by developing new products or services that have positive social or environmental impacts and improving existing products or processes to minimize negative externalities.

- Implement supply-chain strategies to minimize environmental impacts, ensure ethical sourcing practices, and promote social responsibility among suppliers by implementing sustainability standards, conducting supplier assessments, and fostering partnerships with suppliers to drive continuous improvement.

Sustainable Shared Value Creation

Business Sustainability Strategic Plans

Business sustainability requires the establishment of strategies and practices that contribute to short-, medium-, and long-term financial ESP and nonfinancial ESG sustainability performance, focusing on economic viability. This section presents strategic planning for business sustainability, including how stakeholders' perception of sustainability reports and metrics influences those strategic plans and actionable steps to developing business sustainability strategic plans.[28] Strategic sustainability planning enables business organizations to focus on the profit-with-purpose mission of maximizing its positive impacts on all stakeholders, including shareholders, employees, communities, customers, society, and the environment, and to minimize the negative impacts on multi-stakeholders. In case of nonexistence of and/or inadequate "Statement of Purpose" and "strategic sustainability planning," the board of directors, in collaboration with management, should develop the Statement of Purpose and strategic sustainability planning. The Statement of Purpose should include the mission, which reflects the organization's strategic sustainability planning in achieving short-, medium-, and long-term sustainable performance. Companies are now adopting the corporate mission of profit-with-purpose and strategic sustainability planning to create shared value for all stakeholders by shifting their goals to create shareholder value while fulfilling their social, environmental, and governance responsibilities. The Statement of Purpose, along with strategic sustainability planning, should define objectives for survival in the short term, continuity of business in the medium term, and strategic sustainability planning in the long term. In collaboration with management, the board of directors should also design strategic sustainability planning to achieve new objectives by designing business continuity plans, long-term strategic plans, and crisis management strategies.

Effective development and implementation of a strategic plan for business sustainability involves setting goals, strategies, and actions to ensure the long-term financial viability and success of the organization while considering environmental and social outcomes. The proper framework for establishing robust and comprehensive sustainability strategic plans requires:

1. **Assessment of the Existing Business Environment**: An effective strategic plan demands the evaluation of the current state of business in terms of ESP and ESG sustainability performance in determining environmental impacts, social responsibilities, and economic factors by identifying strengths, weaknesses, opportunities, and threats (SWOT analysis) associated with sustainability performance.
2. **Stakeholder Engagement**: Engage with stakeholders, including shareholders, employees, customers, suppliers, creditors, and communities, to understand their

needs, expectations, concerns, and priorities regarding sustainability in identifying key issues and sustainability initiatives.

3. **Establish Sustainability Goals**: Establish clear and measurable sustainability goals aligned with the organization's mission of profit-with-purpose, values, and long-term vision and feedback from stakeholders. These goals should cover economic, environmental, and social aspects, including enhancing product sustainability, reducing carbon emissions, improving workplace diversity, and contributing to communities.

4. **Integration into Business Strategy**: Integrate sustainability factors of planning, performance, risk, and disclosure into the organization's overall business strategy to ensure that sustainability goals are embedded into main strategic areas such as product development, supply-chain management, operations, marketing, and human resources.

5. **Implementation Strategic Plan**: Effective implementation of strategic plans requires determining specific actions, responsibilities, timelines, and resources to achieve sustainability goals.

6. **Resource Allocation**: Effective strategic plans require the allocation of appropriate and sufficient resources, including budget, personnel, and technology, to support the implementation of sustainability initiatives.

7. **Monitoring and Measurement**: Ongoing evaluation and monitoring of ESP and ESG KPIs related to environmental performance, social impact, and financial outcomes ensure the achievement of the adopted strategic plans.

8. **Continuous Improvement**: Continuous assessment and improvement of key sustainability performance by encouraging innovation, collaboration, and learning contribute to the effective achievement of sustainability strategic plans.

9. **Communication and Reporting**: Proper communication of sustainability initiatives and efforts to stakeholders through sustainability reports, websites, social media, and other channels demonstrates commitment to sustainability strategic plans and builds trust with stakeholders.

10. **External Collaboration and Advocacy**: Engagement with industry associations, government agencies, not-for-profit organizations, and other stakeholders ensures collaboration on sustainability initiatives and advocates for policies that support sustainable business practices.

Summary

Business organizations worldwide now recognize the importance of shared value creation and sustainability performance and the link between financial ESP and nonfinancial ESG sustainability performance with the profit-with-purpose mission to create shared value for all stakeholders. Justifications for business sustainability are moral obligation, social responsibility, maintaining a good reputation, ensuring sustainability, environmental consciousness, licensing to operate, and creating shared value for all stakeholders. In creating shared value for all stakeholders, corporations identify potential social, environmental, governance, and ethical issues and integrate them into their strategic planning and supply-chain management. There are many factors why a company should integrate sustainability performance into its supply-chain management, including the pressure of the labor movement, the development of moral values and social standards, the development of business education, and the change in public opinion about the role of business, environmental matters, governance, and ethical scandals. Companies that are, or aspire to be, leaders in sustainability are challenged by raising public expectations, increasing innovation, continuous quality improvement, effective governance measures, high standards of ethics and integrity, and heightened social and environmental problems. The emerging mission of profit-with-purpose corporations suggests that public companies have the dual mission of profit-making function of creating shareholder value while protecting the interests of other stakeholders through their social benefit function. It appears there is a move away from pure shareholder primacy to stakeholder primacy of profit-with-purpose corporations. It appears that European and Asian companies are moving closer to the concept of stakeholder primacy with the profit-with-purpose mission than their counterparts in North America.

Globalization has provided incentives and opportunities for business organizations, stakeholders, and executives to develop sustainability strategic plans to impact their business sustainability initiatives and strategies and integrate them into their supply-chain management. Corporations can choose from various sustainability strategic plans and initiatives regarding the scope, extent, and type of sustainability strategies that focus on different issues, functions, areas, and supply-chain management that drive positive environmental, social, and economic outcomes while also enhancing long-term competitiveness and resilience. Organizations of all types and sizes can integrate the suggested sustainability strategic plan framework consisting of the stewardship theory implementation, continuous improvements of both ESP and ESG sustainability performance, shared value creation, and sustainability disclosures into their corporate culture business model in effectively achieving their missions and goals of creating shared value for all stakeholders.

Key Points

- The main objective of business organizations has evolved from profit maximization to increasing shareholder wealth. This objective has changed in recent years, considering the recent developments in corporate governance and business sustainability to create shared value for all stakeholders.

- To effectively achieve this new objective, corporations are expanding their performance to both financial/quantitative ESP and nonfinancial/qualitative ESG sustainability performance.
- Companies are now adopting the corporate mission of profit with the purpose of creating shared value for all stakeholders by shifting their goals to create shareholder value while fulfilling their social, environmental, and governance responsibilities.
- Public companies must clearly define their "purpose" of creating shared value for all stakeholders.
- In collaboration with C-suite officers, the board of directors should publish a "Statement of Purpose" to create shared value for all stakeholders, which shareholders approve.
- Integrate the profit-with-purpose concept into the article of incorporation.
- Accept the mission of profit-with-purpose in creating shared value for all stakeholders.
- Establish the right balance between making a profit for shareholders and generating social and environmental impacts.
- Focus on ensuring employees, customers, and suppliers' safety, health, and well-being in the aftermath of the 2020 COVID-19 pandemic.

Review Questions

1. **What has the purpose of business shifted to in recent decades?**
2. **Why is the concept of shared value important?**
3. **What is the significance of the 2019 Business Roundtable's Statement on the Purpose of a Corporation?**
4. **What is the significance of having a clear Statement of Purpose for a company?**
5. **What are some benefits of integrating sustainability into corporate culture and business strategies?**
6. **Why is it important for companies to have ethical practices?**
7. **How can companies enhance the reliability and credibility of sustainability reports?**
8. **How can businesses achieve shared value creation?**
9. **Why is stakeholder engagement crucial in sustainability planning?**
10. **How does the concept of shared value creation impact corporate governance?**

11. **Why is it important for companies to integrate social and environmental considerations into business decision-making?**
12. **What is the significance of the European Union's Corporate Sustainability Due Diligence Directive proposal?**
13. **What are some global trends in sustainability reporting?**
14. **How does the concept of shared value challenge traditional business practices?**
15. **How can companies effectively communicate their sustainability efforts to stakeholders?**

Discussion Questions

1. **How has the purpose of business shifted in recent decades?**
2. **What role do corporate directors and executives play in developing strategies for business sustainability?**
3. **What are the main objectives of strategic planning for business sustainability?**
4. **How do stakeholders' perceptions of sustainability reports influence strategic plans?**
5. **What are some examples of nonfinancial ESG sustainability performance activities?**
6. **How does the concept of stakeholder primacy differ from shareholder primacy?**
7. **What is the role of the board of directors in promoting business sustainability?**
8. **What is the significance of integrating financial ESP and nonfinancial ESG sustainability performance?**
9. **What are some challenges in adopting a profit-with-purpose mission?**
10. **What are the benefits of establishing a clear corporate purpose statement?**
11. **What is the role of management in achieving the profit-with-purpose mission?**
12. **What are some key performance indicators (KPIs) for measuring sustainability performance?**
13. **What are some emerging trends in business sustainability?**
14. **What are the primary components of a sustainability strategy?**
15. **How can companies balance financial performance with social and environmental responsibilities?**

Multiple-Choice Questions

1. **What are the two main components of the profit-with-purpose mission?**
   A) Financial returns and customer satisfaction
   B) Financial economic sustainability performance (ESP) and nonfinancial environmental social and governance (ESG) sustainability performance
   C) Product innovation and market expansion
   D) Cost reduction and profit maximization

2. **What is the role of corporate directors and executives in business sustainability?**
   A) Focusing on short-term financial goals
   B) Developing and implementing strategies that integrate both financial and nonfinancial sustainability goals
   C) Reducing transparency in sustainability reporting
   D) Limiting stakeholder engagement

3. **Why is stakeholder engagement crucial in sustainability planning?**
   A) It reduces operational costs
   B) It helps in understanding stakeholder preferences and expectations, which informs the development of effective sustainability strategies
   C) It focuses solely on financial performance
   D) It limits transparency and reduces regulatory compliance

4. **How does the concept of shared value creation impact corporate governance?**
   A) It reduces operational risks
   B) It extends the fiduciary duties of the board of directors to all stakeholders, ensuring that corporate resources and activities create shared value
   C) It focuses solely on financial performance
   D) It limits stakeholder engagement and reduces transparency

5. **What are the primary components of a sustainability strategy?**
   A) Reducing operational costs and increasing shareholder wealth
   B) Establishing sustainability goals, integrating them into the business strategy, implementing action plans, and continuously monitoring and improving performance
   C) Focusing solely on financial performance
   D) Limiting stakeholder engagement and reducing transparency

6. **How can companies balance financial performance with social and environmental responsibilities?**
    A) By focusing solely on short-term financial goals
    B) By developing and implementing strategies that integrate financial ESP with nonfinancial ESG sustainability performance, ensuring long-term success and shared value creation
    C) By reducing transparency in sustainability reporting
    D) By limiting stakeholder engagement and reducing costs

7. **Why is it important for companies to have a well-defined purpose?**
    A) Reducing transparency and limiting stakeholder engagement
    B) A well-defined purpose helps guide business strategies, aligns with stakeholder expectations, and promotes long-term sustainability
    C) Focusing solely on financial performance
    D) Minimizing regulatory compliance and reducing costs

8. **What are some best practices for companies aiming to achieve a profit-with-purpose mission?**
    A) Developing a clear purpose statement, integrating sustainability into business strategies, establishing KPIs, ensuring transparent reporting, and engaging stakeholders
    B) Reducing operational costs and increasing shareholder wealth
    C) Focusing solely on financial performance
    D) Limiting stakeholder engagement and reducing transparency

9. **What is the significance of integrating financial ESP and nonfinancial ESG sustainability performance?**
    A) It reduces operational risks
    B) It ensures comprehensive sustainability performance by balancing financial success with social and environmental responsibilities
    C) It focuses solely on financial performance
    D) It limits stakeholder engagement and reduces transparency

10. **What are some challenges in adopting a profit-with-purpose mission?**
    A) Balancing the interests of shareholders with those of other stakeholders, ensuring transparency in sustainability reporting, and effectively integrating sustainability into business strategies
    B) Reducing operational costs and increasing shareholder wealth
    C) Focusing solely on financial performance
    D) Limiting stakeholder engagement and reducing transparency

11. **What are the benefits of establishing a clear corporate purpose statement?**
    A) Reducing transparency and limiting stakeholder engagement
    B) Providing a clear direction for the organization, ensuring alignment with stake-holder interests, and promoting long-term sustainability
    C) Focusing solely on financial performance
    D) Minimizing regulatory compliance and reducing costs

12. **What is the role of management in achieving the profit-with-purpose mission?**
    A) Focusing on short-term financial goals
    B) Developing strategies, engaging stakeholders, driving innovation, and ensuring transparent communication of sustainability performance
    C) Reducing transparency in sustainability reporting
    D) Limiting stakeholder engagement

13. **What is the significance of the European Union's Corporate Sustainability Due Diligence Directive proposal?**
    A) It aims to integrate sustainability into business decision-making and address inequalities in power dynamics by emphasizing stakeholder interests
    B) It focuses solely on financial performance
    C) It reduces transparency and limits stakeholder engagement
    D) It minimizes regulatory compliance and reduces costs

14. **What are some global trends in sustainability reporting?**
    A) The move toward adopting a profit-with-purpose mission, increased stakeholder engagement, and enhanced sustainability reporting and assurance
    B) Reducing operational costs and increasing shareholder wealth
    C) Focusing solely on financial performance
    D) Limiting stakeholder engagement and reducing transparency

15. **How does the concept of shared value challenge traditional business practices?**
    A) It reduces operational risks
    B) It promotes the idea that businesses should generate economic value while also creating societal value by addressing social and environmental issues
    C) It focuses solely on financial performance
    D) It limits stakeholder engagement and reduces transparency

16. **What role do corporate directors and executives play in developing strategies for business sustainability?**
    A) Focusing on short-term financial goals

B)   Developing strategies that integrate both financial and nonfinancial sustainability goals

C)   Reducing transparency in sustainability reporting

D)   Limiting stakeholder engagement

17.   **What are the four primary attributes of business sustainability?**

A)   Stakeholder theory, long-term performance, multidimensional nature of sustainability performance, and complementarity of sustainability dimensions

B)   Financial performance, short-term profits, regulatory compliance, and limited stakeholder engagement

C)   Ethical conduct, governance structure, financial stability, and social responsibility

D)   Economic growth, environmental impact, social responsibility, and governance compliance

18.   **How can businesses balance short-term and long-term performance?**

A)   By focusing solely on short-term profits

B)   By focusing on long-term performance instead of just meeting periodic financial targets

C)   By reducing transparency in financial disclosures

D)   By limiting stakeholder engagement

19.   **What are some examples of nonfinancial ESG sustainability performance?**

A)   Ethical workplace, customer satisfaction, just and safe working conditions, and workplace diversity

B)   Financial stability, short-term profits, regulatory compliance, and limited stakeholder engagement

C)   Economic growth, environmental impact, social responsibility, and governance compliance

D)   Profitability, market share, competitive advantage, and innovation

20.   **What are some global initiatives promoting sustainability reporting?**

A)   The Global Reporting Initiative (GRI), the Sustainability Accounting Standards Board (SASB), and the European Union's Corporate Sustainability Reporting Directive (CSRD)

B)   The World Bank, International Monetary Fund (IMF), and World Trade Organization (WTO)

C)   The United Nations, World Health Organization (WHO), and International Labour Organization (ILO)

D)   The International Finance Corporation (IFC), Asian Development Bank (ADB), and African Development Bank (AfDB)

21. **What is the significance of the International Sustainability Standards Board (ISSB)?**
    A) It focuses solely on financial performance
    B) It establishes sustainability accounting and reporting standards to ensure consistent and comparable sustainability disclosures
    C) It reduces regulatory compliance and limits stakeholder engagement
    D) It promotes short-term profits and minimizes the impact of sustainability initiatives

22. **What are some key performance indicators (KPIs) for sustainability?**
    A) ESG ratings, financial performance, impact metrics, stakeholder engagement, and regulatory compliance
    B) Market share, competitive advantage, innovation, and profitability
    C) Short-term profits, regulatory compliance, limited stakeholder engagement, and reduced transparency
    D) Economic growth, environmental impact, social responsibility, and governance compliance

23. **What are the benefits of integrating sustainability into corporate culture?**
    A) It reduces transparency and limits stakeholder engagement
    B) It promotes long-term performance, enhances reputation, and creates a positive impact on society and the environment
    C) It focuses solely on financial performance
    D) It minimizes regulatory compliance and reduces costs

24. **How can companies enhance the reliability and credibility of sustainability reports?**
    A) By obtaining assurance on sustainability reports from credible external sources
    B) By focusing solely on financial performance
    C) By reducing transparency and limiting stakeholder engagement
    D) By minimizing regulatory compliance and reducing costs

25. **What is the stakeholder theory in business sustainability?**
    A) A theory that focuses solely on financial performance
    B) A theory that focuses on protecting the interests of all stakeholders and achieving long-term and enduring financial and nonfinancial performance
    C) A theory that reduces regulatory compliance and limits stakeholder engagement
    D) A theory that minimizes the impact of sustainability initiatives

26. **What are the responsibilities of corporate directors?**
    A) To focus solely on short-term profits
    B) To oversee corporate affairs and ensure the company's sustainable performance

Multiple-Choice Questions

C) To reduce transparency and limit stakeholder engagement

D) To minimize regulatory compliance and reduce costs

27. **How do public companies contribute to market efficiency?**

A) By enhancing liquidity and enabling price discovery

B) By reducing transparency and limiting stakeholder engagement

C) By focusing solely on short-term profits

D) By minimizing regulatory compliance and reducing costs

28. **What is the significance of the stakeholder engagement in sustainability planning?**

A) It reduces transparency and limits stakeholder engagement

B) It helps in understanding stakeholder preferences and expectations, which informs the development of effective sustainability strategies

C) It focuses solely on financial performance

D) It minimizes regulatory compliance and reduces costs

29. **What are some global trends in sustainability reporting?**

A) The move toward adopting a profit-with-purpose mission, increased stakeholder engagement, and enhanced sustainability reporting and assurance

B) Reducing operational costs and increasing shareholder wealth

C) Focusing solely on financial performance

D) Limiting stakeholder engagement and reducing transparency

30. **How does the concept of shared value challenge traditional business practices?**

A) It reduces operational risks

B) It promotes the idea that businesses should generate economic value while also creating societal value by addressing social and environmental issues

C) It focuses solely on financial performance

D) It limits stakeholder engagement and reduces transparency

Notes

1 Much of the discussion in this chapter comes from Rezaee, Z. (2021). *Business Sustainability: Profit-With-Purpose Focus, Business Expert Press*, July 2021 and Chapters 3 and 4 of Rezaee, Z. (2024). *The Sustainable Business Blueprint: Planning, Performance, Risk, Reporting and Assurance*. Routledge/Taylor and Francis.

2 Business Roundtable (BRT). (2019). Statement on the Purpose of a Corporation. August 19, 2019. https://opportunity.businessroundtable.org/wp-content/uploads/2019/09/BRT -Statement-on-the-Purpose-of-a-Corporation-with-Signatures-1.pdf

3 Sjafiell, Beate, and Mahonen, Jukka. (April 12, 2022). Corporate purpose and the EU Corporate Sustainability Due Diligence Proposal. The ECGI Blog.

4 Dubois, Edouard, and Saribas, Ali. (2020). Making corporate purpose tangible – a survey of investors. Harvard Law School Forum on Corporate Governance. https://corpgov.law .harvard.edu/2020/06/19/making-corporate-purpose-tangible-a-survey-of-investors/

5 Dubois, Edouard, and Saribas, Ali. (2020). Making corporate purpose tangible – a survey of investors. Harvard Law School Forum on Corporate Governance. https://corpgov.law .harvard.edu/2020/06/19/making-corporate-purpose-tangible-a-survey-of-investors/

6 Benoit, Robe, Delaunay, and Dunn. (2019). French legislation on corporate purpose." Harvard Law School Forum on Corporate Governance. June 8, 2019. https://corpgov.law .harvard.edu/2019/06/08/french-legislation-on-corporate-purpose/

7 Benoit, Robe, Delaunay, and Dunn. (2019). French legislation on corporate purpose. Harvard Law School Forum on Corporate Governance. June 8, 2019. https://corpgov.law.harvard .edu/2019/06/08/french-legislation-on-corporate-purpose/

8 World Economic Forum (WEF). (2020). Measuring stakeholder capitalism towards common metrics and consistent reporting of sustainable value creation. White Paper, September 2020.   https://www.wlrk.com/docs/WEF_IBC_Measuring_Stakeholder_Capitalism_ Report_2020.pdf

9 Porter, M.E., and Kramer, M.R. (2011). Creating shared value. *Harvard Business Review*, January–February, 62–77.

10 Business Roundtable (BRT). (2019). Statement on the Purpose of a Corporation. August 19, 2019. https://opportunity.businessroundtable.org/wp-content/uploads/2019/09/BRT -Statement-on-the-Purpose-of-a-Corporation-with-Signatures-1.pdf

11 Vodovoz, I., Robinson, C., and Sullivan, K. (September 22, 2020). DeloittESGnow – enhancing trust in ESG Disclosures. *Heads Up* 27 (20). https://dart.deloitte.com/USDART/home/ publications/deloitte/heads-up/2020/deloittESGnow-enhancing-trust-in-esg

12 BlackRock. (2018). Investment stewardship's approach to engagement on long-term strategy, purpose, and culture. https://www.blackrock.com/corporate/literature/publication/ blk-annual-stewardship-report-2018.pdf.

13 Business Roundtable (BRT). (August 19, 2019). Business Roundtable redefines the purpose of a corporation to promote "an economy that serves all Americans". https://www.businessroundtable.org/business-roundtable-redefines-the-purpose-of-a-corporation-to-promote-an-economy-that-serves-all-americans.

14 Business Roundtable. One year later: Purpose of a corporation. https://purpose.businessroundtable.org/

15 The International Financial Reporting Standards (IFRS) Foundation. (2020). Consultation paper on sustainability reporting. September 2020. https://cdn.ifrs.org/-/media/project/ sustainability-reporting/consultation-paper-on-sustainability-reporting.pdf

16 Porter, M.E., and Kramer, M.R. (2011). Creating shared value. *Harvard Business Review*, January–February, 62–77.

Notes

17 Porter, M.E., and Kramer, M.R. (2011). Creating shared value. *Harvard Business Review*, January–February, 62–77.

18 KPMG. (2022). Delivering on the promise of value creation. 2022 Market Insights Survey. https://assets.kpmg/content/dam/kpmg/xx/pdf/2022/03/delivering-on-the-promise-of -value-creation.pdf

19 Ng, A.C., and Rezaee, Z. (2015). Business sustainability performance and cost of equity capital. *Journal of Corporate Finance* 34, 128–149.

20 KPMG. (2020). Long-term growth amid talent and digital issues. https://home.kpmg/xx /en/home/insights/2020/09/ceo-are-building-a-path-to-long-term-growth-for-their-busi- nesses.html

21 KPMG. (2020). Long-term growth amid talent and digital issues. https://home.kpmg/xx /en/home/insights/2020/09/ceo-are-building-a-path-to-long-term-growth-for-their-busi- nesses.html

22 Rezaee, Z. and Fogarty, T. (2019). *Business Sustainability, Corporate Governance, Organizational Ethics.* Wiley.

23 Rezaee, Z. and Fogarty, T. (2019). *Business Sustainability, Corporate Governance, Organizational Ethics.* Wiley.

24 Business Roundtable (BRT). (2019). Statement on the Purpose of a Corporation. August 19, 2019. https://opportunity.businessroundtable.org/wp-content/uploads/2019/09/BRT Statement-on-the-Purpose-of-a-Corporation-with-Signatures-1.pdf

25 Business Roundtable (BRT). (2019). Statement on the Purpose of a Corporation. August 19, 2019. https://opportunity.businessroundtable.org/wp-content/uploads/2019/09/BRT Statement-on-the-Purpose-of-a-Corporation-with-Signatures-1.pdf

26 US. Securities and Exchange Commission. (November 3, 2021). Shareholder proposals: Staff Legal Bulletin No. 14L (CF). Division of Corporation Finance Securities and Exchange Commission. SEC.gov | Shareholder Proposals: Staff Legal Bulletin No. 14L (CF)

27 Seeman, Axel, Hardcastle, Dale, Diers, Deike, and Han, Jacqueline (March 1, 2021). The expanding case for ESG in private equity. Global Private Equity Report. Bain and Company. https://www.bain.com/insights/esg-investing-global-private-equity-report-2021/

28 Much of materials in this section come from Rezaee, Z. (2024). *The Sustainable Business Blueprint: Planning, Performance, Risk, Reporting and Assurance.* Routledge/Taylor and Francis, Chapter 4.

Chapter 4
Business Sustainability Models

Shareholder Primacy and Governance Versus Stakeholder Primacy and Governance

---

Learning Objectives

- Learn a profit-with-purpose mission to create shared value for all stakeholders.
- Understand moving away from the shareholder primacy model and moving toward the stakeholder primacy model.
- Understand impact investing to generate desired financial returns for shareholders while achieving social and environmental impacts.
- Learn measures of both financial ESP performance and nonfinancial ESG sustainability performance.
- Learn reporting of both financial ESP performance and nonfinancial ESG sustainability performance to all stakeholders.

Introduction

The amount of environmental, social, and governance (ESG) funds available to US investors increased substantially in 2019 to $20.6 billion, about four times more than the funds invested in ESG in 2021.[1] The Global ESG assets through sustainability investment by socially responsible investors are expected to exceed $53 trillion by 2025.[2] The World Economic Forum (WEF) states that a business organization is more than an economic unit generating wealth for shareholders and should attempt to have social and environmental impacts.[3] Business organizations are expected to fulfill human, environmental, and societal aspirations as part of the broader social system of achieving the desired return for shareholders while having social and environmental impacts.[4] Thus, the purpose of business organizations has transformed from profit-maximization and shareholder wealth creation to the generation of shared value for all stakeholders. There are two distinct models of shareholder primacy and stakeholder primacy, each with its attributes and purposes.[5] The shareholder primacy model focuses on shareholder value creation and thus makes the board of directors' fiduciary responsibility only to shareholders in protecting their

DOI: 10.4324/9781003487081-4

interests with the main mission of creating value primarily for shareholders. This shareholder primacy model, also known as the US capitalism system, is criticized for focusing on generating short-term profits for shareholders while compromising long-term sustainability performance that creates shared value for all stakeholders and promotes innovation, growth, and social and environmental impacts. Corporations can create the right balance between wealth and wealth-maximization for shareholders under the shareholder primacy model while achieving welfare welfare-maximization for all stakeholders under the stakeholder primacy model.

The Business Roundtable (BRT), in 2019, announced the adoption of a new "Statement on the Purpose of a Corporation," signed by 181 high-powered chief executive officers (CEOs), which recommends the move away from the shareholder primacy concept toward the stakeholder primacy concept that promotes sustainability by creating shared value for all stakeholders.[6] Corporate profit-with-purpose and stakeholder considerations have gained worldwide recognition in the business community in generating shared value for all stakeholders. Stakeholder primacy encourages companies to place stakeholders at the heart of their purpose. A shift in corporate purpose from shareholder primacy to stakeholder primacy, reinforced by the US Business Roundtable's "Statement on the Purpose of a Corporation." This focus, combined with public pressure for public companies to engage on social, environmental, and political topics (e.g., human capital, diversity, climate change, immigration, gun control, gender pay equity), encourages corporate America to advance toward business sustainability and public companies worldwide to move toward the stakeholder primacy model. This chapter presents shareholder primacy and stakeholder primacy models and corporate governance under both models.

Shareholder Primacy Model and Shareholder Governance

Shareholder Primacy Model

The shareholder primacy model asserts that the primary purpose of a business entity is to create shareholder wealth and maximize shareholder value. This model suggests that the protection of the interests of shareholders should be the top priority for corporations. Thus, corporate directors and executives should focus on generating profits and increasing corporate value, which ultimately benefits the shareholders. This shareholder primacy model, also known as the US corporate governance model, makes the board of directors judiciary responsible only to shareholders in protecting their interests. Thus, corporate activities are managed to create shareholder value. This corporate governance model has been criticized for focusing on generating short-term profits for shareholders while compromising long-term sustainability performance that creates shared value for all stakeholders and promotes innovation, growth, and social and environmental impacts.[7]

Shareholder primacy is an owner-centric form of corporate governance that focuses on maximization of shareholder wealth before considering the interests of other stakeholders, such as employees, customers, society, community, consumers, and the environment. Corporations as legal entities are incorporated under state law with many privileges, enabling them to raise public capital, operate within the framework of applicable laws and rules, and create wealth for their owners. Under the agency's view of the relationship between owners and management, a main concern is that directors and executives might use their discretion to advance their interests at the expense of shareholders. Sufficient corporate governance measures should be developed and implemented to minimize the potential conflicts of interest and a fundamental tension between the need to grant directors and executives adequate discretion to fulfill their duties while preventing possible opportunistic behavior. The primacy model assumes that shareholders own the corporation and should be run for their sole benefit. This model has been the dominant organizing framework for corporate governance since the 1980s in the United States.

The capitalist system in the United States has traditionally contributed to the nation's economic growth and prosperity. However, like any other system, it has its challenges, as many may believe the capitalist system has not benefited society.[8] With the recent focus on environmental and social issues worldwide, many business organizations and their board of directors are paying attention to the growing interest and demand by socially responsible investors and regulators to focus on the sustainability factors of performance, risk, and disclosure, and consider them in their business and strategic decision-making. Profit-oriented business organizations and their board of directors address these sustainability factors in many of their corporate decisions, including financial economic sustainability performance and nonfinancial environmental, ethical, social, and governance sustainability performance, their relationships with current or potential employees, customers, suppliers, their ability to attract capital and investor interest and their ability to recruit, develop, and retain a talented and motivated workforce. Under the shareholder primacy model, corporate social responsibility (CSR) and nonfinancial ESG activities are often seen as secondary to the primary goal of creating shareholder value. Thus, ESG activities come at the expense of shareholder returns. Business organizations should prepare for new sustainability strategic planning to respond effectively to the request from stakeholders for improvement in nonfinancial ESG activities and performance, as well as the demand by shareholders for improving financial economic sustainability performance in terms of total shareholder return (TSR). The US capital markets driven by the shareholder primacy and capitalism

Shareholder Primacy Model and Shareholder Governance

model have been perceived as promoting shareholder wealth-maximization without creating an inclusive and equitable economy for all Americans. Many corporate leaders, including the board of directors and management, have stronger incentives to give substantial weight to the interests of shareholders with minimal or no incentive to advance stakeholders' interests beyond that to what would benefit the shareholder.

In summary, the shareholder primacy model suggests that the primary responsibility of a corporation is to maximize shareholder value with minimal efforts to protect the interests of other stakeholders, including employees, customers, suppliers, and the broader community. Some of the important aspects and attributes of the shareholder primacy model: (1) business organizations should focus on strategies, actions and decisions that maximize shareholder value by generating the highest possible returns for shareholders through maximizing profits, increasing share prices, and paying dividends; (2) the primary fiduciary duties of the board of directors and executives are to shareholders; (3) the focus on maximizing shareholder wealth can indirectly contribute to overall economic growth and societal well-being that benefit other stakeholders; (4) advancing shareholder interests can contribute to allocate capital efficiently by investing in projects that generate the highest return on investment; (5) prevent conflicts of interest by aligning the interests of management with those of shareholders; and (6) mere focus on maximizing shareholder value can lead to negative consequences of short-termism, neglect of interest of other stakeholders, and potential for unethical behavior.

Shareholder Governance

The shareholder aspect of corporate governance is based on the premise that shareholders provide financial capital to the corporation, which exists for their benefit. It is driven by the agency theory that corporate directors and executives' fiduciary duties are to shareholders who have a residual claim on the company's assets and cash flows. Shareholders (principals) provide financial capital to the company, which is run by management (agents). The principal–agent problem exists because corporations are separate entities from their owners – management needs physical capital (investment funds), and investors need skilled human capital (management) to run the company. According to the principal-agent theory, also called the shareholder model of corporate governance, the primary objective of the company is to maximize shareholder wealth and thus, the role of corporate governance is to ensure the enhancement of shareholder wealth and to align the interests of management with those of the shareholders. The principal–agent problem arises from two factors: the separation of ownership and control and, most importantly, incomplete contracts or costly enforceable contracts between the agents and principals, known as agency costs. Shareholder governance consists of the mechanisms, measures, and processes through which shareholders can exercise their voting rights of electing the board of directors to represent them, participate in decision-making, make investment decisions, and hold corporate directors and management accountable for protecting their interests.

The corporate governance structure consists of internal and external mechanisms intended to effectively align the behavior and interests of management (agents) with the desires of the principals (shareholders). The agency problem exists when the interests of management and shareholders are not in accord and when there are difficulties in verifying management activities. Agency costs also arise when there is an "information asymmetry" between management and shareholders and when the company's board of directors fails to fulfill its fiduciary duties of effectively carrying out its assigned oversight role. The agency problem can never be perfectly solved in the real world, and agency costs cannot be eliminated. If complete contracts were feasible and efficiently enforceable, there would be no agency costs, in the sense that investors would have known exactly what management was doing with their funds, and management would know investors' expectations. However, complete contracts are neither feasible nor enforceable, resulting in the occurrence of "residual contract rights" of making decisions based on the rights not specified in the contract or on unforeseen circumstances. The residual contract rights may cause asymmetric information problems as management possesses information not disclosed or available to investors, which may result in management entrenchment.

Shareholder aspect governance is designed to reduce the agency costs and align the interests of management with those of investors through (1) providing incentives and opportunities for management to carry out its function effectively and maximize shareholder wealth by providing executive compensation plans, ownerships, or stock options; (2) strengthening shareholder rights to monitor, control, and discipline management through enforceable contracts or legal protection; (3) promoting shareholder democracy; (4) improving the vigilance of the board's oversight function; (5) holding directors accountable and liable for the fulfillment of their fiduciary duties; and (6) improving the effectiveness of both internal corporate governance mechanisms (board of directors, internal controls) and external corporate governance mechanisms (external Audit, monitoring, and regulatory functions). Shareholders, as owners of public companies, should be attentive and protect their investments by attending shareholders' annual meetings (in person and virtually) to vote on corporate governance issues as reflected in management and shareholders' resolutions. Shareholders play a crucial role in corporate governance through their voting rights and engagements in meetings and discussions with the board of directors and management. These engagements enable shareholders to submit their governance proposals at the annual meetings.

Shareholder Primacy Model and Shareholder Governance

Shareholders play an important role in corporate governance by electing directors who appoint management to make day-to-day business decisions for public companies. In addition, shareholders vote on many important issues that can create value for them. Generally, at annual shareholder meetings, shareholders vote for or against candidates for director positions, obtain detailed information regarding executive compensation plans, put forth proposals for consideration by other shareholders, and attend special shareholder meetings to vote on important corporate structure matters (mergers and acquisitions). Shareholders can vote at the meetings in person or "by proxy," including online, by mail, or by phone. Shareholders play an important role in corporate governance by exercising their voting rights and engaging in meetings and discussions with the board and management. This engagement becomes increasingly crucial when shareholders submit their proposals at the companies' annual meetings.

Agency/shareholder theory focuses on risk sharing and agency problems between shareholders and management by suggesting that the interests of principals (owners) and their agents (executives) often need to be aligned. Thus, in the context of agency theory, corporate governance's role is to align management's interests with those of shareholders. Moral hazards can occur in the presence of information asymmetry where the agent (management) acting on behalf of the principal (shareholders) knows more about its actions and/or intentions than the principal does due to a lack of effective corporate governance in properly monitoring management. The implications of agency/shareholder theory for corporate governance are that management incentives and activities often focus on short-term earnings targets and self-serving of maximizing executive compensation rather than improving long-term performance in creating shareholder value. Thus, corporate governance measures should be in place to ensure that management focuses on creating shareholder value.

Directors have fiduciary duties of care and loyalty that they must uphold. These duties require the directors to use informed, deliberate decision-making and act disinterestedly and independently when making decisions. They are required to use good faith and judgment to act in the best interest of the company and the stockholders they represent. Directors should be well-advised and properly informed, using all material information. They must be comfortable with all processes, keep confidential information confidential, weigh risks and rewards and compare them to alternatives, and respond appropriately to all issues. Finally, they must act in good faith and decide what they believe is in the company's best interest. A big responsibility that directors must deal with is effective oversight over the company and its risk management. Protocols to monitor and avoid risk and comply with laws and regulations must be implemented to avoid a breach of fiduciary duties.

A good board process creates an appropriate framework for any situation while recording how situations were handled and serving as evidence for the director's completion of the fiduciary duties. This is all very important because if the director is sent to court, the burden is now on the plaintiff to provide evidence of gross negligence regarding a director's fiduciary duties due to the business judgment rule. This rule, reliance on company records, indemnification, expense advancement, exculpation of certain personal liabilities, and directors' and officers' (D&O) liability insurance, helps directors satisfy their fiduciary duties and protect them from possible accusations of breach.

In summary, effective shareholder governance is crucial for maintaining a balance of power between shareholders, directors, and management within corporations, ensuring that the interests of shareholders are aligned with the long-term sustainability of the company, and promoting overall corporate responsibility and accountability. Some of the aspects and attributes of effective shareholder governance are: (1) shareholders possess certain rights, including voting on electing directors and key issues and receiving information about the company's financial performance that enable them to participate in corporate governance; (2) shareholders participation in Annual General Meetings (AGMs): to discuss important matters, voice concerns and express their views on corporate decisions, vote on resolutions, and receive updates from the management regarding the strategic plans; (3) shareholders can vote to elect directors to, represent their interests and oversee the company's management; and (4) shareholders have the right to propose resolutions that are put to the vote during AGMs that can influence corporate policies and practices and address ESG sustainability issues. Directors represent shareholders and have fiduciary duties of care and loyalty to protect the interests of shareholders. These duties require the directors to use informed, deliberate decision-making and use good faith and independent judgment to act in the best interest of the company and its shareholders.

Stakeholder Primacy Model and Stakeholder Governance

The primary purpose of companies has evolved from profit-maximization to shareholder wealth enhancement to the creation of shared value for all stakeholders with the mission of profit-with-purpose. Business organizations are now facing pressure from social activists and stakeholders to pay attention to the interests of customers, suppliers, employees, society, and the environment, among others, to create shared value for all stakeholders. Thus, stakeholder governance measures are intended to protect the interests of all stakeholders who have a stake (interest) in the company, as well as their risks. The World Economic Forum highly recommends that companies move from the traditional model of "shareholder capitalism" to the model of "stakeholder capitalism" and supports the stakeholder governance concept in the context of the stakeholder primacy model.[9] The stakeholder primacy model focuses on the broader view of the company as the nexus of contracts among all stakeholders with the common goal of creating shared value. Under the stakeholder primacy model, public companies must be socially responsible, environmentally conscious, and good citizens, granted the use of the nation's physical and human capital, which must be managed in the public interest. Thus, the performance of public companies is measured in terms of key financial indicators (earnings, market share, stock price), social indicators (employment, customer satisfaction, fair trading with suppliers), ethical indicators (proper business culture, business code of conduct), and environmental indicators (antipollution, preservation of natural resources).

Stakeholder Primacy Model

The stakeholder primacy model considers the interests of all stakeholders, including shareholders, and the creation of shared value for all stakeholders. The stakeholder primacy model focuses on the impact investing concept of generating desired financial returns on shareholders' investments while protecting other stakeholders' interests and achieving social and environmental impacts. Under the stakeholder primacy model, while shareholders have the right to protect their investments, they also benefit in the long term, where their company is sustainable in creating shared value for all stakeholders. Stakeholder welfare creation rather than shareholder wealth creation is promoted under stakeholder capitalism. Stakeholders are individuals or groups who affect the company's strategic decisions, operations, and performance, as well as its decisions or activities. Traditionally, shareholders have been the primary users of the company's financial reports, which reflect the company's financial condition and the results of operations. While shareholders are still the primary recipients of the company's reports on economic performance, stakeholders are now becoming more engaged and interested in the company's multiple-bottom-lines (MBLs) performance on various economic, governance, ethical, social, and environmental issues. Shareholders' initiatives, proposals, and resolutions on environmental and social issues are being considered by the board of directors and incorporated into the corporate governance structure.

The stakeholder primacy model has gained support after the 2007–2009 global financial crisis and the move toward business sustainability. This model requires (1) identification of all stakeholders who affect and are affected by the organization's business and affairs, including investors, creditors, customers, employees, suppliers, society, and the environment; (2) determination of rights, authorities; responsibilities, and accountability of each stakeholder; (3) development of a systematic process to ensure proper accountability for the stewardship of the organization's resources and capitals; and (4) establishment of a fair system of rewards based on the risk taken by stakeholders. Under the stakeholder theory of corporate governance, the primary objective is to achieve sustainable financial and non-financial performance by creating shared value for all stakeholders. Some of the aspects and attributes of the stakeholder primacy model are: (1) balancing interests of all stakeholders by recognizing that business organizations create shared value for all stakeholders including shareholders and their impact extends beyond shareholders to encompass employees, customers, suppliers and the wider community; (2) engagement of a diverse set of stakeholders in decision-making processes to ensure that decisions involve all concerned stakeholders, reflect a broader range of perspectives, and consider the potential impacts on a variety of stakeholders; (3) focus on the long-term sustainability of a company and its stakeholders by improving by relationships with employees, investors, customers, suppliers, communities, society and the environment; (4) compliance with the principles of corporate social responsibility by taking take actions on a voluntary basis beyond what is required by law to benefit society; (5) promotion of responsible business practices that go beyond mere compliance with laws, rules, regulations, and standards; (6) recognition of the importance of considering societal and environmental concerns and impacts by adopting adopt sustainable and environmentally friendly and socially responsible practices; (7) using globally accepted sustainability reporting guidelines and frameworks (GRI, SASB, ISSB) to disclose the companies ESP and ESG sustainability performance; and (8) adherence to stakeholder governance measures presented in the next section.

Several initiatives have been undertaken in moving away from shareholder primacy and toward stakeholder primacy under this new corporate governance model, including:[10]

1. The board's fiduciary duty should be extended to all stakeholders, and the board of directors should be accountable to all stakeholders, not just shareowners.
2. Corporate purpose statements should specifically state that corporations benefit society positively by creating shared value for all stakeholders.
3. Multiple stakeholders, including employees, should be represented on corporate boards.
4. Large corporations should be required to be organized under federal charters to facilitate governance reform accountability that requires responsibility to all stakeholders.
5. Legislative acts and regulatory mandates.

Stakeholder Primacy Model and Stakeholder Governance

Stakeholder Governance

Shareholder governance advocates that shareholders are authorized to direct and monitor the company's business and affairs by exercising their right to elect directors, who then appoint management to run the company for their benefit. Stakeholder governance consists of governance measures, mechanisms, practices, and processes used to protect the interests of all stakeholders by managing the company's relationships and interactions with various stakeholders. Stakeholder governance is a process of managing an organization for the benefit of all of its stakeholders by considering the interests and perspectives of various stakeholders. Stakeholders consist of individuals, groups, or entities such as shareholders, creditors, employees, customers, suppliers, communities, and governmental bodies, among others, that have an interest or stake in the organization, and they assume risks as they are affected by its decisions and actions. Unlike the shareholder governance model presented in the previous section, which focuses primarily on shareholders, stakeholder governance considers the interests of a broader range of stakeholders when making decisions rather than primarily focusing on maximizing shareholder value under the traditional approach in corporate governance. Stakeholder governance is a holistic and sustainable approach to corporate governance that recognizes that a company's success is linked to the well-being of various stakeholders. Stakeholder governance effectiveness has been the main focus of business organizations and their stakeholders, including shareholders, employees, suppliers, customers, and communities. Stakeholder governance recognizes the importance of business survival and continuity in the short term and sustainable value creation for all shareholders in the long term as a corporate strategy.

Stakeholder governance represents a broader trend in corporate governance practices and discussion by emphasizing a more inclusive and sustainable approach to corporate governance. Some of the important aspects and attributes of stakeholder governance are: (1) identification of all stakeholders that have stake in the company and take risk including shareholders, creditors, employees, customers, suppliers, society and the environment; (2) active involvement and engagement of all concerned stakeholders by seeking input, feedback, and collaboration from them to understand their interests and concerns and ensure a more comprehensive and diverse perspectives of decision-makings and actions; (3) Creating a right balance among interests of all stakeholders by finding solutions that address their needs and concerns; (4) improving transparent and open communication with stakeholders by providing clear and accessible information about the company's strategic planning, activities, and impacts; (5) focus on the social and environmental responsibilities of the company by taking initiatives that contribute positively to society and the environment; (6) understanding that the success of a company is intertwined with the well-being of its stakeholders by focusing on sustainable business practices and creation of sustainable shared value for all stakeholders; (7) implementation of governance mechanisms for ongoing engagement with all stakeholders through regular meetings, surveys, feedback channels, and other means to ensure proper communication and responsiveness to stakeholder concerns; (8) focus on addressing stakeholder expectations by being adaptable and responsive to evolving circumstances; and (9) holding corporate decision-makers including directors and executive accountability for their decisions and actions to all stakeholders including shareholders.

The primary goal of corporate governance is not simply to reduce agency costs but to create a proper balance of power sharing among all stakeholders participating in corporate, including shareholders, directors, management, employees, customers, and communities, among others, driven by the responsibility to create and enhance long-term shared value for all stakeholders. The stakeholder model of corporate governance focuses on the broader view of the company with purpose and profit as the nexus of contracts among all corporate governance participants with the common goal of creating shared value for all stakeholders. The stakeholder model concentrates on the maximization of wealth for all stakeholders, including (1) contractual participants such as shareholders, creditors, suppliers, customers, and employees; and (2) social constituents including the local community; society and global partners; local, state, and federal governments; and environmental matters. Under stakeholder governance, public companies must be socially responsible, good citizens, and agents of using the nation's physical and human capital, managed in the public interest to leave a better environment for the next generations. Thus, the performance of public companies is measured in terms of key financial indicators (earnings, market share, stock price), social indicators (employment, customer satisfaction, fair trading with suppliers), ethical indicators (proper business culture, business code of conduct), and environmental indicators (antipollution, preservation of natural resources).

Stakeholders have a reciprocal relationship and interaction with a firm in that they contribute to its value creation, and the firm's performance affects their well-being. Stakeholder theory applies to all managerial processes in that the synergy and integration among all elements of the business model and its processes are essential in achieving overall sustainable performance objectives. From the stakeholder's perspective, an organization is part of a network of groups that work together to achieve the network/system goals. However, management may take actions to improve sustainability performance that benefit stakeholders (shareholders) who have the power to influence its compensation. The application of stakeholder theory to corporate governance and, thus, management processes suggests that a company should be viewed as a nexus of all stakeholders. Corporate stakeholders

Stakeholder Primacy Model and Stakeholder Governance

are shareholders, creditors, customers, suppliers, employees, government, competitors, the environment, and society. Under stakeholder theory, management's role is to improve sustainable performance and create shared value for all stakeholders. The stakeholder governance paradigm requires a new set of guiding principles driven by shared value concepts, new governance functions redefining the fiduciary duties of directors and executives to all stakeholders, and a new set of corporate governance measures to ensure its effectiveness.

The stakeholder governance concept focusing on stakeholders has recently been debated among policymakers, regulators, investors, the business community, and the accounting profession, with both discussion of the positive impacts of benefiting all stakeholders and the imposition of additional costs on shareholders and society. However, the World Economic Forum advocates the stakeholder governance concept promoted by stakeholder capitalism and has established the principles to protect all stakeholders' interests, including shareholders, employees, customers, suppliers, governments, and society. The International Business Council (IBC) of the World Economic Forum, in collaboration with the Big-Four accounting firms, has released its final recommendations for a set of globally accepted, standardized, and industry-oriented environmental, social, and governance sustainability performance metrics and disclosures. These recommendations are intended to provide guiding principles for focusing on the ESG sustainability factors of performance, risk, and disclosures on governance, people, planet, and prosperity.

Stakeholder governance principles guide corporate gatekeepers and participants, from the board of directors to executives, investors, legal counsel, financial advisors, and auditors, to discharge their responsibility effectively and fulfill their accountability. Stakeholder governance guiding principles are advancing and intended to provide a basic framework and foundation for effective governance in protecting the interests of all stakeholders, and as such, they apply to all types and sizes of organizations. The primary oversight function of the board of directors under stakeholder governance is to protect multi-stakeholders' interests by appointing competent, accountable, ethical, and responsible executives to manage the business for the benefit of all stakeholders. Regulators worldwide should promulgate proactive, cost-efficient, effective, and scalable rules and regulations to protect the interests of all stakeholders. Internal and external governance mechanisms should be established to achieve the organization's purposes, mission, vision, values, and goals. Internal mechanisms consist of a vigilant board of directors overseeing the organization's purpose, mission, objectives, and strategies, executives' commitments to implement proper strategies to minimize the negative impacts and maximize positive impacts of the organization's activities, operations, and performance. External mechanisms established by policymakers, regulators, and standard setters can play an important role in stakeholder governance, such as establishing applicable laws, regulations, rules, and standards intended to benefit all stakeholders and protect their interests.

The new stakeholder governance paradigm recognizes the importance of short-term and long-term sustainable value creation for all shareholders by viewing governance as coordination and collaboration among all corporate governance participants, from shareholders to boards of directors, executives, and other stakeholders to achieve financial ESP and nonfinancial ESG sustainability performance in creating shared value for all stakeholders. The emerging new stakeholder governance enables global business organizations to realize their responsibility for the safety, health, and well-being of shareholders, employees, customers, and suppliers better. It also redefines its business purpose of achieving financial ESP and nonfinancial ESG sustainability performance. The new stakeholder governance paradigm requires a new coherent set of guiding principles provided by the WEF and driven by a shared value concept, new governance functions redefining the fiduciary duties of directors and executives to all stakeholders, and a new set of internal and external governance mechanisms.

Stakeholder governance defines governance participants' roles and responsibilities, including the board of directors, executives, auditors, and investors, and has been the main focus of business organizations and their stakeholders. The new paradigm for corporate governance recognizes the importance of short-term performance, including business survival and continuity, and long-term performance in creating shared value for all stakeholders. The new paradigm views corporate governance as coordination and collaboration among all corporate governance participants, from shareholders to boards of directors, executives, and other stakeholders, to achieve financial and nonfinancial sustainability performance in creating shared value for all stakeholders. It provides a road map for all corporate governance participants, including shareholders, to be attentive in monitoring their investments, boards of directors in providing effective and engaged oversight, executives in diligently implementing short, medium, and long-term sustainable business strategies, and other corporate gatekeepers (auditors, legal counsel, financial analysts) in protecting interests of all stakeholders.

Comparison of Shareholder Governance and Stakeholder Governance

Corporate governance has traditionally been viewed under the shareholder primacy model as a process of aligning the interests of management with those of shareholders and ensuring compliance with all applicable laws, rules, regulations, standards, and best practices to create shareholder value. Corporate governance under the stakeholder primacy model can be defined as a process of aligning the interests of management with those of stakeholders and making sure management works for the best interests of all stakeholders in creating shared value for them. Corporate governance under both shareholder primacy and stakeholder primacy determines the roles and responsibilities of corporate governance participants, including the board of directors, executives, regulators, auditors, and investors. Corporate governance provides a framework for all corporate governance participants, including shareholders, to be attentive in monitoring their investments, boards of directors in providing effective and engaged oversight, executives in diligently implementing short, medium, and long-term sustainable business strategies, and other corporate gatekeepers (auditors, legal counsel, financial analysts) in protecting interests of all stakeholders. Corporate governance measures are intended to achieve the mission of profit-with-purpose in creating shared value for all stakeholders. Stakeholder governance is a system of governance in decision-making in which the interests of various stakeholders are considered. In the traditional shareholder corporate governance model, the focus is often on maximizing shareholder value.

In contrast, stakeholder governance recognizes that businesses have responsibilities to a broader set of stakeholders, including creditors, employees, customers, suppliers, communities, and the environment, in addition to shareholders. Proper implementation of stakeholder governance consists of various practices, including establishing stakeholder advisory boards, integrating stakeholder perspectives into strategic decision-making processes, and conducting regular stakeholder consultations. Many companies adopt the stakeholder governance framework to improve their reputation, mitigate risks, build stronger relationships with stakeholders, and contribute to their long-term success and sustainability.

The three components of corporate governance structure relevant to both shareholder primacy and stakeholder primacy models are principles, functions, and mechanisms.[11] The corporate governance principles and mechanisms are basically similar under both shareholder and stakeholder primacy models. Corporate governance principles set forth guidelines about the roles and responsibilities of companies, their boards, management, and stakeholders, as well as their actions, behavior, and interactions with others. Corporate governance principles are: (1) honesty in establishing a trusting relationship among all corporate governance participants (directors, management, auditors, financial advisors, legal counsel, employees, customers, and government); (2) resilience in ensuring sustainable and enduring processes that are easily recuperate from setbacks and abuse; (3) responsiveness in establishing timely and appropriate responses to the concerns, requests, or desires of all stakeholders including investors, customers, employees, auditors, suppliers; (4) transparency of ensuring corporate disclosures are fair, accurate, reliable, and understandable by stakeholders; (5) value-adding philosophy of ensuring all corporate governance participants add value to the company's well-being and prosperity; (6) ethical behavior of promoting ethical conduct for all corporate governance participants throughout the company; and (7) independence of determining the extent to which the corporate governance processes minimize or avoid conflicts of interests and self-dealing actions of directors, officers, auditors, legal counsel, financial analysts, investment bankers, and other key personnel.[12] Key governance principles under stakeholder governance are (1) inclusivity of involving all stakeholders with a legitimate stake and interest in the organization; (2) transparency of communicating truthfully and openly all decision-making processes, outcomes, and disclosures regarding both financial ESP and nonfinancial ESG performance to all stakeholders; (3) equity of given fair consideration to all stakeholders, rather than prioritizing one group over another; (4) long-term orientation of emphasizing sustainable practices and long-term shared value creation for all stakeholders; (5) responsiveness of responding to all events and engaging with stakeholders, incorporating their feedback and addressing their concerns; and (6) ethics and values of promoting businesses to operate in alignment with ethical principles and values that benefit all stakeholders.

Corporate governance mechanisms, both internal and external, are designed to prevent, detect, and correct such abuses.[13] Internal mechanisms include a vigilant board of directors, responsible management, effective internal controls, and a robust system of checks and balances with related policies and procedures. External mechanisms are applicable laws, regulations, rules, and standards, the capital markets, the market for corporate control, the labor market, and stakeholder monitoring.

Corporate Governance Functions

Corporate governance reflects corporate culture, accountability, and leadership in response to emerging challenges and moves toward business sustainability. There is an increasing interest in corporate governance because of new initiatives about business sustainability, concerns about insufficient response to emerging challenges, poor corporate culture, the lack of accountability and transparency, and the self-serving behavior of some large corporations. Thus, corporate governance functions need to be identified and examined in determining the roles, responsibilities, and accountability of all corporate governance gatekeepers, from the board of directors to executives, auditors, regulators, legal counsel, financial analysts, and investors under both shareholder and stakeholder primacy models. The commonly used corporate governance functions are oversight, managerial, compliance, internal Audit, legal and financial advisory, external auditing, and monitoring.[14]

Comparison of Shareholder Governance and Stakeholder Governance

The remainder of this section examines the attributes of the seven corporate governance functions under both the shareholder governance and the stakeholder governance models as summarized in Exhibits 4.1–4.7.[15]

Oversight Function

The oversight function of corporate governance is granted to the board of directors elected by shareholders to represent and protect their interests by overseeing managers to ensure they are acting in the best interests of the company and its shareholders. The board of directors is ultimately responsible for business affairs and making strategic decisions. It has a fiduciary duty to initiate and oversee managerial strategies, decisions, and actions to achieve the corporate mission of profit with purpose. The board of directors should provide direction and oversight to management to manage the company's day-to-day operations for the benefit of all stakeholders. The primary oversight function of the board of directors is to (1) appoint the most competent and ethical chief executive officer (CEO) and approve the hiring of other senior executives, including the chief financial officer (CFO); (2) oversee reliable reporting of financial ESG sustainability and nonfinancial ESG sustainability performance; (3) design executive compensation schemes that are linked to sustainable performance; (4) promote the mission of profit-with-purpose, understand the business of the company and actively engage in corporate strategic decisions; (5) oversee business risk assessment and management; (6) oversee the effectiveness of internal controls; and (7) ensure the alignment of management interests with those of shareholders and protect interests of other stakeholders (employees, creditors, customers, suppliers, communities, government, environment, society).

The board should also provide oversight, insight, and foresight function on the achievement of both financial economic sustainability performanceand nonfinancial environmental, social, and governance sustainability performance driven by financial, human, social, manufacturing capital as well as innovation, culture, corporate governance, and ESG initiatives. The board's role under stakeholder primacy, as opposed to the shareholder primacy model, is to oversee the managerial function of focusing on long-term sustainability performance and effectively communicating sustainability performance information to all stakeholders. Under stakeholder governance, the oversight function of the board of directors remains essential in protecting the interests of all stakeholders beyond just shareholders. The board should be informed and understand the stakeholders' objectives and rationales for focusing on sustainability factors of performance, risk and disclosure, managerial, strategic planning, sustainable operational performance, and executive compensation in promoting long-term corporate value. The board should also provide oversight, insight, and foresight function on achieving financial ESP and nonfinancial ESG performance driven by

Exhibit 4.1 Comparison of the Board of Directors under the Shareholder Governance and the Stakeholder Governance

Shareholder Governance	Stakeholder Governance
Oversight of the organization's affairs in creating shareholder value.	Oversight of the organization's affairs in creating shared value for all stakeholders.
Oversee management decisions and actions to improve financial performance.	Oversee management decisions and actions in improving financial ESP and nonfinancial ESG sustainability performance.
Pursue the mission of profit-maximization and shareholder wealth creation.	Pursue the mission of profit with purpose.
Protect the interests of shareholders.	Balance stakeholder interests by ensuring that the interests of all stakeholders are considered in the decision-making process.
Representative of shareholders to protect their interests.	Representative of all stakeholders in protecting shared value
Establish a tone at the top to promote the achievement of long-term performance.	Establish a tone at the top to promote the achievement of short-, medium-, and long-term sustainability performance and business continuity.
Proactive oversight of strategic decisions.	Proactive and reactive oversight of strategic decisions to set the company's strategic direction in a manner that reflects its values, purpose, and long-term sustainability.
Promote Accountability	Promote accountability and transparency.
Generous and large director compensation	Significant cuts in director compensation
Strategy-driven oversight activities	Purpose/mission-driven oversight activities
Shareholder-primacy focus	Stakeholder-primacy focus
Improve investor confidence in financial reports.	Rebuild trust in corporate disclosures through both financial and nonfinancial reports.
Primary focus on the achievement of financial performance	Focus on achievement of financial and nonfinancial ESG performance
Oversee financial risks	Oversee the assessment and management of risks facing the organization, including financial, reputation, strategic, social responsibility, and environmental sustainability.
Establish and oversee business codes of conduct.	Ensure compliance with relevant laws, regulations, and ethical standards by overseeing the development and Implementation of policies and practices that promote ethical behavior and responsible corporate citizenship.
Oversee financial reporting and auditing processes.	Oversee financial and nonfinancial reporting, auditing, and assurance processes.
Oversee shareholders' engagements and involvement in corporate affairs and activities.	Oversee stakeholder engagement initiatives and respond appropriately to their concerns, suggestions, and feedback.

Comparison of Shareholder Governance and Stakeholder Governance

Exhibit 4.2 Comparison of the Managerial Function under the Shareholder Governance and the Stakeholder Governance

Shareholder Governance	Stakeholder Governance
Focus on short-term performance.	Focus on business continuity and sustainable performance.
Achievement of profit-maximization and shareholder wealth creation.	Achievement of profit-with-purpose in creating shared value for all stakeholders.
Executive (CEO and CFO) certification of financial statements and internal controls over financial reporting.	Executive (CEO and CFO) certification of both financial and nonfinancial reports and internal controls over financial reporting.
Financial risk assessment and management.	Financial and nonfinancial risk assessment and management.
Meetings with shareholders.	Meeting with stakeholders, including shareholders.
Shareholder engagement.	Stakeholder engagement.
Financial goals oriented.	Financial and nonfinancial goals-oriented.
Lean management and Budgeted performance.	Continuous improvement performance.
Business growth model.	Business recovery, continuity, and transformation.
Innovation to improve operational effectiveness and efficiency.	Innovation and adaptation to meet the evolving needs and expectations of stakeholders, including developing new products or services that address social or environmental challenges and financial and operational goals.
Financial Capital Focus.	Financial, human, social, and environmental capita focus.
Accountability and evaluation of achieving financial performance.	Accountability and evaluation of achieving stakeholder-related objectives and for the overall financial ESP and nonfinancial ESG sustainability performance of the organization in delivering shared value to stakeholders.
Transparent communication with shareholders to provide accurate and reliable financial information.	Transparent communication with stakeholders to provide timely and accurate ESP and ESG information about organizational performance, policies, and decisions.

financial, human, social, and manufacturing capitals, as well as innovation, culture, corporate governance, and ESG initiatives. The financial and nonfinancial key performance indicators should be identified, measured, and disclosed through metrics reflecting the corporate value, long-term investment, and innovation on ESG initiatives.

Fxhihit 4.1 contrasts the oversight function under shareholder and stakeholder governance models. The prominent differences in the oversight function between shareholder governance and stakeholder governance models are: (1) the board of directors represents the

Exhibit 4.3 Comparison of the Compliance Function under the Shareholder Governance and the Stakeholder Governance

Shareholder Governance	Stakeholder Governance
Rebuild public trust and shareholder confidence in public financial information and capital markets.	Rebuild public trust and stakeholder confidence in public financial information, ESG information, and capital markets.
Shareholder-centric compliance policies and procedures.	Stakeholder-focused compliance policies and procedures.
Regulations promoting the shareholder primacy concept.	Regulations promoting the stakeholder primacy concept.
Financial regulations, policies, and procedures.	Financial and nonfinancial regulations pertaining to financial, social, environmental, and human capital.
Regulation and standards for fair presentation of financial reports.	Regulations pertaining to continuing orderly and fair function of the securities markets relevant to corporate disclosures, including financial and nonfinancial reports.
Fair and full corporate disclosures relevant to financial activities and performance.	Corporate disclosure with full transparency and broad, timely, and accurate disclosures of both financial and nonfinancial performance.
Compliance with financial risk assessment and management.	Compliance with financial risk assessment and management.
Shareholder engagement in compliance processes.	Stakeholder engagement in compliance processes.
Monitor and report compliance with all applicable financial laws, rules, regulations, standards, and best practices.	Monitor and report compliance with all applicable financial, social, environmental, and governance laws, rules, regulations, standards, and best practices.

Comparison of Shareholder Governance and Stakeholder Governance

interests of all stakeholders including shareholders; (2) directors should have understanding, knowledge and expertise to bring different perspectives to the board, including representatives from employees, communities, and environmental or social advocacy organizations; (3) the board of directors' fiduciary duties under the stakeholder governance are extended to all stakeholders; (4) the board of directors pursues the goal of creating shared value for all stakeholders rather than the mission of shareholder wealth-maximization; (5) the board of directors is actively engaged with stakeholders to understand their interests, concerns, perspectives, and expectations by having regular meetings, surveys, focus groups, and enabling stakeholder representatives attend board meetings; (6) the board of directors focuses on the long-term sustainability of the organization by overseeing both financial economic sustainability performance (ESP) and nonfinancial environmental, social, governance (ESG) performance and reporting; and (7) the board of directs oversees the identification, assessment, and management of sustainability risks presented in Chapter 9 including

Exhibit 4.4 Comparison of the Internal Audit Function under the Shareholder Governance and the Stakeholder Governance

Shareholder Governance	Stakeholder Governance
Focus on internal financial audits.	Focus on financial and nonfinancial audits.
Risk and compliance audits.	Risk, compliance, sustainability, and accountability audits.
Shareholder-oriented risk assessment and management.	Stakeholder-focused risk assessment and management.
Consulting services for management.	Consulting services for all corporate gatekeepers.
Assurance services on financial and internal controls.	Assurance services on financial and nonfinancial information and internal controls.
Compliance reports relevant to applicable regulations, policies, and procedures.	Compliance reports on upcoming regulatory changes relevant to ESG sustainability.
Training sessions for staff in educating them with new technology, regulations.	Training sessions for staff in educating them with new ESG-related technology, regulations.
Using Big Data and data analytics.	Using data science and automating assurance
Minimum internal audit outsourcing.	More internal audit outsourcing.
Functional risk assessment and audit programs.	Enterprise risk assessment and audit programs and risk appetite.
Financial audit planning.	Integrated and comprehensive audit planning of ESP and ESG sustainability.
Monitoring and follow-up on operational, financial, and compliance processes.	Monitoring and follow-up on sustainability processes.
Continuous improvement of ESP operation.	Continuous improvement of ESP and ESG operation.

the potential reputational, regulatory, operational, social, environmental risks associated with different stakeholder issues to ensure appropriate measures are taken to mitigate these risks. The primary oversight function of the board of directors remains to protect the interests of all stakeholders by appointing competent, responsible, accountable, and ethical executives to manage the company for the benefit of all stakeholders.

In the stakeholder governance model, the board of directors is expected to engage more proactively in the oversight function, setting strategic priorities for addressing emerging sustainability initiatives and dealing with global economic and political uncertainties and challenges. The fiduciary duties of the board of directors are expected to be extended to all stakeholders, including shareholders, creditors, communities, customers, suppliers, employees, government, society, and the environment with the move toward a

Exhibit 4.5 Comparison of the Legal and Advisory Function under the Shareholder Governance and the Stakeholder Governance

Shareholder Governance	Stakeholder Governance
Present and analyze relevant financial information	Present and analyze emerging legal and financial challenges.
Compliance monitoring to ensure adherence to relevant financial and legal laws, regulations, and industry standards.	Compliance monitoring to ensure adherence to relevant financial, nonfinancial, and legal laws, regulations, and industry standards.
Manual and electronic legal and financial evidence.	Electronic legal and financial evidence.
Risk assessment and management of risk relevant to legal and financial requirements.	Risk assessment and management of risk relevant to legal financial and nonfinancial requirements.
Assisted in the development and Implementation of shareholder governance policies and procedures, including board structure, director responsibilities, and ethical standards.	Assisted in the development and Implementation of stakeholder governance policies and procedures, including board structure, director responsibilities, and ethical standards.
Shareholder relations include communicating shareholder strategies and shareholder rights and resolving conflicts of interest.	Stakeholder relations include communicating stakeholder strategies and stakeholder rights and resolving conflicts of interest.
Financial planning and analysis by assisting in the development of financial plans, budgets, and forecasts to support strategic decision-making and resource allocation.	Financial and ESG planning and analysis by assisting in the development of financial and ESG plans, budgets, and forecasts to support strategic decision-making and resource allocation.
Risk assessment and management of financial risks, including market volatility, liquidity constraints, and credit exposure, as well as recommending appropriate risk management strategies.	Risk assessment and management of financial and nonfinancial risks, including market volatility, liquidity constraints, reputational risk, climate change challenges, and credit exposure, and recommending appropriate risk management strategies.
Investment management of advising on investment opportunities, asset allocation, and portfolio diversification to optimize returns while managing risks.	Investment management includes advising on investment opportunities, asset allocation, and portfolio diversification to optimize returns while managing risks and focusing on social and environmental impacts.
Assist with financial reporting and ensuring compliance with accounting and financial standards and best practices.	Assist with financial and ESG sustainability reporting to ensure compliance with accounting and financial standards and best practices and integration of ESG information to corporate disclosure systems.

Comparison of Shareholder Governance and Stakeholder Governance

Exhibit 4.6 Comparison of the External Audit Function under the Shareholder Governance and the Stakeholder Governance

Shareholder Governance	Stakeholder Governance
Focus on financial statement audits.	Focus on financial and nonfinancial audits.
Risk-based audit approach.	Risk and compliance-based audit approach.
Financial and internal control audits.	Financial and internal control audits and assurance services on nonfinancial ESG information.
Emphasis on Matters relevant to financial reports.	Critical Audit Matters relevant to financial and nonfinancial issues.
Less are concern issues.	More going concern issues.
Audit planning and execution, including developing an audit plan that outlines the scope, objectives, and methodologies for the audit engagement, identifying and evaluating key risks, performing audit procedures, including testing of financial transactions, reviewing documentation, and interviewing key personnel to gather evidence.	Audit planning and execution on both financial statements and ESG sustainability reports, including developing an audit plan that outlines the scope, objectives, and methodologies for the audit engagement, identifying and evaluating key risks, performing audit procedures, and ingathering sufficient and competent audit evidence.
Reporting and communication of audit opinion on financial statements, internal control over financial reporting ICFR).	Reporting and communication of audit opinion on financial statements, internal control over financial reporting (ICFR), and assurance statement on ESG sustainability reports.
Shareholder engagement of involving shareholders in the understanding of financial and audit processes.	Stakeholder engagement of engaging with various stakeholders, including shareholders,employees, regulators, creditors, and other interested parties, to address inquiries, provide clarification, enhance transparency, and foster trust and confidence in the organization's financial reporting, ESG reporting, and governance processes.

profit-with-purpose mission. The expanded fiduciary duty to all stakeholders requires the board of directors to establish proactive strategic profit-with-purpose missions, goals, and objectives to ensure business continuity and sustainability in creating long-term shared value and oversee managerial decisions and actions in effectively implementing these strategic goals. The board oversight responsibility is extended in overseeing managerial decisions and actions, the assessment and management of sustainability risks presented in Chapter 9, overseeing management stewardship of all resources and capitals described in Chapter 10 and overseeing the accuracy, completeness, and transparency of disclosures of both financial ESP and nonfinancial ESG sustainability performance. The board oversight function is more inclusive, forward-thinking, and focused on creating sustainable shared value for all stakeholders in contributing to the long-term success and resilience of the

Exhibit 4.7 Comparison of the Monitoring Function under the Shareholder Governance and the Stakeholder Governance

Shareholder Governance	Stakeholder Governance
Shareholder-centric.	Stakeholder-centric.
Shareholder primacy.	Stakeholder primacy.
Shareholder monitoring.	Stakeholder monitoring.
Shareholder accountability.	Stakeholder accountability and transparency.
Shareholder democracy.	Stakeholder democracy.
Shareholder engagement is establishing relationships with shareholders in gathering feedback, addressing concerns, and promoting transparency and accountability.	Stakeholder engagement is establishing relationships with stakeholders in gathering feedback, addressing concerns, and promoting transparency and accountability.
Investor activists.	Institutional investor activists
Shareholder communication is about providing timely and accurate information to shareholders regarding the organization's performance, strategic direction, and governance practice.	Stakeholder communication of providing timely and accurate information to stakeholders regarding the organization's performance, strategic direction, and governance practice.
The monitoring system ensures that the organization operates in the best interests of its shareholders, maintains effective controls and processes, and upholds high standards of accountability and transparency.	The monitoring system ensures that the organization operates in the best interests of its stakeholders, maintains effective controls and processes, and upholds high standards of accountability and transparency.

organization and holding management accountable for implementing decisions that align with stakeholder interests and organization goals and objectives.

Managerial Function

The managerial function of corporate governance is assumed by the management team appointed by the board of directors and led by the CEO and other executives. The effective achievement of the managerial function is measured by the alignment of the interests of management with those of stakeholders, including shareholders. Management's primary responsibilities are to pursue the mission of profit-with-purpose, achieve operational efficiency and effectiveness, foster both financial ESP and nonfinancial ESG performance, comply with all applicable laws, rules, regulations, and standards, properly assess risk, and provide fair and true disclosure of financial and nonfinancial information. Exhibit 4.2 contracts the managerial function under shareholder governance and stakeholder governance with following attributes of managerial function under stakeholder governance: (1) management is more actively engaged with stakeholders to understand their needs, concerns,

Comparison of Shareholder Governance and Stakeholder Governance

and expectations by establishing channels for communication including regular meetings, surveys, focus groups, and online platforms, to get feedbacks and consider them in decision-making processes; (2) management focuses on the longer-term strategic performance by adopting an integrated approach to decision-making that considers the interests of all stakeholders including shareholders and seeking consensus-based solutions that maximize overall benefit and create shared value for all stakeholders; (3) management adopts the mission of achievement of profit-with-purpose in creating shared value for all stakeholders; (4) management prioritizes sustainability and responsible business practices in is activities and operations integrating ESG considerations into business strategies including reducing carbon emissions, ensuring ethical supply chain practices, promoting diversity and inclusion, and. preparing accurate and complete financial statements and reports on ESG; (5) management assumes the responsibility for identifying, assessing, and managing sustainability risks including understanding the potential impacts of stakeholder issues and concerns on the organization's strategic decisions, reputation, brand, operations, and implementing risk mitigation measures to address these risks; (6) management's transparent communication with all stakeholders in providing timely and accurate information about organization's financial ESP and nonfinancial ESG performance, policies, and decisions to foster trust and credibility with stakeholders and to build stronger relationships with them based on mutual respect and understanding; (7) managerial accountability and performance evaluation of assuming accountability for achieving stakeholder-related objectives including achieving financial performance, stakeholder satisfaction, social impact and environmental impacts, and compliance with corporate governance principles and ethical standards; and (8) management commitments in promoting innovation and adaptation to meet needs and expectations of stakeholders including developing new products or services that address new technologies to improve efficiency and sustainability of operations, social or environmental challenges and promote best practices in corporate governance and stakeholder engagement.

The recent move toward business sustainability has brought unique opportunities and risks to business operations, practices, and performance that need to be considered by the board of directors and assessed by management. Those in the C-suite, including the CEO, Chief Operating Officer, Chief Compliance Office, Chief Human Resources Officer, Chief Legal Office or General Counsel, and Chief Financial Officer, should coordinate efforts and activities to address challenges, opportunities, and risks affecting employees, customers, and the entire organization. To effectively address these emerging and growing business challenges, opportunities, and risks, the board of directors may form a new executive position of "Chief Sustainability Officer" to be responsible for managing the three sustainability factors of performance, risk, and disclosure.

Finally, the CFO should collaborate with the CEO in preparing and certifying the integrated sustainability reports and disclosing the achievement of the adopted "Statement of Purpose." This integrated sustainability report can disclose the achievement of both financial returns and social and environmental impacts. This integrated report enables shareholders and other stakeholders to learn and assess the company's success in achieving its adopted purpose. This assessment can positively impact investor risk-premium and their willingness to invest in the company's stock. This is the only path toward stakeholder capitalism rather than societal socialism to achieve long-term, durable, and sustainable growth and performance. The challenge is not whether a "Statement of Purpose" is desirable and achievable; rather, the hurdle is whether high-profile corporate executives collaborate to make it happen, including CEOs, CFOs, and institutional investors. Under stakeholder governance, the managerial function plays an essential role in driving organizational sustainability and long-term success by promoting sustainability and responsible business practices, fostering inclusive decision-making, creating shared value for stakeholders, and building strong relationships with all stakeholders based on trust, mutual value creation, transparency, and accountability.

Compliance Function

The compliance function reflects the mandatory regulatory and compliance framework for business organizations to effectively operate within the regulatory framework in achieving financial ESP and nonfinancial ESG sustainability performance to create a shared value for all stakeholders. This regulatory framework comprises laws, rules, regulations, standards, and best practices. Under the stakeholder governance model, policymakers, regulators, and standard-setters should be reactive and proactive in establishing and enforcing cost-effective, efficient, proactive, and scalable rules and regulations to address many emerging opportunities and risks associated with the move toward business sustainability. Regulations should establish a framework within which business organizations can achieve sustainable ESP and ESG performance while following rules. Under stakeholder governance, the compliance function plays an essential role in ensuring that the organization operates in accordance with all applicable and relevant laws, rules, regulations, and standards while addressing the expectations and concerns of various stakeholders and complying with both financial regulations and social and environmental initiatives. With the integration of stakeholder governance and perspectives into compliance efforts and regulatory frameworks, organizations can improve their overall governance structure, build trust with stakeholders, foster a culture of compliance and responsible business conduct that contributes to long-term sustainability and success, and effectively mitigate compliance-related risks.

Comparison of Shareholder Governance and Stakeholder Governance

Exhibit 4.3 compares the compliance function under shareholder and stakeholder govern-ance models. The primary differences in the compliance function between the shareholder governance and stakeholder governance are: (1) establishment of regulations promoting the stakeholder primacy model; (2) development of compliance policies and procedures with consideration for the interests and concerns of all stakeholders including sharehold-ers by identifying key stakeholder expectations relevant to compliance and integrating them into the organization's compliance framework; (3) promotion of holistic compliance risk assessment and management of all sustainability risks presented in Chapter 9 includ-ing financial, operational, reputational, environmental among others that address not only legal and regulatory risks but also risks relevant to stakeholder relations; (4) engagement of stakeholders in compliance processes of gathering insight, input and feedback on com-pliance-related matters; (5) monitoring and reporting compliance activities to ensure ongo-ing compliance with all applicable laws, regulations, standards, and internal policies by conducting audits and reviews, and reporting compliance-related measures to stakehold-ers; (6) enacting nonfinancial regulations pertaining to social, environmental, and human capitals; and (7) enhancing corporate disclosure with full transparency and timely and accurate disclosures of both financial ESP information and nonfinancial ESG performance information.

Internal Audit Function

The internal audit function of corporate governance is assumed by internal auditors who provide both assurance and consulting services to the company in achieving its mission of profit-with-purpose. The roles and responsibilities of internal auditors have expanded to corporate governance, internal control evaluation, and risk assessment in assisting the organization and its members to achieve its goals. Internal auditors perform assurance and consulting services for business organizations in operational efficiency, governance processes, risk management, internal controls, and financial reporting. Assurance reports provided by internal auditors are typically intended for internal use by management and can be extended to assuring financial ESP and nonfinancial ESG sustainability performance reports. Internal auditors are in a unique position to work with the board of directors and management in assessing ESG challenges associated with sustainability risks and oppor-tunities, design appropriate policies and processes to address these challenges, educate employees about these policies and procedures, and ensure compliance with relevant new normal, standards, policies, and procedures.

In 2020, the Committee of Sponsoring Organizations of the Treadway Commission (COSO) issued its new guidance on risk appetite to assess how it can be used in the decision-making processes.[16] The COSO guidance can assist internal auditors in working with management to design and implement strategies and objectives to cope with the challenges of maintaining sustainable performance and business continuity. Understanding and developing appropriate risk appetite is integral to effective corporate governance, strategic planning, and decision-making. Thus, internal auditors should work with management under the oversight of the board of directors to integrate risk appetite into business strategic plans and culture.

Under stakeholder governance, the internal audit function plays an essential role in pursuing the organization's mission of profit-with-purpose, achievement of both financial ESP and nonfinancial ESG sustainability performance, operational effectiveness, safeguarding all sustainability capitals presented in the Chapter 10 and transparency, accountability, and effective risk management as described in Chapters 9 and 11. Exhibit 4.4 compares the internal audit function under both the shareholder governance and stakeholder governance models. The primary differences in the internal function between the shareholder governance and stakeholder governance are: (1) internal auditors assurance services on both financial and nonfinancial performance activities; (2) training sessions for staff in educating them with new ESG-related technology, regulations; (3) performance of risk assessments relevant to all stakeholders by considering their interests and concerns by identifying their expectations related to risk management and incorporating them into the risk assessment processes; (4) engaging stakeholders in the internal audit processes by gathering input and feedback on audit plans, scope, and findings and ensuring that audit reports are transparent, comprehensive, accessible and understandable to all stakeholders; (5) monitoring the implementation of audit recommendations and follows up on any outstanding issues to ensure that remediations and corrective actions are taken in a timely manner; (6) ensuring continuous improvement in performance to improve audit processes and procedures in response to changing stakeholder expectations and emerging risks by using emerging audit methodologies, technology, and regulatory requirements; and (7) assurance services on risk management and governance that benefit all stakeholders.

Legal and Financial Advisory Function

Legal and financial advisors perform legal and financial advisory functions for business organizations by assisting organizations in evaluating business operations' legal and financial consequences. Legal counsel provides legal advice and assists the organization in complying with applicable laws, regulations, rules, and other legal requirements. Legal counsel plays a more important role under the stakeholder governance model by ensuring compliance with emerging regulations relevant to social and environmental initiatives. Financial advisors can assist their companies in developing an appropriate Statement of Purpose under the sustainability initiatives that address the safety, health, and well-being

Comparison of Shareholder Governance and Stakeholder Governance

of all stakeholders, including investors, employees, customers, suppliers, and communities. The Statement of Purpose can focus on ESG factors of performance, risk, and disclosure for investors and their integration into investment decisions that enhance financial returns and mitigate risk. Gender diversity and investment in human capital and employees' safety and health are becoming more important to investors and their advisors.

Corporate legal counsel should evaluate regulatory risks associated with corporate communications with all stakeholders during times of corporate crisis, particularly those disclosures relevant to the health, safety, and well-being of employees, suppliers, and customers. The corporate legal counsel is uniquely positioned to inform and advise the company's board of directors and its board committees, especially the compliance committee and executives, regarding the potential compliance and regulatory risks. The company's general counsel should review the board of directors' fiduciary duty standards to ensure they comply with the new "Statement of Purpose" and the profit-with-purpose mission debated in recent years.

Legal and financial advisory functions under a stakeholder government system play an essential role in ensuring compliance with applicable financial and nonfinancial laws, regulations, and standards, as well as transparency and sound financial and nonfinancial practices. The legal advisory function guides on legal matters relevant to corporate governance, regulatory compliance, and contractual obligations, whereas the financial advisory function offers expertise in strategic planning, financial management, and reporting. Exhibit 4.5 compares legal and financial advisory functions under both shareholder governance and stakeholder governance. The key differences in the legal and advisory function between shareholder governance and stakeholder governance are in the types and methods of promoting and performing legal and advisory functions including: (1) ensuring that the organization adheres to applicable and relevant financial and nonfinancial laws, rules, regulations, and industry standards; (2) identifying and assessing legal risks and implementing strategies to manage and mitigate them by drafting and reviewing contracts, advising on dispute resolution, and assessing liability exposure: (3) advising on legal aspects of stakeholder engagement through communication of strategies, shareholder rights, and resolving conflicts of interest; (4) assisting in the development of financial plans, budgets, and forecasts to support strategic plans and decision-making and resource allocation; (5) advising on investment opportunities, asset allocation, and portfolio diversification to optimize returns while managing risks; and (6) providing guidance and advice on the integration of ESG factors into financial reporting and disclosure practices. Overall, under stakeholder governance, the legal and financial advisory function serves as a liaison between the organization's board of directors, management, and external stakeholders by offering expert legal and financial advice and ensuring compliance with all applicable legal and financial requirements to build trust, foster reputation, enhance accountability, and safeguard the interests of all stakeholders.

External Audit Function

External auditors play an important role in stakeholder governance by lending more credibility to financial reports and ESG sustainability reports. The responsibility of external auditors is to audit financial statements and lend more credibility to the published financial statements of public companies, as well as to audit internal control over financial reporting. Auditors provide professional opinions on presenting the company's financial statements in conformity with generally accepted accounting principles (GAAP) and the effectiveness of internal control over financial reporting (ICFR). In recent years, external auditors have provided assurance statements on ESG sustainability reports to lend more credibility to sustainability reports. External auditors are appointed by the audit committee of the board of directors independently from the organization's management to ensure that auditors can perform their audits objectively, without bias or influence from internal stakeholders. Thus, independent auditors play a vital role in promoting objectivity and accountability, fostering corporate governance, and protecting the interests of stakeholders by providing independent Audits on the reliability and integrity of an organization's financial information and assurance of ESG sustainability reports.

Exhibit 4.6 compares the external audit function under both shareholder governance and stakeholder governance. The main differences in the external audit function between the shareholder governance and stakeholder governance are: (1) performance of financial statement audits and assurance services on nonfinancial ESG disclosures; (2) conducting a comprehensive audit of the organization's financial statements, internal controls, nonfinancial ESG reports and compliance with relevant laws and regulations'; (3) issuing an audit report on financial statements and assurance statement on ESG sustainability reports that communicates their findings, conclusions, and recommendations to the organization's stakeholders; (4) the disclosure of critical Audit matters relevant to both financial and nonfinancial issues; (5) more focus on going concern issues.; and (6) engaging with various stakeholders, including shareholders, regulators, creditors, and other interested parties, to address inquiries, provide clarification, and enhance transparency to foster trust and confidence in the organization's financial reporting, ESG reports and governance processes. The emerging move toward business sustainability can create more opportunities for external auditors to assist their clients in addressing the challenges associated with financial statements and nonfinancial ESG sustainability reports. Audit reports on financial statements and assurance statements on ESG sustainability reports are the most important channels

Comparison of Shareholder Governance and Stakeholder Governance

of communication between auditors and stakeholders and auditors in lending credibility and objectivity to corporate reports. Audits improve financial reporting credibility and reduce information asymmetry between management and shareholders, thus improving investors' confidence in audited financial statements. Assurance statements on ESG can also increase investors' perceived ESG disclosure quality.

Monitoring Function

The monitoring function of corporate governance is the responsibility of stakeholders, including shareholders. Shareholders should monitor their investments, and stakeholders should protect their interests by directly engaging shareholders in looking after their investments. Shareholders play an important role in monitoring public companies to ensure their rights and interests are protected. Corporate sustainability has become an economic and strategic imperative with the potential to create shared value for all stakeholders. Investors should be attentive and proactive in protecting their investments through the monitoring function. Corporate purpose and stakeholder considerations have gained recognition in the business community as stakeholder primacy challenges companies to put stakeholders at the heart of a company's purpose. In stakeholder governance, the monitoring function by stakeholders plays an essential role in overseeing the organization's strategic plans, decisions, and activities to ensure alignment with stakeholder interests and promote accountability and transparency and the organization's mission of profit-with-purpose. Exhibit 4.7 compares the monitoring function under both shareholder governance and stakeholder governance. The primary differences in the monitoring function between shareholder governance and stakeholder governance are: (1) engaging with stakeholders to gather feedback, address needs, and concerns, and promote transparency and accountability by providing timely and accurate information to shareholders regarding the organization's performance, strategic direction, and governance practices; (2) promoting customer relationships of soliciting feedback from customers, clients, and other stakeholders to assess satisfaction levels, identify areas for improvement, and enhance service delivery; (3) fostering community involvements of building and maintaining positive relationships with local communities, advocacy groups, and other external stakeholders to address social and environmental concerns; and (4) engaging in the areas of more focus on stakeholder primacy, monitoring, and accountability. The monitoring function in stakeholder governance serves as an important mechanism for ensuring that the organization operates in the best interests of its stakeholders, maintains effective governance, controls, and processes, and upholds high standards of accountability and transparency.

Summary

Public companies have significantly grown, and their purpose has evolved in the past several decades from profit-maximization to creating shared value for all stakeholders. The mission of profit-with-purpose for business organizations demands a focus on sustainability strategies that have become integral components of the business environment and corporate culture. This emerging trend of moving away from shareholder primacy toward stakeholder primacy and index funding has led to a debate on the implications of common ownership and the main mission of business organizations. Under the stakeholder primacy model, there is spread ownership, and the main mission is to create shared value for all stakeholders. Policymakers, regulators, and society have questioned the fiduciary model of shareholder primacy and advocates moving toward stakeholder primacy. The shareholder primacy model has served investors well in creating value and maximizing their wealth. However, it is criticized for focusing on serving only one group of stakeholders and generating short-term profits at the expense of long-term sustainability, performance innovation, and growth. This model often ignores the social and environmental impacts of corporations. The focus on shareholder wealth creation may not benefit other stakeholders, such as employees, customers, creditors, suppliers, government, society, and the environment. Business organizations are given rights to operate and generate profits for their shareholders, but with these rights come public interests and societal responsibilities of having social and environmental impacts.

The shareholder aspect of corporate governance implies that shareholders, by virtue of their ownership investment in the company, are entitled to direct and monitor the company's business and affairs. Shareholders influence corporate governance by exercising their right to elect directors, who appoint management to run the company. Directors and officers, as agents of the company, act as trustees on behalf of shareholders, and their primary responsibilities and fiduciary duties are to shareholders. While directors' and officers' legal fiduciary duties are only extended to shareholders who invested in the company, they may have many nonfiduciary duties to other stakeholders, who may have various interests and claims to the company's assets and welfare. Shareholders' rights, including the right to elect, the right to put propositions before the annual shareholder meetings, and the right to reliable and accurate financial information, are legally enforceable, and offending directors and officers can be brought to justice through the courts. Corporate purpose is now changing as there is more support for stakeholder governance and stakeholder primacy model in creating shared value for all stakeholders and maximizing stakeholder welfare rather than just creating shareholder value and maximizing shareholder wealth.

Summary

There has been a move toward the stakeholder capitalism and primacy model to ensure the long-term sustainability of business corporations in generating desired financial returns for their shareholders while protecting the interests of all stakeholders. Stakeholders such as employees, creditors, customers, suppliers, social responsibility activists, and communities, who are affected by and can affect the company's success, do not have the right to engage with the company regarding its mission, purpose, strategic plans, performance, and accomplishments. Nonetheless, stakeholders' interests are protected under the contract and tort laws and the stakeholder capitalism and primacy model. Stakeholder capitalism and stakeholder governance are intended to benefit all stakeholders. The stakeholder governance paradigm, including guiding principles, functions, and measures, should assist governance participants from the board of directors to management, accountants, auditors, legal counsel, and stakeholders to address and act in protecting the interests of all stakeholders. Stakeholder governance is driven by the primacy concept, which focuses on creating and protecting shared value for all stakeholders. Business organizations worldwide should modify corporate governance to protect all stakeholders' interests. Business organizations should understand the move towards stakeholder governance with a focus on sustainability factors of performance, risk, and disclosure and integration of these factors into corporate culture and business environment, as well as managerial policies, decisions, and processes to protect the interests of their stakeholders.

Key Points

- Promote a profit-with-purpose mission to create shared value for all stakeholders.
- Consider moving away from the shareholder primacy model and moving toward the stakeholder primacy model.
- Achieve impact investing to generate desired financial returns for shareholders while achieving social and environmental impacts.
- Establish measures of both financial ESP performance and nonfinancial ESG sustainability performance.
- Communicate the achievement of both financial ESP performance and nonfinancial ESG sustainability performance to all stakeholders.

Review Questions

1. **What does the shareholder primacy model assert as the primary purpose of a business entity?**
2. **How does the stakeholder primacy model define the purpose of a business organization?**

3. **What role does the World Economic Forum advocate for companies?**

4. **What was the significance of the Business Roundtable's 2019 Statement on the Purpose of a Corporation?**

5. **What is the primary role of the board of directors under the stakeholder primacy model?**

6. **What is the role of management under the stakeholder governance model?**

7. **How does the compliance function differ between shareholder and stakeholder governance models?**

8. **What is the significance of external audit in stakeholder governance?**

9. **What are the primary goals of corporate governance under the stakeholder primacy model?**

10. **How does the stakeholder governance model redefine the fiduciary duties of directors and executives?**

11. **How can stakeholder engagement improve corporate governance?**

12. **How does the stakeholder primacy model view the company's purpose?**

13. **How should companies measure their performance under the stakeholder primacy model?**

14. **What are the key components of effective corporate governance under both shareholder and stakeholder primacy models?**

15. **What is the importance of the internal audit function under the stakeholder governance model?**

Discussion Questions

16. **What does the shareholder primacy model assert as the primary purpose of a business entity?**

17. **How does the stakeholder primacy model define the purpose of a business organization?**

18. **What role does the World Economic Forum advocate for companies?**

19. **What was the significance of the Business Roundtable's 2019 Statement on the Purpose of a Corporation?**

20. **What is the primary role of the board of directors under the stakeholder primacy model?**

21. **What is the role of management under the stakeholder governance model?**

22. **How does the compliance function differ between shareholder and stakeholder governance models?**

23. **What is the significance of external audit in stakeholder governance?**

24. **What are the primary goals of corporate governance under the stakeholder primacy model?**

25. **How does the stakeholder governance model redefine the fiduciary duties of directors and executives?**

26. **How can stakeholder engagement improve corporate governance?**

27. **How does the stakeholder primacy model view the company's purpose?**

28. **How should companies measure their performance under the stakeholder primacy model?**

29. **What are the key components of effective corporate governance under both shareholder and stakeholder primacy models?**

30. **What is the importance of the internal audit function under the stakeholder governance model?**

Multiple-Choice Questions

1. **What does the stakeholder primacy model emphasize?**
   A) Short-term profit-maximization
   B) Creating value solely for shareholders
   C) Creating shared value for all stakeholders
   D) Minimizing corporate transparency

2. **What organization supports the transition from shareholder capitalism to stakeholder capitalism?**
   A) World Trade Organization
   B) United Nations
   C) World Economic Forum
   D) International Monetary Fund

3. **What are the key responsibilities of the board of directors under the shareholder primacy model?**
   A) Protecting the interests of all stakeholders
   B) Focusing on short-term profits
   C) Overseeing management to maximize shareholder value
   D) Promoting environmental sustainability

4. **What are the two main components of the profit-with-purpose mission?**
   A) Financial returns and customer satisfaction
   B) Financial ESP and nonfinancial ESG sustainability performance
   C) Product innovation and market expansion
   D) Cost reduction and profit-maximization

5. **What is the role of corporate social responsibility (CSR) under the share-holder primacy model?**
   A) It is a primary goal
   B) It is considered secondary to creating shareholder value
   C) It is the main focus of corporate activities
   D) It is integrated into all strategic decisions

6. **What is one key attribute of effective shareholder governance?**
   A) Reducing transparency
   B) Limiting stakeholder engagement
   C) Voting rights for shareholders
   D) Minimizing regulatory compliance

7. **What is the role of corporate governance under the stakeholder primacy model?**
   A) Focusing solely on financial performance
   B) Protecting the interests of all stakeholders and ensuring sustainable value creation
   C) Reducing transparency in sustainability reporting
   D) Limiting stakeholder engagement

8. **What are the primary components of a sustainability strategy?**
   A) Reducing operational costs and increasing shareholder wealth
   B) Establishing sustainability goals, integrating them into the business strategy, implementing action plans, and continuously monitoring and improving performance
   C) Focusing solely on financial performance
   D) Limiting stakeholder engagement and reducing transparency

9. **How can companies balance financial performance with social and environmental responsibilities?**
   A) By focusing solely on short-term financial goals
   B) By developing and implementing strategies that integrate financial ESP with nonfinancial ESG sustainability performance, ensuring long-term success and shared value creation
   C) By reducing transparency in sustainability reporting
   D) By limiting stakeholder engagement and reducing costs

10. **Why is it important for companies to have a well-defined purpose?**
    A) Reducing transparency and limiting stakeholder engagement
    B) A well-defined purpose helps guide business strategies, aligns with stakeholder expectations, and promotes long-term sustainability

C) Focusing solely on financial performance

D) Minimizing regulatory compliance and reducing costs

11. **What is the main objective of the profit-with-purpose mission in business organizations?**

A) To maximize short-term profits

B) To integrate financial success with a commitment to social and environmental impacts

C) To reduce operational costs

D) To limit stakeholder engagement

12. **What is the role of sustainability reporting in achieving business sustainability?**

A) It reduces regulatory compliance costs

B) It provides a platform for the accountability and transparency of sustainability performance

C) It limits stakeholder engagement

D) It focuses solely on financial performance

13. **What is the significance of the stakeholder theory in business sustainability?**

A) It focuses solely on financial performance

B) It protects the interests of all stakeholders and focuses on achieving long-term and enduring financial and nonfinancial performance

C) It reduces regulatory compliance costs

D) It limits stakeholder engagement

14. **What is the impact of effective corporate governance on business sustainability?**

A) It reduces transparency and limits stakeholder engagement

B) It promotes accountability, enhances operational and financial performance, and strengthens stakeholder trust

C) It focuses solely on short-term profits

D) It limits regulatory compliance

15. **Why is it important for companies to disclose sustainability performance?**

A) To demonstrate commitment to transparency and enhance firm value by reducing information asymmetry

B) To limit stakeholder engagement and reduce regulatory compliance costs

C) To focus solely on financial performance

D) To minimize the impact of sustainability initiatives

16. **What are the main objectives of the EU Corporate Sustainability Reporting Directive (CSRD)?**
    A) To reduce transparency and limit stakeholder engagement
    B) To increase transparency in sustainability reporting, enhance sustainability performance, and contribute to long-term economic growth
    C) To focus solely on financial performance and short-term profits
    D) To minimize regulatory compliance and reduce costs

17. **How are sustainability performance and risk management related?**
    A) Sustainability performance focuses solely on financial performance
    B) Effective sustainability performance requires identifying, assessing, and managing sustainability risks to minimize negative impacts and capitalize on opportunities
    C) Sustainability performance reduces transparency and limits stakeholder engagement
    D) Risk management focuses solely on short-term profits

18. **Why is stakeholder engagement crucial in sustainability planning?**
    A) It limits transparency and reduces regulatory compliance
    B) It helps in understanding stakeholder preferences and expectations, which informs the development of effective sustainability strategies
    C) It focuses solely on financial performance
    D) It minimizes the impact of sustainability initiatives

19. **What is the role of voluntary sustainability disclosure?**
    A) It focuses solely on financial performance
    B) It demonstrates a company's commitment to transparency and can differentiate it from less sustainable firms
    C) It reduces regulatory compliance and limits stakeholder engagement
    D) It minimizes the impact of sustainability initiatives

20. **What are some of the emerging trends in business sustainability?**
    A) Integration of sustainability into corporate strategies, increased stakeholder engagement, and enhanced sustainability reporting and assurance
    B) Focus on short-term profits, reduced transparency, and limited stakeholder engagement
    C) Increased regulatory compliance, reduced costs, and minimized sustainability initiatives
    D) Focus solely on financial performance and short-term gains

Multiple-Choice Questions

21. **What are the components of an effective accountability system for corporations?**
    A) Reducing transparency and limiting stakeholder engagement
    B) A well-defined corporate mission, robust governance structure, and transparent disclosures
    C) Focusing solely on short-term profits
    D) Minimizing regulatory compliance and reducing costs

22. **What is the primary focus of long-term sustainability planning?**
    A) To ensure the continuity of business operations and integrate sustainability into the business environment, corporate culture, and strategic plans
    B) To focus solely on financial performance
    C) To reduce transparency and limit stakeholder engagement
    D) To minimize regulatory compliance and reduce costs

23. **What are the benefits of effective corporate governance?**
    A) It promotes accountability, enhances operational and financial performance, and strengthens stakeholder trust
    B) It reduces transparency and limits stakeholder engagement
    C) It focuses solely on financial performance
    D) It minimizes regulatory compliance and reduces costs

24. **How can companies effectively communicate their sustainability efforts to stakeholders?**
    A) By reducing transparency and limiting stakeholder engagement
    B) Through sustainability reports, corporate websites, social media, and public filings such as Form 10-K and proxy statements
    C) By focusing solely on financial performance
    D) By minimizing regulatory compliance and reducing costs

25. **Why is it important for companies to have a well-defined purpose?**
    A) Reducing transparency and limiting stakeholder engagement
    B) A well-defined purpose helps guide business strategies, aligns with stakeholder expectations, and promotes long-term sustainability
    C) Focusing solely on financial performance
    D) Minimizing regulatory compliance and reducing costs

26. **How does the stakeholder governance model redefine the fiduciary duties of directors and executives?**
    A) It extends fiduciary duties to all stakeholders, not just shareholders, and focuses on creating shared value
    B) It focuses solely on financial performance

C) It reduces regulatory compliance and limits stakeholder engagement

D) It minimizes the impact of sustainability initiatives

27. **What are the guiding principles of stakeholder governance?**

A) Inclusivity, transparency, equity, long-term orientation, responsiveness, and ethical conduct

B) Reducing operational costs and increasing shareholder wealth

C) Focusing solely on financial performance

D) Limiting stakeholder engagement and reducing transparency

28. **What is the significance of the stakeholder engagement in sustainability planning?**

A) It reduces transparency and limits stakeholder engagement

B) It helps in understanding stakeholder preferences and expectations, which informs the development of effective sustainability strategies

C) It focuses solely on financial performance

D) It minimizes regulatory compliance and reduces costs

29. **What is the significance of stakeholder governance in achieving business sustainability?**

A) It reduces transparency and limits stakeholder engagement

B) It promotes long-term performance, enhances reputation, and creates a positive impact on society and the environment

C) It focuses solely on financial performance

D) It minimizes regulatory compliance and reduces costs

30. **What are some emerging trends in business sustainability?**

A) Integration of sustainability into corporate strategies, increased stakeholder engagement, and enhanced sustainability reporting and assurance

B) Focus on short-term profits, reduced transparency, and limited stakeholder engagement

C) Increased regulatory compliance, reduced costs, and minimized sustainability initiatives

D) Focus solely on financial performance and short-term gains

Notes

1 Lacurci, G. (2020). Money moving into environmental funds shatters previous record. *CNBC* (January 14, 2020) https://www.cnbc.com/2020/01/14/esg-funds-see-record-inflows-in-2019.html

2 Bloomberg. (2021). Bloomberg Professional Services: ESG assets may hit $53 trillion by 2025, a third of global AUM. *Bloomberg Intelligence* (February 23, 2021). https://www.bloomberg.com/professional/blog/esg-assets-may-hit-53-trillion-by-2025-a-third-of-global-aum/

3 World Economic Forum (2021). About: Our mission (September 7, 2021). https://www.weforum.org/about/world-economic-forum

4 World Economic Forum (2021). About: Our mission (September 7, 2021). https://www.weforum.org/about/world-economic-forum

5 Much of the discussion in this chapter comes from Rezaee, Z. (2021). *Corporate Sustainability: Shareholder Primacy Versus Stakeholder Primacy, Business Expert Press* (July 2021); Rezaee, Z. (2024). *The Sustainable Business Blueprint: Planning, Performance, Risk, Reporting and Assurance.* Routledge/Taylor and Francis, Chapter 2; Rezaee, Z. (2023). Business sustainability approaches: Shareholder primacy and stakeholder primacy. *Indian Accounting Review* 27, (2): 1–24.

6 Business Roundtable (BRT). (2019). Statement on the Purpose of a Corporation. August 19, 2019. https://opportunity.businessroundExhibit.org/wp-content/uploads/2019/09/BRT-Statement-on-the-Purpose-of-a-Corporation-with-Signatures-1.pdf

7 Rezaee, Z. and Fogarty, T. (2019). *Business Sustainability, Corporate Governance and Organizational Ethics.* Wiley.

8 Rezaee, Z. (2021). *Corporate Sustainability: Shareholder Primacy Versus Stakeholder Primacy.* Business Expert Press.

9 Davos Manifesto 2020: The Universal Purpose of a Company in the Fourth Industrial Revolution (December 2, 2019). https://www.weforum.org/agenda/2019/12/davos-manifesto-2020-the-universal-purpose-of-a-company-in-the-fourth-industrial-revolution/.

10 Palladino, L. and Karlsson, K. (2018). Towards "accountable capitalism": Remaking corporate law through stakeholder governance (October). http://rooseveltinstitute.org/wp-content/uploads/2018/10/Towards-%E2%80%98Accountable-Capitalism%E2%80%99-issue-brief.pdf.

11 Rezaee, Z. and Fogarty, T. (2019). *Business Sustainability, Corporate Governance and Organizational Ethics.* Wiley.

12 Rezaee, Z. (2018). *Corporate Governance in the Aftermath of the Global Financial Crisis*, four volumes. Business Expert Press.

13 Rezaee, Z. (2018). *Corporate Governance in the Aftermath of the Global Financial Crisis*, four volumes. Business Expert Press.

14 Rezaee, Z. (2018). *Corporate Governance in the Aftermath of the Global Financial Crisis*, four volumes. Business Expert Press.

15 Rezaee, Z. (2023). Business sustainability approaches: Shareholder primacy and stakeholder primacy. *Indian Accounting Review* 27 (2): 1–24.

16 the Committee of Sponsoring Organizations of the Treadway Commission (COSO). 2020. Applying the COSO ERM framework. https://www.coso.org/erm-framework

Chapter 5
Sustainability Principles, Theories, Research, and Education

Learning Objectives

- Understand business sustainability.
- Provide an overview of the key measures of sustainable performance.
- Learn the sustainability principles.
- Provide an overview of the sustainability standards.
- Be aware of the global implications of sustainability principles, theories, and standards.
- Have an overview of the research and studies related to sustainability.
- Explain how business sustainability impacts education.

Introduction

Conceptually, there are two distinct views on why a firm should focus on both financial economic sustainability performance (ESP) and nonfinancial environmental, social, and governance. Environmental (ESG) sustainability performance with ethics is being integrated into both ESP and ESG dimensions. One view is that a firm exists solely to maximize profits and create values for its shareholders within the realm of law and morality. In this context, a firm's objective is to improve ESP sustainability performance and to engage in ESG sustainability initiatives merely to benefit its public image, prevent government intervention and/or gain government favor, improve its corporate governance effectiveness, obtain industry leadership, improve reputation with customers and society or to improve market share. Under this view, any investment in nonfinancial ESG is considered to be an expense that reduces a firm's bottom line and thus negatively affects shareholder wealth. This view is often referred to as "Finance First" as an investment strategy by investors and a strategic decision by companies to prioritize financial performance and returns as the primary and often the main consideration in decision-making.

Another view is that corporations play an important role in our society in pursuing the mission of profit-with-purpose of creating shared value for all stakeholders, including shareholders, employees, creditors, suppliers, customers, communities, and the environment. In this context, any engagement in nonfinancial ESG sustainability performance is intended

DOI: 10.4324/9781003487081-5

to improve the bottom-line earnings based on the perception that a firm with more effective corporate governance measures that conducts its business ethically and achieves CSR and environmental initiatives with a keen focus on employee and customer satisfaction, is better off financially in the long term. Under this view, any expenditures pertaining to nonfinancial ESG are considered investments that can provide potential returns on investment and ultimately increase long-term financial earnings. This view is often referred to as "Impact First," which is an investment strategy by investors and a strategic decision by companies to prioritize ESG performance while focusing on financial performance.

In recent years, however, there has been a move toward a middle-ground view of "doing well by doing good" by focusing on both financial ESP and nonfinancial ESG sustainability performance. This view is gaining momentum worldwide and is promoted throughout this book. Investors now seek investments that are aligned with their social values (value alignment), for example, by owning stocks only in companies whose activities are consistent with the investor's moral and/or social values. Other investors may also want their investment in portfolio companies that can create more social value (social value creation). Recently, there has been a trend toward impact investing, which started in North America and Europe. Impact investing is defined as accepting a lower return on investment on companies that "do well and do good" by focusing on ESG performance. Many private-wealth arms of global banks, such as Bank of America Private Wealth Management and BNP Paribus, are developing products focused on impact investments. With impact investing, securing the financial return is not the sole objective for investors because they consider social and environmental impacts as well. Thus, impact investing is defined as an investment with financial return as well as nonfinancial impacts on society and the environment. Institutional investors, portfolio, and investment managers usually use ESG sustainability factors for risk assessment, especially in the valuation of intangible assets.

The CFA Institute states, "For investment professionals, a key idea in the discussion of ESG issues is that systematically considering ESG issues will likely lead to more complete analyses and better-informed investment decisions."[1] Theoretically, management's engagement in ESG activities, performance, and disclosure can be viewed as value increasing or value decreasing by investors. On the one hand, companies that effectively manage their business sustainability, improve ESG performance, enhance their reputation, fulfill their social responsibility, and promote a corporate culture of integrity and competency can be financially sustainable in the long term. On the other hand, companies can only survive and generate sustainable performance when they generate profits and cash, which in turn are used to invest in social and environmental initiatives. An intensive and yet inconclusive debate has taken place about whether ESG programs constitute a legitimate activity for corporations to engage in.[2] The costs of these programs are immediate and tangible, but the related benefits may not be realized in the short to medium term, and outcomes are often not easily quantifiable (e.g., CSR initiatives). Sustainability disclosures on ESG are typically considered as externalities beyond the disclosures of ESP and can be viewed positively or negatively by investors and other market participants. Examples of positive externalities are diversity, social impacts, environmental impact, effective governance whereas negative externalities are global warming, CEO duality, climate change, and greenhouse emission. These positive (negative) externalities have been documented to have favorable (unfavorable) effects on the firm's cost of capital and, thus, its market value.[3] Sustainability principles and theories discussed in the next section are intended to explain the possible tension among the five EGSEE dimensions of sustainability performance, in particular, the tension between financial ESP and nonfinancial ESG dimensions.

Sustainability Principles

As business sustainability is gaining increasing attention and recognition as a strategic imperative of being integrated into corporate culture and business environment, its principles are defined by several professional organizations. The five principles of sustainability developed based on the definition of sustainability as "a dynamic equilibrium in the process of interaction between a population and the caring capacity of its environment …" provide guidelines for public companies to effectively manage the social, environmental, and financial aspects of their business.[4] Sustainability principles are guidelines aimed at promoting long-term financial ESP and nonfinancial ESG sustainability performance. They serve as a fundamental framework for individuals, organizations, businesses, and governments to make decisions and take actions that minimize negative impacts on society and the environment while fostering financial well-being, resilience, and positive outcomes for future generations.

The United Nations Global Compact has established ten sustainability principles, and more than 15,000 companies worldwide have adopted and integrated these principles into their strategic planning, decisions, and operations.[5] These ten sustainability principles are classified into four general categories of human rights, labor, environment, and anticorruption, as summarized in Exhibit 5.1, and are relevant to all five EGSEE dimensions of sustainability performance. These ten sustainability principles cover: (1) environmental conservation in protecting natural resources, biodiversity, and ecosystems to minimize pollution, reduce waste, promote sustainable land use practices, and conserve energy and water; (2) social equity of ensuring access to resources, fair treatment, and opportunities for all individuals and communities, regardless of factors such as race, socioeconomic, status gender, ethnicity, or geographic location; (3) intergenerational equity of recognizing the rights and needs of future generations and making decisions that do not compromise their ability to enjoy a high quality of life and meet their own needs; (4) stakeholder engagement of interacting with diverse stakeholders, including businesses, governments, non-governmental organizations, local communities, and indigenous peoples, in decision-making processes to ensure that their interests are considered and their perspectives and needs are incorporated into sustainability initiatives; (5) transparency and accountability of promoting transparency in decision-making processes, operations, and reporting to build trust and accountability among stakeholders; (6) resilience and adaptability of establishing resilience to environmental and social changes including climate change, natural disasters, and economic shifts; (7) economic viability of pursuing economic activities that support long-term and sustainable financial prosperity without compromising the ability of future generations to meet their needs by fostering innovation, investing in sustainable industries, and promoting responsible consumption and production; and (8) circular economy of focusing on the principles of reduce, reuse, and recycle to maximize the efficient use of resources throughout the entire life-cycle of products and services and to minimize waste by redesigning systems and processes to eliminate waste and pollution, while promoting the regeneration of natural systems.

These sustainability principles are derived from two sustainability perspectives: shareholder value maximization and stakeholder/society value creation. These perspectives explain managerial incentives or the assumed level of agency conflicts between management and shareholders/stakeholders and the potential tensions between ESP and ESG performance. According to the traditional "shareholder value maximization" perspective under the shareholder primacy model presented in Chapter 4, management's primary responsibility is to enhance earnings and maximize value for shareholders while minimizing negative impacts on the environment and society. There is a broader perspective of "stakeholder/society value creation" under the stakeholder primacy model, presented in Chapter 4, where management maximizes the sum of the various stakeholders' surpluses. This perspective emphasizes that public companies are responsible for not only generating financial returns for shareholders but also positively contributing to the environment and society in the long run. Under the stakeholder primacy concept, management faces multi-task agency problems, and they need to optimize along the ESP and ESG sustainability dimensions. The ultimate success of business organizations should be measured in terms of their ability and willingness to achieve all five EGSEE dimensions of sustainability performance by adopting these principles of sustainability. These sustainability principles should assist business organizations to:

- Promote the culture of "purpose" rather than "profit," which encourages commitment by all stakeholders, from investors to the board of directors, executives, employees, suppliers, and customers, to create shared value and meaningful impacts for all stakeholders. This sense of business with purpose should improve confidence and create synergies among all stakeholders to pursue the business purpose, which includes making a profit.

- Focus on creating sustainable performance that benefits humans, society, and the environment.

- Adopt sustainability as an integrated component of their mission and recognize that sustainability integrates social, economic, governance, ethical, environmental, and cultural interactions.

- Encourage the discussion of sustainability concepts throughout the company.

- Commit to ongoing assessments of the company's progress toward sustainability.

- Commit to the development and implementation of policies and operating procedures that promote the fulfillment of these principles.

Exhibit 5.1 United Nations Ten Global Compact Principles and Sustainability Performance

Principle	Description	Categories/ Domains	Sustainability Performance
1	The protection of international human rights should be respected and supported.	**Human rights**	**Social**
2	Businesses shall not take part in the abuse of human rights.		
3	Freedom of association and the right to collective bargaining should be supported.	**Labor/Social**	
4	Forced and compulsory labor should be eliminated.		
5	Child labor should be effectively eradicated.		
6	Discrimination in employment and occupation should be abolished.		
7	Businesses should take safety measures against environmental challenges.	**Environment**	**Environmental**
8	Greater environmental responsibility should be promoted.		
9	Businesses should encourage the advancement and distribution of environmentally friendly technology.		
10	Businesses should combat extortion, bribery, and all forms of corruption.	**Anticorruption/ Economic**	**Ethical**

Sustainability Principles

Individuals, organizations, and societies can work toward creating a more sustainable and equitable world for present and future generations by adhering to these sustainability principles and promoting their effectiveness. These principles collectively suggest that sustainability enables businesses to meet the needs of the current generation without compromising the needs of future generations. A combination of these sustainability principles should be used as the foundation and guidelines for business organizations in transforming business sustainability from a greenwashing appearance into a strategic imperative of integrating into the business environment and corporate culture. Specifically, these principles should be used as foundations for the development of sustainability theories, which are explained in the following section.

Sustainability Theories

Business sustainability theories provide guiding principles and frameworks for understanding and implementing sustainable initiatives and practices within organizations. The theories presented in this section guide businesses in integrating financial ESP and nonfinancial ESG sustainability performance and considerations into their strategies, operations, and decision-making processes. The concept of sustainability performance suggests that a firm must extend its focus beyond maximizing short-term shareholder profit by considering the impact of its operations on all stakeholders, including the community, society, and the environment.[6] Several theories, including shareholder/agency, stakeholder, signaling/disclosure, legitimacy, institutional, and stewardship, help to explain the interrelated financial ESP and nonfinancial ESG dimensions of sustainability performance and their integrated link to business models and corporate culture in creating shared values for all stakeholders.[7] This section presents these theories and their implications for business sustainability practice, education, research, and standards.

Shareholder/Agency Theory

Shareholder/agency theory defines the relationship between shareowners (principals) and management (agent) and addresses the potential conflicts of interest between management and shareholders. There may be potential conflicts of interest between owners (shareholders) and agents (management) in a corporate setting when agents are charged with the responsibility of managing the business affairs in the best interest of owners. Shareholder/agency theory addresses how corporations are managed and suggests that the interests of owners and agents are often not aligned. Shareholder/agency theory explains the economic function and valuation implications of sustainability performance in maximizing positive externalities and minimizing negative externalities of sustainability activities that are intended to create shareholder value. This theory suggests that management maximizes the interests of shareholders by engaging in positive net present value (NPV) projects that create shareholder value. This shareholder wealth maximization theory specifies that shareholders are the owners of the firm, and that management has a fiduciary duty to act in the best interest of owners to maximize their wealth.[8]

Shareholder/agency theory focuses on risk sharing and the agency problems between the principal (owner) and agent (management). In the presence of information asymmetry where the agent (management) acts on behalf of the principal (shareholders) and knows more about its actions and/or intentions than the principal, the agent has incentives not to act in the best interest of owners and/or withhold important information from them. With proper monitoring, the principal incurs agency costs of monitoring, bonding, and residual claims to align their interests with those of the agent.[9] Agency theory (viewing management as only accountable to shareholders for creating shareholder value and whose interests may diverge from those of their shareholders) has traditionally been the dominant theory of corporate finance, management, and governance research. While agency theory has been useful in explaining the principle-agent relationship and interest divergence for individualistic utility maximization and motivation, this theory may not adequately address the emerging complex organization structure that is oriented toward business sustainability in protecting the interests of all stakeholders.

The implications of shareholder/agency theory for sustainability performance is that management incentives and activities may be focused on meeting short-term earnings targets and away from achieving sustainable and long-term performance for all stakeholders, including shareholders. Under this theory, nonfinancial ESG sustainability activities, particularly CSR expenditures, are typically viewed as the allocation of firm resources in pursuit of activities that are not in the best financial interests of shareholders, even though they may create value for other stakeholders. At this moment, firms focus only on creating shareholder value and leave decisions about social responsibility to individual investors. Shareholder/agency theory suggests that there is an information asymmetry among stakeholders, as only the senior management typically knows the true representation of financial and nonfinancial reports. Thus, to mitigate the perceived information asymmetry, management may choose to disclose nonfinancial ESG performance information voluntarily. Agency theory postulates that ESG activities can create shareholder value when they increase future cash flows by increasing revenue (better customer satisfaction), reducing costs (reducing waste, better quality and cost-effective products and services, maintaining talented and loyal employees) and reducing risks (comply with regulations, avoid taxes and fines).

Sustainability Theories

Stakeholder Theory

Stakeholder theory and the "enlightened value maximization" concept recognize the maximization of sustainable performance and the long-term value of the firm as the criterion for balancing the interests of all stakeholders.[10] In the context of shareholder wealth-maximization and stakeholder welfare maximization, ESG sustainability efforts may create both synergies and conflicts. The stakeholder theory suggests that sustainability activities and performance enhancement of the long-term value of the firm fulfill the firm's social responsibilities, meet its environmental obligations, and improve its reputation.[11] However, these sustainability efforts may require considerable resource allocation that can conflict with the shareholder wealth maximization objectives, and thus, management may not invest in sustainability initiatives (social and environmental) that result in long-term financial sustainability.

Under the stakeholder theory, all stakeholders have a reciprocal relationship with a company. The stakeholder theory is applicable to business sustainability in the sense that the synergy and integration among all elements of the supply-chain and financial processes are essential in achieving overall sustainable performance objectives. Stakeholders do not only value the firm's sustainability performance but also become aware of such activities and take action to hold the firm responsible. The application of the stakeholder theory to business sustainability suggests that a company should be viewed as a nexus of all constituencies in creating shared values for all stakeholders. This theory suggests the integration of all business activities from the supply chain, inbound and outbound logistics, processes and operations, finished products and customer interface, distribution channels services, and financial reporting processes to achieve sustainability performance in all five EESG dimensions. According to this theory, sustainability performance dimensions (ESP and ESG) are viewed by stakeholders as value-added activities that create shared values for all stakeholders.

Stakeholder theory has been and shall continue to be the prevailing theory of corporate sustainability since 1984 when Freeman published his book *Strategic Management: A Stakeholder Approach*.[12] Mitchell, Agle, and Wood[13] discuss a normative theory of stakeholder identification in explaining why management may consider certain groups (e.g., owners, nonowners) as the firm's stakeholders and a descriptive theory of stakeholders' alliance in describing the conditions under which management may recognize certain groups as stakeholders. One of the most prevailing and broad definitions of a stakeholder is defined by Freeman as "any group or individual who can affect or is affected by the achievement of the organization's objectives."[14] In the context of business sustainability, stakeholders can be classified as internal stakeholders who have a direct interest (stake) and bear risks associated with business activities and external stakeholders. Stakeholders are those who have vested interests in a firm through their investments in the form of financial capital (shareholders), human capital (employees), physical capital (customers and suppliers), social capital (the society), environmental capital (environment), and regulatory capital (government). Stakeholders have reciprocal relations and interactions with a firm in the sense that they contribute to the firm value creation (stake), and their well-being is also affected by the firm's activities (risk). Stakeholder theory, as developed by Freeman, posits that businesses should consider the interests of all stakeholders, including shareholders, creditors, employees, customers, suppliers, communities, and governments when making decisions. By addressing the needs and concerns of diverse stakeholders, businesses can create shared value for all stakeholders while enhancing long-term financial performance. The legitimacy and institutional theories discussed below are closely related to the stakeholder theory in the sense that only those with legitimacy claims and institutional identification can be considered stakeholders. Stakeholders are those who have property/legal claims (shareholders), contractual agreements (creditors, employees, management, suppliers), moral responsibilities (society, customers), and presumed/legal claims (the environment, government, competitors).

Legitimacy Theory

Legitimacy theory is built on a sociopolitical view that suggests that firms are facing social and political pressure to preserve their legitimacy by fulfilling their social contract. This theory justifies the importance of the social and environmental dimensions of sustainability performance. Firms engage in voluntary disclosure activities to obtain legitimacy and thereby fulfill the "social contract" and thus gain the support of society.[15] The legitimacy theory suggests that all stakeholders, including customers, desire social and environmental sustainability performance, and therefore, noncompliance with social norms and environmental requirements threatens organizational legitimacy and its financial sustainability.[16]

Legitimacy theory is important in improving the reputation of the company's products and services as desirable, proper, and of the quality that is acceptable within the social norms and values and is beneficial rather than detrimental to the environment and society. For example, tobacco companies may increase their shareholder wealth, as promoted by the shareholder theory, by selling their products at the risk of being detrimental to the health of customers. Business sustainability should be an integral component of corporate culture, business environment, and strategic decisions and actions, including supply-chain management, particularly when there is a conflict between the corporate goals of maximizing profits and social goals. The existence and persistence of such a conflict require corporations to establish and maintain sustainability strategies, including supply-chain policies,

Sustainability Theories

programs, and practices, to ensure their board of directors and senior executives are setting an "appropriate tone at the top" and taking sustainability and the social interest seriously. Legitimacy theory advocates for designing products and processes that improve a
company's legitimacy in society by eliminating the concept of waste and instead mimicking
natural systems, where materials are continuously recycled or biodegraded, and by emphasizing the importance of product design, material selection, and closed-loop systems in
achieving sustainability and minimizing environmental impacts.

Signaling/Disclosure Theory

The signaling/disclosure theory helps explain management incentives for achieving all five
EGSEE dimensions of sustainability performance and reporting ESP and ESG sustainability
performance, as well as investors' reactions to the disclosure of sustainability performance
information.[17] This theory suggests that firms tend to signal "good news" using various
corporate finance mechanisms, including voluntary reporting of nonfinancial ESG sustainability performance. However, the expected link between a firm's voluntary ESG sustainability performance reporting and the use of these signals is ambiguous. Firm voluntary
reporting may act as a means to signal information about expected future performance.
Alternatively, these signaling mechanisms could be a substitute, suggesting a negative
relationship between the probability of voluntary disclosure and the use of these signals.[18]

The signaling/disclosure theory suggests that firms with good sustainability performance
differentiate themselves from firms with poor sustainability performance. Thus, by sustainability reporting, firms signal their good sustainability performance, which non-sustainable
firms cannot easily mimic. This theory relates to the ability to communicate credibly with
all stakeholders and supply-chain partners regarding synergy, integration, and the resource
dependency of different components of supply-chain management and sending a uniform
signal of achieving all five EGSEE dimensions of sustainability performance.[19]

Institutional Theory

Institutional theory focuses on the role of normative influences in the decision-making
processes that affect organization structure and offers a structural framework that can
be useful in addressing various issues, conditions, and challenges that enable the structure to become institutionalized.[20] The focus is on the social aspects of decision-making,
such as the decision to invest in corporate social responsibility (CSR) expenditures and the
conditions under which the investment decisions on CSR or environmental initiatives are
made and their possible impacts on the environment and society. Institutional theory views
a firm as an institutional form of diverse individuals and groups with unified interests,
transactions, governance, values, rules, and practices that can become institutionalized.

Institutional theory primarily focuses on the rationalization, legitimacy, practicality, and aspects of social structure and related processes in establishing guidelines and best practices in compliance with applicable laws, rules, standards, and norms. Institutional theory posits that the institutional environment and corporate culture can be more effective than external forces (laws, regulations) in impacting organizations' structures and innovation, which would result in technical efficiencies and effectiveness.

Institutional theory suggests that businesses have a responsibility to contribute positively to society and the environment beyond maximizing profits by integrating social, environmental, and ethical considerations into business operations and decision-making processes and by engaging in philanthropy, environmental conservation efforts, ethical sourcing practices, and community engagement programs that promote business reputation. A more pragmatic institutional theory promotes corporate sustainability by viewing a firm as an institution that serves human needs and protects the interests of all stakeholders – from shareholders to creditors, employees, customers, suppliers, society, and the environment. A company as an institution is sustainable as long as it creates shared value for all stakeholders, including shareholders. Thus, the implication of institutional theory for promoting business sustainability is that social and environmental initiatives, corporate measures, and ethical practices will ultimately reach a level of legitimization and best practices where failure to adopt them is considered irresponsible and irrational.

Stewardship Theory

Stewardship theory is derived from sociology and psychology, and views management as custodians of the long-term interests of a variety of stakeholders rather than its own self-serving and short-term opportunistic behavior under agency theory. Stewardship is "the extent to which an individual [manager] willingly subjugates his or her interests to act in protection of others' [stakeholders] long-term welfare [and thus it] is very applicable to the emerging concept of corporate sustainability."[21] Two aspects of this definition, long-term orientation and protection of the interests of all stakeholders are the main drivers of corporate sustainability. Stewardship theory is applicable to corporate sustainability because it considers management strategic decisions and actions as stewardship behaviors that "serve a shared valued end, which provides social benefits to collective interests over the long term."[22] Under stewardship theory, management is the steward of all capitals, from the financial capital provided by shareholders to the human capital offered by employees, the social capital extended by society, and the environmental capital enabled by the environment as presented in Chapter 10. Stewardship theory promotes that businesses should focus on the optimization of all capital and focus on measuring their success not only by financial performance (profit) but also by their impact on the environment (planet), society

Sustainability Theories

(people), and reputation (prosperity). This theory emphasizes the utilization of resources and capital that enables the interconnectedness of economic, environmental, and social factors and encourages businesses to pursue sustainability across all five EGSEE sustainability performance dimensions.

Resource Dependence Theory

Resource dependence theory (RDT) attempts to explain the dynamic of power in interorganizational relations. Organization A might control a resource needed by organization B, creating a situation in which B relies on A. The basis of RDT states that in this situation, A has power over B to the proportional degree that B is dependent upon the resource controlled by A; this is the power dynamic between A and B. Organizations are constantly concerned with the survival of the organization itself while maintaining stability in exchange relationships, such as the aforementioned scenario. However, RDT does not define power as a zero-sum game, as it is possible for B to depend upon A to the same degree that A depends upon B; this is defined as interdependence. Considering these realities leads organizations to strategically plan the use of power and manage the exposure of their dependence.[23] This theory runs on three core concepts: (1) social context, (2) the organization's aim to improve autonomy and explore interests, and (3) the fact that the internal and external actions of organizations are dictated, in part, by power.[24] These core concepts can be regrouped to recognize that an organization's behavior is influenced by external factors that can diminish the proper decision-making of management.[25]

Organizations can manage interdependence, uncertainty, and external power struggles through mergers and acquisitions (M&A) and even through political action. RDT is one of the primary theory-based explanations for the occurrence of M&A. This can help reduce competition by absorbing competitors, reducing dependence upon suppliers and buyers, and increasing diversification, such as not relying on any one organization too heavily. Organizations can also attempt to reduce uncertainty by shaping the regulatory environment in which they operate. Shaping the regulatory environment can be accomplished by influencing legislation through hiring lobbyists to influence politicians' decisions. Doing this effectively allows the organization to create an optimal environment in which it can operate virtually unimpeded.[26]

Strategic Choice Theory

Strategic choice theory (SCT) is a decision-making tool that allows the user to achieve long-term strategic objectives. Strategic choice is different from strategic planning in that strategic choice is an ongoing, cumulative process of progressing toward a leader's or group's goals. At the same time, strategic planning is looked at as an opportunity to fundamentally change the structure or strategy of the organization abruptly. Previously, it was thought and accepted that the external environment was primarily responsible for shaping the internal structure of corporations and organizations; however, research suggests that the use of strategic choice can have a greater effect in the long term.[27]

SCT has three key elements that are used to structure a problem and subsequently to arrive at the perceived "optimal" decision to achieve long-term goals. These three elements include (1) the Decision Area, (2) the Comparison Area, and (3) the Uncertainty Area. The Decision Area is comprised of the different choices that can be made in response to a certain issue. The Comparison Area is used to compare the circumstances of each decision and its individual effects on the organization. The Uncertainty Area considers all of the unknowns in the decision by classifying them into three categories of uncertainty. These are uncertainties related to the environment, guiding values, and related choices.[28] Strategic choice theory can be used to improve the long-term sustainability of corporations or organizations. When a leader within the organization aligns their decision-making with their long-term objective of sustainability, a slow but sure improvement in sustainability will occur. SCT proposes that businesses can achieve sustainability and intended optimal decisions and performance by recognizing and valuing financial and natural resources as assets, investing in resource efficiency and renewable energy, and redesigning products and processes to mimic nature's efficiency and advocating for businesses to prioritize the long-term preservation of natural capital while pursuing economic growth and prosperity.

Social Network Theory

Social network theory (SNT) is used to study how social interactions and relationships affect information flow, the use of personal or media influence, and the ability to initiate a behavioral change within an organization or group. The basic idea is that by applying this theory, the user will be able to understand or even predict the social interactions between different organizations, within a single organization, or between the individual "nodes" in an organization. SNT describes social relationships in the form of "nodes" and "ties." The nodes are singular actors or individuals in the network, while the ties represent the relationships between the individual nodes. This distribution of nodes and ties creates a map of the respective "social network" in which the social influence of an individual or group can be determined. A key distinction that the SNT assumes is that the attributes of an individual node are less influential than the ties that interconnect actors.[29]

Social network analysis (SNA) has emerged from the social network theory, aiming to study the relational characteristics of social events and patterns in the behavior between individuals or organizations within the same social network. Due to its simplicity and practicality,

Sustainability Theories

SNA has received interest from practitioners who are interested in the analysis of the social dynamic within their organization or between their organization and others. SNA has been used in economics, computer science, mathematics, and politics due to its widespread applications and can effectively be used in any circumstance in which social capital exists.[30] This form of analysis allows the user to understand the invisibly woven fabric of a social network. By understanding this dynamic, the user can make decisions with less uncertainty as to how the decision will affect the social network and subsequently cause organizational change. Ultimately, this helps the user interact and make decisions that yield better results than previously thought attainable.

Data-Driven Storytelling Theory

Data-driven storytelling (DDS) theory can be used to illustrate a graphical presentation of the ESG sustainability performance information. This theory emphasizes the importance of crafting narratives around data to effectively communicate insights and engage stakeholders in sustainability factors of planning, performance, risk, and reporting.[31] The effective disclosure of complex ESG performance information requires conveying the story behind ESG metrics in a compelling and understandable manner. The DDS theory enables firms to: (1) tell their ESG success stories effectively; (2) link ESG presentation to the needs and preferences of their stakeholders including investors, customers, employees, and communities; (3) present ESG graphical ESG disclosures around a clear narrative including risks and opportunities, data analysis and insights; (4) utilize graphs, charts, and visuals to support narrative by choosing visuals that effectively illustrate ESG trends, comparisons, and correlations within the company and across companies; (5) provide context for the ESG data to enable the stakeholders understand the importance and relevance of ESG data; and (6) present ESG data within a larger narrative that resonates with stakeholders' values and priorities including industry benchmarks, historical trends, or comparisons with peers or competitors. Companies worldwide can effectively communicate the significance of ESG key performance indicators (KPIs), engage stakeholders in ESG initiatives and activities, and drive positive action toward sustainability and social responsibility goals by applying the principles of DDS to ESG graph presentation.

Integrated Sustainability Theory

The above sub-section addresses the agency/shareholder, stakeholder, signaling, legitimacy, institutional, stewardship, and other sustainability theories to explain the integrated and interrelated dimensions of sustainability performance and their relevance to shared value creation. These theories suggest that companies should focus on the key measures of sustainable performance, such as operational efficiency, supply-chain management, customer satisfaction, talent management, and innovation. These measures are derived from the internal factors of strategy, risk profile, strengths and weaknesses, and corporate culture, as well as the external factors of reputation, technology, competition, globalization, and utilization of natural resources. Companies should use a principles-based and integrated approach in infusing financial and nonfinancial sustainability information into their business model, from purchasing and inbound logistics, production design, and manufacturing processes to distribution and outbound logistics. Integrated sustainability theory provides a comprehensive framework for addressing sustainability challenges, risks, and opportunities and promoting sustainability across economic, social, and environmental dimensions. Businesses can align their strategies and initiatives by considering integrated sustainability theory to contribute to broader efforts to end poverty, protect the planet, and ensure prosperity for all.

The concept of sustainability performance and sustainability theories discussed above suggest that a firm must extend its focus beyond maximizing short-term shareholder profit under the shareholder/agency theory by considering the impact of its operation and entire value chains on all stakeholders, including the community, society, and the environment. Disclosure of the EGSEE dimensions of sustainability performance while signaling the company's sustainability performance and establishing legitimacy with all supply-chain partners poses a cost-benefit trade-off that has implications for investors and business organizations. For example, any environmental initiatives pertaining to reducing pollution levels or saving energy costs may require huge upfront capital expenditures, but in the long run, they will also reduce contingent and actual environmental liabilities. Sustainability information on EESG is typically considered as a set of externalities beyond disclosure of financial performance, which can be viewed positively (e.g., social and environmental initiatives, board diversity and independence) or negatively (e.g., natural resource depletion, pollution, and human rights abuses) by market participants and supply-chain partners. These factors are important determinants of firms' future performance, operational risks, and supply-chain management beyond the factors that are typically included in the basic financial statements.

Taken together, the above-discussed theories are not exclusive, and other sustainability theories have implications for business sustainability. These theories offer different perspectives and approaches to business sustainability, but they share a common goal of promoting long-term financial viability and resilience while minimizing negative impacts on the environment and society. Organizations can draw upon these theories to develop tailored sustainability strategies and activities that align with their values, goals, and stakeholders' expectations. Firms will realize that their main objective function is to create shareholder

Sustainability Theories

value in compliance with agency/shareholder theory while protecting the interests of other stakeholders under the stakeholder theory, contributing to society and human needs in accordance with the institutional theory, securing their legitimacy under the legitimacy theory, differentiating themselves from low ESG/CSR firms through the disclosure/signaling theory, pursuing the long-term interests of a variety of stakeholders as suggested by stewardship theory and using other sustainability theories of the social network, strategic choice a resource dependency to understand or even predict the social interactions between different organizations and to determine the best strategy in achieving long-term sustainable performance. According to the stakeholder theory, sustainability performance dimensions (ESP and ESG) are viewed by stakeholders as value-added activities that create stakeholder value. In compliance with the signaling/disclosure and legitimacy/institutional theories, good firms (high sustainability performance) differentiate themselves from poor firms (low sustainability performance) by signaling their legitimacy as good corporate citizens with corporate transparency and reputation as well as corporate culture. In accordance with the impression management and reputation risk management theories, voluntary disclosures of ESG sustainability performance can be viewed by stakeholders as good corporate citizenship and socially and environmentally responsible image, which enables the firm to create a good impression and manage its reputational risks. Thus, achieving legitimacy under the institutional/legitimacy theory is crucial in assuring that management makes a good impression and properly assesses reputation risks.

The concept and theory of emerging business sustainability requires management to simultaneously consider divergent economic, governance, social, ethical, and environmental issues. Stewardship theory enables management to effectively exercise stewardship over a broader range of financial and nonfinancial assets and capitals, including financial, physical, human, social, and environmental capital. Stewardship, among other theories, enables firms and their management to translate ESG sustainability performance to financial performance, leading to value creation. The relationships between business, society, and the environment are complex and often tense, and management must realize ways to address the potential tension and maximize both ESP and ESG sustainability performance. However, a single, cohesive, and integrated theory of business sustainability is apparently lacking in explaining the multidimensional and apparently conflicting aspects of sustainability performance. Management is generally responsible for stewarding corporate resources, including assets and capital, with an ethical vision toward how to benefit the broader range of stakeholders, including society and the environment. Thus, management should not impose its vision of doing good for society but instead, seek compliance with regulatory measures and the best practices of sustainability in creating shared value for all stakeholders.

These theories, while explaining the possible tensions and constraints imposed on the main business objective of creating shareholder value, have often ignored the integration among various dimensions of sustainability performance. They have used a narrow aspect of sustainability performance that emphasizes either ESP under the shareholder theory or ESG sustainability performance under stakeholder, signaling, legitimacy, and institutional theories. Nonetheless, there is a need for an integrated sustainability theory under which management acts as the steward of strategic capital, financial capital, human capital, social capital, and environmental capital and makes strategic decisions to achieve sustainability performance. Thus, an integrated sustainability theory of combinations of all the above theories is more relevant to business sustainability and can provide a means by which management can engage with all stakeholders and focus on the achievement of both financial ESP and nonfinancial ESG sustainability performance. An integrated sustainability theory can be more suitable for explaining sustainability education, practice, and research. An integrated sustainability theory supports the concept of stakeholder capitalism, which creates long-term sustainable shared value for all stakeholders. Regardless of which theory is more relevant to a particular firm, there should be a set of globally accepted sustainability-related standards to guide business organizations in advancing their sustainability initiatives, as discussed in the next section.

Sustainability Standards

Sustainable business for organizations means not only providing products and services that satisfy the customer and doing so without jeopardizing the environment but also operating in a socially responsible manner. Sustainability standards are guidelines and criteria established to promote financial ESP and nonfinancial ESG sustainability performance and practices in various industries. Sustainability standards provide frameworks for companies, organizations, and governments to assess and improve their sustainability ESP and ESG sustainability performance, and they often address material and relevant global challenges, including economic viability, climate change, biodiversity loss, social inequality, and resource depletion. Sustainability standards are classified into: (1) economic standards of addressing responsible business and financial practices, transparency, and ethical governance by encouraging companies to operate in a financially viable and socially responsible manner; (2) environmental standards of emphasizing the importance of reducing the environmental impact of products, services, and operations by focusing on areas such as energy efficiency, emissions reduction, waste management and water conservation; (3) social standards of addressing working conditions, labor rights, human rights, and community engagement to ensure fair treatment of workers, promote diversity and inclusion, and support local communities; (4) governance standards of managing the organization for benefit of its stakeholders by employing corporate measures (board independence,

Sustainability Theories

executive competency, internal controls) to create shred value for all stakeholders; (5) ethical standards of setting an appropriate tone at the top promoting ethical behavior and practices throughout the organization; and (6) reporting and disclosure standards of presenting sustainability reporting and assurance performance information through annual reports, sustainability reports, and other communication channels. Proper adoption and implementation of sustainability standards can bring several benefits, including transparent financial ESP information, improved reputation, reduced risk, cost savings, access to new markets, and increased competitiveness. Sustainability standards play an essential role in driving global positive economic, environmental, social, and governance outcomes.

The business literature suggests the use of sustainability standards developed by the International Organization for Standardization (ISO) in measuring both financial ESP and nonfinancial ESG sustainability performance, as well as preparing integrated sustainability reporting and obtaining assurance on sustainability performance reports.[32] The ISO standards and certifications can promote compliance with environmental regulations and social standards. Therefore, the ISO enables a consensus to be reached on solutions that meet both the requirements of businesses and the broader needs of society. Pressure to do so comes from customers, consumers, governments, associations, and the public at large. At the same time, far-sighted organizational leaders recognize that lasting success must be built on credible business practices and the prevention of activities such as fraudulent accounting and labor exploitation. A comprehensive set of ISO standards is needed to explain the link between sustainability theories and all five dimensions of sustainability performance. Several standards of the ISO are relevant to the five EGSSE dimensions of sustainability performance.[33] Specifically, ISO 9000 on quality control, ISO 14000 on environmental programs, ISO 20120 for sustainability events, ISO 26000 on corporate social responsibility, ISO 27001 for information security, and ISO 31000 on risk assessment are relevant.[34] ISO standards presented in the following subsections refer to a set of international standards developed by the ISO, an independent, non-governmental international organization to provide guidelines and specifications for products, services, and systems to ensure quality, safety, efficiency, and interoperability across various industries and sectors.

ISO 9000

ISO 9000 is the standard that provides a set of standardized requirements for a quality management system regardless of what the user organization does, its size, or whether it is in the private or the public sector. It is the only standard in the family against which organizations can be certified – although certification is not a compulsory requirement of the standard. The other standards in the family cover specific aspects such as fundamentals and vocabulary, performance improvements, documentation, training, and financial and economic aspects. The ISO 9000 standards are intended to improve the quality of products and services and thus are directly related to enhancing financial ESP. ISO 9000 can also be linked to nonfinancial ESG dimensions of sustainability performance in the sense that it improves the quality of services and products provided by business organizations. ISO 9000 series standards address quality management systems (QMS) and provide guidelines for organizations to ensure transparency, consistency, customer satisfaction, and continuous improvement in their products and services.

ISO 14000

The ISO 14000 family addresses various aspects of environmental management, risk assessment, reporting, and auditing. The very first two standards – ISO 14001:2004 and ISO 14004:2004 – deal with environmental management systems (EMS). ISO 14001:2004 provides the requirements for an EMS, and ISO 14004:2004 gives general EMS guidelines. The other standards and guidelines in the family address specific environmental aspects, including labeling, performance evaluation, life cycle analysis, communication, and auditing. Guidelines provided in ISO 14000 regarding environmental performance, reporting, and auditing are relevant to the environmental dimension of sustainability performance. ISO 14000 series standards focus on EMS and assist organizations in minimizing their environmental impact, complying with regulations, and enhancing environmental sustainability performance.

ISO 20121

ISO 20121, entitled "Sustainability Events," addresses resources, society, and the environment. This standard offers guidelines and best practices to help manage sustainability efforts and events and control their social, economic, and environmental impacts. ISO 20121 offers benefits for integrating its guidelines in all stages of management processes, including corporate infrastructure and supply-chain management that promote best business practices and reputational advantages.

ISO 22000

ISO 22000 standards address food safety by emphasizing food safety management systems and assisting organizations in the food industry to ensure the safety and quality of food products throughout the supply chain.

ISO 26000

ISO 26000 covers a broad range of an organization's activities, from economic to social, governance, ethics, and environmental issues. It is a globally accepted guidance document

Sustainability Theories

for social responsibility that assists organizations worldwide in fulfilling their CSR goals. Social responsibility performance promoted in ISO 26000 is conceptually and practically associated with the development of achieving sustainable performance because the fulfillment of social responsibility necessitates and ensures sustainable development. ISO 26000 provides guidance pertaining to social responsibility and encourages organizations to operate in a socially responsible and ethical manner, contribute to sustainable development, and engage with stakeholders in a transparent and accountable manner. ISO 26000 goes beyond profit maximization by presenting a framework for organizations to contribute to sustainable development and the welfare of society. The core subject areas of ISO 26000 take into account all aspects of the triple-bottom-line's (TBL) key financial and non-financial performance relevant to people, planet, and profit.

People: ISO 26000 encourages companies to recognize human rights as a critical aspect of social responsibility by ensuring that the countries in which they operate demonstrate respect for the political, civil, social, and cultural rights of the citizens.

Planet: ISO 26000 promotes sustainable resource management to ensure that business organizations are not exploiting the environment in which they are operating.

Profit: The primary goal of business organizations has been and will continue to earn profits in a socially responsible way to ensure shareholder value creation and the achievement of the desired rate of return on investment.

ISO 27000

ISO 27000 series standards cover information security management systems (ISMS) and provide guidelines for protecting sensitive information, managing risks, and ensuring data confidentiality, integrity, and availability. Particularly, the purpose of ISO 27001 is to offer organizations guidance on keeping information assets secure by providing guidelines and suggesting requirements for an ISMS. The ISMS is a systematic approach to managing sensitive information, protecting its integrity, and helping identify the risks associated with important information and control activities designed and implemented to manage the risks.

ISO 31000

The ISO 31000 standards set out principles, frameworks, and processes for the management of risks that are applicable to any organization in the public or private sector. It does not mandate a "one-size-fits-all" approach but rather emphasizes the fact that the management of risk must be tailored to the specific needs and structure of the particular organization. Guidelines provided in ISO 31000 are applicable in the assessment and management of risks associated with all five EESG dimensions of sustainability performance. These risks include strategic, financial, compliance, operational, supply chain, cyberattacks, and reputational risks.

Implementation of these ISO standards to various dimensions of sustainability performance and certifications of compliance with these standards promote improvements in the quality of products and services that directly affect earnings, ensure compliance with environmental regulations and social standards, strengthen governance measures and ethical value, and thus improve the effectiveness of sustainability performance. These standards also establish practical foundations that can be developed based on the theoretical framework of sustainability. Sustainability reports reflecting all five EESG dimensions of sustainability performance are deemed to be useful when they are complete and accurate, and ISO certifications ascertain their reliability, objectivity, and credibility. These ISO certifications of sustainability performance provide external assurance about the credibility and legitimacy of the integrated sustainability reports disseminated to all stakeholders.

ISO 37001

The ISO 37001 standards address anti-bribery management systems.[35] Bribery is known as the under-the-table facilitating payments that are common in some countries as a way of advancing business. The Foreign Corrupt Practices Act (FCPA) of 1977 in the United States prohibits corporations from bribing foreign officials to further their business benefits.[36] The FCPA prohibits the management of public companies from engaging in business activities with foreign agents that would aid in acquiring and disposing of business through bribe payments. Bribery in recent years has become an increasingly destructive and difficult challenge for many multinational companies. In addition to the loss of over US$1 trillion due to bribes each year, bribery can increase poverty, reduce quality of life, destroy business operations, and erode public trust.[37] ISO 37001 standards provide guidelines for organizations worldwide to promote an ethical business environment and corporate culture and to fight bribery.

ISO 45000

ISO 45000 series standards focus on occupational health and safety management systems (OHSMS) and assist organizations in creating safe and healthy work environments, preventing accidents and injuries, and complying with relevant regulations. Particularly, the ISO 45001 standards pertain to occupational health and safety.[38] Over 2.78 million people die every year from work-related diseases and accidents, and to combat this problem ISO 45001 sets standards for occupational health and safety management systems and requirements and provides guidelines for organizations worldwide to address this important safety issue. These guidelines enable organizations to reduce the burden of occupational injuries and diseases by providing a framework to improve employee safety, create better and safer working environments and conditions, and reduce workplace risks.

ISO 50000

ISO 50000 series standards focus on energy management systems (EnMS) and provide guidelines for organizations to improve energy efficiency, reduce energy consumption, and lower greenhouse gas emissions. Particularly, the ISO 50001 standards address energy management.[39] One important aspect of sustainability is leaving a better environment for the next generations. ISO 50001 standards provide a framework for organizations worldwide to conserve resources, use energy more effectively and efficiently, and address climate change by developing a sound and robust EnMS.

Other Standards

The ISO standards presented in the above subsections are just a few examples of ISO standards, and the organization develops standards for various other areas, such as risk management, supply-chain management, innovation management, and sustainable development. These ISO standards are voluntary, but many organizations choose to adopt them to demonstrate conformity with best practices, meet customer requirements, and enhance their competitive advantage in domestic and international markets. The ISEAL Alliance is a global association with the goal of improving the credibility and increasing the transparency of sustainability standards. ISEAL works with businesses, governments, researchers, and even other sustainability standard-setters to help increase the efficiency and effectiveness of sustainability standards and to identify opportunities that increase the rate of adoption of these standards in targeted regions around the globe. A key initiative of this organization is to establish global consensus on what constitutes "good practice" in different industries. To do this, ISEAL has consulted with stakeholders to create three "Codes of Good Practice": (1) Standard-Setting Code, (2) Impacts Code, and (3) Assurance Code.[40] The Standard-Setting Code guides setting social and environmental standards, while the Impacts Code assesses the impact of the social and environmental standards. The Assurance Code aims to enable compliance with social and environmental standards that have been implemented within an organization. ISEAL also engages external stakeholders in thinking about and participating in the development of credible sustainability standards.

ASTM International, formerly known as the American Society for Testing and Materials, is an international standard-setting organization that develops and releases sustainability standards for over 90 sectors globally. In total, ASTM has over 12,500 industry-specific standards with 30,000+ volunteer members across 140 countries. ASTM aims to combine these developed sustainability factors with innovative business services to enhance performance and improve consumer confidence in services and products that they use or buy. To accomplish this, ASTM has implemented five strategic goals to guide sustainability progress: (1) Leadership, (2) Global Technical Expertise, (3) Standards and Technical Content Development, (4) Services Provider, and (5) Organizational Vitality.[41]

Implications of Sustainability Principles, Theories, and Standards

Business organizations worldwide are now recognizing the importance of sustainability performance and the link between financial ESP and the nonfinancial ESG dimensions of sustainability performance. Justifications for business sustainability are moral obligation, social responsibility, maintaining a good reputation, ensuring sustainability, being environmentally conscious, having licensing to operate, and creating stakeholder value. Social performance can be viewed by management as nonvalue-adding and nonessential activities that may not necessarily increase shareholder value but should improve the image and reputation of the company as a socially responsible citizen. Sustainability performance, which can be driven by signaling and legitimacy incentives, measures how well a company translates its social goals into practice. Sustainability performance can be achieved through many activities, ranging from focusing on producing to delivering high-quality products and services that are not detrimental to society. The goal is to become a positive contributor to the sustainability of the planet and to improve employee health and well-being beyond compliance with applicable laws, regulations, standards, and common practices.

In creating shared values for all stakeholders, corporations identify the potential social, environmental, governance, and ethical issues of concern and integrate them into their strategic planning and supply-chain management practices. Many factors explain why a company should integrate sustainability performance into its corporate culture, business environment, and supply-chain management. These factors include the pressure of the labor movement, the development of moral values and social standards, the development of business education, and changes in public opinion about the role of business caused by environmental matters, governance, and ethical scandals. Companies that are, or aspire to be, leaders in sustainability are challenged by rising public expectations, increasing innovation, continuous quality improvement, effective governance measures, high standards of ethics and integrity, and heightened social and environmental problems.

Globalization created incentives and opportunities for business organizations and their stakeholders and executives to influence their business sustainability initiatives and strategies. Corporations can choose from a variety of sustainability initiatives and performance with regard to the scope, extent, and type of sustainability strategies that focus on

Sustainability Theories

different issues, functions, and areas. The sustainability program can be designed to mini-mize the conflicts between corporations and society caused by the differences between private and social costs and benefits and to align corporate goals with those of society. Examples of conflicts between corporations and society that are related to environmental issues are pollution, acid rain, global warming, wages paid by multinational corporations in poor countries, and the use of child labor in developing countries. Corporate govern-ance measures, which include the rules, regulations, and best practices of sustainabil-ity programs, can raise companies' awareness of the social costs and benefits of their business activities. The benefits of a sustainability program include addressing environ-mental matters, reducing waste, reducing risk, improving relations with society, and dis-couraging regulatory actions. Sustainability programs enable corporations to take proper actions to promote the social good and advance social goals above and beyond, creating shareholder value or complying with applicable laws and regulations (e.g., antipollution measures). Sustainability programs should also promote a set of voluntary actions that advance the social good and go beyond the company's obligation to its various stakehold-ers. Nonfinancial sustainability activities should be measured and disclosed in the same way as financial activities.

Four implications of sustainability theories and standards are presented in this chapter for businesses that wish to integrate the five EGSEE dimensions of sustainability performance into their strategic decisions and actions. First, the business sustainability framework and its five EGSEE sustainability performance dimensions are driven by and built on the stakeholder theory, which is the process of creating shared values for all stakeholders. Second, the main goal and objective function of business organizations is to maximize firm value. The goal of firm value maximization can be achieved under business sustainability by protecting the interests of all stakeholders, including investors, creditors, suppliers, customers, employees, the environment, and society. Business sustainability promotes the achievement of long-term financial performance that generates enduring future cash flows for investors to maximize their long-term share value and thus maximize overall firm value. Focusing on nonfinancial ESG sustainability performance enables the achievement of long-term firm value maximization by creating value for shareholders while meeting the claims of other stakeholders. The third theme is the time horizon of balancing short-term and long-term performance in all five EGSEE dimensions of sustainability performance. The final theme is the multidimensional nature of sustainability performance in all ESGEE areas. The multidimensional EGSEE sustainability performance is interrelated and should be integrated into supply-chain management.

The International Business Council of the World Economic Forum (WEF, 2018) developed a new paradigm for business sustainability. It suggests a roadmap for corporate governance partnership between corporations and their board of directors and investors, particularly shareholders, to achieve business sustainability performance of long-term investment and growth.[42] The new paradigm focuses on the best practices of business sustainability and corporate governance in forging a meaningful, impactful, and successful private sector solution in advancing business sustainability. The new paradigm suggests focusing on the achievement of long-term performance that generates shared value for all stakeholders. It is expected that the new paradigm will encourage:[43]

1. Public companies and their stakeholders, particularly investors, support tax policies that enable and promote long-term investment.
2. Public companies and their stakeholders, particularly investors, should work toward creating long-term sustainable performance.
3. Close working relationships between government and corporations to obviate the need for regulation and legislation to enforce a longer-term approach.

To achieve this, a collection of key expectations and responsibilities has been created, intended to be used by CEOs and senior leadership to guide corporations and investors into the new paradigm of business sustainability. These expectations charge corporations and investors with the following:[44]

1. Long-term strategy and performance: Discussing and shaping long-term business strategies within corporations and having an open, transparent dialogue with investors regarding said strategy.
2. Engagement: Establishing a relationship with shareholders to understand their perspective on the company's strategy, performance, and governance.
3. Social responsibility and ESG/CSR: Implement high ESG/CSR standards into strategic and operational plans.
4. Risk management: Benchmarking a baseline risk appetite for a corporation and setting standards to comply with legal and regulatory entities. Creating a culture of risk awareness and integrating that into the decision-making process.
5. Monitoring and partnering with management: Maintaining a relationship with management and CEOs to increase the chances of long-term success by monitoring and improving the execution of long-term strategies.
6. Tone at the top: Creating an environment that exudes and values a high level of ethics to guide business practices.

Sustainability principles, theories, and standards explained in this chapter provide rationale and justification for the promotion of sustainability domains. Several domains of sustainability, including economic, social culture, environmental, life, technological, and public policy, are related to sustainability standards and relevant to all five EGSEE dimensions of sustainability performance. These six domains of sustainability are closely linked to the three pillars of planet, people, and profit (TBL) of sustainability, as promoted in ISO 26000 discussed above. For example, the environment and life are associated with the planet pillar, whereas economic and technological domains are linked to the profit pillar, and the social culture and public policy domains are related to the people pillar. Similar to the five EGSEE dimensions of sustainability performance, the six domains of sustainability and related three pillars can be viewed as complementary/completing or conflicting/contra-dicting. This means that business organizations should create the right balance between investing in financial projects that generate profit and non-financial projects (life, social culture, environment) that achieve social and environmental impacts. These sustainability domains can be mapped into the 17 Sustainability Development Goals (SDGs) presented in Chapter 4.[45]

Sustainability Research

Sustainability research consists of a wide range of interdisciplinary studies aimed at under-standing and addressing the complex challenges related to financial ESP and nonfinancial ESG sustainability factors of planning, performance, risk, and disclosure. Researchers investigate issues such as the association between ESP and ESG sustainability perfor-mance, climate change, biodiversity loss, resource depletion, social inequality, and sus-tainable development. Many anecdotal evidence and empirical findings suggest a positive relationship between financial ESP and nonfinancial ESG sustainability performance for companies with strong commitments to governance social and environmental efforts.[46] All five EGSEE dimensions of sustainability performance are important to stakeholders. However, the ESP is regarded as the main objective function for business organizations, primarily because companies have to do well financially in order to do good for society.[47] The 2013 KPMG report suggests the key measures of ESP as financial cash flows, earn-ings and return on investment, nonfinancial operational efficiency, customer satisfaction, talent management, innovation reputation, technology, competition, globalization, and utilization of natural resources.[48] Prior research identifies the six measures of ESP as (1) average return on equity for the current year, (2) sales scaled by total assets, (3) sales growth scaled by total assets, (4) ratio of market to book value of equity, (5) research and development expenses scaled by total assets, and (6) advertising expenses scaled by total assets.[49]

Early sustainability-related research with a primary focus on CSR addresses the rationale for CSR expenditures and the relationship between CSR activities and firm performance.[50]

In compliance with stakeholder theory, CSR/ESG activities are viewed as an integral component of a firm's mission of protecting the interests of all stakeholders, including society and the environment, and as such, ESG expenditures are regarded as investments.[51] Much of the academic literature has focused on CSR and its drivers, performance, and impacts on financial operations earnings and market performance. The extant CSR literature, as reviewed below, suggests that CSR performance is associated with financial performance, how it affects the cost of capital, improves a firm's valuation, impacts stock price crash risk, discloses private information, reduces exposure to risk of conflicts with stakeholders, reduces earnings management and discourages stock short selling and tax avoidance.

Five streams of related research address the various aspects of sustainability. The first stream of research consists of several papers[52] documenting the relevance of green and social initiatives to business by investigating whether it pays to be green and socially responsible and how the business organization should deal with environmental and social issues. This stream of research focuses on the relevance of social and environmental issues to firms' entire value chains, from inbound and outbound logistics to processes and operations, finished products and customer interface, and distribution channels and customer services.

The second stream of research discusses the benefits of sustainability and whether sustainability investments in environmental and social issues pay off in terms of customers' perceptions of products and services. This stream of research[53] often uses the term *sustainable supply chain management* (SSCM) to highlight managerial decisions and actions in achieving financial performance (management of materials, capital flows, production process, and information) and other activities in dealing with environmental and social issues and their comparison with best practices in supply-chain management.

The third stream of research discusses the theoretical framework for business sustainability and its implications for sustainability performance, reporting, and assurance. These studies[54] suggest the use of multiple theories in relating sustainability performance to supply-chain management and other managerial strategies.

The fourth stream of research pertains to the role and use of ISO standards and certifications in improving the quantity and quality of sustainability reporting and assurance. By focusing on the implementation of certification under ISO 14,000 environmental standards, these studies suggest that such certification can promote compliance with environmental regulations and social standards.[55]

These four streams of related research use both conventional financial KPIs, such as earnings and return on investment, and conceptualization KPIs, such as social and

Sustainability Research

environmental performance, in linking sustainability performance to financial performance and supply-chain management.[56] Prior research, while examining several aspects of sustainability performance, reporting, and assurance, has not sufficiently addressed a holistic approach to integrating all five EESG dimensions of sustainability performance into firms' entire value chains, from strategic planning by top-level management to purchasing and inbound logistics, production design and manufacturing process, distribution and outbound logistics and marketing and customer services.

The final stream of research deals with the link between financial and nonfinancial ESG dimensions of sustainability performance and the impact on firms' financial and market performance. Several studies find that corporations that initiate CSR disclosure programs typically exhibit better financial and market performance, as evidenced by reductions in their costs of equity and increases in analyst coverage in the following year.[57] Thus, other studies find that sustainability may result in improved firm performance as proxied by the associations between environmental supply-chain practices and both accounting and market-based financial and operational performance. Overall, these studies report a non-linear relationship between financial and nonfinancial CSR dimensions of sustainability performance, where very small and very large firms are more likely to engage in CSR activities and performance.

Taken together, these five streams of research primarily focus on ESG sustainability issues in an isolated fashion. These studies, while indirectly examining several aspects of business sustainability, have not sufficiently addressed a holistic approach of integrating all five EGSEE dimensions of sustainability performance into corporate culture, business model, management processes, and value chains from the strategic planning of top-level management to purchasing and marketing and customer services. These streams of sustainability research address many emerging sustainability issues, including competition issues (the use of advertising and the arrival of new types of ESG risk with new technology; environmental issues (climate change and regulatory changes for hazardous substances and waste); human rights (labor rights); product responsibility (access, safety, risk, disclosure labeling and packaging); bribery and corruption (financial reporting fraud, financial scandals, money laundering); respect for privacy; ensuring transparency and accountability; institutionalization of ESG; stakeholder engagement; battle for talent; community investment; supply-chain and product safety; social enterprises; and poverty alleviation.

Mandatory and voluntary corporate disclosures provide vital information to the financial markets. The type and extent of voluntary disclosures have recently received considerable attention as more than 40,000 firms worldwide disclose sustainability information on various ESG dimensions of their sustainability performance. Public companies are required to disclose a set of financial statements under the corporate mandatory disclosures regime, and they also disclose other information through corporate voluntary disclosures. Looking from a macroscopic perspective at the issue of effecting widespread business sustainability practices through mandatory or voluntary schemes may give insights into how best to generate clear, concise, and valuable sustainability reporting for different environments. A recent paper by Ioannou and Serafeim[58] seeks to ascertain how these interactions among, in this case, various countries' overall outlooks and contexts influence their leaning toward one dimension of sustainability or another. For example, the researchers found that firms in countries that encourage them to compete tend to focus less on environmental and social concerns, while the same detriments are found in those countries with a majority/plurality of leftist governance. The reasons for the similarity between those two groups, disparate as the two groups may seem to be, lie in the conflicting motivations of the stakeholders in question. The paper suggests that, in the first case, the lower performance in environmental and social matters is due in large part to the increase in competitive efficiencies, while the latter group's actions may be explained by the higher corporate taxes and the subsequent fiscal inability to take on more CSR matters. There is a need for an active balance of the various issues surrounding CSR through a dynamic set of regulations, guidelines, initiatives, and best practices. To that end, there is a great demand for research in this area from the various perspectives of accounting, finance, economics, psychology, sociology, political science, and other disciplines.

Sustainability research typically involves collaboration between scholars, scientists, policymakers, businesses, NGOs, and community stakeholders to develop evidence-based and data-driven solutions to pressing global sustainability challenges by examining ESG factors, generating knowledge, informing decision-making, and fostering innovation. Thus, sustainability research plays an essential role in shaping a more sustainable and resilient future for society and the environment. The key areas of sustainability research cover: (1) financial ESP sustainability and financial viability including the effects of designing products, materials, and systems to minimize waste, maximize resource efficiency, and promote reuse, recycling, and regeneration by exploring research models, strategies, and policies to support the transition to a more sustainable economy; (2) climate change research of examining the causes, impacts, and mitigation strategies related to climate change, assessing greenhouse gas emissions, developing renewable energy technologies, evaluating climate models, and exploring adaptation measures; (3) biodiversity research focuses on examining the diversity of life on Earth and its importance for ecosystem functioning, and conservation efforts aim to protect endangered species, promote sustainable use of natural resources and preserve habitats; (4) corporate social responsibility of investigating the role of businesses in promoting sustainability through CSR, sustainable supply-chain

Sustainability Research

management, environmental management systems, sustainable business models and social issues of poverty, inequality, human rights, and social justice; and (5) research on corporate governance, regulatory policies and corporate strategies by examining sustainability issues, challenges and opportunities that inform policymaking and governance at local, national, and international levels about the effectiveness of environmental regulations and cooperation and coordination among stakeholders.

Business Sustainability Education

Sustainability education is an interdisciplinary field intended to foster knowledge, skills, attributes, and values to contribute to a more sustainable and equitable, socially responsible, environmentally conservative world by promoting formal sustainability education in schools, colleges, and universities and informal education through community programs, public outreach, and awareness campaigns. The global investment community is holding public companies responsible and accountable for their business activities and their financial reporting process. As business schools are the main providers of professional accountants, they play important roles in preparing ethical and competent future business leaders who understand business sustainability. The public, regulators, the accounting profession, and the academic community are taking a closer look at colleges and universities to explore ways to hold these institutions more accountable for achieving their mission of providing higher education with relevant curricula. Therefore, business sustainability education and research have recently been addressed by the global community and accreditation bodies. For example, the Association of Advanced Collegiate School of Business (AACSB) International has established an Ethics/Sustainability Resource Center, and it probes questions like "Do you think business schools should conduct more research on sustainability and how business can contribute to it?" on its website. All respondents, as of July 17, 2012, have responded "Yes" to this question, suggesting there is an urgent need to research sustainability.[59] The AACSB, in its accrediting standards (Standard 9), identifies sustainability as a knowledge area by stating that "society is increasingly demanding that companies become more accountable for their actions, exhibit a greater sense of social responsibility, and embrace more sustainable practices."[60]

The proposed integrated framework for defining the post-2015 UN development agenda suggests a vision built based on the core values of human rights, equality, and sustainability for the entire world's present and future generations. Four key dimensions of the UN integrated framework are inclusive of social development, economic development, environmental sustainability, and peace and security.[61] Despite all progress in business sustainability education development, it appears that research and education in business sustainability are fragmented, and there is a lack of an integrated approach covering all five EGSEE dimensions in many universities.

Business sustainability has been one of the top five emerging education majors in the past decade, as suggested by the Chronicle for Higher Education.[62] Sustainability is also considered one of the hottest and most demanding majors that lead to jobs.[63] Realizing the importance of incorporating sustainability into curriculums, academics are trying to integrate sustainability into higher education. Business sustainability practices require an integrated approach to sustainability reporting and assurance, and sustainability education demands a knowledge base in both financial ESP and nonfinancial ESG sustainability performance and reporting. Despite the importance of sustainability disclosures to corporations and investors and the move toward integrated sustainability reporting and assurance, there is limited research on the integration of sustainability education into the business curriculum. Academics examine the coverage of sustainability education and find that as demand for and interest in sustainability education has increased in recent years, more business schools are planning to provide such education.[64]

Realizing the importance of incorporating sustainability into curricula, academics are trying to integrate sustainability in higher education, including studies focused on business, management, and accounting education. For example, the Association for Advancement of Sustainability in Higher Education (AASHE) (2010) tries to explore the needs of a curriculum that "prepares learners for living sustainably, both professionally and personally, and that explicitly helps the learner deeply understand the iterations, inter-connections, and the consequences of actions and decisions." However, sustainability has to be taught holistically, and different aspects of sustainability have to be covered and linked effectively. An academic study presents a matrix of options for integrating sustainability in management and business education and illustrates how the matrix can be used, using the example of a business school in the Northeastern United States, including lessons learned.[65] The matrix provides a framework for discussion, as well as a framework for action – since it provides faculty, staff, and administrators with options for integrating sustainability and includes advantages, disadvantages, and recommendations for using each option.

Business sustainability practices require an integrated approach to sustainability reporting and assurance, and sustainability education demands a knowledge base in both financial ESP and nonfinancial ESG sustainability performance and reporting. Despite the importance of sustainability disclosures to corporations and investors and the move toward integrated sustainability reporting and assurance, there is limited research on the integration of sustainability education into the business curriculum. Another study examines the coverage of sustainability education and finds that as demand for and interest in sustainability

Business Sustainability Education

education has increased in recent years, more business schools are planning to provide such education.[66] The coverage of sustainability education topics in a separate course or their integration into existing business courses requires the classification of related topics into teaching modules covering both financial ESP and nonfinancial ESG dimensions of sustainability performance. Exhibit 5.1 presents a model of business sustainability education with the main goal of providing cutting-edge sustainability education in all aspects of sustainability including theories, practice and sustainability performance, reporting, and assurance. Many factors, including the availability of teaching resources, cost and benefit feasibility, quality accreditation, technology and innovation, regulatory compliance, and commitment from administrators and faculty, constrain the achievement of sustainability education goals.

North American and European business schools typically offer their sustainability education at the graduate level. Christensen et al. (2007) examine how deans and directors at the top 50 global MBA programs respond to questions about the inclusion and coverage of the topics of ethics, corporate social responsibility, and sustainability at their respective institutions. They find that a majority (about 84%) of business schools require that one or more of the three topics (ethics, corporate social responsibility, and sustainability) be covered in their MBA curriculum, and there is a trend toward the inclusion of sustainability-related courses. More students are interested in these topics, and experiential learning and immersion techniques are used to teach them. Another academic paper reports that only 27% of universities in Australia and New Zealand require students to take one or more ethics, social responsibility, and/or sustainability core courses.[67] Another study also found that institutions of higher education are exploring ways to integrate sustainability into their curriculum.[68] The area of sustainability is often discussed in isolation by business academic leaders with a focus on green reporting in accounting, sustainability development in management, and supply-chain sustainability strategies in marketing and finance. It is also covered in other disciplines, such as social sciences, engineering, and biological sciences, in the context of the global move toward sustainability. A content analysis of a sample of sustainability accounting courses from the websites of universities finds that about 30% of these universities have information about their sustainability accounting education on their websites.[69]

Business sustainability, corporate governance, and professional ethics are taking center stage in the global business environment, and thus, universities and colleges worldwide are offering degree programs and courses on these topics. Currently, more than 450 universities worldwide are offering courses in business sustainability. Business schools play an important and everlasting role in preparing the next generation of business leaders with life-long education and training to promote acting with integrity, upholding the highest levels of ethical conduct, and shouldering the heavy burden of public trust. The next generations of business leaders must understand the importance of ethical conduct, business sustainability, and corporate governance corporations to our society and the complexity of financial reporting. Thus, the business curriculum must reflect courses in ethical behavior, professional accountability, and personal integrity. Exhibit 5.4 presents a sample of these universities with their course offerings and website addresses. More universities are expected to offer such courses and programs.

Academic organizations such as the American Accounting Association (AAA) are supporting the integration of sustainability education into business and accounting curricula. The AAA has recently promoted the integration of sustainability education into the accounting and business curricula. For example, the AAA organized a two-day conference on February 17 and 18, 2023, entitled "Sustainability, ESG, and Accounting: Implications for the Academy and the Profession Conference" and another ESG sustainability education conference in February 2024, entitled "Sustainability, ESG, and Accounting: Implications for the Academy and the Profession: One Year Later."[70] The 2023 and 2024 AAA conferences are intended to bring in regulators, investor executives, and academics together to share best practices in integrating sustainability education into the accounting curriculum, discuss the demand for ESG sustainability education, learn about the existing ESG sustainability-related courses and how to make these courses more relevant and useful to accounting students. The AAA has sponsored a survey to find the demand for and interest in sustainability education and the need for the establishment of a "Sustainability Accounting Section" (SAS). More than 80% of the 463 respondents reported that they are expecting future demand for and interest in business sustainability practice and education to increase, and there is a need to establish a SAS within the AAA.[71]

Overall, sustainability education plays a crucial role in enabling individuals, organizations, and businesses to become informed, engaged, and effective agents of change in building a more sustainable future for present and future generations by providing knowledge, skills, and values needed to address sustainability challenges; education contributes to creating a more resilient and vibrant financial market as well as equitable and thriving society. Some key aspects of sustainability education are: (1) focusing on sustainability education of both financial ESP and nonfinancial ESG sustainability factors; (2) considering sustainability education as a multidisciplinary approach consisting of all relevant disciplines, including environmental science, social sciences, business, economics, ethics, and policy studies; (3) encouraging holistic thinking and interdisciplinary collaboration to address complex sustainability challenges and to provide appropriate sustainability education; (4) emphasizing hands-on, experiential learning approaches such as field trips,

Business Sustainability Education

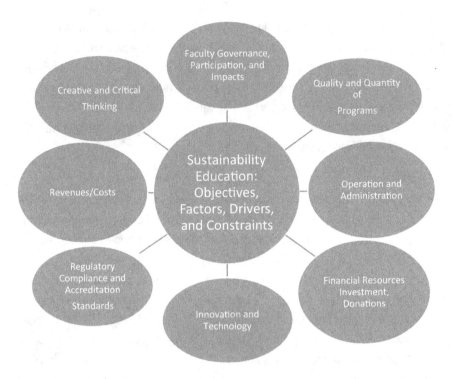

EXHIBIT 5.2   Sustainability Education and Its Attributes

internships, service-learning projects to enable students to engage directly with real-world sustainability issues, develop practical skills, and apply classroom knowledge in authentic settings; (5) promoting critical thinking skills by encouraging students to study sustainability factors and assumptions, evaluate evidence, and analyze complex problems from multiple perspectives and to learn to identify root causes of sustainability challenges and opportunities and to develop innovative solutions through collaborative inquiry and problem-solving activities; and (6) promoting life-long learning and action-oriented learning of emphasizing the importance of taking action to create positive change in local communities and globally by engaging in projects, campaigns, and advocacy efforts aimed at promoting sustainability, raising awareness, and expanding sustainability education throughout life by encouraging life-long learning and continuous personal and professional development and education to stay informed about sustainability issues, update skills, and adapt to changing circumstances.

Sustainability Certifications

All professions have their certification of professionalism, competency, compliance, and ethical conduct, and the field of sustainability is no exception. The business and accounting profession worldwide has adapted over time to many standards and has been shaped by a variety of internal and external factors. One of the most influential factors contributing to the professionalism and refinement of any profession is the certification program. At the same time, there are several certifications in accounting, and the certified public accountant (CPA) is viewed as the highest credential in the accounting profession. Education requirements are typically a prerequisite for almost all certifications. Sustainability certifications cover a wide range of knowledge, skills, and experience, reflecting the growing global emphasis on environmental conservation, social responsibility, and economic viability. The SASB sponsors the Fundamentals of Sustainability Accounting (FSA) Credential.[72] The FSA enables the certificate holders to stand out from their peers as leaders and experts in sustainability, to obtain cutting-edge learning materials on sustainability-related issues, and to be able to assist their organizations in integrating sustainability into their business environment, corporate culture, and managerial strategic plans, decisions, and actions.

The FSA Credential consists of the following three parts:[73]

Part I: The Need for Sustainability Accounting Standards: This part provides candidates with the historical, legal, accounting, and investing context for learning the importance of material sustainability information to the capital markets and why this is relevant for sustainability accounting.

Part II: Understanding SASB Sustainability Accounting Standards: Part II presents the importance and relevance of the industry-focused sustainability standards and why an industry-specific approach to identifying sustainability information is value-relevant.

Part III: Using SASB Standards: Part III describes the implications of industry-specific sustainability standards and related material sustainability information and outlines considerations for using SASB standards for all professionals and organizations regardless of types and sizes.

Certification can be obtained at Level I and Level II; candidate information is available at FSA@sasb.org. As of March 22, 2019, more than 700 candidates have signed up for Level I, and more than 200 in 22 countries have earned the FSA credential.[74] The SASB provides FSA Level 1 learning objectives and curriculum outlines to candidates. Almost all professional certifications in accounting, including the CPA certification, require a bachelor's degree in accounting or business with a concentration in accounting as part of their education requirements. Education requirements of many certifications are related to (1) technical skills such as financial accounting, auditing, management accounting, sustainability taxes, and statistical courses; (2) soft skills such as courses in critical thinking,

Sustainability Certifications

corporate governance, ethics, business sustainability, and organization behavior and communication; and (3) analytical skills in information technology, computer literacy, and analytical reasoning.

All professional business and accounting certifications require candidates to take an exam to prove understanding of a common body of knowledge in the designated certifications, and FSA certification is no exception. Several other organizations provide certification or recognition for aligning their activities with the United Nations SDGs, demonstrating their commitment to addressing global challenges such as poverty, inequality, and climate change. Many accounting and business professional certifications require work experience as either a prerequisite for being eligible to take the exam or to become certified. Thus, work experience in sustainability is very relevant to obtaining FSA credentials. Continuing professional education (CPE) programs are often required to maintain the certification's good standing and are intended to ensure that certificate holders keep abreast with developments in their profession. The effectiveness of CPE programs in sustainability depends on their coverage of emerging issues affecting business sustainability factors of performance, risk, and disclosure. The business schools have recently been faced with increased scrutiny demanding changes in business sustainability, corporate governance measures, risk assessment, cybersecurity, climate change planning, and electronic accounting and auditing processes. To meet these challenges, business students and certificate holders should keep pace with advances and update their technical, analytical, and soft skills. One way to obtain, secure, and document the required skills is through the CPE programs.

Summary

Business sustainability requires business organizations to focus on achieving all five EGSEE dimensions of sustainability performance by taking initiatives to advance social good beyond their interests, compliance with applicable regulations, and enhancement of shareholder wealth. Simply put, business sustainability means enhancing corporations' positive impacts and minimizing their negative effects on society, as well as minimizing harm to society and the environment and creating positive impacts on shareholders, the community, the environment, employees, customers, and suppliers.

Business sustainability has been debated in the literature and has changed business organizations' strategies and practices in focusing on long-term and multidimensional sustainability performance. Corporations' primary goals have refocused from maximizing profit to increasing shareholder wealth. Now, in light of the moves toward business sustainability worldwide, those goals are shifting toward creating shared values for all stakeholders, including shareholders. Companies today face the challenges of adapting proper business models and sustainable supply-chain management strategies and practices to effectively respond to social, ethical, environmental, and governance issues while creating sustainable financial performance and values for their shareholders. Scholars also attempt to adopt an appropriate sustainability theory to explain the relationship between financial ESP and nonfinancial governance, as well as social, ethical, and environmental sustainability performance.

All theories, including agency/shareholder, stakeholder, signaling, institutional, legitimacy, and stewardship, focus on key measures of sustainable performance, such as operational efficiency, customer satisfaction, talent management, and innovation. These theories are derived from internal factors of strategy, risk profiles, strengths and weaknesses, and corporate culture, as well as external factors of reputation, technology, completion, globalization, and utilization of natural resources. These theories and standards help explain companies' objectives, as reflected in management strategies and practices of creating sustainable values for shareholders while protecting the interests of other stakeholders such as creditors, employees, customers, suppliers, government, and society. In conclusion, the sustainability principles, theoretical framework and practical sustainability standards, research, and education suggest that:

1. Sustainability strategies should be integrated into corporate decision-making processes, including strategic decisions on supply-chain management in promoting the achievement of all five EGSEE dimensions of sustainability performance.
2. Companies should use a principles-based approach in integrating both financial ESP and nonfinancial ESG sustainability performance information into their corporate reporting.
3. All theories, including agency/shareholder, stakeholder, signaling, legitimacy, institutional, and stewardship, focus on key measures of sustainable performance such as operational efficiency, customer satisfaction, talent management, and innovation, should be derived from internal factors of strategy, risk profile, strengths and weaknesses, and corporate culture as well as external factors of reputation, technology, competition, globalization, and utilization of natural resources.
4. These theories help in explaining companies' objectives of creating sustainable value for shareholders while protecting the interests of other stakeholders, such as creditors, employees, customers, suppliers, government, and society.
5. Cutting-edge business sustainability education should stem from relevant theories to standards to promote its integration into the relevant components of business curriculums in colleges and universities.

Key Points

- Integration of sustainability performance into business and investment analysis, supply-chain management and decision-making process, business culture, corporate environment, and business policies and practices.

- Incorporation of all five EGSEE dimensions of sustainability performance into scholarly research.

- Integrate sustainability principles into business sustainability research and education to advance the promotion of appropriate disclosure of sustainability performance.

- Collaboration among all stakeholders to enhance the effectiveness of implementing sustainability theories, programs, and development.

- Faculty and administrators in colleges and universities should continue to add business sustainability education as a subject or topic to be integrated into relevant curriculums.

- There are tremendous opportunities for playmakers, regulators, standard-setters, researchers, and academics to establish more effective sustainability guidelines, provide sustainability education, and conduct sustainability research.

Review Questions

1. What is the main focus of the "Finance First" investment strategy?
2. What is the middle-ground view of sustainability performance?
3. What is the stance of the CFA Institute on considering ESG issues in investment decisions?
4. What organization established ten sustainability principles, and how many companies have adopted them?
5. From which perspectives are sustainability principles derived?
6. What is the main implication of shareholder/agency theory for sustainability performance?
7. How does legitimacy theory justify the importance of social and environmental dimensions of sustainability performance?
8. What does institutional theory focus on in the context of business sustainability?
9. What is the primary focus of resource dependence theory (RDT)?
10. What does social network theory (SNT) study?
11. What does integrated sustainability theory suggest for businesses?

12. **What does ISO 9000 focus on?**
13. **What is the purpose of ISO 20121?**
14. **What are the two perspectives from which sustainability principles are derived?**
15. **What factors affect the relative importance of the five EESG dimensions of sustainability performance?**

Discussion Questions

1. **What is the goal of firm value maximization under business sustainability?**
2. **How does the shareholder/agency theory view the primary responsibility of management?**
3. **According to the chapter, what are some benefits of engaging in ESG activities?**
4. **What is the primary focus of the stewardship theory?**
5. **What are the three key elements of the strategic choice theory (SCT)?**
6. **What is data-driven storytelling (DDS) theory used for?**
7. **What does ISO 9000 address?**
8. **What does ISO 26000 provide guidance on?**
9. **How does stewardship theory view management?**
10. **What is the main goal of business sustainability according to the chapter?**
11. **What does ISO 37001 address?**
12. **What are some key aspects of sustainability education?**
13. **What are the four key dimensions of the UN integrated framework for sustainability?**
14. **What does the stakeholder theory emphasize in terms of business activities?**
15. **What is the impact of effective corporate governance on sustainability?**

Multiple-Choice Questions

1. **What are the five dimensions of sustainability performance discussed in this chapter?**
   A) Financial, Operational, Strategic, Ethical, Environmental
   B) Economic, Governance, Social, Ethical, Environmental
   C) Financial, Strategic, Governance, Environmental, Social
   D) Economic, Social, Technological, Environmental, Ethical

2. **What does the legitimacy theory suggest about firms and social contracts?**
   A) Firms should only focus on financial performance
   B) Firms engage in voluntary disclosure activities to obtain legitimacy and fulfill their social contract
   C) Firms should reduce operational transparency
   D) Firms should maximize short-term profits

3. **What is resource dependence theory (RDT) concerned with?**
   A) Reducing operational costs
   B) Managing interdependence and external power struggles
   C) Maximizing short-term profits
   D) Enhancing customer satisfaction

4. **What does social network theory (SNT) study?**
   A) Financial performance metrics
   B) Social interactions and relationships affecting information flow
   C) Operational efficiencies
   D) Market share analysis

5. **What are the benefits of implementing ISO standards in sustainability?**
   A) Promoting compliance with environmental regulations, social standards, and improving the quality of products and services
   B) Reducing transparency and limiting stakeholder engagement
   C) Focusing solely on financial performance
   D) Enhancing short-term profits

6. **What is the focus of ISO 14000 standards?**
   A) Quality management systems
   B) Environmental management systems
   C) Social responsibility
   D) Risk management

7. **What is the purpose of ISO 31000 standards?**
   A) Quality management systems
   B) Social responsibility
   C) Environmental management systems
   D) Risk management

8. **What are the goals of sustainability standards?**
   A) Promoting financial ESP and nonfinancial ESG sustainability performance
   B) Reducing transparency and limiting stakeholder engagement

C) Focusing solely on short-term profits

D) Enhancing market share

9. **What are the core subject areas of ISO 26000?**

A) Human rights, labor practices, environment, fair operating practices, consumer issues, community involvement and development

B) Quality management systems, environmental management systems, risk management

C) Financial reporting, market analysis, operational efficiency

D) Short-term profits, market share, customer satisfaction

10. **What is the significance of impact investing?**

A) Maximizing short-term profits

B) Generating financial returns while also creating positive social and environmental impacts

C) Reducing operational costs

D) Enhancing market share

11. **How does the chapter define sustainability performance?**

A) Maximizing short-term shareholder profit

B) Considering the impact on all stakeholders, including the community, society, and the environment

C) Reducing operational costs

D) Enhancing market share

12. **What is the role of institutional theory in sustainability?**

A) Focusing solely on financial performance

B) Emphasizing the social aspects of CSR and the conditions under which these decisions impact society and the environment

C) Reducing operational costs

D) Enhancing market share

13. **What is the implication of legitimacy theory for business sustainability?**

A) Firms must engage in sustainability practices to maintain societal support and legitimacy

B) Firms should only focus on financial performance

C) Firms should reduce operational transparency

D) Firms should maximize short-term profits

14. **What are the benefits of adopting the stakeholder primacy model for companies?**

A) Improved reputation, risk mitigation, stronger stakeholder relationships, and long-term sustainability

B)   Reducing operational costs and increasing shareholder wealth

C)   Focusing solely on financial performance

D)   Limiting stakeholder engagement and reducing transparency

15.   **What is the focus of ISO 50000 standards?**

A)   Quality management systems

B)   Social responsibility

C)   Energy management systems

D)   Risk management

16.   **What is the significance of stakeholder governance in achieving business sustainability?**

A)   Reduces transparency and limits stakeholder engagement

B)   Promotes long-term performance, enhances reputation, and creates a positive impact on society and the environment

C)   Focuses solely on financial performance

D)   Minimizes regulatory compliance and reduces costs

17.   **What does resource dependence theory (RDT) explain?**

A)   The dynamic of power in interorganizational relations and managing interdependence and external power struggles

B)   The focus solely on financial performance

C)   Reducing transparency in sustainability reporting

D)   Limiting stakeholder engagement

18.   **What are the benefits of implementing ISO standards in sustainability?**

A)   Promoting compliance with environmental regulations, social standards, and improving the quality of products and services

B)   Reducing transparency and limiting stakeholder engagement

C)   Focusing solely on financial performance

D)   Enhancing short-term profits

19.   **What is the focus of ISO 14000 standards?**

A)   Quality management systems

B)   Environmental management systems

C)   Social responsibility

D)   Risk management

20.   **What is the purpose of ISO 31000 standards?**

A)   Quality management systems

B)   Social responsibility

C) Environmental management systems

D) Risk management

21. **What are the goals of sustainability standards?**

A) Promoting financial ESP and nonfinancial ESG sustainability performance

B) Reducing transparency and limiting stakeholder engagement

C) Focusing solely on short-term profits

D) Enhancing market share

22. **What are the core subject areas of ISO 26000?**

A) Human rights, labor practices, environment, fair operating practices, consumer issues, community involvement and development

B) Quality management systems, environmental management systems, risk management

C) Financial reporting, market analysis, operational efficiency

D) Short-term profits, market share, customer satisfaction

23. **What is the significance of impact investing?**

A) Maximizing short-term profits

B) Generating financial returns while also creating positive social and environmental impacts

C) Reducing operational costs

D) Enhancing market share

24. **How does the chapter define sustainability performance?**

A) Maximizing short-term shareholder profit

B) Considering the impact on all stakeholders, including the community, society, and the environment

C) Reducing operational costs

D) Enhancing market share

25. **What is the role of institutional theory in sustainability?**

A) Focusing solely on financial performance

B) Emphasizing the social aspects of CSR and the conditions under which these decisions impact society and the environment

C) Reducing operational costs

D) Enhancing market share

26. **What is the implication of legitimacy theory for business sustainability?**

A) Firms must engage in sustainability practices to maintain societal support and legitimacy

B) Firms should only focus on financial performance

C) Firms should reduce operational transparency

D) Firms should maximize short-term profits

27. **What are the benefits of adopting the stakeholder primacy model for companies?**

A) Improved reputation, risk mitigation, stronger stakeholder relationships, and long-term sustainability

B) Reducing operational costs and increasing shareholder wealth

C) Focusing solely on financial performance

D) Limiting stakeholder engagement and reducing transparency

28. **What is the focus of ISO 50000 standards?**

A) Quality management systems

B) Social responsibility

C) Energy management systems

D) Risk management

29. **What is the significance of stakeholder governance in achieving business sustainability?**

A) Reduces transparency and limits stakeholder engagement

B) Promotes long-term performance, enhances reputation, and creates a positive impact on society and the environment

C) Focuses solely on financial performance

D) Minimizes regulatory compliance and reduces costs

30. **What does resource dependence theory (RDT) explain?**

A) The dynamic of power in interorganizational relations and managing interdependence and external power struggles

B) The focus solely on financial performance

C) Reducing transparency in sustainability reporting

D) Limiting stakeholder engagement

Notes

1 CFA Institute. (2015). Environmental, social, and governance issues in investing: A guide for investment professionals. https://www.cfainstitute.org/-/media/documents/article/position-paper/esg-issues-in-investing-a-guide-for-investment-professionals.ashx.

2 Rezaee, Z. (2016). Business sustainability research: A theoretical and integrated perspective. *Journal of Accounting Literature* 36: 48–64.

3 Ng, A.C., and Rezaee, Z. (2015). Business sustainability performance and cost of equity capital. *Journal of Corporate Finance* 34: 128–149.

4 The Sustainability Laboratory. (2015). Sustainability: Definition and five core principles. http://www.sustainabilitylabs.org/assets/img/SL5CorePrinciples.pdf.

5 UN Global Compact (2013).

6 Brockett, A., and Rezaee, Z. (2012). *Corporate Sustainability: Integrating Performance and Reporting*. Wiley.

7 Rezaee, Z. (2016). Business sustainability research: A theoretical and integrated perspective. *Journal of Accounting Literature* 36: 48–64.

8 Shleifer, A., and Vishny, R. (1997). A survey of corporate governance. *Journal of Finance* 52: 737–783.

9 Jensen, M. (2001). Value maximization, stakeholder theory, and the corporate objective function. *European Financial Management* 7: 297–317.

10 Jensen, M. (2001). Value maximization, stakeholder theory, and the corporate objective function. *European Financial Management* 7: 297–317.

11 Clarkson, P.M., Li, Y., Richardson, G.D., and Vasari, F.P. (2011). Does it really pay to be green? Determinants and consequences of proactive environmental strategies. *Journal of Accounting and Public Policy* 30: 122–144.

12 Freeman, R.E. (1984). *Strategic Management: A Stakeholder Approach*. Pitman.

13 Mitchell, R.K., Agle, B.R., and Wood, D.J. (1997). Toward a theory of stakeholder identification and salience: Defining the principle of who and what really counts. *The Academy of Management Review* 22 (4, October): 853–886.

14 Freeman, R.E. (1984). *Strategic Management: A Stakeholder Approach*. Pitman, 46.

15 Guthriea, J., and Parker, L.D. (1989). Corporate social reporting: A rebuttal of legitimacy theory. *Accounting and Business Research* 19 (76): 343–352.

16 Guthriea, J., and Parker, L.D. (1989). Corporate social reporting: A rebuttal of legitimacy theory. *Accounting and Business Research* 19 (76): 343–352.

17 Grinblatt, M., and Hwang, C. (1989). Signaling and the pricing of new issues. *Journal of Finance* (June 1989): 393–420.

18 Grinblatt, M., and Hwang, C. (1989). Signaling and the pricing of new issues. *Journal of Finance* (June 1989): 393–420.

19 Connelly, B.L., Ketchen, D.J., and Slater, S.F. (2011). Toward a "theoretical toolbox" for sustainability research in marketing. *Journal of the Academy of Marketing Science* 39 (1): 86–100.

20 Meyer, J., and Rowan, B. (1977). Institutionalized organizations: Formal structure as myth and ceremony. *American Journal of Sociology* 83: 340–363.

21 Hernandez, M. (2008). Promoting stewardship behavior in organizations: A leadership model. *Journal of Business Ethics* 80: 121–128.

22 Hernandez, M. (2012). Toward an understanding of the psychology of stewardship. *Academy of Management Review* 37 (2): 172–193.

23 http://webuser.bus.umich.edu/gfdavis/Papers/davis_cobb_09_RSO.pdf.

24 http://webuser.bus.umich.edu/gfdavis/Papers/davis_cobb_09_RSO.pdf.

Notes

25 http://journals.sagepub.com/doi/pdf/10.1177/0149206309343469.

26 http://journals.sagepub.com/doi/pdf/10.1177/0149206309343469.

27 Weil, D. (2005). A strategic choice framework for union decision making. *Journal of Labor and Society* 8 (3): 327–347.

28 Institute for Manufacturing (2016). Strategic choice approach. https://www.ifm.eng.cam .ac.uk/research/dstools/strategic-choice-approach/.

29 Kadushin, C. (2012). The ten master ideas. In *Understanding Social Networks: Theories, Concepts, and Findings*. Oxford University Press.

30 Hirschi, C. (2010). Introduction: Applications of social network analysis. *Procedia Social and Behavioral Sciences* 4: 2–3.

31 Asgari, M. and Hurtut, T. (2024). A design language for prototyping and storyboarding data-driven stories. *Applied Sciences* 14, (4): 1387, 2024.

32 Bansal, P., and Hunter, T. (2003). Strategic explanations for the early adoption of ISO 14001. *Journal of Business Ethics* 46: 289–299.

33 International Organization for Standardization (ISO). (2010). ISO 26000 – Social Responsibility. http://www.iso.org/iso/iso_catalogue/management_and_leadership _standards/social_responsibility/sr_iso26000_overview.htm#sr-1.

34 Rezaee, Z. (2016). Business sustainability research: A theoretical and integrated perspective. *Journal of Accounting Literature* 36: 48–64.

35 International Organization for Standardization (ISO). (2018). ISO 37001 – Anti-bribery Management Systems. https://www.iso.org/iso-37001-anti-bribery-management.html.

36 The Foreign Corrupt Practices Act (FCPA). (1977). Anti-bribery and books & records provisions of the FCPA. https://www.justice.gov/sites/default/files/criminal-fraud/legacy/2012 /11/14/fcpa-english.pdf.

37 International Organization for Standardization (ISO). (2018). ISO 37001 – Anti-bribery Management Systems. https://www.iso.org/iso-37001-anti-bribery-management.html.

38 International Organization for Standardization (ISO). (2018). ISO 45001 – Occupational Health and Safety. www.iso.org/iso-45001-occupational-health-and-safety.html.

39 International Organization for Standardization (ISO). (2018). ISO 50001 – Energy Management. https://www.iso.org/iso-50001-energy-management.html.

40 https://www.isealalliance.org/.

41 https://www.astm.org/.

42 The International Business Council of the World Economic Forum (WEF). (2018). The new paradigm. http://www.wlrk.com/docs/thenewparadigm.pdf.

43 The International Business Council of the World Economic Forum (WEF). (2018). The new paradigm. http://www.wlrk.com/docs/thenewparadigm.pdf.

44 The International Business Council of the World Economic Forum (WEF). (2018). The new paradigm. http://www.wlrk.com/docs/thenewparadigm.pdf.

45 James, P., and Magee, L. (2017). Domains of Sustainability. *Global Encylopedis of Public Administration.* https://www.researchgate.net/publication/313794820_Domains_of _Sustainability

46 Rezaee, Z. (2016). Business sustainability research: A theoretical and integrated perspective. *Journal of Accounting Literature* 36: 48–64.

47 Rezaee, Z. (2016). Business sustainability research: A theoretical and integrated perspective. *Journal of Accounting Literature* 36: 48–64.

48 KPMG. (2013). Beyond quarterly earnings: Is the company on track for long-term success? Spring 2013 Audit Committee Roundtable Report. auditcommittee@kpmg.com.

49 Ng, A.C., and Rezaee, Z. (2015). Business sustainability performance and cost of equity capital. *Journal of Corporate Finance* 34: 128–149.

50 Roman, R., Hayibor, S., and Agle, B. (1999). The relationship between social and financial performance. *Business and Society* 38 (1): 109–125.

51 Freeman, R.E. (1984). *Strategic Management: A Stakeholder Perspective.* Prentice-Hall.

52 Corbett, C.J., and Klassen, R.D. (2006). Extending the horizons: Environmental excellence as key to improving operations. *Manufacturing and Service Operations Management* 8 (1): 5–22.

53 Rao, P., and Holt, D. (2005). Do green supply chains lead to economic performance? *International Journal of Operations and Production Management* 25 (9): 898–916.

54 Carter, C.R., and Easton, P.L. (2011). Sustainable supply chain management: Evolution and future directions. *International Journal of Physical Distribution & Logistics Management* 41 (1): 46–62.

55 Clarkson, P.M., Li, Y., Richardson, G.D., and Vasari, F. P. (2008). Revisiting the relation between environmental performance and environmental disclosure: An empirical analysis. *Accounting, Organizations and Society* 33 (4–5): 303–327.

56 Kleindorfer, P.R., K. Singhal, and Van Wassenhove, L.N. (2005). Sustainable operations management. *Production and Operations Management* 14 (4): 482–492.

57 Dhaliwal, D., Li, O., Tsang, A., and Yang, Y. (2011). Voluntary nonfinancial disclosure and cost of equity capital: The initiation of corporate social responsibility reporting. *The Accounting Review*, 86: 59–100.

58 Ioannou, I., and Serafeim. G. (2010). What drives corporate social performance? International evidence from social, environmental and governance scores. Harvard University Working Paper No. 11-016, Harvard Business School. www.hbs.edu/faculty/Publication%20Files/11 -016.pdf.

59 AACSB International. (2012). Ethics/sustainability resource center. http://www.aacsb.edu /resources/ethics-sustainability/.

60 AACSB International. (2015). Eligibility procedures and accreditation standards for business accreditation. www.aacsb.edu/_/media/AACSB/Docs/Accreditation/Standards /2013-bus-standards-update-jan2015.ashx.

Notes

61 United Nations Global Compact (UNGC). (2014). Guide to Corporate Sustainability. www .unglobalcompact.org/docs/publications/UN_Global_Compact_Guide_to_Corporate _Sustainability.pdf.

62 Fischer, K., and Glenn, D. (2009). Five college majors on the rise. *The Chronicle of Higher Education*. http://chronicle.com/article/5-College-Majors-On-the-Rise/48207/.

63 Gandel, C. (2013). Discover 11 hot college majors that lead to jobs. *US News and World Report*. www.usnews.com/education/best-colleges/articles/2013/09/10/discover-11-hot-college-majors-that-lead-to-jobs?

64 Rezaee, Z., and Homayoun, S. (2014). Integrating corporate sustainability education into the business curriculum: A survey of academics. *Journal of the Academy of Business Education* (Spring): 11–28.

65 Rusinko, C.A. (2010). Integrating sustainability in higher education: A generic matrix. *International Journal of Sustainability in Higher Education* 11 (3): 250–259. https://doi.org /10.1108/14676371011058541.

66 Rezaee, Z., and Homayoun, S. (2014). Integrating business sustainability education into the business curriculum: A survey of academics. *Journal of the Academy of Business Education* 15: 6–83.

67 Rundle-Thiele, S.R., and Wymer, W. (2010). Stand-alone ethics, social responsibility, and sustainability course requirements. *Journal of Marketing Education* 32 (1): 5–12.

68 Rusinko, C.A., and Sama, L.M. (2009). Greening and sustainability across the management curriculum: An extended journey. *Journal of Management Education* 33: 271–275. https:// doi.org/10.1177/1052562908327639.

69 Rezaee, Z. and Homayoun, S. (2014). Integrating corporate sustainability education into the business curriculum: A survey of academics. *Journal of the Academy of Business Education* (Spring 2014): 11–28.

70 American Accounting Association (AAA). (2024). Sustainability, ESG, and accounting: Implications for the academy and the profession: One year later (February 16–17, 2024). Washington DC. https://aaahq.org/Meetings/2024/Sustainability-ESG-Accounting.

71 American Accounting Association (AAA). (2023). Sustainability questionnaire in establishing a "Sustainability Accounting Section" (SAS) within the American Accounting Association (AAA). *AAA Communications*. <info@aaahq.org> https://www.surveymonkey.com/survey-closed/?sm=M1_2F_2FlpY6M_2FdG_2F4Lft0K_2BbbBmSIqsW2FJ9al0 _2FOqmi1O3_2FPdapRshK_2FlERJ9nghOlm_2FJ8wGRklV73x1yatnN1KeOGyMhepp7K7T _2FnEs_2BNvG8_3D, January 31, 2023.

72 Sustainability Accounting Standards Board (SASB). (2019). About the FSA credential. https://fsa.sasb.org/credential/.

73 Sustainability Accounting Standards Board (SASB). (2019). About the FSA credential. https://fsa.sasb.org/credential/.

74 Sustainability Accounting Standards Board (SASB). (2019). The fundamentals of sustainability accounting (FSA) credential (March 22). https://fsa.sasb.org/infographic/.

Chapter 6
Drivers and Sources of Business Sustainability Initiatives

Learning Objectives

- Learn voluntary sustainability initiatives.
- Understand mandatory sustainability requirements.
- Understand the global voluntary and mandatory business sustainability initiatives.
- Explain the objectives of the Global Reporting Initiative (GRI).
- Provide an overview of the drivers and sources of sustainability guidelines.
- Address the sustainable frameworks released by different organizations.
- Provide an overview of the Delaware Act of 2018.
- Explain the purpose of the framework released by the Sustainability Accounting Standards Board (SASB).
- Discuss the objectives of the United Nations Global Compact regarding Sustainability.
- Discuss the purpose of the framework released by the United Nations Sustainable Development Goals (UNSDGs).
- Learn the objectives of the Carbon Disclosure Project (CDP).
- Understand Corporate Sustainability Reporting Directive (CSRD).
- Learn about the European Sustainability Reporting Standards (ESRS).

Introduction

Many public companies now voluntarily manage, measure, recognize, and disclose their commitments, events, and transactions relevant to environmental, social, and governance (ESG) dimensions of sustainability performance. Several mandatory and voluntary initiatives are driven by a combination of internal and external factors, as well as strategic considerations and ethical imperatives to guide business organizations in their sustainability reporting. There is a move toward the establishment of a globally accepted reporting and assurance framework for sustainability information that creates uniformity in objectively reporting both financial economic sustainability performance (ESP) and nonfinancial ESG sustainability performance. Both voluntary and mandatory sustainability initiatives are

DOI: 10.4324/9781003487081-6

driven by: (1) regulatory and legal requirements as global governments are increasingly implementing regulations and laws aimed at addressing ESG issues and noncompliance with these regulations can cause legal risks and penalties; (2) consumer demand as growing awareness among consumers about ESG issues has led to increased demand for sustainable products and services to attract and retain customers; (3) investor Pressure as institutional investors, asset managers, and shareholders are placing greater focus on ESG) factors presented in Chapter 1: (4) cost savings and efficiency improvements as sustainability initiatives can lead to cost savings through improved resource efficiency, energy conservation and waste reduction; (5) stakeholder expectations for businesses to operate responsibly and contribute positively to society and the environment for creating trust and relationships with stakeholders, addressing environmental and social risks, such as climate change, resource scarcity, and supply chain disruptions that can have significant impacts on operations and profitability, and presenting opportunities for innovation and the development of new products, technologies, and business models; and (6) long-term business viability of recognizing the link between ESP and ESG to ensure the long-term viability and resilience in a rapidly changing world and to establish corporate values and culture, reflecting the beliefs and commitments of company leaders, employees, and stakeholders to a more sustainable future. These and other suggestions for developing a set of globally accepted best practices for sustainability performance, reporting, and assurance are presented in this chapter with a focus on drivers of sustainability performance reporting and assurance. This chapter discusses initiatives and drivers of recent moves toward business sustainability performance and integrated sustainability reporting and assurance. Integrated sustainability performance reporting can be promoted through market forces, mandatory sustainability reporting by listing standards of stock exchanges, or a combination of mandatory and voluntary initiatives. The combination of mandatory initiatives, including regulatory requirements and voluntary initiatives such as consumer demand, financial incentives, risk management considerations, and ethical imperatives, drives businesses to adopt sustainability guidelines and frameworks as integral components of their strategies and operations.

Mandatory Business Sustainability Initiatives

Mandatory business sustainability initiatives are those requirements and regulations imposed by governments or regulatory bodies that compel businesses to integrate sustainability factors of planning, performance, risk, and disclosure into their corporate culture, business environment, managerial decisions, and operations. These initiatives aim to address both financial ESP and nonfinancial ESG issues and concerns and ensure that businesses operate in a manner that maximizes shareholder wealth while minimizing negative social and environmental impacts and promoting long-term sustainable development. Global and national stock exchanges have promoted sustainability performance reporting by adopting laws, regulations, and listing standards that specifically mandate sustainability reporting. In recent years, many countries, including Australia, Austria, Canada, Denmark, France, Germany, Hong Kong, Malaysia, Netherlands, Sweden, and the United Kingdom, have adopted mandatory reporting on financial ESP and nonfinancial ESG sustainability performance.[1] It is expected that regulators in other countries will follow suit, moving toward mandatory sustainability performance reporting and assurance. Stock exchanges worldwide either require or recommend that their listed companies report sustainability information (e.g., Singapore Stock Exchange, 2011; Toronto Stock Exchange, 2014; Hong Kong Stock Exchange, 2016), and more than 6000 European companies are required to disclose their nonfinancial GSEE sustainability performance and diversity information for their financial year 2017 and onwards.[2] The 2018 Delaware Act is a voluntary disclosure regime requiring adopted reporting entities to provide reports on their sustainability and related standards and metrics.[3]

Regulators worldwide have addressed ESG-related disclosure requirements. And established mandatory sustainability initiatives relevant to climate change, human capital, and board and workforce diversity, equity, and inclusion. Examples of globally accepted mandatory business sustainability initiatives are "Waste Reduction and Recycling," "Carbon Footprint Reduction," "Water Conservation," and "Compliance with Environmental Regulations." Business organizations should tailor these mandatory sustainability initiatives to their specific industry, size, and operations and update their sustainability initiatives to stay current with ever-increasing standards and best practices. Laws, rules, regulations, and industry standards can drive mandatory initiatives. The risk of noncompliance with mandatory sustainability initiatives can be very costly as the risk of ESG-related litigation compliance regulatory actions and shareholders' demand continues to grow. Companies should effectively and comprehensively review their ESG-related strategy, risk, and disclosure. The global sustainable finance market is expected to grow because of new central banks and regulatory actions and the implementation of more rigorous criteria for ESG-labeled products. Companies should consider relevant opportunities to participate in this market. Financial regulators focus on climate risk management and climate change's effects on financial stability. Financial institutions should assess their current approach to climate risks and opportunities and prepare for new requirements and supervisory expectations.

In the past several decades, growing concerns regarding financial scandals (e.g., Enron, WorldCom, Parmalat, and Satyam), the environmental impact, corporate social responsibility, governance, and ethical behavior of corporations have encouraged policymakers and

Mandatory Business Sustainability Initiatives

regulators to address these concerns by establishing laws and regulations to mitigate their negative impacts. Regulations in the United States require that corporate directors focus on business activities that increase corporate value for the benefit of shareholders. One example in the United States is the passage of the Sarbanes-Oxley Act (SOX) of 2002 to combat financial statement fraud and prevent further occurrences of financial scandals by improving corporate governance and financial reporting and audit processes.[4] SOX and the related Securities and Exchange Commission (SEC) regulations also require public companies in the United States to establish and maintain effective internal controls over financial reporting to combat fraud and irregularities in reporting related to governmental laws and SEC regulations. The SEC, in the past several decades, has issued numerous regulations for disclosure of environmental liabilities, including Releases Number 5170 in 1971, Number 5386 in 1973, the climate change interpretive guidance in 2010, and conflict minerals rules in 2012.[5]

In 2021, the SEC considered releasing its proposed Climate Risk Disclosure Requirements rule by registrants. On March 21, 2022, the SEC released its proposed rule changes requiring registrants to disclose certain climate-related information in their registration statements and periodic reports. The proposed disclosures contain information about climate-related risks that are reasonably likely to impact registrants' financial results and conditions, including disclosure of a registrant's greenhouse gas emissions.[6] On March 6, 2024, the SEC released its Final Rules Regarding Mandatory Climate Risk Disclosures that require: (1) climate risk disclosures be included in a company's SEC filings, such as annual reports and registration statements by making the filings more reliable; (2) disclosure of material climate-related risks faced by a company as well as any governance and processes used by the company to manage climate-related risks by updating Regulation S-K to require; (3) larger registrants, specifically large accelerated filers and accelerated filers, to disclose direct Greenhouse Gas (GHG) emissions (Scope 1) and emissions associated with energy purchases (Scope 2) when those emissions are material; (4) important financial statement footnote disclosures on expenditures resulting from severe weather events and disclosure of disclose capitalized costs, expenses, charges, and losses as a result of such events; (5) a disclosure of material impacts on financial estimates and assumptions; and (6) a level of third-party review subject to attestation standards of those emissions data to increase their veracity and reliability to disclose a quantitative dataset of GHG emissions subject to a gatekeepers' review.[7] These rules are intended to enhance the disclosures needed by investors to make their investment decisions as they benefit from the consistency, comparability, and reliability of these disclosures. Climate change disclosures are aimed at providing investors insight into the financial impact of climate change on companies today for understanding companies' forward-looking disclosures in Regulation S-K.

The SEC is planning to propose further Rules for Human Capital Management (HCM) and Board Diversity Disclosure. In August 2020, the SEC adopted rules to modernize human capital disclosure.[8] In July 2023, the Financial Accounting Standards Board (FASB) issued a proposal to mandate that companies disaggregate the reporting of major operating costs, thus requiring public companies to disclose employee compensation costs included in the income statement.[9]

The European Commission has also been promoting corporate social responsibility (CSR) and its integration into corporate strategic decisions by defining CSR as "a concept whereby companies integrate social and environmental concerns in their business."[10] This definition of CSR suggests that companies should take actions beyond their mandatory requirements toward the promotion of social and environmental benefits. Business sustainability with a keen focus on CSR can "benefit in terms of risk management, cost savings, access to capital, customer relationships, human resource management, and innovation capacity."[11] Disclosure of this information promotes interaction with all stakeholders related to non-financial ESG sustainability performance. Disclosure of nonfinancial ESG sustainability performance demonstrates companies' commitment and move toward achieving the European Union's treaty objectives of "the Europe 2020 strategy for smart, sustainable and inclusive growth including the 75% employment target."[12] At the same time, it facilitates stakeholders' engagements regarding sustainable growth and understanding of risks. It also helps stakeholders build trust in the company by understanding how capitals are allocated, and long-term investment goals are achieved.

On September 29, 2014, the European Commission endorsed the adoption of the Council Directive on disclosure of nonfinancial sustainability information for more than 6000 large public companies for their financial year 2017.[13] The primary objectives of the Directive are to (1) increase transparency in sustainability reporting, (2) increase sustainability performance on social and environmental matters, and (3) contribute effectively to long-term economic growth and employment. In addition to reporting on their operations, covered organizations will need to include information about their supply chain. Affected companies should report their environmental performance, social and employee-related information, human rights policies, anticorruption and bribery issues, and diversity on the board of directors.

In January 2023, the EU Corporate Sustainability Reporting Directive (CSRD) was released, which would require mandatory sustainability reporting for European companies and their counterparts and trading partners worldwide.[14] The CSRD is designed to complement existing sustainability-focused regulations and voluntary frameworks and standards of the Global Reporting Initiative (GRI) and the International Sustainability Standards Board

Mandatory Business Sustainability Initiatives

(ISSB) and will have a global implication. For example, US-domiciled public and private companies with significant EU revenue would be subject to CSRD's reporting requirements. The CSRD requires covered companies to disclose historical and forward-looking information relevant to sustainability matters, including ESG issues and information about sustainability risk management, metrics, and value chain due diligence for EU companies starting July 2023 and onwards. The first sustainability reports in compliance with CSRD requirements covering non-EU companies are not due until 2029, and early compliance is encouraged. Specifically, the CSRD applies to:

1. Large EU-domiciled companies.
2. All EU-listed companies, wherever incorporated.
3. Any public or private company headquartered outside the European Union that has consolidated annual "net turnover" in the European Union exceeding €150 million in each of the last two fiscal years.
4. An EU branch with net revenue exceeding €40 million in the last fiscal year or an EU subsidiary that meets two of the following criteria for the last fiscal year: (a) average of more than 250 employees during the year and (b) annual net turnover of more than €40 million balance sheet over €20 million.

The European Financial Reporting Advisory Group (EFRAG) adopted in July 2023 the European Sustainability Reporting Standards (ESRS) under the CSRD of the European Union.[15] These standards are intended to enhance and harmonize the reporting of ESG factors of performance and risk by companies within the European Union, ensuring greater transparency and consistency in sustainability reporting and assurance. Objectives of ESRS are to (1) improve the transparency of companies' ESP and ESG sustainability performance; (2) ensure consistency and comparability of sustainability information across different companies and sectors; and (3) provide stakeholders, including shareholders, creditors, customers, suppliers, employees, regulators and policymakers, with relevant and reliable sustainability information. These standards focus on providing guidelines for: (1) environmental reporting relevant to environmental matters and areas such as climate change mitigation and adaptation, biodiversity, pollution, water and marine resources, and circular economy; (2) social reporting of issues and matters like customer reputation and satisfaction, employee well-being, diversity and inclusion, human rights, and community impacts; and (3) governance reporting of corporate governance matters relevant to corporate governance structures, measures, functions, business ethics, anti-corruption measures, and risk management. The core guiding principles of these standards are: (1) double materiality of considering both financial materiality relevant to sustainability issues affect the company's financial performance and environmental/social materiality reflecting how the company impacts the environment and society; (2) sector-specific standards of customized requirements for different sectors to address industry-specific sustainability challenges and impacts; and (3) forward-Looking information of focusing on reporting future-oriented data, such as sustainability targets, strategic planning, and trajectories. These standards require mandatory reporting and assurance for all large companies and listed SMEs in the European Union, encompassing a wide range of sectors, and are designed to improved sustainability reporting aids investors and other stakeholders in making informed decisions, enhance companies' reputation and brand value, and meet regulatory requirements and align with EU sustainability goals and policies. Overall, the ESRS aims at providing comprehensive and standardized sustainability reporting and assurance in Europe, reflecting the European Union's commitment to sustainable development and responsible business practices.

In April 2018, the Canadian Securities Administrators (CSA), the organization representing the 13 provincial and territorial securities commissions, published the results of its climate-change-related disclosure review project.[16] This report suggests that:

- Regulators, investors, businesses, and other stakeholders have increased their expectations of board oversight in setting a tone at the top regarding ESG matters, particularly climate change.
- Proxy advisory firms consider the quality and quantity of ESG disclosures when making recommendations.
- Management commitments to improving ESG disclosure in general and climate-related risks in particular are important in promoting business sustainability and should be a management priority.

Another example includes the revision of the Danish Financial Statements Act in Denmark in requiring sustainability reporting, the guidelines for external reporting of ESG sustainability performance by state-owned companies in Sweden, and mandatory integrated reporting under the Grenelle II Act in France and the King Code III in South Africa.[17]

In summary, mandatory sustainability initiatives are those requirements imposed by governments or regulatory bodies and intended to compel businesses to integrate sustainability factors into their operations to address ESG issues, concerns, and challenges and ensure that businesses operate in a manner that minimizes negative social and environmental impacts and promotes long-term sustainable development and financial viability. The mandatory initiatives presented in this section consist of: (1) environmental regulations intended to mitigate environmental pollution, conserve natural resources, and reduce

Mandatory Business Sustainability Initiatives

greenhouse gas emissions including those relevant to emission standards, waste disposal requirements, and energy efficiency; (2) carbon pricing and emissions trading schemes to incentivize businesses to reduce their carbon footprint and to adopt cleaner technologies and practices; (3) corporate governance requirements to promote transparency, account-ability, and ethical behavior including having independent board directors, establish-ing ethics and compliance programs, and disclosing executive compensation details; (4) sustainable reporting requirements to report on their financial ESP and nonfinancial ESG sustainability performance and related metrics to provide stakeholders with transparent information about businesses' sustainability efforts; (5) supply chain transparency regula-tions of requiring businesses to disclose information about their supply chains, including environmental and social risks, labor practices, and human rights impacts; (6) biodiver-sity conservation requirements aimed at protecting biodiversity and ecosystems that may impose restrictions on businesses' activities in environmentally sensitive areas to conduct environmental impact assessments and implement measures to mitigate their impacts on biodiversity; and (7) waste management, reduction and recycling requirements to promote waste reduction, recycling, and circular economy principles to separate waste streams, recycle materials, and minimize landfill disposal through extended producer responsibility (EPR) programs and to ensure sustainable water management practices, including water use efficiency, pollution prevention, and watershed conservation. These mandatory busi-ness sustainability initiatives play a vital role in driving corporate responsibility, advanc-ing the transition toward a more sustainable economy, mitigating environmental and social risks, and maintaining their license to operate and uphold their social license from stakeholders.

Voluntary Business Sustainability Initiatives

Voluntary business sustainability initiatives are actions taken by individuals, professional organizations, and companies that go beyond regulatory requirements to address finan-cial ESP and nonfinancial ESG sustainability factors of planning, performance, risk, and disclosure to promote economic viability, reduce environmental footprint, and enhance social responsibility. These initiatives demonstrate a company's commitment to both ESP and ESG sustainability and involve activities such as promoting financial viability, sup-porting community development, reducing greenhouse gas emissions, minimizing waste generation, and promoting ethical labor practices. Business organizations can take vol-untary initiatives to address their sustainability issues and challenges by establishing a comprehensive framework to guide them in developing their sustainability factors of planning, performance, risk, and disclosure. Voluntary sustainability initiatives refer to business organizations' programs, strategic plans, actions, or projects to address their

ESP and ESG sustainability performance. Several organizations worldwide, including the GRI, International Integrated Reporting Council (IIRC), Sustainability Accounting Standard Board (SASB), the United Nations Global Compact, and ISSB have issued guiding principles and standards regarding voluntary disclosure of sustainability performance information. The effective implementation of these voluntary initiatives can demonstrate corporations' commitments to promote business sustainability, improve corporate credibility and reputation, ensure social and environmental impacts, and prevent excessive mandatory government sustainability initiatives.

Global Reporting Initiative

The GRI was launched in 1997 to bring consistency, complete, and global standardization to sustainability reporting. The evolution of GRI guidelines began with the initial focus on incorporating environmental performance into corporate reporting with its first publication, *Sustainability Reporting Guidelines*, in 2000. The GRI Sustainability Reporting Guidelines are updated periodically to reflect new developments in sustainability reporting. Guideline G4 was released in May 2013 pursuant to the initial guidelines of G1, G2, and G3. The G4 Guideline presents Reporting Principles, Standard Disclosures, and an Implementation Manual for sustainability reporting on economic, governance, social, and environmental sustainability performance metrics, with ethics being integrated into the other four metrics. The G4 Guideline is to be used by all organizations regardless of their type, size, sector, or location.[18] It focuses more heavily on materiality considerations in the reporting process and final report. The intention is to make sustainability reports "more relevant, more credible and more user-friendly" by encouraging companies to center their reports on the organization's goals and the impacts it may have on society and other stakeholders.[19] In this Guideline, the GRI promotes sustainability reporting as a standard practice of disclosing sustainability-related issues that are relevant to companies' businesses and their stakeholders.

The G4 Guideline has two parts. "Reporting Principles and Standard Disclosures" contains the criteria necessary for an organization to prepare its sustainability report "in accordance" with the Guideline, and the "Implementation Manual" instructs practitioners on how to apply the Reporting Principles, how to prepare disclosure information, and how to interpret various concepts in the Guideline. The G4 Guideline also provides a set of steps to follow for preparing a sustainability report, namely (1) how organizations must obtain an overview and understanding of the guidelines; (2) choose their preferred option for compliance ("in accordance") from Core or Comprehensive based on the needs of the organization and its stakeholders; (3) prepare to disclose the General Standard Disclosures, then the

Voluntary Business Sustainability Initiatives

Specific Standard Disclosure (both based on the compliance option selected in step 2); and (4) finally prepare the sustainability report and decide how to disseminate it.[20] G4 introduces 27 new disclosures with a new structure for the guidance documents. G4 provides guidance on how to select material topics and illustrates the boundaries of where these occur. In G4, there are two options, namely core and comprehensive, which concentrate on the process of defining material aspects and boundaries. The revised guidelines emphasize materiality in sustainability reporting and include new and updated disclosures in various areas including governance (G4-34-55), ethics and integrity (G4-56-58), supply chain (G4-12 and G4-EC9), anticorruption (G4-SO3-SO6), energy (G4-EN3-EN7), and greenhouse gas (GHG) emissions (G4-EN15-21).

The Global Sustainability Standards Board (GSSB) was published in 2020 by the GRI and was among the first globally accepted standards for sustainability reporting. These GSSBs were established as independent operating entities under the auspices of GRI. The GSSB is made up of 15 members representing a range of expertise and multi-stakeholder perspectives on sustainability reporting. The GSSB operates under the GSSB Terms of Reference to oversee the development of the GRI Standards according to a formally defined due process.[21] The GSSB works exclusively in the public interest and according to the vision and mission of GRI. The GRI launched its 2021 Universal Standards in October 2021, which represent the most important update on ESG sustainability reporting, from providing GRI guidance to setting standards for sustainability.[22] The 2021 Universal Standards strengthen the basic foundations of all sustainability reporting through GRI, focusing on transparency, due diligence, and material topics that impact the economy, environment, and people for global organizations of all types and sizes. The 2021 updated GRI standards include a consolidated set of standards, including GRI 1 Foundations, GRI 2 General Disclosures, GRI 3 Material Topics, GRI 11 Oil and Gas Sector, GRI 201 Economic Performance, GRI 202 Market Presence, GRI 203 Indirect Economic Impacts, GRI 204 Performance Practices, and GRI 205 Anticorruption.[23]

International Integrated Reporting Council (IIRC)

The IIRC is a global coalition of investors, regulators, standard-setters, public companies, non-governmental organizations (NGOs), the accounting profession, and academia. In April 2013, the IIRC released the draft of its framework consultation on integrated reporting, which provides guidelines for communication with stakeholders.[24] The IIRC's proposed framework addresses fundamental concepts of integrated reporting and its guiding principles on an organization's strategy, governance, performance, and prospects. The IIRC, in its December 2013 Integrated Reporting Framework, promotes a more integrated approach to corporate reporting by improving the quality and quantity of information disseminated to providers of financial capital, including shareholders and other stakeholders.[25]

In late September 2015, the IIRC appointed a new board of directors that is "reflective of the global reach and influence of integrated reporting across a broad range of areas including Africa, North and South America, Asia, Europe, and Oceania." The board consists of experts from areas of banking, finance, government, and retail. According to Paul Druckman, IIRC Chief Executive, over 1000 businesses worldwide use integrated reporting in 27 countries.[26] The IIRC suggests six capitals – (1) financial capital, (2) manufactured capital, (3) intellectual capital, (4) human capital, (5) social and relationship capital, and (6) natural capital – that organizations can utilize in creating shared value for all stakeholders.[27] In compliance with stewardship theory, management is responsible for stewarding corporate resources with an ethical vision toward how to benefit the broader society. Management should not impose its vision of "good" on society, but instead seek compliance with regulatory measures and the best practices of sustainability. However, a stewardship mindset requires that management strategies and actions be focused on the continuous improvement of both financial ESP and nonfinancial GSEE components of sustainability performance in compliance with the integrated sustainability framework of the IIRC.

The IIRC also published a framework known as the Integrated Reporting (IR) Framework, which describes how companies should communicate with their shareholders. An "Integrated Report" promotes transparency and addresses how an organization's performance will benefit both shareholders and stakeholders. The purpose of the report is to be a further extension of a company's external financial reports and is aimed at a specialist audience, such as regulators and lawyers. The IIRC also released a prototype to aid in the compilation of nonfinancial and financial information.

Sustainability Accounting Standards Board (SASB)

The SASB is an independent non-profit organization that aims to establish and release sustainability accounting standards to enable public corporations to disclose material, decision-useful sustainability information to investors.[28] In October 2013, the SASB released its Sustainability Conceptual Framework consisting of objectives, key definitions, and characteristics of sustainability accounting and disclosures, methodology for assessing the materiality of sustainability issues, and structure and harmonization of sustainability accounting standards.[29] The SASB has developed sustainability accounting standards relevant to disclosing material sustainability issues for 88 industries in ten sectors. The SASB establishes and creates sustainability accounting standards suitable for developing measures to disclose material sustainability issues as well. The standards launch the process for mandatory filings to the SEC, such as Form 10-K and 20-F, through the first quarter of 2015. The SASB's objective is to create standards that enable peer-to-peer comparison between companies, which can be useful for investment decisions and capital allocation. Harmonizing the SASB standards with existing disclosure standards avoids additional costs for companies and aligns the SASB's work with global corporate transparency efforts.

United Nations Global Compact

The 2013 *Global Corporate (GC) Sustainability Report* released by the United Nations Global Compact (UNGC) addresses the state of corporate sustainability today and presents the actions taken by companies worldwide in integrating sustainability into their strategies, operations, and culture. The report encourages companies to engage their suppliers in the establishment of more sustainable practices and integration of sustainability into their supply chain processes.[30] The report finds that companies are increasingly focusing on business sustainability and making progress in setting expectations for their suppliers to integrate sustainability into their strategies and practices. Other benefits of sustainability reporting are improved reputation, increased employee loyalty, and customer satisfaction. However, several sustainability challenges could be threatening business value if they are not addressed properly, but these challenges can also be turned into business opportunities.

According to the recent update on global sustainability by the UNGC, over 12,000 organizations in over 160 countries are currently members of the Global Compact, with the majority coming from Europe and Latin America.[31] The new guide presents the performance of member organizations worldwide with respect to the ten principles of the UNGC that are related to human rights, labor, the environment, and anticorruption. The report indicates that investors continue to demand that companies act upon and report sustainability, while companies have found that it is beneficial to integrate corporate responsibility into their business operations. These new initiatives enhance stakeholder relations, improve commitment by the CEO, promote internal information sharing, and provide information for investors.[32]

United Nations Sustainable Development Goals (UNSDGs)

In September 2015, the United Nations (UN) proposed a holistic framework of the Sustainable Development Goals (SDGs) to design indicators and an integrated monitoring framework to address all three dimensions of economic development, social inclusion, and environmental sustainability.[33] The 17 SDGs build on the United Nations Millennium Development Goals of 2000–2015 and involve new areas such as climate change, economic inequality, innovation, sustainable production and consumption, and peace and justice.[34] These SDGs are relevant to three dimensions of sustainability development: economic, social, and environmental development, and thus can be linked to all EGSEE dimensions of sustainability performance. There are 169 targets and 232 indicators that support the SDGs, and they are aligned with GRI G4 performance indicators.[35] Some of the SDGs (e.g., SDGs 5, 10, and 16) are applicable to the nature of life below the water and life on land, and others (e.g., SDGs 14 and 15) are relevant to human rights and equality. Corporations frequently use these goals and link them to sustainability performance from the sourcing of raw materials and inputs for production to product innovations that lead to positive impacts on the environment, health, or society; employee safety, training, and diversity; compliance with ethical principles and human rights standards; and community initiatives in the areas of health and well-being, education, employment, and economic empowerment.

The 17 United Nations SDGs are related to sustainability reporting and assurance as they address economic, social, ethical, governance, and ecological sustainability performance. In November 2016, the International Federation of Accounting (IFAC) published a policy document that considers many of the 17 SDGs relevant to the accounting profession, including those that address quality education, gender equality, economic growth, innovation, production, climate action, and societal issues.[36] The 2017 report of PricewaterhouseCoopers (PwC) suggests that the majority of global firms (over 62%) referred to the SDGs in their reporting.[37]

Social Investment Forum (SIF)

In 2009, the Social Investment Forum (SIF) requested that the Obama Administration take the initiative to restore investor confidence by strengthening mandatory reporting on ESG initiatives.[38] To provide more accountability, the SIF proposed that the SEC require public companies to (1) report annually their sustainability information in compliance with the GRI guidelines and (2) disclose their short-term and long-term sustainability risks in the Management Discussion and Analysis (MD&A) section of their 10-K forms.[39] Furthermore, in March 2013, the United States SASB released its proposed sustainability accounting standards for the healthcare sector (SASB 2013).[40] A 2013 Joint Study by the Investor Responsibility Research Centre Institute (IRRCI) and the Sustainable Investments Institute (Si2) reports that only 1.4% of S&P 500 companies (seven firms) issued a stand-alone sustainability report by mentioning sustainability reporting in their regulatory filing of 10-K reports. In contrast, almost all S&P 500 companies disclosed at least one piece of sustainability information, 74% placed monetary value on their sustainability-related disclosures, and about 44% of the companies linked their executive compensation to some sustainability criteria.[41]

The Carbon Disclosure Project (CDP)

The Carbon Disclosure Project (CDP) is an international, not-for-profit organization that includes 655 institutional investors and collects information from companies on their greenhouse gas emissions and assessment of climate change and water risk and opportunity. The CDP website hosts many functions for the exploration of climate data. The CDP open-data portal allows a user to search for relevant scores, emissions, and other necessary data related to carbon indices and various other climate conditions. Through data sharing and outreach, the CDP's goal is to ensure that resources are used reliably and efficiently to reduce the overall carbon footprint. The Climate Disclosure Standards Board is an organization that hosts multiple NGOs from around the globe. Similar to the CDP, the board intends to improve the dissemination of information regarding the environment through a framework that was released in 2010. On November 6, 2012, the CDP and the Climate Disclosure Standards Board (CDSB) released the XBRL climate change reporting taxonomy.[42] This taxonomy streamlines the process of reporting climate change information so that the information can be more easily promulgated into financial reports and dispersed to the interested parties.

In summary, in June 2011, the Global Initiative for Sustainability Ratings (GISR) developed ESG rating standards with an eye toward maximum harmonization with leading complementary standard-setters, most notably the GRI, the IIRC,[43] the CDP, and SASB.[44] Harmonizing SASB standards with existing disclosure standards avoids additional costs for companies and aligns the SASB's work with global corporate transparency efforts. In April 2013, the IIRC released the draft of its framework consultation on integrated reporting intended to provide guidelines on communication with stakeholders.[45] The IIRC's proposed framework addresses fundamental concepts of integrated reporting and its guiding principles on an organization's strategy, governance, performance, and prospects. The products of the SASB, GRI, and IIRC can be used in complementary ways for the development of a sustainability report for investors and all stakeholders. The SASB provides standards developed to meet materiality standards, supported by the US courts and capital markets, consistent with current US mandatory financial reporting standards. In contrast, GRI and

IIRC provide frameworks for voluntary reporting of relevant, not necessarily material, information internationally.

Delaware Act of 2018

The Delaware Certification of Adoption of Transparency and Sustainability Standards Act (the "Act") was signed into law on June 27, 2018, as described in detail in Chapter 4. The Act represents Delaware's initiative to support sustainability practices by encouraging Delaware-governed entities to disclose their commitment to CSR and Sustainability. The Act is intended to promote sustainability, is voluntary, and applies only to entities governed by Delaware law that choose to become certified as reporting entities. The Act gives entities much flexibility in developing their sustainability strategies and practices to meet their sustainability goals and needs. As of March 22, 2019, only one company (DSM North America, Inc.) has complied with the voluntary provisions of the ACT, whereas about 50% of public companies in the United States have registered in the State of Delaware.

The 2018 Delaware Act is a voluntary disclosure regime requiring adopted reporting entities to provide reports on their sustainability and related standards and metrics. Reporting entities are provided with the flexibility to report on their financial as well as nonfinancial sustainability performance while maintaining their privileged information, trade secrets, or competitively sensitive information. Thus, Delaware entities that decide to disclose their sustainability performance information can obtain certification from the Delaware Secretary of State under the Act as to their transparency in sustainability reporting. This certification demonstrates the entity's commitment to sustainability efforts and compliance with related sustainability standards and measures and serves as a signal to investors, clients, and customers that the entity is taking its sustainability efforts seriously.

The CFA Institute

In recent years, the CFA Institute has promoted the relevance of nonfinancial ESG in investment decision-making. The CFA Institute, in its 2015 report entitled Environmental, Social, and Governance Issues in Investing: A Guide for Investment Professionals states that "For investment professionals, a key idea in the discussion of ESG issues is that systematically considering ESG issues will likely lead to more complete investment analyses and better-informed investment decisions."[46] The CFA Institute suggests that every investor, investment analyst, and portfolio manager should know about and consider the investment opportunities and risks posed by ESG issues and factors. The CFA Institute guide

Voluntary Business Sustainability Initiatives

for investing is divided into three chapters: Chapter 1 presents background information needed to understand ESG considerations in investing, Chapter 2 describes the application of different methods of considering ESG issues, and Chapter 3 provides salient issues in the debate on ESG considerations. The guide explains six methods that investors have used to integrate ESG into investment decisions. These methods are exclusionary screening, best-in-class selection, thematic investing, active ownership, impact investing, and ESG integration. These methods are not intended to be mutually exclusive and are usually used in combinations by both value- and values-motivated investors.

In January 2019, the CFA Institute released an updated ESG policy statement that addresses the growing importance of global ESG and the focus placed on ESG factors of performance, disclosure, and risk by public companies and investment management.[47] This policy statement highlights the CFA positions on the integration of ESG factors into investment decisions by focusing on the quality, relevance, and comparability of the ESG information provided by public companies and how to integrate ESG factors of performance, disclosure, and risk into the investment selection process. The CFA positions suggest that proper consideration of ESG factors by financial professionals can strengthen their fundamental analysis and improve their investment choices. The CFA Institute, in addition to encouraging all investment professionals and financial analysts to use ESG factors in their investment analyses, is developing ESG-focused curricula and educational tools for its members, CFA candidates, and the broader investment management industry. ESG sustainability factors of performance, risk, and disclosure should enable investors to achieve the desired rate of returns on their investment while encouraging their company to engage in activities that generate social and environmental impacts. To fully integrate ESG factors into investment decisions, the integrated sustainability reports providing ESG information need to be standardized, refined, and consistently reported across industry sectors.

European Commission

The European Commission (EC) has been promoting disclosure of nonfinancial ESG with its proposal in April 2013, and then the Parliament voted on the Directive in April 2019 in 2014. Finally, the EC adopted a directive in 2014 that requires more than 6000 European companies to disclose ESG sustainability performance information as well as diversity in their 2017 financial reports and onwards.[48] The primary objectives of the EC Directive are to increase sustainability transparency, improve sustainability performance on environmental and social matters, and contribute effectively to long-term economic growth and employment. All publicly traded companies with at least 500 employees, banks, insurance companies, and public-interest entities as designated by national governments, which overall includes approximately 6000 large companies and groups across the European Union. Specifically, the sustainability reporting companies must disclose environmental performance, social and employee-related matters, human rights policies, anticorruption and bribery issues, and diversity on the board of directors. The affected companies in Europe should also include ESG sustainability information about their suppliers.

On January 10, 2019, the Technical Expert Group on Sustainable Finance (Financial Stability, Financial Services and Capital Markets Union, Banking and Financial Services) published its report on climate-related sustainability disclosures.[49] This report is intended to establish climate-related metrics based on the EU sustainability taxonomy to improve the disclosure of climate-related information. It includes recommendations to update its nonbinding guidelines on nonfinancial ESG reporting with specific reference to climate-related information.

International Sustainability Standards Board (ISSB)

The International Financial Reporting Standards (IFRS) Foundation's consultation on establishing a global nonfinancial ESG reporting framework has highlighted the need for global sustainability reporting standards and received strong support from investors, the corporate sector, accounting professionals, policymakers, regulators, and central banks. These sustainability disclosure initiatives, whether mandatory or voluntary, are intended to reflect the financial, social, and environmental impacts of a company's business operation and, thus, provide relevant and reliable financial and nonfinancial information for all stake-holders, including investors. There are debates among policymakers and scholars that international accounting standard-setters, such as the FASB and International Accounting Standards Board (IASB), should issue accounting standards for proper disclosure of ESG sustainability information. In April 2021, IRFS put out an exposure draft proposing targeted amendments to the Foundation's Constitution to create IFRS sustainability standards. In this exposure draft, the suggested proposals include expanding the Foundation's efforts to create a new board to set sustainability standards, creating the ISSB under IFRS governance, and amending the Foundation's governance structure. The exposure draft also included several pieces about the IFRS Foundation, including its objectives, governance, trustees, and further information about the IASB, the Monitoring Board, and the Interpretations Committee.

The ISSB is a sustainability standard-setting body created by the IFRS Foundation in November 2021. The ISSB's mission is to establish sustainability-related financial reporting standards to satisfy investors' information demands and needs for sustainability reporting.

Voluntary Business Sustainability Initiatives

The primary mission of the ISSB is to establish global sustainability-related disclosure standards that provide investors and other capital market participants with material and relevant sustainability information about companies' factors of planning, performance, risk, and disclosure to enable them to make informed decisions. The ISSB is established to function on four key principles: comprehensive global baseline, consolidation, and building on existing initiatives (e.g., GRI, SASB), informed by the ISSB reporting expert advice and global footprint. In March 2022, the ISSB issued two exposure drafts of proposed general sustainability-related disclosure requirements (IFRS S1) and climate-related disclosure requirements (IFRS S2).

IFRS S1 establishes overall standards for disclosing sustainability-related financial information to provide stakeholders, including investors, with a complete set of sustainability-related financial disclosures. IFRS S2 establishes the requirements for identifying, measuring, and disclosing climate-related risks and opportunities. These two proposals are driven by the recommendations of the Task Force on Climate-Related Financial Disclosures (TCFD) and industry-based disclosure requirements of SASB standards. In June 2023, the ISSB issued its inaugural global sustainability disclosure standards of IFRS S1 and IFRS S2 to establish a common language for disclosing the effect of climate-related risks and opportunities on a company's prospects. IFRS S1 provides a set of disclosure requirements intended to assist companies in communicating with their investors about sustainability-related risks and opportunities. IFRS S2 establishes specific climate-related disclosures and is intended to be used with IFRS S1.

Business sustainability initiatives, both mandatory and voluntary, are intended to shape and influence sustainability factors of planning, performance, risk, and disclosure. These sustainability initiatives address many sustainability factors of: (1) CSR programs to address various social and environmental issues including charitable donations, volunteer programs, and partnerships with not-for-profit organizations to support community development, education, and healthcare; (2) energy efficiency and renewable energy adoption to reduce their carbon footprint and dependence on fossil fuels including implementing smart building technologies, installing solar panels, and upgrading to energy-efficient lighting and appliances; (3) sustainable product design and development by focusing on material selection, product lifespan, and end-of-life disposal, using recycled or biodegradable materials, designing products for easy disassembly and recycling, and offering take-back programs for used products; (4) green supply-chain management of adopting sustainable practices throughout their supply chain to reduce environmental impacts by sourcing materials and components from environmentally responsible suppliers, optimizing transportation routes to minimize emissions, and reducing packaging waste; and (5) transparency and reporting to enhance transparency and reliability of both financial ESP and nonfinancial ESG sustainability performance information to build trust with stakeholders and empower accountability in achieving sustainability goals.

Summary

Business sustainability is an important corporate decision, and its economic consequences are of considerable interest to all stakeholders, including investors, society, the environment, and regulators. Recent developments in mandatory and voluntary sustainability disclosures enable management to exercise judgment when disclosing sustainability information. Anecdotal and academic evidence suggests that more mandatory or voluntary disclosures of sustainability performance information are good practices. There are many drivers of sustainability, including political, economic, cultural, and capital markets. These drivers may affect the implementation of business sustainability activities and programs in various countries. Business sustainability is advancing, and many voluntary and mandatory initiatives are continuing to emerge in promoting sustainability in all five EGSEE performance dimensions. It is expected that as investors demand more nonfinancial sustainability performance information, regulators require disclosure of such information, business organizations produce integrated sustainability reports, and more attention will be paid to business sustainability. Sustainability initiatives, both mandatory and voluntary, are intended to benefit all stakeholders by enabling positive environmental and social impacts and creating value for businesses by improving operational efficiency, reducing costs, enhancing brand reputation, and attracting environmentally conscious customers and investors. Sustainability initiatives discussed in this chapter, whether mandatory or voluntary, are intended to reflect the financial, social, and environmental impacts of a company's business operation and, thus, provide relevant and reliable financial ESP and nonfinancial ESG sustainability performance information for all stakeholders, including shareholders.

Key Points

- Business organizations should increase the quality and quantity of all stakeholder engagements with sustainability development.
- Global mandatory and voluntary business sustainability initiatives have been explored as the basis for influencing business sustainability.
- There is a global need for standardization of sustainability guidelines.
- A set of globally accepted sustainability standards can enable uniformity, consistency, and comparability in sustainability reporting.

- There is a growing demand by investors for relevant and reliable nonfinancial ESG information for making investment decisions.
- Sustainability initiatives, both mandatory and voluntary, enable business organizations to create shared value for all stakeholders.

Review Questions

1. How can an organization generate a desired rate of return for shareholders through sustainability efforts?
2. Where can sustainability information be found?
3. What is the sustainability reporting process?
4. What information must be disclosed in sustainability reporting to ensure the report is reliable and useful?
5. Why should sustainability reports reflect only measurable and verifiable sustainable performance?
6. In which aspect can sustainability disclosures be improved?
7. Why do stakeholders require sustainability assurance?
8. What are the global standards providing assurance guidance for business sustainability now?
9. How to evaluate the level of continuum assurance?
10. How did the global and national stock exchanges promote sustainability performance reporting?
11. What does the GRI promote in its G4 Guideline?
12. What is the purpose of the framework provided by the International Integrated Reporting Council (IIRC)?
13. In compliance with stewardship theory, what is the responsibility of management?
14. What is the purpose of the Global Corporate (GC) Sustainability Report released by the United Nations Global Compact (UNGC)?
15. What does the report released by the United Nations Global Compact indicate?

Discussion Questions

1. Explain the purpose of mandatory business sustainability initiatives.
2. Discuss the evolution of the GRI guidelines.
3. Describe the objectives of the International Integrated Reporting Council (IIRC).

4. **Explain the purpose of the Sustainability Accounting Standards Board (SASB).**

5. **Discuss the purpose of the framework released by the United Nations Sustainable Development Goals (UNSDGs).**

6. **What impact does the disclosure of nonfinancial ESG sustainability performance have on organizations?**

7. **Why is standardization important in sustainability reporting?**

8. **How do mandatory sustainability initiatives drive corporate responsibility?**

9. **What are the key components of the Global Reporting Initiative (GRI) G4 Guideline?**

10. **How does the CFA Institute view the relevance of ESG in investment decisions?**

11. **Discuss the objectives of the Carbon Disclosure Project (CDP).**

12. **What are the key principles guiding the ISSB's mission?**

13. **What is the significance of the 2021 Universal Standards by GRI?**

14. **What are the main components of the SASB's Sustainability Conceptual Framework?**

15. **What are some key considerations for businesses when adopting sustainability guidelines?**

Multiple Choice Questions

1. **Which guideline by GRI was released in May 2013?**
   A. G1
   B. G2
   C. G3
   D. G4

2. **How many new disclosures does the G4 Guideline introduce?**
   A. 10
   B. 15
   C. 20
   D. 27

3. **What are the six capitals suggested by the IIRC?**
   A. Financial, Manufactured, Intellectual, Human, Social and Relationship, Natural
   B. Financial, Environmental, Social, Governance, Human, Economic
   C. Financial, Manufactured, Social, Governance, Intellectual, Environmental
   D. Financial, Environmental, Social, Governance, Intellectual, Human

Multiple Choice Questions

4. **When was the Sustainability Conceptual Framework released by SASB?**
   A.   2010
   B.   2013
   C.   2015
   D.   2018

5. **Which report addresses the state of corporate sustainability today?**
   A.   GRI Sustainability Report
   B.   IIRC Annual Report
   C.   Global Corporate (GC) Sustainability Report by UNGC
   D.   SASB Industry Report

6. **How many Sustainable Development Goals (SDGs) are there?**
   A.   10
   B.   12
   C.   15
   D.   17

7. **Which organization's report suggests integrating sustainability into corporate strategies and operations?**
   A.   GRI
   B.   IIRC
   C.   SASB
   D.   UNGC

8. **Which organization released the climate change reporting taxonomy?**
   A.   GRI
   B.   IIRC
   C.   SASB
   D.   CDP and CDSB

9. **Who promotes the relevance of nonfinancial ESG in investment decisions?**
   A.   GRI
   B.   IIRC
   C.   SASB
   D.   CFA Institute

10. **Which directive requires over 6000 European companies to disclose ESG sustainability performance information?**
   A.   GRI Directive
   B.   IIRC Directive

C. EC Directive

D. SASB Directive

11. **What is the mission of the International Sustainability Standards Board (ISSB)?**

A. To increase short-term profits

B. To establish sustainability-related financial reporting standards

C. To promote global trade

D. To reduce regulatory burdens

12. **What are the key principles guiding the ISSB's mission?**

A. Profit maximization

B. Comprehensive global baseline, consolidation, informed by expert advice, global footprint

C. Market expansion, cost reduction, short-term gains, innovation

D. Regulatory compliance, risk management, financial control, stakeholder engagement

13. **What is one of the main objectives of business sustainability initiatives?**

A. Increasing short-term profits

B. Reducing long-term risks

C. Improving product quality

D. Enhancing brand reputation

14. **What does the SASB Conceptual Framework consist of?**

A. Key definitions and characteristics of sustainability accounting

B. Objectives and methodology for assessing materiality

C. Structure and harmonization of sustainability accounting standards

D. All of the above

15. **Which principles are covered by the UNGC's ten principles?**

A. Financial, Environmental, Social, Governance

B. Human Rights, Labor, Environment, Anti-Corruption

C. Governance, Ethics, Environmental, Social

D. Financial, Economic, Governance, Social

16. **What is the focus of the Global Reporting Initiative (GRI)?**

A. Financial performance

B. Environmental performance

C. Governance performance

D. All of the above

Multiple Choice Questions

17. **What does the G4 Guideline focus more heavily on in the reporting process?**
    A. Profitability
    B. Market share
    C. Materiality considerations
    D. Product innovation

18. **Which organization released the Integrated Reporting (IR) Framework?**
    A. SASB
    B. GRI
    C. IIRC
    D. UNGC

19. **Which organization aims to establish and release sustainability accounting standards?**
    A. GRI
    B. IIRC
    C. SASB
    D. UNGC

20. **What is the role of the Carbon Disclosure Project (CDP) in sustainability reporting?**
    A. Enhancing corporate profits
    B. Improving transparency on greenhouse gas emissions and climate-related risks
    C. Reducing operational costs
    D. Increasing market share

21. **What is the main objective of the Delaware Act of 2018?**
    A. Enhancing financial reporting
    B. Supporting sustainability practices through voluntary disclosure
    C. Reducing tax obligations
    D. Enhancing market competitiveness

22. **What does the European Commission (EC) promote regarding corporate social responsibility (CSR)?**
    A. Financial gains
    B. Short-term profits
    C. Social and environmental concerns integration
    D. Market expansion

23. **When did the EU Corporate Sustainability Reporting Directive (CSRD) come into effect?**
    A. 2015

B. 2018

C. 2020

D. 2023

24. **What is the purpose of the proposed IFRS S1 standard by ISSB?**
    A. To establish specific climate-related disclosures
    B. To provide a set of disclosure requirements for sustainability-related financial information
    C. To reduce financial risks
    D. To enhance market expansion

25. **What is the primary mission of the ISSB?**
    A. To reduce operational costs
    B. To establish sustainability-related financial reporting standards
    C. To increase market share
    D. To improve short-term profits

26. **Which organization provides a framework known as the Integrated Reporting (IR) Framework?**
    A. SASB
    B. IIRC
    C. GRI
    D. UNGC

27. **Which report addresses the actions taken by companies worldwide in integrating sustainability into their strategies, operations, and culture?**
    A. GRI Sustainability Report
    B. IIRC Annual Report
    C. Global Corporate (GC) Sustainability Report by UNGC
    D. SASB Industry Report

28. **What are the objectives of the Carbon Disclosure Project (CDP)?**
    A. To enhance financial performance
    B. To improve transparency on greenhouse gas emissions
    C. To reduce operational costs
    D. To increase market share

29. **Which guideline by GRI was released in May 2013?**
    A. G1
    B. G2
    C. G3
    D. G4

30. **How many new disclosures does the G4 Guideline introduce?**

    A. 10

    B. 15

    C. 20

    D. 27

Notes

1 Rezaee, Z. (2015). *Business sustainability: Performance, compliance, accountability, and integrated reporting.* Greenleaf Publishing Limited.

2 European Commission (2014). Disclosure of nonfinancial information: Europe information: Europe's largest companies to be more transparent on social and environmental issues (September 29). http://ec.europa.eu/ rapid/press-release_STATEMENT-14-291_en.htm.

3 Delaware General Assembly. House Bill 310: An Act to Amend Title 6 of the Delaware Code Relating to the Certification of Adoption of Sustainability and Transparency Standards by Delaware Entities (June 27). https://legis.delaware.gov/BillDetail/26304.

4 Sarbanes-Oxley Act 2002, Pub. L. 107–204, enacted July 30, 2002, adding 15 U.S.C. § 7201 *et seq.* and adding and am sending other provisions of the United States Code, as explained in the notes accompanying 15 U.S.C. § 7201, hereinafter in this portfolio the "Sarbanes-Oxley Act" or "SOX."

5 Rezaee, Z. (2015). *Business sustainability: Performance, compliance, accountability, and integrated reporting.* Greenleaf Publishing Limited.

6 Securities and Exchange Commission (SEC). (2022). SEC proposes rules to enhance and standardize climate-related disclosures for investors (March 21, 2022). https://www.sec.gov/news/press-release/2022-46

7 Securities and Exchange Commission (SEC). (2024). The enhancement and standardization of climate-related disclosures for investors. 17 CFR 210, 229, 230, 232, 239, and 249, [Release Nos. 33-11275; 34-99678; File No. S7-10-22]. Final Rules (March 6, 2024). https://www.sec.gov/files/rules/final/2024/33-11275.pdf

8 Securities and Exchange Commission (SEC). (2020). SEC adopts rule amendments to modernize disclosures of business, legal proceedings, and risk factors under regulation S-K (August 26, 2020). https://www.sec.gov/news/press-release/2020-192

9 Financial Accounting Foundation, Proposed Accounting Standards Update, FASB In Focus (July 31, 2023). https://www.fasb.org/page/PageContent?pageId=/news-media/fasbinfocus/fif-income-statement-reporting-comprehensive-income-expense-disaggregation-disclosures-subtopic-220-40-disaggregation-of-income-statement-expenses.html&bcpath=tff

10 European Commission (2011). Corporate Social Responsibility (CSR). http://ec.europa.eu/growth/industry/corporate-social-responsibility_en.

11 European Commission (2011). Corporate Social Responsibility (CSR). http://ec.europa.eu/growth/industry/corporate-social-responsibility_en.

12 European Commission (2011). Corporate Social Responsibility (CSR). http://ec.europa.eu/growth/industry/corporate-social-responsibility_en.

13 European Commission (2014). Disclosure of nonfinancial information: Europe information: Europe's largest companies to be more transparent on social and environmental issues (September 29). http://ec.europa.eu/ rapid/press-release_STATEMENT-14-291_en.htm.

14 European Commission (EC). (2023). The Corporate Sustainability Reporting Directive (CSRD) (January 5, 2023). https://finance.ec.europa.eu/capital-markets-union-and-financial-markets/company-reporting-and-auditing/company-reporting/corporate-sustainability-reporting_en

15 European Commission (EC). 2023. The Commission adopts the European Sustainability Reporting Standards (July 31, 2023). https://finance.ec.europa.eu/news/commission-adopts-european-sustainability-reporting-standards-2023-07-31_en

16 Canadian Securities Administrators (CSA) (2018). Staff notice 51-354 report on climate change-related disclosure project (April). www.osc.gov.on.ca/documents/en/Securities-Category5/csa_20180405_climate-change-related-disclosure-project.pdf.

17 Investor Responsibility Research Center Institute (IRRCI). (2017). How investors integrate ESG: A typology of approaches (April). https://irrcinstitute.org/wp-content/uploads/2017/04/FinalIRRCiReport_HowInvestorsIntegrateESG.ATypologyofApproaches.pdf.

18 Global Reporting Initiative (GRI). (2013). G4 sustainability reporting guidelines. https://www.globalreporting.org/resourcelibrary/GRIG4-Part1-Reporting-Principles-and-Standard-Disclosures.pdf.

19 Global Reporting Initiative (GRI). (2013). G4 sustainability reporting guidelines. https://www.globalreporting.org/resourcelibrary/GRIG4-Part1-Reporting-Principles-and-Standard-Disclosures.pdf.

20 Global Reporting Initiative (GRI). (2013). G4 sustainability reporting guidelines. https://www.globalreporting.org/resourcelibrary/GRIG4-Part1-Reporting-Principles-and-Standard-Disclosures.pdf, 7–8.

21 Global Sustainability Standards Board (GRI). (2020). https://www.globalreporting.org/standards/gssb-and-standard-setting/

22 Global Reporting Initiative (GRI). (2021). Universal Standards: Setting a new global benchmark for sustainability reporting (October 2021). https://www.globalreporting.org/standards/standards-development/universal-standards/

23 Global Reporting Initiative (GRI). (2021). Universal Standards: GRI Standards (October 2022). https://www.globalreporting.org/how-to-use-the-gri-standards/gri-standards-english-language/.

24 International Integrated Reporting Committee (IIRC). (2013). IIRC consultative draft. 2013. IIRC consultative draft section 3.12; page 19. http://www.theiirc.org/consultationdraft2013/.

25 International Integrated Reporting Committee (IIRC). (2013). IIRC consultative draft. 2013. IIRC consultative draft section 3.12; page 19. http://www.theiirc.org/consultationdraft2013/.

26 International Integrated Reporting Committee (IIRC) (2013). IIRC consultative draft. 2013. IIRC consultative draft section 3.12; page 19. http://www.theiirc.org/consultationdraft2013/.

27 International Integrated Reporting Committee (IIRC). (2013). IIRC consultative draft. 2013. IIRC consultative draft section 3.12; page 19. http://www.theiirc.org/consultationdraft2013/.

28 The Sustainability Accounting Standards Board (SASB). Contact Us. https://www.sasb.org/contact/

29 Sustainability Accounting Standards Board (SASB). (2013). US SASB publishes exposure drafts on health care sector sustainability reporting. http://www.iasplus.com/en/othernews/united-states/2013/sasb-health-care-ed.

30 United Nations (UN). (2013). How investors are addressing environmental, social and governance factors in fundamental equity valuation, United Nations–supported principles for responsible investment (PRI) (February).http://www.unpri.org/viewer/?file=wp-content/uploads/Integrated_Analysis_2013.pdf.

31 United Nations Global Compact (UNGC). (2015). Guide to corporate sustainability. https://www.unglobalcompact.org/docs/publications/UN_Global_Compact_Guide_to_Corporate_Sustainability.pdf.

32 United Nations Global Compact (UNGC). (2015). Guide to corporate sustainability. https://www.unglobalcompact.org/docs/publications/UN_Global_Compact_Guide_to_Corporate_Sustainability.pdf.

33 UN Sustainable Development Goals Report (UNSDGs). (2015). Indicators and a monitoring framework for the Sustainable Development Goals launching a data revolution for the SDGs. http://unsdsn.org/wp-content/uploads/2015/03/150320-SDSN-Indicator-Report.pdf.

34 UN Sustainable Development Goals Report (UNSDGs). (2015). Indicators and a monitoring framework for the Sustainable Development Goals launching a data revolution for the SDGs. http://unsdsn.org/wp-content/uploads/2015/03/150320-SDSN-Indicator-Report.pdf.

35 Global Reporting Initiative (GRI). (2017). Linking the GRI Standards and the European Directive on Non-financial and Diversity Disclosure. https://www.globalreporting.org/standards/resource-download-center/linking-gri-standards-and-european-directive-on-non-financial-and-diversity-disclosure/.

36 International Federation of Accountants. (2016). The 2030 Agenda for Sustainable Development: A snapshot of the accountancy profession's contribution. International Federation of Accountants, New York. https://www.ifac.org/publications-resources/2030-agenda-sustainable-development.

37 PWC. (2017). SDG reporting challenge 2017. Exploring business communication on the Global Goals 2017. https://www.pwc.com/gx/en/sustainability/SDG/pwc-sdg-reporting-challenge-2017-final.pdf.

38 PWC. (2017). SDG reporting challenge 2017. Exploring business communication on the Global Goals 2017. https://www.pwc.com/gx/en/sustainability/SDG/pwc-sdg-reporting-challenge-2017-final.pdf.

39 PWC. (2017). SDG reporting challenge 2017. Exploring business communication on the Global Goals 2017. https://www.pwc.com/gx/en/sustainability/SDG/pwc-sdg-reporting -challenge-2017-final.pdf.

40 Sustainability Accounting Standards Board (SASB). (2013). US SASB publishes exposure drafts on health care sector sustainability reporting. http://www.iasplus.com/en/oth-ernews/united-states/2013/sasb-health-care-ed.

41 International Integrated Reporting Committee (IIRC). (2013). IIRC consultative draft. 2013. IIRC consultative draft section 3.12; page 19. http://www.theiirc.org/consultationdra ft2013/.

42 Climate Change Reporting Taxonomy (CCRT). (2012). Climate change reporting taxonomy, taxonomy architecture and style guide. www.cdproject.net/Documents/xbrl/CCRT-tax-onomy-architecture-and-style-guide-v1-0.pdf.

43 International Integrated Reporting Committee (IIRC). (2013). IIRC consultative draft 2013. IIRC consultative draft section 3.12; page 19. http://www.theiirc.org/consultationdra ft2013/.

44 Climate Change Reporting Taxonomy (CCRT). (2013). Climate change reporting taxonomy (CCRT) due process. https://www.cdproject.net/en-us/news/pages/xbrl-due-process .aspx.

45 International Integrated Reporting Council (IIRC) (2013). Consultation Draft of the International Integrated Reporting Framework (April). www.theiirc.org/consultationdra ft2013.

46 CFA Institute (2015). Environmental, social, and governance issues in investing: A guide for investment professionals https://www.cfainstitute.org/-/media/documents/article/posi-tion-paper/esg-issues-in-investing-a-guide-for-investment-professionals.ashx.

47 CFA Institute (2019). Positions on environmental, social, and governance integration. https://www.cfainstitute.org/-/media/documents/article/position-paper/cfa-institute -position-statement-esg.ashx.

48 .European Commission (2014). Disclosure of nonfinancial information: Europe information: Europe's largest companies to be more transparent on social and environmental issues (September 29). http://ec.europa.eu/ rapid/press-release_STATEMENT-14-291_en.htm.

49 European Commission (EU) (2019). Technical Expert Group on Sustainable Finance: Report on climate-related disclosures. https://ec.europa.eu/info/publications/190110-sustainable -finance-teg-report-climate-related-disclosures_en.

Chapter 7
Financial Economic Dimension of Sustainability

Learning Objectives

- Explain the effect that the achievement of long-term sustainable economic performance has on shareholder value creation.
- Understand the value maximization concept.
- Provide an overview of financial economic sustainability performance.
- Provide an overview of the measures taken in the post-Sarbanes-Oxley (SOX) era to improve the quality of financial reports.
- Understand the financial reporting process.
- Provide an overview of the Forward-Looking Financial Reports.
- Explore the three levels of measurement of shared value and their focuses.
- Learn the characteristics of economic sustainability performance.
- Understand the various components of audited financial statements.
- Understand provisions of the Sarbanes-Oxley (SOX) relevant to financial reporting and auditing processes.
- Learn how the value relevance of voluntary sustainability information is measured.

Introduction

Sustainability performance is vital to business organizations in obtaining desired rates of returns for shareholders while having some environmental and social impacts. Sustainability performance is typically classified into financial economic sustainability performance (ESP) and nonfinancial environmental, social, and governance (ESG) sustainability performance, with ethical performance being integrated into both ESP and ESG dimensions of sustainability performance.[1] Public companies are formed to generate sustainable earnings to create value for their shareholders. Investor confidence in public financial information and capital markets is the key driver of economic growth, prosperity, and financial stability for the nation, and this confidence can be significantly improved by focusing on long-term sustainable economic performance. Economic sustainability performance with a keen focus on long-term financial performance is gaining more attention from investors. In the context of agency theory, where information asymmetry is assumed to be present, financial

DOI: 10.4324/9781003487081-7

short-termism could occur. The agent (management) acting on behalf of the principal (shareholders) has incentives to achieve self-interested short-term financial performance due to the lack of proper monitoring of the agent. When the interests of the agent are not aligned with those of the principal, the agent has incentives to not act in the best interest of long-term financial sustainability performance and/or withhold important sustainability financial information from the principal and the investors. Short-termism is referred to as an excessive focus on a company's quarterly reported financial results rather than on sustainable, enduring, and long-term economic performance. This short-term practice undermines the sustainable economic performance of many companies by encouraging management to emphasize short-term performance by meeting analysts' quarterly earnings forecasts. This chapter presents financial ESP, which is considered the primary function of business organizations in creating value for shareholders.

Financial Economic Sustainability Performance

Transparency in financial and nonfinancial reports has always been part of the conceptual reporting framework regardless of investors' attitudes toward risk (e.g., risk-averse, tolerant of risks, or embraces risk). The financial ESP dimension is the most important component of sustainability in creating shareholder values. The primary goal of any business organization is to maximize firm value by creating shareholder wealth through generating sustainable economic performance throughout the firm life. Business organizations should focus on activities that generate long-term and sustainable corporate performance rather than short-term profit to enhance the overall firm value and increase shareholder wealth. The economic dimension of sustainability performance can be achieved when business organizations focus on long-term sustainability performance and continuous improvement in performance in all areas of effectiveness, efficiency, and productivity. In addition, long-term economic sustainability performance should also be communicated to shareholders through the preparation of high-quality, reliable, relevant, and transparent financial reports that are readily accessible. The ESP is disclosed to shareholders in a set of financial statements prepared by management. These financial statements are typically prepared in compliance with national accounting standards and/or the International Financial Reporting Standards (IFRS). Traditional corporate reporting models reflect financial information disseminated to shareholders, whereas business sustainability covers a broad range of stakeholders and reflects a broader range of multiple-bottom-line EGSEE performance. The ESP dimension is the cornerstone of business sustainability, and its disclosure is the release of information pertaining to the profitability of the company. The ESP dimension of sustainability performance presents long-term financial sustainability as reflected in the audited financial statements, which could contain the following eight documents:

1. Management certifications of financial statements.
2. Management certification of the assessments of the effectiveness of internal control over financial reporting.
3. Independent auditor's report on financial statements.
4. Independent auditor's report on internal control over financial reporting (ICFR).
5. Audited financial statements, including their notes.
6. Management's discussion and analysis (MD&A) of financial condition and results of operations.
7. Five-year summary of selected financial data.
8. Summary of selected quarterly financial data for the past two years.

Audited financial statements, which typically provide information concerning an entity's financial condition and results of operations as a proxy for future business performance, may not provide relevant information to investors and other stakeholders. Investors demand forward-looking financial and nonfinancial information on key performance indicators (KPIs) concerning the entity's EGSEE activities. High-quality financial information reflecting the ESP dimension of performance enables investors to assess the risks and returns associated with their investments. In the post-Sarbanes-Oxley (SOX) era, public companies in the United States presented their audited financial statements and audited ICFR. Section 404(a) of SOX 2002 requires that management certifies the effectiveness of ICFR. This ICFR certification states that management is responsible for designing and maintaining effective ICFR and documenting the effectiveness of internal controls through testing-related control activities. Executive certification of the effectiveness of ICFR indicates that there is only a remote possibility that material misstatements may not be prevented, detected, or corrected on a timely basis. Any material weaknesses detected in internal control must be disclosed in management's report, along with actions taken to correct those material weaknesses.

Section 404(b) of SOX requires that the independent auditor opines on the effectiveness of ICFR. The Public Company Accounting Oversight Board (PCAOB) in the United States has issued auditing standards for independent auditors to audit and opine on ICFR. PCAOB Auditing Standard (AS) No. 2, *An Audit of Internal Control over Financial Reporting Performed in Conjunction with an Audit of Financial Statements*,[2] is superseded by AS No. 5, which makes the audit of ICFR more effective and efficient. PCAOB AS No. 5 requires auditors to use a risk-based approach in the audit of ICFR. The independent auditor's report on ICFR can either be issued separately or be combined with an opinion on the financial statements. The auditor should also render an opinion on the effectiveness of ICFR. Reporting and auditing of financial statements and ICFR is vital to assist shareholders in making appropriate investment and voting decisions. Public companies in the United States are required to publish audited annual financial statements and audited ICFR. Section 404 SOX is intended to improve the effectiveness of the design and operation of internal control over financial reporting.[3] PCAOB AS No. 5 is intended to improve the audit by (1) focusing the audit on the matters most important to internal control, (2) eliminating unnecessary audit procedures, (3) simplifying the auditor requirements, and (4) scaling the integrated audit for smaller companies.

Preparation of reliable, useful, and relevant financial information on the ESP dimension of sustainability performance is a key responsibility of management. Executive certifications of financial and ICFR reports have a global reach in providing accurate and complete information on ESP. However, management may have incentives to mislead investors, and when opportunities are provided, they may attempt to manipulate financial information. The effective and vigilant overseeing of management reporting activities by the board of directors can reduce managerial opportunistic behavior. As the agent of investors, management has more information about ESP and may act inappropriately in withholding such information to investors if the principal (investors) fails to monitor the agent or if the interests of the agent are not aligned with those of the principal.

Financial Reporting Process

Financial reporting is the process of preparing and disseminating financial statements (balance sheet, income statement, statement of owners equity, and cash flow statement) that disclose financial positions, financial results, and financial status for the interested users of financial statements. Users of financial statements can be internal users, such as the board of directors, management, and employees, or external users, including shareholders, creditors, government, customers, suppliers, and other stakeholders. Regulators in the United States, including the SEC and the PCAOB, and standard setters, such as the FASB and the AICPA, addressed the financial reporting issues at the 2018 AICPA Conference on Current SEC and PCAOB Developments.[4] The following financial reporting issues were considered important in enhancing financial disclosure and related controls:

- Ever-increasing risks associated with cybersecurity, Brexit, and the transition away from LIBOR: The SEC has taken several initiatives and released interpretive guidelines that expand on the principles-based disclosure guidance detailing the SEC expectations regarding the effective design and implementation of controls to assure timely disclosure of material cyber risks and breaches. Public companies should re-evaluate the adequacy of their cybersecurity disclosures at fiscal year-end in light of the new

Financial Economic Sustainability Performance

guidance. Management should consider the adequacy of cyber-related controls and procedures into account in the CEO/CFO certification process and disclosures about control effectiveness. The audit committee and external auditors should evaluate the adequacy of the company risk factors, MD&A "known trends and uncertainties," and other Brexit-related disclosures included in Form 10-K (or 20-F) and other periodic and current reports filed in 2019. The risks associated with the global transition away from the London Inter-Bank Offered Rate (LIBOR), which serves as a short-term interest rate benchmark for many commercial and financial contracts, should be assessed by management and overseen by the audit committee.

- "New GAAP" and the end of SAB 118 provisional income tax accounting: New generally accepted accounting principles (GAAP) standards that should get attention of the audit committee, management and external auditors are: (1) the new revenue recognition accounting standard; (2) the new lease accounting standard; (3) the new accounting standard for current expected credit losses, better known as CECL; and (4) the end of the SAB 118 grace period for income tax accounting.

- Non-GAAP financial measures: Non-GAAP financial measure disclosures made in earnings releases, management earnings forecasts, webcast earnings calls, as well as voluntary disclosures on CSR/ESG sustainability performance and other investor presentations should be reconciled with the GAAP-mandated disclosures made in the financial statements filed as part of 10-Ks and 10-Qs, and any discrepancies should be resolved.

- Identification and disclosure of material weaknesses in ICFR and management (CEO, CFO) certification of ICFR should be reviewed by the audit committee and properly disclosed to shareholders.

- Compliance with PCAOB's new auditor reporting standard, including the preparation of new critical audit matters (CAMs) for the fiscal 2019 audit of accelerated filers. CAMs relevant to accounts or disclosures that are material to the financial statements involving "especially challenging, subjective or complex [areas of] auditor judgment" are required to be communicated by the external independent auditor to the audit committee.

Business organizations worldwide are being criticized for primarily focusing on short-term profit maximization and shareholder value enhancement, with minimal attention paid to the impacts of their operations on society and the environment.[5] As business sustainability is gaining attention and being integrated into the corporate culture and business model, there has been a shift from the creation of shareholder value to the development of "sustainable shared value creation" to protect the interests of all stakeholders.[6] The concept of shared value is defined as "policies and practices that enhance the competitiveness of a company while simultaneously advancing the economic and social conditions in the communities in which it operates."[7] Under the shared value creation concept, management focuses on the continuous performance improvement of business operations in generating long-term value while maximizing the positive impacts of operations on society and the environment by measuring sustainable performance in terms of both ESP and GSEE sustainability performance. Thus, corporate objectives have advanced from profit maximization to increasing shareholder wealth and now to creating shared value for all stakeholders.

There has been an ongoing debate in recent years that publicly traded for-profit companies should do more than maximize profit in creating shareholder value and should also engage in ESG sustainability activities that generate social and environmental impacts. Indeed, the impact investing concept of focusing on generating financial returns as well as social and environmental returns is gaining the attention of retail investors, institutional investors, and their asset managers. There are two views regarding the relevance of nonfinancial ESG to for-profit business organizations. At one end, many public companies have already adopted ESG sustainability as a business strategic imperative, integrating it into their business culture, corporate environment, decisions, and supply chain management. On the other hand, some companies view any investment in ESG/CSR sustainability projects as expenses and activities that are inappropriate concerns for for-profit businesses. Yet, some corporations consider ESG/CSR initiatives as greenwashing and branding, or they have started to consider whether and how ESG can affect their operations and thus be relevant to their businesses. Regardless of where corporations are along this spectrum, they can benefit in the long term by focusing on achieving both economic sustainability performance and ESG sustainability performance in creating shared value for all stakeholders.

Sustainable shared value creation, being the primary objective for many business organizations, can be achieved by focusing on the economic dimension of sustainability performance. Corporate management, asset managers, equity analysts, and even shareholders are motivated, and thus, their behaviors are biased toward short-term performance for a variety of reasons.[8] The focus on short-term considerations may have an adverse impact on long-term and sustainable shareholder value creation, reducing the expected value of future returns and, consequently, the current share prices. Stocks can be priced lower than their potential value by overemphasizing short-term considerations, encouraging asset managers to trade more frequently, and forcing long-term investors to be short-changed. This fixation on short-term considerations contributed to the financial scandals of Enron, WorldCom, and other similar companies. Long-term and sustainable shareholder value creation is promoted through developing strategic plans and investments with sound, long-term objectives and linking executive compensation to long-term performance.

Financial Economic Sustainability Performance

The short-termism behavior of many corporate managers is in sharp contrast with the long-term view of sustainable economic performance. The main objective of any business organization is to create shareholder value and thus maximize firm value by establishing a proper balance between economic sustainability performance and other nonfinancial dimensions of sustainability performance. The enlightened value maximization concept of sustainability performance is supported by recent anecdotal evidence that suggests that companies that "see sustainability as both a necessity and opportunity and change their business models in response are finding success."[9] Further sustainability information can lead to a better understanding of the link between management actions and sustainable performance and thus could reduce noise in the corporate reporting process as well as short-termism attributes.

The concept of stakeholder capitalism has emerged in response to the move toward shared value aspects of business organizations with a focus on achieving financial returns and generating social and environmental impacts.[10] The emerging move toward a profit-with-purpose business mission, ESG sustainability, and growing interest in creating long-term shared value for all stakeholders has resulted in a move toward business sustainability. There is a general move toward stakeholder capitalism, which creates long-term sustainable shared value for all stakeholders, from shareholders to creditors, employees, customers, suppliers, regulators, society, and the environment. Public companies, their board of directors, and executives can communicate the commitment to sustainability in creating shared value for stakeholders through integrated sustainability reporting, focusing on measuring and disclosing both financial ESP and nonfinancial GSEE. As described in a paper from the Foundation Strategy Group (FSG), the pursuit and measurement of shared value opportunities on three levels. These three levels are (1) enabling cluster development, (2) redefining productivity in the value chain, and (3) reconceiving products and markets. Each of these levels produces business and social results. In combination, these three levels can lead to increases in revenue, market share, efficient energy use, job creation, and supply chain costs. In order to properly apply these levels, strategies and measurements must be integrated. The four steps to accomplish this are to identify the social issues, make the case for addressing them, track the progress, and evaluate results.[11]

Integrated Financial and Internal Control Reporting

In the post-financial crisis and new regulatory framework era, corporations are searching for more effective, efficient, and feasible ways to improve the quality of their earnings. Sustainability performance can encourage management to focus on achieving long-term sustainable performance and away from the short-termism mentality of meeting or beating analysts' quarterly earnings forecasts. The 2007–2009 financial crisis was preceded by a period of corporate short-term profit-seeking at the expense of long-term sustainable performance.[12] The short-termism focus of corporations and their executives and gatekeepers (e.g., investors and analysts) creates opportunities for managing quarterly earnings and avoiding activities (e.g., R&D) that generate sustainable and long-term performance. Improper earnings management and resulting financial manipulations and scandals at many high-profile public companies, such as Enron, WorldCom, and Global Crossing, at the turn of the 21st century, caused Congress to pass the Sarbanes-Oxley Act of 2002. The Act requires, among other things, certification of financial statements and ICFR by management (CEO and CFO) of public companies.

Integrated financial and internal control reporting (IFICR) is defined in this chapter as the process of preparing both financial statements and ICFR and includes (1) management reporting on and certification of financial statements; (2) management reporting on and certification of ICFR; (3) the independent auditor's opinion on fair and true presentation of financial statements; (4) independent auditor opinion on the effectiveness of ICFR; and (5) the audit committee's review of audited financial statements and both management and auditor reports on ICFR. The effectiveness of IFICR depends on a vigilant oversight function by the board of directors, particularly the audit committee, a responsible and accountable managerial function by senior executives, a credible external audit function by the independent auditor, and an objective internal audit function by internal auditors. IFICR adds value by lending credibility to both financial statements and internal controls, which promotes investor confidence and reinforces public trust in public financial information. IFICR reports are expected to reduce the information risks of financial information being misleading, biased, incomplete, inaccurate, or fraudulent. In this context, audits reduce financial information asymmetries between management and shareholders and thus help investors make more informed decisions that, in turn, make the capital markets more efficient and add to the nation's economic prosperity. The need for IFICR can be attributed to the principal-agent conflict suggested in agency theory, where principals (owners) lack reasons to trust their agents (management) primarily because of differing motives and information asymmetries.

Internal Control Reporting

Legislators, regulators, and the accounting profession have traditionally addressed the establishment and maintenance of internal control systems by public companies, management, and auditors' public reports on internal control systems. The SEC has long been an advocate of internal control reporting but stopped short of making it a requirement for public companies.[13] The SEC (1) initially in its Release No. 13185, in January 1977, proposed a requirement that management maintain an effective internal control system and expressed interest in mandatory internal control reporting to shareholders; (2) advised public companies in February 1978 to make necessary changes in their internal controls and business practices to comply with provisions of the Foreign Corrupt Practices Act (FCPA of 1977) in its Accounting Series Release No. 242;[14] and (3) proposed rules in April 1979 that would have required SEC registrants to issue a management report and auditor opinion on internal accounting controls, and subsequently in June 1980 withdrew these proposed rules.[15]

The American Institute of Certified Public Accountants (1) in its 1978 report to the Commission on Auditor's Responsibilities, recommended auditors report material weakness in internal controls to management or the audit committee as well as management's response to auditors' suggestions for correction of weaknesses; (2) issued the Statement on Auditing Standards (SAS) No. 20 in 1977, which required communication of material weaknesses in internal accounting controls to management; (3) issued an exposure draft in December 1979 that provided guidance on auditors' reports on internal accounting controls based on the review of internal controls; and (4) issued SAS No. 55 in April 1988, and subsequently SAS No. 78, in 1995, which guides auditors in evaluating the internal control structure as part of the audit of financial statements.

The Committee of Sponsoring Organizations of Treadway (COSO), in its first report in 1987, underscored the importance of internal controls in preventing and detecting fraudulent financial activities. The COSO, in its second report in 1992, titled "Internal Control-Integrated Framework," recommended voluntary internal control reporting by both management and independent auditors of public companies.[16] The COSO provided detailed guidance as to what the content of internal control reporting should be, including the nature, objectives, components, the role of management, the audit committee, the independent auditor, and the limitation of internal controls. In 2013, the COSO updated its framework on internal control reporting to make it more relevant for companies to report on their ICFR and more useful to investors in obtaining more information on the integrity and reliability of both internal controls and financial reporting systems. The framework is very strong in design, analysis, assessments, and reporting. The increased focus on operations, compliance, and nonfinancial reporting objectives is also a major improvement.

Section 404 of SOX is intended to improve the effectiveness of the design and operation of internal control over financial reporting. Compliance with Section 404 is now required for a majority of public companies (accelerated filers) for fiscal years ending on or after November

15, 2004.[17] Section 404 requires management to state its responsibility for designing and maintaining adequate internal controls over financial reporting and its assessment of the effectiveness of such control as of the end of the company's most recent fiscal year. Executive certification of internal control over financial reporting requires management to document the adequacy and effectiveness of the internal control through testing-related control activities and specifying inherent limitations. This suggests that when internal control is effective, there is only a remote possibility that material misstatements will not be prevented, detected, and corrected on a timely basis. Any detected material weakness in internal controls must be disclosed in management's report, along with actions taken to correct those significant deficiencies and material weaknesses.

Section 404 of the Act requires the independent auditor to attest to and report on management's assessment of the company's internal control over financial reporting and directs the PCAOB to issue guidance on the auditor report on internal control. The PCAOB issued its AS No. 2, An Audit of Internal Control over Financial Reporting Performance in Conjunctions with an Audit of Financial Statements.[18] PCAOB AS No. 2 establishes guidance for the audit of internal control over financial reporting. In expressing an opinion on internal control over financial reporting, the independent auditor must perform tests of controls to evaluate: (1) management's assessment of the effectiveness of internal control over financial reporting by gathering sufficient competent evidence about both the process used and the conclusion reached by management, and (2) the effectiveness of both the design and operation of internal control over financial reporting. Any deficiencies found in internal control over financial reporting must be evaluated in terms of their possible effects on misstatements of an account balance or disclosure. The PCAOB in 2007 revised and superseded AS No. 2 by issuing AS No. 5 of making internal control reporting and auditing more cost-effective, efficient, and scalable.[19] PCAOB AS No. 5 is intended to improve the audit by (1) focusing the audit on the matters most important to internal control, (2) eliminating unnecessary audit procedures, (3) simplifying the auditor requirements, and (4) scaling the integrated audit for smaller companies.

The independent auditor should issue an opinion on management's assessment of internal control over financial reporting either as a separate report or as a combined report with an opinion on the financial statements. The three possible types of audit opinion on internal control are (1) unqualified opinion when there is no material weakness in internal controls; (2) adverse opinion when significant deficiencies in internal controls can result in one or more material weaknesses; and (3) disclaimer of opinion when the auditor cannot express an opinion due to a scope limitation. PCAOB AS No. 2 mentions some circumstances where management may conclude that the company's internal control over financial reporting

Financial Economic Sustainability Performance

is ineffective, and if the auditor concurs with management's assessment, may issue an unqualified opinion on management's assessment and render an adverse opinion on the effectiveness of internal control over financial reporting. There may be situations where management reports that the company's internal control is effective. when the independent auditor discovers material weaknesses that were not corrected, and they issue an adverse opinion on the effectiveness of the company's internal control over financial reporting.

Management certifications of financial statements and ICFR of public companies in the United States in compliance with Sections 302 and 404 of SOX can contribute to sustainable financial reporting and internal control reporting in the following ways: Benefits of mandatory internal control reporting are:

1. Creation of a more engaged control environment resulting from active participation and commitment by the board of directors, the audit committee, and management.
2. Recognition of continuous monitoring as an integral component of the control process with more thoughtful analysis of monitoring controls.
3. More structure for the year-end closing process and recording of journal entries.
4. Implementation of antifraud programs and activities to prevent, detect, and correct errors, irregularities, and fraud, including responsibility for follow-up to resolve the issues.
5. Better understanding of risks associated with electronics processing and related computer controls and the need to improve both controls and audit procedures to assure that risks associated with the electronic reporting process and information technology (IT) are properly managed.
6. Documentation of controls and the control process that can serve as a basis for continuous monitoring, training, and best practice guidance.
7. Improvements in the concept and definition of internal controls and their relation to the organization with risk management.
8. Better understanding of internal controls concept throughout the organization at every operational level and reporting unit.
9. Improvements in the sufficiency and competency of the audit trail as a basis to support operations and the assessment of the effectiveness of ICFR.
10. Implementation of fundamental controls, including segregation of duties, authorization processes, and periodic reconciliation of accounts.
11. Production of more reliable, credible, and transparent financial reports.
12. Public report on the soundness of accounting and internal control systems in reflecting economic sustainability performance.

Risk Assessment and Financial Sustainability

Technological advances, including the internet, Big Data, and blockchain platforms, enable investors to have real-time online access to a large volume of information with simultaneous verification about public companies, their governance, operations, investment choices, and capital markets. The value relevance of financial information can be influenced by the risk associated with such information. Companies should conduct risk assessments periodically to identify potential risks and design appropriate controls to mitigate their adversarial impacts. The Committee of Sponsoring Organizations (COSO) issued its enterprise risk management (ERM) report in 2004, which provides guidelines for the effective assessment and management of risks associated with financial information and ESP sustainability information in particular.[20] The board of directors, particularly the audit committee, should oversee the company's ERM, and both internal and external auditors should be involved in assessing the risks of natural disasters and the protection of important electronics and other information. The board of directors should oversee the company's risk appetite, access timely information on current and emerging material risk exposures, risk response strategies, and implement effective risk management processes. There are three general approaches to effective board oversight of risk assessment and management:

- Establishing a risk compliance board committee by delegating all responsibilities to such board committees.
- Making the entire board of directors responsible for risk oversight.
- Combination of the first two alternatives by making the whole board responsible along with delegation of specific roles and responsibilities to Board committees.

Forward-Looking Financial Reports

Traditional financial statements, providing historical financial information concerning an entity's financial condition and results of operations as a proxy for future business performance, may not provide relevant information to investors and other stakeholders. Investors demand forward-looking financial and nonfinancial information on KPIs concerning the entity's EGSEE activities. Long-term shareholder value is often used as a proxy for long-term economic performance as measured by stock price, which reflects the cash flow generated over time and is available to shareholders, given no share repurchase or equity issuances. High-quality financial information reflecting the economic dimension of sustainability performance enables investors to assess better the risk and return associated with their investments through more accurate and complete financial information. The economic dimension of sustainability should unambiguously affect the cost of both debt

Risk Assessment and Financial Sustainability

and equity. When a company discloses more information with respect to economic sustainability, both stock and bond investors have better access to information with respect to corporate profitability. Since investors can make better investment decisions when they have more relevant information about corporate profitability, the cost of debt and equity should, therefore, be lower.

Corporate reports are intended to provide investors with relevant, transparent, timely, and reliable information for making sound investment decisions and improving the efficiency of the financial markets. Public companies are required to report a set of financial statements to their shareholders under the corporate mandatory disclosures regime and a set of voluntary disclosures on their product innovations, research and development, and growth and earnings forecasts that are often viewed as forward-looking information. Regulators and standard setters worldwide have shown interest in improving the financial reporting process by focusing on both financial and nonfinancial KPIs.[21]

Investors demand forward-looking financial and nonfinancial information, and companies provide such information to all their stakeholders. PricewaterhouseCoopers (PwC) has presented guidelines for public companies to meet investor demand for forward-looking financial and nonfinancial information.[22] The PwC's guide is based on the following several pillars of corporate effective communication with stakeholders, namely: (1) commitment to adequate resources for proper disclosures and how they are managed; (2) identification of material risks and uncertainties that may affect the company's sustainable performance; (3) development of significant relationships with principal stakeholders to ensure sustainable performance; (4) presentation of data pertaining to trends and factors that are likely to affect the company's prospects; and (5) identification of any material uncertainties threatening the achievement of the company's objectives, goals, and strategic activities.

Value Relevance of Financial Economic Sustainability

Sustainable shareholder value creation, the primary objective for many business organizations, can be achieved by focusing on the economic dimension of sustainability performance, which will be examined in detail in the next section. The focus on short-term considerations has an adverse impact on long-term and sustainable shareholder value creation and reduces the expected value of future returns and, thus, the current share prices. As the number of public companies reporting their sustainability performance is growing worldwide, the value relevance of sustainability performance reports has been addressed by regulators, investors, and the business community. In recent years, there has been an increased focus on integrated sustainability performance reports. Theoretically, management's engagement in sustainability activities, performance, and reports can be viewed as value increasing or value decreasing for investors depending on the costs and benefits of disclosing sustainability performance information. Obviously, companies that effectively manage their business sustainability, improve CSR performance, strengthen their reputation, fulfill their social responsibility, and promote a corporate culture of integrity and competency are sustainable in creating shareholder value. Thus, business sustainability focuses on activities that generate long-term financial performance of firm value maximization as well as voluntary activities that result in the achievement of non-financial sustainability performance that concerns all stakeholders.

The value relevance of voluntary sustainability information is measured by the firm-specific costs and benefits of providing such information. The firm value is expected to increase where the firm-specific benefits of sustainability performance information exceed the costs of providing such information. Market-wide effects of firm sustainability information are important if the net benefit at the firm level affects the entire market, or the net benefit is ignored or not fully internalized by firms. Market-wide effects of voluntary sustainability disclosures can be measured in terms of the impacts on firm valuation. This suggests that investors are willing to pay a premium for firms that engage in sustainability activities by assigning higher valuations to these firms in the financial markets. There are three costs associated with sustainability performance reporting. First, the direct cost of producing sustainability reports and obtaining assurance on the reports. The second cost is the opportunity cost of managerial time and efforts spent on the preparation of sustainability reports. Finally, there are the *proprietary costs* of voluntary disclosures if the firm reveals valuable information, such as information about profitable customers and markets, the revelation of trade secrets, or the exposure of operating or reporting weakness to regulators, unions, investors, customers, suppliers, or competitors.[23] There is also the possibility that the likelihood of litigations is higher when firms voluntarily disclose sustainability information. Thus, the cost–benefit trade-offs in voluntary disclosure of sustainability performance information should be assessed to determine its value relevance.

The primary attributes of financial ESP are: (1) financial stability and viability of maintaining a strong and stable financial position, sustaining effective and efficient operations, managing financial risk, and maintaining a sustainable capital structure that supports long-term growth and development; (2) continuous improvements of achieving consistent and reasonable earnings streams, balancing short-term financial profit with long-term value creation, and ensuring that profit margins are sustainable and competitive; (3) cost efficiency and effectiveness of implementing cost-effective and efficient operations and production processes, identifying and eliminating wastes and unnecessary expenses, and adopting continuous improvement strategies; (5) long-term planning of establishing and

Value Relevance of Financial Economic Sustainability

executing long-term sustainable strategic plans in balancing short-term financial goals with long-term sustainability, and using economic, social, and environmental factors in decision-making; (4) market positioning of developing competitive advantage and a strong market presence, building customer loyalty and brand equity, and differentiating products or services to create unique market position (5) compliance and governance by complying with all applicable laws, rules, regulations, corporate governance standards, and ethical business practices, adhering to financial regulations and reporting requirements, and achieving transparency in financial reporting; (6) job creation and economic prosperity by providing fair employment opportunities and contributing to job creation, supporting local, national and global economic development initiatives, and assessing and minimizing negative impacts on local, national and global economies; and (7) stakeholder value creation by maintaining a positive relationship with shareholders through transparent communication, and balancing the interests of different stakeholders, including shareholders, creditors, employees, customers, and suppliers. Some of the key performance indicators of financial ESP are reported earnings, cash flows, return on assets, growth, research and development, return on investment, total spending on R&D, total spending on information technology, and net investment (capital expenditure less depreciation). These KPIs should be used as benchmarks against which financial ESP is evaluated, and directors and executives are held accountable for generating long-term and sustainable economic performance.

Summary

Under agency theory and the shareholder primacy concept, the primary responsibility of business organizations is to their shareholders in maximizing their wealth. Financial ESP is the most important dimension of sustainability performance in creating shareholder value. Business organizations must be economically and financially sustainable in creating shareholder values to survive and be able to achieve other dimensions of sustainability performance. Financial and internal control reporting systems under the integrated financial and internal control reporting in the post-SOX era must be robust, effective, and reliable in producing and disseminating high-quality financial information to reflect economic sustainability performance properly. The effectiveness of financial and internal control systems requires management to identify significant risks that may cause material misstatements and design control activities to minimize negative impacts. Management is primarily responsible for the achievement of sustainable economic performance, which is achieved through effective reporting of such performance to all stakeholders, particularly the investors. This chapter presents financial and economic sustainability in achieving financial performance to create shareholder value. Business sustainability encourages management to focus on achieving long-term sustainable financial and economic performance and discourages managerial short-term.

Key Points

- Economic sustainability performance has been and will continue to be a vital component of business sustainability performance, as business organizations must be financially stable and perform well financially before contributing to the environment and society.
- Improving financial sustainability performance starts with establishing a proper tone at the top with a commitment to effective economic sustainability performance, reporting, and assurance.
- Management should incorporate financial sustainability development into decision-making, planning, implementation, and evaluation processes.
- Management should expand and redesign corporate financial reporting to sustainability and accountability with a keen focus on supporting the information needs of long-term investors regarding sustainable economic performance.
- Audit strategies on ICFR should be effective, efficient, adequate, and in compliance with applicable accounting and auditing guidelines and standards.

Review Questions

1. **In which areas do investors primarily use sustainability information?**
2. **What are the benefits of web-based corporate reporting?**
3. **How can sustainability development and reporting affect long-term economic performance and thus shareholder value?**
4. **What could occur in the context of the agency theory where information asymmetry is assumed to be present?**
5. **What are some reasons why business organizations worldwide are being criticized?**
6. **How can sustainable shared value creation be achieved?**
7. **Under the shared value creation concept, what is management focusing on?**
8. **What is the main objective of any business organization?**
9. **What is the difference between traditional corporate reporting and business sustainability?**
10. **What positive impact can high-quality financial information have on investors?**

Key Points

11. **How does a firm achieve effective internal control?**
12. **What is one key responsibility of management?**
13. **Discuss the concept of stakeholder capitalism.**
14. **What is the importance of transparency in financial and nonfinancial reports?**
15. **Discuss the significance of high-quality financial information reflecting ESP.**

Discussion Questions

1. **Explain the value maximization concept.**
2. **Discuss the measures taken in the post-Sarbanes-Oxley (SOX) era to improve the quality of financial reports.**
3. **Discuss the concept of shared value and its impact on an organization.**
4. **Examine the characteristics of economic sustainability performance.**
5. **Investigate the primary uses of sustainability information by investors.**
6. **Learn how the value relevance of voluntary sustainability information is measured.**
7. **Why does corporate reporting need to be improved nowadays?**
8. **Why is narrative reporting an important element of corporate communication with stakeholders?**
9. **What is the key driver of economic growth and prosperity in capital markets?**
10. **What can happen when the interests of the agent are not aligned with those of the principal?**
11. **Under the shared value creation concept, what is management focusing on?**
12. **What is the main objective of any business organization?**
13. **What is the difference between traditional corporate reporting and business sustainability?**
14. **What positive impact can high-quality financial information have on investors?**
15. **How does a firm achieve effective internal control?**

Multiple Choice Questions

1. **Which law requires management certification of financial statements and internal control over financial reporting (ICFR)?**
   A) Sarbanes-Oxley Act (SOX)
   B) Dodd-Frank Act

C) Securities Exchange Act

D) Federal Reserve Act

2. **Which component is considered the most important in creating shareholder value?**

A) Environmental performance

B) Social performance

C) Governance performance

D) Economic sustainability performance (ESP)

3. **What do audited financial statements typically provide information about?**

A) Short-term profits

B) Marketing strategies

C) Entity's financial condition and results of operations

D) Employee satisfaction

4. **Which standard requires auditors to use a risk-based approach in the audit of ICFR?**

A) PCAOB Auditing Standard (AS) No. 2

B) PCAOB Auditing Standard (AS) No. 5

C) FASB Standard No. 1

D) IFRS Standard No. 3

5. **What is the primary responsibility of management in terms of financial reporting?**

A) Reducing expenses

B) Preparing reliable, useful, and relevant financial information

C) Marketing the company's products

D) Hiring new employees

6. **What must be included in the management's discussion and analysis (MD&A) of financial condition and results of operations?**

A) Marketing strategies

B) Detailed financial data and analysis

C) Employee demographics

D) Product descriptions

7. **How can sustainable shared value creation be achieved?**

A) By focusing solely on short-term profits

B) By integrating economic, social, and environmental factors in business strategies

C) By minimizing workforce

D) By increasing debt

Multiple Choice Questions

8. **Which component is not typically included in audited financial statements?**
    A) Management certifications of financial statements
    B) Independent auditor's report on financial statements
    C) Detailed marketing strategies
    D) Management's discussion and analysis (MD&A)

9. **What is one of the primary uses of sustainability information by investors?**
    A) To assess risks and returns associated with investments
    B) To market products
    C) To hire new employees
    D) To reduce costs

10. **Which approach is recommended for auditors in PCAOB AS No. 5?**
    A) A standardized approach
    B) A risk-based approach
    C) A random approach
    D) A cost-based approach

11. **What is the main objective of financial economic sustainability performance (ESP)?**
    A) Maximizing short-term profits
    B) Creating long-term sustainable shareholder value
    C) Reducing operational costs
    D) Increasing market share

12. **What is a potential consequence of financial short-termism?**
    A) Long-term sustainable growth
    B) Reduced emphasis on quarterly earnings
    C) Undermining sustainable economic performance by focusing on short-term results
    D) Increased environmental sustainability

13. **What is a key driver of economic growth, prosperity, and financial stability for the nation?**
    A) Investor confidence in public financial information and capital markets
    B) Short-term profit maximization
    C) Reducing workforce
    D) Increasing debt

14. **What is the main purpose of management certifications of financial statements and ICFR?**
    A) Marketing the company's products

B) Ensuring the accuracy and reliability of financial reports

C) Increasing debt

D) Reducing workforce

15. **What is required by Section 404(b) of SOX?**

A) Management certification of the effectiveness of ICFR

B) Independent auditor opinion on the effectiveness of ICFR

C) Employee certification

D) Customer feedback reports

16. **What is the primary function of business organizations in creating value for shareholders?**

A) Maximizing short-term profits

B) Achieving long-term financial sustainability performance

C) Reducing operational costs

D) Increasing market share

17. **What is required for effective integrated financial and internal control reporting (IFICR)?**

A) Reducing workforce

B) Vigilant oversight by the board of directors

C) Marketing strategies

D) Increasing debt

18. **What is the significance of high-quality financial information in the context of financial economic sustainability performance (ESP)?**

A) It reduces shareholder wealth

B) It enables investors to assess risks and returns more accurately

C) It has no impact on investor decisions

D) It increases tax liabilities

19. **What is the key driver of economic growth and prosperity in capital markets?**

A) Short-term profit maximization

B) Investor confidence in public financial information

C) Reducing workforce

D) Increasing debt

20. **What are the key components of economic sustainability performance (ESP)?**

A) Financial stability, continuous improvements, cost efficiency, long-term planning, market positioning, compliance and governance, job creation, stakeholder value creation

B) Employee satisfaction, customer loyalty, brand equity, cost reduction, asset management

C) Marketing strategies, product descriptions, employee demographics, customer feedback

D) Reducing workforce, increasing debt, minimizing taxes, ignoring environmental impacts

21. **What is the role of the board of directors in financial reporting?**

A) Reducing workforce

B) Overseeing management reporting activities to ensure accurate financial information

C) Marketing the company's products

D) Increasing debt

22. **What is the impact of financial short-termism on long-term economic performance?**

A) Enhances long-term growth

B) Undermines sustainable economic performance by focusing on short-term results

C) Has no impact on long-term performance

D) Increases environmental sustainability

23. **What is the main purpose of the management's discussion and analysis (MD&A)?**

A) Marketing strategies

B) Detailed financial data and analysis

C) Employee demographics

D) Product descriptions

24. **What does Section 404(b) of SOX require?**

A) Management certification of the effectiveness of ICFR

B) Independent auditor opinion on the effectiveness of ICFR

C) Employee certification

D) Customer feedback reports

25. **What is the primary goal of business organizations according to the enlightened value maximization concept?**

A) Maximizing short-term profits

B) Balancing economic sustainability performance with other nonfinancial dimensions of sustainability

C) Reducing workforce

D) Increasing debt

26. **What is the primary focus of business organizations in terms of economic sustainability performance (ESP)?**
    A) Short-term profit maximization
    B) Achieving long-term financial sustainability performance
    C) Reducing workforce
    D) Increasing debt

27. **What is the primary responsibility of management in terms of financial reporting?**
    A) Reducing expenses
    B) Preparing reliable, useful, and relevant financial information
    C) Marketing the company's products
    D) Hiring new employees

28. **What is the significance of transparency in financial and nonfinancial reports?**
    A) Reduces shareholder wealth
    B) Enhances credibility and builds stakeholder trust
    C) Has no impact on stakeholder decisions
    D) Increases tax liabilities

29. **What is required for effective integrated financial and internal control reporting (IFICR)?**
    A) Reducing workforce
    B) Vigilant oversight by the board of directors
    C) Marketing strategies
    D) Increasing debt

30. **What is the effect of focusing on long-term sustainable economic performance on shareholder value?**
    A) Decreases shareholder value
    B) Has no impact on shareholder value
    C) Increases shareholder value
    D) Only affects nonfinancial stakeholders

Notes

1 Much of discussions and materials for this section and the next two sections come from Rezaee, Z. (2015). *Business sustainability: Performance, Compliance, Accountability and Integrated Reporting.* Greenleaf Publishing Limited and Rezaee, Z (2024). *The Sustainable*

Business Blueprint: Planning, Performance, Risk, Reporting and Assurance. Routledge/
Taylor and Francis.

2 Public Company Accounting Oversight Board (PCAOB). (2004). Auditing standard No. 2: An audit of internal control over financial reporting performed in conjunction with an audit of financial statements. www.pcaobus.org/Standards/Standards_and_Related_Rules/Auditing_Standard_No.2.aspx.

3 Sarbanes-Oxley Act (SOX) (2002, July 30). www.law.uc.edu/CCL/SOact/soact.pdf.

4 AICPA. (2018). The 2018 AICPA conference on current SEC and PCAOB developments. https://www.aicpa.org/cpeandconferences/conferences/secpcaob.html.

5 Porter, M.E., and Kramer, M.R. (2011). Creating shared value. *Harvard Business Review* (January–February): 62–77.

6 Porter, M.E., and Kramer, M.R. (2011). Creating shared value. *Harvard Business Review* (January–February): 62–77.

7 Porter, M.E., and Kramer, M.R. (2011). Creating shared value. *Harvard Business Review* (January–February): 65.

8 Committee for Economic Development. (2007). Built to last: Focusing corporations onlong-term performance. www.ced.org/docs/report/report_corpgov2007.pdf.

9 Kiron, D., Kruschwitz, N., Haanaes, K., Reeves, M., and Goh, E. (2013). The innovation bottom line: How companies that see sustainability as both a necessity and an opportunity, and change their business models in response, are finding success. *MIT Sloan Management Review.* http://csbf.org.nz/wp-content/uploads/the-innovation-bottom-line.pdf.

10 Klemash, S., J. Smith and R. Doyle. (2019). Stakeholder capitalism for long-term value creation. Harvard Law School on Corporate Governance and Financial Regulation. June 13, 2019. Available at https://corpgov.law.harvard.edu/2019/06/13/stakeholder-capitalism-for-long-term-value-creation/

11 FSG. (2018). Measuring shared value: How to unlock value by linking social and business results. https://www.hbs.edu/faculty/Publication%20Files/Measuring_Shared_Value_57032487-9e5c-46a1-9bd8-90bd7f1f9cef.pdf.

12 Dallas, L.L. (2012). Short-termism, the financial crisis, and corporate governance. University of San Diego, School of Law, Research Paper No. 12-078 (February). *The Journal of Corporation Law* 37 (2): 266–361. http://ssrn.com/abstract=2006556.

13 Securities and Exchange Commission (SEC). (1977). Securities Exchange Act Release No. 13185 (January 19).

14 SEC. (1978). Notification of enactment of Foreign Corrupt Practices Act of 1977. Accounting Series Release No. 242 (Release No. 34-14478, February 16, 43 FR 7752).

15 SEC. (1979). Statement of management on internal accounting control. 17CFR Parts 221, 229, 240, 249; Release No. 34-15772, File No. S7-779 (April).

16 The Committee of Sponsoring Organizations of the Treadway Commission. (1992). Internal control-integrated framework. COSO. Executive summary. http://www.coso.org/publications/executive_summary_integrated_framework.htm.

17 Sarbanes-Oxley Act (SOX). (2002, July 30). www.law.uc.edu/CCL/SOact/soact.pdf.

18 Public Company Accounting Oversight Board (PCAOB). (2004). Auditing Standard No. 2: An audit of internal control over financial reporting performed in conjunction with an audit of financial statements. http://www.pcaob.org/Standards/Standards_and_Related_Rules/Auditing_Standard_No.2.aspx.

19 Public Company Accounting Oversight Board (PCAOB). (2007). Auditing Standard No. 5: An audit of internal control over financial reporting that is integrated with an audit of financial statements (December 19). www.pcaob.org/Standards/Standards_and_Related_Rules/Auditing_Standard_No.5.aspx.

20 Committee of Sponsoring Organizations of the Treadway Commission (COSO). (2004). Enterprise risk management – integrated framework (September), New York.

21 Reilly, D. (2007). Profit as we know it could be lost with new accounting statements. *Wall Street Journal* (May 12): A1. online.wsj.com/public/article/SB1178935201395008 14-m5r4 gJLCTET50No6lq_tulrvFug_20070522.html?mod=blogs.

22 PricewaterhouseCoopers (PwC). (2006). Guide to forward-looking information: Don't fear the future – communicating with confidence (January). www.pwc.com/Extweb/pwcpublications.nsf/docid/E97847126DD93E13802570FA004100D7.

23 Leuz, C. (2004). Proprietary versus non-proprietary disclosures: Evidence from Germany. In *The Economics and Politics of Accounting* (C. Leuz, D. Pfaff, and A. Hopwood, eds.), 164–197. Oxford University Press.

Notes

Chapter 8
Nonfinancial Dimension of Sustainability

Learning Objectives

- Understand the nonfinancial dimension of sustainability performance.
- Provide an overview of each dimension of nonfinancial sustainability performance.
- Learn the best practices of the nonfinancial dimension of sustainability performance dimensions.
- Be aware of the different issues of corporate social responsibility.
- Be aware of the importance of CSR reporting and assurance.
- Provide an overview of initiatives taken toward global environmental concerns.
- Know the general guidelines for implementing ISO 14000.
- Provide an overview of the best practices of environmental KPIs that have been adopted.
- Understand the purpose of Environmental Management Systems (EMS).
- Understand the importance of environmental reporting and disclosure.
- Provide an overview of the environmental assurance and auditing.
- Be aware of environmental best practices.

Introduction

Nonfinancial dimensions of sustainability performance are divided into environmental, social, and governance (ESG) dimensions, with the ethics component integrated into other ESG components. KPMG, in its 2020 audit committee agenda, underscores the emerging challenges of ESG for the audit committees of business organizations.[1] KPMG highlights seven issues that the audit committees should address in the 2020 audit committee agenda, which include matters such as reassessing the scope and quality of ESG/sustainability reports and disclosures, refocusing standards on ethical compliance and whistleblower programs, and helping ensure that internal auditors stay focused on critical risks, specific for nonfinancial disclosures. ESG issues and reporting standards have become important for various stakeholders, from customers to employees, suppliers, regulators, and investors. With the recent move toward business sustainability technological advancements and immediate information in social media. Investors are demanding more

DOI: 10.4324/9781003487081-8

transparent and higher quality relevant financial ESP and nonfinancial ESG reports to make sound investment decisions. Ernst and Young (EY) has also outlined the importance of ESG dimensions for audit committees to understand controls, disclosure requirements, and audits.[2] Nonfinancial ESG sustainability performance dimensions refer to the integration of ESG and ethics factors into business decision-making processes beyond financial metrics. Companies that prioritize nonfinancial ESG sustainability performance recognize that their long-term success depends not only on financial ESP outcomes but also on their ability to manage risks and opportunities related to ESG issues and factors.

Environmental Dimension of Sustainability

The environmental dimension of sustainability performance is vital to business sustainability, and it covers the assessment and management of a company's environmental performance and its environmental impact, including carbon footprint, energy consumption, water usage, waste generation, and pollution. Environmental initiatives may include adopting renewable energy sources, reducing greenhouse gas emissions, conserving resources, implementing sustainable supply-chain practices, and investing in eco-friendly technologies. To effectively compete in the global market, companies worldwide should integrate environmental sustainability into their business strategies and models. Many of the business disasters that occurred over the past decade accentuate that corporate environmental responsibilities are vital to economic sustainability and the well-being of society and future generations. Companies should respond to environmental challenges and turn them into opportunities by changing their environmental management, policies, and practices that safeguard the global environment and improve their environmental performance.

Sustainability performance relevant to the environmental dimension has gained significant attention from investors, regulators, the business community, research scholars, and the accounting profession. The move toward addressing global warming, climate change, and the green economy requires reliable, relevant, and transparent information about the impacts of an organization's activities and operations on the environment beyond what is legislated by law. Corporations can no longer solely focus on corporate profitability while ignoring their impacts on society and the environment. The environmental dimension of sustainability performance considers a business's impact on the environment and its efforts to operate to minimize negative impacts on the environment, conserve resources, foster ecological balance, and promote a better environment for the next generations. This includes creating a better work environment, improving air and water quality, reducing the carbon footprint, maximizing the positive effects of an organization, and minimizing the negative impacts on natural resources and the environment.

Environmental Dimension of Sustainability

Many of the business disasters that occurred in the past decade underscore that corporate environmental policies are vital to economic sustainability and the well-being of society. Environmental sustainability is defined as a process of preserving the quality of the environment in the long term and creating a better environment for future generations while creating shareholder value. In 2010, the SEC released guidance reiterating the relevance and importance of adequate disclosure of material risk associated with climate change by public companies.[3] On March 6, 2024, the SEC released its Final Rules Regarding Mandatory Climate Risk Disclosures that require disclosure of direct Greenhouse Gas (GHG) emissions (Scope 1) and emissions associated with energy purchases (Scope 2) when those emissions are material.[4] Current and future legislation, coupled with society's increasing sensitivity to the environment (especially toward pollution, hazardous waste, human health, and other general environmental concerns), necessitates the need for high-level management to pay attention to their companies' environmental practices and obligations.

The International Standardization Organization (ISO) released ISO 14000, which requires executive management to conduct regular evaluations of the Environmental Management System (EMS) to ensure that the system realizes the set goals and missions of the environmental policies.[5] The main goal for management's review of the EMS is to identify deficiencies and successes to improve environmental practices in the future. A company will benefit economically and socially through the implementation and continuous usage of an EMS that is relevant, accurate, and sustainable in monitoring and developing environmental best practices, missions, and goals. This chapter presents the environmental dimension of EESG sustainability performance with a keen focus on Asia, including environmental key performance indicators (KPIs), global environmental initiatives, environmental management systems, environmental reporting, environmental assurance and auditing, and environmental best practices.

The environmental dimension of sustainability performance includes reducing an organization's carbon footprint, creating a better work environment, and improving the air and water quality of the property and the surrounding community. Many of the business disasters (e.g., BP oil spill) that occurred in the past decade proved that corporate environmental responsibilities are vital to economic sustainability and the well-being of society and future generations. Sustainability disclosures with respect to the environmental dimension are mainly related to effects on natural resources and the environment that could directly or indirectly affect the living conditions of human beings. Strengths in environmental areas include (1) beneficial products and services, (2) anti-pollution policies, (3) recycling, (4) clean energy, (5) sustainability programs, and (6) other environmental strengths. Weaknesses include (1) hazardous waste, (2) regulatory problems, (3) ozone-depleting chemicals, (4) substantial emissions, (5) agricultural chemicals, (6) climate changes, (7) overpopulation, (8) deforestation, (9) natural disasters, (10) agricultural pollution, and (11) excess waste.

Widening sensitivities to the environment (e.g., pollution, hazardous waste, human health, and other general environmental concerns), along with ever-increasing environmental laws and regulations, force corporations to pay attention to their environmental practices and obligations. Reporting environmental performance in the United States in a corporate setting has been built on regulations and societal demand for accurate environmental reporting. Corporations have developed environmental reporting tools through voluntary and enforced standards via various social and governmental initiatives. Environmental initiatives and regulations have far-reaching consequences on how corporations are viewed in society and are held liable for inadequate environmental consideration. Environmental business sustainability created through best practices, regulations, or accounting standards is forcing Corporate America to rethink how business is conducted.

Moreover, corporations are developing or adapting voluntary reporting tools to be compliant with regulatory bodies and to enhance their social responsibility. Developing an environmental strategy for the company is only the beginning. Companies that have large supplier relationships must verify the integrity of the specific suppliers' environmental KPIs to ensure sustainability throughout the value chain. Implementing these practices is voluntary in the United States. However, the increase in environmental regulations has induced the federal government to enforce the regulations through the Environmental Protection Agency (EPA). The EPA is responsible for identifying and enforcing environmental laws and regulations and forcing companies to clean up or to seek recovery costs from cleaning up a contaminated site. Companies that do not comply will be liable for (i) clean-up costs, (ii) reducing or eliminating future contamination, (iii) degradation of natural resources, (iv) societal litigation, and (v) criminal charges. Effective compliance with environmental laws and regulations requires full commitment by companies to initiate environmental management systems and accounting and auditing practices.[6]

The United Kingdom and the United States both have large corporations or conglomerates that operate throughout the globe. The United Kingdom has developed environmental laws that enforce environmental practices, whereas the United States has regulations that govern industries that are involved in the use of natural resources. Although both countries have laws and regulations to ensure public safety now and in the future, neither have standards on how to disclose environmental practices. Furthermore, such disclosure is voluntary but increasing in popularity stemming from societal demand. In the United States, the SEC and the Financial Accounting Standards Board (FASB) have given corporations support in developing reporting standards. However, the major increase in reporting is mainly attributed to the increase in social awareness and governmental regulation.[7] The EPA has influenced the types of KPIs being monitored and used throughout the business world. Moreover, systems have been developed to help report environmental information. The EPA has implemented several environmental regulations to control and monitor environmental degradation, which enables it to enforce the regulations when companies fail to act accordingly.[8]

Environmental sustainability has become a strategic focus of corporations worldwide. The response to environmental challenges and the pursuit of opportunities has resulted in policies and practices that seek to safeguard the environment and improve the well-being of society. Global environmental calamities like the Union Carbide Bhopal chemical leak in 1984 and the (2010) British Petroleum oil spill in the Gulf of Mexico are examples of events that have forever changed the affected environments, ecosystems, corporations, and communities.[9] The BP gas spill, also known as Deepwater Horizon, caught media attention when an oil rig exploded, killed 11 workers, and became the largest oceanic oil spill in history. The spill lasted approximately 90 days, with a total of 4 million barrels of oil being dispersed in the Gulf of Mexico. The spill led to the United States of America filing suit against BP and other responsible culprits. This led to settlements of $90 million for MOEX Offshore LLC, $1 billion for Transocean Offshore, and $14.9 billion for BP exploration and production. The US court system also created a website for all to visit regarding the spill.[10]

Public awareness of both corporate and individual responsibilities has increased, as has stakeholder input. Environmental risk mitigation is an integral part of economic sustainability, both present and future. Increased CO_2 levels from greenhouse gases (coal, oil, and natural gas) are linked to atmospheric temperature, which will affect weather patterns. Volatility in climate patterns increases uncertainty about future demand, supply chains, and the stability of infrastructure. Hence, business policy will evolve as these patterns are better understood. Extreme weather conditions are well understood and responded to in most cases and are generally part of an organization's business continuity plan. Both extreme weather and climate change impact sustainability. Energy and fuel supply uncertainties increase volatility in fossil-fuel markets. Managing one's corporate reputation, customer expectations, and efficiency drives interest more than legal compliance in most cases. Independent ranking agencies rate companies on emissions and goals. Carbon footprints are found in supply chains and are an efficiency and risk measure, which is a liability that demands stakeholder management. Scarce material resources will increase in line with population growth and urbanization. Shareholders have become more educated about these challenges and recognize the corporate investment required to meet long-term sustainability. Several sustainability indices are being developed by agencies such as Bloomberg to provide valuation tools for the measurement and comparison of companies.

The stresses placed on the natural environment over the last century have increased strains and crises worldwide. In addition to the identification of ozone depletion in the late 20th century, the identification of climate change is a manifestation of this deterioration in our natural environment. Initiatives like the Kyoto Protocol, the European Union Emission Trading System (EU ETS), the Carbon Reduction Commitment (CRC), the Montreal Protocol, and the Paris Agreement are all efforts to gain consensus on mechanisms by which to measure impacts on the environment and to set limits on activities deemed detrimental. Specifically, the Kyoto Protocol sets greenhouse gas emission limits and provides signature nations three mechanisms by which to meet the necessary output level, namely emissions trading, clean development mechanisms, and joint implementation.

In addition to the numerous organizations like the Alliance for Global Sustainability that seek to improve the scientific understanding of global environmental challenges as well as the education of a new generation of leaders committed to sustainable development, the International Organization for Standardization established global standards to assist firms in developing adequate environmental management systems. The global success of ISO 9000 quality assurance standards serves as the model for the ISO 14000 series standards. While not mandatory, many organizations are also required by their customers to be ISO 14000 certified prior to conducting business. Meeting ISO 14000 standards is increasingly becoming a prerequisite for competition in the global market. Further, the 14000 series standards can serve as the framework for environmentally sustainable business plans and mission statements, which, if well-built and adhered to, will likely limit a company's future liability and constrain the cost of enforcement. As energy dependence rises, one would expect further visibility and development of ISO standards, which specifically address energy management throughout organizations.

The Sustainability Accounting Standards Board (SASB), in October 2014, released its standard for the chemical industry, which identifies the following sustainability disclosure topics:[11]

- Greenhouse gas emissions are measured in terms of gross global scope 1 emissions, percentage covered under a regulatory program, and long-term and short-term strategy to assess and manage it.
- Energy management is measured in terms of total energy consumed, percentage of grid electricity, and percentage of renewable energy.
- Air quality is measured in terms of air emissions for pollutants.
- Water management is measured in terms of total water withdrawal, percentage recycled, and percentage in regions with high or extremely high baseline water stress.

Environmental Dimension of Sustainability

- Hazardous materials management is measured in terms of the amount of hazardous waste and the percentage recycled.
- Employee health and safety are measured in terms of total recordable injury rate and fatality rate for full-time employees and contract employees.
- Product lifecycle management and innovation are measured in terms of the percentage of products by revenue that contain genetically modified organisms.
- Political spending is measured in terms of the amount of political, lobbying, or tax-exempt group expenditures.
- Operational safety, emergency management, and response are measured in terms of challenges of the safety indicator rate.

Climate change is an important environmental issue that can present significant challenges and opportunities for business organizations, as well as investment risks and opportunities for shareholders, with the potential to affect the long-term success and value of the company. The January 2019 public opinion survey indicates that a record number of Americans care about climate change and global warming, and they believe that climate change is real and humans mainly cause it; this needs to be addressed through policy initiatives such as carbon tax to prevent further damages to the environment.[12] In 2010, the SEC released guidance reiterating the relevance and importance of adequate disclosure of material risk associated with climate change by public companies.[13] Items in filing SEC documents S-K or S-X that trigger climate-related disclosure are items 101, 103, 503(c), and 303. Item 101 pertains to any material capital expenditures on facilities environmental controls during the company's current fiscal year and previous periods where the company finds its material.[14] Item 103 requires a company or its subsidiaries to describe any material legal proceedings in which it may be involved.[15] Item 503(c) gives guidance on what risk factors a company should review and disclose regarding existing or pending regulations on climate change.[16] Item 303 requires public companies to determine the effect any enacted climate change legislation or regulation will have on the company's financial position.[17] The SEC released its final rules on climate change in March 2024 that require additional disclosures of climate change issues.[18] This regulation requires climate-related disclosures in public companies' annual reports and registration statements. As anticipated, these climate change rules are facing multiple legal challenges. Even though the climate-related disclosure rules are on hold while court challenges are heard, public companies should prepare for the possibility that some or all parts of the rules will come into effect. Furthermore, several states (e.g., California) and other countries in Europe are requiring similar disclosures of mandating quantitative and qualitative measures of the climate impact of operations, projected climate-related risks and progress toward sustainability goals.

Exhibit 8.1   Climate Change-Related Risks and Potential Impacts

Risks	Strategic Impacts	Financial Impacts
Physical		
1. Changing weather patterns; 2. Water availability and quality	1. Asset damage; 2. Health and safety; 3. Operational disruptions; 4. Transportation interruptions; 5. Restriction of licenses, availability, and use	1. Asset write-offs; 2. Capital expenditures; 3. Increased costs; 4. Reduced revenues; 5. Increased cost of capital; 6. Market risks
Regulatory		
Current/changing regulations	1. Compliance; 2. Impact on market demand; 3. Restriction of licenses, availability and use; 4. Market restrictions	1. Increased costs; 2. Capital expenditures; 3. Reduced revenues; 4. Asset valuations; 5. Early retirement or write-offs
Reputational		
1. Employees' and investors' attitudes; 2. Regulatory violations; 3. Work conditions	1. Reduced availability of capital; 2. Litigation/penalties; 3. Reduced demand; for goods/ services	1. Asset write-offs; 2. Increased costs; 3. Reduced revenues; 4. Customer satisfaction
Business Model		
1. Changes in demands for products/services; 2. Renewable energy; 3. Energy efficient products	1. Lower demand; 2. Higher costs for transition	1. Lower revenues; 2. Increased costs; 3. Higher cost of capital/ limited access to capital; 4. Asset write-offs

Source: Prepared from Canadian Securities Administrators (CSA): CSA Staff Notice 51–354: Report on Climate Change-Related Disclosure Project. http://www.osc.gov.on.ca/documents/en/.Securities-Category5/csa_201804 05_climatechange-related-disclosure-project.pdf.

Proper disclosures of climate change-related risks, strategic impacts, and financial impacts should be overseen by the board of directors, implemented by management, and reported by public companies. Exhibit 8.1 presents some of the climate change-related risks and their potential financial and strategic impacts.

The climate change and global warming issues have received the attention of policymakers, regulators, and businesses. Investors are concerned about the potential risks of global warming, climate change, and emission-related damages. Regulators, including the SEC,

Environmental Dimension of Sustainability

have addressed climate change and related regulations. Thus, stock exchanges worldwide have launched indices that track the environmental-related parameters of the listed companies. The S&P Dow Jones Indices and Toronto Stock Exchange in 2015 developed three climate change index series.[19] These three indices are:

1. The **S&P/TSX 60 Carbon Efficient Index**, which is intended to measure the performance of companies in the S&P/TSX 60 while overweighting/underweighting those companies that have lower/higher levels of carbon emissions.
2. The **S&P/TSX 60 Carbon Efficient Select Index**, which is designed to measure the performance of companies in the S&P/TSX 60 while excluding those companies with the largest relative carbon footprint.
3. The **S&P/TSX 60 Fossil Fuel Free Index**, which is designed to measure the performance of companies in the S&P/TSX 60 that do not own fossil fuel reserves.

The Fourth National Climate Assessment Report was published in 2018 in two volumes with a focus on the human welfare, environmental, and societal elements of climate change in the context of climate change risks and potential strategic and financial impacts.[20] The report provides examples of actions and best practices in the United States to reduce the risks associated with climate change, increase resilience, and improve livelihoods. This report should be relevant to policy and decision-makers, regulators, utility and natural resource managers, emergency planners and public health officials, and other stakeholders by presenting an examination of the effects of climate change. Some of the findings of this report are:[21]

1. Communities: Climate change creates risks in communities across the United States by presenting growing challenges to human health and safety, the rate of economic growth, and effects on quality of life. Reducing greenhouse gas emissions can substantially mitigate these risks and increase opportunities for healthier communities and economic growth.
2. Economy: Global warming and climate change are expected to cause growing losses to US infrastructure and property and impede the rate of economic growth. Proper substantial and sustained global mitigation and regional adaptation efforts should be made to reverse the rising temperatures, which reduce the efficiency of power generation and increase energy demands that can cause higher electricity costs.
3. Interconnected Impacts: The whole world is now interconnected, and climate change in one place can have cascading impacts that are often difficult to predict, threatening essential services within and beyond the nation's borders.
4. Actions to Reduce Risks: Communities, governments, and businesses are working to avoid substantial damages to the economy, environment, and human health and to

reduce risks from and costs associated with climate change by taking action to lower greenhouse gas emissions and implement adaptation strategies considered necessary over the coming decades.

5. Water: The quality and quantity of water available for use by people and ecosystems worldwide are being affected by climate change, increasing risks and costs to agriculture, energy production, industry, recreation, and the environment.

6. Health: The detrimental impacts of climate change on extreme weather and climate-related events, air quality, and the transmission of disease through insects and pests, food, and water increasingly threaten the health and well-being of humans.

7. Indigenous Peoples: Climate change increasingly threatens indigenous communities' livelihoods, cultural identities, economies, and health by disrupting interconnected social, physical, and ecological systems.

8. Ecosystems and Ecosystem Services: Ecosystems and the benefits they provide to society are being adversely affected by climate change, and without substantial and sustained reductions in global greenhouse gas emissions, transformative impacts on some ecosystems will continue to occur.

9. Agricultural and Food: Rising temperatures, extreme heat, drought, wildfire on rangelands, and heavy downpours are expected to disrupt agricultural productivity worldwide increasingly. In the United States, increases in challenges to livestock health and declines in crops are expected.

10. Infrastructure: The aging and deteriorating infrastructure is further stressed by increases in heavy precipitation events, coastal flooding, heat, wildfires, and other extreme events, as well as changes to average precipitation and temperature. Climate change will continue to degrade infrastructure performance with the potential for cascading impacts that threaten the economy, national security, essential services, and health and well-being in the absence of efforts to reverse this trend.

11. Oceans and Coasts: Coastal communities and the ecosystems that support them are increasingly threatened by the impacts of climate change, and without significant reductions in global greenhouse gas emissions and regional adaptation measures, many coastal regions will be transformed by putting ocean and marine species at risk.

12. Tourism and Recreation: Outdoor recreation, tourist economies, and quality of life are positively affected by the healthy natural environment that could be degraded by the impacts of climate change in many ways.

BlackRock Investment Stewardship (BIS) considers climate risk to be a key component of our "Environmental Risks and Opportunities" engagement priority.[22] Sound practices in relation to the material environmental factors inherent to a company's business model can be a signal of operational excellence and management quality. Environmental factors relevant to the long-term economic performance of companies are typically industry-specific,

Environmental Dimension of Sustainability

although in today's dynamic business environment, some, such as regulation and technological change, can have a broader impact. Corporate reporting should help investors and others understand the company's approach to these factors, how risks are integrated, and how opportunities are realized.

The Task Force on Climate-Related Financial Disclosures (TCFD) recommendations were finalized in June 2017, and they are intended to enable stakeholders to understand companies' exposure to climate-related risks and carbon-related assets. The TCFD is organized into four specific categories and encourages corporate climate change disclosures in the areas of governance, strategy, risk management and metrics, and targets related to:[23]

- Governance: The organization's governance measures to address climate-related risks and opportunities.
- Strategy: Business strategies relevant to the actual and potential impacts of climate-related risks and opportunities.
- Risk Management: The processes designed and implemented to identify, assess, and manage climate-related risks.
- Metrics and Targets: The metrics and targets are designed to assess and manage relevant climate-related risks and opportunities effectively.

To help reduce the environmental footprint, corporations are adopting formal evaluation processes to measure its impact on the planet. Various environmental KPI measures are being developed and adopted. The best practices of the adopted environmental KPIs are:

- Production and delivery of environmentally safe products by using biodegradable, non-toxic, and naturally derived materials in the production.
- Efficient and effective utilization of scarce natural resources like power, energy, and scarce natural materials.
- Efficient and effective use of recycled materials.
- Low-carbon-footprint model towns.
- Leveraging technology to maximize utilization of scarce resources and replacement of nonrenewable resources.
- Effective and efficient utilization of non-waste technologies.
- Minimization of the use of harmful and unsafe materials and products.
- Assessment and management of environmental risks, including providing appropriate insurance for risks and environmental remediation and disposal efforts.

- Environmental reporting that discloses environmental risk assessment and management, compliance with environmental requirements, and measurement of environmental liabilities.
- Environmental external auditing and assurance on environmental reports.

The EMS within a corporation are programs established by the corporation to improve the environmental performance of the company. EMS programs allow companies to achieve environmental goals based on the company's control of its processes. EMS programs maintain themselves through mission statements and company policies. These policies and goals are available to all the stakeholders. It is believed that when a company can control its environmental impact through goals, the company will improve its environmental performance. Most companies benefit from EMS programs through energy savings.

The management team is responsible for determining the policies and goals for the EMS programs. Once the goals and policies have been established, a plan is developed to attain the goals set by the corporation. The company must then implement the plan and develop a monitoring system to determine the effectiveness and completion of the goals and policies. This ultimately comes to the review by management to further develop goals and policies. The documentation for EMS programs is specifically based on ISO 14000 standards. ISO 14001 is the leading standard for EMS programs. It requires extensive documentation as well as regular review of the documentation by executive management.

The corporation has established its EMS programs and has applied for ISO 14000 certification. The company will then be audited regarding its goals and policies. Once the company gains certification, they will be subject to periodic reviews. Some benefits of becoming certified include new market customers, increased employee morale, increased efficiency, and a better public image. Some of the best practices and goals of an effective EMS are:

- Appropriate tone at the top is set by the board of directors and senior executives to provide the leadership and commit adequate resources necessary for responsible environmental management.
- The compliance board committee and/or compliance officers are assigned the primary responsibility for the environmental performance of the operations within their control.
- Proper education of all employees regarding environmental laws, regulations, and best practices.
- Development of environmental policies and procedures in compliance with environmental rules and regulations.

Environmental Dimension of Sustainability

- Assignment of qualified officers and staff in charge of compliance with environmental policies to advance the corporation's knowledge of environmental protection.
- Assessment and management of environmental risks and evaluation of environmental performance on the ongoing monitoring process.
- Certification of compliance with established operating environmental procedures to ensure maintenance of environmental regulatory compliance and responsible environmental management.
- Establishment of an environmental audit program to ensure periodic reviews of environmental KPIs are in operation.
- Proper disclosure of environmental policies and procedures, reporting, and auditing to all stakeholders.

Environmental KPIs should be managed, measured, and reported in compliance with the GRI reporting framework. Environmental reporting is often referred to as "green accounting" or "green reporting." Environmental information can be included in the corporate annual reports, provided in Management Discussion and Analysis (MD&A), or presented in a standalone environmental report. Environmental information has traditionally been disclosed in both annual reports and MD&A. The GRI framework developed a set of principles to establish whether the type of information the company wants to report will be included in the sustainability report.[24] The basic principles are as follows:

> Materiality: The organization should report information that has the greatest impact on short- and long-term operations, societal impacts, and environmental influences, fulfilling all dimensions of EGSEE. The materiality of reporting sustainability information should reflect the organization's overall mission, vision, strategies, stakeholder welfare, society impacts, and environmental issues.

> Stakeholders: The reports should disclose all major stakeholders' expectations and address any concerns or interests. A stakeholder is any entity (living or not yet born) that can be affected by an organization's operations.

> Sustainability context: The objective is to disseminate sustainability information across all areas of EESG performance, which can be prepared in a format that best reflects all of these areas.

> Completeness: The report should reflect all areas of EGSEE in order to properly and transparently reflect the organization's overall sustainability performance.

There are a growing number of companies worldwide that are now issuing separate environmental reports. For example: "2,500 organizations in some 60 countries around the world now measure and disclose their greenhouse gas emissions and climate change strategies through the climate disclosure project (CDP), and over 1300 organizations published a GRI-based report in 2009."[25] There are numerous reporting and certification processes and guidelines to help develop proper reporting tools for government agencies and other stakeholders. Industry-led initiatives such as ISO 14000, ISO 26000, and Leadership in Energy and Environmental Design (LEED) are all certification processes in the United States and globally that can be used to track sustainable business development. These initiatives require companies to develop environmental management systems, as discussed in the previous section, but they do not require mandatory environmental accounting and reporting. A more convincing argument for encouraging the issuance of separate environmental reports is that the existing annual reports presenting financial statements are already very complicated and complex. The addition of environmental disclosures in the annual reports would further increase the complexity of financial statements. More importantly, by producing a separate environmental report, the organization can signal that it considers and values environmental disclosures as important as financial information.

The Statement of Financial Accounting Standards (SFAS No. 5) on contingent gains or contingent losses discusses how potential gains and losses are accounted for on financial statements. Financial Reporting Standard 12 (FRS-12), issued in September 1998, sets the principles for accounting provisions, contingent liabilities, and contingent assets. In most cases, organizations faced with transforming their environmental management activities will be faced with reporting environmental provisions, contingent liabilities, and contingent assets. FRS-12 guidelines will help an organization to deal with and accurately report in accordance with generally accepted accounting principles (GAAP) and difficult accounting situations when dealing with environmental reporting. A provision is a type of liability where timing is uncertain, arises from preceding transactions, and where the measurement of economic effect is difficult to estimate. A contingent asset also arises from past events. The FRS-12 guidelines from provisions state that provisions can be recognized when a legal or constructive contract is present, payment may occur, and the amount of payment can be reasonably estimated. The estimate must be the best estimate with no exceptions.[26]

The TCFD released its report of final recommendations that present a framework for companies to develop more effective climate-related financial disclosures through their existing reporting processes initially on June 29, 2017, and its second status report on June 5, 2019.[27] The TCFD provides voluntary, consistent climate-related financial risk disclosures for use by companies in presenting their climate-related information to investors, lenders, insurers, and other stakeholders. These recommendations are intended to assist companies and other organizations in implementing the TCFD recommendations by providing over 300 relevant insights, tools, and resources. These resources consist of existing legislation and regulations, frameworks, standards, guidance, research papers, tools, and webinars. The TCFD encourages companies to use its recommendations as a framework for reporting on climate-related risks and opportunities by continually improving the quality and usefulness of their climate-related financial disclosures.

Moreover, an organization seeking an EMS must develop the necessary tools to report and track environmental performance. Through scientific advancement — e.g., global climate modeling, modeling ecosystems, and alternative energy sources — society's awareness regarding the impact of humans on the environment has increased. This has multiplied the costs and obligations that organizations will have to bear. Environmental laws and regulations will increase as well and will force organizations to take a more hands-on approach to voluntary environmental challenges. Voluntary disclosures of environmental information allow for diversity and discrepancies in the format, structure, and content of environmental reports, whereas mandatory standardized environmental reporting would promote comparability and uniformity in environmental disclosures.

Environmental assurance and auditing is a broad term used to encompass environmental compliance, assessments of risks, and company environmental sustainability and audits. ISO 14010 is a systematic verification process that evaluates the effectiveness of the EMS. The audit will provide assurance that the company is complying with regulations, reducing insurance costs, and appropriately assessing the operational environmental liabilities. There is a growing trend to have the sustainability report assured in part or as a whole as the value of these efforts becomes embedded in business strategy and stakeholder value. To ensure that the company is always improving its risk reduction efforts, a third-party independent assurance provider can be hired to provide assurance reports on compliance with applicable environmental rules, laws, and regulations. The third-party assurance provider can examine chemical hazards and security vulnerabilities, facilitate and apply the appropriate risk analysis technique for the risks identified, and recommend, prioritize, and review options to manage risk to a level appropriate for each company's specific risk tolerance. Guidelines were released to aid in the audit process for environmental audits to have a proper structure. The International Organization for Standardization released ISO 19011, which can be accessed through the site. Several other standards are related to the environment, such as the ISO 14000 series, which are also accessible on the organization's website and are discussed later in the book.[28]

Best practices are standards set informally through methods or processes that have proven successful over time. Generally, common sense plays a role in developing best practices and standards, such as ISO 9000 and ISO 14000, which are examples of voluntary best practices. Environmental best practices are standards such as ISO 14000 that establish an

EMS in the organization to fully integrate environmental best practices that would lead to an environmentally sustainable organization. Some organizations choose to report, based on KPIs, on an annual or quarterly basis on company-specific missions, goals, and accomplishments. Some examples are CO_2 output, energy consumption, recycled material, raw material used, recycled material used, employee health in the workplace, and so forth. However, useful internal KPIs such as ISO 14000 can set global standards for management to use to become leaders in environmental sustainability. For example, Target Corporation discloses environmental initiatives on the planet section of the corporate responsibility report. Target identifies six areas that it aids in improving. These areas are the climate, chemicals, deforestation, water, sustainable operations, and sustainable products.

In 1996, the ISO created the ISO 14000 standards to help organizations globally develop adequate environmental management systems. The ISO was established in 1946 to encourage the development and execution of uniform standards through international trade. ISO 9000 standards on quality assurance and quality management are the best-known, and it has over 1 million certified members.[29] Globalization is creating competitive pressures throughout all globally competitive companies and is a driving force behind the staggering number of companies being certified in ISO 9000. ISO 14000 standards are not mandatory. However, they are essential tools and guidelines to help organizations manage, monitor, and comply with external stakeholder demands on their environmental actions as well as government laws and regulations. This certification will ensure that organizations meet the forthcoming environmental challenges faced by businesses and societies worldwide by providing standards globally set for EMS. Organizations view the ISO 14000 standards as a way to improve environmental performance while reducing its impact on the environment and as a tool for organizations to use instead of reacting to governmental laws and regulations. ISO 14000 certification can also help prevent future government litigation or the passage of laws and regulations and minimize their exposure to environmental costs enforced by governing bodies such as the EPA. Since the ISO 14000 standards are not mandatory and are strictly voluntary, environmental groups, governments, legal representatives, accountants, and other stakeholders should become familiar with the ISO 14000 standards and their impact.

ISO 14000 standards have six specific guidance areas that help an organization deal with environmental resolution, as the previous section discusses. ISO 14000 standards are becoming a necessity in competing in the global market and are helping organizations to develop environmentally sustainable business plans, missions, and goals. For example, Apple has eliminated toxic chemicals and substances from its products, such as arsenic, brominated flame retardants (BFRs), mercury, phthalates, and polyvinyl chloride (PVC), reduced the size of packaging for its computers by 40%, and offers complete recycling

Environmental Dimension of Sustainability

programs for old computers.[30] Many organizations are becoming more vocal in their environmental achievements and will continue to satisfy the growing concern about environmental sustainability. Globally, other standards comply with or are compatible with ISO 14000 in developing an EMS. One such system is the British standard 7750, which helps describe an EMS in that particular region.

However, there are some objections to the efficacy of continued compliance with ISO 14000 after a company or a facility has been certified.[31] Studies have shown that certified organizations or facilities do not have better environmental performance than noncertified organizations or facilities.[32] However, a study conducted by Deepa Aravind and Petra Christmann shows that while there is little difference in the average performance between facilities that have or have not been certified, facilities that have a high-quality implementation with the full commitment of management do have higher post-environmental performance.[33] This illustrates the need for a regular auditing system that eliminates conflict of interest while implementing proper interim monitoring systems to ensure ISO 14000 compliance and commitment. Despite some technical drawbacks, ISO 14001 certification helps organizations comply with government regulations and various waste reduction schemes and reduce overall emissions.[34]

Leadership in Energy and Environmental Design or LEED was developed in 2000 by the US Green Building Council (USGBC) to provide building construction projects (existing building transformation or new construction) with a framework and a quantification process for developing sustainable-green-design buildings, construction, or maintenance projects. LEED certification is useful in assessing if the organization is following environmentally sustainable development projects, which is audited and documented accurately. LEED measures:[35]

- Sustainable Sites: Reduce the site's impact on the local ecosystem.
- Water Efficiency: Water use reduction inside and outside of the complex.
- Energy and Atmosphere: Sustainable design and energy monitoring systems.
- Materials and Resources: Recycled materials, sustainable, grown, and harvested.
- Indoor Environmental Quality: Improve indoor air quality.
- Locations and Linkages: Transportation efficiency to locations.
- Awareness and Education: Provide necessary information about the use of green buildings.
- Innovation in Design: Improve the building's efficiency beyond what is necessary by LEED.

These categories will lower the costs of operating the building, reduce waste, conserve energy and water, improve indoor and living quality, and reduce or eliminate GHG emissions. The certification process can also qualify for tax incentives from the United States Government.[36] It is based on a point system.[37] In general, the levels of certification are as follows: Certified (40–49), Silver (50–59), Gold (60–79), and Platinum (greater than 80 points), with Platinum certification being the highest achievement. Such certification can help an organization document and achieve tangible, sustainable development with monetary value. The certification can be a part of an organization's ISO 14000 standard system development to create a sustainable business.

The key environmental issues that impact our world today, the increase in the world's population and climate change, have become the challenges of our time. The increased need to reduce greenhouse gases in the atmosphere and the lack of natural resources make corporations vulnerable. Natural resources include water, energy, metals, scarce natural materials, and forest products. Best practices are evolving and companies are becoming increasingly proud to share their efforts, meet regulations, and proactively lead the way in these practices. Noncompliance can be very costly, as was evidenced in the nearly US$20 billion BP oil spill in the Gulf of Mexico.

There are many opportunities and challenges pertaining to environmental performance, reporting, and assurance. The 2014 revision of ISO 14001 addresses the following emerging changes in environmental management systems:[38]

1. Strategic environmental management: The company's strategic plans and processes play an important role in the effective management of environmental performance. Proper environmental strategies can be mutually beneficial to the company and the environment. Effective strategies should identify and consider both opportunities and challenges facing the company in meeting its environmental responsibilities and ensuring sustainable environmental performance.
2. Leadership: Proper leadership and tone at the top demonstrating a commitment to sustainable environmental performance is the key to successful environmental management systems.
3. Protecting the environment: Business organizations are expected to protect the environment by maximizing their positive impacts and minimizing the negative effects of their activities on the environment. Examples are prevention of pollution, protection of biodiversity and ecosystems, sustainable resource use, greenhouse gas initiatives, and climate change mitigation and adaptation.
4. Environmental performance: Business organizations should strive to continuously improve their environmental performance by strengthening their environmental

management systems and policy commitments to sustainable environmental performance.

5. Lifecycle thinking: Business organizations need to not only manage their environmental aspects but also extend their environmental management systems and related controls and impacts to the environment.

6. Communication: Business organizations should utilize environmental reporting as a channel of communication with all internal and external constituencies about their commitments to the environmental aspects of their business, effective management of environmental activities, and fulfillment of environmental responsibilities.

7. Documentation: Technological advances enable business organizations to effectively and digitally document their environmental performance, reporting, and assurance.

Social Dimension of Sustainability

The social dimension of sustainability performance focuses on a business's impact on society and relationships with employees, communities, and broader societal well-being by emphasizing integrating social goals into the business environment, corporate culture, and managerial decisions and practices that benefit all stakeholders of business organizations. Social performance reflects an organization's social goals and alignment with the interests and values of the society in which it operates. The social dimension of sustainability performance can encompass many issues ranging from ensuring the high quality of products and services that are not detrimental to society to improved employee health and well-being and enhanced customer satisfaction to adding a positive contribution to the sustainability of the planet and the quality of life for future generations. The social dimension of sustainability performance has become more relevant in recent years in response to the perceived inequality and injustice in the workplace. This section addresses social issues such as labor practices, human rights, diversity and inclusion, employee well-being, community engagement, and customer satisfaction. Social initiatives may include promoting fair labor practices, ensuring workplace safety, fostering diversity and inclusion, supporting local communities through philanthropy and volunteerism, and maintaining ethical relationships with suppliers and customers. Corporations have shifted their primary goals from profit-maximization to creating value for all stakeholders, including shareholders while fulfilling their social responsibilities. Particularly, the corporate social responsibility (CSR) program is designed to minimize conflicts between corporations and society caused by differences between private and social costs and benefits and to align corporate goals with those of society. CSR requires business organizations to take initiatives to advance some social good beyond their own interests and compliance with applicable regulations. This section presents the social dimension of sustainability performance, reporting, and assurance.

The social dimension of sustainability is an ethical or ideological issue that suggests that entities, regardless of type and size, have a responsibility to protect the society in which they operate. Such responsibility varies across countries and is influenced significantly by the culture's socioeconomic attributes. Social performance measures how well an entity has translated its social goals into practice and is measured through the principles, actions, and corrective measures implemented. Social performance, or the social bottom line, is about making an organization's social mission a reality and aligned with the interests of society by adding accepted social values and fulfilling social responsibility. Not all companies present meaningful reports on their social performance to shareholders and the general public. A governing body providing regulations or standards for disclosures on social responsibility will enhance the transparency, accuracy, and usefulness of such reports.

CSR has emerged as an important area of challenges and opportunities for corporations worldwide. Corporations are facing challenges in responding to CSR issues and the perceived pressure of localization and globalization in determining their CSR policies and procedures. Employee-related CSR initiatives are derived from and directed toward improving social, political, and economic opportunities for existing and potential employees, contract workers, society, and other stakeholders. These initiatives range from empowering employee participation in making strategic decisions, improving employee benefits, wages, and work conditions, giving voice to customer satisfaction, and being a good citizen. These initiatives include addressing specific issues of diversity in terms of female participation, ethnic makeup, or linguistic capabilities, among others. Product and marketing-related CSR initiatives and activities are gaining considerable attention from customers, suppliers, manufacturers, government, and society. Consumer-driven CSR includes product and process innovations, environmental issues, promotions, advertising, and distribution policies and practices.

Social performance measures how well a company has translated its social goals into practice. Social performance is about making the company's social mission a reality and aligning with the interests of society. Variables in the social area are associated with the existence of corporate policies that are mainly community service-related or geared toward improving social conditions. The strength of social measures includes (1) charitable giving, (2) innovative giving, (3) support for housing, (4) support for education, (5) other community strengths, (6) promotion of minorities, (7) diversity of the board of directors, (8) work/life benefits, (9) contracting with women and minorities, (10) employment of the disabled, (11) gay and lesbian policies, and (12) other diversity strengths. Concerns include (1) investment controversies, (2) negative economic impact, (3) tax disputes, (4) other community concerns, (5) diversity controversies, (6) minority nonrepresentation, and (7) other diversity concerns.

Social Dimension of Sustainability

Business organizations typically strive to promote social responsibility among all their stakeholders. They focus their efforts on building and maintaining a diverse community of extremely engaged employees and establishing good relationships with vendors and contractors. Businesses often offer global philanthropic activities in the United States and other countries, particularly in those communities where the company has affiliate operations. Business organizations can contribute to their communities by engaging in social and philanthropic activities such as the World Food Program, which formed a school feeding program and other community involvements.

ISO 26000 covers a broad range of an organization's activities, from economic to social, governance, and ethical and environmental issues.[39] ISO 26000 is a globally accepted guidance document for social responsibility that assists organizations worldwide in fulfilling their CSR goals (ISO 2010). Social responsibility performance promoted in ISO 26000 is conceptually and practically associated with the development of achieving sustainable performance because the fulfillment of social responsibility necessitates and ensures sustainable development. ISO 26000 goes beyond profit-maximization by presenting a framework for organizations to contribute to sustainable development and the welfare of society. The core subject areas of ISO 26000 consider all aspects of the triple bottom line's (TBL) key financial and nonfinancial performance relevant to people, planet, and profit. The following provisions of ISO 26000 are designed to help business organizations operate in a socially responsible manner by guiding on:

- Concepts, frameworks, terms, and definitions pertaining to CSR.
- Background, trends, characteristics, and best practices of socially responsible organizations.
- Principles, standards, and best practices relevant to CSR.
- Policies, procedures, and best practices for integrating, implementing, and promoting CSR.
- Engagement of all stakeholders, including shareholders, in socially responsible activities.
- Disclosure of information and nonfinancial KPIs related to social responsibility.

Social performance and responsibilities are obligations to respond effectively to societal and stakeholder concerns by integrating social considerations into business strategic decisions, activities, and operations through voluntary initiatives that go above and beyond regulatory requirements and philanthropic activities. Many factors have encouraged companies to engage in CSR activities, including consumer activism, corporate malfeasances, improper corporate behavior and actions (Enron, WorldCom, Parmalat), and socially responsible investing (SRI).

Social performance involves three components: (1) the identification of the domains of an organization's social responsibility, (2) the development of processes to evaluate stakeholder demands, and (3) the implementation of programs to manage social issues.[40] An organization's social responsibility can be classified into four categories, namely economic, legal, ethical, and discretionary responsibilities.[41]

- **Economic responsibilities**: Entities of all types and sizes must produce goods and services that society needs and wants. Unless businesses fulfill their economic function, they will neither have the resources to perform other roles nor will they survive long enough to be an agent for any form of societal change.
- **Legal responsibilities**: Society grants business entities the right to pursue their economic goals but explicitly requires companies to fulfill these goals within the framework of legal requirements.
- **Ethical responsibilities**: Society also has expectations for business entities that are above and beyond legal requirements. Ethical responsibilities require corporations to engage in business practices in a manner consistent with societal values in such matters as fair employment and the environmental impact of production.
- **Discretionary responsibilities:** Socially desirable actions taken by business entities that are beyond their economic, legal, and ethical obligations. Corporations have discretions over the type, timing, and extent of their involvement in discretionary social performance, which may include activities such as philanthropy and community leadership.

Organizations can no longer isolate their operations from the wider society and environment in which they operate, and thus they should effectively measure their social performance to maintain their sustainability. Measuring social performance implies the evaluation of principles, actions, outputs, some elements of outcome, and corrective measures. Social activities include improving reputation, brand value, employee satisfaction, crisis management, environmental preservation, and philanthropic activities. Emphasizing the results and their impact, social performance should include an analysis of the declared objectives of institutions, the effectiveness of their systems and services in meeting these objectives, related outputs (for example, reaching larger numbers of very poor households), and success in effecting positive changes in the lives of mankind.

KPIs are quantifiable measurements that reflect the critical success factors of an organization and help them define and measure progress toward organizational goals. Whatever

KPIs are selected, they must reflect the organization's goals, be recognized as key determinants of its success, and be quantifiable (measurable). Key performance indicators usually are long-term considerations. KPIs for social responsibility play a key role in evaluating social responsibility initiatives. Social activities can be measured through social contribution, strategic partners, community outreach, involvement, and time spent volunteering. Proper measurement of the KPIs pertaining to social activities and responsibilities enables organizations to effectively report their social performance and fulfill their social responsibilities. Commonly used social KPIs include building responsible networks, diversity, supporting the community, and social impact activities (social investment, employee voluntarism, strategic partners, leadership fellows, reputation, brand value, and good relations with the community).

Several models and best practices of CSR have been presented to hold business organizations accountable for fulfilling their CSR. Stehi suggests a three-level model for corporate social performance, which reflects business organizations' behavior toward society as (1) a social liability as demanded by regulatory constraints and market mechanisms; (2) a social responsibility beyond the legal and market requirement to benefit society; and (3) social accountability to all stakeholders, including shareholders, employees, customers, creditors, suppliers, government, the environment, and society.[42] Carroll developed a CSR conceptual model that consists of four dimensions: economic, legal, moral, and philanthropic responsibilities.[43] The first dimension is economic responsibility, which includes a commitment to the desired return on investment for shareholders and creditors, job opportunities and proper compensation for employees, exploration of new resources, promotion of technology and innovation, and the production and offering of high-quality and safe services and products. The legal dimension of CSR responsibility includes compliance with all applicable laws, rules, regulations, policies, and standards. The moral dimension of CSR represents engagement in social activities above and beyond the legal requirements and personal benefits by maximizing social benefits and minimizing costs to society. The philanthropic dimension of CSR suggests that involvement in activities and programs that provide financial and nonfinancial assistance to the community tends to be less strategic than other forms of CSR involvement in terms of adding social and business values.

CSR best practices are designed to minimize the conflicts between corporations and society and to align corporate goals with those of society. Conflicts are caused by differences between private and social costs and benefits, examples of which are related to environmental issues (pollution, acid rain, global warming), wages paid by multinational corporations in poor countries, and child labor in developing countries. Corporate governance measures, which include rules, regulations, and best practices of CSR programs, can raise companies' awareness of the social costs and benefits of their business activities. These CSR models and best practices assist business organizations in developing their own CSR programs to achieve and enhance their social performance. The Organization of Economic Co-operation and Development (OECD) defines the purpose of a CSR program as "to encourage the positive contributions that multinational enterprises can make to economics, environmental, and social progress and to minimize the difficulties to which their various operations may give rise."[44] This definition focuses on two important aspects of a CSR program, namely the creation of social value through corporate activities (social value-added activities) and the avoidance of conflicts between corporate goals and societal goals (societal consensus).

The primary concepts of CSR programs are:

- CSR programs are important ingredients of business sustainability, and companies must strive to make a footprint on CSR.
- One of the most important investments a company can make is in its CSR programs, including its employees, investors, customers, and communities.
- Philanthropic programs are important in aiding those who are less fortunate, and thus, they are a common theme among companies with a global reach.

These CSR programs are not without costs, and they should be viewed as corporate investments in employees, communities, and society, which should generate long-term and sustainable financial performance. However, there are two differing views regarding the relationship between investing in CSR programs and firm financial performance: (1) socially responsible behavior is costly due to increases in expenses but no increase in benefits, and (2) a positive association exists between CSR and firm performance because CSR programs and activities enhance employee morale and productivity, attract and retain high-quality employees, generate a positive corporate image, enhance product evaluation via an overall evaluation of the firm, and improve a firm's access to sources of capital.

Business organizations worldwide are now recognizing the importance of quality as it relates to CSR and the link between profitability and social behavior. Justifications for CSR are moral obligation, maintaining a good reputation, ensuring sustainability, keeping their license to operate, and creating shared value. In a shared value approach, corporations identify potential social issues of concern and integrate them into their strategic planning. There are many factors determining why a company should follow CSR, such as the pressure of the labor movement, the development of moral values and social standards, the development of business education, and the change in public opinion about the role of

Social Dimension of Sustainability

business. Companies that are, or aspire to be, leaders in CSR are challenged by rising public expectations, increasing innovation, continuous quality improvement, and heightened social and environmental problems. Companies should fulfill their social responsibility due to public image, consumer movements, government requirements, investors' education, tax benefits, better relations with stakeholders, employee satisfaction, a sense of pride, and an appropriate way to improve quality.

Globalization creates incentives and opportunities for multinational corporations (MNCs) and their stakeholders and executives to influence their CSR initiatives and strategies of the headquarters as well as subsidiaries. MNCs can choose from a variety of CSR initiatives regarding the scope, extent, and type of CSR strategies that focus on different issues, functions, areas, and stakeholders that vary across their subsidiaries. Given that scarce resources also constrain MNCs, they must be selective when deciding on the scope, extent, and type of CSR initiatives. Subsidiaries' CSR initiatives typically have distinct "home country" characteristics that are pursued across subsidiaries. Nonetheless, global/local CSR initiatives often vary depending on the type of initiatives and the CSR strategies that are being pursued. International Organization for Standardization (ISO) 26000 covers a broad range of an organization's activities, from economic to social, governance, ethics, and environmental issues.[45] ISO 26000 is a globally accepted guidance document for social responsibility that assists organizations worldwide in fulfilling their CSR goals (ISO 2010). Social responsibility performance promoted in ISO 26000 is conceptually and practically associated with the development of achieving sustainable performance because the fulfillment of social responsibility necessitates and ensures sustainability development. ISO 26000 goes beyond profit-maximization by presenting a framework for organizations to contribute to sustainable development and the welfare of society. The core subject areas of ISO 26000 consider all aspects of the TBL key financial and nonfinancial performance relevant to people, planet, and profit.

The ISO 26000 standards are voluntary and aspirational rather than prescriptive, providing a framework for incorporating CSR issues into business and investment decision-making and ownership practices. Compliance with ISO 26000 standards is expected to lead not only to a more sustainable financial return but also to a close alignment of the interests of businesses and investors with those of the global society at large. Management should develop and maintain proper CSR programs that provide a common framework for the integration of CRS issues and activities that consist of:

- Integration of CSR issues into the business and investment analysis and decision-making process.

- Incorporation of CSR issues and activities into business and investment policies and practices.

- Promotion of appropriate disclosure on CSR issues and performance.

- Collaboration among all stakeholders to enhance the effectiveness of implementing CSR programs.

- Promotion of product innovation and quality, customer retention and attraction, and employee satisfaction and productivity through CSR programs.

- Periodic disclosures of both financial and nonfinancial KPIs relevant to CSR activities to all stakeholders.

In summary, the social dimension of sustainability performance requires business organizations to take initiatives to advance some social good beyond their interests and compliance with applicable regulations. Simply put, CSR means enhancing corporations' positive impacts and minimizing their negative effects on society, as well as minimizing harm to society and the environment and creating positive impacts on the community, environment, employees, customers, and suppliers. CSR has emerged as an important area of challenges and opportunities for the business community and the accounting profession worldwide. Particularly, multinational corporations are facing challenges in responding to CSR issues while balancing localization and globalization realities in determining CSR policies and procedures for their headquarters and, more importantly, for their subsidiaries abroad with different political and cultural norms. In the globalized world, the long-term value and success of businesses are inextricably linked to the integration of economic, social, environmental, and governance issues into corporate management and operations. The main drivers for implementing CSR strategies have been risk management on the one hand and ethical considerations on the other hand. For instance, the Global Head of KPMG Sustainability Services, Wim Bartels, stated in the survey that "In a world of changing expectations, companies must account for the way they impact the communities and environments where they operate."[46] Corporate social responsibility is the key condition for a continued global market economy, and companies will need to accept and implement this condition if they are to keep their license to operate.

Employee-related CSR initiatives are derived from and directed toward improving social, political, and economic opportunities for existing and potential employees, contract workers, society, and other stakeholders. Initiatives range from empowering employee participation in strategic decisions to improving employee benefits, wages, and work conditions, as well as being a good citizen. These initiatives address specific issues of diversity in terms of female participation ethnic, or linguistic capabilities.

Human capital management (HCM) is becoming an important investment and CSR issue. Business organizations need to address whether they contribute to society, whether they create a diverse workforce, whether they provide health and safety labor relations with their employees, and whether they provide proper training and opportunities for their employees – the most important capital in the ever-changing and advancing automated world. The BIS team has identified human capital management as one of our engagement priorities with companies in which we invest on behalf of our clients.[47]

The board of directors should consider the following HCM issues:[48]

1. Overseeing policies and procedures intended to protect employees (e.g., whistleblowing, codes of conduct, employee fair compensation) and management accountability and reporting to assess their implementation.
2. Overseeing the process through which the components of a company's HCM strategy ensure a healthy culture and collegial work environment and prevent unwanted behaviors.
3. Overseeing and monitoring the integration of HCM risks into risk management processes.
4. Promoting diversity in the workplace.
5. Linking HCM performance to executive compensation to promote board and management accountability.
6. Considering visiting workplaces and factories to independently assess the culture and operations of the company and its relations with employees.

Management should consider the following HCM issues:[49]

1. Establishing policies and procedures to encourage employee engagement, participation outcomes, and key drivers (e.g., wellness programs, safe environment, support of employee networks, training and development programs, and stock participation programs).
2. Designing processes for ensuring employee health and safety and complying with occupational health and safety policies.
3. Implementing voluntary and involuntary turnover on various dimensions (e.g., seniority of roles, tenure, gender, and ethnicity).
4. Preparing data on gender and other diversity characteristics as well as addressing compensation gaps across different employee demographics and proper disclosure in corporate reporting.
5. Establishing programs to engage organized labor and their representatives.
6. Implementing systems and processes to oversee matters related to the supply chain (including contingent workers, contractors, and subcontractors).

The SEC rules of disclosure requirements of human capital are outdated since items 101 and 102 of Regulation S-K were relevant at the time when property, plant, and equipment constituted the majority of the total assets for public companies, and there was a closer link between recorded assets and a company's market value. In recent years, human capital and intellectual property have often been the main drivers and sources of revenue-generating performance for companies. As such, they represent a much higher proportion of the justification for a firm's market value, even though they are often not recorded in total assets. The SEC chairman believes that public companies should consider human capital as an investment, not a cost, and provide sufficient information relevant to their human capital that is viewed as material information by a reasonable investor in making informed investment and voting decisions.[50]

Product and marketing-related CSR initiatives and activities are gaining attention from customers, suppliers, manufacturers, government, and society. Consumer-driven CSR includes product and process innovations, life cycle and footprint assessments, promotion, advertising, and distribution policies and practices. Implementing CSR initiatives will improve product quality, functionality, transparency, and corporate philanthropy, as well as offer the potential to build brand loyalty (for example, Timberland, Interface, and Patagonia).

CSR supply-chain covers the entire input and output process, which includes buying raw materials from socially responsible suppliers, designing and producing products that are not detrimental to society or harmful to customers, and marketing and selling products that minimize the use of scarce resources (e.g., smaller and environmentally conscientious packaging). CSR processing and production activities, including permits to operate (licenses for mine sites), are becoming integral components of supply chains. Organizations that undertake CSR programs not only integrate them into their production process but also influence CSR initiatives for a variety of stakeholders in their supply-chain process (suppliers and customers).

Legislation regarding CSR is a hot topic as the world continues to advance. Several prominent pieces of legislation have been enacted to support the expansion of CSR. These include Section 1502 of the Dodd-Frank Act, the Supply Chains Act, SB 861, and HB 425. Section 1502 is designed to limit the exploitation of minerals that could finance the Democratic Republic of the Congo. This section mandates that a report be written to show compliance with this law. The report must contain a private sector audit, company certification, the measures used to be diligent, and any conflict related to disclosure. The state of California passed the Supply Chains Act. This act applies to companies that file a California tax return, do business in California, and have global revenues in excess of US$100 million. This act requires disclosure of supply-chain addresses, supplier audits, companies with antislavery laws, accountability standards, and training protocols.[51]

Social Dimension of Sustainability

Corporations are no longer isolated from their stakeholders, particularly in the wider society in which they operate. They affect the welfare of their stakeholders, and they are affected by their stakeholders' interests and demands. Social responsibility doesn't refer to any responsibility *to* stakeholders but designates a responsibility *by* stakeholders. "Ethical" investing, the "green" consumer movement, and the growth of "vigilante consumerism" are examples of how such "conscientious stockholding" can influence the way a business operates. Hence, social responsibility is fully compatible with corporate governance and culture.

Stakeholders, which include individuals and groups, are beginning to affect CSR. The stakeholder principle is the relationship between the business and the consumer (investor, creditor). This principle is addressed in ISO 26000, which is discussed earlier in the text, and AA 1000, which will be discussed here.[52] AA 1000, released by AccountAbility, is a framework for CSR that is based on inclusivity, materiality, responsiveness, and impact. Each of these revolve around reflection, measurement, and monitoring of CSR activity. The framework allows ease of integration with other well-known principle-based approaches to CSR and can be used on the international, national, or sectoral levels. The framework aids in effective corporate governance through increased efficiency, allocation, and measurement of operations while increasing the relevance of decisions made by upper management.[53] Stakeholder engagement is also necessary for CSR in businesses. Stakeholders can range from business partners to governments, suppliers, NGOs, and local communities. Each particular stakeholder category contains types of engagements and issues relevant to those engagements.[54]

Companies worldwide have created their CSR programs that aim to balance their operations with the concerns of external stakeholders such as customers, unions, local communities, NGOs, and governments. Social and environmental consequences are weighed against economic gains. Although the field of CSR has grown exponentially, the debate still exists about the legitimacy and value of corporate responses to CSR concerns. The relationship between corporate social responsibility and financial performance is generally positive, varying between highly positive and moderately positive.[55] Socially responsible practices such as minority hiring, and managerial principles have a greater effect on financial performance than environmental responsibility. Social responsibility and financial performance affect each other in a "virtuous cycle": successful firms spend more because they can afford to, and such spending helps them to become more successful.

Corporate decision-makers must consider a range of social and environmental matters if they are to maximize long-term financial returns rather than short-term profits. An initial challenge in testing the relationship between corporate social responsibility and financial performance is identifying those companies/services that have adopted corporate social responsibility and have issued a sustainability report. This is because corporate social responsibility reflects an approach to internal decision-making, the presence or absence of which may not easily be determined by external observers. Also, a sustainability report provides information to external stakeholders about the conduct of a company, allowing consumers, employees, investors, and others to make informed decisions when dealing with the company. Importantly, the preparation of a sustainability report also provides company management with information about social and environmental performance, facilitating improved decision-making.

In summary, there are two differing views regarding the relationship between CSR and firm financial performance:

1. Socially responsible behavior is costly due to increased expenses but no increase in benefits.
2. A positive association between CSR and firm performance because CSR will:
   a. Enhance employee morale and productivity.
   b. Attract and retain high-quality employees.
   c. Generate a positive corporate image.
   d. Enhance product evaluation via an overall evaluation of the firm.
   e. Improve a firm's access to sources of capital.
   f. Promote reputation and trust.
   g. Attract and motivate talent.
   h. Create new business opportunities.
   i. Provide a more secure and sustainable working environment.

Social Responsibility is an ethical or ideological theory that suggests that entities, regardless of type and size, have a responsibility to protect the society in which they operate and that such responsibility varies across countries and is influenced significantly by the culture's socioeconomic attributes. Social performance measures how well an entity has translated its social goals into practice and is measured through the principles, actions, and corrective measures implemented. Social performance, or the social bottom line, is about making an organization's social mission a reality and aligned with the interests of society by adding accepted social values and fulfilling social responsibility. Not all companies present meaningful reports on their social performance to shareholders and the public. A governing body providing regulations or standards for disclosures on social responsibility will enhance the transparency, accuracy, and usefulness of such reports.

Social Dimension of Sustainability

Companies generally issue CSR/sustainability reports on an annual basis, which would enable them to integrate CSR/sustainability reporting with their annual financial reporting process and/or report. CSR reporting on social performance is key to building stakeholder buy-in and support for the goals and ongoing social achievements. External reporting of social performance in corporate annual reports is becoming widespread, largely because of public and regulatory pressures. There are many ways to report on social performance, though there are no standard methods, and the companies have to choose from among several generally accepted alternatives. In most cases, companies start with the basics – choosing to follow a theory of social performance disclosure, deciding on the method of annual report presentation, and deciding upon the annual activities for disclosure, which can vary widely among companies. An important goal of CSR is to exhibit a commitment to social performance and to embrace responsibility for the company's actions. Taking responsibility for its impact on society necessitates that a company account for its actions. Social accounting, a concept describing the communication of social activities and actions to particular interest groups within society and to society at large, is an integral element of CSR.

Social accounting emphasizes the notion of corporate accountability. Reporting guidelines or standards have been developed to serve as frameworks for social accounting, auditing, and reporting. In some nations, legal requirements for social accounting, auditing, and reporting exist despite some difficulties in meaningful measurements of social and environmental performance. Many companies worldwide disclose audited annual reports that cover Sustainable Development and CSR issues ("Triple Bottom-Line Reports"), but the reports vary widely in format, style, and content. Combining financial and CSR reporting into one report enables organizations to disclose their initiatives in integrating good corporate citizenship into their business. In some parts of Europe, CSR reporting has become mandatory for public companies, and investors have come to want and expect greater accountability. The majority of companies there responded by creating annual integrated financial and CSR reports. Today's investors and consumers require a high level of transparency, so anything less can do more harm than good to corporate reputation. If CSR reporting is integrated into financial reporting, it moves it out of the realm of marketing and back into its rightful place as solid, straightforward, honest reporting on accomplishments and mistakes. More companies should adopt this method because it forces them to approach all of their reporting from a more holistic point of view. Adequate corporate social responsibility disclosure has important implications for the credibility of the capital markets in transition economies. The goal of CSR is to embrace responsibility for the company's actions and encourage a positive impact through its activities on the environment, consumers, employees, communities, and stakeholders. Ideally, CSR reporting should be integrated into financial reporting. The integrated sustainability reporting would enable organizations worldwide to demonstrate a coherent approach to understanding the inter-actions of all the EESG sustainability dimensions on their performance.

Governance Dimension of Sustainability Performance

Corporate governance is an important dimension of sustainability performance and will continue to be the theme of the 21st century to address the existence and persistence of financial scandals, business misconduct, the 2017–2019 global financial crisis, and the 2020 global COVID-19 pandemic. Corporate governance measures, both internal (independent board) and external (rules and regulations), have been established by policymakers, regula-tors, and corporations in terms of best practices to effectively manage corporations and promote economic stability, public trust, and investor confidence in public financial reports. Corporate governance can be defined in several ways; first, it is a process of managing the organization for the benefit of its stakeholders. Second, it is a process of aligning manage-ment interests with those of shareholders. Third, it is a process of compliance with a set of laws, rules, regulations, and standards relevant to the operation of public companies. Governance sustainability performance reflects how well corporate governance partici-pants, from the board of directors to executives, financial advisors, accountants, auditors, and legal counsel, fulfill their responsibilities in creating shared value for all stakeholders and protecting their interests.

Corporate governance performance reflects the way business organizations manage and operate to generate shared value for all stakeholders and govern and how their decision-making processes contribute to sustainable practices. Corporate governance plays an essential role in shaping business organizations' policies, strategies, and actions that influ-ence their environmental and social impact. The corporate governance structure consists of principles that guide corporate participants and gatekeepers in fulfilling their respon-sibilities and corporate governance functions that define the roles and responsibilities of corporate participants from directors to executives, auditors, legal counsel, and financial advisors; and mechanisms that determine corporate governance measures.

In a dynamic financial system, reliable financial information and effective corporate gov-ernance are essential for global economic development and growth. In the aftermath of the 2007–2009 global financial crisis, countries worldwide have taken initiatives to improve their corporate governance by establishing more robust corporate governance measures to strengthen their regulatory frameworks to promote economic stability, public trust, and investor confidence in their financial reporting. The globalization of capital markets and the demand for investor protection in response to financial scandals worldwide, such as Enron, WorldCom, Parmalat, Ahold, and Satyam, also require consistency and uniformity in regulatory reforms and corporate governance practices. Business organizations focus on governance practices that ensure transparency, accountability, integrity, and ethical behavior in all aspects of their operations. Corporate governance Initiatives may include having a diverse and independent board of directors, establishing robust corporate governance structures and policies, promoting shareholder rights, managing conflicts of interest, and adhering to ethical standards and regulatory compliance.

Corporate governance has evolved as a central issue with regulators and public companies in the wake of the 2007–2009 global financial crisis. Corporate governance is defined from a legal perspective as measures that enable and ensure compliance with all applicable laws, rules, regulations, and standards. From the agency theory perspective, corporate governance is defined as the process of aligning management interests with those of shareholders in creating shareholder value.[56] Companies normally undergo a series of corporate governance reforms aimed at improving the effectiveness of their governance, internal controls, and financial reports. Effective corporate governance promotes accountability, improves the reliability and quality of financial information, and prevents fraudulent behavior from management. Poor corporate governance adversely affects the company's potential, performance, financial reports, and accountability and can pave the way for business failure and financial statement fraud. Corporate governance, including the oversight function assumed by the board of directors, managerial function delegated to management, internal audit function conducted by internal auditors, external audit function performed by external auditors, and compliance function enforced by policymakers, regulators, and standard-setters are vital to the quality of financial information. Corporate reputation, customer satisfaction, ethical workplaces, corporate social responsibility, and environmental initiatives are nonfinancial drivers of sustainable economic performance and long-term growth, which are addressed in this chapter and the following chapters under the nonfinancial dimensions of sustainability performance. Business sustainability requires that the company be managed effectively through robust corporate governance mechanisms.

Effective corporate governance can improve business sustainability, corporate culture, corporate strategic decisions, sustainable performance, reliable financial reports, and prospects and growth. The existence and persistence of differences in global economic structure, financial systems, and corporate environment causes countries to adopt their corporate governance reforms and measures. However, globalization, cross-border trade, and capital formation necessitate a convergence in corporate governance measures and regulatory reforms. The emerging global corporate governance reforms are shaping capital market structure worldwide and altering their competitiveness and the protection provided to investors. Globalization and technological advances have promoted global convergence in corporate governance. The move toward convergence in corporate governance has become substantially more prevalent in the aftermath of the 2007–2009 global financial crisis. Corporate governance participants must structure the process to ensure that the goals of both shareholder value creation and stakeholder value protection for public companies are achieved.

The corporate governance structure is shaped by internal and external governance mechanisms as well as policy interventions through regulations. Corporate governance mechanisms are viewed as a nexus of formal and informal contracts that are designed to align the interests of management with those of the shareholders. The effectiveness of both internal and external corporate governance mechanisms depends on the cost/benefit trade-offs among these mechanisms. It is related to their availability, the extent to which they are being used, whether their marginal benefits justify their marginal costs, and the company's corporate governance structure. Several corporate governance reforms (e.g., the Sarbanes-Oxley Act of 2002 and Dodd-Frank Act of 2010) have changed the relationship between shareholders, management, and boards in the United States by creating an appropriate "balance of authority" exercised by boards, management, and shareholders in the corporate decision-making process and governance. Directors are now accountable to a wide range of stakeholders, including shareholders, creditors, employees, customers, suppliers, government, and communities in which the corporation operates.

In recent years, the corporate governance dimension of sustainability has received considerable attention as investors are holding directors and executives more responsible and accountable for the achievement of both financial ESP and nonfinancial ESG sustainability performance. Investors consider the use of nonfinancial ESG sustainability metrics to incentivize directors and executives to focus on overall sustainability. Corporate governance best practices promote business sustainability by engaging investors, directors, and executives to focus on sustainability in many ways, including:

1. Making long-term sustainability investment strategies of focus on long-term and sustainable investments rather than short-term ones.
2. Setting the tone at the top by engaging in sustainability initiatives by electing at least one director with sustainability interests and skills and creating a board sustainability committee consisting of directors with adequate sustainability expertise.
3. Making executive commitments to promoting sustainability performance by demanding sustainability performance from executives, including a sustainability performance

Governance Dimension of Sustainability Performance

target clause in the executive compensation contract rewarding sustainability executive leadership and punishing managerial short-termism.

4. Making sustainability investment initiatives and innovations as priorities of corporate governance.

5. Integrating sustainability performance reporting and assurance into Corporate reporting is an integral component of corporate governance.

Ethical Dimension of Sustainability

The ethics dimension is an important aspect of business sustainability that addresses the moral principles and values guiding business practices with regard to environmental, social, and economic impacts. It reflects a company's responsibility and activities to conduct its operations in a manner that ensures profitability and longevity while considering the well-being of society and the planet. Ethics, in the generic term, is driven by a combination of individual and/or family values, moral principles, religious beliefs, cultural norms, and best practices. An individual's values are derived from moral principles that a person was taught or instilled with as being right or wrong, whereas an individual's choices are the actions taken to do what is right or wrong. Ethics is defined as "a process by which individuals, social groups, and societies evaluate their actions from a perspective of moral principles and value."[57] The corporate culture of integrity, competency, mutual respect, fairness, diversity, equity, and inclusion creates an ethical environment that provides incentives and opportunities for individuals to conduct their activities ethically while penalizing and disciplining them if they engage in unethical conduct. Corporate culture should create an ethical business environment in which all stakeholders are encouraged and empowered to do the right thing and discouraged from engaging in unethical activities.

The current financial crisis was partially caused by a number of ethical lapses made by both organizations and individuals involved in the mortgage markets, including mortgage originators, financial intermediaries, and mortgage borrowers. These lapses collectively contributed to the financial crisis, resulted in a global economic meltdown, and threatened the sustainability of individuals, businesses, and governments. The crisis and related financial scandals have caused policymakers, regulators, and ethics advocates to question to what extent ethics and corporate culture affect the business process. Another question posed is whether ethics performance should be reflected in overall corporate reporting. Exhibit 8.1 shows the triangle of business ethics, consisting of (1) ethics sensitivity, (2) ethics incentives, and (3) ethical behavior.[58] This ethics triangle should be integrated into other dimensions of sustainability performance, as illustrated in Exhibit 8.2. Ethics sensitivity is

EXHIBIT 8.2   The triangle of business ethics. Source: Rezaee, Z. (2007). *Corporate Governance Post-Sarbanes-Oxley Act: Regulations, Requirements, & Integrated Processes.* Wiley., New Jersey, USA

defined as the moral principles, workplace factors, gamesmanship, loyalty, peer pressure, and job security that influence one's ethical decisions and are derived from the organization's ethical culture. The ethics sensitivity element suggests an organization consists of diverse individuals representing a variety of value systems and ethical theories. An individual in an organization works in collaboration and coordination with others to fulfill his or her responsibilities. Gamesmanship, loyalty, peer pressure, and other factors influence one's ethical decisions and actions.

Ethics incentives encompass rewards, punishments, and requirements for behaving either ethically or unethically. Examples of ethics incentives are the tone at the top an organization sets with respect to ethical conduct, various professional codes of conduct (e.g., the AICPA code of conduct), and ethics rules (e.g., the SEC's ethics rule for principal financial officers). Incentives for ethical behavior come from several sources, including (1) individual-based incentives, (2) organization-based incentives, (3) market-based incentives, (4) profession-based incentives, and (5) regulatory-based incentives. The ethical behavior element suggests that the company's directors and executives should set a tone at the top of demonstrating through their actions as well as their policies, a firm commitment to ethical behavior throughout the company and a culture of trust within the company. Setting the right tone at the top is very important in promoting an ethical culture; actions often speak louder than words.

Ethics are broadly described in the literature as (1) moral principles about right and wrong and (2) honorable behavior reflecting values or standards of conduct. Honesty, openness, responsiveness, accountability, due diligence, and fairness are core ethical principles. Business ethics is a specialized study of moral righteousness. An appropriate code of

Ethical Dimension of Sustainability

ethics that sets a proper tone at the top of promoting ethical and professional conduct and establishing the moral structure for the entire organization is the backbone of effective corporate governance. Corporate culture and compliance rules should provide incentives and opportunities to maintain their honesty. Attributes of an ethical corporate culture or an integrity-based culture refer to employee responsibility, freedom to raise concerns, and managers modeling ethical behavior and expressing the importance of integrity. The company's directors and executives should demonstrate through their actions, as well as their policies, a firm commitment to ethical behavior throughout the company, and a culture of trust within the company. Although the "proper tone at the top" is very important in promoting an ethical culture, actions often speak louder than words.

Some important aspects of the ethics dimension of business sustainability are: (1) stakeholder well-beings of considering the interests and welfare of all stakeholders, including shareholders, creditors, employees, customers, suppliers, local communities, and future generations affected by a company's operations; (2) fairness, diversity and equity of commitment to ethical sustainability strive to ensure fairness, diversity and equity in a company's operations including promoting diversity, fair treatment of employees, avoiding actions that contribute to social inequalities, and ensuring equitable access to opportunities; (3) tone at the top for promoting competency and an ethical behavior and action throughout the company; (4) environmental impact to minimize the environmental footprint by implementing practices that conserve resources, mitigate climate change and reduce pollution by investing in renewable energy, implementing sustainable supply-chain practices and adopting eco-friendly technologies; (5) social responsibility of prioritizing social impact and financial gain by engaging in initiatives that support community development, improve the quality of life for individuals and communities affected by business operations, and promote social justice while achieving financial performance; (6) transparency and accountability of business practices and operations as well as disclosure of relevant information pertaining to economic performance, environmental impact, social programs; (7) focus on long-term perspective of business decisions, considering the potential consequences of actions not only in the short term but also in the long-term by creating a right balance between gaining immediate profits and achieving long-term sustainability and societal well-being; (8) ethical leadership of promoting ethical sustainability within an organization by fostering a culture of integrity, responsibility, and accountability that promotes and encourage the company's values, behaviors, and priorities; and (9) compliance and ethical standards of promoting and requiring compliance with all relevant and applicable laws, rules, regulations, and ethical standards governing business operations and even striving to exceed minimum requirements and uphold higher ethical standards. These aspects of the ethical dimension of business sustainability should be integrated into both the ESP and

ESG dimensions of business sustainability performance. These ethical aspects emphasize the importance of conducting business in a manner that respects ethical principles, promotes societal well-being, and ensures the long-term viability of both the business and the planet to improve reputation and stakeholder trust and contribute to building a more sustainable and equitable world.

Ethics reporting is the process of disclosing an organization's ethics performance and related assurance. A standalone ethics reporting and assurance is not commonly practiced because of lack of proper and adequate reporting and assurance standards. The process of ethics reporting needs to be established, standardized, and practiced. Ethics KPIs need to be developed to enable an organization to measure its success in reaching its ethical goals or objectives. The KPIs can be useful as a benchmark for assessing an organization's compliance with its internally established codes of ethical conduct and external laws, rules, regulations, and standards. Proper use of the KPIs enables an organization to define its ethical culture and goals and establish metrics to measure its ethical performance. The ethics KPIs are classified into corporate culture and its ethical values, ethics codes of conduct and their enforcement, and ethics performance and the process of promoting ethical behavior. Ethics reporting should promote the practice of not only complying with applicable laws and regulations but also the culture and the commitment to doing the right thing and providing relevant, timely, useful, and reliable ethics information. Organizational or corporate culture is an essential component of ethical sustainability performance in determining the shared values, beliefs, norms, and behaviors that characterize how people within an organization or a company interact with each other and conduct business. It is often described as the "personality" of an organization and affects how employees perceive their work environment, make decisions, and collaborate with others. Corporate culture can have a significant impact on various aspects of an organization, including employee satisfaction, performance, innovation, and, ultimately, its success. Organizations of all types and sizes should establish an ethical organizational culture. Organizational culture describes a range of beliefs and behaviors that shape how individuals (directors, executives, and employees) interact and manage outside business transactions. Organizational culture affects every aspect of an organization's operations, including investing and financing activities, from hiring, supply chain, production, business hours, customer satisfaction, workplace environment, and commitment to all stakeholders. As such, culture can be applied to distinctive customs and traditions that people practice and that are sufficiently important to distinguish them from others. Corporate culture and compliance rules should provide incentives and opportunities for most ethical individuals to preserve their honesty and integrity and provide measures for monitoring, penalizing, and correcting the minority of unethical individuals.

Ethical Dimension of Sustainability

Corporate culture determines three factors that are most important in affecting people's behavior: incentives, opportunity, and choices. Incentives are perhaps the most essential determinant of business ethics. Individuals within the company (managers and employees) tend to act according to the incentives provided to them through the performance evaluation process. Opportunity defines conditions that enable individuals to act in certain manners. For example, when opportunities exist, wrongdoers will take advantage and behave opportunistically. Thus, effective corporate governance, internal controls, and enterprise risk management can reduce the opportunities for unethical conduct. Individuals always make choices available to them when making decisions or taking action. No single phrase captures the ethical relevancy of good corporate culture better than the "tone at the top," which promotes the corporate culture of integrity and competency. The key elements of corporate culture are: (1) values and beliefs that shape corporate culture, reflect the company's mission, vision, and long-term objectives and guide decision-making and behavior within the organization; (2) norms and practices that govern how work is conducted within the company including communication styles, dress codes, work hours, and approaches to problem-solving; (3) employee behavior and engagement of how employees interact with each other, approach their work, and respond to challenges by providing a sense of purpose, autonomy, and recognition for contributions; (4) cultural incentives and opportunities of a positive culture, which fosters collaboration, teamwork, and a sense of belonging, and a negative culture that can lead to conflict, disengagement, and turnover; (5) leadership style of directors and top executives that could influence the attitudes and behaviors of employees throughout the organization; (6) customer focus of determining the commitment to customer satisfaction and service excellence and being considered as a customer-centric culture prioritize meeting customer needs and delivering high-quality products or services; (7) ethical standards of promoting competency, honesty, integrity, and accountability: and (8) diversity and inclusion of fostering a sense of belonging for employees from different backgrounds, experiences, and perspectives. In summary, corporate culture is a fundamental aspect of organizational identity and has a profound impact on employee behavior and performance as well as the overall success of the company. Cultivating a positive, relevant, and supportive culture requires ongoing effort and commitment from the company's board of directors, top executives, and employees.

Taken together, nonfinancial ESG sustainability initiatives are increasingly recognized as critical drivers of long-term value creation, influencing factors such as brand reputation, employee retention, customer loyalty, risk management, and access to capital. Companies that effectively integrate ESG considerations into their business strategies are better positioned to navigate evolving market trends, regulatory requirements, and stakeholder expectations, ultimately contributing to a more sustainable and resilient global economy.

Additionally, investors, customers, and other stakeholders are increasingly seeking information on companies' ESG performance to inform their decision-making and allocation of resources. Therefore, transparent reporting on nonfinancial ESG metrics has become essential for companies to build trust and demonstrate their commitment to sustainability and responsible business practices.

Internal Control and Nonfinancial Sustainability

The Committee of Sponsoring Organizations (COSO) released its report in 1992, titled "Internal Control-Integrated Framework," which recommends voluntary internal control reports by both management and independent auditors of public companies.[59] COSO provided detailed guidance on the content of internal control reports, including the nature, objectives, and components of internal control; the role of management, the audit committee, and the independent auditor; and the limitations of internal control. Many components of the COSO internal control framework, such as control environment, activities, communication, risk assessment, and monitoring, are applicable and relevant to nonfinancial ESG dimensions of sustainability performance. The COSO Internal Control-Integrated Framework can be used to assess and manage risks associated with both financial ESP and nonfinancial ESG dimensions of sustainability performance to improve reliability and confidence in sustainability information. The COSO framework objectives of enhancing the reliability of financial reports, improving operational effectiveness and efficiency, and ensuring compliance with all applicable laws, rules, and regulations are applicable to both financial ESP and nonfinancial ESG dimensions of sustainability performance. For example, enhancing the reliability of financial reports is the most applicable objective to the financial ESP dimension of sustainability, whereas the other two objectives (compliance and operation effectiveness) are more relevant to nonfinancial ESG dimensions of sustainability performance.

Summary

Stakeholder wealth-maximization can be achieved only when business organizations focus on all five EGSEE dimensions of sustainability. This chapter presents nonfinancial ESG dimensions of sustainability performance reporting and assurance with a practical emphasis on social and environmental aspects. Given that a company is the property of its owners and not stakeholders, the owners have the right to decide how to handle their property as either for profit or for social good, or both if they desire. However, there has been a move in recent years to a middle-ground view of "doing well by doing good" by focusing on both financial and nonfinancial sustainability performance. Companies that are doing well financially have more slack resources to undertake social and environmental activities. Companies that are managed more effectively through robust corporate governance measures, run ethically, and pay attention to their social and environmental initiatives are more sustainable in the long term.

Corporate social responsibility requires that business organizations take social initiatives beyond their contractual requirements and comply with regulatory reform. Environmental sustainability is a process of preserving the quality of the environment in the long term and leaving a better environment for future generations while creating shareholder value for the current generation. Environmental sustainability has become a strategic focus of corporations worldwide because of climate change and global warming. The responses to the global environmental challenges and the pursuit of opportunities have advanced policies and practices that seek to safeguard the environment and improve the well-being of society. Many organizations, including the International Organization for Standardization, have established global standards to assist organizations in developing adequate CSR programs and environmental management systems, environmental auditing, and reporting.

Key Points

- Various incentives and pressures driven by socially and environmentally responsible investors and activists have encouraged companies to focus on their nonfinancial governance, social, ethical, and environmental performance, reporting, and assurance.
- Business organizations should integrate environmental initiatives and guidelines established by professional organizations into corporate culture, business environment, and strategic decisions.
- ISO 14000 standards are relevant to the development of environmental management systems, environmental risk assessment, and environmental auditing and reporting.
- External and independent verification of environmental reports lends objectivity and credibility to environmental sustainability reports.
- Business organizations should pay attention to product innovation and quality, customer retention and attraction, employee satisfaction and productivity, socially responsible citizenship, and environmentally conscious operation.
- CSR sustainability requires taking proper initiatives to further social good above and beyond your interests, as well as the requirements of compliance and legal obligations.
- CSR activities and practices are promoted to respond to stakeholder expectations, including minimizing negative impacts of operations on society or the environment

while maximizing positive impacts on the community customers, employees, suppliers, and society.

- Commitment to corporate conscience, citizenship, and social performance adds to bottom-line earnings.
- CSR initiatives are intended to enhance corporations' positive impacts and minimize negative effects on society.

Review Questions

1. **What are the key components of the environmental dimension of sustainability?**
2. **What is the role of Environmental Management Systems (EMS) in sustainability?**
3. What is the significance of ISO 14000 in environmental management?
4. What role does governance play in sustainability?
5. What are the benefits of transparent ESG reporting for companies?
6. How does sustainability reporting enhance corporate reputation?
7. What are the challenges of integrating ESG into business strategies?
8. What are the three pillars of sustainability performance?
9. What is the significance of the environmental dimension of sustainability?
10. How does ISO 14000 contribute to environmental sustainability?
11. Explain the challenges of sustainability reporting.
12. How does stakeholder engagement influence corporate sustainability?
13. What are the benefits of transparent ESG reporting for investors?
14. What is the significance of the governance dimension of sustainability?
15. **Explain the concept of "doing well by doing good" in the context of sustainability.**

Discussion Questions

1. **What are the key components of the environmental dimension of sustainability?**
2. **Explain the role of Environmental Management Systems (EMS) in sustainability.**
3. Discuss the significance of ISO 14000 in environmental management.
4. What role does governance play in sustainability?

5. **What are the benefits of transparent ESG reporting for companies?**
6. **How does sustainability reporting enhance corporate reputation?**
7. **What are the challenges of integrating ESG into business strategies?**
8. **What are the three pillars of sustainability performance?**
9. **What is the significance of the environmental dimension of sustainability?**
10. **How does ISO 14000 contribute to environmental sustainability?**
11. **Explain the challenges of sustainability reporting.**
12. **How does stakeholder engagement influence corporate sustainability?**
13. **What are the benefits of transparent ESG reporting for investors?**
14. **What is the significance of the governance dimension of sustainability?**
15. **Explain the concept of "doing well by doing good" in the context of sustainability.**

Multiple Choice Questions

1. **What is the primary benefit of integrating ESG into business strategies?**
   A) Short-term profit-maximization
   B) Enhanced long-term value
   C) Increased market volatility
   D) Reduced operational costs

2. **What does CSR stand for?**
   A) Corporate Sustainability Reporting
   B) Corporate Social Responsibility
   C) Corporate Strategic Resources
   D) Corporate Social Risks

3. **What is a significant challenge in environmental reporting?**
   A) Lack of stakeholder interest
   B) Reliable and transparent data
   C) High profitability
   D) Marketing complexity

4. **What does EMS stand for in sustainability management?**
   A) Environmental Management Systems
   B) Energy Management Systems
   C) Economic Management Systems
   D) Environmental Marketing Systems

5. **Which organization released the ISO 14000 standards?**
   A) United Nations
   B) International Organization for Standardization (ISO)
   C) World Health Organization (WHO)
   D) World Trade Organization (WTO)

6. **Which environmental initiative focuses on renewable energy sources?**
   A) ISO 14000
   B) Carbon footprint reduction
   C) Social KPIs
   D) Financial auditing

7. **Which factor is essential in environmental sustainability?**
   A) High employee turnover
   B) Resource conservation
   C) Increased advertising
   D) Financial leverage

8. **Which of the following is an environmental KPI?**
   A) Employee satisfaction
   B) Water usage
   C) Market share
   D) Customer loyalty

9. **Which aspect is included in the social dimension of sustainability?**
   A) Financial auditing
   B) Employee well-being
   C) Product development
   D) Marketing strategies

10. **What does the SEC require companies to disclose regarding environmental risks?**
    A) Marketing strategies
    B) Financial leverage
    C) Direct Greenhouse Gas emissions
    D) Employee turnover rates

11. **What is the focus of environmental KPIs?**
    A) Social well-being
    B) Financial growth
    C) Environmental impact
    D) Marketing strategies

Multiple Choice Questions

12. **What is the purpose of environmental reporting?**
    A) Financial analysis
    B) Marketing strategies
    C) Disclosing environmental impacts
    D) Employee engagement

13. **What is the significance of the governance dimension in sustainability?**
    A) Short-term profit-maximization
    B) Ensuring long-term ethical practices
    C) Reducing product quality
    D) Enhancing marketing strategies

14. **What is the primary goal of EMS?**
    A) Increase market share
    B) Enhance financial performance
    C) Improve environmental practices
    D) Boost employee turnover

15. **What is the role of environmental assurance?**
    A) Reduce marketing costs
    B) Ensure compliance with environmental regulations
    C) Increase financial leverage
    D) Enhance product quality

16. **What does the environmental dimension of sustainability focus on?**
    A) Product innovation
    B) Market expansion
    C) Environmental impact
    D) Financial growth

17. **Which of the following is included in environmental reporting?**
    A) Employee turnover rates
    B) Marketing strategies
    C) Greenhouse Gas emissions
    D) Financial leverage

18. **What is the primary focus of governance in sustainability?**
    A) Financial performance
    B) Ethical business practices
    C) Product innovation
    D) Marketing strategies

19. **What is the significance of stakeholder engagement in ESG?**
    A) Reduce operational costs
    B) Enhance product features
    C) Build trust and improve relationships
    D) Increase financial leverage

20. **Which of the following is an environmental KPI?**
    A) Market expansion
    B) Employee health
    C) Water usage
    D) Product innovation

21. **What does ISO 14000 primarily address?**
    A) Financial performance
    B) Employee engagement
    C) Environmental management systems
    D) Product quality

22. **What is the role of corporate governance in sustainability?**
    A) Increasing short-term profits
    B) Reducing operational costs
    C) Ensuring ethical business practices
    D) Enhancing product quality

23. **Which ISO standard is relevant for environmental management?**
    A) ISO 9000
    B) ISO 14000
    C) ISO 26000
    D) ISO 31000

24. **Which of the following is a benefit of transparent ESG reporting?**
    A) Increased market volatility
    B) Higher short-term profits
    C) Enhanced stakeholder trust
    D) Reduced operational costs

25. **Which of the following is included in social KPIs?**
    A) Carbon footprint
    B) Market expansion
    C) Labor practices
    D) Financial growth

Multiple Choice Questions

26. **Which of the following is a key benefit of ISO 14000 certification?**
    A) Increase marketing costs
    B) Enhance environmental performance
    C) Reduce employee morale
    D) Lower product quality

27. **Which of the following is an element of social KPIs?**
    A) Energy consumption
    B) Employee health and safety
    C) Carbon footprint
    D) Financial auditing

28. **Which of the following is a benefit of transparent ESG reporting?**
    A) Enhanced stakeholder trust
    B) Increased market volatility
    C) Reduced operational costs
    D) Higher short-term profits

29. **What is the purpose of corporate social responsibility (CSR)?**
    A) Increase advertising costs
    B) Achieve short-term profits
    C) Advance social good beyond company interests
    D) Enhance financial leverage

30. **What is the role of social KPIs in sustainability?**
    A) Measure environmental impact
    B) Assess social goals and alignment with societal values
    C) Enhance product quality
    D) Reduce marketing costs

Notes

1 KPMG. (2020). On the 2020 audit committee agenda Board Leadership Center. Summer 2020 Audit Committee Roundtable report. https://boardleadership.kpmg.us/content/dam/boardleadership/en/pdf/2019/on-the-2020-audit-committee-agenda.pdf

2 EY Center for Board Matters (2020). What audit committee should consider at the end of 2020 and beyond (September 8, 2020). https://assets.ey.com/content/dam/ey-sites/ey-com/en_us/topics/board-matters/ey-what-audit-committees-should-consider-at-the-end-of-2020-and-beyond.pdf.

3 The Securities and Exchange Commission (SEC) (2010). Commission guidance regarding climate change. Release No.33-9106; 34-61469. https://www.sec.gov/rules/interp/2010/33-9106.pdf.

4 Securities and Exchange Commission (SEC). (2024). The enhancement and standardization of climate-related disclosures for investors. 17 CFR 210, 229, 230, 232, 239, and 249, [Release Nos. 33-11275; 34-99678; File No. S7-10-22]. Final Rules, March 6, 2024. Available at https://www.sec.gov/files/rules/final/2024/33-11275.pdf.

5 International Standardization Organization (ISO). ISO 14000 Family: Environmental Management. https://www.iso.org/iso-14001-environmental-management.html.

6 EPA. Introduction: Environmental enforcement and compliance. http://www.epa.gov/region9/enforcement/intro.html.

7 Holland, Leigh, and Foo, Yee Boon. (2003). Differences in environmental reporting practices in the UK and the US: The legal and regulatory context, Department of Accounting and Finance, De Montfort University, The Gateway, Leicester LE1 9BH, UK (April 15), 1–18.

8 Environmental Protection Agency (EPA). Regulations. www.epa.gov/laws-regulations/regulations.

9 Environmental Protection Agency (EPA). Deepwater Horizon – BP Gulf of Mexico oil spill. https://www.epa.gov/enforcement/deepwater-horizon-bp-gulf-mexico-oil-spill (accessed October 25, 2018).

10 Environmental Protection Agency (EPA). Deepwater Horizon – BP Gulf of Mexico oil spill. https://www.epa.gov/enforcement/deepwater-horizon-bp-gulf-mexico-oil-spill (accessed October 25, 2018).

11 The Sustainability Accounting Standards Board (SASB). (2014). Chemicals sustainability accounting standard. http://www.sasb.org/wp-content/uploads/2013/09/rt_pcp_standards_combined.pdf.

12 Schwartz, J. (2019). Global warming concerns rise among Americans in new poll. *New York Times.* https://www.nytimes.com/2019/01/22/climate/americans-global-warming-poll.html.

13 Securities and Exchange Commission (SEC). (2010). 17 CFR parts 211, 231, and 241: Commission guidance regarding disclosure related to climate change; final rule. *Federal Register* 75 (25, February 8). www.sec.gov.

14 Securities and Exchange Commission (SEC). (2010). 17 CFR parts 211, 231, and 241: Commission guidance regarding disclosure related to climate change; final rule. *Federal Register* 75 (25, February 8), 6295–6296. www.sec.gov.

15 Securities and Exchange Commission (SEC). (2010). 17 CFR parts 211, 231, and 241: Commission guidance regarding disclosure related to climate change; final rule. *Federal Register* 75 (25, February 8), 6293. www.sec.gov.

16 Securities and Exchange Commission (SEC). (2010). 17 CFR parts 211, 231, and 241: Commission guidance regarding disclosure related to climate change; final rule. *Federal Register* 75 (25, February 8), 6296. www.sec.gov.

17 Securities and Exchange Commission (SEC). (2010). 17 CFR parts 211, 231, and 241: Commission guidance regarding disclosure related to climate change; final rule. *Federal Register* 75 (25, February 8), 6296. www.sec.gov.

Notes

18 Securities and Exchange Commission (SEC). (2024). The enhancement and standardization of climate-related disclosures for investors. 17 CFR 210, 229, 230, 232, 239, and 249, [Release Nos. 33-11275; 34-99678; File No. S7-10-22]. Final Rules, March 6, 2024. Available at https://www.sec.gov/files/rules/final/2024/33-11275.pdf

19 TMX Group. (2015). Three new climate change index series launched by S&P Dow Jones Indices and Toronto Stock Exchange (October 29). https://www.tmx.com/newsroom/press-releases?id=374&year=2015.

20 US Global Change Research Program. (2018). Fourth national climate assessment (NCA4). https://nca2018.globalchange.gov/downloads/NCA4_Report-in-Brief.pdf.

21 US Global Change Research Program. (2018). Fourth national climate assessment (NCA4). https://nca2018.globalchange.gov/downloads/NCA4_Report-in-Brief.pdf.

22 The BlackRock Investment Stewardship (BIS). (2018). Protecting andf enhancing our clients' assets for the long term. https://www.blackrock.com/corporate/literature/publication/blk-commentary-engaging-on-climate-risk.pdf.

23 The Task Force on Climate-Related Financial Disclosres (TCFD). (2018). Status report. https://www.fsb-tcfd.org/.

24 Global Reporting Initiative (GRI). (2010). *GRI Sustainability Reporting Guidelines*, Version 3.0. http://www.globalreporting.org/reporting framework.

25 GRI and CDP. (2010). Linking up GRI and CDP: How do the Global Reporting Initiative reporting guidelines match with the carbon disclosure project questions? www.globalreporting.org; www.cdproject.net.

26 ICAEW. FRS 12 provisions, contingent liabilities and contingent assets. https://www.icaew.com/technical/financial-reporting/uk-gaap/uk-gaap-standards/frs-12-provisions-contingent-liabilities-and-contingent-assets.

27 Task Force on Climate-related Financial Disclosures (TCFD) (2019). Second TCFD status report publication (June 5, 2019). https://www.fsb-tcfd.org/. The TCFD recommendations can be found at https://www.fsb-tcfd.org/wp-content/uploads/2017/12/FINAL-TCFD-Annex-Amended-121517.pdf

28 International Organization for Standardization. ISO 19011: 2018. https://www.iso.org/standard/70017.html.

29 ISO 9001 certifications top 1 million mark, food safety and information security continue meteoric increase (October 25, 2010). http://www.iso.org/iso/pressrelease.htm?refid=Ref1363.

30 MacBook Pro and the environment. www.apple.com/macbookpro/environment.html.

31 O'Rourke, D. (2003). Outsourcing regulation: Analyzing nongovernmental systems of labor standards and monitoring. *Policy Studies Journal*, 31: 1–29.

32 Damall, N., and Sides, S. (2008). Assessing the performance of voluntary environmental programs: Does certification matter? *Policy Studies Journal* 36: 95–117.

33 Aravind, Deepa, and Christmann, Petra (2011). Decoupling of standard implementation from certification: Does quality of ISO 14001 implementation affect facilities' environmental performance? *Business Ethics Quarterly* 21: 1 (January). ISSN 1052-150X.

34 Aravind, Deepa, and Christmann, Petra (2011). Decoupling of standard implementation from certification: Does quality of ISO 14001 implementation affect facilities' environmental performance? *Business Ethics Quarterly* 21: 1 (January). ISSN 1052-150X.

35 What LEED measures. http://www.usgbc.org/DisplayPage.aspx?CMSPageID=1989.

36 What LEED delivers. http://www.usgbc.org/DisplayPage.aspx?CMSPageID=1990.

37 http://www.usgbc.org/ShowFile.aspx?DocumentID=8868.

38 ISO 14000 (2014). Revision of ISO 14001 Environmental Management Systems, updated July 2014. ISO/TC 207/SC 1. www.iso.org/iso/tc207sc1home.

39 International Organization for Standardization (ISO) (2010). ISO 26000, Social responsibility. http://www.iso.org/iso/iso_catalogue/management_and_leadership_standards/social_responsibility/sr_iso26000_overview.htm#sr-1.

40 Carroll, Archie B. (1979). A three-dimensional conceptual model of corporate performance. *The Academy of Management Review* 4 (4): 497–505.

41 Carroll, Archie B. (1979). A three-dimensional conceptual model of corporate performance. *The Academy of Management Review* 4 (4): 497–505.

42 Sethi, S.P. (1975). Dimensions of corporate social performance: An analytical framework. *California Management Review* 17 (3, Spring): 58.

43 Carroll, A.B. (1999). Corporate social responsibility: Evolution of a definitional construct. *Business and Society* 38 (3): 268–295.

44 Organisation of Economic Co-operation and Development (OECD) (2003). Guidelines for multinational enterprises. www.oecd.org.

45 International Organization for Standardization (ISO) (2010). ISO 26000, Social responsibility. http://www.iso.org/iso/iso_catalogue/management_and_leadership_standards/social_responsibility/sr_iso26000_overview.htm#sr-1.

46 KMPG International. (2008). KPMG International survey of corporate responsibility reporting 2008. http://www.kpmg.com/Global/IssuesAndInsights/ArticlesAndPublications/Pages/Sustainability-corporate-responsibility-reporting-2008.aspx.

47 The BlackRock Investment Stewardship (BIS). (2018). https://www.blackrock.com/corporate/literature/publication/blk-stewardship-priorities.pdf.

48 The BlackRock Investment Stewardship (BIS). (2018). https://www.blackrock.com/corporate/literature/publication/blk-stewardship-priorities.pdf.

49 The BlackRock Investment Stewardship (BIS). (2018). https://www.blackrock.com/corporate/literature/publication/blk-stewardship-priorities.pdf.

50 Clayton, J. (2018). Remarks for telephone call with SEC Investor Advisory Committee Members by the Chairman of the SEC (February 8). https://www.sec.gov/news/public-statement/clayton-remarks-investor-advisory-committee-call-020619.

51 Clayton, J. (2018). Remarks for telephone call with SEC Investor Advisory Committee Members by the Chairman of the SEC (February 8). https://www.sec.gov/news/public-statement/clayton-remarks-investor-advisory-committee-call-020619.

Notes

52 Deloitte. Stakeholder engagement – keys to success. https://www2.deloitte.com/au/en /pages/risk/solutions/stakeholder-engagement-keys-success-sustainability-csr-training .html (accessed October 24, 2018).

53 AccountAbility (2018). AA 1000 accountability principles 2018. https://www.account-ability.org/wp-content/uploads/2018/05/AA1000_ACCOUNTABILITY_PRINCIPLES_2018 _Single_Pages.pdf.

54 PricewaterhouseCoopers. (2016). Stakeholder engagement: How we engage. www.pwc .com/gx/en/corporate-responsibility/assets/stakeholder-engagement.pdf.

55 Mcknight, L. (2011). Companies that do good also do well. Market Watch, *Wall Street Journal (Digital Network)*. http://www.marketwatch.com/story/companies-that-do-good -also-dowell-2011-03-23.

56 Rezaee, Z. (2007). *Corporate Governance Post Sarbanes-Oxley: Regulations, Requirements, and Integrated Processes*. Wiley.

57 Cordiero, W.P. (2003). The only solution to the decline in business ethics: ethical managers. *Teaching Business Ethics* 7 (3): 265–277.

58 Rezaee, Z. (2018). *Corporate Governance and Business Ethics*. Wiley.

59 Committee of Sponsoring Organizations of the Treadway Commission (COSO). (1992). Internal Control Integrated Framework (AICPA). New York. https://www.coso.org/Pages /default.aspx

Chapter 9
Business Sustainability Risks

Learning Objectives

- Explain the effect that the achievement of long-term sustainable economic performance has on shareholder value creation.
- Understand the value maximization concept.
- Provide an overview of financial economic sustainability performance risk.
- Provide an overview of the measures taken in the post–Sarbanes-Oxley (SOX) era to improve the quality of financial reports.
- Understand the financial reporting process and related risks.
- Provide an overview of Forward-Looking Financial Reports.
- Understand all types of business sustainability risks.
- Learn risk assessment and management in mitigating risks.

Introduction

Sustainability risks reflect potential adverse impacts of business strategies, activities, products, and services on the financial health, the environment, society, and well-being of current and future generations.[1] Business organizations are experiencing sustainability risks related to economic events, financial activities, and environmental aspects, including climate change and resource depletion, supply chain disruptions, regulatory compliance, social inequality, and ethical considerations. Sustainability risks represent the probability that an organization is not meeting its sustainability performance targets of not achieving financial economic sustainability performance (ESP) and nonfinancial environmental, social, and governance (ESG) sustainability performance. Sustainability risks reflect the potential adverse effects of business activities on the environment and society. Sustainability risks are conditions that can negatively impact business organizations' ability to meet their present and future needs while maintaining economic, environmental, and social sustainability. Sustainability risks can arise from various sources and may affect different ESP and ESG dimensions of sustainability performance. Identifying, assessing, and managing sustainability risks is vital for promoting resilience and sustainable development. Many

DOI: 10.4324/9781003487081-9

organizations have established the position of Chief Information Systems Officers (CISOs) to identify, assess and manage sustainability risks presented in this chapter.

The 2020 Government Accountability Office (GAO) report indicates that many of the surveyed institutional investors integrate ESG factors of performance and risk into their portfolio decisions to better understand risks associated with financial performance and information.[2] Investors generally use ESG disclosures provided by public companies to monitor management and assessment of ESG risks and make investment and voting decisions. This chapter explains the scope of business sustainability risks, risk management, and mitigation. This chapter also discusses enterprise risk management (ERM) and the COSO ERM framework in assessing and managing business sustainability risks. The most important risks relevant to business sustainability are strategic, operational, reputational, and financial risks. Strategic risk is the probability that an organization will fail to achieve its strategic sustainability plans and goals (e.g., focus on climate change and reducing GHG emissions). This risk should be identified, assessed, and managed to minimize its negative effects on operational and financial performance and build up on the opportunities provided by addressing this risk. The operation risk is relevant to financial ESP and nonfinancial ESG sustainability performance. The operation risk should be assessed at all levels of business activities and integrated into all sustainability performance dimensions, starting from operating activities across operational units, operation technology, supply chain, and information technology to other functional areas.

All financial ESP and nonfinancial ESG sustainability performance dimensions are affected by customer satisfaction, business reputation, and the employee workplace. The company's reputation and related risks should be assessed and managed continuously, and any damage to the reputation should be minimized. The financial risk of issuing materially misstated financial reports is detrimental to corporations' financial viability and sustainability. Sustainability reports are expected to be value-relevant to both external and internal users of such reports. Cyber hacking and security breaches of information systems are becoming a reality for many businesses (e.g., Sony, Target, Morgan Chase), and their risk assessment and controls demand significant IT investment and commitment by directors and offices to prevent their occurrences. Sustainability risks can be classified into several general categories: environmental, social, governance, market, regulatory, economic, and supply chain risks. Assessing, managing, and mitigating sustainability risks requires adopting sustainable business practices and integrating ESG initiatives into decision-making processes. Businesses that effectively manage and mitigate sustainability risks are better able to create long-term shared value for their stakeholders, have desirable social and environmental impacts, and contribute to a more sustainable future. This chapter presents sustainability risks as depicted in Exhibit 9.1 and is explained in the next section.

Sustainability Risks

Sustainability risks reflect potential adverse impacts of both financial ESP and nonfinancial ESG factors that can have detrimental effects on the long-term sustainability and performance of economies, businesses, and individuals. Sustainability risks have recently gained the attention of policymakers, regulators, businesses, and investors as more robust sustainability initiatives have been implemented. Sustainability risks can be classified into economic, financial, environmental, governance, compliance, regulatory, and social risks discussed in this section. Investors typically consider sustainability risks when integrating financial ESP and nonfinancial ESG sustainability performance into their investment decisions. Investors are now considering nonfinancial ESG risks and opportunities in their investment strategies and decisions as the majority of responded investors believe that consideration of nonfinancial ESG sustainability issues reduces investment risk, and other drivers are enhancing performance and avoiding firms with unsustainable performance and unethical conduct.[3] Transparent nonfinancial ESG disclosure, effective and honest relationship between investors and the board, and understanding of the organization's culture are the key points for a better understanding of financial performance in the past and prediction of the same in the future.[4] Among several sustainability risks, investors consider are strategic, economic, financial, regulatory non-compliance, cyberbanking, reputational, changes in consumer preferences, and operational social unrest risks. These and other sustainability risks are presented in this section.

These risks are interrelated and, thus, should be properly assessed and managed. For example, an excessive strategic risk can also cause operations, financial, compliance, and reputational risks. The compliance risk directly or indirectly associated with business sustainability, including non-compliance with regulatory reforms, health and safety, human rights and labor laws, corporate governance measures, anti-bribery, and environmental risks, can vary among organizations and across countries. For example, environmental risks can include direct effects (e.g., emissions trading cost exposures) and indirect consequences (e.g., energy price increases and accompanying reporting and compliance costs) of non-compliance with environmental laws, rules, and regulations. Business organizations also assess and manage their financial risk of producing and disclosing materially misstated financial reports. Minimizing the reputational risk is vital to the success of sustainability programs and related performance, as stakeholder satisfaction is essential to sustainable business. To effectively manage sustainability risks, business organizations adopt enterprise risk management policies and practices, conduct robust and thorough ESP and ESG assessments, engage with stakeholders, and integrate sustainability factors of performance and disclosure into their decision-making processes to mitigate risks and

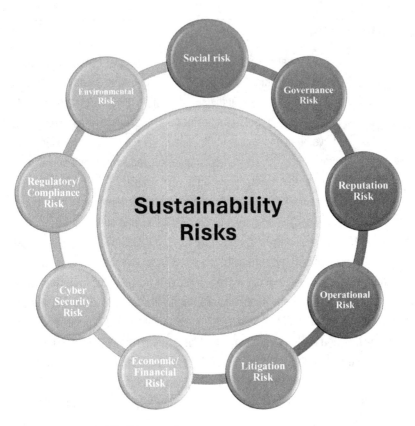

EXHIBIT 9.1   Sustainability Risks

ensure long-term shared value creation for all stakeholders. Investors also consider sustainability opportunities and risks when making their investment decisions. The following subsection examines nine sustainability risks in detail, as depicted in Figure 9.1.

Environmental Risks

Environmental risks include factors such as climate change, resource scarcity, pollution, and ecosystem degradation. Businesses that heavily rely on natural resources or operate in environmentally sensitive areas face risks relevant to regulatory changes, physical impacts (e.g., extreme weather events), and reputational damage due to unsustainable practices. Climate change risk generally is the failure to address the potential adverse effects of climate change on various aspects of business, society, the economy, and the environment that have been caused by changing climate patterns of extreme weather events, sea-level rise, and rising temperatures. Climate change is often caused by human activities that increase the concentration of greenhouse gases in the atmosphere, which could trigger global warming and related changes in weather patterns. The risk results from the physical impacts of climate change. The global initiatives relevant to climate change are real, and the expected transitions to a net-zero carbon economy could put more pressure on the economic sustainability of many countries and their business organizations. Climate change risks include the detrimental effects of (1) the threat of global greenhouse gas (GHG) emissions; (2) the physical risk of rising temperatures of about 1.8°F since the mid-20th century; (3) natural disasters of catastrophic flooding, wildfires, storms, and droughts; (4) extreme weather events (hurricanes, droughts, floods, wildfires, and heatwaves); (5) rising sea levels that can lead to damages to coastal communities, infrastructure, and eco-systems; (6) legal and liability risks associated with climate change; and (7) other climate changes and environmental related issues that could have detrimental effects on business operations. Several initiatives can be taken to assess, manage, and mitigate climate change risks, including realizing the changing climate, reducing greenhouse gas emissions, setting emission reduction targets, adopting sustainable business practices to address climate change, integrating climate risk assessment and management into their strategic planning processes, establishing and implementing international agreements that address climate change risks, incorporating climate risk considerations into investment decisions and recognizing the importance of climate-related financial disclosures.

The initial 2019 Carbon Disclosure Project (CDP) survey and subsequent surveys in 2020 and 2021 show that 215 of the world's largest public companies could suffer financial losses of about $1 trillion of climate-related risk in the next five years.[5] The recent 2021 survey revealed that over 13,000 companies (64% of global market capitalization) and over 11,000 cities disclosed their environmental data. This represents a 35% growth when compared to last year, and it just shows how seriously organizations took the survey results from 2019.[6] However, this is not a surprise considering the CDP's five-year strategy of accelerating the rate of change, which focuses on improving transparency, tracking the reported results, and implementing strategies.[7] The CDP climate change programs are intended to mitigate climate change risk and reduce greenhouse gas emissions. The climate change risk can be assessed and managed, and its negative impacts can be minimized if business organizations:

1. Acknowledge that climate change poses risks to their operational effectiveness, financial market stability, and financial sustainability.
2. Adopting sustainable business practices that establish emission reduction targets.
3. Integrate climate risk assessments into their strategic planning processes.
4. Explore the integration of climate risk into all aspects of business, from operational to financial and supply chain.
5. Integrate climate change into their strategic planning, decisions, corporate culture, and business environment.

Sustainability Risks

6. Assess the adequacy and effectiveness of internal controls in responding to climate risks.
7. Disclose the climate risk properly and transparently to all stakeholders.
8. Comply with international agreements and regulations aimed at addressing climate change risks.
9. Recognize the importance of climate-related financial disclosures and incorporate climate risk considerations into investment decisions.

Proper disclosure of climate change by business organizations is important in addressing the global climate change risk. This disclosure can be included in financial reports, sustainability reports, or a separate report by management to inform stakeholders about the organization's efforts to address and adapt to climate change and related risks. In March 2022, the Securities and Exchange Commission (SEC) proposed new rules for disclosing climate-related financial risks in SEC filings by requiring public companies to discuss their climate risk management and disclose greenhouse gas emissions in their annual reports.[8] The SEC, in Mach 2024, released its final rules that require public companies to: (1) disclose information related to their climate-related risks, impacts, and strategies including greenhouse gas emissions, climate-related risks to operations and supply chains, and the potential financial impacts of climate change on the company's business; (2) integrate climate-related disclosures into existing SEC reporting frameworks, such as Form 10-K, Form 20-F, and Form 40-F; (3) establish standardized reporting metrics and disclosures to enhance consistency and comparability across companies and industries to enable investors better assess and compare companies' climate-related risks and performance; (4) assess the materiality of their climate-related risks and impacts and disclose information that is material to investors including evaluating the significance of climate-related factors on the company's financial condition, operating performance, and prospects; and (5) disclose information about their governance structures, internal controls, and management processes related to climate-related risks and opportunities to enable investors to evaluate how companies are managing and addressing climate-related issues at the board and executive levels.[9]

The success of the global economy, despite the increase in zero pure carbon, depends on governments, companies, and households working together to eliminate or absorb carbon. Simple methods can take steps such as measurement and annual reporting. Much progress has been made in measurement and reporting, but public companies do not disclose this information. Also, a small number of private companies do this, and there is no specific framework or method for measurement and reporting. Carbon emission information is essential given the critical weather conditions. The first but necessary step is to require public and private companies to publish carbon emission reports. Carbon emissions alone will not solve climate crises, but they will help accelerate this, as companies are encouraged to change their emissions from previous years by releasing carbon emissions reports.

Regulatory/Compliance Risks

Regulatory sustainability risks stem from noncompliance with applicable laws, rules, regulations, and standards governing financial, environmental, social, and governance practices. Changes in regulations, stricter enforcement, or emerging legal requirements can expose businesses to fines, penalties, litigation, and operational restrictions. Failure to anticipate and adapt to regulatory changes can undermine business operations and competitiveness. Regulatory sustainability risks refer to the challenges and potential negative impacts that arise from non-compliance with both ESP and ESG regulations and standards. These risks can have significant consequences for businesses, including legal penalties, reputational damage, operational disruptions, and financial losses. Regulatory sustainability risks encompass a wide range of issues, including environmental regulations, climate change regulations, labor laws, human rights standards, supply chain regulations, data privacy and cybersecurity regulations and corporate governance requirements. To effectively mitigate regulatory sustainability risks, businesses should stay informed about relevant laws, rules and regulations, conduct regular compliance assessments, adopt robust corporate governance structures, establish effective internal controls and monitoring mechanisms, and implement policies and procedures to ensure adherence to regulatory requirements. Business organizations should also engage with stakeholders, including regulators, industry associations, and advocacy groups, to stay abreast of emerging regulatory trends and proactively address sustainability risks in their operations and supply chains. By effectively assessing and managing regulatory sustainability risks, business organizations can enhance their financial viability operational resilience, protect their reputation, and create long-term shared value for all stakeholders.

Technological advances and globalization require business organizations to comply with local, national, and international laws, rules, regulations, standards, and best practices. Compliance risks are failures to comply with these local, national, and international laws, rules, regulations, and standards relevant to many issues ranging from financial reporting standards to climate change, social responsibility, and financial activities.[10] Compliance risk is the company's failure to comply with applicable laws, rules, and regulations relevant to its operation that can have significant financial, legal, and reputational consequences. Many companies are experiencing the challenges of complying with the ever-increasing regulatory measures, and non-compliance with these regulations may cause significant risks of interruption, paying fines, and/or discontinuing their business operation. Major

Sustainability Risks

components of compliance risk are failure to comply with (1) regulatory compliance; (2) data privacy and security policies and procedures; (3) internal policies and procedures to ensure operational efficiency and ethical conduct; (4) financial compliance with financial regulation and accounting standards; (5) anti-money laundering and counter-terrorism financing to prevent illegal financial activities; and (6) ESG mandatory and voluntary initiatives by conducting ESG statement inventory, providing regular training on ESG matters, reviewing and clarifying ESG policies, maintaining accurate records, and assess the ESG compliance policies and disclosures to avoid misrepresentation and greenwashing.

Compliance risks need to be assessed and managed, and their negative impacts on financing, investing, and operating activities be minimized. Many companies have created either a board compliance committee or an executive position as compliance and risk officers to achieve this objective. The compliance committee usually comprises executives who can assist the compliance officer in making important decisions regarding compliance with many obligations, regulations, and laws. Even though the company's strategic risks, goals, and tasks differ from one organization to another, the main goal of the committee, as well as the compliance officer, remains the same. Chief Financial Officer, Chief Accounting Officer, HR Director, IT Director, and General Counsel are some key executives who should be inside the compliance committee and try to reduce any potential compliance risk. The committee should work with leaders and managers from different departments to minimize and maintain complete control over the risk. Some organizations do not have a compliance committee, only a compliance officer. While the compliance officer does not work directly on emerging issues, he or she works closely with other executives and managers and navigates them throughout the compliance process. With the greater number of responsibilities assigned to only one person to oversee, there is a greater chance of compliance risk becoming a serious threat, and organizations must be aware of it.

Governance, risk management, and compliance reporting (GRC) have evolved to mitigate the rising economic challenges. GRC refers to the strategy the organization implements when dealing with these three components while also assisting the company in achieving its goals and meeting its objectives. It comprises a set of practices that must be followed to ensure that risks are reduced and visibility of the same is increased, business objectives are met, segregation among the departments is minimal, costs are lower, and information is gathered more efficiently and used more appropriately. Specifically, compliance risk has increased due to the widening business complexity, the need to reduce risk exposure, and the mission to improve the firm's performance. Companies and their board of directors and top executives should pay considerable attention to compliance risks or face consequences such as fines, public scrutiny, regulatory intervention, or discontinuation of their operations.

Cybersecurity Risks

An ever-increasing number of cyberattack incidents is detrimental to companies' operations and business sustainability. Cybersecurity risks are potential threats and vulnerabilities that could compromise the integrity, confidentiality, and availability of an organization's information systems, data processing, electronic data, and digital assets. Many factors can cause these risks, including malicious actors, human error, technical weaknesses, and internal or external factors. Effective and robust cybersecurity risk assessment and management is vital for businesses to protect against cyber threats and safeguard sensitive information. Some severe cybersecurity risks are: (1) data breaches by unauthorized individuals gain access to sensitive or confidential information including customer data, financial records, or intellectual property causing financial losses, reputational damage, regulatory fines, and legal liabilities; (2) phishing consisting of fraudulent emails, messages, or websites designed to trick individuals into disclosing sensitive information, such as login credentials, financial details, or personal data; (3) malware attacks involving viruses, worms, ransomware, and spyware, poses a significant cybersecurity risk to businesses that infect systems, steal data, disrupt operations, and extort ransom payments; (4) insider threats and security damages posed by employees, business partners or contractors who misuse their access privileges to intentionally or unintentionally harm the organization; (5) third-party risks caused by vendors, suppliers, and service providers for various products and services, including supply chain attacks, data breaches at vendor organizations, or inadequate security practices by third-party partners; and (6) ineffective and inadequate authentication mechanisms and access controls that make systems and data vulnerable to unauthorized access and misuse including default or weak passwords, lack of multi-factor authentication, and improper configuration of access permissions increase the risk of unauthorized access by malicious actors.

Cybersecurity risk is the potential harm caused by unauthorized access, use, disruption, modification, destruction, or disclosure of information, networks, and systems that are material to individuals, businesses, and governments. Risks related to data breaches and cyberattacks can have detrimental effects of disrupting operations and compromising sensitive information. Technological advances enable hackers to access information systems, creating significant challenges for individuals, organizations, and governments. Destructive cyberattacks, like the ones of Sony Pictures, Target, Yahoo, JPMorgan, Chase, Uber, Home Depot, Equifax, and Facebook, have been devastating and are recorded as the most damaging cyberattacks outside the norms of cyber practices. Technological advancements have turned cyber security into the top agenda of public companies' boards of directors and executives. For example, the Equifax cyber breach is one of the largest data breaches in history, affecting nearly half of the population in the United States (about 143 million Americans).[11] There are many reasons and aspects of these cyberattacks and related cybersecurity risks, including threats of malware of software viruses, ransomware, and spyware, deceptive emails or messages, vulnerabilities or weaknesses in software, employees or individuals with access to sensitive information, hackers gaining access to sensitive data, and lack of a robust incident response plan. To mitigate cybersecurity risks, business organizations should implement robust and comprehensive security measures, including regular software updates, the use of encryption technologies, employee training, network monitoring, and a proactive and adaptive cybersecurity posture. To effectively assess, manage, and mitigate cybersecurity risks, organizations should implement comprehensive and robust cybersecurity measures, including proactive and robust security policies and procedures, encryption and data protection mechanisms, employee training and awareness programs, regular vulnerability assessments and penetration testing, intrusion detection and prevention systems, incident response and recovery plans, and collaboration with cybersecurity experts and industry peers. The mitigation of cybersecurity risks enables business organizations to protect critical assets, enhance their resilience, and maintain trust with customers, partners, and stakeholders.

Cyber hacking can be detected and prevented using effective and efficient cybersecurity processes and procedures driven by information security management systems (ISMS). Cybersecurity standards enable organizations to manage the security of assets such as financial information, human capital, intellectual property, employee information, or information entrusted to the entities by third parties.[12] ISMS is a systematic approach to managing sensitive information and maintaining its integrity and confidentiality. ISMS can also help identify the risks to valuable information and design appropriate controls to reduce the risk. It includes measures, people, processes, and information technology systems by applying a risk management process. These standards are available to help any size and type of organization, whether small, medium, or large businesses in any industry. There are several policies and procedures for managing sensitive data in companies. The purpose of this system is to minimize the risk of safety violations.

ISMS can be implemented in various ways, such as using comprehensive customer data methods that usually deal with employee behavior and company data. ISMS could be different from organization to organization because not all are subject to the same risk. Regardless, some of the same policies, regulations, procedures, and workflows should be implemented to prevent information asset theft and limit potential setbacks caused by it. Controls set by the organizations must be followed and reviewed regularly for efficiency to ensure that controls go along with the company's objectives. To ensure controls are effective, organizations must separate the data by its value and importance and appropriately use risk assessment to determine the right set of controls for each set of organizational data. Rather than just creating ISMS and continuing with their everyday operations, organizations should strive to incorporate it by making it part of the company's culture, training their employees, and raising their awareness about potential threats and risks.[13] One of the best ways to effectively implement ISMS while demonstrating to your clients that a strong set of controls is being executed is by following ISO/IEC 27001:2013. Even though it is not mandatory, most organizations decide to follow this set of effective requirements while obtaining certification to ISO/IEC 27001:2013 and, in that way, build up their stakeholders' confidence in the organization.[14] Some key benefits include reduced risk of cyberattacks while securing the information in any given form, faster response to security threats, a central framework managing all the information in one place, and improving the company's culture while raising its reputation.

In March 2022, the SEC proposed legislation to reduce cyber risks and increase the standardization of public company disclosure and risk management for cybersecurity, and on July 26, 2023, adopted rules requiring registrants, including foreign private issuers, to disclose material cybersecurity incidents they experience as well as material information regarding their cybersecurity risk management, strategy, and governance on an annual basis.[15] In the past several years, the SEC has been actively considering cybersecurity threats to financial markets and protecting sensitive information. The SEC rules address (1) disclosure requirements of disclosing material information related to cybersecurity risks and incidents; (2) guidance on cybersecurity disclosures to assist public companies in preparing disclosures about cybersecurity risks and incidents; (3) internal controls and policies for establishing and maintaining internal controls and procedures to ensure disclosures of adequate information pertaining to cybersecurity risks; (4) board oversight of the establishment of cybersecurity policies and procedures of cybersecurity risk assessment and management; and (5) examination and enforcement to assess the implementation of adequate cybersecurity measures and risk management by public companies.

Economic/Financial Risks

Economic and financial sustainability risks are risks associated with financial and economic factors such as market volatility, inflation, currency fluctuations, economic downturns, and financial instability. Businesses that fail to address economic risks of changing market conditions, anticipate economic shocks, or manage financial risks effectively may experience reduced profitability, financial losses, and even bankruptcy. Economic and financial sustainability risks are threats and challenges that may undermine an organization's long-term financial health, stability, and viability. These risks can arise from various internal and external factors, including economic downturns, market volatility, material financial misstatements, financial mismanagement, and structural weaknesses. Effectively managing economic and financial sustainability risks is essential for businesses to ensure financial viability, resilience, profitability, and shared value creation over time for all stakeholders. Financial risk is related to investments in unsustainable activities or exposure to liabilities associated with environmental or social issues. Is the probability that investors and users of corporate financial statements receive materially misstated financial reports that will adversely affect their financial and investment decisions?

Financial risks are often triggered by economic instability, market uncertainties, and fluctuations in commodity prices that can negatively affect businesses and industries. Receiving materially misstated information is usually due to management incompetence, weak internal controls, a rapidly changing environment, or poor accounting systems and information recording, and organizations should try to devote additional attention to all of these factors. It is important to understand that not only investors and outside users could be affected by false or incomplete accounting information, but also executives and internal users, having their decision-making and strategic goals based on the wrong or insufficient information, not understanding the full scope of the situation, and leading an organization to the disastrous outcome. Nonfinancial dimensions of sustainability performance, including ESG, can also affect financial performance. The financial risk of issuing materially misstated financial reports negatively affects investors' confidence and public trust in financial information and, thus, is detrimental to the overall sustainability of corporations.

Some of the common economic and financial sustainability risks are: (1) market volatility: Market volatility caused by fluctuations in asset prices, interest rates, exchange rates, and other financial variables that can affect a company's financial viability including revenues, expenses, and profitability, creating uncertainty, risk aversion, and reduced investor confidence; (2) economic downturns of recessions or economic contractions that could pose significant risks to businesses by reducing consumer spending, declining sales, revenue losses, credit defaults, and liquidity challenges; (3) financial instability caused by vulnerabilities within the financial system, weaknesses in banking institutions, capital markets, and credit markets, that can lead to systemic crises, disruptions and financial risks; (4) credit and counterparty risks of non-payment of loans, bonds, or trade receivables that can lead to default on derivatives contracts, swaps, or other financial instruments; (5) liquidity shortages risks of lack sufficient cash or liquid assets to meet short-term financial obligations resulted from poor cash flow management, excessive debt levels, unexpected cash outflows, or disruptions in funding markets, leading to financial distress or bankruptcy; (6) currency and exchange rate risks arise from fluctuations in foreign exchange rates that can impact the value of assets, liabilities, revenues, and expenses denominated in foreign currencies; (7) commodity price risks associated with exposure to fluctuations in the prices of raw materials, energy resources, or agricultural products that are essential inputs for production or operations; and (8) regulatory and policy risks relevant to changes in laws, regulations, taxation, or government policies that affect business operations, investments, and financial markets. To mitigate economic and financial sustainability risks, organizations should adopt proactive, efficient and prudent risk management practices, including financial planning, stress testing, hedging strategies, diversification of investments, scenario analysis, and maintaining adequate reserves of liquidity and capital. Furthermore, businesses should be vigilant about macroeconomic trends, regulatory developments, and geopolitical risks that could impact their operations and financial performance. By effectively managing economic and financial sustainability risks, organizations can improve their financial health and enhance their resilience, competitiveness, and long-term value creation for stakeholders.

Sustainability reporting can be used as a tool for more effective risk assessment and management to identify opportunities and risks associated with financing, investing, and operating activities. Thus, more transparent sustainability disclosures on financial ESP and nonfinancial ESG sustainability performance create opportunities to identify and correct operational inefficiencies, reputational damages, and financial risks that would improve financial economic performance. Best practices of sustainability suggest that companies which ignore their financial ESP and nonfinancial ESG sustainability performance issues and responsibilities would encounter the risk of: (1) not maintaining sustainability in the long term; (2) being subject to higher scrutiny and intervention by regulators; (3) losing their license to operate; (4) having less of an analyst following and forecasting, that may affect their market valuation; (5) not attracting socially responsible investors with long-term horizons; (6) encouraging managerial practices of not committing to the long-term sustainability of multidimension stakeholders; (7) not setting an appropriate tone at the top by directors and executives in promoting sustainability and ethical, accountable, socially, and environmentally responsible behavior and practices; (8) losing customer and customers reputation and their confidence in products and services; (9) not being able to attract and retain most qualified and talented human capital and workforce; (10) incurring a higher cost of capital both in debt and equity; and (11) prevent proper growth and development.

Litigation Risks

Litigation risk is the probability that a company becomes suggest of legal proceedings that could result in adverse outcomes, including financial losses, damage to reputation, or other negative consequences. Litigation risk can arise from various sources and for various reasons, including changes in laws and regulations that may impact business operations and compliance. And could involve civil, criminal, or regulatory actions. Risks arise from changes in laws and regulations that may impact business operations and compliance. Litigation risks could arise in ESG reporting issues because of the lack of compliance with applicable ESG-related laws, rules, regulations, and standards. The rise in litigations occurs because of the lack of compliance and the newly increased availability of ESG sustainability information. Financial reports outside users are now able to see information that was not previously disclosed, use it, and drive conclusions based on it. For example, when using scenario analysis to understand future business performance through various potential climate-based scenarios, disclosing these results and analysis, or lack thereof, gives way to possible litigation issues. This explains the current rise in litigations and makes companies aware of both potential benefits and risks regarding nonfinancial ESG sustainability reporting.

Risks could come from inadequate climate-based scenarios or working papers regarding scenario analysis and could be used to commence litigation. Inaccurate or misleading material information from these scenarios and lack of adequate attention to environmental, social, and governance measures can also pose an immense potential litigation risk. Investors and other stakeholders are looking for transparent and sufficient information that can be utilized for effective decision-making. Information and disclosures of a company should include all material matters to prevent the risks of litigation resulting from inadequate reports and inappropriate assumptions used in preparing ESG sustainability reports. These risks stem from a lack of preparation for future events, such as the COVID-19 pandemic, giving rise to a potentially misleading set of financial statements. Business organizations can implement several strategies to manage litigation risk, including risk assessment and management policies and procedures, comprehensive and robust compliance programs, retaining legal counsel, obtaining adequate insurance coverage, focusing on ethical business practices, adopting proactive measures to address and prevent potential issues before they escalate into legal disputes. A robust and effective ongoing legal reviews, and compliance audits. can contribute to minimizing litigation risk.

Operational Risks

Operational sustainability risks pertain to challenges within the company's operations, business processes and supply chain, including supply chain disruptions, cybersecurity breaches, data privacy violations, product defects, and accidents. Ineffective and inadequate risk management practices, inefficient operations, and lack of contingency planning can disrupt business continuity and lead to financial and reputational damage. Operational risk is the failure of internal processes, systems, people, and external events to generate desired outcomes and production that can cause potential challenges for business organizations to conduct their business and operations successfully. Operational risks can be triggered by a lack of resources, such as materials, water, minerals, and energy sources, and often are relevant to both financial ESP and nonfinancial ESG sustainability performance dimensions. Operational risk should be integrated into all sustainability performance dimensions as well as operating activities across operational units, information technology, operation technology, supply chain, and other functional areas. One of the important challenges for business organizations in implementing their strategic sustainability planning is effective collaboration and integration across operational business units and key functional areas. Operational risks are relevant to both conventional financial key performance indicators (KPIs), such as earnings and return on investment, and nonfinancial KPIs, such as social, environmental, and natural performance. Risks such as internal or external fraud, employee mistakes, business processes, controls-related risks, and technology risks are only some operational risks that can highly influence financial and nonfinancial KPIs. After these risks are identified, they need to be accurately assessed and managed, and their negative impacts on both financial ESP and nonfinancial ESG should be minimized. Operational risks are related to the business operation's impact on sustainability performance, including those risks pertaining to IT, supply chain, and production facilities. Strategic sustainability planning can be used as a tool for more effective risk assessment and management and in identifying challenges and opportunities associated with operations. The more transparent disclosure of operational risk, the lower the risk of regulatory actions, higher employee satisfaction, higher customer confidence, and more effective management activities and practices within the organization.

Some of the important aspects of operational risk are (1) inadequacies or failures in internal processes, systems, and controls that may result in financial loss or harm to the organization's sustainability; (2) failure of employees triggered by inadequate training, employee turnover, misconduct that can impact operational performance and create vulnerabilities; (3) failures or disruptions in information technology systems that can have material detrimental operational and financial consequences; and (4) inadequate or non-compliance with applicable laws, rules, regulations and industry standards that can result in legal and regulatory actions with potential financial penalties, operational disruptions and reputational damage. As business sustainability and its reporting evolve, the board of directors and executives will have to give considerable attention to operational risk management and its overall effectiveness and efficiency. Even though many organizations implement the ERM approach, there are some organizations that, in addition to it, use the operational risk management (ORM) perspective, which comes with fewer risks compared to ERM. That is why ORM is considered a subset of ERM, excluding strategic, reputational, and financial risks.[16] ORM strictly focuses on day-to-day operations and minimization of operations-related risks while trying to implement the right set of controls that could aid in risk prevention.

One of the most effective approaches to ORM is by dividing risks into groups and, in that way, diminishing the risk. If implemented correctly, ORM can create stronger stakeholder confidence, better business risk anticipation, more accurate financial forecasting, more efficient operations on a daily level, improved quality of the product/service and its recognition, as well as providing executives with better visibility of the processes. Using the ERM and ORM in managing operational risk requires identifying, assessing, and mitigating potential risks by implementing effective and strong internal controls, risk management frameworks, monitoring systems, and adequate insurance coverage. A robust and comprehensive management of operational risk contributes to the success of an organization and its business sustainability.

Reputation Risks

Reputational sustainability risks arise from negative perceptions of a company's decisions, actions, behaviors, or performance in relation to sustainability factors of planning, performance, and disclosures. These risks can result from customer dissatisfaction, environmental incidents, social controversies, unethical conduct, or failure to meet stakeholder expectations. Reputational damage can erode stakeholder and, particularly, customer trust, deter investors, and impact employee morale, leading to financial losses and long-term harm to the brand. Reputation is the most important asset for any profit and non-profit organization; it can be earned through much effort and dedication over many years and can be easily destroyed overnight. Reputational risk is the potential for damage to the reputation of an individual, company, or institution that can have adverse consequences on its brand, business operations, and customer trust. Reputation risk may result from the perception of customers, employees, investors, regulators, and the public. A negative reputation can cause business loss, sustainability damage, legal or regulatory issues, and challenges in attracting and retaining talent. Sustaining a good business reputation and meeting and exceeding the expectations of corporate stakeholders, from investors to creditors, customers, employees, suppliers, community, society, and the environment is a major challenge for many businesses. Reputational risks are growing increasingly and present a significant risk to the financial and operational of a company.

Many factors can contribute to reputational risk, including problems with products or services, quality control challenges, supply chain disruptions, unethical behavior, noncompliance with applicable laws, rules, regulations, and legal issues, loss of customer data triggered by cyberattacks, executive misconduct, and leadership failures. The business sustainability performance of financial ESP and nonfinancial ESG is relevant to business reputation, customer satisfaction, suppliers, the ethical workplace, upholding high ethical standards, and compliance with regulations. Reputational risks can be triggered by (1) brand damage of perceived or actual negative impacts on the environment, society, or ethical behavior and (2) consumer activism of ill-informed awareness and activism among consumers pertaining to sustainable practices. The company's reputation risk should be evaluated and managed on an ongoing basis, and any damage to the reputation must be minimized. The social risk theory suggests that every company faces an unavoidable reputational risk relevant to CSR initiatives. Research shows that many companies better understand the importance of social risks and their impact on reputation, but they do not necessarily report them openly.[17] Public companies pay close attention to risks affecting their shareholders, such as financial risks and those risks that are perceived as most prevailing. From the perspective of CEOs, one of the biggest threats to reputation in the technology-evolving world is the threat of online reviews and unwanted search results. Based on multiple research projects, most executives believe this factor can significantly affect an organization's earnings. Even though reputation risk is highly unpredictable, unwanted search results are even more common. Organizations try to deal with it by implementing search engine optimization (SEO) and, in that way, regulating what potential customers could find online. Hand in hand with the organization's reputation image goes the CEO's reputation. Having an ethical person at the top of the company representing it correctly and with integrity can significantly decrease reputation risks. Additional factors and events that organizations must tackle on time are usually related to negative articles, social media, services and pricing, data loss, and regulation changes.[18] Reputational risk management is an important integral component of overall risk assessment and management strategies for organizations that requires a robust, comprehensive, and proactive approach to maintain trust and credibility.

Governance Risks

Governance risks involve challenges related to corporate governance, strategies, ethics, transparency, and compliance with regulations and standards. Ineffective corporate governance structures, lack of board oversight, ineffective and incompetent management, conflicts of interest, and unethical behavior can lead to legal penalties, shareholder activism, loss of investor confidence, and damage to stakeholder trust. Strategic risk is the potential uncertainties and threats caused by unsound strategic decisions made by individuals or organizations. Unlike other risks, such as operational or financial risks that are more tangible and measurable, strategic risks are typically more subjective. They are associated with consequences of choices regarding business decisions in achieving intended goals, objectives, and the allocation of resources. Important aspects of strategic risks are: (1) ever-increasing technological advances that can create challenges and opportunities for organizations and their failure I to adapt or invest sufficiently in IT; (2) changes in market conditions such as the emergence of new competitor and shifts in consumer preferences and the risk of not responding or adjusting to these changes; (3) new rules and regulations and changes in government policies can pose a strategic risk of non-compliance; (4) failing to innovate or adapt to new trends of establishing market positioning can pose a strategic risk; (5) risks associated with poor working conditions, unfair labor practices, and violations of human rights; (6) risks related to the displacement of communities triggered by industrial activities, development projects, or environmental changes; (7) risks caused by unequal distribution of resources, opportunities, and benefits within societies. Effective management of strategic risks, including proper oversight function by the board of directors and proper planning and adaptability, can contribute to business success and sustainability. Strategic risk management is an integral component of enterprise risk management that enables organizations to manage their strategic risks effectively and better position themselves to adapt to changes, capitalize on opportunities, and achieve long-term and sustainable success. Business organizations are taking many initiatives and guidelines, including board risk oversight function, managerial strategies, adequate IT investment, and cybersecurity infrastructure to ensure the integrity of IT systems and the effectiveness of cyber-infrastructure in minimizing cybersecurity risk and dealing with potential cyberattacks and cybersecurity breaches.

The achievement of both financial ESP and nonfinancial ESG sustainability performance requires business organizations to assess and manage all risks, particularly those that threaten strategic sustainability planning. There are several strategic risks triggered by business sustainability performance, reporting, and assurance, including threats to survival and achievement of long-term performance, business continuity, uncertainty with marketing position and volatility in security prices, risks relevant to strategic investments, stakeholder communications, investor relations, abnormal changes in consumer demand, and changes in global trends. Technology advancements and globalization underscore the importance and relevance of these risks. Executives consider new technology risks, including social media, data mining, and analytics, to be the most disruptive for the business model and can highly affect business strategic sustainability. The risk and compliance board committee should oversee the managerial approach in assessing and managing the risk and determine the risk tolerance and a plan of action to respond to the risk quickly and efficiently.[19] Business continuity and threats to survival, especially since the pandemic started, are among the main risks to consider. In this new world where organizations highly rely on their software and business processes being online, factors such as software failure, and data non-compliance can trigger governance and operational risks. In addition to technology failure, human vulnerability and human-made mistakes could play a huge role in business continuity, affecting business strategic goals. Due to the accelerated lifestyle and progress in almost all scientific and technology fields, it is not a surprise that global trends also happen at a faster pace. Considering the speed at which the information travels, companies may be under threat or, if they react appropriately, have an advantage in reaching their strategic goals. While these strategic risks provide many challenges, they may also create opportunities for possible improvements in investing, financing, and operating activities to create shared value for all stakeholders. Strategic risks affecting strategic sustainability planning should be identified, assessed, and managed with a keen focus on minimizing their negative effects and building up on the opportunities provided by addressing these risks. Recent research highlights the importance of ERM in assessing and managing the strategic risk relevant to sustainability performance implementation and sustainability reporting to address the importance of strategic risk assessment and management on the quality and quantity of sustainability reporting and assurance.[20]

Social Risks

Social sustainability risks are potential adverse impacts of business decisions and activities on communities, societies, and individuals. These risks can stem from a range of factors, including economic inequality, labor exploitation, human rights abuses, discrimination, community displacement, and cultural erosion, among others. Some common examples of social sustainability risks: (1) discrimination and inequality based on race, gender, sexual orientation, ethnicity, religion, or other factors that can cause social tensions and unequal opportunities within communities and workplaces manifested in hiring practices, access to resources and services, and promotion policies; (2) labor exploitation issues of forced labor, unsafe working conditions, child labor, and insufficient wages; (3) human rights abuses arise from violations of human rights, including freedom of speech, assembly, and association, and abuses related to political repression, torture, and arbitrary detention that pose significant social sustainability risks; (4) community displacement of urban development, large-scale infrastructure projects, or natural resource extraction activities that can lead to the displacement of communities, resulting in disruptions to livelihoods, cultural heritage, and social cohesion; (5) health and safety concerns of no or poor access to healthcare, unsafe working conditions, or exposure to environmental pollutants that can jeopardize the health and well-being of individuals and communities; (6) supply chain risks of complex and opaque supply chain processes that can increase the likelihood of social sustainability risks such as exploitation of workers, environmental degradation, and human rights violations; and (7) cultural preservation risks stem from rapid urbanization, globalization, and mass tourism that can threaten indigenous cultures, traditions, and languages.

Social sustainability risks pertain to issues associated with human rights, labor practices, community relations, and diversity and inclusion. Failure to address these risks can result in negative publicity, labor disputes, supply chain disruptions, and legal liabilities. Social risks relevant to issues such as poor working conditions, child labor, forced labor, discrimination, and can damage a company's reputation and brand value and trigger legal consequences. Effective assessment and management of social sustainability risks require a comprehensive and robust approach to engaging stakeholders from multiple sectors, including businesses, governments, civil society organizations, and communities, in addressing social issues, including fostering inclusive economic development, implementing and enforcing robust labor laws and regulations, promoting respect for human rights, supporting community-driven initiatives, and ensuring transparency and accountability throughout governance structures and supply chain processes.

Sustainability Risk Assessment and Management

Business organizations should adopt a proactive approach to effectively address their sustainability risks by integrating sustainability considerations into strategic planning, risk management processes, and decision-making frameworks. Effective sustainability risk assessment and management involves identifying, assessing, mitigating, and monitoring sustainability risks across the organization, engaging with stakeholders, and fostering a culture of accountability, transparency, and continuous improvement. By assessing and managing sustainability risks effectively and comprehensively, businesses can enhance resilience, seize opportunities, and contribute to long-term value creation for all stakeholders. Sustainability risk assessment and management are integral components of overall sustainability strategic planning and practices, which enable business organizations to identify, assess, and manage the potential economic, social, and environmental risks and opportunities associated with their operations. Identification of sustainability risks discussed in the previous section is the first step in the sustainability risk assessment, management, and control. Effective and comprehensive sustainability risk assessment and management require the use of an integrated approach in evaluating the relationships between economic, governance, environmental, and social factors to develop a risk mitigation strategy to minimize risks and maximize opportunities for long-term business resilience and success. The approach to effective assessment and management of sustainability risks consists of the identification of risks, development of risk evaluation tools and metrics, integration with ERM, performing scenario analyses, materiality assessment, development of risk mitigation and management strategies, engagement of stakeholders, compliance with regulations and standards, and conducting the review, adaptability, and continuous improvement.

The Committee of Sponsoring Organizations (COSO) ERM framework is an excellent guide in assessing and managing sustainability risks.[21] All eight components of the COSO ERM framework should be considered including: (1) internal environment of setting the tone at the top of an organization in promoting sustainability factors of performance, risk, and disclosure; (2) objective setting of achieving short-, median-, and long-term strategic sustainability planning; (3) risk identification of risk exposures relevant to sustainability issues; (4) risk assessment of determining risk root cause, sensitivity analyses of the drivers, and pathways of organizational risks; (5) risk responses of addressing the drivers of sustainability risks; (6) control activities designed to manage sustainability risks; (7) information and communication of the organization's responses and efforts in assessing and managing sustainability risks and proper communication with all affected stakeholders; and (8) monitoring of ensuring that an organization in achieving its sustainability objectives, managing related sustainability risks and monitoring and evaluating its sustainability activities.[22]

The COSO ERM framework also suggests several tips for raising sustainability awareness in the organization, including (1) getting leadership (the board of directors and executives) involved by embedding sustainability into corporate culture and business environment, making sustainability part of strategic planning; (2) engaging stakeholders (investors, employees, suppliers, customers) in sustainability initiatives and activities; (3) integrating sustainability into the business strategies; (4) identifying, assessing and managing material sustainability risks; (5) looking for sustainability achievements and quick wins; (6) properly communicating sustainability good, bad, and ugly stories; (7) selecting appropriate measurement tools by using balanced scorecards.[23]

The COSO revised its 1992 issue of "Internal Control-Integrated Framework" in 2013 and then in 2022 to address internal controls for both financial and nonfinancial ESG activities. The COSO 2023 internal control framework, Achieving Effective Internal Control over Sustainability Reporting (ICSR), was published in March 2023 to tailor internal controls for sustainability reporting.[24] Business organizations can promote a culture of sustainability and accountability, revisit their mission of profit-with-purpose, integrate the COSO internal control framework to both financial reporting and sustainability reporting, and focus on the assessment and management of risks associated with financial ESP and nonfinancial ESG sustainability performance.

It is important to understand that sustainability risk management is not a matter of only one component but effectively dealing with multiple threats and risks. To expand on the previously given tips, the board of directors and executives must lead by example and try to implement the right sustainability measures in the corporate culture while being held accountable for their actions or lack thereof. By creating the right culture, objectives, and strategy, organizations should try to present to their stakeholders what they stand for and what aptitude organizations with implemented long-term sustainability strategies have. Organizations should give their lower-level stakeholders and employees an opportunity to

Sustainability Risk Assessment and Management

express their concerns, ideas, preferences, and critiques and, by listening and executing, engage them in a value-adding process. When working on long-term sustainability goals, rather than focusing strictly on long-term strategy, organizations should try to achieve short-term goals and show often and consistently that they are serious about the organization's sustainability. Finally, progress in achieving sustainability should be measured accordingly and frequently to ensure the organization is on the right track.[25]

The International Organization for Standardization (ISO) published its new standard, ISO 31000: Risk Management – Principles and Guidelines, in 2009, which provides principles and guidelines on risk management.[26] The ISO released ISO 31010: Risk Management Assessments Techniques in 2019, providing new risk management guidelines and risk assessment techniques.[27] These ISO 31000 and ISO 31010 risk guidelines and assessment techniques assist business organizations in developing, implementing, maintaining, assessing, monitoring, and continuously improving their risk management system in minimizing the negative effects of strategic, operations, financial, compliance, and reputation risks.[28] These ISO 31000 risk guidelines assist business organizations in developing, implementing, maintaining, assessing, monitoring, sustaining, and continuously improving their risk management system in minimizing the negative effects of strategic, operational, financial, compliance, environmental, and reputation risks.[29] These risks are interrelated and, thus, should be properly assessed and managed. For example, an excessive strategic risk can also cause operations, financial, compliance, and reputational risks. The compliance risk directly or indirectly associated with business sustainability, including noncompliance with regulatory reforms, health and safety, human rights and labor laws, corporate governance measures, anti-bribery, and environmental risks, can vary among organizations and across countries. For example, environmental risks can include direct effects (e.g., emissions trading cost exposures) and indirect consequences (e.g., energy price increases and accompanying reporting and compliance costs) of noncompliance with environmental laws, rules, and regulations. Business organizations should also assess and manage their financial risk of producing and disclosing materially misstated financial reports. Minimizing the reputational risk is vital to the success of sustainability programs and related performance, as stakeholder satisfaction is essential to sustainable business.

In summary, effective business sustainability risk assessment and management requires identifying, assessing, managing and mitigating potential risks that may affect the long-term financial viability, resilience, and reputation of a business in both financial ESP and nonfinancial ESG sustainability performance. The guiding principles for the process of business sustainability risk evaluation consists of: (1) Identifying potential risks (e.g., environmental, governance, social, economic, operational, reputation) presented in the previous section that could affect the ESP and ESG sustainability of the business; (2) assessing the identified risks in terms of their likelihood of occurrence and potential impact on the business by gathering data, conducting risk assessments, and using qualitative and quantitative methods to evaluate the severity and significance of each risk; (3) prioritizing risks based on their potential impact, likelihood of occurrence and their alignment with the organization's strategic planning, objectives and values; (4) managing and developing mitigation strategies to reduce the likelihood and impact of these risks by implementing preventive measures, diversifying operations, investing in technology and innovation, building resilience, and developing contingency plans; (5) integrating risk responses into all aspects of decision-making within the organization, including strategic planning, investment decisions, product development, and supply chain management by considering the ESP and ESG implications of business activities and ensuring that sustainability risks and opportunities are adequately addressed; (6) continuous monitoring and reviewing sustainability risks to trace changes in risk factors, assess the effectiveness of mitigation measures, and adjust strategies as needed; (7) engaging with stakeholders, including shareholders, creditors, employees, customers, investors, suppliers, and communities by learning about their perspectives and concerns to build trust and credibility with stakeholders; (8) risk reporting of transparently communicating ESP- and ESG-related sustainability risks, responses, efforts and performance to stakeholders through reporting mechanisms such as sustainability reports, annual filings, and stakeholder engagement platforms.

Summary

The nine risks relevant to sustainability factors of planning performance and disclosures should be identified, assessed, managed, monitored, controlled and reported to all stakeholders to minimize their negative impacts on financial, investment, operational, environmental, and social activities. Business sustainability requires a complete understanding of sustainability factors of planning, performance, risk and disclosure. Several risks are relevant to both financial ESP and nonfinancial ESG business sustainability performance, including strategic, operations, economic, environmental, compliance, financial, climate change, litigation, compliance reputation, social, and cybersecurity. These risks can adversely affect business operations, finance the investing activities of business organizations, and destabilize capital markets. Proper assessment, management, control, and disclosure of those risks are becoming increasingly important and play an effective role in achieving both financial ESP and nonfinancial ESG sustainability performance in creating shared value for all stakeholders. Effective assessment and management of sustainability risks require the use of proactive measures, including conducting risk assessments, implementing robust governance frameworks, adopting sustainable business practices, and developing resilience strategies. By following the guiding principles and steps and integrating them into their risk assessment and management processes presented in this chapter, businesses can improve their financial viability, operational effectiveness, and resilience in creating long-term shared value for all stakeholders and contributing to a more sustainable future.

Key Points

- Business sustainability factors of planning, performance, risk, and disclosure should be integrated into investment objectives and decisions.
- By addressing sustainability risks presented in this chapter, individuals and organizations can contribute to a more sustainable and resilient future.
- The use of ERM for assessing and managing sustainability risks discussed in this chapter can turn sustainability challenges and risks into sustainability opportunities and performance.
- Move toward sustainability reporting and risk assessment that underscores the importance of an adequate ERM in improving the effectiveness of both financial ESP and nonfinancial ESG sustainability performance.
- ISO 31000: Risk Management – Principles and Guidelines was used in 2009, which provides principles and guidelines on risk management.
- Properly disclose assessment and management sustainability risks and their possible impacts on operational, investment, and financial activities and related performance.

Review Questions

1. Why is addressing sustainability risks essential for businesses?
2. How do sustainability risks impact financial economic sustainability performance (ESP)?
3. What is strategic risk in the context of sustainability?
4. What is the importance of customer satisfaction in sustainability performance?
5. What are the categories of sustainability risks outlined in the chapter?
6. How do regulatory/compliance risks impact business sustainability?
7. How can businesses mitigate climate change risks?
8. How do social risks affect business sustainability?
9. Why is stakeholder engagement important in managing social risks?
10. How can businesses effectively manage governance risks?
11. How can economic/financial risks be mitigated?

12. **What is operational risk, and how does it affect sustainability?**
13. **What is reputational risk, and why is it significant?**
14. **What role does cybersecurity play in business sustainability?**
15. **How can businesses address cybersecurity risks?**

Discussion Questions

1. **What are the implications of not properly assessing and managing sustainability risks for stakeholders?**
2. **Discuss the importance of integrating ESG factors into portfolio decisions by institutional investors, as highlighted by the 2020 GAO report.**
3. **Explain the concept of strategic risk in the context of business sustainability and provide examples.**
4. **How do customer satisfaction and business reputation impact sustainability performance? Discuss the relationship between these factors.**
5. **Discuss the significance of cybersecurity risk assessment and management for businesses in the modern digital age.**
6. **What are environmental risks, and how can they affect businesses operating in environmentally sensitive areas?**
7. **What impact do the findings of the Carbon Disclosure Project (CDP) surveys have on businesses, particularly in terms of financial losses from climate-related risks?**
8. **What is the role of a compliance officer in managing regulatory risks, and how do they ensure adherence to relevant laws and standards?**
9. **How do cybersecurity risks impact businesses, and what measures can be taken to mitigate these risks?**
10. **What are economic and financial sustainability risks, and how can they undermine an organization's long-term financial health?**
11. **Identify and discuss common economic and financial sustainability risks that businesses face.**
12. **Define operational sustainability risks and explain how they can impact business processes and supply chains.**
13. **Provide examples of operational risks and discuss how they can affect a business's sustainability performance.**
14. **How can businesses effectively manage reputational risks to maintain a good business reputation and meet stakeholder expectations?**
15. **How do sustainability risks intersect with financial, social, and environmental factors, and what are the implications for long-term business success?**

Multiple-Choice Questions

1. **Why is addressing sustainability risks essential for businesses?**
   A) To reduce operational costs
   B) To ensure resilience, protect their reputation, and create shared value over the long term for all stakeholders
   C) To increase short-term profits
   D) To dominate the market

2. **What is the role of Chief Information Systems Officers (CISOs) in managing sustainability risks?**
   A) Increasing sales
   B) Identifying, assessing, and managing sustainability risks related to information systems
   C) Managing marketing strategies
   D) Overseeing financial reporting

3. **What are the most important risks relevant to business sustainability?**
   A) Marketing, Sales, Advertising, Customer Service
   B) Strategic, Operational, Reputational, Financial
   C) Product Development, Manufacturing, Logistics, Retail
   D) Human Resources, Training, Development, Recruitment

4. **What is operational risk in the context of sustainability performance?**
   A) Risk associated with marketing strategies
   B) Risk relevant to financial ESP and nonfinancial ESG sustainability performance
   C) Risk related to product development
   D) Risk of employee dissatisfaction

5. **What are the consequences of issuing materially misstated financial reports?**
   A) Increased operational efficiency
   B) Detrimental effects on corporations' financial viability and sustainability
   C) Improved customer satisfaction
   D) Enhanced market reputation

6. **How can sustainability risks be classified?**
   A) Marketing, Sales, Advertising, Customer Service
   B) Environmental, Social, Governance, Market, Regulatory, Economic, Supply Chain
   C) Product Development, Manufacturing, Logistics, Retail
   D) Human Resources, Training, Development, Recruitment

7. **What are some potential climate change risks for businesses?**
   A) Increased short-term profits
   B) Detrimental effects of global greenhouse gas emissions, extreme weather events, rising sea levels
   C) Enhanced market reputation
   D) Improved customer satisfaction

8. **What is the role of a compliance officer in managing compliance risks?**
   A) Increasing sales
   B) Navigating the compliance process and ensuring adherence to laws and standards
   C) Managing marketing strategies
   D) Overseeing product development

9. **What are cybersecurity risks, and how do they impact businesses?**
   A) Risks related to employee turnover
   B) Potential threats and vulnerabilities that could compromise information systems, data processing, and digital assets
   C) Risks associated with marketing strategies
   D) Risks related to product development

10. **What are economic and financial sustainability risks?**
    A) Risks associated with product development
    B) Risks associated with financial and economic factors such as market volatility, inflation, currency fluctuations, economic downturns, financial instability
    C) Risks related to employee turnover
    D) Risks of increased marketing costs

11. **Identify and discuss common economic and financial sustainability risks that businesses face.**
    A) Increased sales
    B) Market volatility, economic downturns, financial instability, credit and counter-party risks, liquidity shortages, currency and exchange rate risks, commodity price risks
    C) Improved customer satisfaction
    D) Enhanced market reputation

12. **What are operational sustainability risks?**
    A) Risks related to marketing strategies
    B) Risks pertaining to challenges within a company's operations, business processes, and supply chain

C) Risks associated with employee turnover

D) Risks of increased product development costs

13. **What are reputational sustainability risks?**

A) Risks related to marketing strategies

B) Risks arising from negative perceptions of a company's decisions, actions, behaviors, or performance

C) Risks associated with employee turnover

D) Risks of increased product development costs

14. **Discuss the potential impacts of supply chain disruptions on a business's sustainability performance.**

A) They have no impact

B) They can lead to operational delays, increased costs, and reduced product quality

C) They improve customer satisfaction

D) They enhance market reputation

15. **What are the potential adverse impacts of business strategies on the environment and society?**

A) Positive impacts only

B) Negative impacts such as pollution, resource depletion, and social inequality

C) No impact

D) Improved customer satisfaction

16. **Why is it important to integrate sustainability risks into strategic planning?**

A) To reduce marketing costs

B) To enhance long-term business resilience and success

C) To increase short-term profits

D) To improve product development

17. **What are some common economic and financial sustainability risks?**

A) Increased sales

B) Market volatility, economic downturns, financial instability, credit and counter-party risks, liquidity shortages, currency and exchange rate risks, commodity price risks

C) Improved customer satisfaction

D) Enhanced market reputation

18. **What is the significance of the SEC's proposed new rules for disclosing climate-related financial risks?**

A) They have no significance

B) They require public companies to discuss climate risk management and disclose greenhouse gas emissions

C) They reduce operational efficiency

D) They increase short-term profits

19. **What are social sustainability risks?**

A) Risks related to employee turnover

B) Risks arising from business decisions and activities impacting communities, societies, and individuals

C) Risks associated with marketing strategies

D) Risks of increased product development costs

20. **What are the potential consequences of failing to address social sustainability risks?**

A) Increased operational efficiency

B) Negative publicity, labor disputes, supply chain disruptions, legal liabilities

C) Improved customer satisfaction

D) Enhanced market reputation

21. **What are some key aspects of effective sustainability risk assessment and management?**

A) Ignoring stakeholder engagement

B) Identifying, assessing, mitigating, and monitoring sustainability risks across the organization

C) Reducing transparency

D) Increasing short-term profits

22. **What are some strategies businesses can use to manage litigation risk?**

A) Increase marketing costs

B) Implement risk assessment and management policies, retain legal counsel, obtain adequate insurance, focus on ethical practices

C) Improve customer satisfaction

D) Enhance market reputation

23. **What does ISO 45000 address?**

A) Quality management systems

B) Social responsibility

C) Occupational health and safety management systems

D) Risk management

24. **What is the significance of effective corporate governance on sustainability?**

A) Promotes accountability, enhances operational and financial performance, strengthens stakeholder trust

B) Reduces transparency

C) Focuses solely on financial performance

D) Minimizes regulatory compliance

25. **What are the benefits of integrating sustainability into corporate culture?**

A) Enhances long-term financial performance and creates shared value for all stakeholders

B) Limits stakeholder engagement

C) Focuses solely on financial performance

D) Minimizes regulatory compliance

26. **What does ISO 37001 address?**

A) Quality management systems

B) Social responsibility

C) Anti-bribery management systems

D) Risk management

27. **What does resource dependence theory (RDT) explain?**

A) The dynamic of power in interorganizational relations and managing interdependence and external power struggles

B) Focuses solely on financial performance

C) Reducing transparency

D) Limiting stakeholder engagement

28. **Why is it important for companies to disclose sustainability performance?**

A) To demonstrate commitment to transparency and enhance firm value by reducing information asymmetry

B) To limit stakeholder engagement

C) To reduce regulatory compliance costs

D) To focus solely on financial performance

Notes

1 Much of discussion in this chapter comes from Rezaee, Z. (2024). *The Sustainable Business Blueprint: Planning, Performance, Risk, Reporting and Assurance.* Routledge/Taylor and Francis, Chapter 7.

2 United States Government Accountability Office (GAO). (2020). Report to the Honorable Mark Warner US Senate. Public Companies Disclosure of Environmental, Social and Governance Factors and Options to Enhance Them (July 2020). https://www.gao.gov/assets/710/707949.pdf

3 PricewaterhouseCoopers (PwC). (2014). Sustainability goes mainstream: Insights into investor views (May). http://www.pwc.com/us/en/pwc-investor-resource-institute/index.jhtml.

4 Harvard Law School Forum on Corporate Governance. (2020). Institutional investor survey. https://corpgov.law.harvard.edu/2020/03/25/institutional-investor-survey-2020/#:~:text=Morrow%20Sodali's%20survey%20explores%20how%20ESG%2C%20as%20a,an%20appetite%20for%20a%20separate%20vote%20on%20sustainability.

5 CDP. (2019). World's biggest companies face $1 trillion in climate change risks (June 4, 2019). https://www.cdp.net/en/articles/media/worlds-biggest-companies-face-1-trillion-in-climate-change-risks.

6 CDP. (2021). CDP reports record number of disclosures and unveils new strategy to help further tackle climate and ecological emergency (October 14, 2021). https://www.cdp.net/en/articles/media/cdp-reports-record-number-of-disclosures-and-unveils-new-strategy-to-help-further-tackle-climate-and-ecological-emergency.

7 CDP. (2021). Our five-year strategy: Accelerating the rate of change. https://www.cdp.net/en/info/about-us/our-five-year-strategy.

8 Securities and Exchange Commission (SEC). (March 2022). SEC proposes rules to enhance and standardize climate-related disclosures for investors (Marh 21, 2022). athttps://www.sec.gov/news/press-release/2022-46.

9 Securities and Exchange Commission (SEC). (2024). The enhancement and standardization of climate-related disclosures for investors. 17 CFR 210, 229, 230, 232, 239, and 249, [Release Nos. 33-11275; 34-99678; File No. S7-10-22]. Final Rules, March 6, 2024. Available at https://www.sec.gov/files/rules/final/2024/33-11275.pdf.

10 Corporate Sustainability: Integrating Performance and Reporting. Brockett and Rezaee. https://books.google.com/books?hl=en&lr=&id=EK1NFc8kWZIC&oi=fnd&pg=PP13&dq=Operations+Risk+egsee+sustainability+performance&ots=8wiMqc3Hig&sig=OtcLSX8reP_VQNrju9zJnT-X_q0#v=snippet&q=Operations%20Risk%20&f=false.

11 Sternberg, L.J. (2017). Surviving the Equifax data breach. https://blog.aicpa.org/2017/09/surviving-the-equifax-data-breach.html#sthash.Stida706.dpbs.

12 ISO 27001 – Information security management. http://www.iso.org/iso/home/standards/management-standards/iso27001.htm.

13 Klassen, Matt. (2018). Cherwell. What is an information security management system (ISMS) & how should it be implemented? https://www.cherwell.com/security-management/library/blog/what-is-an-information-management-security-system/.

14 ISO/IEC 27001: 2013. (2013). Information technology – security techniques – information security management systems – requirements. https://www.iso.org/standard/54534.html.

15 Securities and Exchange Commission (SEC). (2023). SEC adopts rules on cybersecurity risk management, strategy, governance, and incident disclosure by public companies (July 26, 2023). https://www.sec.gov/news/press-release/2023-139.

16 Risk Management. Auditboard. What is operational risk management? The overview. https://www.auditboard.com/   blog/operational-risk-management/#:~:text=Examples

%20of%20operational%20risk%20include%3A%201%20Employee%20conduct,as%20 natural%20catastrophes%206%20Internal%20and%20external%20fraud.

17 Jacob, C. (2012). The impact of financial crisis on corporate social responsibility and its implications for reputation risk management. *Journal of Management and Sustainability.* (August 10, 2020). https://heinonline.org/HOL/Page?handle=hein.journals/jms2&id=491 &collection=journals&index=.

18 Sickler, Jonas. (2021). ReputationManagement.com. What is reputational risk and how to manage it. https://www.reputationmanagement.com/ blog/reputational-risk/.

19 Deloitte. (2013). Exploring strategic risk. https://www2.deloitte.com/ content/dam/Deloi tte/global/Documents/Governance-Risk-Compliance/dttl-grc-exploring-strategic-risk.pdf.

20 Integrating sustainability reporting into enterprise risk management and its relationship with business performance: A conceptual framework. *Journal of Cleaner Production* 208: 415–425 (January 20, 2019). https://www.sciencedirect.com/science/article/abs/pii/ S0959652618331366.

21 Committee of Sponsoring Organizations of the Treadway Commission (COSO). (2013). Demystifying sustainability risk (May 2013). https://www.coso.org/documents/COSO -ERM%20Demystifying%20Sustainability%20Risk_Full%20WEB.pdf.

22 Committee of Sponsoring Organizations of the Treadway Commission (COSO). (2013). Demystifying sustainability risk. (May 2013). https://www.coso.org/documents/COSO -ERM%20Demystifying%20Sustainability%20Risk_Full%20WEB.pdf.

23 Committee of Sponsoring Organizations of the Treadway Commission (COSO). (2013). Demystifying sustainability risk (May 2013). https://www.coso.org/documents/COSO -ERM%20Demystifying%20Sustainability%20Risk_Full%20WEB.pdf.

24 The Committee of Sponsoring Organizations of the Treadway Commission (COSO). (2023). Achieving effective internal control over sustainability reporting (ICSR). https://www.sus-tainability-reports.com/coso-releases-new-achieving-effective-internal-control-over-sus-tainability-reporting-icsr-supplemental-guidance/.

25 The Committee of Sponsoring Organizations of the Treadway Commission (COSO). (2023). Achieving effective internal control over sustainability reporting (ICSR). https://www.sus-tainability-reports.com/coso-releases-new-achieving-effective-internal-control-over-sus-tainability-reporting-icsr-supplemental-guidance/.

26 International Organization for Standardization (ISO). (2009). ISO 31000: Risk Management – Principles and Guidelines, 2009. ISO. www.iso.org (Accessed July 31, 2011).

27 International Organization for Standardization (ISO). (2019). ISO 31010: Risk Management – Risk Assessment Techniques, 2019. ISO. www.iso.org (Accessed October 6, 2021).

28 International Organization for Standardization (ISO). (2019). ISO 31010: Risk Management – Risk Assessment Techniques, 2019. ISO. www.iso.org (Accessed October 6, 2021).

29 International Organization for Standardization (ISO). (2019). ISO 31010: Risk Management – Risk Assessment Techniques, 2019. ISO. www.iso.org (Accessed October 6, 2021).

Chapter 10
Business Sustainability Capital

Learning Objectives

- Understand the contribution of various types of capital (financial, natural, social, human, manufactured, and reputational) to business sustainability.
- Recognize the importance of effectively utilizing and optimizing these capitals to enhance financial viability, environmental and social outcomes, reputation, and relationships with stakeholders.
- Comprehend the interconnectedness of different forms of capital and their collective impact on organizational financial health and viability, resilience, and shared value creation for stakeholders.
- Grasp the concept of management as the steward of strategic, financial, human, social, and environmental capital, actively working for the benefit of all stakeholders, including shareholders.
- Learn proper measurement of all capitals.

Introduction

Business organizations have traditionally utilized financial capital to generate profit and create value for shareholders. The recent move toward adopting business sustainability encourages organizations to pay attention to other types of capital in creating shared value for all stakeholders.[1] The magnitude of environmental, social, governance (ESG) sustainability-focused investment was $37.8 trillion at the end of 2020 and is predicted to reach $53 trillion by 2025.[2] Investors investing and holding ESG funds require that corporations define their purpose of generating desired financial returns and achieving social and environmental impacts. Achievement of financial ESP and nonfinancial ESG sustainability performance requires business organizations, their board of directors, and executives to utilize financial and nonfinancial capital presented in this chapter effectively. Business sustainability capital refers to the various forms of capital, including financial, natural, social, human, manufactured, and reputation, that a company relies on to operate sustainably over the long term in creating shared value for all stakeholders. Each of these capitals contributes to the overall financial success and resilience as well as social and environmental impacts of a business in a rapidly changing world.

DOI: 10.4324/9781003487081-10

Types of Sustainability Capitals

Business organizations have traditionally utilized financial capital, both equity and debt capital, in their financing, investing, and operating activities to make a profit for investors with little attention to other types of capital in creating shared value for all stakeholders that also provide resources and capital to them. The recent move toward sustainability requires business organizations to utilize all types of financial capital (equity, debt) and nonfinancial (reputational, human, social, and environmental) to generate shared value for all stakeholders. Sustainability capitals represent all various aspects crucial for achieving long-term economic, environmental, and social goals. These capitals are interconnected and play a role in sustaining financial viability and maintaining and enhancing the well-being of both present and future generations.

The International Integrated Reporting Council (IIRC) suggests six capitals: (1) financial capital, (2) manufactured capital, (3) intellectual capital, (4) human capital, (5) social and relationship capital, and (6) natural capital, which organizations can utilize in creating shared value for all stakeholders.[3] Management is the steward of strategic, financial, human, social, and environmental capital and the active and long-term oriented steward of all stakeholders, including shareholders. Some capitals are interrelated, but all collectively create shared value for all stakeholders. Exhibit 10.1 presents the structure of sustainability capital and all related capital, including strategic, financial, human operational, social, environmental, reputational/trust, intellectual, and manufacturing capital.

The focus on sustainability capital enables management to effectively exercise stewardship over a broader range of business capital (financial, environmental, social, and reputational) to ensure business continuity and sustainability of nonfinancial human capital in protecting the safety, health, and well-being of investors, employees, customers, and suppliers. The relationship between business, society, and the environment is complex and often tense, and it has become more relevant in recent years because management is now required to be a good steward of all capital, including financial, human, environmental, and social. The following subsections present several sustainability capitals in alphabetical order, as illustrated in Exhibit 10.1. The relevance and importance of business sustainability capitals underscore their interconnectedness and collective impact on organizational financial health and viability, resilience, reputation, and shared value creation for stakeholders. By effectively utilizing, managing, and integrating these capitals into business strategies, decisions and actions, companies can enhance their financial viability and competitive advantage, mitigate risks, and contribute positively to society and the environment, thus ensuring long-term prosperity and shared value for all stakeholders.

EXHIBIT 10.1 Sustainability Capitals

Financial Capital

Financial capital represents the monetary resources provided by investors or internally generated, available to a company for investment, expansion, operation, and risk management. Financial capital includes financial resources of equity, debt, retained earnings, and grants that can be used for operations and investments. Integrating sustainability into business operations can lead to cost savings through energy efficiency, utilization of natural resources, waste reduction, and operational improvements. Furthermore, sustainable businesses with sustainability-centric practices can often attract investors who prioritize ESG criteria and enable them to access capital at favorable terms that enhance long-term financial performance. Financial/economic capital consists of assets, monetary resources, and wealth that business entities, governments, and individuals use to generate earnings and support economic and business activities. Financial capital represents financial and economic resources, including infrastructure, financial systems, and wealth, to generate sustainable economic development and to balance economic growth with social and environmental considerations; for business organizations, financial capital refers to equity and debt capital. Debt capital consists of borrowing money through loans or bonds, paying interest, and the return of principal at maturity. Equity capital represents ownership in a company's shares by shareholders who have a claim on the company's assets and earnings. Efficient allocation of financial capital is important for economic efficiency and development. Effective financial capital management is vital for economic stability and growth. Effective and reliable financial management practices, efficient and transparent financial markets, and prudent and robust regulatory frameworks are important in efficiently allocating economic and financial resources.

Financial economic sustainability performance can be achieved by continuously improving capital productivity by optimizing supply chains, cost reengineering focused on reducing operating, production, and compliance costs, improving employee productivity and efficiency, and focusing on activities that create long-term, enduring, and sustainable financial performance. Focusing on economic sustainability can also create opportunities for business innovation and growth by promoting sustainable products and services, new customer relationships, and new markets through environmentally friendly and socially acceptable products and services. Economic sustainability performance is measured in terms of long-term accounting-based measures (return on equity, sales), market-based measures (stock returns, market-book value), and long-term investments (R&D and advertising), and is disclosed through a set of financial statements disseminated to shareholders in assessing the risk and return associated with their investments. When discussing financial capital, it is important to distinguish between financial and economic capital; where financial capital focuses on assets needed to provide goods and services, economic capital represents the estimated funding for potential future losses.[4]

Financial capital includes cash, money and currency, bank deposits, real estate, investments, loan and debt instruments, and business ownership. Financial capital is a critical driver of economic growth, prosperity, and development by facilitating investment in productive activities, enabling innovation, and creating jobs. Sufficient financial capital is essential for businesses and individuals to start or expand operations, make investments, and generate income. Financial markets, including banking systems, stock exchanges, financial institutions, and bond markets, play an important role in allocating and distributing financial capital. Governments and central banks also play an essential role in financial capital, which is influenced by the country's monetary policies, interest rates, regulatory frameworks, and social norms, including issues of wealth distribution, income inequality, and access to financial services. Economic capital is commonly referred to as investment capital consisting of debt and equity, but what is more important is that companies prefer raising financial capital by using equity rather than debt since it is less risky for them. One of the key ratios for determining how much and in which way the company is leveraged is the debt-to-equity ratio. This ratio is specifically important to investors when determining the riskiness of the business.[5]

Human Capital

Human capital represents the capabilities and competencies of people within the organization. It encompasses the education, expertise, skills, knowledge, creativity, and health of an organization's workforce resulting from investing in employee training, health, and well-being that can enhance productivity, effectiveness, innovation, and employee satisfaction. A productive, skilled, and motivated workforce is vital for driving organizational prosperity growth and adapting to changing market conditions. Human capital represents the education, knowledge, skills, abilities, and other intangible assets possessed by individuals that can contribute to their productivity and economic value. Human capital is an important component of an individual's overall capabilities that can contribute to economic growth and development through education, training, and health investment. Human capital is an asset of skills processes by the labor force that can be utilized to generate other assets by investing in people's education, health, skills, and overall well-being. The Organization for Economic Cooperation and Development (OECD) defines human capital as "the knowledge, skills, competencies and other attributes embodied in individuals or groups of individuals acquired during their life and used to produce goods, services or ideas in market circumstances."[6] Human capital (HC) is defined as attributes of labor that increase productivity and is viewed as an investment in labor, including education, training, skills, capacity, health, and ability to adapt to achieve productive capacity goals, maintain innovation, and create economic value. As part of nonfinancial ESG sustainability, human capital factors are relevant and material to investors. Human capital supports sustainable development by enhancing the capabilities and quality of life of individuals who contribute to business sustainability and success.

The important components of human capital are education, skills and knowledge, training, health and well-being, creativity and innovation, expertise and experience. Investment in human capital by focusing on improving education, healthcare, and workforce training can lead to long-term economic benefits and prosperity. Widely considered the most important asset in today's business world, human capital is still not disclosed as it should. The recent move toward business sustainability and integrated sustainability reporting demands nonfinancial ESG disclosure. Stakeholders would also want to know more about human capital factors and how organizations handle them to determine if the human capital is adding to the company's long-term value. In 2018, the Embarkment Project for Inclusive Capitalism (EPIC), put together by the Coalition for Inclusive Capitalism and Ernst & Young, after defining talent as one of the key components of the long-term value creation, produced a set of metrics regarding human capital disclosure and what they call human value to propose a disclosure solution to the organizations and allow investors and other stakeholders to easily compare major factors including human capital deployment, organizational culture, and employee health across the organizations. A specific set of metrics was developed for each one of the major factors, and these include, but are not limited to, workforce cost, training, learning and development, workforce composition and diversity, lifestyle management, access to healthcare and insurance, performance and well-being, ethics, and integrity, alignment with purpose and values, teaming, and adaptability.[7] However, areas that were most commonly disclosed include diversity and inclusion, employee development, safety, and compensation practices, as well as other voluntarily disclosed areas such as employee engagement efforts, strategy employee turnover, culture, recruiting practices, mental health, pay equity, and succession planning. In addition, only 43% of the companies provided one or more quantitative metrics, while the other 57% did not include even one in their reports and strategy, strictly focusing on qualitative language and non-value-adding information. Therefore, even though the new SEC requirements were made to satisfy the demand for transparency and improve the understanding of how human capital adds to overall business value and strategy, only several companies are effectively managing their human capital and properly reporting human capital activities and performance.[8]

Human capital is becoming more important as a valuable and productive asset for public companies, while employees are becoming important stakeholders for several reasons. Corporate boards increasingly prioritize human capital due to market shifts, worker expectations, and ESG demands. Topics like culture, hybrid work, diversity, and well-being are now on-board agendas. The pandemic accelerated these discussions, but digital transformation and talent competition were already driving change. Regulatory drivers and investor expectations call for more human capital disclosure. Boards need to widen their view of workforce risk, enhance oversight, and address upcoming shifts like worker expectations and human–technology collaboration.[9]

Human capital is vital to business sustainability, economic growth, and prosperity for several reasons. First, employee participation in corporate governance and production and service processes is essential as employee productivity improves corporate performance. Second, employees become shareholders by investing in the company's shares through 401(K), 529 plans, and direct investment, and thus they have a vested interest in the company. Third, employees in many countries are given the opportunity to engage in corporate governance and to be represented on the board of directors of public companies (e.g., Germany). Finally, the COVID-19 pandemic has caused business organizations to assess the human capital risk by making the safety, health, and well-being of employees, customers, and suppliers a prerequisite for reopening and continuation of business. Human capital issues are relevant to the company's human resources management and are key assets to delivering long-term value. These issues affect the company's bottom line through employee productivity, labor relations, and the health and safety of employees. Human capital is an important asset that contributes significantly to long-term and sustainable value creation and protection. There is a need for proper identification, measurement, recognition, and reporting of human capital. One of the greatest concerns regarding human capital is whether or how companies should get their stakeholders, especially their employees, involved in making important corporate-level decisions rather than pursuing the shareholder primacy model in which the benefits of shareholders are maximized. Some advantages of shared governance (also known as co-determination) include better coordination, information flows between board and employees, employees' loyalty and motivation, implicit contracts enforcement, and alignment of shareholders' and employees' interests.

Unlike in most European countries, the shareholder primacy model is more popular in the United States. As shareholders' benefits are maximized, no workers are involved in corporate governance and decision-making, and riskier investments are usually made. Even with the help of the labor union, worker bargaining power is still low if the issues are beyond the terms and conditions of the National Labor Relations Act (NLRA). Amendments to labor laws should be made on both state and federal levels to help workers express their opinions and voice their concerns through participation in the board of directors. Recently, there have been proposals from the Reward Work Act and the Accountable Capitalism Act to mandate one-third to 40% of board seats to be assigned to employees. These proposals encourage the stakeholder theory to replace the shareholder primacy model even though implementing a co-determination policy can be challenging in the United States.[10] Business organizations recognize the importance of human capital management and disclosures intended to attract, develop, and retain a skilled and motivated workforce as part of their broader context of ESG initiatives in promoting ethical and sustainable practices in managing human resources.

Natural/Environmental Capital

Natural capital refers to natural resources such as air, water, land, minerals, biodiversity, and ecosystems, which are crucial for sustainable development, survival, environmental stewardship, business growth, and economic prosperity. Business organizations depend on natural resources for their activities, operations, supply chain processes, and business sustainability. Maintaining and preserving natural capital is crucial for long-term business success and viability to ensure the availability of resources for current and future production and mitigate environmental risks such as climate change and resource scarcity. The environmental/natural capital is relevant to the environmental impacts of the operation either through the use of natural resources and non-renewable assets as an input to the supply chain production or through harmful releases into the environment that could affect bottom-line financial earnings. Sustainable business practices are intended to preserve and regenerate natural capital to ensure a healthy environment. Environmental capital is crucial to business organizations' long-term sustainability, growth and innovation, and worldwide economic prosperity, leaving a better environment for the next generations. Environmental/natural capital reflects natural resources and ecosystems that provide valuable goods and services to humans because nature has intrinsic value and is important in supporting human well-being and existence. Natural capital encompasses a wide range of resources and services, including air and water quality, biodiversity, soil fertility, and other natural resources available to an organization. Natural resources consist of both renewable resources like plants and clean air and non-renewable assets like oil and gas. Environmental capital reflects the impact of an organization's operation on the environment, including negative values such as contamination, pollution, and desertification, as well as positive impacts on the environment through preservation and reproduction.

Natural capital is a part of the environment, including fertile soils, geology, air quality, clean water, and all living organisms, which affect the triple bottom line of people, profit, and the planet. Organizations should preserve the environment and try to leave a better one for the next generations. It is important to understand that even though the organizations affect the environment the most, with their responsible or irresponsible behavior, the consumers are the key element here. Without the support of consumers, organizations would not be able to earn enough revenue to be profitable. That is why consumers need to demand a certain standard, but it is also crucial for organizations to adhere to it by training their employees and strictly following rules and regulations.[11]

Environmental capital often refers to the ecosystems and natural resources that provide crucial services to societies and contribute to the well-being of human communities and ecosystems in supporting economic and social activities. The important components of environmental/ natural capital consist of (1) biodiversity of different species, genetic diversity, and ecosystems; (2) ecosystem services, including clean air and water, pollination of crops by insects, cultural and recreational services, regulation of climate; (3) renewable resources that can be regenerated naturally including sunlight, forests, wind and water that should be managed responsibly; (4) non-renewable resources including fossil fuels (coal, oil, and natural gas) and minerals that are finite resources and their use can have material environmental impacts; (5) air and soil quality that contributes to the air purification and agriculture and food production; (6) water and climate resources including rivers, lakes, and aquifers, forests and oceans that are essential for human survival, agriculture, and industrial processes and their effective management is vital for sustaining natural capital. Assessing and managing environmental capital is essential for sustainable development. Human activities, including agriculture, industrialization, and urbanization, can affect environmental capital, and any over-exploitation of resources, excessive pollution, deforestation, and climate change can degrade environmental capital. Any initiatives and efforts to promote environmental sustainability, including strategies to conserve and restore environmental capital, measures to protect biodiversity, reduce pollution, promote sustainable resource management, and address climate change, can preserve environmental capita. The environmental strategies should ensure that current and future generations can continue to benefit from the important services provided by the environment. Thus, individuals, businesses, governments, and organizations should understand and recognize the importance of integrating environmental considerations into decision-making processes. Effective recognition and management of environmental/ capital is important for economic growth and sustainable development. Conservation and sustainable management of natural capital are vital for maintaining the well-being of current and future generations. Any degradation of natural capital triggered by deforestation, over-exploitation of resources, and pollution can negatively affect society and the environment.

Social Capital

Social capital is an important asset that reflects the value of the networks of relationships among individuals, communities, and social groups based on norms of trust, reciprocity, social relationships, interactions, and cooperation between individuals and communities. Social capital is built on shared values, common norms, and behaviors and can be earned through (1) bonding social capital of the close relationships among individuals who share similar values, identities, or experiences; (2) building social capital across groups by developing relationships and connections with different individuals, groups, diverse communities, organizations, or networks; and (3) linking by creating associations and ties between and across groups who share similar values and purposes. Social capital is defined by the OECD as "networks together with shared norms, values, and understandings that facilitate cooperation within or among groups."[12] In this definition, the networks are broadly considered real-world links between groups or individuals, including friends, family, colleagues,

Types of Sustainability Capitals

and local, national, and international communities. The shared values reflect respect for people's safety, security, health, and well-being of others. The important elements of social capital are norms and values, trust, networks and connections, community engagements, and reciprocity. These elements create networks of relationships and strong ties among individuals, social groups, and communities. Social capital impacts individuals and businesses by creating economic development social networks to exchange information, resources, support, and community well-being. Establishing and sustaining social capital requires continuous investments in relationships, community building, social trust, and communication. Establishing strong relationships with investors, employees, customers, suppliers, and local communities improves trust, cooperation, reputation, and goodwill. Business organizations with strong social capital are better equipped and able to address challenges, build brand loyalty and reputation, and access new markets.

Social capital is relevant to the company's management of relationships with key outside stakeholders, including suppliers, customers, local communities, the public, and the government. Social capital is relevant to human rights, responsible business practices, local economic development, customer privacy, and other social matters. In recent years, the perceived social injustice and unrest have made social capital more relevant and important to business organizations. Social capital involves the effective functioning of social groups through interpersonal relationships, a shared sense of identity, understanding, norms, values, trust, cooperation, and reciprocity. Social capital is a measure of the value of resources, both tangible (e.g., public spaces, private property) and intangible (e.g., actors, human capital, people), and the impact that these relationships have on the resources involved in each relationship and on the larger groups. It is generally seen as a form of capital that produces public goods for a common purpose.

Social capital has been used to explain the improved performance of diverse groups, the growth of entrepreneurial firms, superior managerial performance, enhanced supply chain relations, the value derived from strategic alliances, and the evolution of communities, including the positive impacts of human interaction. The positive impacts of social capital are tangible or intangible factors such as useful information, future opportunities, innovative ideas generated from personal relationships, and networks outside and within an organization that enable a productive work environment that adds to the bottom-line earnings. Social capital is a set of shared values that enables individuals to work together to effectively achieve a common purpose and goal that helps them all. Social capital can be attributed to the factors and characteristics that describe how people are able to band together in society to live harmoniously. In business, social capital can contribute to a company's success and sustainable performance by promoting shared values, mutual respect, and common goals.

Social capital is not a new term, and the relationships that compose it are crucial for long-term sustainability. Even though one can see and understand how important social capital really is, managers and organizations tend to ignore the importance and relevance of social capital. Management has often focused on efficiency and profit, forgetting the human side. This way of thinking can be costly since social awareness is one of the most important topics in the 21st century. Like with reputational capital, employees find it hard to stay with an organization that does not support their core beliefs and values. If an organization is not careful about the social aspect of the business processes, its operations, and relationships within and outside the organization, long-term sustainability will be almost impossible. In today's world, when information travels faster than ever before, and a small incident can ruin years of hard work, it is important to highlight social awareness or discuss it and implement it in daily operations and relationships. Social awareness must become a part of the organization's culture to enhance the creation of social capital and support long-term sustainability. In recent years, the Internet has promoted social capital by enabling significant means of social connections such as social networking, social media, online relationships, and reviews, as well as allowing an infinite number of individuals and groups to collaborate in achieving a common purpose. For businesses, social capital can contribute to sustainable business success by developing a sense of common goals, mutual respect, and shared value.

Manufactured Capital

Manufactured Capital refers to physical assets such as infrastructure, buildings, equipment, machinery, and technology that are produced and utilized to contribute to shared value creation for all stakeholders. Efficient utilization of resources, investment in technological innovation, continuous improvement, and maintenance is vital for optimizing manufactured capital. Sustainable and robust practices in manufacturing and operations can reduce waste, improve efficiency, and lower costs over time. The manufactured capital is vastly broad and consists of issues relating to financial, environmental, human, and social integration into the company's value-creation and protection processes. Manufactured capital usually refers to the financial resources and assets invested in producing goods, including funds available for buying equipment, machinery, technology, raw materials, labor, and other factory overhead costs relevant to the manufacturing process. Manufactured capital is often referred to as built capital, which represents the infrastructure, buildings, manufacturing, and physical assets that support economic activities and community life. Thus, manufactured capital investments consist of financial, physical, technological, and human capital. The effectiveness of manufactured capital is typically measured by operational effectiveness, maximum utilization of resources, and return on investment (ROI).

Manufactured capital is a key component of industrial economies, where the production of tangible goods plays a significant role. It represents the financial foundation that enables companies to set up and operate manufacturing facilities, develop new technologies, and expand production capacities. Manufacturing capital deals with issues of resource recovery, product innovation, use phase and disposal of products, and efficiency and responsibility in the design that determines accountability and stewardship for the broad base of capital (financial, manufactured, intellectual, human, social, and relationship, and natural) and emphasize their interdependencies. Manufactured capital is often interchangeable with operational capital in describing activities and related resources relevant to customer relationships, trademarks and trade names, supplier relationships, franchises, and licenses. A business organization establishes the value of relationships with its customers. Employees can contribute to the maintenance of manufacturing capital that can be used in producing goods and services and thus contribute to the long-term sustainability of the business. With global warming being one of the most important topics of the 21st century, organizations specifically pay attention to the manufacturing processes and their toxicity and try to follow industrial ecology policies. As the Earth's population grows daily, the manufacture of new products and materials does so, too. Emphasis is put on training the employees or, more recently, automating the manufacturing process and toxic gas and material emissions since those are two of the biggest concerns. Innovative technologies, such as augmented reality and 3D printing, are only some instruments implemented before mass production.[13]

Operational capital usually refers to the financial resources needed to fund the day-to-day operations and pay for various operational expenses, including raw materials, labor, rent, utilities, and other ongoing costs for conducting business activities. A firm's operational capital reflects an organization's resources in producing goods and services demanded by their constituencies and stakeholders that are not detrimental to society and the environment. The key components of operational capital are cash flow and cash management, working capital (the difference between current assets and current liabilities), inventory management, cost management, benefits management, operating expenses, and contingency funds. The corporate culture of integrity and competency plays a significant role in establishing policies, procedures, and processes to maximize operational capital. Effective management of operational capital is crucial for maintaining business sustainability, economic growth, and prosperity. Inadequate operational capital can create challenges of lack of business continuity and ongoing concern, liquidity problems, difficulties in meeting obligations, and delays in payments, among others, whereas excess operational capital may indicate inefficient use of resources.

Business organizations should balance managing their operational capital with effective and efficient use of scarce resources to ensure smooth daily operations and long-term financial health. The board of directors, as the representative of shareholders, should design directions for operational efficiency and effectiveness and guide management to implement and maintain policies and procedures to achieve both financial economic sustainability performance and nonfinancial environmental, ethical, social, and governance performance in creating shared value for all stakeholders including shareholders, creditors, employees, customers, suppliers, communities, society, and the environment. The board of directors should oversee that the organization is pursuing the goal of sustainable performance and compliance with all applicable laws, rules, regulations, standards, and best practices. While the board of directors should avoid micromanaging operations, it should provide strategic directions for management to continuously improve efficiency and effectiveness. Effective corporate governance measures should be implemented to promote vigilant oversight function by the board of directors, effective managerial function by management, and accountable and responsible actions by other corporate gatekeepers, including auditors and financial advisors. All the measures and actions should be proactively planned. Well-run and vigilant boards usually schedule major topics that they must discuss at a certain time of the year. This is important because it gives the board some time to think about the consequences and concerns regarding the upcoming topic. Additionally, board committees, particularly the audit committee, should be engaged in better and more efficient decision-making. By strictly following decision protocols and ensuring the right governance culture, organizations can strive for long-term financial and nonfinancial sustainability while enhancing their organizational capital.[14]

Intellectual Capital

Intellectual capital refers to the intangible assets that contribute to a company's bottom-line earnings, long-term sustainability performance, business continuity, survival, and competitive advantage. Intellectual capital presents resources and intangible assets consisting of organizational investments and processes in developing intellectual capital, the expertise of employees, and all the effort knowledge contained within the organization. Intellectual capital consists of non-material resources that are not easily measurable but essential for a business's success and innovation. Intellectual capital of knowledge, innovation, and intellectual property can be classified into three main components: human capital, customer/relational capital, and organizational/structural capital presenting structural capital, including the non-physical infrastructure, processes, and databases and information technology platforms of the organization that enables other capitals, including operational,

Types of Sustainability Capitals

financial, and human, to function effectively. Structural capital consists of policies, processes, patents, trademarks, the organization's image, information infrastructure, proprietary software, databases, information technology platforms, innovation, and research and developments. One of the questions that arises when it comes to intellectual capital is how organizations measure it. There have been multiple approaches to this question, but only two stand out: component and holistic methods. Component method separates given elements of the intellectual capital, measures them, and then calculates the total value. On the other side, a holistic approach focuses on the market value and based on that, determines the intellectual capital value. Both methods have been criticized, but newer research tries to answer past criticisms by combining these two methods.[15] Something important to note is that an organization's size plays a significant role in determining the disclosed amount of intellectual capital, based on the research conducted in 2020. The bigger the organization is, the higher its disclosed capital could be. This provides large organizations with an opportunity to disclose potentially higher intellectual capital and minimize their business risk in case they are in debt. Profitability and leverage also positively affect the disclosure amount of intellectual capital, but these two components do not affect it as much as the company's size.[16]

Business recovery and transformation are essential strategic planning for coping with growing challenges caused by the COVID-19 pandemic. Under the board of directors' oversight, executives and management teams of business organizations should consider all possibilities and scenarios under which an organization can survive, recover, and continue sustainable performance by utilizing existing information technology. Business risk assessment and supply chain management can play important roles in recovery. Many business organizations have made significant modifications and adjustments to business operations and practices, using intellectual capital and information technology in response to challenges brought on by the COVID-19 pandemic. These organizations are also changing their communication, reporting, and control systems, using their intellectual capital, information technology, and virtual platforms. The finance function is better positioned to evaluate the available intellectual capital and virtual platforms and make suggestions for their adoption. Intellectual capital should be considered a strategic asset contributing to an organization's long-term success and sustainability.

Reputational/Trust Capital

Reputational capital, also known as trust and cultural capital, reflects the intangible value an organization earns through trust, credibility, and positive perception with its stakeholders and constituencies, including customers, employees, suppliers, investors, and society.

Reputational capital represents the trust, goodwill, and positive reputation built over time through consistent ethical practices, positive behavior, and commitments to delivering on promises that can improve relationships and contribute to long-term success and sustainable business. Important components of reputational capital are cultural heritage, traditions, knowledge and creativity, brand image, credibility, customer satisfaction, ethical workplace, credibility, trustworthiness, corporate social responsibility, and employee relations. Reputational capital is an asset built over a long time and can be challenging to rebuild once damaged; thus, its sustainability is essential for maintaining diverse identities and enhancing a sense of community. It plays an essential role in attracting and maintaining talented employees, creating customer satisfaction and attraction, building professional relationships with suppliers, and maintaining positive relationships with other stakeholders. Business organizations should invest in activities and strategies that create and sustain their reputational capital, including competent and ethical business practices, corporate social responsibility initiatives, fairness, and transparent communication disclosures.

The evolution of trust in the stakeholder era of capitalism has grown increasingly difficult to manage. Research examines global governance and the rule of law with the changing face of leadership, ethical technology, and more.[17] Corporations are structured to make trust and reputational strength difficult to achieve. The business purpose should be molded into an applied enterprise instead of a static set of promises. Corporations should begin investing in aligned and effective governance, leadership, employee engagement, and ethical sourcing for green investment decisions and responsible tax policies to build up their reputation and trust capital. A good reputation with stakeholders, including shareholders, employees, creditors, customers, suppliers, and communities, can take many years to build and can be easily and immediately destroyed with unintentional mistakes and irregularities and intentional fraud to deceive stakeholders.

One of the main reasons reputation has been so easily affected in recent years, is that every piece of information about an organization can be found online. A big part of an organization's reputation depends on online reviews written by customers and partners. According to research, 97% of new consumers look at the reviews online and consider an organization's reputation before engaging in any relationship with them. Good online reviews are worth a lot, but bad reviews can have an even stronger effect on consumers. Statistics show that after reading a negative review, 60% of the potential customers decided not to use the service or business.[18] Some organizations even hire teams to write positive reviews for them and, in that way, raise their review score.[19] Search engine optimization is also one of the things that organizations invest in highly to improve their reputation, attract more

Types of Sustainability Capitals

consumers, and bring in better potential employees. Anecdotal evidence and scholarly research suggest that many factors can positively or negatively affect reputation. Indeed, the reputation–reality gap, changing beliefs and expectations, and weak internal coordination are the three major factors responsible for a potential organization's reputation downfall.[20] It is important for an organization to treat each relationship with caution but also to stick to its core values regardless of challenges and opportunities.

Corporate culture plays a crucial role in trust capital. Speaking of culture, Wilcox states:

> There are, however, three proverbial certainties that have developed around corporate culture: (1) We know it when we see it – and worse, we know it most clearly when its failure leads to a crisis. (2) It is a responsibility of the board of directors, defined by their "tone at the top." (3) It is the foundation for a company's most precious asset, its reputation. Several business metrics, such as worker retention, customer satisfaction, legal issues, etc., can be used to assess a company's culture.[21]

Regarding the popularity of shareholder primacy in the United States, management aims to maximize shareholders' benefits. This principal-agent model usually leads to the misalignment of interests, which can be detrimental to trust or reputational capital. Therefore, a reduction in the power of shareholders or an increase in the power of other stakeholders, especially employees, can be the solution to problems related to integrity in corporate cultures.[22] Moreover, stakeholders now require more transparent communication, which challenges the board of directors to maintain a balance between transparency, confidentiality, and independence.[23]

Strategic Capital

Strategic capital reflects management strategic planning and consists of strategic plans, decisions, and actions. Strategic planning is establishing purpose and mission, making decisions, taking action in documenting and communicating plans throughout the organization to those affected by actions, evaluating compliance with actions, and holding individuals accountable. The strategic plans enable organizations to document their purpose, mission, values, and vision and establish goals and action plans to implement them. The economic order, stakeholder expectations, corporate culture, and business environment are changing in the post-COVID-19 era, and how business organizations define their purpose and measure the achievement of their success is changing, too. Purpose determines why the organization exists, its mission, who the stakeholders are, and its objectives and strategies for achieving them. The main objective function of any business organization is to create shared value for all stakeholders, including shareholders, creditors, customers, suppliers, employees, government, society, and the environment. Changes in the purpose, mission, objectives, and strategies for business organizations in the aftermath of the COVID-19 crisis are important for the organization's long-term sustainability. Without a clear purpose and mission, organizations are finding it difficult not only to manage the pressures from outside stakeholders but also to re-establish their core values to deal with the current crisis. Organizations not only have to understand all potential issues and challenges regarding long- and short-term sustainability, but prioritization among the objectives becomes a major factor in challenging times like this. How businesses operate and the circumstances under which the operation process is done have drastically changed since the pandemic and will be considered key components when discussing future objectives.

Every company should have its unique purpose determined in its charter of incorporation to maximize its positive impacts on all stakeholders, including society and the environment, and to minimize the negative impacts on multi-stakeholders. In case of nonexistence and/or inadequate "Statement of Purpose," all executives in the c-suite under the oversight function of the board of directors and approval by majority shareholders should establish an appropriate stakeholder-inclusive "Statement of Purpose." The purpose of profit maximization and shareholder wealth creation has changed to create shared value for all stakeholders. To effectively achieve this new purpose, corporations are expanding their performance to both financial/quantitative ESP and nonfinancial/qualitative environmental, ethical, social, and governance (EESG) sustainability performance. Sustainability has become an economic and strategic imperative with the potential to create business opportunities and risks.

The mission reflects the organization's determination to stay with its purpose and its short-, medium-, and long-term achievement. Companies are now adopting the corporate mission of profit to create shared value for all stakeholders by shifting their goals to create shareholder value while fulfilling their social, environmental, and governance responsibilities. Corporate objectives have sustainably changed in the post-COVID-19 pandemic to survival in the short term, medium-term continuity, and long-term sustainability. The board of directors pays more attention to the well-being, safety, and health of their employees, customers, and suppliers.

Strategic capital is very broad and can encompass political and technological capital. Political capital refers to the institutions, governance structures, and political systems that can affect decision-making and are vital for achieving sustainability goals. Technological capital represents technological advancements that can contribute to ESP's and ESG's sustainability performance by improving efficiency and addressing environmental issues and challenges. One of the additional factors to consider is the increased technology usage

Types of Sustainability Capitals

due to COVID-19. Even before the pandemic, the way organizations operated was creating an enormous amount of data. With most companies going completely online, data creation is higher than ever. The rise of online data not only represents the potential opportunity for better strategic decisions and capital allocation but also poses a risk of leakage of data and/or exposure of confidential information and strategic objectives. The rise of the data analytics field and its implementation in a considerable number of business processes in recent years just shows how dependable companies are on it and how most of the strategic decisions will be made in the future.

In the aftermath of recent financial crises, it is not uncommon for investors to lose confidence in firms. The board of directors can rebuild trust by focusing on more long-term goals. While the board has fiduciary duties to carry out, they often fall prey to pressures of obtaining immediate results, which may deviate from the long-term picture. Instead, strategies should be implemented so they would allow the firm to withstand short-term pressures. The board's priorities should be more focused on the governance of strategic capital. That can be achieved by delegating duties that do not require the board's full attention to the committees, allowing the board to focus on the company's priorities. To rebuild trust, directors must always act in the company's best interests, even if it means disagreeing with shareholders and risking reelection. Effective communication with shareholders should be established in order to understand their concerns, ideas, feedback, and any potential disconnection in their views. Strategic capital reflects the organization's value, vision, culture, purpose, mission, goals, objectives, plans of action, and accountability and can reflect strategic financial, human, social, and intellectual capital.

Summary

Management has traditionally assumed stewardship of an organization's resources and capital in making strategic decisions that protect the interests of all stakeholders. As the steward of all business capital, management should focus on long-term interests and sustainability goals. Multi-stakeholders' well-being is relevant and applicable to corporate governance in the post-COVID-19 era, as business organizations are more concerned about the safety, health, and well-being of their employees, customers, suppliers, and other stakeholders. Management, as the steward of business resources and related capital discussed in this chapter, has the primary role of improving sustainability performance, managing related risks, and maximizing utilization of all capital from strategic to financial, reputational, manufactured, human, social, and environmental to create shared value for all stakeholders. Stakeholder interests in a firm are equity capital, human capital, social capital, and compliance capital. Thus, management is the steward of strategic, financial, human, social, and environmental capital and the active and long-term oriented steward of all stakeholders, including shareholders.

Key Points

- Management should consider all capital, from strategic to financial, reputational, manufactured, social, environmental, and human, in creating accountability and stewardship for all capital and stakeholders.

- As the steward of business resources, management has the primary role of improving sustainability performance and managing related risks, maximizing utilization of all capital from strategic to financial, reputational, manufactured, human, social, and environmental to create shared value for all stakeholders.

- Management should assess and manage all capital affecting the bottom-line earnings and minimize contingent and actual corporate liabilities.

- All nine sustainability capitals presented in this chapter are crucial to achieving ESP and ESG sustainability performance by recognizing that these different forms of capital are interconnected and interdependent and collectively contribute to financial success and stability and ensure social and environmental impacts.

- A holistic and integrated approach to business sustainability enables the synergies and trade-offs between these capitals to achieve a balanced and resilient financial system.

- Business organizations, policymakers, and investors should use the holistic capital framework to guide their policies, strategies, and decision-making processes toward more sustainable outcomes.

Review Questions

1. **What is financial capital in the context of business sustainability?**
2. **What is the role of natural capital in business sustainability?**
3. **What are the components of manufactured capital?**
4. **What is intellectual capital, and how does it affect business sustainability?**
5. **What is political capital in the context of business sustainability?**
6. **What are the benefits of investing in human capital?**
7. **How can businesses build and sustain social capital?**
8. **What are some key components of operational capital?**
9. **Why is reputational capital challenging to rebuild once damaged?**
10. **How does technological capital contribute to business sustainability?**

11. **How does financial capital include debt and equity?**
12. **What role does strategic planning play in business sustainability?**
13. **What is the significance of integrating environmental considerations into decision-making processes?**
14. **What is the impact of strong social capital on businesses?**
15. **How does the stakeholder theory relate to human capital?**

Discussion Questions

1. **How do stakeholders contribute to business sustainability?**
2. **What are the learning objectives related to business sustainability capital?**
3. **What is the significance of ESG-focused investment according to the chapter?**
4. **How does financial capital contribute to business sustainability?**
5. **Why is investment in human capital important for long-term business sustainability?**
6. **How does natural capital impact business sustainability?**
7. **Why is preserving natural capital important for business organizations?**
8. **What are the main elements of social capital?**
9. **What is manufactured capital and why is it important?**
10. **What are some key components of operational capital?**
11. **What are the main components of intellectual capital?**
12. **What is reputational/trust capital and why is it significant for businesses?**
13. **How can businesses build and sustain their reputational capital?**
14. **How has the COVID-19 pandemic impacted the focus of corporate objectives?**
15. **Why is technological capital important for business sustainability?**

Multiple-Choice Questions

1. **Who are considered stakeholders in the context of business sustainability?**
   A) Only shareholders and employees
   B) Shareholders, employees, society, the environment, customers, suppliers, and the government
   C) Customers and suppliers only
   D) Only society and the environment

2. **What are the six capitals suggested by the International Integrated Reporting Council (IIRC)?**

A) Financial, manufactured, intellectual, human, social and relationship, natural

B) Financial, marketing, sales, human, social and relationship, natural

C) Financial, intellectual, human, sales, marketing, natural

D) Financial, manufactured, sales, marketing, human, natural

3. **How does human capital contribute to business sustainability?**

A) By focusing on short-term profits

B) Through education, skills, knowledge, training, health, and well-being of the workforce

C) By increasing marketing spend

D) By reducing operational costs

4. **What are the main elements of social capital?**

A) Financial resources and market share

B) Norms and values, trust, networks and connections, community engagements, and reciprocity

C) Technology and innovation

D) Sales and marketing strategies

5. **What are some key components of operational capital?**

A) Marketing budget and brand image

B) Cash flow and cash management, working capital, inventory management, cost management, benefits management, operating expenses, and contingency funds

C) Sales strategies and customer loyalty programs

D) Social media presence and online reviews

6. **What is the significance of technological capital?**

A) It has no impact on sustainability

B) It contributes to improving efficiency, addressing environmental issues, and enhancing both financial and environmental sustainability performance

C) It only affects marketing strategies

D) It is only relevant for large companies

7. **What impact did the COVID-19 pandemic have on corporate objectives?**

A) No impact

B) Shifted focus to the well-being, safety, and health of employees, customers, and suppliers, emphasizing long-term sustainability and resilience

C) Increased focus on short-term profits

D) Reduced focus on environmental sustainability

Multiple-Choice Questions

8. **What is the importance of preserving natural capital for businesses?**
   A) To increase marketing budgets
   B) To ensure the availability of resources for current and future production, and mitigate environmental risks
   C) To reduce operational costs
   D) To increase short-term profits

9. **How can businesses build and sustain social capital?**
   A) By increasing marketing budgets
   B) By investing in relationships, community building, social trust, and communication with stakeholders
   C) By reducing operational costs
   D) By focusing on short-term profits

10. **What is the significance of efficient utilization of manufactured capital?**
    A) To increase marketing spend
    B) To reduce waste, improve efficiency, and lower costs over time
    C) To focus on short-term profits
    D) To reduce employee turnover

11. **How does intellectual capital affect business sustainability?**
    A) It has no impact
    B) It contributes to long-term sustainability and competitive advantage through intangible assets like knowledge, innovation, and intellectual property
    C) It only affects marketing strategies
    D) It is only relevant for large companies

12. **What is the importance of integrating environmental considerations into decision-making processes?**
    A) It has no significance
    B) It is important for economic growth and sustainable development
    C) It only affects marketing strategies
    D) It reduces operational costs

13. **How can companies measure intellectual capital?**
    A) By using only qualitative methods
    B) By using component methods and holistic methods
    C) By increasing marketing spend
    D) By focusing on short-term profits

14. **Why is it crucial to preserve natural capital for businesses?**
    A) To increase marketing budgets

B) To ensure the availability of resources for current and future production

C) To focus on short-term profits

D) To reduce employee turnover

15. **How does reputational capital benefit businesses?**

A) It has no impact

B) It helps attract and retain talented employees, create customer satisfaction, and build professional relationships

C) It only affects marketing strategies

D) It reduces operational costs

16. **What are the main elements of social capital?**

A) Financial resources and market share

B) Norms and values, trust, networks and connections, community engagements, and reciprocity

C) Marketing strategies and customer loyalty

D) Social media presence and online reviews

17. **What is financial capital in the context of business sustainability?**

A) Only marketing budgets

B) Monetary resources provided by investors or internally generated for investment, expansion, operation, and risk management

C) Only customer satisfaction

D) Only brand loyalty

18. **What are the components of intellectual capital?**

A) Financial resources and market share

B) Human capital, customer/relational capital, and organizational/structural capital

C) Marketing strategies and customer loyalty

D) Social media presence and online reviews

19. **What is the role of social capital in business sustainability?**

A) To increase marketing spend

B) To create economic development, social networks, and community well-being

C) To focus on short-term profits

D) To reduce operational costs

20. **Why is it important to preserve natural capital?**

A) To increase marketing budgets

B) To ensure the availability of resources for current and future production and mitigate environmental risks

Multiple-Choice Questions

C) To focus on short-term profits

D) To reduce employee turnover

21. **How does technological capital contribute to business sustainability?**

A) It has no impact

B) It contributes to improving efficiency, addressing environmental issues, and enhancing both financial and environmental sustainability performance

C) It only affects marketing strategies

D) It reduces operational costs

22. **What are the main components of human capital?**

A) Financial resources and market share

B) Education, skills, knowledge, training, health, and well-being

C) Marketing strategies and customer loyalty

D) Social media presence and online reviews

23. **What is the impact of strong social capital on businesses?**

A) It has no impact

B) It helps address challenges, build brand loyalty, and access new markets

C) It only affects marketing strategies

D) It reduces operational costs

24. **How can companies measure intellectual capital?**

A) By using only qualitative methods

B) By using component methods and holistic methods

C) By increasing marketing spend

D) By focusing on short-term profits

25. **How does natural capital impact business sustainability?**

A) It has no impact

B) It provides essential resources for long-term business success and environmental stewardship

C) It only affects marketing strategies

D) It reduces operational costs

26. **Why is it important to preserve natural capital?**

A) To increase marketing budgets

B) To ensure the availability of resources for current and future production and mitigate environmental risks

C) To focus on short-term profits

D) To reduce employee turnover

27. **What are some examples of financial capital components?**
    A) Customer satisfaction and brand loyalty
    B) Equity, debt, retained earnings, and grants
    C) Marketing strategies and sales growth
    D) Online reviews and social media presence

28. **What is strategic capital?**
    A) Short-term financial gains
    B) Management's strategic planning, decisions, and actions reflecting the organization's purpose, mission, values, goals, and action plans
    C) Only marketing strategies
    D) Only customer service initiatives

29. **What is the role of cultural capital in business sustainability?**
    A) It has no impact
    B) It includes brand image, customer satisfaction, and ethical workplace, contributing to long-term business success
    C) It only affects marketing strategies
    D) It reduces operational costs

Notes

1 Much of the discussion in this chapter comes from Rezaee, A. (2021). *Corporate Sustainability: Shareholder Primacy Versus Stakeholder Primacy*, Chapter 2, Business Expert Press. New York, New York, USA and Rezaee, Z. (2024). *The Sustainable Business Blueprint: Planning, Performance, Risk, Reporting and Assurance.* Routledge/Taylor and Francis, Chapter 6.

2 Bloomberg Intelligence. (2021). ESG assets may hit $53 trillion by 2025, a third of global AUM. *Bloomberg.* (September 2021). https://www.bloomberg.com/professional/blog/esg-assets-may-hit-53-trillion-by-2025-a-third-of-global-aum/#:~:text=Assuming%2015 %25%20growth%2C%20half%20the%20pace%20of%20the,trillion%20in%202018%2 0from%20%2422.8%20trillion%20in%202016.

3 International Integrated Reporting Council (IIRC). (2013). Integrated reporting capitals. https://integratedreporting.ifrs.org/wp-content/uploads/2013/03/IR-Background-Paper -Capitals.pdf

4 Investopedia. (2019). Understanding financial capital vs. economic capital. https://www .investopedia.com/ask/answers/031715/what-difference-between-financial-capital-and -economic-capital.asp#:~:text=Key%20Takeaways%201%20Financial%20capital%20is %20a%20broad,is%20referring%20to%20financial%20capital%2C%20not%20economic %20capital.

5 The Balance. (2021). What is financial capital?. https://www.thebalance.com/what-is -financial-capital-3305825#:~:text=Key%20Takeaways%201%20Financial%20capital

Notes

%20is%20money%2C%20credit%2C,debt%2C%20equity%2C%20and%20specialty %20capital.%20More%20items...%20

6 Organization of Economic Co-operation and Development (OECD). (2018). Human capital – the value of people. https://www.oecd.org/insights/humancapital-thevalueofpeople.htm

7 Embarkment Project for Inclusive Capitalism. (2017). https://assets.ey.com/content/dam /ey-sites/ey-com/en_ca/topics/transaction-advisory-services/ey-the-embankment-projec t-for-inclusive-capitalism-report.pdf

8 Batish, Amit, Gordon, Andrew, Kepler, John D., Larcker, David F., Tayan, Brian, Yu, Courtney. (2021). Stanford closer look series. Human capital disclosure – What do companies say about their "most important asset"?. https://www.gsb.stanford.edu/faculty-research/pub lications/human-capital-disclosure-what-do-companies-say-about-their-most

9 Restoration: The Role Stakeholder Governance Must Play in Recreating a Fair and Sustainable American Economy – A Reply to Professor Rock by Leo E. Strine, Jr.

10 Harvard Law School Forum on Corporate Governance. (2019). Worker representation on US corporate boards. https://corpgov.law.harvard.edu/2019/12/30/worker-representation -on-u-s-corporate-boards/#:~:text=Thus%2C%20a%20federal%20legislation%20solution ,one%2Dthird%20of%20board%20seats.

11 AllThingsNature. (2021). What is environmental capital? https://www.allthingsnature.org/ what-is-environmental-capital.htm

12 Organization of Economic Co-operation and Development (OECD). (2001). The well-being of nations: The role of human and social capital, OECD Publishing, Paris. https://doi.org/10 .1787/9789264189515-en.

13 Cox, Domonique. (2020). GUD capital. *Manufacturing Operating Capital*. https://gudcapital .com/manufacturing-working-capital/

14 Useem, Michael. (2006). How well-run boards make decisions. *Harvard Business Review*. https://hbr.org/2006/11/ how-well-run-boards-make-decisions

15 Jardon, Carlos M., and Martinez-Cobas, Xavier. (2021). Measuring intellectual capital with financial data. *PLoS ONE*. https://eds.b.ebscohost.com/eds/pdfviewer/pdfviewer?vid=4 &sid=72353f80-0469-4eb4-81ef-e1cf8d3977a6%40pdc-v-sessmgr03

16 Septiana and Subowo. (2020). The effect of the firm's size, profitability, and leverage on the intellectual capital disclosure with audit committee as moderator. *Accounting Analysis Journal*. https://eds.b.ebscohost.com/eds/pdfviewer/pdfviewer?vid=3&sid=dde47c95-82 c7-4614-ac42-1f7e017286d7%40sessionmgr102

17 Harvard Law School Forum on Corporate Governance. (2020). The evolution of trust in the era of stakeholder capitalism. https://corpgov.law.harvard.edu/2020/04/23/the-evolution -of-trust-in-the-era-of-stakeholder-capitalism/

18 Campbell, Kent. (2021). Reputation X. 2021 Online reputation management statistics. https://blog.reputationx.com/online-reputation-management-statistics

19 Schaer, Brianne. (2021). Reputation X. What is reputation capital? https://blog.reputationx .com/what-is-reputation-apital#:~:text=Definition%20of%20reputation%20capital%20

Reputation%20capital%20is%20the,products%20and%20services%2C%20stock%2
0price%2C%20and%20company%20valuation.

20 Eccles, Robert G. Newquist, Scott C., and Schatz, Roland. (2007). Reputation and Its Risks. *Harvard Business Review*. https://hbr.org/2007/02/reputation-and-its-risks

21 Harvard Law School Forum on Corporate Governance. (2020). Corporate purpose and culture. https://corpgov.law.harvard.edu/2020/02/21/corporate-purpose-and-culture/

22 Harvard Law School Forum on Corporate Governance. (2019). The effects of shareholder primacy, publicness, and "privateness" on corporate cultures. https://corpgov.law.harvard.edu/2019/09/23/the-effects-of-shareholder-primacy-publicness-and-privateness-on-corporate-cultures/

23 Harvard Law School Forum on Corporate Governance. (2020). Corporate purpose and culture. https://corpgov.law.harvard.edu/2020/02/21/corporate-purpose-and-culture/

Notes

Chapter 11
Business Sustainability Reporting and Assurance

Learning Objectives

- Present various types and definitions of corporate reporting.
- Provide an overview of financial and nonfinancial key performance indicators (KPIs).
- Understand the role of sustainability reporting.
- Provide an overview of sustainable assurance.
- Be aware of the important principles of integrated reporting.
- Address the global status of sustainability performance reporting.
- Explain the best practices of sustainability reporting and assurance.
- Understand the impact investing concept of required financial returns and desired social and environmental impacts.
- Learn integrated sustainability reporting and assurance.

Introduction

Sustainability reporting and effectively and transparently communicate organizations' financial economic sustainability performance (ESP) and nonfinancial environmental, social, and governance (ESG) sustainability to their stakeholders. The sustainability reporting process involves providing information about the organization's financial ESP (profit) and nonfinancial ESG (impact on the planet, people, and governance practices and prosperities). Sustainability reporting is an integral component of corporate accountability and responsibility. Global business organizations are currently dealing with the challenges of adapting a proper sustainability reporting framework to present both financial ESP and nonfinancial ESG sustainability performance effectively. Business sustainability has recently evolved from focusing on short-term ESP and fulfillment of corporate social responsibility (CSR) to achieving long-term financial ESP and nonfinancial ESG sustainability performance in creating shared value for all stakeholders. Many public companies in Europe and Asia are now required to disclose their nonfinancial ESG sustainability performance information. It is expected that public companies in other countries will follow suit in requiring the disclosure of sustainability information on both financial ESP and nonfinancial ESG. The disclosure requirement of ESG is intended to support investors, consumers, policymakers, and other

DOI: 10.4324/9781003487081-11

interested stakeholders in evaluating the risks and opportunities associated with nonfinancial ESG sustainability performance. A third-party assurance provider should assure sustainability reports to ensure their objectivity, impartiality, and independence. This chapter presents both mandatory and voluntary sustainability reporting and assurance.[1]

Corporate Reporting

Corporate reporting, either mandatory on ESP information and/or voluntary on ESG sustainability performance information, is essential to the financial markets and economic growth. It is value-relevant to investors and other stakeholders when assessing opportunities and risks associated with their investment. The type and extent of ESG voluntary reporting have recently received considerable attention as many public companies worldwide disclose information on various ESG dimensions of their sustainability performance. Corporate reporting, mandatory on ESP and/or voluntary on ESG, is intended to provide investors and other stakeholders with useful, transparent, reliable, and relevant financial and nonfinancial information in making sound investment decisions. Public companies in the United States have traditionally disclosed a set of financial statements to their shareholders under the corporate mandatory disclosure regime and have recently provided voluntary corporate disclosures on ESG information. Anecdotal evidence suggests that investors value meaningful and reliable voluntary disclosures and use them to make investment decisions. They also utilize mandatory disclosures to verify voluntary disclosures.[2]

Management has incentives and is typically required to disclose mandatory financial ESP information, but it may, on a voluntary basis, disclose ESG information. Investors and other corporate stakeholders may view mandatory ESP information and voluntary ESG information as complementary or contradictory. Voluntary ESG disclosures are based on management discretion of what information to disclose, for what purposes, and to what extent to disclose such information. Sustainability ESG disclosures are largely not mandated, and management may opportunistically determine its disclosure strategies and practices. However, there has been an ongoing debate in the business community that conventional financial reports do not portray a comprehensive and complete picture of a company's financial health, sustainability, and risk factors. Thus, corporate reporting should reflect both financial ESP and nonfinancial ESG sustainability performance. Sustainability reporting measures, classifies, and recognizes financial ESP and nonfinancial ESG sustainability performance and discloses such information to all stakeholders. Investors and other external stakeholders, including suppliers, customers, governments, society, and the environment, can now have more transparent information about companies' commitment to sustainability and long-term performance. Management can use sustainability reporting to improve managerial and strategic decisions by integrating sustainability into the business environment, corporate culture, and supply-chain management. Sustainability performance reporting and assurance can provide management and stakeholders with improved confidence in the credibility and trustworthiness of sustainability information.

Sustainability reporting and assurance on nonfinancial ESG sustainability performance information requires the proper measurement, accurate and reliable disclosure of sustainability performance, and effective assessment of sustainability risks. Several organizations worldwide, including the Global Reporting Initiative (GRI), International Integrated Reporting Council (IIRC), Sustainability Accounting Standards Board (SASB), and International Sustainability Standards Board (ISSB), have issued guidelines regarding voluntary/mandatory disclosure of sustainability information. There are two ESG reporting regimes: mandatory (European, some Asian, and South African countries) and voluntary/semi-mandatory (US and some other countries). Disclosure of sustainability performance information is expected to affect the firm's performance and corporate governance. Investors typically have incomplete financial ESP and nonfinancial ESG sustainability performance, and thus, they may not be aware of the firm governance effectiveness, ethical culture, and social and environmental commitments. Lack of knowledge on the part of investors reduces the firm's investor base, which in turn makes risk sharing incomplete and inefficient and may cause stocks of these firms to be out of line with their market's fundamentals.

Furthermore, the costs and benefits of sustainability reporting are often uncertain, and the extent to which sustainability disclosures lead to the release of private information on firms' governance, environmental, and social initiatives is unknown. Stakeholders may attempt to pressure and/or motivate firms to disclose sustainability information about their social, governance, and environmental activities. However, releasing such information may lead to the disclosure of private information that could be detrimental to business survival. Managers tend to analyze the costs/benefits of obtaining sustainability disclosure to improve sustainability disclosures and how these disclosures are integrated and observed by capital markets.

Mandatory Sustainability Reporting

Mandatory sustainability reporting is the requirement imposed on business organizations by regulators and standards-setters worldwide to disclose information about their ESP and ESG sustainability performance. Mandatory sustainability reporting requirements typically cover various sustainability topics, from long-term financial outcomes to environmental impact, labor conditions, human rights, social practices, and governance. Investors have recognized the importance of sustainability disclosures in their decision-making, and regulators have mandated sustainability requirements and standards. Sustainability reporting regulations often imposed by government or regulatory bodies on business organizations are intended to improve accountability, transparency, and the integration of sustainability initiatives and considerations into business practices. For example, in recent decades, many countries, including Australia, Austria, Canada, Denmark, France, Germany, Malaysia, Netherlands, Sweden, Hong Kong, and the United Kingdom, have adopted mandatory reporting on nonfinancial ESG sustainability performance.[3] Regulators in other countries are expected to follow suit, moving toward mandatory sustainability performance reporting and assurance. Stock exchanges worldwide either require or recommend that their listed companies report sustainability information (e.g., Singapore Stock Exchange, 2011; Toronto Stock Exchange, 2014; Hong Kong Stock Exchange, 2015), and more than 6000 European companies are required to disclose their nonfinancial ESG sustainability performance and diversity information for their financial year 2017 and onwards.[4] The Hong Kong Exchange has announced that an integrated sustainability and corporate governance report will be required for Hong Kong-listed companies starting in 2015.[5] This guide requires environmental, social, and governance information. The Hong Kong Exchange encourages an issuer to identify and disclose additional ESG issues and KPIs relevant to its business. An issuer may adopt a higher level of ESG reporting based on international guidance standards, such as IIRC and GRI. In the United States, the Securities and Exchange Commission (SEC) released its proposed rule for climate change on March 21, 2022. It issued its final related rules in March 2024 that require public companies to disclose certain climate-related risks that are considered to have material impacts on their business, results of operations, or financial condition, as well as other climate-related financial statement metrics such as greenhouse gas emissions.[6]

The global standard-setters, including the European Union's Non-Financial Reporting Directive (NFRD), which requires certain large European companies to disclose nonfinancial ESG information, are driving global efforts toward mandatory sustainability reporting. In September 2014, The European Commission adopted the Council of the Directive on disclosure of nonfinancial sustainability information for more than 6000 companies for their financial year 2017.[7] This directive provides non-binding guidelines in facilitating nonfinancial environmental, social, anticorruption, and diversity information disclosure by large public companies either as a separate or integrated report along with financial information. The primary objectives of the directive are to (1) increase transparency in sustainability reporting in the areas of environmental, social, governance, employee-related issues, human rights policies, and anticorruption and bribery issues; (2) increase sustainability performance on social and environmental matters; and (3) contribute effectively to long-term economic growth and employment. In January 2023, the EU Corporate Sustainability Reporting Directive (CSRD) was issued, requiring mandatory sustainability reporting for European companies that could apply to their counterparts and trading partners worldwide.[8] The CSRD is intended to complement existing sustainability-focused regulations, voluntary frameworks and standards of the GRI and the ISSB, and will have a global implication. The CSRD requires covered companies to disclose historical and forward-looking information relevant to sustainability matters, including ESG issues and information about sustainability risk management, metrics, and value chain due diligence for EU companies. The European Sustainability Reporting Standards (ESRS) were adopted by the European Financial Reporting Advisory Group (EFRAG), in July 2023, under the CSRD of the European Union.[9] These standards are intended to enhance and harmonize the reporting of ESG factors by companies within the EU, ensuring greater transparency and consistency in sustainability reporting.

Mandatory sustainability reporting requirements typically focus on identifying and disclosing material ESG sustainability issues considered most relevant to business organizations and their stakeholders. Noncompliance with mandatory sustainability reporting may cause penalties or other consequences, as regulatory bodies oversee financial and corporate reporting and usually monitor and enforce compliance. Sustainability reporting regulations are evolving as sustainability reporting practices have advanced. Mandatory ESG sustainability reporting can encourage positive environmental, social, and governance practices among business organizations and contribute to shared value creation for all stakeholders and the broader goals of sustainable development, generating desired financial performance and having social and environmental impacts. Mandatory ESG sustainability reporting is expected to be integrated with mandatory financial reporting to provide a more comprehensive and holistic approach to corporate reporting. The International Financial Reporting Standards (IFRS) Foundation's consultation on establishing a global nonfinancial ESG reporting framework has released global sustainability reporting standards.[10] These sustainability disclosure initiatives, whether mandatory or voluntary, are intended to reflect the financial, social, and environmental impacts of a company's business operation and, thus, provide relevant and reliable financial and nonfinancial information for all stakeholders, including investors. It is expected that international accounting standard-setters, including the Financial Accounting Standards Board (FASB), International Accounting Standards Board (IASB), and the International Sustainability Standards Board of the IFRS issue accounting standards for proper measurement, recognition, and disclosure of ESG sustainability information, which is discussed in the next section.

In summary, mandatory sustainability initiatives refer to rules, regulations, standards, policies, or requirements imposed by governments, governing bodies, standard-setters or organizations to promote social justice environmentally friendly practices, reduce carbon emissions, conserve resources, and mitigate the impacts of climate change and global warming. These initiatives are often intended to address various aspects of sustainability, including social justice and equity, the efficient use of natural resources, energy efficiency, waste reduction, water conservation, biodiversity protection, and social responsibility. These mandatory initiatives, as discussed in Chapter 6, are relevant to: (1) renewable energy initiatives of setting targets for the use of renewable energy sources such as hydroelectric power, wind, and solar; (2) carbon pricing mechanisms including carbon taxes or cap-and-trade systems to reduce greenhouse gas emissions; (3) energy efficiency standards relevant to buildings, appliances, vehicles, and industrial processes to reduce greenhouse gas emissions and energy consumption; (4) waste management regulations to implement recycling and waste reduction; (5) sustainable procurement standards relevant to the procurement of goods and services such as compliance with fair labor practices and using environmentally friendly materials; and (6) biodiversity conservation regulations to protect endangered species, natural habitats, and ecosystems from degradation and destruction due to human activities.

Overall, corporate sustainability reporting regulations and standards require companies to disclose information about their ESG activities, efforts, and performance. These reporting requirements are intended to promote responsible business practices, transparency, accountability, and compliance with mandatory sustainability initiatives summarized in the previous paragraph. These requirements enable stakeholders, including shareholders, creditors, consumers, employees, and communities, to make informed decisions. Companies may use established reporting frameworks and standards, such as ISSB, GRI, SASB, the Task Force on Climate-related Financial Disclosures (TCFD), or the IIRC, to guide their sustainability reporting compliance and efforts. Mandatory corporate sustainability reporting can vary by jurisdiction, industry, and company size and play a vital role in promoting corporate responsibility accountability, enhancing stakeholder trust, advancing the transition to more sustainable and responsible business practices and driving sustainability performance improvements. At the same time, some countries have made sustainability reporting mandatory, and others have encouraged companies to integrate sustainability into their existing financial reporting practices through voluntary reporting frameworks, as explained in the next section.

Corporate Reporting

Voluntary Sustainability Reporting

Voluntary sustainability reporting is the practice of disclosing ESG information voluntarily by choosing to disclose such information on a voluntary basis rather than being required to do so by regulations or guidelines. These sustainability reports are often published alongside financial reports with the purpose of providing stakeholders with comprehensive information about the company's sustainability efforts and impacts. Business organizations typically initiate voluntary sustainability reporting as part of their commitment to sustainable business practices and to demonstrate their commitment to corporate responsibility. Voluntary sustainability reporting provides a platform and mechanism for business organizations to communicate with stakeholders on a broad range of economic, social, environmental, and governance matters and share their sustainability efforts, initiatives, and achievements. In recent years, many companies in the United States and other countries have issued voluntary integrated sustainability reports on both financial ESP and nonfinancial ESG sustainability performance. Voluntary disclosures, such as management earnings forecasts and nonfinancial ESG, are often released by management on a discretionary basis. Voluntary ESG sustainability reporting demonstrates an organization's commitment to ethical and sustainable business practices by contributing positively to society, minimizing environmental impact, and building trust and reputation with stakeholders, including investors, customers, employees, and suppliers. Voluntary reporting is gaining global attention and acceptance as a best practice in corporate reporting and governance.

Currently, there are several voluntary sustainability reporting initiatives to guide business organizations worldwide in disclosing their ESG performance information. These initiatives provide frameworks and structured processes for companies to communicate their ESG sustainability efforts and activities to their stakeholders. Several global organizations, including GRI, the IIRC, the SASB, the Value Reporting Foundation (VRF), ISSB, the United Nations Global Compact (UNGC), the International Organizations for Standardization (ISO, 26,000), have issued guidelines and frameworks for regarding voluntary reporting of ESG sustainability information. Many public companies worldwide have used and are using these frameworks in producing stand-alone integrated sustainability reports, and companies choose these guidelines that align best with their stakeholder expectations, business models, and industry specifications. These voluntary sustainability initiatives are essential for enhancing transparency and accountability and contributing to the long-term value creation for all stakeholders. For example, the fourth generation (G4) of the GRI Guidelines covers economic, governance, social, and environmental performance, as well as globally accepted sustainability standards emphasizing both financial ESP and nonfinancial ESG sustainability performance.

In 2011, the GRI developed Version 4.1, or the fourth generation (G4) of guidelines, which covers economic, governance, social, and environmental performance, and in 2016 established globally accepted sustainability standards (GASS) which focus on financial and nonfinancial sustainability disclosures. GASS creates a coordinated set of guidelines for businesses and organizations to correctly and consistently report their impacts related to sustainability measures. The reports of these impacts help cater to the needs of stakeholders, investors, and policymakers.[11] In October 2021, The GRI launched its 2021 Universal Standards, representing the most important update on ESG standards for sustainability reporting.[12] The 2021 Universal Standards strengthen the basic foundations of all sustainability reporting through GRI, focusing on transparency, due diligence, and material topics that impact the economy, environment, and people for global organizations of all types and sizes. The 2021 updated GRI standards include a consolidated set of GRI standards, including GRI 1 Foundations, GRI 2 general disclosures, GRI 3, Material Topics, GRI 11, Oil and Gas Sector, GRI 201 Economic Performance. GRI 202 Market Presence, GRI 203 Indirect Economic Impacts, GRI 204 Performance Practices, and GRI 205 Anticorruption.

The International Integrated Reporting Council launched its first Integrated Reporting (IR) framework in December 2013 and is defined by the IIRC as "a concise communication about how an organization's strategy, governance, performance, and prospects, in the context of its external environment, lead to the creation of value over the short, medium, and long term."[13] The IIRC states that integrated reporting differs from financial reporting by focusing on:[14]

1. Improving both the quality and quantity of financial and nonfinancial information available to providers of financial capital to enable a more efficient and productive allocation of capital.
2. Promoting a more cohesive and efficient approach to corporate reporting that discloses all material information of value over time for all stakeholders.
3. Enhancing accountability and stewardship for the broad base of capitals (financial, manufactured, intellectual, human, social and relationship, and natural) and emphasizing their interdependencies.
4. Supporting integrated thinking, decision-making and actions with a keen focus on the creation of value over the short, medium, and long term.

The IIRC integrated reporting is developed based on the following seven guiding principles:[15]

1. Strategic Focus and Future Orientation: This principle determines whether and how the organization's strategy enables the creation of value in the short, medium, and long terms. The integrated sustainability report should provide objective and unbiased KPIs relevant to both financial ESP and nonfinancial ESG sustainability performance.

Corporate Reporting

2. Connectivity of Information: An integrated report should present information on all the interrelated and interdependent factors that affect the organization's ability to create value over time systematically and holistically.

3. Stakeholder Relationships: The focus is on creating shared value for all stakeholders, and thus, the consideration of stakeholder relationships is crucial.

4. Materiality: Stakeholders should be provided with material financial and nonfinancial Information about the organization's ability to create value over the short, medium, and long term. The materiality of sustainability issues and disclosures should be assessed based on the threshold of what is considered to be important to investors (shareowners) and other stakeholders.

5. Conciseness: An integrated report should be concise in disclosing relevant information to all stakeholders.

6. Reliability and Completeness: An integrated report should be complete in presenting all material positive and negative issues and be reliable in presenting information. There should be a proper balance between disclosing financial economic sustainability performance information and nonfinancial ESG sustainability performance information.

7. Consistency and Comparability: An integrated report should present the informational content on a consistent basis over time and in a manner that enables comparisons with other reporting organizations. Sustainability information, both financial ESP and nonfinancial ESG sustainability performance, should be consistently reported to enable comparability among firms in the same industry and across time.

Business organizations, when using the IIRC's integrated reporting to present their material sustainability performance information, should consider the above seven guiding principles and include the suggested eight elements in their sustainability reports. These elements are business model consisting of all the six capitals (financial, manufactured, intellectual, human, social and relationship, and natural); organizational overview and external environment; corporate governance; strategy and resource allocation; all five EGSEE dimensions of sustainability performance; outlook; risks and opportunities; and basis of preparation and presentation.[16] Integration of the seven guiding principles and eight components of the integrated reporting should contribute to the shared value-creation process and enable business organizations to utilize all six types of capital in setting strategic objectives strategies to reach the stated objectives, policies and procedures for achieving sustainable performance, measures to assess performance and related risks and opportunities, and means of reporting performance. The IIRC's integrated reporting framework has recently gained momentum worldwide, particularly in Europe and Asia, and has become mandatory for listed companies in South Africa.[17]

The IIRC issued the IR framework that suggests processes for making a comprehensive sustainability reports framework that merges financial ESP and nonfinancial ESG sustainability performance information into an "integrated" format that is relevant to all corporate stakeholders. The 2021 revision for the IIRC welcomes the identifying metrics that support effective and long-term sustainability value creation and shows the universal need for financial and nonfinancial ESG standards.[18] The 2021 IIRC's international framework provides (1) the foundation for understanding and reporting on multi-faceted value drivers based on financial ESP and nonfinancial ESG information and (2) the principles and key concepts relevant to "what to report" and "how to report" sustainability performance disclosures, and (3) guidelines on sustainability assurance statements that are essential to confidence in both ESP and ESG corporate reporting and most effective when applied against metrics and narrative disclosures.

The Sustainability Accounting Standards Board was founded in 2011 with the mission to establish and maintain industry-specific sustainability disclosure standards for listed companies in the United States.[19] In November 2018, SASB published a complete set of 77 industry standards. These standards provide a complete set of globally applicable industry-specific standards that identify the minimal set of financially material sustainability topics and their associated metrics for the typical company in an industry. SASB's process is focused on financially material sustainability disclosures consistent with standards required for mandatory 10-K or 20-F SEC filings. The SASB standards are intended to provide investors with complete material sustainability information across all its ESGEE dimensions. The standards are composed of both qualitative and quantitative performance disclosures.

In October 2018, the SASB approved its sustainability standards, and they were released in November 2018.[20] These standards are aimed toward 77 specific industries and intended to assist companies in preparing and disclosing useful, relevant, and financially material sustainability information to investors. These industry-focused sustainability standards are developed based on the premise that the primary business objective is to improve financial performance and create value for shareholders because, traditionally, the firm's market value has been determined by financial performance. However, in recent years, in many industries, capitals other than financial (i.e., human, strategic, reputation, manufacturing, social, and environmental) have played important roles, as more than 80% of market capitalization in these industries is made up of intangible assets.[21] SASB's Sustainable Industry Classification System® (SICS®) classifies sectors and industries into 11 sectors and 77 industries based on their business model and resource intensity, their sustainability impacts, and their sustainability innovation potential. Thus, every sector and related industries have its own unique set of sustainability accounting standards in the SASB system.

The SASB sustainability framework consists of important sustainability dimensions in the five broad categories of environment, social capital, human capital, business model and innovation, and leadership and governance. These sustainability dimensions reflect financial returns as well as environmental and social impacts resulting from the production of goods and services that create shared value for all stakeholders. A set of 26 sustainability issues and topics are classified under these five sustainability dimensions as follows:[22]

1. Environment: This environmental dimension reflects the environmental impacts resulting from either the use of natural resources and nonrenewable resources in the production process or through harmful releases into the environment that may affect the company's financial condition or operating performance. The topics relevant to the environmental dimension are air quality, greenhouse gas (GHG) emissions, energy management, waste and hazardous material management, water and wastewater management, and ecological impacts.

2. Social capital: The social capital dimension represents the expectation that every business should contribute to society in return for a social license to operate. It reflects the company's relationships with its employees and key outside parties, such as customers, local communities, the public, and the government. This dimension addresses sustainability issues and topics pertaining to human rights, customer privacy, data security, protection of vulnerable groups, local economic development, access to and quality of products and services, access and affordability, and responsible business practices in marketing, including selling practices and product labeling.

3. Human capital: The human capital sustainability dimension addresses the proper utilization of human capital in the effective management of a company's human resources (employees and individual contractors). This dimension includes sustainability topics and issues that affect the productivity of employees, work conditions, ethical work settings, management of labor relations, and management of the health and safety of employees, employee engagement and participation, the ability to create a safety culture, and diversity and inclusion.

4. Business model and innovation: This sustainability dimension reflects the holistic approach of the integration of environmental, human, governance, and social issues in a company's value-creation process in creating shared value for all stakeholders. Sustainability issues and topics relevant to this dimension are product design and life-cycle management, supply-chain management, business model resilience, resource recovery and other innovations in the production process, material sourcing and efficiency, and the physical impact of climate change.

5. Leadership and governance: The leadership and governance sustainability dimension addresses the governance and leadership of a company. Sustainability topics and issues relevant to this dimension are business ethics, management of the legal and regulatory environment, compliance with all applicable laws, rules, regulations and standards, resolution of conflicts of interest, corruption and bribery, and anti-competitive behavior.

The SASB Conceptual Framework promotes the following sustainability guiding principles:[23]

1. Potential to affect corporate value: Sustainability topics that can or do affect operational and financial performance through revenues and costs, assets and liabilities, and cost of capital or risk profile should be identified, measured, and reported.
2. Investor interest: Sustainability issues that are likely to be interesting to investors should be identified by assessing if a topic emerges from the mixture of information available through the existence of, or potential for, impacts on financial performance and risk.
3. Relevant across an industry: Sustainability topics systemic to an industry and/or represent risks and opportunities unique to the industry that are likely to apply to many of the industry's companies should be included in sustainability reports.
4. Actionable by companies: Sustainability issues, topics, and trends that can be translated into industry-specific topics within the control or influence of individual companies should be considered.
5. Reflective of stakeholder consensus: There should be a consensus among companies and investors that each disclosure topic is reasonably likely to constitute material information for industry-specific companies and stakeholders.
6. Quantitative: Financial ESP and nonfinancial ESG sustainability performance should be measured quantitatively to be recognized and reported. Thus, key performance indicators relevant to both financial ESP and nonfinancial ESG sustainability performance need to be classified, measured, recognized and reported. Some examples of measurable KPIs pertaining to financial ESP are reported earnings, return on assets, growth in earnings, and research and development.
7. Balance: There should be a proper balance between disclosing financial ESP information and nonfinancial ESG sustainability performance information. The integrated sustainability report should provide objective and unbiased KPIs relevant to both financial ESP and nonfinancial ESG sustainability performance.
8. Consistency: Sustainability information, both financial ESP and nonfinancial ESG sustainability performance, should be consistently reported to enable comparability among firms in the same industry and over time.

Corporate Reporting

The Sustainability Accounting Standards Board has developed industry-specific standards for sustainability disclosure.[24] The SASB establishes sustainability accounting standards based on SEC reporting, which mandates material disclosures for many industries in ten sectors as part of mandatory filings with the SEC. The SASB provides a set of industry-specific sustainability accounting standards aimed at assisting companies in disclosing material sustainability information to investors. These standards are tailored to the unique sustainability opportunities and risks of companies across various industries by focusing on: (1) industry-specific guidelines for over 77 industries, ranging from financials to health-care, technology, transportation among others; (2) materiality threshold of disclosing sustainability information that is material to a company's financial performance or condition to enable investors assess the potential impact of ESG factors on a company's long-term value; (3) a set of disclosure topics for each industry, organized into five categories of environmental, social capital, leadership and governance, human capital, and business model and innovation; (4) specific metrics and guidance on how companies can measure, manage, recognize and report relevant sustainability information relevant to carbon emissions, product safety, data privacy, labor practices, board diversity, and supply-chain management; and (5) integration with financial reporting including annual reports, Form 10-K filings, and other financial disclosures to provide investors with a more comprehensive understanding of a company's performance, risks, and opportunities. SASB standards have gained recognition as an effective framework for disclosing financially material sustainability information, adoption by companies, investors, and regulators worldwide, and are now being integrated into the sustainability standards of the ISSB.

The International Sustainability Standards Board as a non-profit organization, was created by the IFRS in 2021 and, by August 2022, integrates the VRF, GRI, SASB, IIRC as a primary sustainability organization in establishing frameworks and standards for sustainability reporting.[25] The ISSB has issued two standards (IFRS S1 and IFRS S2) that improve accountability, trust, and confidence in sustainability matters and create a framework for disclosing sustainability performance information, including the risks and opportunities associated with climate change.[26] IFRS S1 provides disclosure requirements for companies to communicate sustainability-related risks and opportunities to their investors. IFRS S2 establishes specific guidelines relevant to climate-related disclosures and is intended to be used with IFRS S1. ISSB's sustainability reporting standards are akin to IRFS standards to ensure the interconnectedness of corporate reporting tailored to industry-specific details as part of general reporting and emission control targets to be set by entities themselves based on their situation and reporting of progress with reference to those standards. ISSB/IFRS S1 and S2 are designed to establish a global baseline for corporate disclosures by establishing a set of standards to be adopted across several jurisdictions in the next few years. The S1 and S2 rules have garnered global support from 64 jurisdictions to date, with 19 national regulators already consulting on adoption of the recommendations under jurisdictional law. The IFRS S2 Climate-related Disclosures rules are based on the structure and recommendations of the Task Force on Climate-Related Financial Disclosures, which has defined climate reporting globally since the release of its recommendations in 2017. Several disclosure processes to comply with the IFRS S2 standards require organizations to: (1) perform a mapping between their TCFD disclosure with the data points required in IFRS S2; (2) establish a strategy for data gathering to close any gaps that were identified in compliance with S2; (3) consolidate the interoperability and efficiency across leading climate standards (e.g., CSRD, SEC Climate and the California Climate Bills) by avoiding duplication of effort; (4) developing an implementation roadmap w to deliver multiple reporting obligations efficiently of compliance with S2; and (5) communicate the new requirements of both S1 and S2 throughout the organization and value chain, providing upskilling to key stakeholders and developing new processes to capture key data, and disclose them effectively.

These voluntary sustainability reporting initiatives are intended to promote sustainability ESG disclosures that are: (1) transparent in demonstrating a commitment to accountability by disclosing information about the company's sustainability performance, goals, initiatives, and efforts; (2) stakeholder-centric of engaging stakeholders, including shareholders, creditors, customers, employees, suppliers, communities, and NGOs, to assess risks and opportunities associated with ESG and understand their concerns and expectations; (3) informative regarding risk management in providing information about ESG risks and opportunities; (4) companies can better manage these risks, build resilience, and improve long-term performance; (5) value-relevant in enabling companies identify opportunities to create value through sustainability initiatives of innovation in product design, cost savings from resource efficiency, improved relationships with stakeholders and enhanced employee productivity and retention, and assured environmentally friendly efforts, effective corporate governance and fostered trust and reputation in society. Many companies choose to align their voluntary sustainability reporting with internationally recognized standards and frameworks, such as the Global Reporting Initiative), the Sustainability Accounting Standards Board, the Task Force on Climate-related Financial Disclosures, or the IIRC, to enhance credibility and comparability of their reports.

These voluntary reporting initiatives provide a platform and reporting framework for companies to disclose their sustainability goals, track progress, and continuously improve their sustainability performance, demonstrating a commitment to long-term value creation for all stakeholders and responsible business practices. Voluntary sustainability reporting

Corporate Reporting

initiatives and guidelines allow companies flexibility in the type, content and format of their sustainability reports, and they are becoming norms and expectations among investors, consumers, regulators, and other stakeholders. These voluntary sustainability reports are a proactive approach that enables companies to improve ESP and ESG sustainability performance, demonstrate leadership, foster trust and reputation, and contribute to the transition toward a more sustainable, accountable, and responsible global economy and business.

Financial and Nonfinancial Key Performance Indicators

Corporate reporting presented in the previous section is often referred to as sustainability performance reporting, corporate social responsibility, or "multiple-bottom-line" reporting and reflects the role of corporations in society and the disclosure of their accountability to all stakeholders. Corporate reporting focuses on both financial and nonfinancial key performance indicators to ensure corporations are held accountable to all stakeholders and fulfill their responsibility in managing their affairs fairly and transparently. In recent years, both mandatory and voluntary sustainability initiatives have been developed to promote business sustainability and to advance sustainability from greenwashing and branding to a business imperative since investors demand, regulators require, and companies report their sustainability performance information. Corporate success stories can be measured and disclosed through key performance indicators. KPIs can be prepared for both financial and nonfinancial activities to present a company's progress toward achieving its goals. KPIs should reflect a company's strategic mission and goals and how these goals are measured and achieved. KPIs should communicate key activities used by the board of directors and officers in managing an organization, such as achieving the desired return on investment for shareholders, maximizing customer satisfaction or attracting and retaining the best and most talented employees. The extent and types of both financial and nonfinancial KPIs can vary among companies, their peers, industries, and countries, with one overriding determinant of being relevant to the company and its operations. For example, KPIs most relevant to the petroleum industry are exploration success rate, refinery capacity and utilization, reserve resources and related replacement costs. In contrast, for the banking industry, the most common KPIs are deposits and assets under management, loans and loan loss provisions, capital adequacy, and asset quality. The number of KPIs depends on the type and size of the business and its strategy, mission, goals, and activities, with at least one KPI for each major activity and sometimes multiple KPIs for each of the five EGSEE dimensions of sustainability performance. The guiding principles for the relevant KPIs are their linkage to corporate strategies, precise definitions, and measurements, intended purposes, benchmarks, sources, interpretations, assumptions, and limitations. KPIs should be forward-looking to identify, measure, and disclose trends, drivers, and factors relevant to stakeholders, particularly investors' assessment of current and future ESP and ESG sustainability performance dimensions and their association with sustainability risks and opportunities. The Balanced Scorecard, as a strategic management system, can be used to relate financial KPIs to nonfinancial KPIs and their integrated link to business strategy using a multidimensional set of financial and nonfinancial performance metrics.

Integrated Sustainability Reporting

Corporate reporting in the past two decades has evolved from the focus of financial reporting of economic performance to sustainability reporting of all five EGSEE dimensions of sustainability performance. The true measure of success for corporations should be determined not only by their reported earnings but also by their governance, social responsibility, ethical behavior, and environmental performance. Business sustainability has received considerable attention from policymakers, regulators, and the business and investment community over the past decade and is expected to remain the main theme for decades to come. Sustainability theories, standards, policies, programs, activities, risk management, and best practices presented in the previous chapters of this book should assist business organizations worldwide with the integration of the five EGSEE dimensions of sustainability performance into their management processes in order to improve their KPIs as well as the quality of financial and nonfinancial sustainability information disseminated to their stakeholders.

The concept of sustainability performance suggests that management must extend its focus beyond maximizing short-term shareholder profit by considering the impact of its operation and entire value chain on all stakeholders, including the community, society, and the environment. Disclosure of EGSEE dimensions of sustainability performance while signaling management's commitment to sustainability and establishing legitimacy with all constituencies poses a cost-benefit trade-off with implications for investors and business organizations. In creating stakeholder value, management should identify potential social, environmental, governance, and ethical issues of concern and integrate them into their strategic planning and managerial processes. There are many reasons and justifications for why management should integrate sustainability performance into its processes and practices, including the pressure of the labor movement, the development of moral values and social standards, and the change in public opinion about the role of businesses in environmental matters, governance, and ethical scandals. Companies which are, or aspire to be, leaders in sustainability are challenged by rising public expectations, ever-increasing innovation, continuous quality improvement, effective governance measures, high standards of ethics and integrity, and heightened social and environmental problems. Thus, management should develop and maintain proper sustainability programs that provide a common framework for the integration of all five EGSEE dimensions of sustainability into their management processes consisting of:

- Establishment of financial and nonfinancial KPIs relevant to all five EGSEE dimensions of sustainability performance that support management's strategic decisions and actions.
- Integration of financial and nonfinancial sustainability KPIs into the business and investment analysis, supply-chain management, and decision-making process.
- Communication of the company's management sustainability strategies, practices, and expectations to major stakeholders, including suppliers and customers, to mitigate risks and foster corporate values and culture.
- Continuous assessment of the company's sustainability initiatives and related managerial processes to monitor and improve sustainability performance and identify challenging areas and risks that need further improvements.
- Promotion of product innovation and quality, customer retention and attraction, employee satisfaction, talent attraction, and productivity through management sustainability processes.
- Development of environmental, social, ethical, and governance initiatives that will impact the company's ability to generate sustainable financial performance for shareholders and create value for all stakeholders.
- Development of integrated sustainability reports to ensure that relevant financial and nonfinancial sustainability performance information is disclosed to all stakeholders.
- Periodic certifications of both financial and nonfinancial sustainability KPIs, issuance of integrated sustainability reports and securing external assurance reports on all five EGSEE dimensions of sustainability performance.

The global trend toward business sustainability performance, reporting, and assurance encourages and rewards companies that focus on financial ESP and nonfinancial ESG dimensions of sustainability performance and disclose their sustainability performance in sustainability reports with assurance. Taken together, the persistent challenges of maintaining sustainability have been the proper identification, measurement, recognition, reporting, and assurance of financial and nonfinancial KPIs. Examples of these challenges and solutions, according to a 2018 report by BSR, are:[27]

1. Multiple Reporting Framework: Frameworks are the backbone of sustainability and reporting. When several frameworks are being applied at once, it can cause confusion and lead to errant reporting. The solution to this challenge is the Corporate Reporting Dialogue, which reconciles differences between reporting frameworks. The use of multiple frameworks under this method is preferable to a single framework.

2. Volume and Rankings: Requests for information can lead to problems regarding materiality disclosure of material matters, time spent to respond, and value of disclosure. The solution is to provide all necessary information in one report so additional inquiries would not need to be made.

3. Multiple Target Audiences: The need to address multiple audiences with a single sustainability report proves to be a challenge due to differing expectations. The solution is to break down the report into categories based on the audience to address concerns. These categories include social issues, investor type, and privacy.

4. Increasing Depth of Expertise: It is difficult to issue a sustainability report that addresses the expertise of the issues at hand. To address this issue, the reports should be segmented by other frameworks, such as the UNGP's Human Rights framework. These should be listed separately from the report.

5. Differing Definitions of Materiality: Using the materiality threshold can be confusing to companies and investors. It is difficult to measure materiality when it comes to sustainability and in many regulatory environments, including the United States, material information is required to be disclosed in mandatory filings. Therefore, the use of the word "material" for other purposes in other disclosures may expose firms to litigation. In order to address this issue, the term *relevance* should be substituted for materiality in voluntary sustainability reports.

6. Sustainability Reporting Strategy: Multiple requests for change can result in reactive changes rather than proactive ones. The solution to this challenge is to establish multiyear strategies that address the requests in a timely manner while being ahead of the demands of consumers of the reports.

Sustainability reporting is essential for promoting transparency, accountability, and responsible business practices by providing stakeholders with the information they need to assess an organization's economic performance and impact on society and the environment and make informed decisions. Policymakers, regulators, investors, and consumers recognize the importance of sustainability disclosures in evaluating organizations' long-term viability, sustainability, and resilience. Effective, robust, and comprehensive sustainability reporting involves communicating an organization's economic, governance, environmental, and social impacts accurately, reliably, and transparently to all its stakeholders. Management should design, implement, and maintain proper sustainability reporting processes and

Integrated Sustainability Reporting

strategies that provide a common ground for the integration of sustainability into the corporate culture, business environment, strategic plans, and supply-chain that consist of:

- Utilizing all capital from strategic to financial, reputational, human, manufactured, social, environmental, and compliance to ensure accountability and stewardship for all capital as presented in Chapter 10.
- Presenting environmental disclosure as required by the SEC 2024 new rules, including the carbon footprint of reporting on greenhouse gas emissions and efforts to reduce them and reporting natural resource usage of water and energy consumption.
- Disclosing of social issues, work environment, and diversity, including labor practices, human rights, and community impact.
- Disclosing of governance matters, including corporate governance structure under the stakeholder primacy governance model presented in Chapter 4, including board fiduciary duties, composition and diversity, risk management, and ethical business practices.
- Engaging with stakeholders, including shareholders, creditors, customers, employees, suppliers, and communities, to understand their sustainability concerns and expectations.
- Integration of continuous improvement strategies for both financial ESP and nonfinancial ESG sustainability performance into the business environment, corporate culture and investment analysis, supply-chain management, and decision-making process.
- Establishing a tone at the top commitment by the company's board of directors and executives to the effective and robust application of sustainability best practices in managing sustainability issues, including environmental, human rights, and social issues across the operations and supply chains.
- Establishing robust and measurable sustainability targets and goals aligned with the profit-with-purpose mission and present progress toward achieving these goals and targets.
- Developing a long-term and sustainable relationship with all stakeholders. Collaboration among all stakeholders to enhance the effectiveness of implementing sustainability programs and development, including strategies for creating shared value for all stakeholders, is important in developing such relationships.
- Developing sustainable supply-chain management strategies for identifying and selecting suppliers that focus on achieving their sustainability performance by integrating sustainability into all aspects of business, including the supply chain from purchasing and inbound logistics, production design, and manufacturing processes to marketing, distribution, outbound logistics, and customer services.

- Communicating the company's sustainability strategies, practices, and expectations to major stakeholders, suppliers, and customers to mitigate risks and foster corporate values and culture. Failure to address sustainability issues (e.g., human rights, social, and environmental) can create the risk of litigation and damage to brand value and reputation, particularly as supply chains relevant to materials and labor have shifted to emerging markets. Tell your sustainability story in plain language to ensure the report is understandable and comprehensive, providing valuable and relevant information.
- Preparing an integrated sustainability report reflecting both material ESP and ESG sustainability performance and obtaining assurance statements on the sustainability report from third-party assurance providers to enhance the reliability and credibility of sustainability information.

Sustainability Assurance

Assurance providers play an important role in lending credibility to sustainability reports on ESP and ESG dimensions of sustainability performance. Objectivity, reliability, transparency, credibility, and usefulness of sustainability reports are important to both internal and external users of the reports and can be enhanced by providing assurance on sustainability reports. Sustainability assurance can be provided internally by internal auditors or external assurance providers. While internal auditors are well qualified to assist management in the preparation and assurance of sustainability reports, external users of sustainability reports may demand more independent and objective assurance of sustainability reports. This type of assurance can be provided by certified public accountants (CPAs), professional assurance providers, or equivalently accredited individuals, groups, or institutes. Current auditing standards are intended to provide reasonable assurance on financial and internal control reports prepared by management. However, the degree of reliance placed on non-financial information, such as sustainability reporting, is not clear. Assurance standards on different dimensions of sustainability performance reports vary in terms of rigorousness and general acceptability. For example, auditing standards governing reporting and assurance on economic activities presented in the financial statements are well established, widely accepted and practiced. Assurance standards on other dimensions of sustainability, including governance, ethics, social, and environmental standards, have yet to be fully developed and globally accepted.

An integrated model for assurance on both ESP and ESG dimensions of sustainability performance reporting is desirable. Auditing standards published by the Public Company Accounting Oversight Board (PCAOB) are relevant to the economic dimension of sustainability in auditing financial statements and internal controls over financial reporting. Two recent standards released by the International Auditing and Assurance Standards Board (IAASB), namely the International Standard on Assurance Engagements "Other Than Audits or Reviews of Historical Financial Information" 3000 (ISAE 3000) and ISAE 3410 (Assurance Engagements on Greenhouse Gas Statements) can be used for each dimension of EGSEE sustainability.[28] This integrated model provides the policy guideline with practical and educational implications for employing EGSEE reporting and auditing. In 2017, the AICPA issued the AICPA Guide: "Attestation Engagements on Sustainability Information Guide (Including Greenhouse Gas Emissions Information)." The growth of sustainability reporting use and its potential to raise important assurance issues related to sustainability reporting will be very important in the future.

Recognition of the growing number of assurance services seems apparent from the issuance of assurance practice guidance statements published by influential bodies such as AccountAbility,[29] the Global Reporting Initiative,[30] and the European Federation of Accountants.[31] Two important sources of guidance on the assurance of sustainability reporting, each released in 2003, are provided by AccountAbility's AA1000 and the IAASB's International Standard on Assurance Engagement (ISAE) 3000. The AA1000 assurance standards provide guidelines for an assurance engagement by assurance providers from outside the accounting profession, while ISAE 3000 guides an assurance engagement for members of the accounting profession. The International Standards on Assurance Engagements (ISAE) 3000 (issued by the IAAS Board in 2004), the AICPA's Attestation Standards (AT Section 101), CICA section 5025 and AA1000 Assurance Standards (AS) (issued in 2008 by AccountAbility (AA)) guide assurance on nonfinancial dimensions of sustainability.[32]

External assurance is an important part of integrated sustainability reporting, as assurance providers verify the information contained in the reports and publish those conclusions so that others, generally less experienced in the particular dimensions in which said assurance providers have expertise, may be assured that the practices faithfully confirm the statements made by management. The G4 Guideline states that assurance providers must:

- Be independent of the organization and therefore able to reach and publish an objective and impartial opinion or conclusions on the report.
- Be demonstrably competent in both the subject matter and assurance practices.
- Apply quality control procedures to the assurance engagement.
- Conduct the engagement in a manner that is systematic, documented, evidence-based, and characterized by defined procedures.

- Assess whether the report provides a reasonable and balanced presentation of performance, taking into consideration the veracity of the data in the report as well as the overall selection of content.

- Assess the extent to which the report preparer has applied the Guidelines in the course of reaching his conclusions.

- Issue a written report that is publicly available and includes an opinion or set of conclusions, a description of the responsibilities of the report preparer and the assurance provider, and a summary of the work performed to explain the nature of the assurance conveyed by the assurance report.[33]

Numerous bodies have developed methodologies and standards for external assurance for global, regional, and country-specific audiences. Many of these bodies come in the form of trade associations of accountants, engineers, and other professionals who come together to write standards that will raise the quality of their respective industries.[34] As reporting becomes more nuanced, there will be somewhat of a reckoning for companies. Those who have not been disclosing their issues well may see a downtick in their equity capital as investors realize there are more liabilities than previously thought. Conversely, those who receive good marks from external assurance providers may see an uptick in their value as investors find that there is less risk than previously perceived. One of the benefits of having external assurance is that companies will be forced to deal with issues previously unforeseen (perhaps even by the companies themselves) and improve their procedures accordingly. Those who use this as an opportunity to grow will be rewarded accordingly in general, while those who do not will suffer. From an overall market perspective, this will help the product and security markets to become more efficient and, all else being equal, more profitable to those with the best practices. The sustainability assurance framework can be developed to provide sustainability assurance on both financial ESP and nonfinancial ESG sustainability performance dimensions reports. It can be classified into distinct sections or reports based on the degree of assurance and content as follows:

I. Positive and reasonable assurance on financial statements reflecting financial economic sustainability performance.

II. Positive and reasonable assurance on internal control over financial reporting (ICFR), as related to the economic dimension of sustainability performance.

III. Negative and limited assurance on sustainability reports pertaining to the nonfinancial ESG dimensions of sustainability performance.

IV. Materiality assessment of both financial ESP and nonfinancial ESG sustainability performance disclosures.

Sustainability Assurance

Sustainability assurance statements are reports issued by business organizations to provide stakeholders with assurance regarding the accuracy, objectivity, and reliability of their sustainability reports on both ESP and ESG dimensions of sustainability performance. These statements are usually prepared by independent third-party assurance providers, including audit firms or specialized sustainability consultants, and they aim to enhance the credibility, objectivity, and transparency of an organization's sustainability performance reports. The sustainability assurance statement typically includes the following components and paragraphs: (1) an introductory paragraph of outlining the purpose and scope of the assurance engagement, explaining the responsibilities of both the organization and the assurance provider including the responsibilities of management in preparing the sustainability report and the responsibilities of the assurance provider in conducting the assurance engagement and specifying the reporting period covered by the sustainability report being assured; (2) a scope paragraph of specifying the criteria against which the organization's sustainability performance is evaluated including international standards such as the GRI, SASB, ISSB standards, or other relevant frameworks; (3) an assurance scope of defining the scope of the assurance engagement, including the specific aspects of the sustainability report that were subject to assurance procedures; (4) an assurance methodology paragraph of describing the methodology used by the assurance provider to assess the organization's sustainability performance including details of sampling techniques, data verification procedures, interviews conducted, and any other relevant assurance procedures; (5) assurance findings and conclusion paragraph of presenting findings based on the assurance procedures performed, any material discrepancies or areas of concern identified during the assurance engagement, and the conclusion reached regarding an overall assessment of the reliability and accuracy of the organization's sustainability report; (6) an assurance Limitations paragraph of outlining any limitations or constraints encountered during the assurance engagement to assist stakeholders understand the scope and boundaries of the assurance provided; (7) an assurance opinion paragraph of expressing an opinion on the organization's sustainability report that could range from unqualified (meaning the report is reliable and transparent) to qualified or adverse (suggesting significant issues, deficiencies, noncompliance or limitations); (8) assurance statement date and signatures section, which is dated and signed by the responsible assurance providers confirming their independence and compliance with relevant professional standards. Sustainability assurance statements play an essential role in lending more credibility to sustainability reports to build trust and confidence among stakeholders by providing independent verification of an organization's sustainability performance and disclosures. The sustainability assurance statement demonstrates a commitment to transparency, reliability, objectivity and accountability in addressing ESG issues.

Sustainability Disclosure Metrics and Ratings

Sustainability disclosure metrics are measures and critical indicators that organizations can use to communicate their ESG factors of planning, performance, risk, and impacts to all affected stakeholders. These metrics are essential for disclosing accuracy, transparency, accountability, and sustainability practices. Sustainability disclosure metrics should apply to companies in all industries to demonstrate a commitment to achieving a comprehensive methodology that applies to all companies and is suitably adapted for each industry. Sustainability disclosure metrics should use a combination of quantitative-structured and qualitative-unstructured data in developing ESG sustainability rankings and scores. Nonfinancial ESG and financial ESP metrics should be used as benchmarks against which ESG sustainability performance is evaluated, and these metrics are often disclosed by a company to internal and external stakeholders. Some of these metrics can be industry-specific, others relate to socioeconomic factors or macroeconomic matters and can vary across businesses and industries. Sustainability disclosure metrics tend to vary from business to business and from industry to industry. The existing management discussion and analysis (MD&A) disclosures are the starting point for developing sustainability disclosure metrics. However, they may need to adjust to industry specifics or sustainability matters unrelated to finances.

Public companies can be evaluated based on their sustainability performance and practices. Sustainability ratings are opinions of professional organizations and individual experts on the relative standing of a company's sustainability performance and practices as well as compliance with designated sustainability standards and guidelines and best practices relevant to other companies in the same industry, country or internationally. Sustainability ratings are intended to serve as a benchmark in providing credible and independent assessments of the quality and quantity of a company's corporate governance and suggestions for further improvements as well as proper information to stakeholders regarding the extent of a company's sustainability performance, reporting and assurance. Several professional organizations, including the Global Initiative for Sustainability Ratings (GISR), have developed ESG rating standards to demonstrate maximum agreement with leading, complementary standard-setters.

These ratings reflect sustainability performance, reporting assurance, risk disclosures, and financial impacts. These ratings differentiate companies with a high rating as a proxy for superior sustainability from those with a low rating as a proxy for inferior sustainability performance. Thus, high ratings can assist corporations in raising public funds, improving reputation/image/credibility, enhancing valuation, enabling listing or continued listing on stock exchanges, and ensuring transparent relationships with shareholders and other non-shareholding stakeholders. Many stock exchanges worldwide have developed and implemented sustainability measures, including indices, to provide guidance to the investors, or the listed companies themselves. Currently, there are 25 sustainability-related indices around the world that are operational. Some of the leading stock exchanges that have such indices include the New York Stock Exchange (NYSE), Bombay Stock Exchange (BSE), Nasdaq, London Stock Exchange, Euronext, Australian Securities Exchange, and Shanghai Stock Exchange, among others.

These agencies offer a variety of ranking services to the market. For example, Bloomberg, FTSE Russell, the CDP, and MSCI offer sustainability rankings on the composite ESG and each component of environmental, social, and governance. Alternatively, EcoVadis offers specialized raking on supply-chain sustainability. Thomson Reuters and BlackRock initially created Refinitiv in 2018 and sold it to the London Stock Exchange. Vigeo-Eiris, a rating agency, was recently acquired by Moody's, whereas Morningstar acquired a 40% stake in Sustainalytics in 2017. Obtaining sustainability ratings and rankings by disclosure of financial ESP and nonfinancial ESG sustainability performance information is very relevant and beneficial to shareholders in comparing sustainability standings of public companies and in making sound investment and voting decisions. Other stakeholders also benefit from public disclosures of sustainability rankings and scores.

Companies typically use these ratings and rankings to showcase their sustainability efforts and often are greenwashing to attract socially responsible investors. Sustainability ranking organizations use methodologies that can vary among rating agencies, and thus, companies may be assessed based on different criteria depending on the evaluations that emerge over time. However, several costs associated with public disclosure of sustainability information should be considered by public companies and their directors and officers. First, the direct cost of producing sustainability reports, obtaining assurance on sustainability reports and submitting these reports to the sustainability rating organizations. The second cost is the opportunity cost of managerial time and efforts sent on sustainability disclosures and their public rankings. Finally, proprietary costs of submitting sustainability information to external ranking organizations and the disclosure risk when the firm reveals valuable information, such as information about profitable customers and markets, the revelation of trade secrets, or the exposure of operating, organization, or reporting weakness to competitors, unions, regulators, investors, customers, suppliers and/or other stakeholders.

Summary

Conventional corporate reports do not effectively present sustainability information and corporate accountability to all stakeholders. Future corporate reporting should disseminate high-quality financial and nonfinancial information relevant to all five EGSEE dimensions of sustainability performance to enable corporate stakeholders to make sound decisions in protecting their stakes and interests in the company. All relevant information pertaining to the five EGSEE dimensions of sustainability performance can be incorporated into one report commonly known as the "integrated report." This integrated report can be prepared in compliance with the guidelines of G4 of the GRI or other globally accepted frameworks (IIRC, SASB), be forward-looking and present both the financial and nonfinancial KPIs discussed in this chapter. Integrated sustainability reporting and assurance has made steady progress worldwide during the past decade, and it is expected that the mandatory reporting of ESG sustainability in Europe will lead to global acceptance.

Key Points

1. Corporate reports should be comprehensive and relevant in portraying both financial and nonfinancial information on all five EGSEE dimensions of sustainability performance to all stakeholders.
2. Corporate reporting should be aligned with communication strategy and improve relationships with all key stakeholders.
3. Sustainability managers have more incentives to focus on financial sustainability performance that can create tangible shareholder value (return on investment) than social investment with less tangible outcomes.
4. Sustainability managers should use the balanced scorecard to link nonfinancial KPIs to financial KPIs and their integrated impacts on achieving the organization's objectives in creating sustainable value for all stakeholders.
5. Management should ensure the incorporation of sustainability development into decision-making, planning, implementation, and evaluation processes.
6. Expand and redesign corporate reporting to sustainability and accountability with a keen focus on supporting the information needs of long-term investors regarding sustainable performance as well as performance in environmental, social, governance and ethics.

Review Questions

1. Why is sustainability reporting considered an integral component of corporate accountability and responsibility?
2. What is the role of third-party assurance in sustainability reports?
3. What are the two ESG reporting regimes mentioned in the text?
4. What are some sustainability topics covered by mandatory sustainability reporting requirements?
5. How does voluntary sustainability reporting benefit businesses?
6. What does the SASB sustainability framework consist of?
7. What is the focus of the ISSB's IFRS S2 Climate-related Disclosures rules?
8. What are some examples of environmental KPIs listed in the text?
9. What does sustainability performance suggest about management's focus?
10. What is sustainability assurance?
11. What are the components of a typical sustainability assurance statement?
12. What is the purpose of sustainability ratings?
13. What does Bloomberg's ESG data offer?
14. What does the International Integrated Reporting Council (IIRC) framework focus on?
15. What are some key points for effective sustainability reporting and assurance?

Discussion Questions

1. Why is sustainability reporting important for businesses?
2. What does financial capital include?
3. How does human capital contribute to business sustainability?
4. What are the main components of operational capital?
5. Why is technological capital significant for business sustainability?
6. What is the role of sustainability reporting?
7. What are the components of social capital?
8. What is the importance of integrating environmental considerations into decision-making processes?
9. What is strategic capital?
10. How does natural capital impact business sustainability?
11. Why is investment in human capital important for long-term business sustainability?

12. **What is the role of social capital in business sustainability?**
13. **What is the significance of efficient utilization of financial capital?**
14. **What are the main components of human capital?**
15. **Why is it crucial to preserve natural capital for businesses?**

Multiple Choice Questions

1. **Why is sustainability reporting considered an integral component of corporate accountability and responsibility?**
   A) Because it focuses solely on financial performance
   B) Because it reflects both financial and nonfinancial sustainability performance
   C) Because it is voluntary
   D) Because it is mandated by law

2. **What does financial capital include?**
   A) Equity, debt, retained earnings, and grants
   B) Marketing budgets and sales revenue
   C) Human resources and intellectual property
   D) Environmental impact assessments

3. **How does human capital contribute to business sustainability?**
   A) Through education, skills, knowledge, training, health, and well-being of the workforce
   B) By increasing marketing spend
   C) Through short-term profits
   D) By focusing on cost-cutting

4. **What are the main components of operational capital?**
   A) Marketing budget and brand image
   B) Cash flow and cash management, working capital, inventory management, cost management, benefits management, operating expenses, and contingency funds
   C) Sales strategies and customer loyalty programs
   D) Social media presence and online reviews

5. **Why is technological capital significant for business sustainability?**
   A) It has no impact on sustainability
   B) It contributes to improving efficiency, addressing environmental issues, and enhancing both financial and environmental sustainability performance
   C) It only affects marketing strategies
   D) It reduces operational costs

6. **What is the role of sustainability reporting?**

   A) To effectively and transparently communicate organizations' financial economic sustainability performance (ESP) and nonfinancial environmental social and governance (ESG) sustainability to their stakeholders

   B) To focus only on short-term profits

   C) To reduce marketing budgets

   D) To focus solely on operational costs

7. **What are the components of social capital?**

   A) Tangible assets like machinery and buildings

   B) Norms and values, trust, networks and connections, community engagements, and reciprocity

   C) Financial resources and market share

   D) Marketing strategies and customer loyalty

8. **What is the importance of integrating environmental considerations into decision-making processes?**

   A) It has no impact

   B) It is important for economic growth and sustainable development

   C) It only affects marketing strategies

   D) It reduces operational costs

9. **What is strategic capital?**

   A) Short-term financial gains

   B) Management's strategic planning, decisions, and actions reflecting the organization's purpose, mission, values, goals, and action plans

   C) Only marketing strategies

   D) Only customer service initiatives

10. **How does natural capital impact business sustainability?**

    A) It has no impact

    B) It provides essential resources for long-term business success and environmental stewardship

    C) It only affects marketing strategies

    D) It reduces operational costs

11. **Why is investment in human capital important for long-term business sustainability?**

    A) To enhance productivity, innovation, and employee satisfaction

    B) To increase marketing spend

    C) To focus on short-term profits

D) To reduce operational costs

12. **What is the role of social capital in business sustainability?**
    A) To create economic development, social networks, and community well-being
    B) To increase marketing spend
    C) To focus on short-term profits
    D) To reduce operational costs

13. **What is the significance of efficient utilization of financial capital?**
    A) To increase marketing spend
    B) To ensure economic efficiency and development
    C) To focus on short-term profits
    D) To reduce employee turnover

14. **What are the main components of human capital?**
    A) Tangible assets like machinery and buildings
    B) Education, skills, knowledge, training, health, and well-being
    C) Financial resources and market share
    D) Marketing strategies and customer loyalty

15. **Why is it crucial to preserve natural capital for businesses?**
    A) To ensure the availability of resources for current and future production and miti-gate environmental risks
    B) To increase marketing spend
    C) To focus on short-term profits
    D) To reduce operational costs

16. **What are the benefits of sustainability performance reporting and assurance?**
    A) To increase marketing budgets
    B) To provide management and stakeholders with improved confidence in the cred-ibility and trustworthiness of sustainability information
    C) To focus on short-term profits
    D) To reduce operational costs

17. **What are some examples of financial KPIs?**
    A) Customer satisfaction and brand loyalty
    B) Revenues earned, resources consumed, costs recognized, capital raised, and financial risk assessed
    C) Marketing strategies and sales growth
    D) Online reviews and social media presence

18. **What is integrated sustainability reporting?**

A) Reporting only financial performance

B) Reporting all five EGSEE dimensions of sustainability performance in a comprehensive manner

C) Reporting only governance practices

D) Reporting marketing strategies

19. **What should management do to integrate sustainability performance into its processes?**

A) Increase marketing budgets

B) Establish financial and nonfinancial KPIs, integrate these KPIs into decision-making, communicate sustainability strategies, and continuously assess and improve sustainability performance

C) Focus solely on short-term profits

D) Reduce operational costs

20. **Why is external assurance important for sustainability reports?**

A) To increase marketing spend

B) To enhance the reliability and credibility of sustainability information for both internal and external stakeholders

C) To focus on short-term profits

D) To reduce operational costs

21. **What are sustainability disclosure metrics?**

A) Only financial performance indicators

B) Measures and indicators used to communicate ESG factors of planning, performance, risk, and impacts to stakeholders

C) Only governance practices

D) Only marketing strategies

22. **What are some leading stock exchanges that have sustainability-related indices?**

A) Only New York Stock Exchange

B) New York Stock Exchange, Bombay Stock Exchange, Nasdaq, London Stock Exchange, Euronext, and Australian Securities Exchange

C) Only London Stock Exchange

D) Only Euronext

23. **What is the role of the Global Reporting Initiative in sustainability reporting?**

A) To provide guidelines and frameworks for the voluntary reporting of ESG sustainability information

B) To focus solely on financial performance

C) To reduce operational costs

D) To increase marketing spend

24. **What are the five broad categories of the SASB sustainability framework?**

A) Financial, marketing, operational, technological, and reputational

B) Environment, social capital, human capital, business model and innovation, and leadership and governance

C) Only governance practices

D) Only marketing strategies

25. **What is the role of corporate reporting in the context of sustainability?**

A) To focus solely on short-term profits

B) To provide investors and stakeholders with transparent, reliable, and relevant financial and nonfinancial information

C) To increase marketing spend

D) To reduce operational costs

26. **What is the purpose of the EU Corporate Sustainability Reporting Directive (CSRD)?**

A) To increase short-term profits

B) To increase transparency in sustainability reporting and contribute to long-term economic growth and employment

C) To reduce marketing spend

D) To focus solely on operational costs

27. **What are some examples of environmental KPIs?**

A) Customer satisfaction and brand loyalty

B) Disclosure of gigajoules of total energy consumed, metric tons of total CO_2 emitted, and risk exposure to climate changes

C) Marketing strategies and sales growth

D) Online reviews and social media presence

28. **What does sustainability performance suggest about management's focus?**

A) Management must focus solely on short-term shareholder profit

B) Management must extend its focus beyond maximizing short-term shareholder profit by considering the impact of its operations on all stakeholders

C) Management must increase marketing spend

D) Management must reduce operational costs

29. **What is sustainability assurance?**

A) A process of reducing marketing spend

Multiple Choice Questions

B) A process of providing credibility to sustainability reports through verification by independent third-party assurance providers

C) A process of focusing on short-term profits

D) A process of reducing operational costs

30. **What are the components of a typical sustainability assurance statement?**

A) Financial resources and market share

B) Introductory paragraph, scope paragraph, assurance methodology, findings and conclusion, limitations, assurance opinion, and statement date and signatures

C) Marketing strategies and customer loyalty

D) Online reviews and social media presence

Notes

1 Much of the discussion in this chapter comes from Rezaee, Z. (2021). *Corporate Sustainability: Shareholder Primacy Versus Stakeholder Primacy.* Business Expert Press, Chapter 2, and Rezaee, Z. (2024). *The Sustainable Business Blueprint: Planning, Performance, Risk, Reporting and Assurance.* Routledge/Taylor and Francis, Chapter 6

2 Ernst &Young (EY). (2014). Disclosure effectiveness: What investors, company executives and other stakeholders are saying. https://www.eyjapan.jp/library/issue/us/gaap-weekly -update/pdf/GAAP-2014-11-25-03.pdf

3 Rezaee, Z. (2015). *Business Sustainability: Performance, Compliance, Accountability and Integrated Reporting.* Greenleaf Publishing Limited.

4 European Commission. (2014). Disclosure of non-financial information: Europe information: Europe Council, the European Economic and Social, environmental issues. http://ec.europa .eu/internal_market/accounting/non-financial_reporting/index_en.htm (retrieved March 29, 2016).

5 Hong Kong Stock Exchange (HKEx). (2015, January 13) Appendix 27 Environmental, social and governance reporting guide. http://www.hkex.com.hk/eng/rulesreg/listrules/mbrules /documents/appendix_27.pdf

6 Securities and Exchange Commission (SEC). (2022). SEC proposes rules to enhance and standardize climate-related disclosures for investors (March 21, 2023). https://www.sec .gov/news/press-release/2022-46 and SEC final Rules (2024). The enhancement and standardization of climate-related disclosures for investors, https://www.sec.gov/files/ rules/final/2024/33-11275.pdf

7 European Union (EU) Directive 2014/95/EU. Directive 2014/95/EU of the European Parliament and of the Council amending Directive 2013/34/EU as regards disclosure of non-financial and diversity information by certain large undertakings and groups. https:// eur-lex.europa.eu/legalcontent/EN/TXT/PDF/?uri=CELEX:32014L0095&from=EN

8 European Commission (EC). (2023). The Corporate Sustainability Reporting Directive (CSRD) (January 5, 2023). https://finance.ec.europa.eu/capital-markets-union-and-financial-markets/company-reporting-and-auditing/company-reporting/corporate-sustainability-reporting_en

9 European Commission (EC). (2023). The Commission adopts the European sustainability reporting standards (July 31, 2024). https://finance.ec.europa.eu/news/commission-adopts-european-sustainability-reporting-standards-2023-07-31_en

10 The International Financial Reporting Standards (IFRS). (2020). Consultation paper on sustainability reporting (September 2020). https://cdn.ifrs.org/-/media/project/sustainability-reporting/consultation-paper-on-sustainability-reporting.pdf

11 Global Reporting Initiative (GRI). (2016). The global standards for sustainability reporting. Global Reporting Initiative: Standards. https://www.globalreporting.org/standards/

12 Global Reporting Initiative. (2021). Universal Standards. Available at https://www.globalreporting.org/standards/standards-development/universal-standards/

13 The International Integrated Reporting Committee (IIRC). (2013). The international framework (December): p. 7. www.theiirc.org/international-ir-framework.

14 The International Integrated Reporting Committee (IIRC). (2013). The international framework (December): p. 2. www.theiirc.org/international-ir-framework.

15 The International Integrated Reporting Committee (IIRC). (2013). The international framework (December): p. 5. www.theiirc.org/international-ir-framework.

16 The International Integrated Reporting Committee (IIRC). (2013). The international framework (December): p. 5. www.theiirc.org/international-ir-framework.

17 KPMG International. (2013). The KPMG survey of corporate responsibility reporting 2013. www.kpmg.com/Global/en/IssuesAndInsights/ArticlesPublications/corporate-responsibility/Documents/corporate-responsibility-reporting-survey-2013-exec-summary.pdf.

18 International Integrated Reporting Council (IIRC). (2021). The international framework. https://integratedreporting.ifrs.org/wp-content/uploads/2021/01/InternationalIntegratedReportingFramework.pdf

19 Sustainability Accounting Standards Board (SASB). The need for SASB. www.sasb.org/sasb/need.

20 Sustainability Accounting Standards Board (SASB). (2018). Current standards (November). https://www.sasb.org/standards-overview/download-current-standards/.

21 Sustainability Accounting Standards Board (SASB). (2018). Current standards (November). https://www.sasb.org/standards-overview/download-current-standards/.

22 Sustainability Accounting Standards Board (SASB). (2018). Current standards (November). https://www.sasb.org/standards-overview/download-current-standards/.

23 Sustainability Accounting Standards Board (SASB). (2017). SASB conceptual framework. www.sasb.org/wp-content/uploads/2017/02/SASB-Conceptual-Framework.pdf.

24 Sustainability Accounting Standards Board (SASB). (2022). SASB standards overview. https://sasb.ifrs.org/standards/?lang=en-us

25 International Sustainability Standards Board (ISSB). (2021). https://www.ifrs.org/groups/international-sustainability-standards-board/

26 International Financial Reporting Standards (IFRS). (2023). ISSB issues inaugural global sustainability disclosure standards (June 26, 2023). https://www.ifrs.org/news-and-events/news/2023/06/issb-issues-ifrs-s1-ifrs-s2/#:~:text=The%20ISSB%20Standards%20are%20designed%20to%20ensure%20that,be%20used%20in%20conjunction%20with%20any%20accounting%20requirements.

27 BSR. (2018). A practitioner's view of sustainability reporting: Challenges and solution (January). https://www.bsr.org/reports/BSR_A_Practitioners_View_of_Sustainability_Reporting_Challenges_and_Solutions.pdf.

28 International Federation of Accountants (IFAC). (2011). The International Standard on Assurance Engagements, "Other Than Audits or Reviews of Historical Financial Information," 3000 (ISAE 3000). Available at www.iaasb.org (accessed May 27, 2016).

29 AccountAbility. (2003). AA1000 Assurance Standard Practitioners Note. AccountAbility, London.

30 Global Reporting Initiative (GRI). (2002). Sustainability reporting guidelines on economic, environmental, and social performance. Global Reporting Initiative, Amsterdam.

31 Fedération des Experts Comptables Européens (FEE). (2002). Providing assurance on sustainability reports. Discussion Paper, Fedération des Experts Comptables Européens, Brussels.

32 Brockett, A., and Rezaee, Z. (2012). *Corporate Sustainability: Integrating Performance and Reporting.* Wiley.

33 Global Reporting Initiative (GRI). (2013). The external assurance of sustainability reporting. www.globalreporting.org.

34 Global Reporting Initiative (GRI). (2013). Carrots and sticks. UNEP, GRI, KPMG, and the Centre for Corporate Governance in Africa. www.globalreporting.org.

Chapter 12
Emerging Issues in Sustainability Factors

Learning Objectives

- Provide an overview of the best practices for sustainability performance reporting and assurance.
- Understand the methodology for generating a proper sustainability report.
- Understand the conditions required for the effective implementation of sustainability.
- Have an overview of the sustainability risk assessment.
- Be aware of the internal control risks.
- Understand the impact of climate change and global warming on business operations.
- Learn sustainability guidelines provided by global professional organizations.
- Describe investment strategies and impact investing strategies.
- Learn the role of technological innovations in enhancing sustainability performance, reporting, and assurance.
- Understand the integration of sustainability in supply-chain management.
- Learn the effectiveness of sustainability reporting frameworks and initiatives.
- Understand the role of sustainability in corporate governance.
- Understand the financial implications of sustainability investments.
- Learn global sustainability initiatives and trends and their impacts on businesses.

Introduction

Business organizations are under scrutiny by regulators and investors worldwide to focus on both financial economic sustainability performance (ESP) and nonfinancial environmental, social, and governance (ESG) sustainability performance in creating shared value for all stakeholders. The corporation's purpose has evolved over the past several decades from profit maximization to shareholder wealth maximization to creating shared value for all stakeholders with the mission of profit-with-purpose.[1] The profit-with-purpose mission can be achieved when corporations focus on generating desired financial returns for their shareholders and achieving social and environmental impacts. while protecting the interests of other stakeholders, including customers, employees, suppliers, communities,

DOI: 10.4324/9781003487081-12

society, and the environment. This chapter focuses on several emerging aspects of business sustainability, including investors' interest in ESG sustainability, the emergence of benefit corporations, supply-chain sustainability, biodiversity accounting and finance, ESG sustainability, and the initial public offerings (IPO) process.

Shareholder Interest in Sustainability

A growing number of investors, including shareholders, are now interested in obtaining sustainability performance information by considering impact investing with a keen focus on financial ESP and nonfinancial ESG sustainability performance in assessing the risks and opportunities associated with ESG efforts. Shareholder interest in sustainability has been growing in recent years as awareness increases about ESG factors of planning, performance, risk, and disclosure that can impact a company's long-term performance and resilience. There are several reasons for shareholders to show more interest in sustainability, including: (1) risk management of ESG issues including climate change, human rights violations, resource scarcity, and labor practices that can pose significant risks to companies; (2) long-term value creation opportunities, understanding that sustainable business practices can lead to improved financial performance over time by reducing costs, enhancing brand reputation, attracting talent, and fostering innovation; (3) consumers, employees, and stakeholder expectations that are important for maintaining customer loyalty, attracting talent, and securing social license to operate; (4) regulatory and legal pressures relevant to labor rights, environmental protection, and corporate governance are compelling companies to adopt more sustainable practices and investors to assess their outcomes; (6) transparency and accountability, as stakeholders are demanding greater transparency and accountability from companies regarding their environmental and social impacts because noncompliance can result in legal and financial penalties and reputational damage. Shareholder interest in sustainability reflects a broader recognition of the link between ESP and ESG components of sustainability performance to address sustainability risks and opportunities associated with ESG in maintaining sustainability.

Business sustainability factors and ESG criteria are now more commonly integrated into the executive incentive plans of S&P 500 firms, witnessing a 23% surge in 2022 bringing the overall prevalence to 70%.[2] Diversity and inclusion and carbon footprint metrics have experienced the most substantial expansion. Investors place high importance on human capital management and environmental concerns, prompting companies to include these metrics in their plans to demonstrate their dedication to ESG objectives. Human capital management metrics currently hold the most vital position, but environmental metrics are also gaining traction, primarily due to pressure from institutional investors and growing awareness of climate change implications.[3]

The impact investment strategy suggests that investors demand a desired rate of return on their investment while they would like to see their companies have social and environmental impacts as well. Prior research provides mixed results regarding the link between financial/market performance and ESG factors of performance, risk, and disclosure.[4] The quality and reliability of public information, both financial ESP and nonfinancial ESG sustainability performance, improve the integrity and efficiency of capital markets. The quality of sustainability disclosures also improves market liquidity by reducing information asymmetry across traders. Sustainability disclosures are expected to affect market liquidity when such disclosures cause information asymmetry that induces adverse selection into share markets. Nonfinancial ESG sustainability disclosures are expected to be value-relevant to both external and internal users of such disclosures. Investors and other stakeholders, including employees, suppliers, customers, the environment, governments, and society, can have more transparent information about ESG performance, which enables them to make more informed decisions. ESG sustainability disclosures can also improve internal management practices by enabling companies to implement their strategic sustainability planning and establish better relationships with investors, customers, suppliers, employees, regulators, society, and the environment.

Investors, including shareholders and bondholders, expect to receive financial ESP information to ensure the desired rate of return on their investments and nonfinancial ESG sustainability information to gauge social and environmental impacts. Based on standardized sustainability reporting and assurance, investors consider sustainability information value-relevant when it is relevant, reliable, and transparent. Investors prefer to receive sustainability ratings, rankings, indexes, and matrixes assured by independent third parties and often consider them when making investment decisions. Investors seek these standardized and assured sustainability disclosures in assessing a company's strategic planning for securing sustainability and its drivers of long-term economic growth and prosperity. The content and format of sustainability disclosures and metrics have been debated and considered among public companies, investors, regulators, and standard-setters. Transparent, qualitative, and quantitative sustainability metrics that are measurable, meaningful, verifiable, generally acceptable, and applicable are value-relevant to retail and institutional investors.

More than 1300 institutional investors worldwide, representing $59 trillion in assets under management, have signed on to the UN Principles of Responsible Investing, which seek to integrate sustainability factors of planning, performance, disclosure, and risk into their investment objectives.[5] Asset managers, like BlackRock, State Street, and Vanguard, are now investing in sustainability-centric companies. Business organizations play a vital economic role by creating jobs, fostering innovation, and providing essential goods and

Shareholder Interest in Sustainability

services. Investors buy their shares and expect desired financial returns when they invest in business organizations. Shareholders are better off when their companies are economically sustainable and generate earnings and cash in the long term. Business sustainability is important to investors in obtaining sustainable returns on their investment, and companies maximize firm value and, thus, shareholder wealth. Shared value creation for all stakeholders can be promoted within the wealth-maximization framework for shareholders to pursue the goal of profit-with-purpose for corporations. Corporations can balance the wealth maximization for shareholders under the shareholder primacy concept while achieving welfare maximization for all stakeholders under the stakeholder primacy concept.

Investor perception regarding the relative importance of ESP and ESG sustainability performance with respect to each other and their contribution to the overall firm's long-term value maximization is affected by whether ESP and ESG are viewed as complementary or conflicting factors. Sustainability performance dimensions (ESP and ESG) can be considered complementary since firms must be financially prominent in the long run to perform well in other sustainability activities (e.g., social and environmental). Economically viable and financially profitable firms are in better positions financially, have more resources to create jobs and wealth, and better fulfill their social and environmental responsibilities. In addition, firms that are committed to corporate social responsibility (CSR), environmental obligations, and effective governance can also be sustainable in generating long-term financial performance. However, it is also possible that investors view these dimensions as conflicting, and a trade-off exists between investing in environmental, CSR, and corporate governance initiatives or business activities that maximize economic profits. Focusing on ESP and ESG sustainability performance enables long-term firm value maximization by creating value for shareholders while meeting the claims of other stakeholders. Sustainability performance pertaining to ESG could improve the relevance and precision of the performance signal and thus result in more informationally efficient stock prices.

In the context of sustainability, current earnings contribute limited useful information for predicting future dividends, and thus, investors must rely on alternate information to secure expected returns on investment in their valuation model. Impact investing, focusing on both financial returns on investment and social and environmental impacts, becomes more critical to investors. However, a growing number of investors are now considering impact investing with a keen focus on financial return and ESG sustainability factors and integrating nonfinancial ESG sustainability factors into their investment strategies.[6] Institutional investors and socially responsible investors have recently shown much interest in business sustainability. Thus, management should recognize this continuous interest in sustainability and its possible impact on the cost of capital. The 2021 survey conducted by the Institutional Shareholder Services (ISS) reveals that:[7]

- The majority of respondents (62.5%) report that ESG factors of performance risk and disclosure have been more relevant to them since the beginning of the COVID-19 pandemic.
- The governance dimension of ESG sustainability is considered the most important ESG factor (86% of respondents) in their investment analysis and stewardship activities.
- The most important drivers of focus on ESG investments in response to the COVID-19 pandemic are client and stakeholder demand, racial inequality and diversity, and regulatory changes.
- Less than half of the respondents (44.1%) expect future ESG ratings to integrate sustainability factors such as diversity and inclusion, workplace safety, treatment of employees, and supply-chain labor dynamics into sustainability rating disclosures.
- More than one-third (37.5%) of respondents have either already added or intend to add new staff to manage ESG-related issues during and in the aftermath of the COVID-19 pandemic.

In summary, investors' interest in and the use of sustainability information by investors has been a growing trend because they increasingly recognize the importance and relevance of ESG factors in assessing the opportunity for long-term performance and risks of their investments. Sustainability disclosures relevant to a company's environmental and social impacts and governance structure can be used by investors to assess the risks and opportunities associated with ESG initiatives and make more informed decisions. Investors use sustainability ESP and ESG information in many ways including: (1) opportunity for investment in long-term ESP and ESG performance as reported by public companies about their long-term financial viability, management of environmental and social issues, and ability to generate sustainable returns over time; (2) risk assessment of analyzing ESG factors to identify potential risks that may impact a company's financial performance, including assessing climate-related risks, regulatory compliance, and supply-chain vulnerabilities; (3) impact investing of achieving desired rates of return on investment while obtaining some social and environmental impacts by aligning financial goals with positive societal or environmental outcomes; (4) investors prefer to engage with companies to promote better sustainability practices, including communicating with company directors and management, voting on ESG-related issues during annual meetings, and involving with shareholder resolutions on sustainability matters; (5) compare and evaluate companies' ESG factors with peers and industry norms based on consistent metrics; (6) compliance assessment of companies' compliance with sustainability-related applicable laws, rules, regulations, and standards; and (7) stakeholder engagement, relationships, and influence that could affect companies' long-term performance, sustainable success, growth, and prosperity.

Shareholder Interest in Sustainability

Board of Directors and Business Sustainability

Corporate directors and executives face new challenges and expectations as they are now expected to address financial health, climate change, and workforce wellness while navigating technology's opportunities and risks. Adaptability and change are keys to success in this dynamic landscape, focusing on impact investing, stakeholder engagement and relationships, ESG factors and considerations, risk assessment and management, growth and innovation, diversity, equity, and inclusion, transparent communication, and fostering a responsible corporate culture. A company's board of directors is essential in overseeing and impacting business sustainability practices and performance. The board is responsible for providing strategic direction and governance, overseeing sustainability efforts, and its decisions can significantly affect a company's sustainability initiatives and accomplishments.

The board of directors, as representatives of shareholders, has traditionally been responsible for protecting the interests of shareholders by overseeing corporate governance, financial reporting, and auditing processes under the shareholder primacy model presented in Chapter 4. The only fiduciary duty of the board of directors under the shareholder primacy model has been to shareholders. Under the emerging stakeholder primacy model, with recent events of perceived social injustice and a move toward diversity, inclusion, and environmental initiatives, the board of directors has assumed fiduciary responsibility to all stakeholders, as discussed in Chapter 4 of the stakeholder primacy model. The current move toward the stakeholder primacy model and recent events, presented in Chapter 4, encourage public companies and their board of directors to: (1) renew interest in the company's mission of profit-with-purpose in defining its purpose in society in providing goods and services that are not detrimental to society and meet basic needs and innovation; (2) holding the board of directors fiduciary responsible to all stakeholders; (3) focus the board's interest in both financial ESP and nonfinancial ESG sustainability performance; (4) address the value of human and social capital and related changes in the nature of work and the workplace; (5) explore social matters, including issues of racial and gender equality and social justice; (6) focus on environmental initiatives and climate change; (7) oversee the assessment and management of all sustainability risks presented in Chapter 9; and (8) hold management responsible for managing all sustainability capitals (financial, human, social, environmental) presented in Chapter 10.

Management and Business Sustainability

The substantial growth in the use of both financial ESP and nonfinancial ESG by investors in making investment decisions encourages business organizations, their board of directors, and management to pay attention to sustainability strategies. Proper attention to all four sustainability factors of planning, performance, risk, and disclosure and effective practices for sustainability strategies enables management to communicate sustainability success stories to all stakeholders, including shareholders. Lack of focus on business sustainability and poor sustainability practices causes management to miss opportunities to adopt robust and comprehensive sustainability strategies to create shared value for all stakeholders. Business organizations, their board of directors, and executives should develop financial ESP and nonfinancial ESG sustainability performance and continuous improvement, consisting of board oversight, strategic alignment, executive monitoring, risk assessment and management, and performance evaluation in promoting and advancing business sustainability. One way to improve the transparency and quality of corporate reporting is through voluntary disclosures on ESG information and related key performance indicators (KPIs). Sustainability KPIs information on products, strategies, plans, forecasted performance, and nonfinancial ESG is gaining momentum. Management plays an important role in corporate reporting, and stakeholders, including shareholders, can view its engagement in both financial ESP issues and nonfinancial ESG activities. Management is willing, able, and capable of producing integrated sustainable performance reporting for all stakeholders.

Management plays an important role in ensuring the effective implementation of sustainability strategic planning and that the company operates economically, environmentally, and socially responsibly, including integrating sustainability principles and factors into the core business strategy, corporate culture, decision-making processes, and daily operations. The top management team in the C-suite is led by the chief executive officer (CEO) in collaboration with other executives, including the chief financial officer (CFO), the controller, the treasurer, and other senior executives who are responsible for managing the organization for the benefit of its stakeholders. Management's primary responsibilities are to achieve operational efficiency and effectiveness, comply with all applicable laws, rules, regulations, and standards, properly assess risk, and fair and true disclosure of both financial ESP and nonfinancial (ESG) sustainability performance information.

Management, under the oversight function of the company's board of directors, is primarily responsible for the development of strategic plans, operational efficiency and effectiveness, compliance with all applicable laws, rules, regulations, and standards, and preparation of reliable financial ESP and nonfinancial ESG reports. The effective fulfillment of management responsibility creates sustainable performance and protects the interests of all stakeholders, including shareholders. Management is responsible for achieving financial ESP and nonfinancial ESG sustainability performance, effectively assessing the related risks, and properly disclosing sustainability financial and nonfinancial information. Those in

Management and Business Sustainability

the C-suite, including the CEO, CFO, Chief Operating Officer, Chief Compliance Officer, Chief Human Resources Officer, Chief Legal Officer or General Counsel, and Chief Sustainability Officer (CSO), should coordinate their efforts and activities to address the emerging move toward business sustainability. Management, under the oversight function of the board of directors, should prioritize a proper balance between investing in human capital and physical and financial capital and oversee managerial strategic plans for implementing investment and allocating resources to various capitals. In collaboration with other executives and overseeing the board of directors, the CFO should consider all possibilities and scenarios under which an organization can survive, recover, and continue sustainable performance. Business risk assessment and supply-chain management can play important roles in recovery. Particularly, the finance function led by the CFO should reevaluate the critical finance processes, including working capital and cash flows, accounts receivable, accounts payable, investment activities, operation cycle, financing activities, financial reporting, filing with regulators, and financial communications with investors.

An integrated sustainability report, reflecting both financial ESP and nonfinancial ESG sustainability performance information prepared by management under the board of directors' oversight function can improve the quality and quantity of the firm's communication and financial reporting with all internal and external stakeholders. First, ESG sustainability disclosures and ratings can improve transparency, enabling more effective monitoring of management to act in the best interest of all stakeholders. Second, increased ESG sustainability disclosures can enable stakeholders (e.g., institutional investors, analysts, creditors, government, suppliers, society, and employees) to develop their own independent and informed views on firms' sustainable performance in all areas of economic, environmental, social, ethical, and governance activities. Third, a focus on sustainability performance encourages management to pursue firm value maximization that benefits all stakeholders, and disclosure of sustainability performance and ratings affects stock prices. Fourth, more transparent sustainability disclosures on long-term economic and ESG performance create opportunities to identify and correct operational inefficiencies and reputational and financial risks that would improve economic performance and thus increase firm value. Finally, market-wide effects of firm sustainability disclosures are also important if the net benefits of issuing sustainability reports at the firm level affect the entire market or if the net benefit is ignored or not fully internalized by firms. Market-wide effects of voluntary sustainability disclosures can be measured in terms of the impact on cost of capital, liquidity, and firm valuation.

Business sustainability enables management to establish synergy and congruence between cost and performance management and integrate sustainability into the business environment, corporate culture, and supply-chain processes. The concept of cost management suggests that management maximizes the utilization of scarce resources to generate revenue and deliver high-quality value to customers to improve performance. The concept of performance management suggests that management strikes a proper balance between short-term and long-term ESP and a trade-off between financial/quantitative ESP and nonfinancial/qualitative ESG sustainability performance. The integrated cost management and performance management concepts under business sustainability suggest that a firm must extend its focus beyond maximizing short-term shareholder profit by considering the impact of its operations on the long-term interests of all stakeholders, including shareholders, creditors, customers, employees, the community, society, and the environment.

Management best sustainability practices suggest the integration of cost management and performance management in promoting the following aspects of sustainability performance:

- Design and implement a company-specific statement of purpose that defines goals and mission and explains how the operations are conducted in producing goods or services.
- Focus on policies and procedures that promote the achievement of financial ESP and nonfinancial ESG sustainability performance.
- Establish managerial policies and procedures to deal with issues of diversity, social justice, and treatment of complaints from employees, customers, and suppliers.
- Assess and manage all sustainability risks from reputational to operational, financial, environmental, and compliance, as presented in Chapter 9.
- Prepare and disseminate an integrated sustainability report presenting both financial ESP and nonfinancial ESG sustainability performance information to all stakeholders.
- Follow developments and trends in both financial ESP and nonfinancial ESG disclosure, including guidelines by professional organizations and standard-setters (GRI, IIRC, SASB), and regulators.
- Ensure employees', customers', and suppliers' safety, health, and well-being in the aftermath of the COVID-19 pandemic.
- Focus on a long-term sustainable strategy to create shared value for all stakeholders.
- Assess how current crises can be addressed to minimize their long-term impacts.

Proper management of both financial ESP and nonfinancial ESG can contribute to sustainability success, and a lack of commitment to sustainability by directors and officers can result in an unsustainable business environment and ongoing concern. The most challenging and problematic practice for sustainability success is the lack of a profit-with-purpose mission and strategy for achieving sustainability.

Chief Sustainability Officer

Effective achievement of both financial ESP and nonfinancial ESG sustainability performance dimensions demands "tone-at-the-top" commitments to business sustainability strategies and actions. Commitment from the board of directors and top executives is essential in effectively coordinating all sustainability strategies and activities and successfully implementing sustainability strategies. Businesses are more likely to achieve their ESG targets when their sustainability leader reports directly to a CEO committed to sustainability initiatives. A CSO is a top-level executive responsible for leading and overseeing sustainability initiatives, efforts, and strategies. The role of a CSO has become increasingly important as businesses integrate sustainability into their overall business strategy, corporate culture, business environment, and operations. Chief Sustainability Officers who are empowered and report to CEOs can drive positive organizational change. To effectively address the company's sustainability initiatives and factors, the board of directors may form a new executive position of "Chief Sustainability Officer" to be responsible for (1) promoting achievement of both ESP and ESG sustainability performance; (2) assessing and managing the ESG-related risks; (3) ensuring compliance with all applicable rules, regulations, and standards to protect the safety and well-being of all stakeholders, particularly customers, suppliers, and employees; (4) managing business continuity; (5) preventing possible disruption in the supply chain; (6) effectively communicating sustainability information. to all stakeholders; and (7) complying with all the growing government guidelines and regulations.

In recent years, there has been an urgent need for the CSO position to be established for C-suite executives of business organizations. The role of the CSO includes:

- Participation with other executives in preparing the "statement of purpose" for the company.
- Developing and implementing the organization's sustainability strategy involves working with other top executives to set goals, define key performance indicators, and align sustainability initiatives with the company's overall business goals and objectives.
- Have a profit-oriented mentality and practice establishing and implementing sustainability policies and procedures to achieve economic viability and prosperity, environmental impact, social responsibility, governance effectiveness, and ethical business conduct.
- Implement the concept of profit-with-purpose by focusing on allocating resources more wisely, managing waste and CO_2 emissions responsibly, acting as a good citizen, and celebrating diversity among workers to support sustainability initiatives, and

investing in technologies, infrastructure, and programs that contribute to sustainability goals.

- Engage with various stakeholders, including shareholders, employees, customers, suppliers, and communities, by building relationships, understanding stakeholder expectations, and finding ways to reach out to new stakeholders or increase participation and communication with existing ones.

- Demonstrate flexibility in new endeavors that seek to increase the company's future growth prospects.

- Communicate effectively to other officers and employees about best practices in sustainability and enforce compliance with them.

- Learn to leverage company strengths, such as technology, manpower, expertise, resources, and market positions, by evaluating the effectiveness of existing initiatives, identifying areas for improvement, and staying informed about emerging sustainability initiatives, trends, and best practices.

- Engaging in long-term strategy and performance involves discussing and shaping long-term business strategies within corporations and having an open, transparent dialogue with investors regarding said strategy.

- Establishing a relationship with shareholders to understand their perspective on the company's strategy, performance, and governance, and leading efforts to assess and improve sustainability performance continuously.

- Implement sustainability standards into strategic and operational plans by collaborating with other executives and external advocacy groups and partnerships to promote sustainability within the company, the industry, and broader society.

- Ensuring compliance with environmental regulations and managing sustainability-related risks are part of the CSO's responsibilities, as well as staying informed about evolving regulations and proactively addressing potential risks to the company.

- Benchmarking a baseline risk appetite for a corporation, setting standards to comply with legal and regulatory initiatives, creating a culture of risk awareness, and implementing that into the decision-making processes.

- Maintaining a relationship with top executives and employees increases the chances of long-term success by monitoring and improving the execution of long-term strategies. This includes fostering a culture of sustainability within the organization, educating employees about sustainability goals, encouraging their participation in initiatives, and integrating sustainability into training and development programs.

- Setting a tone at the top by creating an environment that values high ethics to guide business practices and commits to balancing economic success with environmental and social responsibility.

Management and Business Sustainability

Business Sustainability and Supply-Chain Management

Supply-chain sustainability refers to the integration of environmentally and socially responsible practices throughout the entire supply chain, from sourcing raw materials to distributing finished products. It involves minimizing the negative environmental and social impacts associated with producing and distributing goods while maximizing positive contributions. Technological advances, globalization, and the move toward business sustainability have disrupted traditional supply-chain models and created an evolving landscape of supply-chain strategies, emphasizing the shift from focusing solely on cost and efficiency to considering risk and resilience. A sustainable supply chain requires companies to contemplate more localized sourcing, increased transparency, and digital technology to enhance supply-chain visibility and resilience. Developing the right balance between efficiency and resilience is a complex task, requiring data-driven decision-making and human judgment. The role of boards in overseeing and guiding supply-chain strategies is crucial in achieving a sustainable supply-chain management system.

Business sustainability has become a strategic imperative for corporations worldwide in integrating financial ESP and nonfinancial ESG sustainability performance into their business environment, corporate culture, supply-chain management, and operational models, creating shared value for all stakeholders. Global public companies are adopting proper supply-chain sustainability (SCS) strategies and practices to respond effectively to the move toward integrating nonfinancial ESG sustainability performance and financial ESP and creating shared value for their shareholders. The transition toward clean energy has heightened awareness of critical minerals like cobalt, copper, lithium, and nickel and their use in SCS strategies and practices. Management should assess the control over critical mineral supply chains. Using critical minerals in SCS requires understanding ownership structures, governance issues in producer countries, and economic/geopolitical risks.

Supply-chain management (SCM) is defined in the context of business sustainability as managing the flow of products and services in the supply chain and converting raw materials into final products with a keen focus on maximizing customer value and earnings while achieving social and environmental impacts. The 2015 United Nations Global Compact defines supply-chain sustainability as "focusing on effective governance practices to ensure delivery of high quality of goods and services with utmost economic, social and environmental positive impacts."[8] The focus on SCS during and in the aftermath of the COVID-19 pandemic is relevant and important for several reasons.[9] First, the implication of SCS with a keen focus on performance management and cost management enables companies to set a tone at the top through their board of directors and top executives in managing all business capital, including financial, strategic, operational, human, reputation, social, and environmental. Second, SCS can improve the corporate environment, business culture, infrastructure, and business models that could achieve desired financial returns for shareholders while generating positive social and environmental impacts. Third, the integration of business sustainability and continuous improvement into SCS provides opportunities for corporations, their board of directors, and top executives to maximize customer value and improve product and service quality. Fourth, public companies can integrate both financial ESP and nonfinancial ESG sustainability performance dimensions into their supply-chain management, from purchasing and inbound logistics and production design and manufacturing to outbound marketing distribution, delivery, logistics, and customer services. Finally, the focus on continuous improvement, cost management, performance management, and SCS strategies enables companies to comply with all applicable laws, rules, regulations, standards, and best practices to improve the overall quality and quantity of SCS.

The best practices of SCS are evolving as more business organizations integrate cost management, performance management, lean management, and continuous improvements of financial ESP and nonfinancial ESG sustainability performance into their business environment, corporate culture, and supply chain. These best practices suggest integrating the sustainability continuous performance improvement concept presented in the next section, focusing on both financial ESP and nonfinancial ESG sustainability performance into SCS strategies, policies, and procedures. Management should design, implement, and maintain proper SCS strategies that provide a common ground for integrating both financial ESP and nonfinancial ESG into their supply-chain management. Key attributes and aspects of SCS are: (1) supply-chain transparency of understanding and improving the sustainability of the supply chain, and providing visibility into manufacturing processes, suppliers, and the potential impact of the supply chain on the environment and communities; (2) ethical sourcing of ensuring that raw materials and components are sourced ethically, considering factors such as human rights, fair labor practices, and avoiding the use of materials that can cause environmental harm; (3) risk assessment and management of identifying, evaluating, and mitigating potential risks associated with sustainability issues in the supply chain, and assessing the impact of regulatory initiatives, climate change, and other factors that could impact the stability and sustainability of the supply chain; (4) reducing the environmental impact of adopting SCS practices that minimize the environmental footprint of the supply chain, minimizing waste, using renewable energy sources, reducing greenhouse gas emissions, minimizing waste, and optimizing logistics and transportation to lower energy consumption; (5) circular economy practices of designing products and packaging for reuse, recycling, or repurposing that could reduce waste and encourage a more sustainable use of resources throughout the supply chain; (6) supplier engagement and collaboration of collaborating and working closely with suppliers to set and achieve sustainability goals, provide support, and encourage the adoption of sustainable practices; (7) compliance with applicable regulations and standards of complying with relevant sustainability standards and regulations, adhering to fair trade standards, environmental certifications, and other industry-specific guidelines; (8) social responsibility of focusing on social responsibility issues within their supply chains to create positive impacts on the communities, ensure fair labor practices, safe working conditions, and respect for human rights; (9) continuous improvement of conducting an ongoing process of improvement, regular assessments, audits, and feedback mechanisms; and (10) technology and innovation of leveraging technology and innovation, and using data analytics, blockchain, and other technologies to address the environmental and social impact of products throughout the supply chain.

Supply-chain sustainability challenges should be identified, evaluated, and turned into sustainable opportunities by business organizations, their board of directors, and executives. Examples of these challenges are the following:

1. Lack of proper definition of the profit-with-purpose mission that contributes to the creation of shared value for all stakeholders.
2. Inadequate focus on lean management and continuous improvement strategies.
3. Lack of integration of supply-chain sustainability into business sustainability, hindering the achievement of both financial ESP and nonfinancial ESG sustainability performance.
4. Ineffective communication and disclosure of the importance and relevance of supply-chain sustainability to all stakeholders, including investors, customers, employees, and suppliers.
5. Insufficient guidelines and robust policies and procedures for achieving supply-chain sustainability.
6. Disconnection of supply-chain sustainability with continuous improvement and other sustainability-related strategies.
7. Non-existence of tone at the top by the board of directors and commitment by executives to supply-chain sustainability and related strategies.
8. Ineffective and inadequate assessment and management of risks associated with supply-chain sustainability.
9. Lack of monitoring of the progress toward achieving supply-chain sustainability.
10. Lack of focus on the ten key aspects of supply-chain sustainability discussed in the previous pages.
11. Insufficient use of continuous improvement strategies, cost management, and performance management in the supply-chain sustainability system.

In summary, supply-chain strategies are evolving from focusing on cost and efficiency to resilience in the face of unexpected disruptions, with digital technology playing a pivotal role in enabling this transformation. Boards must actively oversee these changes to ensure the company's supply-chain aligns with its mission and strategy. Companies prioritizing SCS can contribute to environmental and social well-being and benefit from cost savings, enhanced brand reputation, and increased customer loyalty.

Business Sustainability of Mergers and Acquisitions

Mergers and Acquisition (M&A) deals have also increased substantially in recent years as worldwide M&A deals in 2021 reached $6.2 trillion and are expected to be higher in global volume in 2022.[10] The ESG sustainability factors of planning, performance, risk, and disclosure and their effects on investment and M&A decisions are becoming increasingly important to businesses and investors. Disclosures of ESG performance can provide value-relevant information about investment risks and opportunities pertaining to M&A transactions. However, how the M&A deal-makers, including the board of directors, and executives of acquirer and target firms, consider the ESG factors needs to be examined. A survey of corporate executives and asset managers found that ESG factors are relevant and important to M&A decision-makers as they perform ESG due diligence on ESG assessment for investment opportunities and risk.[11] The 2022 M&A trends survey conducted by Deloitte reveals that more than 70% of respondents report that their organizations consider ESG metrics in the valuations of target firms and portfolio reassessment.[12] The 2023 Deloitte poll results indicate that about 50% of private equity investors (PEIs) and 44% of corporates use ESG clauses in deal contracts and conduct some form of ESG pre-deal due diligence.[13] The ESG issues critical to the M&A due diligence processes are climate change, greenhouse gas emissions (GHG), labor standards, and human rights. M&A deals significantly impact stakeholders, suppliers, and customers of both acquirers and targets and the economy. It is expected that ESG factors of planning, performance, risk, and disclosure have a significant impact on M&A deal-making in several ways:

1. Expansion of ESG-Oriented M&A: Companies are considering ESG factors when evaluating potential acquisitions and looking for synergies in ESG profiles. ESG-related risks and opportunities drive some transactions, especially in response to climate change and transition risks.
2. Financial Sector Involvement: Financial institutions are expanding their ESG services and analytical capabilities, helping businesses incorporate ESG into M&A decision-making.

3. Valuation, Due Diligence, and Contracts: ESG performance increasingly affects company valuations, due diligence processes, and contract terms. Investors are willing to pay premiums for companies with strong ESG records.

4. Financing: ESG risks impact creditworthiness, with credit rating agencies integrating ESG into ratings. Sustainability-linked financing is emerging, potentially lowering the cost of capital for companies that improve their ESG performance.

5. Investor and Stakeholder Engagement: Companies are addressing ESG synergies and opportunities in investor communications, engaging stakeholders on ESG matters, and demonstrating how ESG will impact long-term performance.

6. Regulatory Risks: Evolving ESG, human capital, and cybersecurity disclosures may introduce new regulatory risks affecting M&A. Recent legislation and potential new regulations could create opportunities in renewables and impact supply chains.

7. ESG Activism: Activist investors use ESG issues to rally shareholder support for broader strategic changes, including M&A. Regulatory changes may encourage activism against companies slow to adapt to new ESG standards.

8. Post-Merger Governance and Integration: ESG considerations are shaping post-acquisition governance structures, with oversight responsibilities being transferred and delegated. Integration efforts must align with ESG goals and policies to avoid negative impacts.

The full impact of ESG on M&A is still unfolding, and it will depend on ongoing developments in regulations, disclosures, and the evolving priorities of companies, investors, and regulators. Using ESG considerations in M&A deals has become increasingly important as businesses recognize the relevance of integrating sustainability and responsible business practices into their strategic planning. Sustainability ESG factors of planning, performance, risk, and disclosure are now considered critical elements that can impact the success and long-term value of M&A transactions. Some of the ESG considerations that should be incorporated into M&A deals are (1) due diligence of assessing the target company's environmental practices, including its waste management, carbon footprint, resource usage, compliance with environmental regulations, social practices, diversity and inclusion, employee relations, community engagement, board composition, internal controls, executive compensation, and adherence to ethical business practices; (2) risk assessment and management of identifying potential ESG-related risks (regulatory compliance, litigation risks, and reputational risks) that could affect the target company's financial performance and reputation. This includes assessing issues associated with ESG; (3) integration planning of setting targets and milestones for incorporating sustainable practices, ensuring a smooth transition that preserves or enhances ESG performance, aligning cultures, engaging employees from target and acquired organizations to promote a culture of sustainability, diversity, and ethical business conduct; (4) post-merger monitoring and reporting of tracking progress on sustainability initiatives, diversity metrics, and other relevant indicators, and enhancing stakeholder confidence and support for long-term value creation; (5) regulatory compliance of ensuring that the combined entity complies with ESG-related regulations; and (6) stakeholder engagement of considering the interests of various stakeholders including investors, employees, customers, suppliers, and communities. Integrating ESG considerations into M&A deals requires understanding that sustainable and responsible business practices contribute to long-term business success. Companies should incorporate planning, performance, risk, and disclosure of sustainability factors into their M&A strategies to enhance resilience, reputation, and overall business value.

Business Sustainability and Benefit Corporation

Benefit Corporations (BCs) have recently been incorporated under corporate law in many states in the United States to provide flexibility to social entrepreneurs to achieve the dual objectives of doing well and doing good by focusing on creating shared value for and protecting the interests of all stakeholders. It is expected that BCs will gain more acceptance as business organizations pay more attention to their continuity and sustainability in addressing their financial position and ensuring the safety, health, and well-being of their employees, customers, and suppliers. This section presents the evolution, relevance, status, and future of BCs. The BC is an alternative legal entity that addresses the requirements of entrepreneurs and investors for creating shareholder value while protecting the interests of identified stakeholders, including society, by filling a gap between conventional corporations (CCs) and non-profits and giving social entrepreneurs flexibility to achieve the dual objectives of doing well and doing good. BCs have recently emerged in the United States as an alternative business entity for entrepreneurs who want to make a profit and give back something to society. In CCs, the primary goal is to create shareholder value, and the main fiduciary duty of their boards of directors is to protect shareholders' interests, often without regard for the needs of other stakeholders (social or environmental). In contrast, the fiduciary duty of the boards of directors of BCs is to protect the interests of all identified stakeholders. However, BCs are still taxed under the same corporate taxation laws and held to the same level of accountability and transparency as CCs. The existence and persistence of high-profile corporate scandals triggered by greed on the part of corporate directors and officers cause the investment community and society to embrace the creation of BCs that protect the interests of all stakeholders.

Benefit corporations are initially formed as legal entities by legislation in nine states.[14] Since August 1, 2013, the Delaware General Corporation Law has authorized the formation of public BCs.[15] As of this writing, more than 40 states have adopted the establishment of BCs.[16] Pursuing a mixed commercial and social mission creates a unique research opportunity for business organizations to obtain desired financial returns for their shareholders while achieving social and environmental impacts. Benefit corporations are a new business structure that enables for-profit organizations to earn profits for their owners while considering society, the environment, employees, customers, and suppliers in decision-making. Benefit corporations are legally for-profit entities incorporated as CCs under state law that have also chosen to adopt other ESG missions in their articles of incorporation. BCs are intended to minimize the conflicts between corporations and society caused by differences between private and social costs and benefits and to align corporate goals with those of society under both the state corporate model and the benefit statute. Examples of conflicts between corporations and society are related to environmental issues (pollution, acid rain, global warming), wages paid by multinational corporations in poor countries, and child labor in developing countries. BCs, in pursuing their mission of protecting the interests of all stakeholders, can raise companies' awareness of the social costs and benefits of their business activities.

The major characteristics of the BC form are (1) a requirement of a corporate purpose to create a material positive impact on society and the environment with a commitment to pursuing a social and/or environmental mission and profit-making objectives; (2) this mission is integrated into governing documents that are legally obligated to consider the impact of its decisions on various stakeholders; (3) an expansion of the duties of directors to require the consideration of nonfinancial stakeholders as well as the financial interests of shareholders; (4) the main objective is to balance profit-making with positive impacts on society and the environment; (5) focus on impact investing to generate financial returns for investors while having social and environmental impacts; (6) BCs are established as legal entities in many jurisdictions, and their legal structure incorporates the requirement to consider the interests of stakeholders beyond shareholders with specific requirements and reporting obligations; (7) requirements to meet their social and environmental goals and to publish regular reports presenting their performance in fulfilling their mission; (8) a requirement to consider the impact of their decisions on various stakeholders including investors, employees, customers, communities, and the environment; (9) independent third-party assessments to verify and validate their social and environmental performance through certification from organizations like B Lab to demonstrate commitment to high standards; (10) flexibility in their governance structures, enabling them to adopt governance practices that align with their mission and values; (11) creation of trust among investors and consumers who are increasingly interested in supporting businesses that prioritize social and environmental impacts; and (12) an obligation to report on overall social and environmental performance using a comprehensive, credible, independent, and transparent third-party standard.

Expected benefits of BCs include (1) the attention and market share of socially conscious investors; (2) the power of business resources to solve social and environmental challenges; (3) more trust in businesses by the public, shareholders, potential employees, and customers; (4) improved business, operational, and investment efficacy; (5) the generation of desired financial returns for investors while protecting the interests of other stakeholders including employees, customers, suppliers, society, and the environmental; and (6) disclosure requirements that will improve assessing, managing, and minimizing strategic, operational, financial, reputational, and compliance risks.

Biodiversity Accounting and Finance

Companies worldwide face risks from biodiversity loss. Regulators require and highly encourage multinational firms to increase attention to biodiversity, and companies have a powerful incentive to view biodiversity as a key business issue. Biodiversity accounting and finance are gaining the attention of businesses and investors. These fields of business address the integration of biodiversity, including natural resources, environmental considerations, and ecosystem services, into accounting and finance disciplines, as well as accounting, business, and finance decisions. Biodiversity accounting and finance focus on business sustainability, including protecting nature and biodiversity, ensuring the sustainable use of natural resources, and preserving the environment while achieving economic prosperity, growth, and development.

Biodiversity accounting, also known as natural capital accounting or ecosystem accounting, is an approach that seeks to measure, monitor, and account for the value of biodiversity and ecosystems in economic and policy decision-making. This concept recognizes that biodiversity and healthy ecosystems provide a wide range of benefits and services to society, often referred to as ecosystem services. These services include clean water, climate regulation, food production, recreation, and cultural values. Biodiversity accounting evaluates, measures, and quantifies the value of biodiversity and ecosystem services in financial terms and reports biodiversity performance. Biodiversity accounting provides value-relevant financial information pertaining to the natural capital generated by ecosystems to better understand the contributions of biodiversity and natural systems to the global economy, businesses, and investment decision-making.

Biodiversity finance enables the financial resources, mechanisms, and instruments to support biodiversity conservation and sustainable resource management. It involves various financial approaches to generate funds for conserving ecosystem services such as clean water, pollination, climate regulation, and genetic resources, and integrating biodiversity considerations into financial decision-making. Sources of biodiversity finance include socially responsible investments, such as social stocks, green and sustainable bonds, government budgets, philanthropic donations, international aid, ecosystem service payments, biodiversity offset programs, sustainable business practices, impact investing, risk assessment, and sustainable supply-chain management.

Biodiversity accounting and finance are related to business sustainability and can have several implications for regulators, investors, businesses, and academics, including the following:

1. Policymakers, regulators, and standard-setters should be concerned about ecosystems, nature, climate change, and the environment and provide guidelines for regulatory compliance to preserve nature, protect the environment, and set standards for businesses to integrate biodiversity into their corporate culture, supply chain, operations, performance, and reporting.
2. Investors should assess biodiversity risks and opportunities by identifying and mitigating risks associated with climate change, environmental changes, regulatory pressures, and reputational issues. Investors should also consider the opportunities associated with biodiversity and ecosystems, new markets, sustainable and green investments, and governmental grants and incentives.
3. Businesses should take advantage of the benefits provided by using natural resources, biodiversity, and ecosystem services to maintain the sustainability of these ecosystem services for future generations.
4. Research should be conducted in the areas of ownership and depletion of natural resources, valuation methods for green and sustainable development, bonds and stocks, examination of stakeholder expectations, social trust, the preservation of biodiversity and ecosystems, and the sustainable use of natural resources.

Sustainability Reporting and Assurance

The content and format of sustainability reporting are also evolving toward being online and in real-time. The eXtensible Business Reporting Language (XBRL) format is being used in financial, tax, and statutory reporting, and researchers are exploring its relevance to sustainability reporting. Continuous auditing techniques are being applied to audit the automated financial reporting process, and their applications in providing continuous assurance on sustainability reporting are examined in this chapter. The XBRL platform for sustainability reporting and the outline of the implementation methods for using XBRL-based architectures for sustainability reporting are viewed by many as the future of corporate reporting and assurance services. Several stock exchanges worldwide require their listed companies to disclose sustainability performance information. The best practices for business sustainability developments, programs, and performance are being initiated, and their reporting and assurance are being established. This chapter discusses the best practices for sustainability performance, reporting, and assurance in actions, as well as the future of business sustainability worldwide.

Future Trends in Sustainability Reporting

Sustainability reporting has evolved from voluntarily disclosing some aspects of sustainability performance, such as CSR, in annual reports to issuing standalone voluntary sustainability reports on EGSEE dimensions of sustainability performance to integrating both financial and nonfinancial dimensions of sustainability performance into corporate reporting. The future of sustainability reporting will be either a mandatory standalone or an integrated report on all five EGSEE dimensions of sustainability performance, along with the use of XBRL in sustainability reporting. The use of XBRL-formatted reporting is an important step in applying XBRL to all dimensions of sustainability performance reporting. Several professional organizations are now developing sustainability taxonomies and related instances that both providers and users of sustainability performance and assurance reports can effectively adopt. Future sustainability reporting will be market-driven and/or regulatory-mandated integrated reports, using XBRL in all dimensions of sustainability performance reporting by applying several existing taxonomies for financial and nonfinancial information relevant to the dimensions of sustainable performance. Many professional organizations, including GRI, IIRC, SASB, and ISSB, are in the process of developing business sustainability information systems that capture and consolidate the details necessary to prepare reports externally as well as monitor and control internally by using XBRL to facilitate the integration, consolidation, and audit trail of both conventional financial and emerging nonfinancial information.

Both mandatory and voluntary corporate disclosure provide investors and stakeholders with reliable, relevant, useful, and transparent financial and nonfinancial information for making sound decisions. Global public companies are generally required to disclose a set of financial statements under the corporate mandatory disclosures regime, and they disclose other financial and nonfinancial information through voluntary corporate disclosures. Business sustainability disclosure is the communication of organizational performance on material matters relating to financial, environmental, social, and governance activities. Information regarding an organization's sustainability has been disclosed through various channels, including external websites, social media channels, intranet sites, marketing materials, internal signage and postings, presentations, and newsletters.

The eXtensible Business Reporting Language format, a derivative language of the Extensible Markup Language (XML), has recently gained considerable attention and is becoming an integral component of corporate reporting.[17] XBRL is a consortium consisting of a series of technical specifications intended to make business information more accessible and more easily communicated electronically. XBRL also facilitates the timely and accurate analysis of both internal and external business information. Companies and users of business reports can electronically search, download, and analyze information that is "tagged" electronically. XBRL also facilitates the timely and accurate analysis of both internal and external business information. The primary benefits of XBRL are the ability to retrieve and analyze data, facilitate interparty interactions without human interference, and formalize labels, definitions, and interpretations. XBRL defines and tags data using standard definitions, which provide a mechanism for consistent structure and the use of the XBRL *US GAAP Financial Reporting Taxonomy* and/or other taxonomies (such as the IFRS Taxonomy) or extended (customized) tags based on either national or international accounting standards. The Securities and Exchange Commission (SEC) has encouraged public companies to tag financial statement information on the EDGAR reporting system using XBRL since 2005, as approximately 9600 public companies are filing XBRL-formatted information with the SEC.[18] Since 2009, the SEC has required that public companies that use US GAAP file their financial statements in the XBRL format.

XBRL can provide the technological foundation for the communication of both financial and nonfinancial information to stakeholders. The five EGSEE dimensions of sustainability performance can be integrated into XBRL GL instance documents that contain tagged KPIs on both financial and nonfinancial information. However, no single taxonomy exists at present that can cover the world's diverse needs for financial and nonfinancial sustainability reporting, but XBRL enables companies to define proper taxonomies and incorporate them into corporate reporting.

The development of taxonomies for sustainability performance encourages corporations to disclose both material ESP and GSEE sustainability to reflect the true values of corporate performance. Management has more latitude in choosing the type, content, and timing of such disclosures to reflect both their ESP and GSEE sustainability performance. The establishment of taxonomies for five dimensions of sustainability performance provides material indicator taxonomies for both financial FSP and nonfinancial GSEE dimensions of sustainability performance and disclosure, helping companies, their directors, and officers in making sound decisions to enhance shared value for all stakeholders.

The format and content of integrated sustainability performance reporting are evolving rapidly. Although guidelines for sustainability reporting (e.g., GRI, IIRC, SASB, ISSB) are helpful, currently, there is no single taxonomy that can address ESP and ESG dimensions of sustainability performance. Following the standards and guidelines of these professionals and other organizations, we develop our material indicator taxonomies. The development of the XBRL taxonomy for EGSEE sustainability reports represents an important milestone in implementing the concept of EGSEE sustainability reporting. While the use of XBRL facilitates the standardization of EGSEE sustainability reporting, many challenges must be addressed as the financial reporting paradigm shifts from a paper-based to an information-based model. A variety of XBRL taxonomies have been proposed for use in EGSEE reporting to harmonize the document structure for online communication by organizations. The EGSEE taxonomy will enable organizations to communicate sustainability information in the XBRL format much faster and more efficiently.

The mandatory use of XBRL-formatted financial reporting indicates that applying XBRL to the five EGSEE dimensions of sustainability performance as well would allow for effective and efficient analysis by all participants (board of directors, management, auditors, legal counsel, financial analysts, regulators, and investors) involved in the corporate reporting process. The tags of EGSEE sustainability taxonomies describe each of the five EGSEE dimensions of sustainability performance data with labels that are both human- and machine-readable, showing their relation to other sustainability data elements and applying sustainability frameworks (e.g., GRI G4).

XBRL-tagged sustainability reports, when made publicly available, can be used by all stakeholders interested in sustainability information. The global acceptance of XBRL-formatted sustainability reports requires the proper development of taxonomies for each of the five EGSEE dimensions of sustainability performance. Several organizations and interest groups are currently developing XBRL taxonomies, namely: GRI; the Governance, Risk Management, and Compliance (GRC); the Central Scoreboard for Corporate Social Responsibility (CSC); the Carbon Disclosure (CDP); the Climate Disclosure Standards Board (CDSB); the Climate Change Reporting Taxonomy (CCRT); The Integrated Scoreboard – Financial, Environmental, Social, and Corporate Governance (IS-FESG); and the IIRC. CCRT is a joint project of the CDP and the CDSB, and it is currently working to provide a single CCRT in the XBRL format.[19]

The essence of EGSEE reporting using XBRL is the integrated presentation of nonfinancial information and the relationships among different types of sustainability performance dimensions. A single EGSEE report can provide financial and nonfinancial sustainability information of interest to various stakeholders, and XBRL makes it possible to provide

Future Trends in Sustainability Reporting

users with the tools that enable them to analyze and compare performance dimensions. A single EGSEE report using XBRL can provide all relevant information for a mutual conversation and ongoing dialogue between a company and all of its stakeholders, thereby adding a much greater dimension to the idea of EGSEE reporting.

Exhibit 12.1   Summary of Financial and Nonfinancial Reporting Taxonomies and Related Standards

Description	Location	Organization	Version	Sustainability Performance Dimension
IFRS Taxonomy 2018 files and support materials	https://www.ifrs.org/issued -standards/ifrs-taxonomy/ ifrs-taxonomy-2018/.	IFRS Foundation/ IASB	January 2018	Financial/ economic
2018 US GAAP Financial Reporting Taxonomy	https://xbrl.us/xbrl -taxonomy/2018-us-gaap/.	FASB US GAAP	2018	Financial/ economic
Management's Discussion and Analysis Taxonomy	https://xbrl.us/sec-reporting /taxonomies/.	US GAAP	2015	Financial/ economic
GRI Taxonomy Architecture & Style Guide	https://www.globalreporting .org/resourcelibrary/ GRI-Taxonomy-2014 -Implementation-Guide.pdf.	GRI and Deloitte Netherlands	2014	Nonfinancial (governance, social, environmental)
Central Scoreboard for Corporate Social Responsibility (CCI)	http://www.aeca.es/es/ gaap/rsc/2010-05-31/CCI -XBRL-Description.doc.	AECA	2010-05-31	Nonfinancial (environmental and social)
World Intellectual Capital Initiative (WICI)	http://www.wici-global.com /taxonomy.	WICI	V1.0 2010	Nonfinancial (environmental, social, and governance)
Governance, Risk, and Complaince (GRC)	https://www.xbrl.org/ TaxonomyRecognition/GRC %20Summary.htm.	Open Compliance and Ethics Group	2009	Nonfinancial (governance and ethics)
Carbon Disclosure Project (CDP)	https://www.cdp.net/en/ research/xbrl.	CDP/CDSB	06/5/2012	Nonfinancial (environmental)
Climate Change Reporting Taxonomy (CCRT)	https://www.cdproject.net /Documents/xbrl/CCRT -taxonomy-architecture-and -style-guide-v1-0.pdf.	CDP/CDSB	V 1.0 06/11/2012	Nonfinancial (environmental)
Integrated Scoreboard of Financial, Environmental, Social and Corporative Governance (IS-FESG)	http://www.aeca.es/es/ fr/gaap/csr/2012/IS-FESG -XBRL-Summary.pdf.	AECA	V 2.1, 2012-01-25	Financial and Nonfinancial (financial, environmental, social, and governance)

Future Trends in Sustainability Assurance

Sustainability reporting is mandatory in Europe and other jurisdictions. Thus, the reliability, objectivity, transparency, and credibility of sustainability reports can be improved by providing assurance for these reports. Unlike audit reports on the economic dimension of sustainability performance in the context of audit reports on financial statements and internal control over financial reporting, assurance opinions on nonfinancial GSEE dimensions of sustainability information are neither standardized, regulated, nor licensed. Several professionals, including internal auditors, external auditors, and other service providers, can offer assurance on nonfinancial sustainability information. International accounting firms have developed expertise in sustainability reporting and assurance, and they are well-equipped and trained to provide sustainability assurance services on financial and nonfinancial dimensions of sustainability performance reports. A more standardized, integrated, and audited process is required to make sustainability reports on EGSEE performance comparable, commonly acceptable, and relevant to all corporate stakeholders.

Accounting and auditing standards have long been established for financial reporting and auditing.[20] Standards also exist for measuring, recognizing, reporting, and auditing GSEE sustainability performance, but these are new and few by comparison. The standards include GRI and AA1000, which were issued in 2008 by AccountAbility (AA). There is an AA1000 assurance standard, as well as ISO standards and accounting profession standards for auditing sustainability metrics. The AICPA Assurance Executive Committee (ASEC) Sustainability Assurance and Advisory Task Force developed application guidance assurance services.[21] The AICPA issued Statement of Position (SOP) No. 13-1, which supersedes SOP No. 03-2, Attest Engagements on Greenhouse Gas Emissions Information, specifying how to apply the attestation standards for a review engagement to the specific subject matter of Greenhouse Gas (GHG) Protocol emissions information.[22] The SOP No. 03-2 is an essential resource that examines or reviews and provides guidance on performing and reporting relating to information about a GHG emissions inventory or a baseline GHG inventory, as well as a schedule or an assertion relating to information about a GHG emission reduction in connection with the recording of the reduction with a registry or a trade of that reduction or credit.[23] The SOP No. 13-1 provides guidance on the types of analytics and inquiries that might be performed in a review engagement on Greenhouse Gas Emissions Information. Consequently, performing analytics and inquiries alone with respect to GHG emissions information might not yield sufficient evidence for the limited assurance conclusion to be formed (otherwise known as "negative assurance" in the United States).

Several existing assurance standards have been developed for both financial and nonfinancial dimensions of sustainability performance information. Sustainability assurance reports prepared based on the AICPA Assurance framework and SOP No. 13-2 can be used to address the completeness, mapping, consistency, or structure of EESG sustainability information and includes planning, performing evidence-gathering procedures, and reporting audit findings on all five EGSEE dimensions of sustainability performance in an integrated audit report or a separate audit report on individual EGSEE dimensions. The end product of a sustainability assurance engagement is the sustainability report, reflecting the auditor's either positive or negative opinion in the context of either reasonable or limited assurance on sustainability performance reports.

In general, the extent of test procedures performed differs between levels of assurance. Depending on the standards applied, these levels of assurance may have been described differently, but their implications are essentially similar. The highest level of assurance is described as reasonable (ISAE 3000), examination (AT 101), or audit (CICA 5025) level of assurance. The lower level of assurance can be described as limited (ISAE 3000), moderate (AT 101), or review (CICA 5025) level assurance.[24] A reasonable assurance engagement provides a positive opinion on whether the subject matter is, in all material respects, appropriately stated, and the work performed is, of course, greater than under limited assurance engagement. A limited assurance engagement provides what is called a negative opinion: "nothing has come to our attention to cause us to believe that the subject matter is not, in all material aspects, appropriately stated." A limited assurance engagement requires a lower level of work and consists primarily of inquiry and analytical procedures.

The content and format of the sustainability assurance report that should be addressed to either the entity's board of directors, management, or intended user may vary and, in general, should include the following:[25]

1. Reference to sustainability information presented by management.
2. The assurance provider should use the criteria as a benchmark in assessing the effectiveness, efficiency, completeness, reliability, and transparency of sustainability EGSEE performance.
3. Responsibilities of management and assurance: Management is primarily responsible for the preparation, content, completeness, and reliability of information in sustainability reports. The assurance provider is responsible for the assurance conclusion provided on the reports.
4. The scope of work done by the assurance provider should include the criteria used, analytical procedures, inquiries, and other evidence-gathering procedures performed to test for assessing the risk of material misstatements in sustainability reports. Evidence-gathering should be documented and used as a basis for reaching sustainability conclusions.

The assurance service providers should take the following steps:[26]

1. Obtain an understanding of the organization's five EGSEE sustainability performance measures.
2. Obtain an understanding of the organization's current and prospective sustainability initiatives.
3. Perform analytical procedures designed to enhance the understanding of the relations among different components of EGSEE sustainability performance and identify areas of high risk that might affect the reliability of financial statements.
4. Conduct an assessment of sustainability risk.
5. Encourage communication among the audit engagement team members regarding the EGSEE sustainability dimension that might affect the risks of material misstatement of financial statements.
6. Test the effectiveness of the internal control system used to collect, compile, process, and disclose EGSEE sustainability performance.
7. Perform audit procedures to gather sufficient and appropriate evidence on reported sustainability information.
8. Interview the board of directors, management, and other personnel charged with the preparation of EGSEE sustainability reports.
9. Confirm certain sustainability information with outside parties where applicable (donations, environmental initiatives).
10. Review important documents relevant to the business sustainability mission, objectives, strategies, policies, and procedures.
11. Decide on the type and level of assurance that can be given on each dimension of EGSEE sustainability performance.

Corporate Governance and Business Sustainability

Investors demand forward-looking financial and nonfinancial information, and companies have strived to provide such information. Traditionally, public companies have focused on achieving their economic objective of making a profit and enhancing shareholder wealth by engaging in operating, investment, and financing activities to provide and distribute goods and services. This narrow focus on achieving economic performance has been criticized for ignoring other social, ethical, and environmental responsibilities of corporations. The multiple bottom lines (MBL) objectives of economic, social, ethical, and environmental (ESEE) performance have been advocated by global business and investment communities.[27] With the MBL objectives, the primary goal is to achieve economic performance by creating shareholder value while giving proper consideration to other measures and performance, including social, ethical, and environmental (SEE). Sustainability performance and account-ability reporting have gained new interest during the recent financial crises and the result-ing global economic meltdown, which have sparked widening concerns about whether big businesses (banks and carmakers) are sustainable in the long term in contributing to the economic growth and prosperity of the nation.

The ever-increasing erosion of public trust and investor confidence in the sustainability of large businesses, the widening concern about social responsibility and environmen-tal matters, the overconsumption of natural resources, the global government bailout of big businesses, and the perception that governments cannot solve all problems of busi-nesses underscores the importance of having a keen focus on sustainability performance and accountability reporting. The literature and interest in accountability and its con-nection with social responsibility and sustainability are growing. The Institute of Supply Management (ISM), in partnership with 500 companies, has developed "Principles of Sustainability and Social Responsibility." In addition, the International Organization for Standardization (ISO) developed ISO 26000 on business sustainability. Furthermore, more than 8000 organizations worldwide (including Fortune 500) have adopted Global Reporting Initiatives (GRI) for sustainable performance reporting.[28]

Globalization and economic, social, and technological developments in the twenty-first century demand a new type of corporate accountability reporting, reflecting KPIs on both financial and nonfinancial information. The latest financial scandals and the subprime mortgage market crisis have raised questions and concerns about corporate accountability in recent years. It appears that public companies and their gatekeepers are not effectively fulfilling their fiduciary duties and professional responsibility to promote accountability, compliance, and transparency. An effective sustainability performance and accountability reporting model reflecting all aspects of business (e.g., economic, social, environmental, ethical, and governance) in addressing the interests of all stakeholders is the bedrock of the capital market and business strategies. Significant opportunities exist for businesses to improve the value-relevance of their corporate reporting to better meet the needs of global investors and enhance investors' understanding of their MBL sustainable performance.

In today's business environment, global businesses face scrutiny and profound pressure from lawmakers, regulators, the investment community, and their various stakeholders to focus on sustainability measures and accept accountability and responsibility for their MBL of EGSEE performance.[29] Organizations worldwide recognize the importance of sustain-ability performance in creating shared value for all their stakeholders, from shareholders to creditors, customers, suppliers, employees, government, society, and the environment. Over 14,000 public companies worldwide are now issuing sustainability reports on some or all five EGSEE dimensions of sustainability performance, and this trend is expected to continue well into the future. More than 6000 European companies will be required to disclose their environmental, social, and governance sustainability as well as diversity information for their 2017 financial reporting and onwards.[30] Hong Kong-listed companies are required to disclose environmental, social, governance, and diversity sustainability in their 2005 annual reports and onwards.[31]

Business organizations have traditionally reported their performance in economic affairs, but their main focus on financial results has become insufficient. In recent years, stakeholders, investors, regulators, global organizations, and the public at large have increasingly demanded information on both financial and nonfinancial KPIs in this platform of MBL accountability and sustainability reporting. Sustainability performance and accountability reporting have gained new interest during the recent financial crises and the resulting global economic meltdown, which have sparked widening concerns about whether or not big businesses (e.g., banks and carmakers) are sustainable in the long term in contributing to the economic growth and prosperity of the nation. The ever-increasing erosion of public trust and investor confidence in the sustainability of large businesses, the widening concern about social responsibility and environmental matters, the overconsumption of natural resources, the global government bailout of big businesses, and the perception that the government cannot solve all problems in the business world underscore the importance of having a keen focus on sustainability performance and accountability reporting. The United Nations Global Compact, in its 2013 Global Corporate Sustainability Report, while underscoring the importance of business sustainability, calls on corporations worldwide to integrate ten principles of sustainability pertaining to the environment, human rights, fair labor, and anticorruption into their strategies and operations.[32]

Companies should strive to maintain good CSR in their everyday practices to minimize information asymmetry among all of their stakeholders. If a company withholds information about its practices, whether intentionally in efforts to minimize its effect on the bottom line or unintentionally as a result of not performing due diligence on its processes, this may result in increased perceived risk of the venture, decreased share price, concerns regarding the management's ability to lead the company, or even so-called black swan events – unforeseen events that have a major, and usually negative, impact on the company and could be avoided if more attention were paid. Thus, good CSR is important for a company to have in the short run to ensure viability in the ever-changing marketplace. However, to build a strong company in the long run, business sustainability must be put into practice to prepare for the future and mitigate the unforeseen or inescapable events that may occur even when a company follows CSR principles rigorously. One of the key

Corporate Governance and Business Sustainability

features of putting business sustainability into practice is that when faced with problems from multiple stakeholders, a sustainable company can pivot its position to answer the problem in the best manner possible.

Sustainability performance is typically classified into financial and nonfinancial performance and grouped into five dimensions: economic, governance, social, ethical, and environmental, abbreviated as EGSEE.[33] Although business sustainability continues to evolve, several dimensions of sustainability performance pertaining to social and environmental initiatives have gained widespread global acceptance. These initiatives include an ethical workplace, customer satisfaction, just and safe working conditions, nondiscriminatory fair wages, workplace diversity, environmental preservation, clear air and water, the minimum age for child labor, safe and quality products, concern for the environment, and fair and transparent business practices. Each industry has its own applicable set of sustainability financial and nonfinancial KPIs. Each business organization must carefully identify its own social and environmental responsibilities, given the context of the business culture in which it operates. The list of financial and nonfinancial sustainability KPIs depends on a variety of factors: industry, legal regimes, cultural diversity, corporate mission and strategy, corporate culture, political infrastructure, and managerial philosophy. Despite these disparate sustainability performance dimensions and their KPIs, sustainability has become an integral component of business. This section describes each of the EGSEE sustainability performance dimensions and their related KPIs. The true measure of success for corporations should be determined not only by their reported earnings but also by their governance, social responsibility, ethical behavior, and environmental performance. Business sustainability has received considerable attention from policymakers, regulators, and the business and investment community over the past decade, and it is expected to remain the main theme for decades to come.

The global trend toward business sustainability performance, reporting, and assurance encourages and ultimately rewards companies that focus on five EGSEE dimensions of sustainability performance and strike the right balance between the triple bottom line of profit, people, and planet. Business sustainability can be successfully achieved when the following best practices are considered by companies worldwide:

1. Sustainability tone at the top in engaging in sustainability initiatives: The board of directors, as representatives of shareholders, should consider the opportunities and challenges, including risks, offered by the global move toward sustainability, and place sustainability issues at the top of the board agenda. This can be accomplished in three ways. First, socially responsible investors place a need in proxy proposals for the election of at least one director with sustainability interests and skills.

Second, the creation of a Board Sustainability Committee consisting of directors with adequate sustainability expertise. Third, the entire board of directors is required to engage in sustainability issues and initiatives, be held accountable for achieving sustainable performance, and provide the needed sustainability leadership. The board culture should be guided toward sustainability leadership, and the mindset of directors should be directed toward sustainability and sustainable strategic decisions to create shared value for all stakeholders and away from short-term value creation for only shareholders.

2. Executive Commitments for Promoting Sustainability: Corporate executives, particularly CEOs and CFOs, should be fully committed to achieving all five dimensions of sustainability performance by moving away from greenwashing sustainability and moving toward sustainability as a strategic imperative. This can be achieved either through active oversight function of the board of directors demanding sustainable performance from executives, adding a sustainability performance target clause in executive compensation contracts. or for the labor market to reward sustainable executive leadership and punish managerial short-termism.

3. Long-term sustainability investment strategies: Individual investors, as well as institutional investors, should focus on long-term and sustainable investments rather than short-term market movements, including sustainability investment initiatives and innovations.

4. Integration of sustainability performance reporting and assurance into corporate reporting.

5. Adopting a broad definition of corporate sustainability as a process of achieving all five EGSEE dimensions of sustainability performance in creating shared value for all stakeholders by generating revenue for shareholders and protecting the interests of other stakeholders.

Business Sustainability and Management Accounting

Traditionally, organizations have reported their performance on economic affairs, and their focus solely on financial results has become complicated, irrelevant, and less valuable to all stakeholders, including shareholders. In recent years, stakeholders, global organizations, and the public have increasingly demanded information on both financial ESP and nonfinancial ESG sustainability KPIs in the platform of accountability and integrated sustainability reporting. Given the growing global attention to corporate sustainability, management accountants should contribute to the sustainability business processes, monitor the progress toward sustainability, and link nonfinancial GSEE to financial sustainability from both qualitative and quantitative perspectives. The role of business corporations in our society has evolved from profit maximization to creating shareholder value and, in recent years, to creating shared value for all stakeholders. Firm performance is measured not only by financial income but also by the mechanisms through which business success and sustainability are measured in terms of nonfinancial sustainability key performance indicators pertaining to environmental, social, governance, and ethical activities.

Corporations worldwide are now recognizing the importance of both financial and non-financial performance and their links to profitability and social goals. Justifications for improved sustainability include enhancing financial sustainability and moral obligation, maintaining a good reputation, ensuring CSR, keeping their license to operate, and creating value for all stakeholders. In a shared value approach, corporations identify potential sustainability issues of concern and integrate them into their strategic planning. There are many reasons why a company should focus on sustainability, such as the pressure of the labor movement, the development of moral values and social standards, the development of business education, and the change in public opinion about the role of business. Companies that are, or aspire to be, leaders in sustainability are challenged by rising public expectations, increasing innovation, continuous quality improvement, and heightened social and environmental problems.

Cost management and performance management practices have recently received considerable attention in management and financial accounting and the business community. Cost management is defined in the context of enterprise sustainability as a process of planning and controlling the costs of products and services to promote maximum utilization of scarce resources in generating revenue and delivering high-quality and environmentally safe products and services to customers. Performance management, in the context of sustainability, consists of all business activities that generate financial ESP and nonfinancial ESG sustainability performance to maximize firm value and create shared value for all stakeholders. Management accountants should assess the integrated effects of both economic factors and managerial incentives on cost behavior and sustainability performance. Business sustainability can build a bridge between managerial accounting and financial accounting by focusing on both internal information systems (cost management) and external information systems (performance management), as these two functions are interrelated and integrated. Management accountants can provide insights into managerial initiatives for advancing corporate sustainability, from greenwashing and business branding to creating opportunities for revenue generation, cost management, business growth, and product and service innovation.

Business sustainability enables management accountants to establish synergy and congruence between the two managerial concepts of cost management and performance management and integrate sustainability into the business environment, corporate culture, and supply-chain processes. The concept of cost management suggests that management maximizes the utilization of scarce resources to generate revenue and deliver high-quality value to customers to improve performance. The concept of performance management suggests that management strikes a proper balance between short-term and long-term ESP as well as a trade-off between financial/quantitative ESP and nonfinancial/qualitative ESG sustainability performance. The integrated cost management and performance management concepts under business sustainability suggest that a firm must extend its focus beyond maximizing short-term shareholder profit by considering the impact of its operations on the long-term interests of all stakeholders, including shareholders, creditors, customers, employees, the community, society, and the environment. Management accountants can help suppliers improve their sustainability performance and enhance their social and environmental accounting in terms of proper measurement, risk assessment, internal controls evaluation, and adequate disclosure. Furthermore, management accountants should design compensation schemes that are linked to sustainability performance to motivate employees to work toward long-term and sustainable goals by cultivating integrated thinking.

Several recent reports released by Chartered Global Management Accountants (CGMA) suggest that companies underutilize the knowledge and skills of their management accountants in advancing sustainability programs and developments and in reporting the impacts of environmental, social, ethical, and governance factors on financial performance. These reports suggest the following ways in which management accountants can assist their organizations in achieving sustainable performance and success:

1. Identify nonfinancial sustainability initiatives, including the environmental and social trends that will affect the company's ability to create stakeholder value over time.
2. Link business sustainability challenges to the company's strategy, business model, operations, and performance.
3. Assess and explain the impact of these sustainability issues, including challenges and concerns.
4. Develop both financial and nonfinancial KPIs that support the achievement of sustainability strategies and goals.
5. Apply management accounting tools and techniques, including balanced scorecards, scenario planning of natural resource availability, data analytics, lifecycle costing, and carbon footprinting, to integrate sustainability into the decision-making processes.
6. Produce integrated/sustainability reports that include data on sustainability impacts in all business decisions, including supply chains, budgeting and pricing decisions, cost analysis, investment appraisals, and strategic planning.

Business Sustainability and Management Accounting

7. Develop a sustainability reporting strategy that integrates all five dimensions of sustainability performance into strategic planning, decisions, and operations.[34]

Globalization created incentives and opportunities for multinational corporations (MNCs) and their stakeholders and executives to influence their sustainability initiatives and strategies of the headquarters as well as subsidiaries around the world. MNCs can choose from a variety of sustainability initiatives regarding the scope, extent, and type of strategies that focus on different issues, functions, areas, and stakeholders. Management should develop and maintain proper sustainability programs that provide a common framework for the integration of sustainability into their strategies and operations, which consist of:

- Integration of sustainability developments and programs into the business and investment analysis and decision-making processes.
- Incorporation of all five EGSEE dimensions of sustainability performance into business and investment policies, activities, and practices.
- Promotion of appropriate reporting of sustainability performance.
- Collaboration among all stakeholders enhances the effectiveness of implementing sustainability programs.
- Promotion of product innovation and quality, customer retention and attraction, employee satisfaction, and productivity through sustainability programs.

Business sustainability enables management accountants to examine enterprise sustainability performance, reporting, and assurance and their integration into strategy, governance, risk assessment, cost management, performance management, and the reporting process of disclosing governance, ethics, social, environmental, and economic sustainable performance. A business organization's success in the effective achievement of all five EGSEE dimensions of sustainability performance demands commitment from the board of directors and top executives to effectively coordinate all sustainability strategies and activities and successfully implement these strategies. There is an urgent need for the establishment of the position of CSO among the C-suite executives of business organizations.

Internal Auditors and Business Sustainability

Internal auditors can play an important role in assisting management in measuring, assessing, and improving sustainability performance, as well as assessing the risks and opportunities associated with sustainability performance. The Institute of Internal Auditing (IIA) encourages internal auditors to engage in business sustainability by:[35]

1. Obtaining a holistic understanding of the organization's sustainability strategy and performance.
2. Assessment of the utilization of all six types of capital, including financial, reputational, strategic, operational, human, social, and environmental.
3. Close working relationships and interactions with a broad range of internal and external stakeholders promote sustainability.
4. Connectivity and reliability of both qualitative and quantitative financial and nonfinancial information.
5. Assess materiality for all sustainability risks from strategic to operational, financial, reputational, and compliance.
6. Evaluate internal control activities relevant to both financial ESP and nonfinancial GSEE dimensions of sustainability.

Internal auditors can provide consulting services to the board of directors in setting an appropriate tone at the top in promoting business sustainability and assist management in implementing sustainability strategic plans and incorporating sustainability into managerial decisions, actions, and performance. Internal auditors can also provide sustainability assurance regarding the completeness, accuracy, and reliability of sustainability information by assisting management to:

1. Obtain consistency over disclosure of both financial ESP and nonfinancial GSEE dimensions of sustainability performance reporting.
2. Vouch for inputs, processes, outputs, and outcomes of managerial sustainability initiatives.
3. Communicate sustainability-related initiatives to everyone within the organization.
4. Assist management with sustainability materiality assessment.
5. Assist management with the assessment of sustainability-related control activities.
6. Lend credibility to sustainability reports.

Materiality Assessment and Business Sustainability

The materiality process determines the most relevant and significant issues for an organization and its stakeholders. Thus, sustainability reports should reflect all relevant material performance information that could influence stakeholders' decision-making processes regarding all five EGSEE dimensions of sustainability. This materiality concept is relatively well-defined in financial reporting of financial sustainability performance dimensions but has yet to be defined for nonfinancial GSEE dimensions of sustainability performance. The four commonly used thresholds of materiality in sustainability reporting are (1) relevance to an organization's operations, investment, and financing activities; (2) the qualitative

Business Sustainability and Management Accounting

importance of the activities; (3) the quantitative significance of activities; and (4) the capability of affecting users' decisions.

Materiality is typically shaped by professional judgment, and its qualitative and quantitative measures for all EGSEE dimensions of sustainability performance require the proper use of professional judgment. Business organizations should focus on important and material issues for their stakeholders when reporting on their EGSEE dimensions of sustainability performance. Unlike financial reports, which are primarily prepared in detail for the purpose and benefit of shareholders, sustainability reports are intended to provide relevant and material sustainability performance information. Thus, sustainability reports should be concise and relevant, with a focus on only material issues that reflect the company's EGSEE performance and assist its stakeholders in understanding and assessing such performance. A more reasonable materiality standard should be established for all EGSEE dimensions of business sustainability.

Materiality guidelines and thresholds are fairly developed for financial reporting, but their applications in sustainability reporting are not well established. Comprehensive and globally accepted materiality guidelines for all five EGSEE dimensions of sustainability performance need to be developed. The International Standard for Assurance Engagements (ISAE) 3000 provides some guidance as to the extent and type of sustainability disclosures and the assessment and attestation of such disclosures.[36] The GRI, in its Sustainability Reporting Guidelines Version 3 (G3), defines materiality in relation to sustainability reporting.[37] The information in a report should cover topics and indicators that reflect the organization's significant economic, environmental, and social impacts or that would substantively influence the assessments and decisions of stakeholders. Thus, the sustainability report should present all important sustainability information that reflects the organization's significant financial ESP and nonfinancial ESG performance that could influence the assessment of decisions of stakeholders.

The SASB standards focus on the materiality concept to ensure that important sustainability factors of performance, disclosure, and risk matter most to investors. The SASB identifies the minimum set of sustainability factors and issues that could be material to companies and their investors within a given industry. Materiality in the context of sustainability means what is important and meaningful to all stakeholders and what sustainability issues and factors could influence investors' assessment of sustainability information. The SASB definition of materiality is very broad and covers a wide range of sustainability factors and issues that could be material to investors. The European Sustainability Reporting Standards (ESRS) under the Corporate Sustainability Reporting Directive (CSRD) of the

European Union require double materiality, considering both financial materiality relevant to how sustainability issues affect the company's financial performance, and environmental/social materiality reflecting how the company impacts the environment and society.[38]

Business Sustainability for New Ventures and IPOs

Business sustainability performance and reporting are as important to new ventures and IPOs as they are to well-established and mature business organizations. New business ventures and IPOs often face more challenges in attracting new investors to invest in their businesses. One pool of potential investors is the socially responsible investment funds (SRI). The United Nations Principles of Responsible Investing (UN PRI) was initiated in 2005 to encourage global investors to integrate ESG in their investment decisions.[39] The UN PRI covers many jurisdictions, including the United States, the United Kingdom, and Canada and has over 1100 signatories representing more than US$32 trillion in assets under management. Investors consider various sustainability issues in both financial, economic, and nonfinancial ESG sustainability in their investment analysis, as SRI increased by more than 22% to $3.74 trillion in managed assets during the 2010–2012 period.[40] Academic research, in general, finds a positive relation between firm value and the stakeholder welfare scores constructed to measure the extent to which firms meet the expectations of their stakeholders, including the SRI funds.[41] Nonfinancial ESG sustainability performance is more relevant to entrepreneurs and joint ventures that have reached the maturity and survival stage. Business sustainability makes it easier for emerging growth companies (EGCs) to make it to their IPO, thus providing these companies with access to significant funding opportunities related to public capital markets.

Business sustainability and IPOs are two interconnected concepts in the modern corporate landscape for several reasons. First, business sustainability, as defined in the previous chapters, refers to the ability of a company to thrive over the long-term in financial performance while considering its impact on society, the environment, and its stakeholders. Sustainable businesses are intended to meet present needs without compromising the ability of future generations to meet their own needs by focusing on environmental stewardship, social responsibility, and economic viability. Similarly, an IPO is the process by which a private company becomes publicly traded by offering its shares to the public with the purpose of creating a growth trajectory and becoming a sustainable company. Second, IPOs can provide companies with substantial capital infusion, which can be used to fund sustainability financial ESP and nonfinancial ESG initiatives, including investments in biodiversity, eco-friendly practices, renewable energy, supply-chain optimization for reduced carbon footprint, or research and development of sustainable products and technologies.

Business Sustainability and Management Accounting

Third, fostering investor expectations as publicly traded companies are subject to greater scrutiny and accountability, they have to answer to a broader set of stakeholders, including shareholders and regulatory bodies. This scrutiny causes IPOs to adopt sustainable practices, as investors increasingly consider ESG factors in their investment decisions. Fourth, integrating sustainability into business operations can contribute to long-term financial performance and resilience by effectively managing environmental and social risks to enhance investor confidence and support sustained market performance post-IPO. Fifth, IPO companies with strong sustainability credentials may attract greater investor interest, command higher valuations in the public markets, and enjoy competitive advantages in terms of brand reputation, customer loyalty, and market positioning. Sixth, publicly traded companies are subject to vigorous regulations and reporting requirements, including those related to sustainability disclosures that show commitments to transparency and responsible business practices, which can enhance investor trust and confidence. Finally, while IPOs provide companies with access to capital and liquidity, integrating sustainability factors into their business models and operations can contribute to long-term value creation, investor confidence, and market resilience, and can enjoy sustained growth and competitive advantage in the public markets.

Global Collaboration and Leadership for Sustainability

Global collaboration and leadership for sustainability are vital for addressing pressing and emerging environmental, social, and economic challenges worldwide. The 2015 research conducted by MIT Sloan Management Review, the Boston Consulting Group, and the United Nations Global Compact indicates that an increasing number of companies are collaborating with their suppliers, industry alliances, peers, and even competitors, as well as government and non-government entities to become more sustainable.[42] This suggests that all stakeholders need to integrate efforts to focus on achieving all five EGSEE dimensions of sustainability performance, addressing sustainability challenges, and creating new product and market opportunities. The report suggests that sustainability has and will continue to move to the center of business as evidenced by: (1) 39% of responding companies are publicly reporting their sustainability efforts, and this is expected to increase by 15% in the next four years; (2) the number of companies that utilize financial and nonfinancial sustainability KPIs and effective governance structures toward sustainability has increased by 6% in the past four years; (3) the number of companies that consider sustainability as a top management agenda item has increased substantially to 65% in 2014 compared to 46% in 2010; and (4) the number of companies with no focus on sustainability has significantly decreased in the past four years.[43]

The study also looked at board engagement as a driver of sustainability success. Overall, 86% of respondents believe that the board of directors should play a strong role in driving their company's sustainability efforts. However, only 42% of respondents see their boards as moderately or more engaged with the company's sustainability agenda. This disconnect affects performance: in companies whose boards are perceived as active supporters, 67% of respondents rate collaborations as very or quite successful. In companies whose boards are not engaged, the reported rate of success is less than half that. The report also suggests the type and extent of collaborations may vary among companies but, at the minimum, can include:[44]

1. Developing sustainability standards and promoting best practices in business sustainability.
2. Sharing information about best practices for sustainability to foster discoveries or communicate externally about sustainability performance.
3. Empowering all stakeholders to engage in business sustainability by creating value.
4. Sharing in investments to save costs or reduce risks and create value.

In summary, several aspects of global collaboration and leadership for sustainability are: (1) shared sustainability goals and agreements, as many countries, organizations, and stakeholders worldwide need to align on common sustainability goals and objectives such as the United Nations Sustainable Development Goals (SDGs) or regional initiatives relevant to water management, biodiversity conservation, or renewable energy adoption; (2) integration of diverse expertise, resources, and perspectives to facilitate knowledge sharing, capacity building, and coordinated action on global sustainability issues among governments, international organizations, NGOs, businesses, and civil society; (3) global collaborative efforts that can promote the transfer of sustainable technologies and best practices across borders, particularly from developed to developing countries, to accelerate the adoption of sustainable agriculture practices, cleaner energy sources, resilient infrastructure, and waste management solutions; (4) developed countries and international financial institutions providing financial support, grants, loans, and investment opportunities to developing nations for implementing sustainable development projects and achieving the SDGs in the foreseeable future; (5) international collaboration facilitating sustainability knowledge sharing, education, training, and technology transfer to enhance the resilience of communities, businesses, and governments in addressing sustainability challenges; (6) global cooperation facilitating the development of common frameworks for sustainable finance, environmental protection, carbon pricing, and corporate responsibility to create a conducive environment for sustainable development and trade; (7) global collaboration fostering advocacy efforts, public awareness campaigns, and citizen engagement initiatives

Global Collaboration and Leadership for Sustainability

to mobilize support for sustainability initiatives and actions; and (8) establishment of global mechanisms for monitoring progress, reporting on sustainability indicators, and providing assurance on sustainability reports to promote transparency, data sharing, and independent verification mechanisms to ensure accountability and trust among stakeholders. Thus, global collaboration for sustainability requires concerted efforts and collective action at local, national, regional, and international levels to achieve sustainable development goals, address shared challenges, and create a more equitable and resilient future for all stakeholders worldwide.

The Process of Moving toward Global Sustainability Performance Reporting and Assurance

An effective process of moving toward global sustainability performance reporting and assurance requires a firm commitment from the board of directors and the top management team to advance business sustainability. A proper tone at the top in promoting sustainability performance reporting and assurance consists of the following actions:

1. Establishing a task force and steering committee to explore the need for sustainability initiatives.
2. Considering best practices for sustainability by benchmarking peer companies.
3. Engaging all relevant stakeholders in the development of sustainability strategies, programs, and processes.
4. Developing sustainability key performance indicators (KPIs) in all EGSEE dimensions of sustainability performance.
5. Assessing materiality thresholds for all dimensions of sustainability performance.
6. Developing sustainability reporting principles and criteria.
7. Collecting data on all sustainability performance dimensions.
8. Preparing sustainability reports.
9. Obtaining assurance on sustainability reports.
10. Making continuous improvements in sustainability performance reporting and assurance.
11. Adopting sustainability reporting rules developed by the International Sustainability Standards Board (ISSB) for the IFRS Sustainability Disclosure Standards to harmonize sustainability reporting and data in a complex regulatory environment.
12. The mandatory EU Corporate Sustainability Reporting Directive (CSRD) could also affect sustainability reporting for non-EU companies with significant operations or business and financial ties to the EU.
13. Develop an integrated sustainability reporting model to adhere to multiple regulations, especially for companies captured by several regulatory regimes with operations in different countries.

14. Adopting various levels of sustainability assurance required across regulations worldwide.

15. Designing comprehensive and robust governance mechanisms to support the implementation of materiality and risk aspects of sustainability reporting and assurance.

Double Fraud in Sustainability Reporting

A growing number of business organizations have made statements on financial ESP and nonfinancial ESG sustainability performance, including climate-related issues, and incorporated them into their sustainability reports. Stakeholders, and especially investors, are interested in the risks and opportunities associated with ESG initiatives and performance and are seeking additional information on the impacts of climate change on the business environment and corporate culture, as well as their current and future financial results, to understand the risks businesses face. However, investors are experiencing a significant challenge of greenwashing that could damage the trust in the sustainability environment and reporting. Double fraud in financial ESP and nonfinancial ESG sustainability performance refers to the simultaneous occurrence of deceptive practices in both financial and nonfinancial reporting by a company. Double fraud refers to situations when a company engages in fraud in both ESP and ESG reporting. This means the company is misleading stakeholders about both its financial health and its commitment to sustainable and ethical practices, including social and environmental impacts. Financial ESP reflects how a company reports its economic and financial activities, focusing on long-term sustainability and economic viability to create wealth for shareholders. Fraud in financial ESP reporting may involve providing false or exaggerated information about a company's environmental impact, social initiatives, or governance practices. For example, a company might falsely claim to have reduced carbon emissions or misrepresent its labor practices and corporate governance standards. Nonfinancial ESG sustainability measures a company's commitment to environmental protection, social responsibility, and governance practices, which generate environmental and social impacts. Fraud in nonfinancial ESG sustainability reporting may involve providing false or exaggerated information about a company's environmental impact, social initiatives, or governance practices. For example, a company might falsely claim to have reduced carbon emissions or misrepresent its labor practices and corporate governance standards.

Business organizations may claim to reduce their carbon footprint by changing operations so that the organization's activities release less carbon. Specifically, some companies have stated that they have set strategic targets such as "net zero" emissions and disclosing carbon offset programs. However, many companies do not explain how they achieve these targets, how they assess and manage the risks of the process, and how they provide assurance for the results related to these targets. Moreover, the fact that climate change has not yet been included in the financial statements at the desired level is concerning. Double fraud can severely undermine investor confidence, damage the company's reputation, and lead to legal and regulatory consequences. It can mislead stakeholders into believing the company is more sustainable and financially healthy than it is, potentially leading to poor investment decisions and misallocation of resources. The Association of Certified Fraud Examiners (ACFE) and Grant Thornton (Auditing Firm) published a paper in 2022 on "Managing Fraud Risks in an Evolving ESG Environment," focusing on the ESG fraud taxonomy to conduct an ESG fraud risk assessment and develop related internal control procedures and activities to mitigate ESG fraud risks.[45] Examples of double fraud in sustainability reporting include: (1) overstating financial performance, where a company might inflate its financial results to appear more profitable while simultaneously exaggerating its ESG achievements to attract socially conscious investors; and (2) greenwashing and financial misreporting, where a company could engage in greenwashing by falsely claiming environmental initiatives and at the same time manipulate its financial statements to hide losses or inflate profits, inflating the value of carbon credits, using modern slavery for production, and making illegal political donations.

Identification, prevention, and detection of double fraud in sustainability reporting are essential to:

- **Investor Protection**: Detecting and preventing double fraud is crucial for protecting investors from receiving misstated financial and nonfinancial information and for ensuring they have accurate information for decision-making.
- **Regulatory Compliance**: Ensuring companies adhere to financial and ESG reporting standards and comply with all applicable laws, rules, regulations, and standards that help maintain market integrity and trust.
- **Sustainable Development**: Accurate reporting on both financial and ESG metrics is essential for promoting genuine sustainable development and corporate responsibility.
- **Understanding Double Fraud**: helps stakeholders, including investors, regulators, and policymakers, to better evaluate the true performance and sustainability of a company, thereby fostering a more transparent and accountable business environment.

Some cases of double fraud are:

- **Volkswagen Emissions Scandal (Dieselgate)**: In 2015, Volkswagen was found to have installed software in diesel engines to cheat emissions tests. The software allowed the vehicles to emit lower levels of pollutants during testing than they did in real-world driving conditions. This deceit affected around 11 million cars worldwide. The scandal led to significant legal penalties, a massive recall of vehicles, and severe reputational damage. It highlighted the need for stricter oversight in environmental claims by corporations.

- **Enron Scandal**: Enron used complex financial structures to hide liabilities and inflate profits. This large-scale accounting fraud misled investors and employees about the company's financial health, directly relating to governance. The scandal led to Enron's bankruptcy, significant losses for investors, the demise of Andersen Auditing firm, and the establishment of the Sarbanes-Oxley Act to improve corporate governance and financial practices, regulating the accounting profession.

- **Wells Fargo Fake Accounts Scandal**: Wells Fargo employees created millions of unauthorized bank and credit card accounts. To meet aggressive sales targets, employees opened accounts without customer consent, which is a breach of trust and social governance. The bank faced hefty fines, congressional hearings, and a loss of customer trust. The scandal underscored the importance of ethical practices and effective governance, and ethical conducts in financial institutions.

- **Toshiba Accounting Scandal**: Toshiba was found to have overstated its profits by approximately $1.2 billion over seven years. The company engaged in improper accounting practices to inflate profits and mislead investors, which is a governance issue. The scandal led to the resignations of top executives, a significant drop in the company's stock price, and a reevaluation of corporate governance standards in Japan.

- **BP Deepwater Horizon Oil Spill**: In 2010, BP's Deepwater Horizon oil rig exploded, causing one of the worst environmental disasters in history. The company was found to have ignored safety protocols and environmental concerns, which are key components of environmental and governance practices. BP faced substantial fines, cleanup costs, and long-term reputational damage. The disaster highlighted the importance of environmental responsibility and robust safety governance.

The pervasiveness of double fraud in recent decades has caused the SEC to enforce financial and nonfinancial fraud committed by public companies. The SEC has recently launched the Climate and ESG Task Force within the Division of Enforcement to develop initiatives to proactively identify ESG-related misconduct consistent with increased investor reliance on climate and ESG-related disclosure and investment.[46] Some of the examples of Enforcement Actions Related to ESG Issues are:

- Goldman Sachs Asset Management (2022), where advisors fail to comply with ESG investment policies.

- BNY Mellon (2022), Presenting misleading ESG information.
- Nikola (2021), fraud involving alternative fuel vehicles.

These cases illustrate the broad spectrum of ESG fraud, encompassing environmental deception, social misconduct, and governance failures. They underline the importance of transparency, ethical practices, and stringent regulatory frameworks to prevent such fraudulent activities and protect stakeholders' interests. In response to the problem of greenwashing and double fraud, which are largely a result of uncertainty and variable definitions, policymakers, regulators, businesses, financial and accounting institutions, investor coalitions, and sustainability standard-setting organizations (SASB, ISSB) have accelerated their deliberations on the standardization of sustainability disclosure and reporting, including ESP and ESG taxonomies.

Sustainability Best Practices

Sustainability best practices encompass a wide range of sustainability strategies and initiatives aimed at ensuring long-term economic viability, minimizing environmental impact, and promoting social responsibility. Ceres was among the first groups of public companies to establish its vision for corporate sustainability leadership in its Roadmap to Sustainability in 2010, which contains 20 specific expectations for corporate sustainability leadership in four areas: governance, stakeholder engagement, performance, and disclosure.[47] All these areas of sustainability activities have been assessed and managed annually in the past decade. The best practices in business sustainability consist of nine recommendations highlighted under three strategies to guide business organizations toward more effective and robust ESG sustainability as follows:[48]

Strategy #1: Formalize sustainable business integration

1. Demonstrate accountability for achieving sustainable performance.
2. Develop the sustainability business cases and strategies.
3. Cultivate collaboration between sustainability, investor relations, and governance teams, including the board of directors and executives.

Strategy #2: Identify what to disclose and where to disclose

1. Focus investor-directed disclosures on what is material, but don't ignore emerging issues and trends in sustainability.
2. Disclose decision-useful information, both quantitatively and qualitative, to stakeholders.

3. Disclose sustainability information consistently where investors are already looking and using such information.

Strategy #3: Implement a proactive investor engagement strategy

1. Use language that investors understand and value about sustainability.
2. Leverage the C-suite and board of directors as key messengers and advocates for moving toward sustainability.
3. Diversify investor engagement strategies to involve investors with sustainability initiatives.

These recommendations for sustainability best practices are still relevant in: (1) promoting environmental conservation and resource management through reducing, reusing, and recycling (3Rs), implementing waste reduction strategies, promoting the reuse of materials, and maximizing recycling efforts to minimize resource consumption and landfill waste; (2) adopting renewable energy by transitioning to renewable energy sources such as solar, wind, hydro, and geothermal to reduce dependence on fossil fuels, mitigate climate change, and achieve carbon neutrality, and investing in on-site renewable energy generation, grid modernization, and energy storage systems to enhance resilience and reliability of energy supply; (3) engaging in CSR activities such as philanthropic and community development projects, and charitable giving to support social causes, improve quality of life, and address societal needs, adopting fair labor practices, promoting diversity and inclusion, and ensuring safe working conditions to protect the rights and well-being of employees and stakeholders; (4) designing and constructing buildings with sustainable materials, green technologies, and energy-efficient systems to minimize energy consumption, enhance indoor air quality, and reduce carbon emissions; (5) adopting a culture of continuous improvement and innovation to drive sustainability performance., develop innovative solutions to complex environmental and social challenges, identify opportunities for optimization, stay competitive in a rapidly evolving market, and contribute to global sustainability goals; (6) engaging with stakeholders, including shareholders, creditors, employees, customers, NGOs, and local communities to understand their needs, expectations, and concerns, gather feedback, and foster collaboration on sustainability initiatives.

Through the integration of these sustainability best practices into the business environment, corporate culture, and operations, business organizations can enhance their long-term financial performance, environmental stewardship, and social impact, thus contributing to a more sustainable and resilient future for society and the planet. The emerging concept of profit-with-purpose corporations suggests that public companies have the dual mission of the profit-making function of creating shareholder value while protecting the

Global Collaboration and Leadership for Sustainability

interests of other stakeholders through their social benefit function. It appears there is a move away from pure shareholder primacy to stakeholder primacy for profit-with-purpose corporations. It appears that European and Asian companies are moving closer to the concept of stakeholder primacy than their counterparts in North America.

Sustainability Opportunities and Challenges

Business sustainability presents both opportunities and challenges for business organizations across various sustainability dimensions, including environmental, social, and economic governance. While sustainability presents significant opportunities for businesses, communities, the environment, and society, it also poses challenges that require collective action, leadership, innovation, and commitment from all stakeholders. Recent moves toward green initiatives, along with mandatory ESG sustainability reporting in Europe and Asia and voluntary disclosure of ESG sustainability in other countries, including the United States, have created many challenges and opportunities for business organizations and public companies in particular. Some of the sustainability opportunities are as follows:

- Build awareness of sustainability challenges and programs – both within the company and among stakeholders, including investors.
- Identify and analyze material issues and create alignment within the organization to ensure an integrated response.
- Invest in and focus on tangible and measurable sustainability outcomes instead of positions on rating lists.
- Obtain adequate *capacity* and *expertise* to comply with multiple sustainability regulations and standards to deal with the demands of new regulations, as well as the right skill set for specialized areas, e.g., Scope 3 emissions or biodiversity.
- Understand overlapping disclosure topics that can find efficiencies in sustainability reporting and assurance processes and practices.
- Formulate a strategy once tangible sustainability measures are established.
- Incorporate the sustainability strategy into the overall corporate strategy, including a clear business case or proof of value.
- Conduct materiality assessments by considering the nuances in how these should be executed under key regulations such as ISSB and CSRD, with the required double materiality approach of assessing the impact of company activities and conduct on people and the planet, and the financial effect of social and environmental issues for wider users of sustainability disclosures.
- Engage investors and a broad range of stakeholders to discuss the company's sustainability strategy and progress.

- Promotion of sustainability can drive innovation in products, services, and business models, creating opportunities for market differentiation and competitive advantage, and attracting environmentally and socially conscious consumers.

- Implementation of sustainable practices such as energy efficiency, waste reduction, and resource optimization can lead to significant cost savings, improved operational efficiency, and reduce long-term business risks.

- Encourage the growing demand for sustainable products and services to create opportunities to enter new markets and customer segments. Such opportunities include the circular economy, renewable energy adoption, and eco-friendly alternatives, which offer avenues for business growth and expansion into sustainable markets.

- Integrate sustainability into business strategies and operations to proactively address sustainability issues by complying with evolving regulations, mitigating compliance risks, and avoiding legal penalties to anticipate regulatory changes, adapt to market trends, and enhance resilience to environmental and social risks.

- Enhance brand reputation and customer loyalty by demonstrating a commitment to sustainability, building trust with stakeholders, and fostering customer loyalty through prioritizing environmental stewardship, social responsibility, and ethical business practices.

Some of the persistent sustainability challenges are:

- The complexity and interconnectedness of sustainability issues, such as climate change, biodiversity loss, and social inequality, require coordinated action at local, national, and global levels that necessitate holistic approaches and collaboration across multiple stakeholders. Addressing these issues can be challenging.

- Balancing short-term financial goals with long-term sustainability objectives can be challenging for companies that face resistance to change from stakeholders focused solely on short-term profits. This makes it difficult to prioritize sustainability initiatives.

- Implementation of sustainable practices often requires upfront investments, resource allocation, and trade-offs between competing priorities, which could be a challenge for companies with limited access to capital, technology, and expertise.

- Management of sustainability across complex supply chains can be challenging because of issues such as transparency, traceability, ethical sourcing, and risk assessment and management.

- Encouragement of behavioral change and engagement of stakeholders in sustainability initiatives can be challenging, requiring cultural shifts, communication, and education due to resistance to change, lack of awareness, and competing interests among stakeholders.

Global Collaboration and Leadership for Sustainability

Summary

The concept of a purpose-with-profit organization model is gaining momentum as society holds businesses accountable for generating financial revenues and achieving social and environmental impacts. In the past two decades, investors have shown increasing interest in nonfinancial sustainability information that impacts long-term viability and the well-being of the company in creating shareholder value. With the advent of social media and new technological developments, investors can easily obtain the necessary information they need from different sources beyond traditional financial reporting. The number of business organizations providing sustainability information regarding their financial and nonfinancial EGSEE performance is on the rise and might be an indication that the traditional financial reporting model should be more inclusive of relevant nonfinancial sustainability information disclosures. Business sustainability performance reporting in terms of integrated reporting has extended the type and amount of financial and nonfinancial information that business organizations provide to their stakeholders regarding their EGSEE sustainability.

The integrated reporting provides the foundation for the communication of both financial and nonfinancial information to stakeholders. The content, format, and method of disseminating sustainability reporting have been evolving, and the optimal disclosure of sustainability information varies across countries and companies. However, a balance between financial economic sustainability performance and other nonfinancial GSEE dimensions of sustainability performance can lead to a competitive advantage as stakeholders value sustainability disclosures. Reliable and useful sustainability information on all five EGSEE dimensions of sustainability performance enables all stakeholders to make sound decisions regarding operating, financing, and investment activities. The use of the XBRL platform and continuous auditing improves the relevance and credibility of sustainability reports. There is still room for more progress toward advancing business sustainability with many challenges and opportunities. It is expected that sustainability performance reporting and assurance will continue to make progress.

Key Points

- Sustainability should be integrated into day-to-day management decision processes, particularly operational, financing, capital investment decisions, and supply-chain management.
- Identification of all stakeholders who are affected and who will affect business sustainability and its success is the first step toward achieving long-term sustainability.
- There are primary stakeholders and secondary stakeholders. Primary stakeholders are visible and are able to influence corporate decisions, whereas secondary stakeholders

are disconnected from the company due to a lack of interest and remoteness. Typical stakeholders include shareholders, creditors, customers, suppliers, employees, regulators, the environment, and the community.

- Achievement of successful business sustainability performance requires a firm commitment from the board of directors, and executives to an integrated and comprehensive approach to promoting sustainability.

- Business sustainability, integrated thinking, and integrated reporting are key components of business strategy and strategic decisions.

- Directors' and executives' commitment to integrated thinking, performance, and reporting are vital in creating sustainable value for all stakeholders.

- A balance between all these five dimensions of sustainability performance can lead to competitive advantage and long-term, enduring value creation for all stakeholders.

- Sustainability reporting should reflect the business organization's sustainability performance in all five dimensions of economic, governance, social, ethical, and environmental (EGSEE) activities.

- External assurance on sustainability reports improves their reliability, credibility, and effectiveness in achieving the organizational objectives of creating value for all stakeholders.

- Tone-at-the-top commitment to sustainability leadership requires organizations to define their sustainability mission, strategic objectives, and actions, and integrate their processes to promote sustainability throughout the organization and its link to sustainable financial performance.

- Sustainability performance in all five EGSEE dimensions is an important driver for building corporate citizenship of trust, retaining talented employees and satisfied customers, and rewarding shareholders.

- Business sustainability development enables organizations to integrate sustainability principles with everyday business operations, processes, and performance.

- The success and effectiveness of business sustainability are determined by integrating sustainability into all facets of business operations, measurements, performance reporting, and assurance.

Review Questions

1. **How has the role of corporations changed over the past several decades?**
2. **Why are shareholders increasingly interested in sustainability performance information?**
3. **How does impact investing influence business sustainability?**

4. What role do institutional investors play in promoting business sustainability?
5. How has the stakeholder primacy model influenced corporate governance?
6. How can integrating sustainability into corporate reporting improve transparency?
7. Why is supply-chain sustainability (SCS) important for businesses?
8. How do mergers and acquisitions (M&A) integrate ESG factors?
9. How do benefit corporations (BCs) differ from conventional corporations?
10. How does the eXtensible Business Reporting Language (XBRL) contribute to sustainability reporting?
11. Why is materiality assessment important in sustainability reporting?
12. How do governance practices affect business sustainability?
13. How can management accountants contribute to business sustainability?
14. What challenges do companies face in achieving supply-chain sustainability?
15. What are the components of a typical sustainability assurance statement?

Discussion Questions

1. How has the purpose of corporations evolved over the past several decades?
2. Why are shareholders increasingly interested in sustainability?
3. What is impact investing and how does it relate to sustainability?
4. What role do standardized sustainability reporting and assurance play for investors?
5. What responsibilities do corporate directors and executives have in sustaining business sustainability?
6. What role does management play in achieving business sustainability?
7. What best practices should management follow for sustainability success?
8. Why is it important for companies to adopt supply-chain sustainability (SCS) strategies?
9. What are some key aspects of supply-chain sustainability (SCS)?
10. How do mergers and acquisitions (M&A) integrate ESG factors into their processes?
11. What benefits do benefit corporations (BCs) offer compared to conventional corporations?
12. How does the eXtensible Business Reporting Language (XBRL) contribute to sustainability reporting?
13. Why is materiality assessment important in sustainability reporting?

14. **How do governance practices affect business sustainability?**

15. **How can management accountants contribute to business sustainability?**

Multiple Choice Questions

1. **What has the corporation's purpose evolved into over the past several decades?**
   A) Profit maximization
   B) Shareholder wealth maximization
   C) Creating shared value for all stakeholders with a mission of profit-with-purpose
   D) Marketing innovation

2. **Why are shareholders increasingly interested in sustainability performance information?**
   A) For marketing purposes
   B) Due to risk management, long-term value creation, regulatory pressures, transparency, and accountability
   C) To reduce operational costs
   D) To increase short-term profits

3. **How does impact investing influence business sustainability?**
   A) It focuses solely on short-term profits
   B) It encourages companies to adopt sustainable business practices by demanding a return on investment while also expecting positive social and environmental impacts
   C) It reduces the need for sustainability disclosures
   D) It increases marketing costs

4. **What role do institutional investors play in promoting business sustainability?**
   A) They focus solely on short-term profits
   B) They demand sustainability performance information and integrate ESG factors into their investment strategies
   C) They reduce the need for sustainability disclosures
   D) They increase marketing expenses

5. **How has the stakeholder primacy model influenced corporate governance?**
   A) It encourages boards to focus solely on shareholder interests
   B) It encourages boards to protect the interests of all stakeholders and address social and environmental initiatives
   C) It reduces the need for sustainability disclosures
   D) It increases marketing expenses

6. **How can integrating sustainability into corporate reporting improve transparency?**
   A) By reducing the amount of disclosed information
   B) By providing comprehensive information on financial ESP and nonfinancial ESG performance
   C) By increasing marketing expenses
   D) By decreasing operational costs

7. **Why is supply-chain sustainability (SCS) important for businesses?**
   A) It reduces the need for sustainability disclosures
   B) It integrates environmentally and socially responsible practices throughout the supply chain, minimizing negative impacts and maximizing positive contributions
   C) It increases marketing expenses
   D) It decreases operational costs

8. **How do mergers and acquisitions (M&A) integrate ESG factors?**
   A) By focusing solely on short-term profits
   B) By performing ESG due diligence, considering ESG metrics in valuations, incorporating ESG clauses in contracts, and engaging stakeholders on ESG matters
   C) By reducing marketing expenses
   D) By increasing operational costs

9. **How do benefit corporations (BCs) differ from conventional corporations?**
   A) BCs focus solely on shareholder value
   B) BCs focus on creating shared value for all stakeholders, balancing profit with social and environmental goals
   C) BCs reduce the need for sustainability disclosures
   D) BCs increase marketing expenses

10. **How does the eXtensible Business Reporting Language (XBRL) contribute to sustainability reporting?**
    A) It reduces the amount of disclosed information
    B) It facilitates timely and accurate analysis of business information and enables companies to define proper taxonomies for sustainability performance
    C) It increases marketing expenses
    D) It decreases operational costs

11. **Why is materiality assessment important in sustainability reporting?**
    A) It reduces the amount of disclosed information
    B) It determines the most relevant and significant issues for an organization and its stakeholders

C) It increases marketing expenses

D) It decreases operational costs

12. **How do governance practices affect business sustainability?**

A) They focus solely on short-term profits

B) They ensure companies address financial health, climate change, workforce wellness, stakeholder engagement, ESG factors, risk management, growth, innovation, and diversity

C) They reduce the need for sustainability disclosures

D) They increase marketing expenses

13. **How can management accountants contribute to business sustainability?**

A) Focusing solely on short-term profits

B) Identifying nonfinancial sustainability initiatives, linking sustainability challenges to company strategy, developing KPIs, and assisting in sustainability reporting and strategic planning

C) Reducing marketing expenses

D) Increasing operational costs

14. **What challenges do companies face in achieving supply-chain sustainability?**

A) Lack of proper definition of the profit-with-purpose mission, inadequate focus on lean management, lack of integration of supply-chain sustainability into business sustainability, ineffective communication, insufficient guidelines, and lack of tone at the top

B) Reducing marketing expenses

C) Increasing operational costs

D) Decreasing brand reputation

15. **What are the components of a typical sustainability assurance statement?**

A) An introductory paragraph, scope paragraph, assurance methodology, findings and conclusion, limitations, assurance opinion, statement date, and signatures

B) Increased marketing expenses

C) Decreased brand reputation

D) Higher operational costs

16. **What is the role of the Chief Sustainability Officer (CSO) in promoting sustainability?**

A) Focusing solely on short-term profits

B) Leading sustainability initiatives, assessing and managing ESG-related risks, ensuring compliance, managing business continuity, and communicating sustainability information

Multiple Choice Questions

C) Reducing marketing expenses

D) Increasing operational costs

17. **What is the impact of the COVID-19 pandemic on supply-chain sustainability?**

A) It has reduced the need for sustainability disclosures

B) It has highlighted the importance of supply-chain transparency, resilience, and sustainability

C) It has increased marketing expenses

D) It has decreased operational costs

18. **What is the importance of human capital management in business sustainability?**

A) It increases marketing expenses

B) It enhances financial performance, brand reputation, talent attraction, and innovation

C) It reduces operational costs

D) It decreases brand reputation

19. **What is the role of the board of directors in overseeing sustainability initiatives?**

A) To focus solely on short-term profits

B) To provide strategic direction and governance for sustainability efforts

C) To reduce marketing expenses

D) To increase operational costs

20. **What is the significance of biodiversity accounting?**

A) It focuses solely on short-term profits

B) It integrates biodiversity considerations into accounting and finance disciplines

C) It reduces the need for sustainability disclosures

D) It increases marketing expenses

21. **What is the purpose of sustainability assurance?**

A) To reduce the amount of disclosed information

B) To provide verification and credibility to sustainability reports

C) To increase marketing expenses

D) To decrease operational costs

22. **What does a materiality assessment ensure in sustainability reporting?**

A) Reduced need for transparency

B) Rolovant and significant issues are reported

C) Increased marketing expenses

D) Decreased operational costs

23. **What are benefit corporations (BCs)?**

   A) Corporations focusing solely on shareholder value

   B) Corporations that balance profit with social and environmental goals

   C) Corporations that reduce the need for sustainability disclosures

   D) Corporations that increase marketing expenses

24. **What role do institutional investors play in promoting sustainability?**

   A) They focus solely on short-term profits

   B) They integrate ESG factors into their investment strategies

   C) They reduce the need for sustainability disclosures

   D) They increase marketing expenses

25. **What are the benefits of adopting a multiple bottom lines (MBL) approach?**

   A) It focuses solely on short-term profits

   B) It helps achieve economic, social, ethical, and environmental performance

   C) It reduces the need for sustainability disclosures

   D) It increases marketing expenses

26. **What challenges should be addressed in achieving supply-chain sustainability?**

   A) Reducing the amount of disclosed information

   B) Properly defining the profit-with-purpose mission, integrating SCS into business sustainability, and effective communication

   C) Increasing marketing expenses

   D) Decreasing operational costs

27. **What are some examples of environmental KPIs?**

   A) Customer satisfaction and brand loyalty

   B) Disclosure of gigajoules of total energy consumed, metric tons of total CO_2 emitted, and risk exposure to climate change

   C) Marketing strategies and sales growth

   D) Online reviews and social media presence

28. **What does sustainability performance suggest about management's focus?**

   A) Management must focus solely on short-term shareholder profit

   B) Management must extend its focus beyond maximizing short-term shareholder profit by considering the impact of its operations on the long-term interests of all stakeholders

   C) Management must increase marketing expenses

   D) Management must reduce operational costs

Multiple Choice Questions

29. **What impact does the integration of ESG factors have on M&A deals?**

    A)   Reduces the need for sustainability disclosures

    B)   Increases the importance of ESG due diligence and valuation

    C)   Increases marketing expenses

    D)   Decreases operational costs

30. **What are the benefits of adopting a multiple bottom lines (MBL) approach?**

    A)   It focuses solely on short-term profits

    B)   It helps achieve economic, social, ethical, and environmental performance

    C)   It reduces the need for sustainability disclosures

    D)   It increases marketing expenses

Notes

1 Much of the discussion in this chapter comes from Rezaee, Z. (2024). *The Sustainable Business Blueprint: Planning, Performance, Risk, Reporting and Assurance.* Routledge/ Taylor and Francis, Chapter 12.

2 Bebchuk, L., and Tallarita, R. (2022). The perils and questionable promise of ESG-Based compensation. *Journal of Corporation Law* 48: 37–75.

3 Bebchuk, L., and Tallarita, R. (2022). The perils and questionable promise of ESG-based compensation. *Journal of Corporation Law*, 48 (2022): 37–75.

4 Rezaee, Z. (2016). Business sustainability research: A theoretical and integrated perspective. *Journal of Accounting Literature* 36 (June 2016): 48–64

5 Rezaee, Z., and Rezaee, N. (2021). *Business Sustainability: Investor, Board and Management Perspective.* Business Expert Press (August 2021).

6 Rezaee, Z. and Rezaee, N. (2021). *Business Sustainability: Investor, Board and Management Perspective.* Business Expert Press (August 2021).

7 Sounders, Maura. (2020). Survey analysis: ESG investment pre-and post-pandemic. Institute of Shareholder Services (ISS). https://www.issgovernance.com/file/publications/ ISS-ESG-Investing-Survey-Analysis.pdf.

8 United Nations Global Compact (UN Global Compact). (2015). Supply chain sustainability: A practical guide for continuous improvement. Second edition. https://www.unglobalcom- pact.org/library/205 (accessed September 3, 2020).

9 Rezaee, Z. (2018). Integrating business sustainability into supply chain management. *International Journal of Finance and Managerial Accounting* 3 (9) (Spring 2018): 1–15.

10 Morgan Stanley. (2022). 2022 M&A outlook: Continued strength after a record year (January 14, 2022). https://www.morganstanley.com/ideas/mergers-and-acquisitions -outlook-2022-continued-strength-after-record.

11 HIS Markit. (2019). ESG on the rise: Making an impact in M&A. https://cdn.ihsmarkit.com/ www/prot/pdf/1120/Mergermarket-ESG.pdf.

12 Deloitte. (2022). The future of M&A: 2022 M&A trends survey (January 2022). https://www2.deloitte.com/content/dam/Deloitte/us/Documents/mergers-acqisitions/us-deloitte-2022-mna-trends-report.pdf.

13 Deloitte. (2023). ESG's evolving role in corporate M&A decisions (March 2023). https://www.slideshare.net/DeloitteUS/private-equity-leads-corporate-deal-teams-on-esg-in-ma?from_action=save.

14 Hiller, J.S. (2013). The benefit corporations and corporate social responsibility. *Journal of Business Ethics* 118: 287–301.

15 Delaware Law Series. (2013). DGCL amended to authorize public benefit corporations (August 14, 2013). http://blogs.law.harvard.edu/corpgov/tag/delaware-law/.

16 Northwest Register Agent. (2020). Benefit corporations aka the "B Corp." https://www.northwestregisteredagent.com/benefit-corporation.html#:~:text=You%20can%20currently%20form%20a%20benefit%20corporation%20in,Island%2C%20South%20Carolina%2C%20Vermont%2C%20Virginia%2C%20and%20Washington%20DC.

17 XBRL. (2013). Corporate reporting evolved: Integrated reporting and the role of XBRL, an issues brief of the XBRL International Best Practices Board. http://xbrl.org/sites/xbrl.org/files/imce/issues_brief_intgrpt2013.pdf.

18 Securities and Exchange Commission (SEC). (2012). Remarks to the IFRS taxonomy annual convention (April 25, 2010). http://www.sec.gov/news/speech/2012/spch042512ms.htm.

19 Climate Change Reporting Taxonomy (CCRT). (2013). Climate change reporting taxonomy (CCRT) due process. www.cdproject.net/en-us/news/pages/xbrl-due-process.aspx.

20 Brockett and Rezaee (2012).

21 American Institute of Certified Public Accountants (AICPA). (2003). Attest Engagements on Greenhouse Gas Emissions Information. Statement of Position 03-2. New York: AICPA.

22 American Institute of Certified Public Accountants (AICPA). (2003). Attest Engagements on Greenhouse Gas Emissions Information. Statement of Position 03-2. New York: AICPA.

23 American Institute of Certified Public Accountants (AICPA). (2003). Attest Engagements on Greenhouse Gas Emissions Information. Statement of Position 03-2. New York: AICPA.

24 Brockett, A. and Rezaee, Z. (2012). *Corporate Sustainability: Integrating Performance and Reporting*. Wiley.

25 Brockett, A. and Rezaee, Z. (2012). *Corporate Sustainability: Integrating Performance and Reporting*. Wiley.

26 Brockett, A. and Rezaee, Z. (2012). *Corporate Sustainability: Integrating Performance and Reporting*. Wiley.

27 Global Reporting Initiative (GRI). (2002). Sustainability reporting guidelines on economic, environmental, and social performance. www.globalreporting.org.

28 Rezaee, Z. (2015). *Business Sustainability: Performance, Compliance, Accountability and Integrated Reporting*. Greenleaf Publishing Limited.

29 Rezaee, Z. (2015). *Business Sustainability: Performance, Compliance, Accountability and Integrated Reporting*. Greenleaf Publishing Limited.

Notes

30 Rezaee, Z. (2015). *Business Sustainability: Performance, Compliance, Accountability and Integrated Reporting.* Greenleaf Publishing Limited.

31 Rezaee, Z. (2015). *Business Sustainability: Performance, Compliance, Accountability and Integrated Reporting.* Greenleaf Publishing Limited.

32 United Nations Global Compact (UN Global Compact). (2013). Global corporate sustainability report 2013. https://www.unglobalcompact.org/docs/about_the_gc/Global_Corporate_Sustainability_Report2013.pdf.

33 Brockett, A. and Rezaee, Z. (2012). *Corporate Sustainability: Integrating Performance and Reporting.* Wiley.

34 White, S. (2015). How management accountants can lead their organizations toward sustainability success (January 6). http://www.cgma.org/Learn/Publications/Pages/Publications.aspx.

35 The Institute of Internal Auditors (IIA). (2015). Enhancing integrated reporting: Internal audit value proposition, p. 9. http://auditoresinternos.es/uploads/media_items/integrated-reporting.original.pdf.

36 The International Standard on Assurance Engagements 3000 (ISAE 3000). (2005). Assurance engagements other than audits or reviews of historical financial information. *ISAE* (January 1), 1–57. www.accountability21.net.

37 Global Reporting Initiative (GRI). (2006). Sustainability reporting guidelines, version 3.0. www.globalreporting.org/NR/rdonlyres/ED9E9B36-AB54-4DE1-BFF2-5F735235CA44/0/G3_GuidelinesENU.pdf.

38 European Commission (EC). (2023). The Commission adopts the European sustainability reporting standards (July 31, 2024). https://finance.ec.europa.eu/news/commission-adopts-european-sustainability-reporting-standards-2023-07-31_en.

39 United Nations Principles of Responsible Investing (UN PRI). (2005). The freshfields report. www.unepfi.org/fileadmin/documents/freshfields_legal_resp_20051123.pdf.

40 Social Investment Forum (SIF). (2012). 2012 report on sustainable and responsible investing trends in the United States. US SIF Foundation: The Forum for Sustainable and Responsible Investment (November).

41 Jiao, Y. (2010). Stakeholder welfare and firm value. *Journal of Banking and Finance* 34 (10): 2549–2561.

42 MIT Sloan Management Review. (2015). Joining forces: Collaboration and leadership for sustainability (January 12). http://sloanreview.mit.edu/projects/joining-forces/?utm_source=SUEnews%201/13/15%20B&utm_medium=email&utm_campaign=susrpt15.

43 MIT Sloan Management Review. (2015). Joining forces: Collaboration and leadership for sustainability (January 12). http://sloanreview.mit.edu/projects/joining-forces/?utm_source=SUEnews%201/13/15%20B&utm_medium=email&utm_campaign=susrpt15.

44 MIT Sloan Management Review. (2015). Joining forces: Collaboration and leadership for sustainability (January 12). http://sloanreview.mit.edu/projects/joining-forces/?utm_source=SUEnews%201/13/15%20B&utm_medium=email&utm_campaign=susrpt15.

45 Association of Certified Fraud Examiners (ACFE) and Grant Thornton. (2022). Managing Fraud Risks in an Evolving ESG Environment. https://www.grantthornton.com.cw/globalas-sets/1.-member-firms/curacao/acfe_gt_esgreport-digital.pdf.

46 Securities and Exchange Commission (SEC). (2024). Enforcement task force focused on climate and ESG issues. Available at https://www.sec.gov/securities-topics/enforcement-task-force-focused-climate-esg-issues.

47 Ceres. (2010). The Ceres roadmap for sustainability. https://www.ceres.org/ceres-roadmap.

48 Ceres. (2019). Change the conversation: Redefining how companies engage investors on sustainability. www.ceres.org and https://corpgov.law.harvard.edu/wp-content/uploads/2019/02/Ceres.pdf.

Notes

Index

Printed in the United States
by Baker & Taylor Publisher Services